David Nye Brown

Reflecting on Art

John Andrew Fisher
University of Colorado, Boulder

MAYFIELD PUBLISHING COMPANY
Mountain View, California
London • Toronto

Library Of Congress Cataloging-In-Publication Data
Fisher, John A. (John Andrew)
Reflecting on art/John A. Fisher.
    p.   cm.
Includes bibliographical references and index.
ISBN 0-87484-821-0
1. Art—Philosophy.   I. Title.
N71.F57   1992
701—dc20   91-44294
                                                                 CIP

Manufactured in the United States of America
10 9 8 7 6 5 4 3 2 1

Mayfield Publishing Company
1240 Villa Street
Mountain View, CA 94041

Sponsoring editor, James Bull; managing editor, Linda Toy; production editor, April Wells-Hayes; copyeditor, Sally Peyrefitte; text and cover designer, David Bullen; art director, Jeanne M. Schreiber; manufacturing manager, Martha Branch; cover image, Virginia Maitland. The text was set in 9.5/12 Sabon and printed on 50# Finch Opaque by Arcata Graphics.

Acknowledgments and copyrights appear at the back of the book on pages 427–428, which constitute an extension of the copyright page.

Preface

This text provides more than enough material for a one-semester introduction to the philosophy of art. It introduces many of the crucial philosophical ideas and issues arising from reflection on the nature and impact of the arts. Because this book focuses as much on the arts as on the traditional subject of aesthetics, it should be of interest to philosophically minded artists and art students as well as to philosophy students with an interest in the arts.

The philosophy of art goes back over two thousand years to the beginning of Western philosophy in the writings of Plato and Aristotle. Art is as challenging to understand and evaluate today as it was in ancient Greek times. Indeed, the issues are much more complex for us, because we have inherited, in addition to a rich and complex history of art, a number of competing theories of art, all with some appeal. Moreover, the growth of romanticism and the avant-garde in the nineteenth and twentieth centuries signaled a shift in much serious art. Many romantic and avant-garde artists meant their work to oppose conventional cultural values, a situation that gives art a role very different from the one it played in earlier societies, such as Renaissance Italy.

The following text comprises a series of discussions of the central issues in the philosophy of art. These discussions are accompanied by supplementary readings selected to represent both classical texts in philosophy of art and important and provocative texts in contemporary art theory and philosophy. The discussions are organized in a logical progression, taking the reader from an initial questioning of art to an exploration of the major theories of art.

This text differs from other texts on aesthetics in three significant ways. First, to emphasize the arts, I have de-emphasized some topics usually covered in the field of aesthetics. Some philosophers use the term "aesthetics" in the traditional way to refer to the study of a special mode of attention that can be directed at both nature and art; other writers merely use the expression as a synonym for "philosophy of art." But even for such writers, the term "aesthetics" often carries with it a certain set of assumptions and concepts. The principal themes of aesthetics (including the word "aesthetics") were largely developed in the eighteenth century: the notion of a special aesthetic experience, the concepts of the beautiful and the sublime, the faculty of aesthetic judgment (taste), and so forth. Although I agree that these concepts are important and interesting, I do not think that they merit a dominant place in an exploration of issues pertaining to the nature and value of the arts in the late twentieth century. Thus I discuss issues, such as public support for the arts and art and morality, generally untouched by standard texts on aesthetics.

Second, many aesthetics anthologies aim to give a taste of all of the main issues and theories in aesthetics and art. Instead of taking this smorgasbord approach, I have chosen to impose a particular order on the material. I chose this order to motivate the study of philosophy of art, to give the reader some idea of why the philosophy of art is interesting and important, and to provide the conceptual tools for thinking clearly about art and art theories. Although the chapters are relatively independent of each other, and no particular chapters are essential, this overall development of thought informs the argument of most chapters.

Third, I have attempted to produce a genuine *introduction* to issues in the philosophy of art. Although most of the topics broached in the chapters could be the subjects of separate books and graduate seminars in philosophy of art, it isn't possible, I believe, to approach them at that level of detail in an introduction. Typically, books on aesthetics, even wide-ranging ones, tend to presuppose a level of sophistication that is appropriate for upper-division or graduate courses. By contrast, I have tried to write for the intelligent layperson and undergraduate. For this reason, I have not been afraid to discuss basic questions that are often overlooked in more sophisticated treatments; my goal is to interest readers and direct them in certain directions, rather than to provide a definitive summary of the current state of scholarship.

Part I begins by clarifying the initial resistance many people feel to intellectual discussions of art. It then moves to some of the important reasons for having a philosophy of art: questions of meaning and justification that occur even to sympathetic observers of the arts (and to artists themselves, such as the great novelist and art theorist Leo Tolstoy). Unlike most books on the arts, mine does not assume without argument that the arts are intrinsically valuable and unproblematic. Of course, like many others, I accept that the arts are among the most valuable products of human culture. But as a philosopher, I know it is not easy to formulate a clear rationale for this fundamental value claim. Especially in the current cultural climate, the status of the arts can no longer remain unquestioned. It is thus a matter of some urgency to reconsider the question of the nature of art, keeping in mind the need to discover, if we can, compelling reasons why art is as valuable as many people assume it is.

Part II moves on to a series of distinctions that need highlighting if the strong claims customarily made for art are to be sustained: distinctions between art and craft and art and entertainment. Part III considers the most important of the traditional and contemporary theories of art: mimetic theory, formalism, and expression theory. Those who prefer a more systematic approach may wish to alter the order of exposition, beginning with Chapter 1 and then going on to the theories of art investigated in Part III. They could then proceed to examine the issues delineated in Part I, treating these as problems to which theories of art may be usefully applied.

The book concludes with two views of the future of art. My own ideas about the nature of art have been greatly influenced by R. G. Collingwood's *Principles of Art*; the general character and movement of thought of my text mirror Collingwood's approach. It is thus appropriate that one of these views is Collingwood's account of what he considers the true mission of art in society.

I wish to express my appreciation to the following people for their thoughtful perusal of and insightful comments on the manuscript of this book: Anthony Coyne, University of North Carolina at Asheville; Thomas Franks, Eastern Michigan University; Herbert Gare-lick, Michigan State University; George Graham, University of Alabama at Birmingham; John McDermott, Texas A&M University; Diane Michelfelder, California Polytechnic State University; Cynthia Rostankowski, Santa Clara University; and Dennis Rothermel, Califor-nia State University, Chico. I am also indebted to my colleagues Dale Jamieson, for his continued encouragement, and Christopher Shields, for conversations on Plato and Aristotle;

to all the students who have participated in my classes in philosophy and the arts throughout the years; and to the University of Colorado for research leaves in Soho and Florence that enabled me to do the research which forms the basis for this book. Those at Mayfield to whom particular thanks are due are Jim Bull for his unfailing support throughout this project; Lans Hays for his initial encouragement; and April Wells-Hayes, Sally Peyrefitte, Pamela Trainer, and Kirstan Price for their conscientious and creative support during the production process. Finally, I am profoundly grateful to my wife, the painter Virginia Maitland, for her inspiring creativity and for teaching me all about the visual arts, and to my infant son for his enthusiasm about the world.

Contents

For Ginger and Russell

Introduction: Definition and Subjectivity—The Ineffability of Art

◀ *Mona Lisa* (ca. 1503–1505) by Leonardo da Vinci, and *Cuts* (1967) by Carl Andre. So many kinds of things are considered art that thinkers have voiced frustration at what R.A. Sharp terms "the apparent impenetrability of a concept of 'art' that embraces both the *Mona Lisa* and piles of bricks."

Come, eyes, see more than you see!
For the world within and the outer world
rejoice as one.

— Robert Duncan, *Variations on Two Dicta by William Blake*

To some people, philosophy of art may sound like an unstable chemical compound, ready to blow apart at any moment. In the popular mind, the arts are associated with subjectivity, sensory experience, and even insanity, whereas philosophy is associated with dry and abstract theorizing. Those familiar with philosophy can add that philosophers attempt to produce objective and rational accounts of phenomena, the very opposite of what many people take to be possible with art. In spite of this seeming incompatibility, philosophers have theorized about the arts since the beginning of philosophy, and some of the most important figures in the history of philosophy — Plato, Aristotle, Hume, Kant, Hegel, Nietzsche — have made significant contributions to the philosophy of art.

Of course, the philosophy of a field need not have the characteristics of that field. The philosophy of law does not itself have the character of a legal system; the philosophy of mathematics does not have the rigor and formal structure of mathematics. Still, articulating a philosophy of art seems to present special problems. Two in particular are given preliminary examination in this chapter. The first is the familiar difficulty of providing any adequate definition of art. (One writer refers to "the apparent impenetrability of a concept of 'art' which embraces both the Mona Lisa and piles of bricks."[1]) The second is the equally familiar notion that works of art depend on the subjective evaluations of audiences. This notion tempts us to reason in the following way: Art essentially depends on the spectator's response; the spectator's response is entirely subjective. Hence, art is entirely subjective. This general skepticism about art finds its most familiar expression in the habitual doubts that many people have about the validity of art criticism. Let's look more closely at these two problems.

CAN ART BE DEFINED?

Before discussing this issue, we must clarify our terminology. In contemporary English, the term "art" is used in two different ways. In its narrow meaning, "art" denotes just the visual arts, that is, paintings, sculpture, drawings, and so on. But in the philosophy of art, the terms "art," "artist," and "work of art" are not associated solely with the visual arts. There is a more important, broader use of the term "art," which is reflected in our ability to refer collectively to literature, music, dance, visual arts, and so on, as "the arts." By conceptually yoking together creative activities in these various media, we imply that they are similar in virtue of being art-making activities. We imply this whenever we refer to composers, poets, or dancers as artists or whenever we say, for instance, that the composer Ludwig van Beethoven was one of the greatest artists who ever lived or that the writer James Joyce is an important artist of the twentieth century. The expression "work of art" is especially open in its application to a broad spectrum of creative products, among them operas, ballets, poems, and the like. This broad sense of "art" (and "artist") is the sense in which thinkers traditionally have discussed the nature and importance of art; philosophy of art examines art in this broad sense.

The broad use of "art" and "artist" closely corresponds to the familiar broad use of the terms "science" and "scientist." Just as biologists, physicists, and geologists are all scientists, and biology, physics, and geology are all sciences, so, too, are poets, painters, and composers artists, and poetry, painting, and music arts. To say this is *not* to say several things: first, it is not to say that such classifications are easy or uncontroversial, even in the sciences. Second, it is not to imply that these classifications are closed and unalterable, even in the sciences. Are parapsychology and creation science, for example, real sciences? Third, it is not to beg the question of whether there is an essence or nature that defines art or science. (I will return to this question in a moment.)

Finally, it is not to imply that the concept of art — from now on I will use the term only in the broad sense — is as clear or uncontroversial as the concept of science. There are serious and long-standing arguments about whether certain activities and media — for example, jazz, furniture making, and movies — deserve to be considered art. These controversies reflect the high status we attach to art; in the words of one philosopher of art, "Nothing equals the value and importance of the arts."[2] Such claims raise the philosophical question of whether we can specify a concept of art that not only is clear and consistent but also can explain this importance.

The question of whether art can be defined has many facets. There are those who say that art cannot be defined, because its very nature is to be original and always changing. Moreover, for every characteristic that traditionally might have been proposed to define art in general or to define subcategories of art, such as "play," "painting," "piece of music," or "dance," there are experimental twentieth-century artworks that lack that characteristic. For many artists, it seems, the content of art has become its own undefinability. (Chapter 5 examines the challenge posed by avant-garde art.) Then there are those who claim that each individual must determine what is and is not art. In a different vein, some claim that there is nothing common to all works of art; the order suggested by our use of the term "art" to cover all the various arts is an artificial order that does not correspond to any real property or set of properties in the world. Is there something that all works of art — whether plays, paintings, or string quartets — have in common, something that makes them works of art and distinguishes them from other activities and artifacts? Some social critics of art charge that the very concept of art draws invidious distinctions between the culture of the elite and the cultures of the lower classes by implying that what the educated and powerful enjoy, being "art," is somehow of a different and more valuable order.

It's easy to see why the problem of how to define art is one of the most important concerns of modern art theory. The many theoretical accounts of art proposed over the centuries have all presupposed that there is a definition of art. Yet, as we have seen, many thinkers, both art theorists and artists, have held that no valid definition can be given. Suppose we cannot define art; would we be defeated before we begin? Does the philosophy of art depend on our being able to give a definition of "art"? I will argue that the answer is no.

Thinkers have traditionally assumed that words that express abstract concepts, for example, such words as "justice," "truth," and "art," are used to refer to some essential property that instances of the concept must exemplify. Thus, an action is just because it exemplifies justice. In a parallel fashion, a piece of music, for instance, is a work of art if it exemplifies the essential property or properties that characterize a work of art. This traditional assumption has been seriously questioned by twentieth-century philosophers. Philosophers under the influence of Ludwig Wittgenstein (1889–1951) have attacked the idea that all objects designated by a common name must exhibit certain common properties. In aesthetics, the philosopher Morris Weitz applies the Wittgensteinian idea of "family resemblances" to explain how we can pick out works of art from other things even though there is no strict logical definition of "art" (see the Readings for this chapter).

In Weitz's view, the search for a definition of art is a search for a set of properties that are separately necessary and jointly sufficient for an item to be art. When, for example, we define a square as a plane figure having four equal sides and four right angles we are saying that having exactly four sides is a necessary condition for something to be a square; if a figure has only three sides or more than four sides, it cannot be a square. Likewise, it is a necessary condition to be a square that a figure have four right angles. Moreover, we are saying that the figure's having all of these properties is sufficient to allow us to apply the term "square" to the figure; if a plane figure is four-sided and has four right angles, it is necessarily a square. If there are necessary and sufficient conditions that define art, then there are properties that every work of art must have and the possession of which guarantees that something is a work of art.

Weitz claims that the concept of art *cannot* be defined in this way, nor can any of art's subconcepts, such as "tragedy," "painting," "opera," and so on. He draws our attention to Wittgenstein's famous discussion of the concept of a game:

> What is common to them all? — Don't say: "there *must* be something common, or they would not be called 'games'" but *look and see* whether there is anything common to all. — For if you look at them you will not see something that is common to *all*, but similarities, relationships . . . a complicated network of similarities overlapping and crisscrossing. (p. 14)

Weitz applies this idea to the concept of art:

> If we actually look and see what it is that we call "art," we will also find no common properties — only strands of similarities. Knowing what art is is not apprehending some manifest or latent essence but being able to recognize, describe, and explain those things we call "art" in virtue of these similarities. (p. 14)

Many philosophers have attacked Weitz's claim that we can find no common property that defines art. These philosophers have suggested various sophisticated definitions that attempt to capture what all works of art have in common (see Chapter 5). But what if Weitz is correct? What are the consequences for philosophy of art?

It seems obvious that Weitz's own view *is* a sort of philosophy of art. It tells us the nature of art: in Weitz's terminology, "art" is an "open" concept not bounded by strict and unchanging conditions of application. The possibility of philosophy of art, then, does not depend on our formulating a set of properties that define art. We can make generalizations about art even if we cannot specify any one thing that all works of art or art activities have in common.

To clarify the issue, we can distinguish what I will call the *naive* problem of defining art from what I will call the *philosophical* problem of defining art. The philosophical problem is just the question of whether we can find a formula that defines necessary and/or sufficient conditions for art. Weitz claims that no such definition can be found. Others disagree, but clearly this is a dispute *within* philosophy of art. The naive problem, by contrast, is fundamental to having a rational discussion about the nature of art; it is the problem of whether we can *agree on examples* of art. If we cannot agree even on the examples, we do not have a common conception of what phenomena we are trying to understand.

The naive problem is resolvable: we can agree on examples of art, although not as clearly as we can agree, for instance, on examples of science. We simply have to appeal to the traditions and institutions of art, keeping an open mind about what to include or exclude. It is true that we are caught in a conceptual circle connecting three concepts: art, artists, and the arts. Art is what artists make; artists are those who participate in the arts; the arts are those cultural activities that exemplify art. Practically speaking, however, there is no great difficulty in specifying our object of study by referring to the European tradition of the arts. This is implicitly what the National Endowment for the Arts (NEA) does when it provides grants to poets but not to gardeners, to symphony orchestras but not to sports teams.

The heart of this approach is to remind ourselves of paradigm cases, cases that exemplify what the expression "art" means, as well as what the subconcepts "poem," "sonata," "tragedy" mean. Such paradigms inevitably include the great masterpieces of the arts. Surely we can agree that the greatest poets, painters, novelists, composers, and playwrights of the past and present are artists and that their finest works are works of art. We agree that Beethoven, Bach, Mozart, Shakespeare, Dostoevsky, Tolstoy, and Michelangelo are paradigm cases of great artists who produced great works of art. So, we can at least start with agreement about plenty of examples. Keeping these examples in mind, perhaps we can eventually produce some account of this phenomenon, either in the form of a theory or a definition of art. In fact, the philosophical problem of how to define art arises because we have an enormous variety of examples that we agree are art but that we cannot easily define.

The crucial question is whether the predicate "___ is art" is arbitrary or not. Are there *truth conditions* for "X is art," that is, conditions that make the statement "X is art" true or false? Weitz argues that although there are no necessary or sufficient conditions for "___ is art," there are criteria of recognition that make it correct to describe something as a work of art: "Thus, mostly, when we describe something as a work of art, we do so under the conditions of there being present some sort of artifact, made by human skill, ingenuity, and imagination, which embodies in its sensuous, public medium — stone, wood, sounds, words, etc. — certain distinguishable elements and relations" (p. 16). Weitz claims that even these features are not strictly necessary, although most works of art exemplify these properties as well as many other typical features.

I would add to Weitz's list of typical features of art that *most* works of art have some sort of intended audience. Moreover, it seems generally true that the audience assumes a special attitude toward the artifact. This attitude or mode of attention is difficult to define, but it seems to be such that multiple experiences of the very same artifact or performance do not diminish that artifact's value or interest to the audience. This gives artworks a universal quality that differentiates them from the momentary interest evoked by a sports contest, for example.

Even though not governed by strict conditions of application, the expression "art" is governed by criteria of application and recognition. Weitz holds that the question of whether to extend the notion of art to novel sorts of work is not arbitrary. As he says about the extension of the concept of a novel to new experimental writings, "What is at stake is no factual analysis concerning necessary and sufficient properties but a decision as to whether the work under examination is similar in certain respects to other works, already called 'novels' . . ." (p. 15). The same is true, according to Weitz, of the concept of art itself; thus, even though the concept of art is perhaps vague, it is not arbitrary.

Private Definitions

Sometimes people react to the controversy surrounding the *philosophical* problem of defining art by offering a private definition of art: This is art if I think it is. Hence, whatever I think is art *is* art! There are two objections to this personal definition. First, "art" is a very public concept, however vague. My thinking that something is a work of art has no more to do with whether the language community that determines the meaning of "art" will count it as art than my thinking that the Empire State Building is a game has anything to do with whether others will consider it a game. Second, there is a blatant circularity in the very idea of this definition. In the case of "art," *what* is it I am attributing to the object if I think it is art? Either I think it is relevantly similar to accepted works of art — in which case we can have a rational debate about that, and I could be wrong — or I think it is the sort of thing I think is ___. But how do I fill in the blank where "art" should go? Remember, art is what I think is art. If I use this alleged definition to fill in the blank, I get this: It is the sort of thing I think is the sort of thing I think is ___. Again, I cannot complete my thought. I am caught in a circle; I can never put any content into my claim that this is art, because my only thought is that this is what I call art. But what *is* that?

A more coherent but still problematic idea is that only artists have the right to determine what is and is not art. Often this idea is put forward because of prejudice against critics, theorists, and even the general public. The idea is that only practitioners can define a field. But "art" isn't a private concept of artists, not even in the way that, of necessity, "science" is determined by scientists. This proposal, in fact, poses all sorts of difficulties. Who are the artists? How do we define those who have the right to determine what is art? Are art students such artists? Are students who take one or two art classes such artists? Does an art student know more about the arts than, say, an art historian? Do teachers of the arts count if they are not themselves commercially successful artists? Will people who have sung or played a musical instrument — which is virtually everyone — count as artists with a right to determine the answer? Are gallery directors, music scholars, poetry editors, dance critics, and faithful members of the audience for the arts not entitled to a valid opinion? When two artists disagree, are they both right?

Finally, there is again the problem of putting content into this definition. What is an artist judging, on this definition, when he or she judges that X is art? That other artists will agree? But *what* are they agreeing about? The only plausible answer seems to be Weitz's: the judgment is that X is relevantly similar to paradigm works of art. But any knowledgeable person can take part in such a discussion, and any unknowledgeable person, even an artist, could be wrong. In this regard, the difference between art and science is that scientists are often the only people expert enough to determine whether new scientific practice conforms to acceptable science. Scientists can function as autonomous experts determining science, whereas, because of the very nature of art, the audience, critics, curators, editors, art historians, and theorists play a substantive role in determining the direction of art.

> What a poem means is as much what it means to others as what it means to the author; and indeed, in the course of time a poet may become merely a reader in respect to his own works.
>
> — T. S. Eliot[3]

Cultural Relativism

Some thinkers are not troubled by our possible failure to reach agreement about what counts as art; rather, this agreement is precisely what worries them. They hold that the concept of art is merely conventional — that it is governed by a convention that identifies a group of artifacts favored by the elite of a society. Let me label this view the cultural-relativist position. The sociologist Herbert Gans formulates a relativist position in his book *Popular Culture and High Culture*. Although Gans does not articulate a view about the concept of "art," he does wish to defend popular culture — which includes popular entertainment forms and media not usually counted as art — against those who attack them as inferior to what Gans labels "high culture." We may assume that high culture includes the world of the arts: the world of original paintings in museums, serious literature, classical music, and so on. Popular culture would include magazines, television programs, and popular music, among other things.

Gans argues for the equality of everyone's choice of cultural products, low-brow as well as high-brow. He makes his point this way:

> There are a number of popular cultures, and they as well as high culture are all *taste cultures* which function to entertain, inform, and beautify life, among other things, and which express values and standards of taste and aesthetics. . . . Taste cultures, as I define them, consist of values, the cultural forms which express these values: music, art, design, literature, drama, comedy, poetry, criticism, news, and the media in which these are expressed — books, magazines, newspapers, records, films and television programs, paintings and sculpture, architecture, and insofar as ordinary consumer goods also express aesthetic values or functions, furnishings, clothes, appliances, and automobiles as well.[4]

A relativist might intend to make one of two very different critiques of the concept of art: (1) He or she might claim that every class or "taste public" has its own art, and those art forms and individual works of art traditionally favored in the high European tradition are only expressions of the values of the elite classes, whereas in fact each taste public has comparably substantial art, which has been overlooked because of prejudice. (2) He or she might claim that the values represented by art — for example, originality, artistic freedom, expression, uniqueness, sophistication, knowledge of the history of an art form, affirmation of humanistic ideals — are themselves only the values of the elite classes and that the values represented by art forms and media of popular culture — for example, escapism, mass production and marketing, artistic anonymity, audience dominance — are just as valid. To emphasize a radical relativism, I have characterized the second position in a way that makes it appear unattractive. In a sense, it is simply an attack on art and a proposal to replace it with a different set of cultural values. A full rebuttal of this view, however, would require the development of a theory of art, both to see what is the value of art and also to see whether it is really true that popular culture does not produce art in the traditional sense.

Those who hold the first position argue that we ought to spread our net more broadly when considering what deserves the status of art; we should look at popular cultural forms, not just those forms validated by habit and tradition. One might argue, for example, that rock videos could be the most important art form of the 1980s. This is plausible; but if the relativist goes on to claim that all popular art forms are just as much art as "high" art forms are, then the relativist appears tempted not only by the questionable idea that something is art merely because it is in a certain form (we will examine this idea in Chapter 6) but also by the far more dubious claim

There were, and perhaps still are, people who used to maintain that the word masterpiece was merely the expression of a personal opinion deriving from whim and fashion. This belief seems to me to undermine the whole fabric of human greatness.

— Sir Kenneth Clark[5]

that all forms are equal. It is one thing to claim that a popular movie (for instance, *It's a Wonderful Life*) has more artistic interest than an art film made by a serious artist or that a jazz performance (for example, John Coltrane's *Giant Steps*) is just as profound as a performance of classical music (for instance, Horowitz's performance of a Chopin etude). It is another to claim that Sousa marches, just because they are marches, have equal claim to the label "art" as any symphony, or that comic books, just by virtue of being comic books, are just as much works of art as novels. It is one thing to be open-minded about various media and forms; it is another to insist a priori that all media and forms are of equal worth. But the relativist is tempted to do precisely this.

Because our paradigms of art come from high art, it does not follow that we must embrace the notion that there are special "art media," which only the high arts exemplify, nor that the music, painting, dancing, and decorating of folk or popular art cannot count as art. To ground the meaning of the concept of art in paradigms from the high arts does not require us to *limit* art to the high arts. Indeed, the need to determine whether the traditional elitism that accompanies the notion of "Art" is justified is a strong reason for trying to develop a systematic theory of art. Such a theory may well show that what we value in traditional masterpieces is alive and well in folk or popular arts or in new art media. For example, it is because many people using an intuitive concept of art have recognized the important artistic similarities between photography, jazz, and movies, on the one hand, and artwork in the high art tradition, on the other, that these newer forms have become increasingly accepted as Art. Only with *some* explicit theory of the nature of art can we rationally debate about what is and isn't art.

CRITICISM AND THE SUBJECTIVITY OF ART

Whereas a scientific theory addresses objects, properties, and events in the external world and is judged according to the accuracy with which it describes them, a work of art can be judged only by how it affects its audience or how well it conforms to the artist's inner life. Or so many people think. It seems undeniable that, in the end, a work of art has to please the sensibilities of its audience. As a result, it may appear that the content and quality of a work of art can be judged only on the basis of how it affects people. If this contention is true, criticism would be nearly impossible, for surely our critical evaluations of art need to be objective — yet how could they be, if they are merely about our variable and idiosyncratic inner lives?

> The time has come to give art, by a pitiless method, the precision of the natural sciences. But the principle difficulty for me is still the style, the indefinable Beauty resulting from the conception itself.
> — Gustave Flaubert[6]

As this dilemma illustrates, the problems of criticism are both deep and interesting. On the one hand, criticism is surely both possible and important; on the other hand, as we have just seen, it is extremely difficult to see why it works. I will not attempt to cover the main problems and theories of criticism; the philosophical problems of criticism are difficult enough to require a separate book (see the Suggested Additional Readings for this chapter), and I do not want to bias our discussion about the nature of art by a concern to defend particular theories of criticism. The following discussion is limited to some preliminary clarifications concerning subjectivity and the basis of elementary critical judgments.

To begin, we may divide criticism into three components. Critics — and that includes all of us some of the time — issue *descriptions* of works of art, *interpretations* of works of art, and *evaluations* of the quality of works of art. Of these three activities, description is usually conceived to be objective, at least insofar as it is logically distinct from interpretation. Unfortunately, sometimes it isn't. These examples show that even description of an artwork can be problematic:

- Sometimes even to describe the figures in a painting we must know or guess what the picture is about, what the painter intended to portray.
- It is not always evident what notes really belong in a piece of music. Sometimes scholars argue that the composer really intended to write down different or additional notes.
- The recent cleaning of Michelangelo's frescoes on the Sistine Chapel ceiling has caused a storm of controversy over whether the frescoes really have bold and bright colors (pinks, greens, oranges) or whether the colors were originally somber, covered by a deliberately added haze.

But just to say what notes are in a piece of music, or what figures are in a painting, or what colors are in the Sistine Chapel fresco is to engage in mere description; it is to give an account of the elements, forms, and properties of a piece, an account that everyone can verify in their experience of the piece.

Controversy about criticism really begins with interpretation and evaluation. Most works of art allow multiple interpretations. These interpretations — which say what a work is really about or what it means — go beyond the factual elements of the piece determinable at the level of description; that is, several interpretations are usually compatible with all the facts available from objective descriptions of the work.[7] Those who seek certainty in their beliefs find this situation unacceptable. What makes an interpretation correct or incorrect? We can eliminate some interpretations because they do not fit the objectively determinable features. But of the remaining interpretations we may not be able to select the best one, or we may select it not because it is objectively the best but because it appeals to us or illuminates the work in some way.[8]

The aspect of criticism most often thought to be completely subjective is evaluation. If I judge a work of art as mediocre, and you think it is great, then it *pleased* you more than it did me. You liked it and I didn't, but, as the saying goes, in matters of taste there is no dispute. People who "don't know much about art but know what they like" often invoke this egalitarian position. If we seriously accept this position, however, we must face radical relativistic consequences. Everyone's critical or aesthetic judgments (that is, assertions that an artwork is a good or bad one) would be equally valid. Because nearly every work of art can evoke the full spectrum of positive and negative responses (for instance, some people prefer supermarket novels to the novels of Dostoevsky, or muzak to Beethoven), any estimation about the quality of some artwork — as greater and more worthy of study, preservation, and public praise than another artwork — would be totally irrational.

The great philosopher Immanuel Kant (1724–1804) considered the inconsistency of our beliefs about aesthetic evaluation such a paradox that he labeled it the "antinomy of taste."[11] It is an antinomy because on the one hand we are inclined to view critical judgments as subjective, but on the other hand, we aren't at all prepared to accept the consequences of a universal relativism of taste. Every work would be as good as every other work, a drawing by me just as good as one by Leonardo, if I or someone else likes it as much.

> [Interpretation] is the revenge of the intellect upon the world. To interpret is to impoverish, to deplete the world — in order to set up a shadow world of "meanings."
>
> — Susan Sontag[9]

> Then comes the disgusted comment, "a work of art means anything, everything — that is, nothing — and what is the use of discussing it?" No use whatever if the object of the discussion is to carry a motion by unanimous vote, or to establish a fact as a physicist establishes a formula.
>
> — Alfred Harbage[10]

It is certainly true that descriptions and evaluations of art will never approach the precision of the objective measurements of mathematics and science. Still, as Kant pointed out, our passionate disagreements about our interpretations of art shows that we assume our responses and criticisms, though subjective, have a certain objective validity, that is, that our criticisms have a claim to be correct, to be true descriptions of what the work of art is. It is also true that we believe that some people — for example, the artist — have much more informed responses than others do. This, too, implies that not all opinions are equally valid.

Hume's Solution

About forty years before Kant, the famous Scottish philosopher David Hume (1711–1776) offered one of the most influential solutions to this problem in "Of the Standard of Taste" (see the Readings). Hume realized that our thinking about art is influenced by aesthetic skepticism, as I call it. Hume characterized this as "a species of philosophy, which cuts off all hopes of success" in the attempt to find a *Standard of Taste*; a rule by which the various sentiments of men may be reconciled; at least a decision afforded confirming one sentiment, and condemning another" (p. 19). The skeptic's argument is based on what he claims to be the character of judgments of taste, which, although they appear to be about the external object — for example, that this drink tastes better than that one — are really mere expressions of subjective preferences. As such, they are neither correct nor incorrect. Hume formulates the skeptic's reasoning:

> The difference . . . is very wide between judgment and sentiment. All sentiment is right; because sentiment has a reference to nothing beyond itself, and is always real, wherever a man is conscious of it. But all determinations of the understanding are not right; because they have a reference to something beyond themselves, to wit, real matter of fact; and are not always conformable to that standard. Among a thousand different opinions which different men may entertain of the same subject, there is one, and but one, that is just and true: and the only difficulty is to fix and ascertain it. On the contrary, a thousand different sentiments, excited by the same object are all right; because no sentiment represents what is really in the object. (p. 19)

To the eighteenth-century thinker, the fundamental aesthetic judgment is that something is beautiful. According to Hume, to understand the skeptical position is to realize that it holds that "beauty is no quality in things themselves: it exists merely in the mind which contemplates them; and each mind perceives a different beauty. . . . To seek the real beauty, or real deformity, is as fruitless an inquiry, as to pretend to ascertain the real sweet or real bitter" (p. 19). It's worth noting that such a position supports the radical relativism considered earlier.

Hume finds this consequence absurd: "Whoever would assert an equality of genius and elegance between Ogilby and Milton, or Bunyan and Addison, would be thought to defend no less an extravagance, than if he had maintained a mole-hill to be as high as Teneriffe, or a pond as extensive as the ocean. . . . The principle of the natural equality of tastes . . . appears . . . a palpable absurdity, where objects so disproportioned are compared together" (p. 20). But how are we to account for the fact that some evaluations are much more valid or correct than others unless we treat beauty, and other critical characterizations, as real properties of the objects we are evaluating?

To solve this puzzle along Humean lines we need to distinguish two different concepts of "subjectivity." We need to distinguish these two claims:

1. Our responses to artworks are not about real (objective) characteristics of the artworks.
2. We cannot reach a valid agreement about our responses.

If we think for a moment about the alleged property of beauty, we can understand the relation of these two claims. It is natural to suppose that beauty cannot be a real property of things, because there is such variability and disagreement about what is beautiful; in short, proposition 2 seems to imply proposition 1. This is connected to the view that the real characteristics of the world ought to be such that we can define and measure them so as to make a decisive determination of their presence. If we cannot reach any agreement concerning our responses to a particular situation, then our responses are subjective rather than objective. But the important question is whether (1) implies (2). If we are convinced that X is not an objective property of objects, does it follow that we cannot agree on the presence of X? The short answer is no.

> Although we may disagree about a theory, the impact of a masterpiece is something about which there is an astonishing degree of unanimity.
> — Sir Kenneth Clark[12]

Since the time of the philosopher John Locke, philosophers have distinguished primary qualities from secondary qualities. Primary qualities are objectively determinable properties, such as the weight or shape of an object; subjective properties are sensory qualities, such as colors, sounds, tastes, and so forth. Secondary qualities result from the interaction of our senses with physical causes in the external world, such as light and sound waves. The interesting point about secondary qualities is that they appear to be real properties of objects. In spite of what science tells us, we universally treat our world as if it really is full of color, sound, and so forth. Our ability to do this is predicated on the agreement we can achieve about most secondary qualities. For example, we can define the property of being blue as the property something has of causing a normal observer under standard conditions to say it is blue.

Hume's solution to the subjectivity of aesthetic or critical evaluations amounts to insisting that our inability to agree about such judgments has been overstated. It is the nature of aesthetic preference to allow for different reactions to items that are similar to each other; but it doesn't follow from this that a broad agreement about items of greatly different aesthetic quality is impossible. Hume suggests that rules of composition and other aesthetic canons are ultimately based on "what has been universally found to please in all countries and in all ages," and that our individual abilities to judge what is beautiful are founded upon "the common sentiments of human nature" (p. 20). In short, we can consider beauty as analogous to a secondary quality whose detection is very delicate and subtle. Hume is not claiming that our judgments of aesthetic qualities are about qualities *in* the objects. Nonetheless, we may make valid judgments about objects; when we claim that an artwork has positive aesthetic features, we are claiming that it has a disposition to please others.

> The perception of *why* Shakespeare, or Dante, or Sophocles holds the place he has is something which comes only very slowly in the course of living.
> — T. S. Eliot[13]

Hume explains disagreement about beauty as based on ignorance, prejudice, and so forth. Most people are much more competent to judge everyday secondary qualities than to make the more taxing estimates of artworks. We ignore this fact when we take seriously everyone's opinion, however it was arrived at. Hume draws an analogy with wine tasting: some people are able to taste minute qualities of various substances in wines, whereas others fail to notice. Whose judgments of wine tastes should carry more weight? By analogy, "delicacy of imagination," as Hume calls it, is required to judge art.

Hume, in fact, gives a number of rules to differentiate critics with proper abilities from those who lack such. The goal is to find those best able to discover what is pleasing to human nature. Hume's account rests upon his belief that

> amidst all the variety and caprice of taste, there are certain general principles of approbation or blame, whose influence a careful eye may trace in all operations of the mind. Some particular forms or qualities, from the original structure of the internal fabric are calculated to please, and others to displease; and if they fail of their effect in any particular instance, it is from some apparent defect or imperfection of the organ. . . . If, in the sound state of the organ, there be an entire or a considerable uniformity of sentiment among men, we may thence derive an idea of the perfect beauty. (p. 21)

What seems right about Hume's idea is that our critical judgments clearly have reference beyond ourselves to a more general response. We all know that when we praise or condemn an artwork we are implicitly appealing to the agreements of others. And if Hume's theory may strike us as overoptimistic about the existence of a common human nature and about the resulting nearly universal principles of taste (p. 25), we still can retain the main outlines of his solution. We must be sensitive, knowledgeable, and consistent in our comparisons between artworks of the same kind, and we must apply principles that have generally been found to describe the best, that is, the most pleasing, artworks *within our culture*. Under such conditions, we might not even particularly like something but realize that it is a good or even great artwork of its kind. To issue an evaluation of an artwork is not, on this account, the same as merely saying, "I like it."[14]

READINGS FOR CHAPTER 1

Morris Weitz, "The Role of Theory in Aesthetics"
David Hume, "Of the Standard of Taste"

The Role of Theory in Aesthetics

Morris Weitz

From *The Journal of Aesthetics and Art Criticism.* Vol. XV, no. 1, 1956. Copyright 1956 by The American Society for Aesthetics. Reprinted by permission of the publisher.

Theory has been central in aesthetics and is still the preoccupation of the philosophy of art. Its main avowed concern remains the determination of the nature of art which can be formulated into a definition of it. It construes definition as the statement of the necessary and sufficient properties of what is being defined, where the statement purports to be a true or false claim about the essence of art, what characterizes and distinguishes it from everything else. Each of the great theories of art—Formalism, Voluntarism, Emotionalism, Intellectualism, Intuitionism, Organicism—converges on the attempt to state the defining properties of art. Each claims that it is the true theory because it has formulated correctly into a real definition the nature of art; and that the others are false because they have left out some necessary or sufficient property. Many theorists contend that their enterprise is no mere intellectual exercise but an absolute necessity for any understanding of art and our proper evaluation of it. Unless we know what art is, they say, what are its necessary and sufficient properties, we cannot begin to respond to it adequately or to say why one work is good or better than another. Aesthetic theory, thus, is important not only in itself but for the foundations of both appreciation and criticism. Philosophers, critics, and even artists who have written on art, agree that what is primary in aesthetics is a theory about the nature of art.

Is aesthetic theory, in the sense of a true definition or set of necessary and sufficient properties of art, possible? If nothing else does, the history of aesthetics itself should give one enormous pause here. For, in spite of the many theories, we seem no nearer our goal today than we were in Plato's time. Each age, each art-movement, each philosophy of art, tries over and over again to establish the stated ideal only to be succeeded by a new or revised theory, rooted, at least in part, in the repudiation of preceding ones. Even today, almost everyone interested in aesthetic matters is still deeply wedded to the hope that the correct theory of art is forthcoming. We need only examine the numerous new books on art in which new definitions are proffered; or, in our own country especially, the basic textbooks and anthologies to recognize how strong the priority of a theory of art is.

In this essay I want to plead for the rejection of this problem. I want to show that theory—in the requisite classical sense—is *never* forthcoming in aesthetics, and that we would do much better as philosophers to supplant the question, "What is the nature of art?" by other questions, the answers to which will provide us with all the understanding of the arts there can be. I want to show that the inadequacies of the theories are not primarily occasioned by any legitimate difficulty such e.g., as the vast complexity of art, which might be corrected by further probing and research. Their basic inadequacies reside instead in a fundamental misconception of art. Aesthetic theory—all of it—is wrong in principle in thinking that a correct theory is possible because it

13

radically misconstrues the logic of the concept of art. Its main contention that "art" is amenable to real or any kind of true definition is false. Its attempt to discover the necessary and sufficient properties of art is logically misbegotten for the very simple reason that such a set and, consequently, such a formula about it, is never forthcoming. Art, as the logic of the concept shows, has no set of necessary and sufficient properties, hence a theory of it is logically impossible and not merely factually difficult. Aesthetic theory tries to define what cannot be defined in its requisite sense. But in recommending the repudiation of aesthetic theory I shall not argue from this, as too many others have done, that its logical confusions render it meaningless or worthless. On the contrary, I wish to reassess its role and its contribution primarily in order to show that it is of the greatest importance to our understanding of the arts. . . .

The problem with which we must begin is not "What is art?" but "What sort of concept is 'art'?" Indeed, the root problem of philosophy itself is to explain the relation between the employment of certain kinds of concepts and the conditions under which they can be correctly applied. If I may paraphrase Wittgenstein, we must not ask, What is the nature of any philosophical x? or even, according to the semanticist, What does "x" mean? a transformation that leads to the disastrous interpretation of "art" as a name for some specifiable class of objects; but rather, What is the use or employment of "x"? What does "x" do in the language? This, I take it, is the initial question, the begin-all if not the end-all of any philosophical problem and solution. Thus, in aesthetics, our first problem is the elucidation of the actual employment of the concept of art, to give a logical description of the actual functioning of the concept, including a description of the conditions under which we correctly use it or its correlates.

My model in this type of logical description or philosophy derives from Wittgenstein. It is also he who, in his refutation of philosophical theoriz-

ing in the sense of constructing definitions of philosophical entities, has furnished contemporary aesthetics with a starting point for any future progress. In his new work, *Philosophical Investigations*,[1] Wittgenstein raises as an illustrative question, What is a game? The traditional philosophical, theoretical answer would be in terms of some exhaustive set of properties common to all games. To this Wittgenstein says, let us consider what we call "games": "I mean board-games, card-games, ball-games, Olympic games, and so on. What is common to them all?—Don't say 'there *must* be something common, or they would not be called "games"' but *look and see* whether there is anything common to all. — For if you look at them you will not see something that is common to *all*, but similarities, relationships, and a whole series of them at that. . . ."

Card games are like board games in some respects but not in others. Not all games are amusing, nor is there always winning or losing or competition. Some games resemble others in some respects — that is all. What we find are no necessary and sufficient properties, only "a complicated network of similarities overlapping and crisscrossing," such that we can say of games that they form a family with family resemblances and no common trait. If one asks what a game is, we pick out sample games, describe these, and add, "This and *similar things* are called 'games'." This is all we need to say and indeed all any of us knows about games. Knowing what a game is is not knowing some real definition or theory but being able to recognize and explain games and to decide which among imaginary and new examples would or would not be called "games."

The problem of the nature of art is like that of the nature of games, at least in these respects: If we actually look and see what it is that we call "art," we will also find no common properties — only strands of similarities. Knowing what art is is not apprehending some manifest or latent es-

---

[1] L. Wittgenstein, *Philosophical Investigations* (Oxford, 1953), tr. by E. Anscombe; see esp. Part I, Sections 65–75. All quotations are from these sections.

sence but being able to recognize, describe, and explain those things we call "art" in virtue of these similarities.

But the basic resemblance between these concepts is their open texture. In elucidating them, certain (paradigm) cases can be given, about which there can be no question as to their being correctly described as "art" or "game," but no exhaustive set of cases can be given. I can list some cases and some conditions under which I can apply correctly the concept of art but I cannot list all of them, for the all-important reason that unforeseeable or novel conditions are always forthcoming or envisageable.

A concept is open if its conditions of application are emendable and corrigible; i.e., if a situation or case can be imagined or secured which would call for some sort of *decision* on our part to extend the use of the concept to cover this, or to close the concept and invent a new one to deal with the new case and its new property. If necessary and sufficient conditions for the application of a concept can be stated, the concept is a closed one. But this can happen only in logic or mathematics where concepts are constructed and completely defined. It cannot occur with empirically-descriptive and normative concepts unless we arbitrarily close them by stipulating the ranges of their uses.

I can illustrate this open character of "art" best by examples drawn from its sub-concepts. Consider questions like "Is Dos Passos' *U.S.A.* a novel?" "Is V. Woolf's *To the Lighthouse* a novel?" "Is Joyce's *Finnegan's Wake* a novel?" On the traditional view, these are construed as factual problems to be answered yes or no in accordance with the presence or absence of defining properties. But certainly this is not how any of these questions is answered. Once it arises, as it has many times in the development of the novel from Richardson to Joyce (e.g., "Is Gide's *The School for Wives* a novel or a diary?"), what is at stake is no factual analysis concerning necessary and sufficient properties but a decision as to whether the work under examination is similar in

certain respects to other works, already called "novels," and consequently warrants the extension of the concept to cover the new case. The new work is narrative, fictional, contains character delineation and dialogue but (say) it has no regular time-sequence in the plot or is interspersed with actual newspaper reports. It is like recognized novels, A, B, C . . . , in some respects but not like them in others. But then neither were B and C like A in some respects when it was decided to extend the concept applied to A to B and C. Because work N + 1 (the brand new work) is like A, B, C . . . N in certain respects— has strands of similarity to them—the concept is extended and a new phase of the novel engendered. "Is N 1 a novel?" then, is no factual, but rather a decision problem, where the verdict turns on whether or not we enlarge our set of conditions for applying the concept.

What is true of the novel is, I think, true of every sub-concept of art: "tragedy," "comedy," "painting," "opera," etc., of "art" itself. No "Is X a novel, painting, opera, work of art, etc.?" question allows of a definitive answer in the sense of a factual yes or no report. "Is this *collage* a painting or not?" does not rest on any set of necessary and sufficient properties of painting but on whether we decide—as we did!—to extend "painting" to cover this case.

"Art," itself, is an open concept. New conditions (cases) have constantly arisen and will undoubtedly constantly arise; new art forms, new movements will emerge, which will demand decisions on the part of those interested, usually professional critics, as to whether the concept should be extended or not. Aestheticians may lay down similarity conditions but never necessary and sufficient ones for the correct application of the concept. With "art" its conditions of application can never be exhaustively enumerated since new cases can always be envisaged or created by artists, or even nature, which would call for a decision on someone's part to extend or to close the old or to invent a new concept. (E.g., "It's not a sculpture, it's a mobile.")

What I am arguing, then, is that the very expansive, adventurous character of art, its ever-present changes and novel creations, makes it logically impossible to ensure any set of defining properties. We can, of course, choose to close the concept. But to do this with "art" or "tragedy" or "portraiture," etc., is ludicrous since it forecloses on the very conditions of creativity in the arts. . . .

The primary task of aesthetics is not to seek a theory but to elucidate the concept of art. Specifically, it is to describe the conditions under which we employ the concept correctly. Definition, reconstruction, patterns of analysis are out of place here since they distort and add nothing to our understanding of art. What, then, is the logic of "X is a work of art"?

As we actually use the concept, "Art" is both descriptive (like "chair") and evaluative (like "good"); i.e., we sometimes say, "This is a work of art," to describe something and we sometimes say it to evaluate something. Neither use surprises anyone.

What, first, is the logic of "X is a work of art," when it is a descriptive utterance? What are the conditions under which we would be making such an utterance correctly? There are no necessary and sufficient conditions but there are the strands of similarity conditions, i.e., bundles of properties, none of which need be present but most of which are, when we describe things as works of art. I shall call these the "criteria of recognition" of works of art. All of these have served as the defining criteria of the individual traditional theories of art; so we are already familiar with them. Thus, mostly, when we describe something as a work of art, we do so under the conditions of there being present some sort of artifact, made by human skill, ingenuity, and imagination, which embodies in its sensuous, public medium—stone, wood, sounds, words, etc.—certain distinguishable elements and relations. Special theorists would add conditions like satisfaction of wishes, objectification or expression of emotion, some act of empathy, and so on; but these latter conditions seem to be quite adventitious, present to some but not to other spectators when things are described as works of art. "X is a work of art and contains *no* emotion, expression, act of empathy, satisfaction, etc.," is perfectly good sense and may frequently be true. "X is a work of art and . . . was made by no one," or . . . "exists only in the mind and not in any publicly observable thing," or . . . "was made by accident when he spilled the paint on the canvas," in each case of which a normal condition is denied, are also sensible and capable of being true in certain circumstances. None of the criteria of recognition is a defining one, either necessary or sufficient, because we can sometimes assert of something that it is a work of art and go on to deny any one of these conditions, even the one which has traditionally been taken to be basic, namely, that of being an artifact: Consider, "This piece of driftwood is a lovely piece of sculpture." Thus, to say of anything that it is a work of art is to commit oneself to the presence of *some* of these conditions. One would scarcely describe X as a work of art if X were not an artifact, or a collection of elements sensuously presented in a medium, or a product of human skill, and so on. If none of the conditions were present, if there were no criteria present for recognizing something as a work of art, we would not describe it as one. But, even so, no one of these or any collection of them is either necessary or sufficient.

The elucidation of the descriptive use of "Art" creates little difficulty. But the elucidation of the evaluative use does. For many, especially theorists, "This is a work of art" does more than describe; it also praises. Its conditions of utterance, therefore, include certain preferred properties or characteristics of art. I shall call these "criteria of evaluation." Consider a typical example of this evaluative use, the view according to which to say of something that it is a work of art is to imply that it is a *successful* harmonization of elements. Many of the honorific definitions of art and its sub-concepts are of this form. What is at stake here is that "Art" is construed as an evaluative term which is either identified with its criterion or justified in terms of it. "Art" is defined in terms of its evaluative property, e.g., successful harmonization. On such a view, to say "X is a work of art" is (1) to say something which is taken to *mean* "X is a successful harmonization" (e.g., "Art *is* significant form") or (2) to say something praiseworthy *on the basis* of its successful harmonization. Theorists are never clear whether it is (1) or (2) which is being put forward. Most of them, concerned as they are with this evaluative use, formulate (2), i.e., that feature of art that *makes* it art in the praise-sense, and then go on to state (1), i.e., the definition of "Art" in terms of its art-making feature. And this is clearly to confuse the conditions under which we say something evaluatively with the meaning of what we say. "This is a work of art," said evaluatively, cannot mean "This is a successful harmonization of elements"—except by stipulation—but at most is said in virtue of the art-making property, which is taken as a (the) criterion of "Art," when "Art" is employed to assess. "This is a work of art," used evaluatively, serves to praise and not to affirm the reason why it is said.

The evaluative use of "Art," although distinct from the conditions of its use, relates in a very intimate way to these conditions. For, in every instance of "This is a work of art" (used to praise), what happens is that the criterion of evaluation (e.g., successful harmonization) for the employment of the concept of art is converted into a criterion of recognition. This is why, on its evaluative use, "This is a work of art" implies "This has P," where "P" is some chosen artmarking property. Thus, if one chooses to employ "Art" evaluatively, as many do, so that "This is a work of art and not (aesthetically) good" makes no sense, he uses "Art" in such a way that he refuses to *call* anything a work of art unless it embodies his criterion of excellence.

There is nothing wrong with the evaluative use; in fact, there is good reason for using "Art" to praise. But what cannot be maintained is that theories of the evaluative use of "Art" are true and real definitions of the necessary and sufficient properties of art. Instead they are honorific definitions, pure and simple, in which "Art" has been redefined in terms of chosen criteria.

But what makes them—these honorific definitions—so supremely valuable is not their disguised linguistic recommendations; rather it is the *debates* over the reasons for changing the criteria of the concept of art which are built into the definitions. In each of the great theories of art, whether correctly understood as honorific definitions or incorrectly accepted as real definitions, what is of the utmost importance are the reasons proffered in the argument for the respective theory, that is, the reasons given for the chosen or preferred criterion of excellence and evaluation. It is this perennial debate over these criteria of evaluation which makes the history of aesthetic theory the important study it is. The value of each of the theories resides in its attempt to state and to justify certain criteria which are either neglected or distorted by previous theories. Look at the Bell-Fry theory again. Of course, "Art is significant form" cannot be accepted as a true, real definition of art; and most certainly it actually functions in their aesthetics as a redefinition of art in terms of the chosen condition of significant form. But what gives it its aesthetic importance is what lies behind the formula: In an age in which literary and representational elements have become paramount in painting, *return* to the plastic ones since these are indigenous to painting. Thus, the role of the theory is not to define anything but to use the definitional form, almost epigrammatically, to pinpoint a crucial recommendation to turn our attention once again to the plastic elements in painting.

Once we, as philosophers, understand this distinction between the formula and what lies behind it, it behooves us to deal generously with the traditional theories of art; because incorporated in every one of them is a debate over and argument for emphasizing or centering upon some particular feature of art which has been neglected or perverted. If we take the aesthetic theories literally, as we have seen, they all fail; but if we reconstrue them, in terms of their function and point, as serious and argued-for recommendations to concentrate on certain criteria of excellence in art, we shall see that aesthetic theory is far from worthless. Indeed, it becomes as central as anything in aesthetics, in our understanding of art, for it teaches us what to look for and how to look at it in art. What is central and must be articulated in all the theories are their debates over the reasons for excellence in art — debates over emotional depth, profound truths, natural beauty, exactitude, freshness of treatment, and so on, as criteria of evaluation — the whole of which converges on the perennial problem of what makes a work of art good. To understand the role of aesthetic theory is not to conceive it as definition, logically doomed to failure, but to read it as summaries of seriously made recommendations to attend in certain ways to certain features of art.

Of the Standard of Taste

David Hume

The great variety of Taste, as well as of opinion, which prevails in the world, is too obvious not to have fallen under every one's observation. Men of the most confined knowledge are able to remark a difference of taste in the narrow circle of their acquaintance, even where the persons have been educated under the same government, and have early imbibed the same prejudices. But those who can enlarge their view to contemplate distant nations and remote ages, are still more surprised at the great inconsistence and contrariety. We are apt to call *barbarous* whatever departs widely from our own taste and apprehension; but soon find the epithet of reproach retorted on us. And the highest arrogance and self-conceit is at last startled, on observing an equal assurance on all sides, and scruples, amidst such a contest of sentiment, to pronounce positively in its own favor.

As this variety of taste is obvious to the most careless inquirer, so will it be found, on examination, to be still greater in reality than in appearance. The sentiments of men often differ with regard to beauty and deformity of all kinds, even while their general discourse is the same. There are certain terms in every language which import blame, and others praise; and all men who use the same tongue must agree in their application of them. Every voice is united in applauding elegance, propriety, simplicity, spirit in writing; and in blaming fustian, affectation, coldness, and a false brilliancy. But when critics come to particulars, this seeming unanimity vanishes; and it is found, that they had affixed a very different meaning to their expressions. In all matters of opinion and science, the case is opposite; the difference among men is there oftener found to lie in generals than in particulars, and to be less in reality than in appearance. An explanation of the terms commonly ends the controversy: and the disputants are surprised to find that they had been quarrelling, while at bottom they agreed in their judgment. . . .

It is natural for us to seek a *Standard of Taste*; a rule by which the various sentiments of men may be reconciled; at least a decision afforded confirming one sentiment, and condemning another.

There is a species of philosophy, which cuts off all hopes of success in such an attempt, and represents the impossibility of ever attaining any standard of taste. The difference, it is said, is very wide between judgment and sentiment. All sentiment is right; because sentiment has a reference to nothing beyond itself, and is always real, wherever a man is conscious of it. But all determinations of the understanding are not right; because they have a reference to something beyond themselves, to wit, real matter of fact; and are not always conformable to that standard. Among a thousand different opinions which different men may entertain of the same subject, there is one, and but one, that is just and true: and the only difficulty is to fix and ascertain it. On the contrary, a thousand different sentiments, excited by the same object, are all right; because no sentiment represents what is really in the object. It only marks a certain conformity or relation between the object and the organs or faculties of the mind; and if that conformity did not really exist, the sentiment could never possibly have being. Beauty is no quality in things themselves: it exists merely in the mind which contemplates them; and each mind perceives a different beauty. One person may even perceive deformity, where another is sensible of beauty; and every individual ought to acquiesce in his own sentiment, without pretending to regulate those of others. To seek the real beauty, or real deformity, is as fruitless an inquiry, as to pretend to ascertain the real sweet or real bitter. According to the disposition of the organs, the same object may be both sweet and bitter; and the proverb has justly determined it to be fruitless to dispute concerning tastes. It is very natural, and even quite necessary, to extend this axiom to mental, as well as bodily taste; and thus common sense, which is so often at variance with philosophy, especially with the sceptical kind, is found, in one instance at least, to agree in pronouncing the same decision.

But though this axiom, by passing into a proverb, seems to have attained the sanction of common sense; there is certainly a species of common sense, which opposes it, at least serves to modify and restrain it. Whoever would assert an equality of genius and elegence between Ogilby and Milton, or Bunyan and Addison, would be thought to defend no less an extravagance, than if he had maintained a mole-hill to be as high as Teneriffe, or a pond as extensive as the ocean. Though there may be found persons, who give the preference to the former authors; no one pays attention to such a taste; and we pronounce, without scruple, the sentiment of these pretended critics to be absurd and ridiculous. The principle of the natural equality of tastes is then totally forgot, and while we admit it on some occasions, where the objects seem near an equality, it appears an extravagant paradox, or rather a palpable absurdity, where objects so disproportioned are compared together.

It is evident that none of the rules of composition are fixed by reasonings *à priori*, or can be esteemed abstract conclusions of the understanding, from comparing those habitudes and relations of ideas, which are eternal and immutable. Their foundation is the same with that of all the practical sciences, experience; nor are they any thing but general observations, concerning what has been universally found to please in all countries and in all ages. Many of the beauties of poetry, and even of eloquence, are founded on falsehood and fiction, on hyperboles, metaphors, and an abuse or perversion of terms from their natural meaning. To check the sallies of the imagination, and to reduce every expression to geometrical truth and exactness, would be the most contrary to the laws of criticism; because it would produce a work, which, by universal experience, has been found the most insipid and disagreeable. But though poetry can never submit to exact truth, it must be confined by rules of art, discovered to the author either by genius or observation. If some negligent or irregular writers have pleased, they have not pleased by their transgressions of rule or order, but in spite of these transgressions: they have possessed other beauties, which were conformable to just criticism; and the force of these beauties has been able to overpower censure, and give the mind a satisfaction superior to the disgust arising from the blemishes. Ariosto pleases; but not by his monstrous and improbable fictions, by his bizarre mixture of the serious and comic styles, by the want of coherence in his stories, or by the continual interruptions of his narration. He charms by the force and clearness of his expression, by the readiness and variety of his inventions, and by his natural pictures of the passions, especially those of the gay and amorous kind: and, however his faults may diminish our satisfaction, they are not able entirely to destroy it. Did our pleasure really arise from those parts of his poem, which we denominate faults, this would be no objection to criticism in general: it would only be an objection to those particular rules of criticism, which would establish such circumstances to be faults, and would represent them as universally blamable. If they are found to please, they cannot be faults, let the pleasure which they produce be ever so unexpected and unaccountable.

But though all the general rules of art are founded only on experience, and on the observation of the common sentiments of human nature, we must not imagine, that, on every occasion, the feelings of men will be conformable to these rules. Those finer emotions of the mind are of a very tender and delicate nature, and require the concurrence of many favorable circumstances to make them play with facility and exactness, according to their general and established principles. The least exterior hinderance to such small springs, or the least internal disorder, disturbs their motion, and confounds the operations of the whole machine. When we would make an experiment of this nature, and would try the force of any beauty or deformity, we must choose with care a proper time and place, and bring the fancy to a suitable situation and disposition. A perfect serenity of mind, a recollection of thought, a due attention to the object; if any of these circumstances be wanting, our experiment will be fallacious, and we shall be unable to judge of the catholic and universal beauty. The relation, which nature has placed between the form and the sentiment, will at least be more obscure; and it will require greater accuracy to trace and discern it. We shall be able to ascertain its influence, not so much from the operation of each particular beauty, as from the durable admiration which attends those works that have survived all the caprices of mode and fashion, all the mistakes of ignorance and envy.

The same Homer who pleased at Athens and Rome two thousand years ago, is still admired at Paris and at London. All the changes of climate, government, religion, and language, have not been able to obscure his glory. Authority or prejudice may give a temporary vogue to a bad poet or orator; but his reputation will never be durable or general. When his compositions are examined by posterity or by foreigners, the enchantment is dissipated, and his faults appear in their true colors. On the contrary, a real genius, the longer his works endure, and the more wide they are spread, the more sincere is the admiration which he meets with. Envy and jealousy have too much place in a narrow circle; and even familiar acquaintance with his person may diminish the applause due to his performances: but when these obstructions are removed, the beauties, which are naturally fitted to excite agreeable sentiments, immediately display their energy; and while the world endures, they maintain their authority over the minds of men.

It appears, then, that amidst all the variety and caprice of taste, there are certain general principles of approbation or blame, whose influence a careful eye may trace in all operations of the mind. Some particular forms or qualities, from the original structure of the internal fabric are calculated to please, and others to displease; and if they fail of their effect in any particular instance, it is from some apparent defect or imperfection in the organ. A man in a fever would not insist on his palate as able to decide concerning flavors; nor would one affected with the jaundice pretend to give a verdict with regard to colors. In each creature there is a sound and a defective state; and the former alone can be supposed to afford us a true standard of taste and sentiment. If, in the sound state of the organ, there be an entire or a considerable uniformity of sentiment among men, we may thence derive an idea of the perfect beauty; in like manner as the appearance of objects in daylight, to the eye of a man in health, is denominated their true and real color, even while color is allowed to be merely a phantasm of the senses.

Many and frequent are the defects in the internal organs, which prevent or weaken the influence of those general principles, on which depends our sentiment of beauty or deformity. Though some objects, by the structure of the mind, be naturally calculated to give pleasure, it is not to be expected that in every individual the pleasure will be equally felt. Particular incidents and situations occur, which either throw a false light on the objects, or hinder the true from conveying to the imagination the proper sentiment and perception.

One obvious cause why many feel not the proper sentiment of beauty, is the want of that *delicacy* of imagination which is requisite to convey a sensibility of those finer emotions. This delicacy every one pretends to: every one talks of it; and would reduce every kind of taste or sentiment to its standard. But as our intention in this Essay is to mingle some light of the understanding with the feelings of sentiment, it will be proper to give a more accurate definition of delicacy than has hitherto been attempted. And not to draw our philosophy from too profound a source, we shall have recourse to a noted story in Don Quixote.

It is with good reason, says Sancho to the squire with the great nose, that I pretend to have a judgment in wine: this is a quality hereditary in our family. Two of my kinsmen were once called to give their opinion of a hogshead, which was supposed to be excellent, being old and of a good vintage. One of them tastes it, considers it; and, after mature reflection, pronounces the wine to be good, were it not for a small taste of leather which he perceived in it. The other, after using the same precautions, gives also his verdict in favor of the wine; but with the reserve of a taste of iron, which he could easily distinguish. You cannot imagine how much they were both ridiculed for their judgment. But who laughed in the end? On emptying the hogshead, there was found at the bottom an old key with a leathern thong tied to it.

The great resemblance between mental and bodily taste will easily teach us to apply this story. Though it be certain that beauty and deformity, more than sweet and bitter, are not qualities in objects, but belong entirely to the sentiment, internal or external, it must be allowed, that there are certain qualities in objects which are fitted by nature to produce those particular feelings. Now, as these qualities may be found in a small degree, or may be mixed and confounded with each other, it often happens that the taste is not affected with such minute qualities, or is not able to distinguish all the particular flavors, amidst the disorder in which they are presented. Where the organs are so fine as to allow nothing to escape them, and at the same time so exact as to perceive every ingredient in the composition, this we call delicacy of taste, whether we employ these terms in the literal or metaphorical sense. Here then the general rules of beauty are of use, being drawn from established models, and from the observation of what pleases or displeases, when presented singly and in a high degree; and if the same qualities, in a continued composition, and in a smaller degree, affect not the organs with a sensible delight or uneasiness, we exclude the person from all pretensions to this delicacy. To produce

these general rules or avowed patterns of composition, is like finding the key with the leathern thong, which justified the verdict of Sancho's kinsmen, and confounded those pretended judges who had condemned them. Though the hogshead had never been emptied, the taste of the one was still equally delicate, and that of the other equally dull and languid; but it would have been more difficult to have proved the superiority of the former, to the conviction of every bystander. In like manner, though the beauties of writing had never been methodized, or reduced to general principles; though no excellent models had ever been acknowledged, the different degrees of taste would still have subsisted, and the judgment of one man been preferable to that of another; but it would not have been so easy to silence the bad critic, who might always insist upon his particular sentiment, and refuse to submit to his antagonist. But when we show him an avowed principle of art; when we illustrate this principle by examples, whose operation, from his own particular taste, he acknowledges to be conformable to the principle; when we prove that the same principle may be applied to the present case, where he did not perceive or feel its influence: he must conclude, upon the whole, that the fault lies in himself, and that he wants the delicacy which is requisite to make him sensible of every beauty and every blemish in any composition or discourse.

It is acknowledged to be the perfection of every sense or faculty, to perceive with exactness its most minute objects, and allow nothing to escape its notice and observation. The smaller the objects are which become sensible to the eye, the finer is that organ, and the more elaborate its make and composition. A good palate is not tried by strong flavor, but by a mixture of small ingredients, where we are still sensible of each part, notwithstanding its minuteness and its confusion with the rest. In like manner, a quick and acute perception of beauty and deformity must be the perfection of our mental taste; nor can a man be satisfied with himself while he suspects that any excellence or blemish in a discourse has passed him unobserved. In this case, the perfection of the man, and the perfection of the sense of feeling, are found to be united. A very delicate palate, on many occasions, may be a great inconvenience both to a man himself and to his friends. But a delicate taste of wit or beauty must always be a desirable quality, because it is the source of all the finest and most innocent enjoyments of which human nature is susceptible. In this decision the sentiments of all mankind are agreed. Wherever you can ascertain a delicacy of taste, it is sure to meet with approbation; and the best way of ascertaining it is, to appeal to those models and principles which have been established by the uniform consent and experience of nations and ages.

But though there be naturally a wide difference, in point of delicacy, between one person and another, nothing tends further to increase and improve this talent, than *practice* in a particular art, and frequent survey or contemplation of a particular species of beauty. When objects of any kind are first presented to the eye or imagination, the sentiment which attends them is obscure and confused; and the mind is, in a great measure, incapable of pronouncing concerning their merits or defects. The taste cannot perceive the several excellences of the performance, much less distinguish the particular character of each excellency, and ascertain its quality and degree. If it pronounce the whole in general to be beautiful or deformed, it is the utmost that can be expected; and even this judgment, a person so unpractised will be apt to deliver with great hesitation and reserve. But allow him to acquire experience in those objects, his feeling becomes more exact and nice: he not only perceives the beauties and defects of each part, but marks the distinguishing species of each quality, and assigns it suitable praise or blame. A clear and distinct sentiment attends him through the whole survey of the objects; and he discerns that very degree and kind of approbation or displeasure which each part is naturally fitted to produce. The mist dissipates which seemed formerly to hang over the object; the organ acquires greater perfection in its operations, and can pronounce, without danger of mistake, concerning the merits of every performance.

In a word, the same address and dexterity which practice gives to the execution of any work, is also acquired by the same means in the judging of it.

So advantageous is practice to the discernment of beauty, that, before we can give judgment on any work of importance, it will even be requisite that that very individual performance be more than once perused by us, and be surveyed in different lights with attention and deliberation. There is a flutter or hurry of thought which attends the first perusal of any piece, and which confounds the genuine sentiment of beauty. The relation of the parts is not discerned: the true characters of style are little distinguished. The several perfections and defects seem wrapped up in a species of confusion, and present themselves indistinctly to the imagination. Not to mention, that there is a species of beauty, which, as it is florid and superficial, pleases at first; but being found incompatible with a just expression either of reason or passion, soon palls upon the taste, and is then rejected with disdain, at least rated at a much lower value.

It is impossible to continue in the practice of contemplating any order of beauty, without being frequently obliged to form *comparisons* between the several species and degrees of excellence, and estimating their proportion to each other. A man who has had no opportunity of comparing the different kinds of beauty, is indeed totally unqualified to pronounce an opinion with regard to any object presented to him. By comparison alone we fix the epithets of praise or blame, and learn how to assign the due degree of each. The coarsest daubing contains a certain lustre of colors and exactness of imitation, which are so far beauties, and would affect the mind of a peasant or Indian with the highest admiration. The most vulgar ballads are not entirely destitute of harmony or nature; and none but a person familiarized to superior beauties would pronounce their members harsh, or narration uninteresting. A great inferiority of beauty gives pain to a person conversant in the highest excellence of the kind, and is for that reason pronounced a deformity; as the most finished object with which we are acquainted is naturally supposed to have reached the pinnacle of perfection, and to be entitled to the highest applause. One accustomed to see, and examine, and weigh the several performances, admired in different ages and nations, can alone rate the merits of a work exhibited to his view, and assign its proper rank among the productions of genius.

But to enable a critic the more fully to execute this undertaking, he must preserve his mind free from all *prejudice*, and allow nothing to enter into his consideration, but the very object which is submitted to his examination. We may observe, that every work of art, in order to produce its due effect on the mind, must be surveyed in a certain point of view, and cannot be fully relished by persons whose situation, real or imaginary, is not conformable to that which is required by the performance. An orator addresses himself to a particular audience, and must have a regard to their particular genius, interests, opinions, passions, and prejudices; otherwise he hopes in vain to govern their resolutions, and inflame their affections. Should they even have entertained some prepossessions against him, however unreasonable, he must not overlook this disadvantage; but, before he enters upon the subject, must endeavor to conciliate their affection, and acquire their good graces. A critic of a different age or nation, who should peruse this discourse, must have all these circumstances in his eye, and must place himself in the same situation as the audience, in order to form a true judgment of the oration. In like manner, when any work is addressed to the public, though I should have a friendship or enmity with the author, I must depart from this situation, and, considering myself as a man in general, forget, if possible, my individual being, and my peculiar circumstances. A person influenced by prejudice complies not with this condition, but obstinately maintains his natural position, without placing himself in that point of view which the performance supposes. If the work be addressed to persons of a different age or nation, he makes no allowance for their peculiar views and prejudices; but, full of the manners of his own age and country, rashly condemns what seemed admirable in the eyes of those for whom alone the discourse was calculated. If the work be executed for the public, he never sufficiently enlarges his comprehension, or forgets his interest as a friend or enemy, as a rival or commentator. By this means his sentiments are perverted; nor have the same beauties and blemishes the same influence upon him, as if he had imposed a proper violence on his imagination, and had forgotten himself for a moment. So far his taste evidently departs from the true standard, and of consequence loses all credit and authority.

It is well known, that, in all questions submitted to the understanding, prejudice is destructive of sound judgment, and perverts all operations of the intellectual faculties: it is no less contrary to good taste; nor has it less influence to corrupt our sentiment of beauty. It belongs to *good sense* to check its influence in both cases; and in this respect, as well as in many others, reason, if not an essential part of taste, is at least requisite to the operations of this latter faculty. In all the nobler productions of genius, there is a mutual relation and correspondence of parts; nor can either the beauties or blemishes be perceived by him whose thought is not capacious enough to comprehend all those parts, and compare them with each other, in order to perceive the consistence and uniformity of the whole. Every work of art has also a certain end or purpose for which it is calculated; and is to be deemed more or less perfect, as it is more or less fitted to attain this end. The object of eloquence is to persuade, of history to instruct, of poetry to please, by means of the passions and the imagination. These ends we must carry constantly in our view when we peruse any performance; and we must be able to judge how far the means employed are adapted to their respective purposes. Besides, every kind of composition, even the most poetical, is nothing but a chain of propositions and reasonings; not always, indeed, the justest and most exact, but still plausible and specious, however disguised by the coloring of the imagination. The persons introduced in tragedy and epic poetry must be represented as reasoning, and thinking, and concluding, and acting, suitably to their character and circumstances; and without judgment, as well as taste and invention, a poet can never hope to succeed in so delicate an undertaking. Not to mention, that the same excellence of faculties which contributes to the improvement of reason, the same clearness of conception, the same exactness of distinction, the same vivacity of apprehension, are essential to the operations of true taste, and are its infallible concomitants. It seldom or never happens, that a man of sense, who has experience in any art, cannot judge of its beauty; and it is no less rare to meet with a man who has a just taste without a sound understanding.

Thus, though the principles of taste be universal, and nearly, if not entirely, the same in all men; yet few are qualified to give judgment on any work of art, or establish their own sentiment as the standard of beauty. The organs of internal sensation are seldom so perfect as to allow the general principles their full play, and produce a feeling correspondent to those principles. They either labor under some defect, or are vitiated by some disorder; and by that means excite a sentiment, which may be pronounced erroneous. When the critic has no delicacy, he judges without any distinction, and is only affected by the grosser and more palpable qualities of the object: the finer touches pass unnoticed and disregarded. Where he is not aided by practice, his verdict is attended with confusion and hesitation. Where no comparison has been employed, the most frivolous beauties, such as rather merit the name of defects, are the object of his admiration. Where he lies under the influence of prejudice, all his natural sentiments are perverted. Where good sense is wanting, he is not qualified to discern the beauties of design and reasoning, which are the highest and most excellent. Under some or other of these imperfections, the generality of men labor; and hence a true judge in the finer arts is observed, even during the most polished ages, to be so rare a character: strong sense, united to delicate sentiment, improved by practice, perfected by comparison, and cleared of all prejudice, can alone entitle critics to this valuable character; and the joint verdict of such, wherever they are to be found, is the true standard of taste and beauty.

But where are such critics to be found? By what marks are they to be known? How distinguish them from pretenders? These questions are embarrassing; and seem to throw us back into the same uncertainty from which, during the course of this Essay, we have endeavored to extricate ourselves.

But if we consider the matter aright, these are questions of fact, not of sentiment. Whether any particular person be endowed with good sense and a delicate imagination, free from prejudice, may often be the subject of dispute, and be liable to great discussion and inquiry: but that such a character is valuable and estimable, will be agreed in by all mankind. Where these doubts occur, men can do no more than in other disputable questions which are submitted to the understanding: they must produce the best arguments that their invention suggests to them; they must acknowledge a true and decisive standard to exist somewhere, to wit, real existence and matter of fact; and they must have indulgence to such as differ from them in their appeals to this standard. It is sufficient for our present purpose, if we have proved, that the taste of all individuals is not upon an equal footing, and that some men in general, however difficult to be particularly pitched upon, will be acknowledged by universal sentiment to have a preference above others.

But, in reality, the difficulty of finding, even in particulars, the standard of taste, is not so great as it is represented. Though in speculation we may readily avow a certain criterion in science, and deny it in sentiment, the matter is found in practice to be much more hard to ascertain in the former case than in the latter. Theories of abstract philosophy, systems of profound theology, have prevailed during one age: in a successive period these have been universally exploded: their absurdity has been detected: other theories and systems have supplied their place, which again gave place to their successors: and nothing has been experienced more liable to the revolutions of chance and fashion than these pretended decisions of science. The case is not the same with the beauties of eloquence and poetry. Just expressions of passion and nature are sure, after a little time, to gain public applause, which they maintain for ever. Aristotle, and Plato, and Epicurus, and Descartes, may successively yield to each other: but Terence and Virgil maintain an universal, undisputed empire over the minds of men. The abstract philosophy of Cicero has lost its credit: the vehemence of his oratory is still the object of our admiration.

Though men of delicate taste be rare, they are easily to be distinguished in society by the soundness of their understanding, and the superiority of their faculties above the rest of mankind. The ascendant, which they acquire, gives a prevalence to that lively approbation with which they receive any productions of genius, and renders it generally predominant. Many men, when left to themselves, have but a faint and dubious perception of beauty, who yet are capable of relishing any fine stroke which is pointed out to them. Every convert to the admiration of the real poet or orator, is the cause of some new conversion. And though prejudices may prevail for a time, they never unite in celebrating any rival to the true genius, but yield at last to the force of nature and just sentiment. Thus, though a civilized nation may easily be mistaken in the choice of their admired philosopher, they never have been found long to err, in their affection for a favorite epic or tragic author.

But notwithstanding all our endeavors to fix a standard of taste, and reconcile the discordant apprehensions of men, there still remain two sources of variation, which are not sufficient indeed to confound all the boundaries of beauty and deformity, but will often serve to produce a difference in the degrees of our approbation or blame. The one is the different humors of particular men; the other, the particular manners and opinions of our age and country. The general principles of taste are uniform in human nature: where men vary in their judgments, some defect or perversion in the faculties may commonly be remarked; proceeding either from prejudice, from want of practice, or want of delicacy: and there is just reason for approving one taste, and condemning another. But where there is such a diversity in the internal frame or external situation as is entirely blameless on both sides, and

leaves no room to give one the preference above the other; in that case a certain degree of diversity in judgment is unavoidable, and we seek in vain for a standard, by which we can reconcile the contrary sentiments.

A young man, whose passions are warm, will be more sensibly touched with amorous and tender images, than a man more advanced in years, who takes pleasure in wise, philosophical reflections, concerning the conduct of life, and moderation of the passions. At twenty, Ovid may be the favorite author, Horace at forty, and perhaps Tacitus at fifty. Vainly would we, in such cases, endeavor to enter into the sentiments of others, and divest ourselves of those propensities which are natural to us. We choose our favorite author as we do our friend, from a conformity of humor and disposition. Mirth or passion, sentiment or reflection; whichever of these most predominates in our temper, it gives us a peculiar sympathy with the writer who resembles us.

One person is more pleased with the sublime, another with the tender, a third with raillery. One has a strong sensibility to blemishes, and is extremely studious of correctness; another has a more lively feeling of beauties, and pardons twenty absurdities and defects for one elevated or pathetic stroke. The ear of this man is entirely turned towards conciseness and energy; that man is delighted with a copious, rich, and harmonious expression. Simplicity is affected by one; ornament by another. Comedy, tragedy, satire, odes, have each its partisans, who prefer that particular species of writing to all others. It is plainly an error in a critic, to confine his approbation to one species or style of writing, and condemn all the rest. But it is almost impossible not to feel a predilection for that which suits our particular turn and disposition. Such performances are innocent and unavoidable, and can never reasonably be the object of dispute, because there is no standard by which they can be decided.

For a like reason, we are more pleased, in the course of our reading, with pictures and characters that resemble objects which are found in our own age and country, than with those which describe a different set of customs. It is not without some effort that we reconcile ourselves to the simplicity of ancient manners, and behold princesses carrying water from the spring, and kings and heroes dressing their own victuals. We may allow in general, that the representation of such manners is no fault in the author, nor deformity in the piece; but we are not so sensibly touched with them. For this reason, comedy is not easily transferred from one age or nation to another. A Frenchman or Englishman is not pleased with the *Andria* of Terence, or *Clitia* of Machiavel; where the fine lady, upon whom all the play turns, never once appears to the spectators, but is always kept behind the scenes, suitably to the reserved humor of the ancient Greeks and modern Italians. A man of learning and reflection can make allowance for these peculiarities of manners; but a common audience can never divest themselves so far of their usual ideas and sentiments, as to relish pictures which nowise resemble them.

But here there occurs a reflection, which may, perhaps, be useful in examining the celebrated controversy concerning ancient and modern learning; where we often find the one side excusing any seeming absurdity in the ancients from the manners of the age, and the other refusing to admit this excuse, or at least admitting it only as an apology for the author, not for the performance. In my opinion, the proper boundaries in this subject have seldom been fixed between the contending parties. Where any innocent peculiarities of manners are represented, such as those above mentioned, they ought certainly to be admitted; and a man who is shocked with them, gives an evident proof of false delicacy and refinement. The poet's *monument more durable than brass*, must fall to the ground like common brick or clay, were men to make no allowance for the continual revolutions of manners and customs, and would admit of nothing but what was suitable to the prevailing fashion. Must we throw aside the pictures of our ancestors, because of their ruffs and farthingales? But where the ideas of morality and decency alter from one age to another, and where vicious manners are de-

scribed, without being marked with the proper characters of blame and disapprobation, this must be allowed to disfigure the poem, and to be a real deformity. I cannot, nor is it proper I should, enter into such sentiments; and however I may excuse the poet, on account of the manners of his age, I can never relish the composition. The want of humanity and of decency, so conspicuous in the characters drawn by several of the ancient poets, even sometimes by Homer and the Greek tragedians, diminishes considerably the merit of their noble performances, and gives modern authors an advantage over them. We are not interested in the fortunes and sentiments of such rough heroes; we are displeased to find the limits of vice and virtue so much confounded; and whatever indulgence we may give to the writer on account of his prejudices, we cannot prevail on ourselves to enter into his sentiments, or bear an affection to characters which we plainly discover to be blamable.

The case is not the same with moral principles as with speculative opinions of any kind. These are in continual flux and revolution. The son embraces a different system from the father. Nay, there scarcely is any man, who can boast of great constancy and uniformity in this particular. Whatever speculative errors may be found in the polite writings of any age or country, they detract but little from the value of those compositions. There needs but a certain turn of thought or imagination to make us enter into all the opinions which then prevailed, and relish the sentiments or conclusions derived from them. But a very violent effort is requisite to change our judgment of manners, and excite sentiments of approbation or blame, love or hatred, different from those to which the mind, from long custom, has been familiarized. And where a man is confident of the rectitude of that moral standard by which he judges, he is justly jealous of it, and will not pervert the sentiments of his heart for a moment, in complaisance to any writer whatsoever.

Of all speculative errors, those which regard religion are the most excusable in compositions of genius; nor is it ever permitted to judge of the civility or wisdom of any people, or even of single persons, by the grossness or refinement of their theological principles. The same good sense that directs men in the ordinary occurrences of life, is not hearkened to in religious matters, which are supposed to be placed altogether above the cognizance of human reason. On this account, all the absurdities of the Pagan system of theology must be overlooked by every critic, who would pretend to form a just notion of ancient poetry; and our posterity, in their turn, must have the same indulgence to their forefathers. No religious principles can ever be imputed as a fault to any poet, while they remain merely principles, and take not such strong possession of his heart as to lay him under the imputation of *bigotry* or *superstition*. Where that happens, they confound the sentiments of morality, and alter the natural boundaries of vice and virtue. They are therefore eternal blemishes, according to the principle above mentioned; nor are the prejudices and false opinions of the age sufficient to justify them. . . .

SUGGESTED ADDITIONAL READINGS

Marcia Eaton, *Basic Issues in Aesthetics* (Belmont, Calif.: Wadsworth, 1988).
Herbert J. Gans, *Popular Culture and High Culture* (New York: Basic Books, 1974).
Paul Hernadi, ed., *What Is Criticism?* (Bloomington: Indiana University Press, 1981).
Lawrence W. Levine, *Highbrow/Lowbrow: The Emergence of Cultural Hierarchy in America* (Cambridge, Mass.: Harvard University Press, 1988).
R. A. Sharpe, "Is 'Art' a Partisan Concept?" Chap. 1 in *Contemporary Aesthetics: A Philosophical Analysis* (New York: St. Martin's Press, 1983).

NOTES

1. R. A. Sharp, *Contemporary Aesthetics: A Philosophical Anaylsis* (New York: St. Martin's Press, 1983), p. vii.
2. Sharp, *Contemporary Aesthetics*, p. vii.
3. T. S. Eliot, *The Use of Poetry and the Use of Criticism* (London: Faber & Faber, 1964), p. 130.
4. Herbert J. Gans, *Popular Culture and High Culture: An Analysis and Evaluation of Taste* (New York: Basic Books, 1974), pp. 10ff.
5. Kenneth Clark, *What Is a Masterpiece?* (New York: Thames & Hudson, 1981), p. iv.
6. Quoted by Darko Suvin, "The Mirror and the Dynamo," in *Radical Perspectives in the Arts*, ed. Lee Baxandall (Baltimore: Penguin Books, 1972), p. 68.
7. It is now a widely accepted view of philosophy of science that there are always multiple scientific theories and hypotheses consistent with all the observational facts available to a finite observer. In short, scientific theories are also underdetermined by the possible facts at our disposal.
8. For a discussion of the interrelation of interpretation and evaluation, see Marcia Eaton, *Basic Issues in Aesthetics* (Belmont, Calif.: Wadsworth, 1988), pp. 105–12.
9. Susan Sontag, *Against Interpretation* (New York: Farrar, Straus & Giroux, 1966), p. 7.
10. Alfred Harbage, *As They Liked It: A Study of Shakespeare's Moral Artistry* (Philadelphia: University of Pennsylvania Press, 1972), pp. 31–32.
11. Immanuel Kant, *Critique of Judgment*. See "Analytic of the Beautiful."
12. Clark, *What Is a Masterpiece?*, p. 9.
13. Eliot, *Use of Poetry*, p. 35.
14. For a fuller discussion of the antinomy of taste and Kant's solution, see John A. Fisher and Jeffry Maitland, "The Subjectivist Turn in Aesthetics," *The Review of Metaphysics* 27, no. 4 (June 1974): 726–51.

Part I Why Philosophy of Art?

THE VALUE QUESTIONS   The aim of Part I is to show that to think intelligently about art, we need a theory or philosophy of art. The interrelated issues articulated in Part I all revolve around the value of the arts. This value, which justifies so much, needs in turn to be justified. In Chapter 2, I point out that advanced societies assume that the arts have the very highest importance and value, yet it is difficult to find an account of art that explains this importance. There is no clear definition of art, nor of the value of the arts. One could say about "art" what Saint Augustine said about "time": I know well enough what it is, provided that nobody asks me.

General theories or philosophies of art have been proposed over the centuries, but how are we to evaluate them? How are we to determine which theory is the best, most correct, or most illuminating? Philosophers who think about the nature of art have seldom examined this question. The problems about art brought up in Part I serve as tests to apply to proposed theories of art. Can a given theory resolve, or at least address, these fundamental issues? If it cannot, how *is* it to be evaluated?

Chapter 3 sharpens the question of the value of art by differentiating art's aesthetic value from less puzzling, nonartistic values, such as its historical value. We could have begun the investigation just as easily with Chapter 4, which raises the issue of the relation of art to moral value. Traditionally it was assumed that the arts improve or uplift their audience, that we are better for having read poetry or hearing music. It was the failure of the arts to fulfill this obvious requirement that led Plato to attack them. In recent times, however, this assumption has been disputed, and many artists have asserted that art is independent of morality, indeed, that artworks can disregard or even contradict moral and other social values. What is art that it can transcend values that otherwise are held to be valid and binding? With the growth of the avant-garde during the last century, art has claimed an even more radical independence: it need be neither pleasurable nor even intelligible to the layperson. What is the importance of art that it can parallel science in being a specialized form of investigation understood by only a few? Can art even be defined? Is there any essential idea that both the masterpieces of art throughout history and the revolutionary works of our own time have in common?

In the last analysis, theories are judged by their ability to explain. This applies equally to theories of art. How does a particular theory of art define art? Can it explain the unity of art: what, if anything, do all the arts, or artworks, have in common? Can it explain the nature of art, why we create it and why it is so valuable?

CHAPTER 2

Tolstoy's Challenge — The Status and Costs of Art

◀ *Turandot*, Metropolitan Opera production (1987) by Franco Zeffirelli. Puccini's popular opera *Turandot* (1926) is about a mythical Chinese princess (Turandot) who chops off the heads of suitors who cannot answer her riddles. Tolstoy considers operas themselves to be riddles: "[That] nowhere, except in theaters, do people walk about in such a manner, in pairs, with tinfoil halberds, and in slippers; that no one ever gets angry in such a way, or is affected in such a way, or laughs in such a way, or cries in such a way . . . is beyond the possibility of doubt."

That works of art have the highest cultural value is largely an unquestioned and unexplained presupposition of modern civilization. Even people who don't go to art museums or classical music concerts have been taught to accept the worth of these and other art institutions. A well-rounded education, we believe, is incomplete if it fails to give the student the skills and knowledge necessary to appreciate the arts. It is axiomatic both that the arts add to our lives and that it is better to preserve and display works of art than to ignore or destroy them. We know, or think we know, that the art of the past is intrinsically valuable even if we are less sure about the art of our own time. The preservation and promotion of the arts and of the skills and materials necessary to appreciate them is an ideal so natural that it is seldom subjected to scrutiny, and when it is, people find it difficult to approach the issue in a rational way.

CULTURAL INERTIA?

Art is often assumed to be so significant that it can redeem those who create or support it, even if they are guilty of actions deserving condemnation. Ernest Hauser expresses this attitude in condoning the actions of the Renaissance papacy on the basis of its support of art:

> But though the Holy See did have its share of scandal, and people frequently suffered from its oppression, it often played the leading role in the defense of Western civilization, and its contribution to Italian culture is inestimable. Not only did the popes create one of the world's great libraries and art collections, but their maligned nepotism, by showering church revenues upon some favorite nephew . . . spawned a brood of princely dynasties that vied with one another in sponsoring the arts.[1]

This attitude is a modern one; the arts were not always thought of in such an elevated way. Each art had to struggle for such high status, many of them during the Renaissance. In describing the rise of the visual arts in Florence, Vincent Cronin reminds us that "at the beginning of the fifteenth century the visual artist — whether painter or goldsmith, sculptor or architect — played a humble role in Florence. A craftsman strictly controlled by the regulations of his guild, he eked out a living painting baskets and tournament banners." But by the end of the century, "he had become the intimate friend of leading citizens, his idiosyncrasies were tolerated, he had come to be recognized not only as a skilled technician but as a thinker, a discoverer, an inventor, to such a degree that in his own lifetime Michelangelo was called 'divino'."[2] Even earlier, the Tuscan poets Dante and Petrarch had been treated as great men of their time. After the Renaissance, a similar status was extended to dramatists and musicians;

Shakespeare, Mozart, and Beethoven were considered profound geniuses by thinkers of the nineteenth century. For many people, art had acquired the attributes of a religion. The arts, which had once served church and state, came to be seen as deeply important in themselves. Whereas once Michelangelo's Sistine Chapel fresco of the Creation existed for the sake of the chapel, to us it seems that the chapel exists for the sake of the fresco.

We have inherited this exalted view of the arts without knowing whether its intellectual underpinnings are still acceptable today, that is, without knowing whether the arguments, values, and justifications once used to elevate the arts above their original humble status would still appear plausible in the twentieth century.

For example, consider the concept of beauty. One important reason for the rise in status of the visual arts in the Renaissance was the fact that Florentine Neoplatonist philosophers rediscovered and championed the concept of beauty. Influenced by the Greek philosopher Plato (427–347 B.C.), these enormously influential philosophers considered beauty to be a real metaphysical quality underlying reality.[4]

It is doubtful that a defense of art in these same terms would be persuasive today. Most thinkers since Immanuel Kant (1724–1804) have contended that the experience of beauty is a subjective response, not the perception of an exalted, objective property of reality. Moreover, much art, particularly twentieth-century art, has repudiated beauty as an essential goal for art. No doubt beauty is an important and distinctive feature of *some* art, but it would be very difficult in the late twentieth century to ground the importance of all art on beauty. This is one reason why we need to rethink the basis of our belief in the importance and meaning of art.

> In the course of the nineteenth century, as a consequence of the Enlightenment secularization of culture, two novel value institutions emerged, the Nation and Art.
>
> — Morse Peckham[3]

TOLSTOY'S CHALLENGE

Such reflections on the limitations of the ideas originally used to justify the arts motivate us to search for an adequate contemporary philosophy of art, but they do not strictly force us to develop one. One may think that the position of the arts in our society must be based on something other than cultural inertia, but to work out what that basis is would be merely a matter of unnecessary intellectual curiosity. It is against such complacent attitudes that the great nineteenth-century Russian novelist Leo Tolstoy (1828–1910) directs his brilliant and often harsh discourse on the nature art of art, *What is Art?* (see the Readings).

In his book Tolstoy often appears to attack art in general, but in reality he is only attacking what, in his view, was mistakenly considered art in the nineteenth century. He believes that art is enormously important but that society has forgotten why. We tend to accept everything that is labeled "art" as art, and thus of great value; to Tolstoy, however, it may not be art at all. In *What is Art?*, Tolstoy presents his own theory of art, an early version of the expression theory of art (see Chapter 11). According to his theory, much "art" of his day was not true art at all; conversely, much that was not considered art was, in Tolstoy's eyes, true art. Real art is as essential to society as food and water, but false or counterfeit art is of no value at all.

Tolstoy makes us consider his revolutionary ideas by appealing to the requirements of rationality. In the first chapter of *What is Art?*, Tolstoy reminds us of the cost of the arts, even art that is repulsive, mediocre, or self-indulgent. He reminds us that the resources required to support and produce art must be compensated by the benefits it yields. More explicitly, Tolstoy's argument can be formulated this way:

1. Art has costs; that is, it uses resources.
2. We can rationally allocate these resources only to whatever yields some valuable result.

From this it follows that it would be irrational to provide the resources unless the arts have some positive value. Tolstoy's reasoning also presupposes the following further principle of comparable worth:

3. The value of the result of an activity should be roughly comparable *in importance* to the value of the resources it uses.

This does not mean that the value of the arts can be measured in the same terms as are the resources they require. Whereas the latter can often be measured in economic terms, the value of art, it may be said, cannot be. Nonetheless, we can still insist that what we get out of the arts ought to be just as important as what we put into them.

The conclusion of this line of thought is that we must supply some account of the value of art commensurate with the resources used in its creation, performance, and conservation. Of course, our account of the value of art could turn out to be incorrect, in which case we ought to try to find a better one. What would be truly irrational is to maintain that no account of the rewards of art is required. Society may be mistaken in its reasons for supporting an activity, for example, the constant production of increasingly devastating systems of expensive weapons, but no one would propose that supporting such an activity requires no reason at all.

The brilliance of Tolstoy's discussion lies in his application of commonsense principles of value to art. The example he chooses is an opera that he portrays as worthless. Nevertheless, it entails high costs, particularly human costs. Tolstoy reminds us that many people are involved in an opera performance and that, at least in his day, many of them, both performers and backstage workers, were treated as a mere means to an end. The end, according to Tolstoy, is just the glorification of the leading participants. Here then is an example of a so-called work of art that has very high human costs and offers no apparent compensation.

Tolstoy's description of an extremely artificial opera is rhetorically effective, but it opens him up to the following objection: He has taken an example of *bad* art and used it to argue that all art needs justification. The argument wouldn't seem nearly as persuasive if he had chosen an example of great art! This objection aptly points out that Tolstoy's argument works well because he has chosen an example of art that the reader is unlikely to be able to defend. But even if we grant that great art has great value, the basic point of Tolstoy's reasoning cannot be evaded. The objection seems to suggest that art in general is justified by the great masterpieces of art; it is worthwhile for society to support art because of what it gets out of the best examples of art. This position, however, invites further questions of a Tolstoyan sort: What is the difference between great art and ordinary art? What properties does great art have that makes it great and which makes it rational to support the rest of art? Thus, we are still required to explain the importance of art, that is, the masterpieces of art, to society.

What makes Tolstoy's challenge more than an intellectual puzzle is the fact that in our time, as in Tolstoy's Russia, millions of people lack the basic human needs for food, shelter, and medical care. If resources are scarce, it seems mandatory to have some understanding of why they should be spent on activities and institutions that are frankly of marginal importance to many citizens. Nevertheless, until recently the challenge that Tolstoy raised has not been much discussed. One can single out three reasons why. The first is that the status of art has simply been taken for granted. The second involves a general truth about art, namely, that the finished work or performance creates an illusion of effortless perfection. The endless rewrites, the chisel strokes, the years of rehearsal, the months or years of labor are erased in the finished product, which is not meant to be appreciated for the work that went into its creation. The stage sets, which have to be designed and built out of real materials and moved around by an army of stage technicians, are viewed in the end as illusions, a backdrop for the action. We appreciate art without thinking about its various costs; nonetheless, it has them.

The third reason is that in our society it is common to treat the arts as just another cultural arena, like sports or leisure activities, and to suppose that the "justification" question is adequately answered by the free choice and enjoyment of the people involved. However natural many people find this assumption, it does not account for why the arts should have a much higher status than other special interest activities, nor does it address the constant need to provide subsidies, both public and private, to make art possible or to make it available to more than a few people. In short, this view does not provide any grounds for considering the arts a *public good* — like science, education, public libraries, and the preservation of nature — something worth supporting even when it does not turn a profit.

Consider, as an example, summer music festivals. These festivals feature classical music concerts and often include music education for young performers, as well as performances of less familiar contemporary music and specially commissioned new pieces of music.[5] Even though tickets are expensive, such festivals always need further support to pay their bills. Unlike ordinary forms of entertainment and leisure activities, these activities do not make a profit; they cannot generate enough money from entrance fees to be self-supporting. Private donations, business donations, and governmental subsidies (for example, grants from the National Endowment for the Arts) must provide further subsidies. The story is the same for other arts institutions, such as museums, theaters, dance troupes, and so on. The model of producers doing something just because they choose to and are adequately paid, and of consumers who simply enjoy the product and pay for the activity by buying tickets, books, records, or the products advertised, applies well to professional sports and entertainment but very poorly to most serious art.

At its heart, the proposal that art represents just another cultural arena bases the "justification" of art on the pleasure or enjoyment of the participants. Certainly in modern advanced societies, the arts do provide pleasure to large numbers of people. It is tempting, therefore, to argue that the pleasure of these many people justifies the costs of the arts. This proposal must be taken seriously. (We will return to this idea in Chapter 3.) But it is beset by both practical and theoretical objections. On a theoretical level, it seems to grant too much to opponents of art; it suggests that art has no value that transcends the pleasures of its audience. It thus seems doubtful that the proposal could satisfactorily meet Tolstoy's challenge, because it posits no unusual value or values that art uniquely provides. On a practical level, the thrust of this suggestion is to force art to pay for itself. Why should those who do not gain pleasure from art support the costs of giving pleasure to art lovers? But if there were no subsidies, the number of artworks produced and made accessible to the public would probably be significantly smaller, for many people who now enjoy the arts are in no position to pay for the real, nonsubsidized costs of such institutions as symphony orchestras and art museums.

It is important to keep in mind what Tolstoy's strategy does *not* attempt to argue. Tolstoy's argument does not imply that we cannot give a justification of art, only that we need to give one. Nor does the argument imply that there has to be just one answer; there could be a variety of values that art exemplifies. Tolstoy's own expectation seems to be that when we try to explain why art is valuable we will have a difficult time giving a satisfactory answer. Anticipating the customary appeal to beauty, he argues (in Chapter 4 of *What is Art?*) that the concept of beauty cannot effectively be used to defend the arts. He proposes a dilemma: Either beauty is an entirely subjective concept, or else it is uselessly mysterious, a completely unmeasurable and unknowable quality on whose definition no two thinkers have ever agreed. In this way, Tolstoy paves the way for his own position, namely, that the function of art is expression of feeling. Tolstoy believes that this function is as vital to society as the communication of facts and ideas through language. But he also finds that much that is counted as art, even great art, fails to perform this function.

We have noted important qualifications we need to keep in mind when we consider his conclusion that art needs justification. We must now note the broad application of Tolstoy's reasoning. His argument does not apply only to expensive performing arts; to a certain extent, it applies to all of the arts. Nor is the issue merely one of public or governmental support of the arts.

Every art form uses some resources. Who provides those resources? Among the obvious sources are the paying audience, taxpayers, individual donors, and corporations and foundations that provide grants. But first and foremost, artists themselves subsidize their own activities by devoting their labor and their personal resources to purchase the materials, instruments, rehearsal space, and so on to make producing the artworks possible. One way that many artists subsidize the arts is by accepting a reduced standard of living, at least in our society. The image of a poet, painter, or musician starving in an attic may be an attractive fantasy to some, but it is at odds with what most citizens want for themselves. The great avant-garde jazz player Ornette Coleman complains about the music business: "It's just that in vying for profit . . . everything has to be included, including the toilet paper. You can't get it free and you've got to use it. I know that money's not the solution. But if I could make money with what I'm doing, then that's even better for them because they could feel less guilty about it."[6] Does it make sense, if artworks have real importance, for the majority of artists to be treated as economically marginal, in stark constrast to the other professions society considers valuable, such as doctors, lawyers, corporate executives?

> No honest poet can ever feel quite sure of the permanent value of what he has written: he may have wasted his time and messed up his life for nothing.
> — T. S. Eliot[7]

Even lonely poets devoting their spare time to writing poetry are using at least one precious resource: their lives. It is not a question of freedom to choose whatever career they want; the question, rather, is what is the *good* of this career? Perhaps the poet will say that being a poet gives him or her a sense of self-worth that makes life worthwhile. It is a plausible answer, but it presupposes that there is something worthwhile about being a poet and thus that poetry is something that embodies important values.

PUBLIC SUBSIDIES

At its simplest, Tolstoy's challenge is to give an explanation of the importance of art, an importance that justifies the prominence of the arts and the various costs and sacrifices they entail. One way to see the force of Tolstoy's challenge is to consider the debate over public subsidies of the arts. In a democracy, in which expenditures need to be justified, support for the arts with money derived from taxation is bound to raise Tolstoy's challenge. In the United States, the founding of the National Endowment for the Arts (NEA) in 1965 has spurred many Americans to think about the importance of the arts and their role in a democracy. (See Ellison's introduction to *Buying Time* and the NEA Financial Statement for 1990 in the Readings.)

One can divide the NEA's activities into two areas: support for art already created and support of new art. Under the former heading, the general goals are to preserve and make accessible artworks in various media. Under the latter, the general goal is to make possible the creation of artworks that would not otherwise have been created. To achieve this end, the NEA gives modest grants to artists to support them for a period of time while they compose music, write poems, choreograph dances, and so forth. Grants to arts organizations, symphony orchestras, opera and dance organizations, and theaters and museums help meet both goals; that is, these organizations make both new and old artworks accessible to the public. These organizations are necessary both to preserve our artistic heritage and to create a new heritage of art of our own time.

What difference do public subsidies make? Although the arts would not disappear without them, artworks would certainly be less widely available. Perhaps even more important is that grants give artists the freedom to produce work that is not commercial, work that can thus be more challenging and original. It is worth noting that until very recently the practice in the United States — at the NEA, for example — had been to give grants to artists without dictating what the artists are to create. (Opposition to this practice is increasing. See Chapter 12.) Artists have also been supported, in a sense, in totalitarian countries, but because such governments view art as just another tool of the state, the artists have often been subjected to severe constraints on what they can produce. In effect, government support means government control, a result that not only is intrinsically undesirable but also arguably replaces the promotion of real art with the promotion of propaganda.

The most conspicuous publicly subsidized artworks are works of public art, that is, art that is commissioned to be placed in public sites. Every developed society has produced such art — indeed, public artworks are among the most important elements defining the character of such great cities as Rome, Paris, or Washington, D.C. But in our society, art in public places has often led to acrimonious controversy. The controversies seem to be a consequence of the disparity between our populist traditions, in which the majority of the public determines what is permanently on view in public places, and the fact that our most eminent and advanced artists (the ones most likely to be commissioned) create artworks that many members of the public do not understand — at least at first glance. As a society, we want to honor our best art rather than the lowest common denominator, commercial art, but if the public has little understanding or taste for the best art our society produces, this motive comes into conflict with public taste.

> People are entitled to their opinion; but prejudice, even if it is shared by a majority, ought not to be the reason to destroy a work of art.
>
> — Richard Serra[8]

A sensational example of just such a controversy occurred over Richard Serra's sculpture *Tilted Arc* (see Figures 2.1, 2.2, and 2.3). In 1979, Serra, a prestigious American sculptor, was commissioned by the federal government to build a sculpture for permanent installation in the Federal Plaza in Manhattan. *Tilted Arc* was the result. This long steel wall is entirely consistent with Serra's previous work; moreover, its concept was approved

FIGURE 2.1 Richard Serra's *Tilted Arc* was commissioned in 1979 by the Federal government to stand in Federal Plaza in Manhattan. It was installed in 1981. It aroused so much opposition that hearings were held in 1984 to decide whether to relocate it. In 1989, over the protests of the artist, the government dismantled and removed it in an all-night maneuver; its removal was as controversial as the sculpture itself.

by the General Services Administration (GSA), which had commissioned Serra. Nonetheless, after *Tilted Arc* was installed in 1981, objections were raised. Many people considered it an ugly obstruction; workers in the buildings surrounding the plaza resented its presence. Public hearings were held, and petitions to remove it were signed.[9] The very heated controversy — in which the artworld seemed to be pitted against government workers — eventually led the GSA to order the relocation of *Tilted Arc* to some other site. Serra fought this in the courts, claiming that to move the sculpture would be to destroy it, because it was designed in relation to that exact site. He also appealed to the moral right of artists to object to modification or destruction of their work (an idea accepted in European countries, but not yet in the United States). Serra lost his appeals, the sculpture was dismantled, and the pieces were placed in storage. Serra feels that his sculpture has been brutally destroyed. His chief adversary, the regional director of the GSA, William Diamond, declared, "Now the plaza returns rightfully to the people."[10]

Subsidizing new artworks and making accepted artworks more widely available make sense only if art is valuable. In an age of budget deficits, some question whether art is important enough to merit public subsidies. There is even an important tradition, going back to the philosopher Plato, of suspecting that the arts are a bad influence with no positive value at all. (See Ellison, in the Readings, and Plato, in the Readings for Chapter 3.)

Because of the importance attached to economics and practicality in our society, defenders of public support for the arts often approach the issue on economic grounds. Sir Peter Hall's forceful plea (see the Readings) for government subsidies for the theater in Britain, for

FIGURE 2.2 *Tilted Arc* being removed at night.

FIGURE 2.3 Site after removal of *Tilted Arc*.

example, is based in part on the claim that the arts pay off financially. Even though theater has always been expensive and in need of subsidy, according to Hall, serious noncommercial theater provides indirect revenue, first as an important tourist attraction and second as a training ground that fosters the high quality of British acting in commercial films and on TV. The trouble with such justifications is that they depend on treating live drama as a means to other commercial ends, not as something valuable in its own right.

Peter Hall goes beyond this economic defense when he appeals to the veneration of the British heritage and the importance of appreciating Shakespeare. With this argument he appears to argue in a circle, as he does when he worries that there is a danger that without government support we will "cut out . . . the audience of tomorrow — and with them the plays of tomorrow." But *why* is Shakespeare important, and why is it important to continue to have new plays? Tolstoy has challenged us to show in a noncircular way why it is important to promote either sort of art. (Interestingly, Tolstoy wrote a pamphlet attacking Shakespeare's *King Lear*.) Neither the art of the future nor the art of the past is exempt from this challenge.

The point that we need a noncircular justification of the arts applies also to the position Leonard Bernstein supports (see the Readings). Bernstein (see Figure 2.4) argues persuasively that we will never gain true public support for and involvement with the arts until as a nation we do a much better job educating the public in the arts. He contends that the public will retain the attitude that the arts are light entertainment "until we become not only an art-producing people, but an art-consuming people; and that means a people *prepared* to receive the aesthetic product; and *that* means an *educated* people" (p. 64). He points out, for example, that few Americans can read music — so how can we expect them to understand a Brahms symphony or a Mozart piano sonata, much less appreciate the classical music of our own time? This line of reasoning leads to the conclusion that public funds for the arts ought first to be allocated to education in the arts. Because most Americans lack an understanding of the arts, it is no wonder that support for public subsidies for the arts, which Hall defends, is less than unanimous. Plausible and important as this point is, it is nonetheless logically dependent on first finding justification for the claim that the arts *are* so important that we ought to find ways to educate the public to understand and appreciate them better.

Political scientist Edward Banfield takes a position opposite from that of Hall. Banfield questions whether government should provide any funds for the arts (see the Readings) and he attacks most of the defenses of such funding as specious. In general he holds that "a justification for government support of art must rest on the inherent rather than the incidental values associated with it" and points out that "art is a quite unsuitable means of serving the public interest in the ways claimed." Noting that economic defenses often tout the fact that the arts attract tourists and their money to art centers, he argues that "attracting tourists to one city and away from another does not serve the public interest" (p. 63). He is understandably harsh on the "pleasure defense":

> Giving people pleasure has never been considered a proper function of the U.S. government, except as it may be supposed to affect, for good or for ill, aspects of life that are the proper concern of government. Only as an individual's enjoyment of art is correctly perceived by the public as affecting the well-being of the collectivity does it matter to the public interest. (p. 63)

Given this point, it may seem ironic that Banfield grounds much of his attack on the funding of avant-garde art, which he finds repulsive and often meaningless. This art is often

FIGURE 2.4 Leonard Bernstein, American composer and conductor (1918–1990).

difficult, and certainly it does not seem aimed at providing pleasure. Rather than asking why we should fund the production of mere pleasure, perhaps we should ask why we should fund difficult and sometimes offensive work. Should all the art that is properly subsidized by public monies be pleasing and uncontroversial?

Has Banfield adequately faced the question of the nature of art? He correctly suggests that the theoretical underpinnings of public support for the arts are murky and confusing — as he implies, there is no current definition of art that is accepted by even a working majority of thinkers. But his attack on contemporary art, which often seems to be his real animus, suggests he holds that art ought to be morally elevating in an old-fashioned sense. Since twentieth-century art has largely rejected this goal (see Chapter 4) in favor of what artists no doubt think are more complex and subtle explorations, Banfield finds it an easy target to attack.

Consider his attack on the influential abstract painter Ad Reinhardt (1913–1967). Reinhardt was critical of traditional ideas about painting. In the 1950s he developed a series of black-on-black geometric paintings that expressed his desire for very pure painting for its own sake. Banfield quotes Reinhardt's description of his painting as "a pure, abstract, non-objective, timeless, spaceless, changeless, relationless, disinterested painting, an object that is self-conscious (no unconsciousness), ideal, transcendent, aware of nothing but art" (p. 63).

One might be intrigued or critical of such ideas, but Banfield's interpretation seems willfully blind to Reinhardt's positive aims. Banfield insists that such art "implicitly conveys a message, whose tendency is to degrade human beings. It says that man and all that concerns him, including art itself, do not matter" (p. 62). It is difficult to make sense out of this gloss as an interpretation of either Reinhardt's paintings or writings. Banfield appears to require art to have particular human content and to present a certain picture of human nature. Art that ignores such positive edifying content, in favor (say) of art for art's sake, Banfield considers humanly degrading.

> To America one school-master is worth a dozen poets, and the invention of a machine is of more importance than a masterpiece by Raphael.
>
> — attributed to Benjamin Franklin

If art does not provide conventional moral content, perhaps it at least offers an aesthetic experience. Even if this is so, Banfield argues, government support is unjustified. He does not believe that the government should be subsidizing enjoyment or pleasure — supposing that this is the value of aesthetic experience — and if art is somehow more important, even if "art significantly affects the quality of society . . . it would not follow that government might properly subsidize it" (p. 63). At this point the argument turns on notions of the proper role of the arts and of government in a democracy. Still, we can see how crucial it is to know what art is and what positive functions (inherent or instrumental) it can serve in a society. Even in a case such as medical care, the value of which is accepted by everyone, there are still debates about whether citizens have a right to it and whether it should be subsidized by the government. How much more confusing must be the case of the arts, which are appreciated by only a fraction of the citizens and whose nature has always been a subject of philosophical argument! Nonetheless, given the history and status of the arts in our tradition, it seems unreasonable to claim that the burden of proof lies on the proponents of the arts to prove to the satisfaction of every skeptic that the arts have a universal value. It is arguable that many other activities funded by government, including fundamental scientific research, would also fail to be justified by such high standards.

Banfield goes on to describe the proper functions of government: "to protect the individual in the exercise of certain inalienable rights and to establish the preconditions for the development of competent citizenry" (p. 63). Those who know the arts will probably be surprised at the assumption that art does not have anything significant to do with either of these functions. Indeed, the theories of art that we will look at in Part III specifically claim that in one way or another art is an important part of a deeper understanding of life. Of course, much turns on the notion of a "competent citizen." Banfield's formulation is useful because it makes one consider whether citizens who know nothing of the masterpieces of artistic history or of the arts of their own culture are fully "competent." (See also the excerpt by Hilary Putnam in the Readings for Chapter 3.)

In the end, proponents of art have the task of indicating how the arts enrich the lives of those who experience them and how a society that has art is better off than one that lacks art. These difficult explanations are fundamental, and they illustrate the thrust of Tolstoy's strategy. We cannot successfully justify public support for the arts unless we can provide a convincing account of the nature and value of art that is independent of its limited practical uses. If such an account could be provided, if proponents of public support for the arts could produce a plausible theory of art that shows how it enriches our lives or is intrinsically valuable, they would be able to rationalize both public and private support for art without referring to its economic benefits. Some theories of art appear to do this better than others. But the important point is that even to begin approaching the issue, we must explore and evaluate different theoretical accounts of the arts.

Tolstoy's challenge suggests that one of the features of an adequate theory of art is that it should explain the value of art. This is not to beg the question of whether it does have value. It may turn out — just as Plato argued — that the true account shows that art has no intrinsic or social value. This would be a very surprising result, and one that Tolstoy would not have accepted. No doubt it would be naive to think that we will be able to come up with an unambiguous answer to Tolstoy's challenge. Many competing theories of art have been proposed and vigorously defended over the centuries. Each of the major theories of art that we will consider attributes a different nature to art, and with each nature goes a different set of values embodied by art. The important point is that traditional theories of art don't just say what art is, but also why it is valuable. Contemporary philosophical discussions of art theories sometimes ignore this issue. But if the argument presented in this chapter is correct, doing so is a mistake; one of the most important tasks of an adequate theory of art should be to provide an explanation of why art is important.

RIGHTS AND OBLIGATIONS

Finally, I want to discuss a contemporary issue closely related to Tolstoy's challenge. As Tolstoy points out, the arts have a very high status. This status leads us to do a number of things: to respect and value artworks above ordinary artifacts, to analyze and report on the arts extensively, to donate resources to support the ongoing activities of the arts, and to protect and preserve artworks. Tolstoy's challenge in its barest form is to provide a justification for the status that accounts for all these activities. A contemporary cultural controversy that illustrates the importance of this challenge is the public debate over colorizing black-and-white movies. This controversy involves the issue of respect and preservation of artworks in their original form. (The issue of colorization is thus connected to the removal and/or destruction of Richard Serra's sculpture *Tilted Arc*, for both involve the question of whether artists have a right to control the way their artworks are treated.)

The debate was precipitated by the development of computer technology that can add artificial color to a videotape version of a black-and-white movie. Video network entrepreneurs have begun to use this technology to broadcast artificially colorized versions of classic black-and-white movies, for example, John Huston's *The Maltese Falcon*. The members of the Directors Guild, including Woody Allen and the late John Huston, have fought against what they see as a destruction and misrepresentation of their work. Congressional hearings, at which both sides testified, were held in 1987, and legislation concerning various artists' "rights" is being considered.

> One cannot have a society in which the artists are so regarded that their work can simply be changed at will by other people.
>
> — Woody Allen[11]

Those in favor of colorization argue that television producers can present movies in whatever way they want to because they have purchased broadcast rights. Besides, movies are entertainment, and the public's taste is all that counts here, not the original creators' desires. Few people deny that most viewers no longer watch black-and-white movies; so, colorization is the only way to introduce new audiences to these movies. On the other side, the directors view themselves as artists arguing not only for the integrity of their own work but also on behalf of the other creative artists involved in making movies: writers, actors, scenic designers, photographers, and lighting directors. The directors insist that these movies are works of art, that the movies' creators are artists, and that they and their movies deserve protection out of respect for the artists and the works of art involved. They also insist that colorizing black-and-white movies significantly vulgarizes and misrepresents their work. At the hearings, Huston testified, "[*The Maltese Falcon*] is only one film and I am only one director and these are only a few of the artists who will be subjected to an eternal, unjustified public humiliation, joyfully presented as entertainment by the vandals who we of the directors guild oppose today." Allen added, "You'll always be able to give practical reasons. . . . But the overriding reason is a moral reason. . . . You can't have a culture where people can go in at will and mutilate artists' work no matter what excuse they give."

If we assume for the sake of argument that at least some movies should be considered works of art and that colorization does affect the original black-and-white movie — one of the most controversial points — we arrive at a sharp conflict between the rights of ownership and the special status of artworks. This status seems to imply that outstanding artworks become a sort of public good and that no one has a *right* to alter or destroy them, not even their owners. Consider any great painting. Do you accept that a rich individual has the right to buy it and destroy it or alter its character? If not, why? What is there about great works of art that obligates us, even if we are the legal owners, to preserve rather than harm them? If I own a classic car, I may just decide to destroy it on a whim, as a gesture indicating my wealth. I may be unwise, since the car has a market value, but beyond that have I done something that is somehow wrong? Would it be different if instead I destroyed or altered a work of art?

> The people which ceases to care for its literary inheritance becomes barbaric.
>
> — T. S. Eliot[12]

There is a parallel concern in the case of artworks that, in a sense, cannot be destroyed: pieces of music and literary works. In such cases, we could say that the publisher has an *obligation* not to alter or distort the words of a poem or novel, and the performer not to alter the notes of music or the text of a play. We might ask, Who or what would this be an obligation *to*? To the artwork? To the artist? To the public? No matter how we answer this question, if we are inclined to feel that artworks merit preservation and a respect that outweighs the prerogatives of private property, we seem required to provide an explanation of what there is about these works that merits this very special status. This is Tolstoy's challenge in a different guise.

READINGS FOR CHAPTER 2

Leo Tolstoy, from *What is Art?*
Peter Hall, "Should Theater be Subsidized? A Ringing 'Yes' Vote"
Edward Banfield, from *The Democratic Muse*
Leonard Bernstein, "On Education"
Ralph Ellison, Introduction to *Buying Time*
NEA Financial Summary, 1990

from *What is Art?*

Leo Tolstoy

Chapter One

Take up any one of our ordinary newspapers and you will find a part devoted to the theater and music. In almost every number you will find a description of some art exhibition, or of some particular picture, and you will always find reviews of new works of art that have appeared, of volumes of poems, of short stories, or of novels.

Promptly, and in detail, as soon as it has occurred, an account is published of how such and such an actress or actor played this or that role in such and such a drama, comedy, or opera, and of the merits of the performance, as well as of the contents of the new drama, comedy, or opera, with its defects and merits. With as much care and detail, or even more, we are told how such and such an artist has sung a certain piece, or has played it on the piano or violin, and what were the merits and defects of the piece and of the performance. In every large town there is sure to be at least one, if not more than one, exhibition of new pictures, the merits and defects of which are discussed in the utmost detail by critics and connoisseurs.

New novels and poems, in separate volumes or in the magazines, appear almost every day, and the newspapers consider it their duty to give their readers detailed accounts of these artistic productions.

For the support of art in Russia (where for the education of the people only a hundredth part is spent of what would be required to give every one the opportunity of instruction), the government grants millions of rubles in subsidies to academies, conservatories, and theaters. In France twenty million francs are assigned for art, and similar grants are made in Germany and England.

In every large town enormous buildings are erected for museums, academies, conservatories, dramatic schools, and for performances and concerts. Hundreds of thousands of workmen — carpenters, masons, painters, joiners, paperhangers, tailors, hairdressers, jewelers, molders, typesetters — spend their whole lives in hard labor to satisfy the demands of art, so that hardly any other department of human activity, except the military, consumes so much energy as this.

Not only is enormous labor spent on this activity, but in it, as in war, the very lives of men are sacrificed. Hundreds of thousands of people devote their lives from childhood to learning to twirl their legs rapidly (dancers), or to touch notes and strings very rapidly (musicians), or to draw with paint and represent what they see (artists), or to turn every phrase inside out and find a rhyme to every word. And these people, often very kind and clever, and capable of all sorts of useful labor, grow savage over their specialized and stupefying occupations, and become one-sided and self-complacent specialists, dull to all the serious phenomena of life and skillful only at rapidly twisting their legs, their tongues, or their fingers.

But even this stunting of human life is not the worst. I remember being once at the rehearsal of one of the most ordinary of the new operas which are produced at all the opera houses of Europe and America.

I arrived when the first act had already begun. To reach the auditorium I had to pass through the stage entrance. By dark entrances and passages I was led through the vaults of an enormous building, past immense machines for changing the scenery and for lighting, and there in the gloom and dust I saw workmen busily engaged. One of these men, pale, haggard, in a dirty blouse, with dirty, work-worn hands and cramped fingers, evidently tired and out of humor, went past me, angrily scolding another man. Ascending by a dark stair, I came out on the boards behind the scenes. Amid various poles and rings and scattered scenery, decorations, and curtains, stood and moved dozens, if not hundreds, of painted and dressed-up men, in costumes fitting tight to their thighs and calves, and also women, as usual, as nearly nude as might be. These were all singers, or members of the chorus, or ballet dancers, waiting their turns. My guide led me across the stage and, by means of a bridge of boards across the orchestra (in which perhaps a hundred musicians of all kinds, from kettledrum to flute and harp, were seated), to the dark pit-stalls.

On an elevation, between two lamps with reflectors, and in an armchair placed before a music stand, sat the director of the musical part, baton in hand, managing the orchestra and singers, and, in general, the production of the whole opera.

The performance had already begun, and on the stage a procession of Indians who had brought home a bride was being presented. Besides men and women in costume, two other men in ordinary clothes bustled and ran about on the stage; one was the director of the dramatic part, and the other, who stepped about in soft shoes and ran from place to place with unusual agility, was the dancing master, whose salary per month exceeded what ten laborers earn in a year.

These three directors arranged the singing, the orchestra, and the procession. The procession, as usual, was enacted by couples, with tinfoil halberds on their shoulders. They all came from one place and walked round and round again, and then stopped. The procession took a long time to arrange: first, the Indians with halberds came on too late; then, too soon; then, at the right time, but crowded together at the exit; then they did not crowd, but arranged themselves badly at the sides of the stage; and each time the whole performance was stopped and started again from the beginning. The procession was introduced by a recitative delivered by a man dressed up like some variety of Turk, who, opening his mouth in a curious way, sang, "Home I bring the bri-i-ide." He sings and waves his arm (which is of course bare) from under his mantle. The procession begins, but here the French horn, in the accompaniment of the recitative, does something wrong; and the director, with a shudder as if some catastrophe had occurred, raps with his stick on the stand. All is stopped, and the director, turning to the orchestra, attacks the French horn, scolding him in the rudest terms, as cabmen abuse each other, for taking the wrong note. And again the whole thing begins again. The Indians with their halberds again come on, treading softly in their extraordinary boots; again the singer sings, "Home I bring the bri-i-ide." But here the pairs get too close together. More raps with the stick, more scolding, and a recommencement. Again, "Home I bring the bri-i-ide," again the same gesticulation with the bare arm from under the mantle, and again the couples, treading softly with halberds on their shoulders, some with sad and serious faces, some talking and smiling, arrange themselves in a circle and begin to sing. All seems to be going well, but again the stick raps, and the director, in a distressed and angry voice, begins to scold the men and women of the chorus. It appears that when singing they had omitted to raise their hands from time to time in sign of animation. "Are you all dead, or what? Cows that you are! Are you corpses, that you can't move?" Again they start "Home I bring the bri-i-ide," and again, with sorrowful faces, the chorus women sing, first one and then another of them raising their hands. But two chorus girls speak to each other — again a more vehement rapping with the stick. "Have you come here to talk? Can't you gossip at home? You there in red breeches, come nearer. Look toward me! Begin!" Again, "Home I bring the bri-i-ide." And so it goes on for one, two, three hours. The whole of such a rehearsal lasts six hours on end. Raps with the stick, repetitions, placings, corrections of the singers, of the orchestra, of the procession, of the dancers — all seasoned with angry scolding. I heard the words "asses," "fools," "idiots," "swine," addressed to the musicians and singers at least forty times in the course of one hour. And the unhappy individual to whom the abuse is addressed — flutist, hornblower, or singer — physically and mentally demoralized, does not reply and does what is demanded of him. Twenty times is repeated the one phrase, "Home I bring the bri-i-ide," and twenty times the striding about in yellow shoes with a halberd over the shoulder. The conductor knows that these people are so demoralized that they are no longer fit for anything but to blow trumpets and walk about with halberds and in yellow shoes, and that they are also accustomed to dainty, easy living, so that they will put up with anything rather than lose their luxurious life. He therefore gives free vent to his churlishness, especially as he has seen the same thing done in Paris and Vienna, and knows that this is the way the best conductors behave, and that it is a musical tradition of great artists to be so carried away by the great business of their art that they cannot pause to consider the feelings of other artists.

It would be difficult to find a more repulsive sight. I have seen one workman abuse another for not supporting the weight piled upon him when goods were being unloaded, or, at haystacking, the village elder scold a peasant for not making the rick right, and the man submitted in silence. And, however unpleasant it was to witness the scene, the unpleasantness was lessened by the consciousness that the business in hand was needful and important, and that the fault for which the head man scolded the laborer was one which might spoil a needful undertaking.

But what was being done here? For what, and for whom? Very likely the conductor was tired out, like the workman I passed in the vaults; it was even evident that he was; but who made him tire himself? And for what was he tiring himself? The opera he was rehearsing was one of the most ordinary of operas for people who are accustomed to them, but also one of the most gigantic absurdities that could possibly be devised. An Indian king wants to marry; they bring him a bride; he disguises himself as a minstrel; the bride falls in love with the minstrel and is in despair, but afterwards discovers that the minstrel is the king, and everyone is highly delighted.

That there never were, or could be, such Indians, and that they were not only unlike Indians, but that what they were doing was unlike anything on earth except other operas, was beyond all manner of doubt; that people do not converse in such a way as recitative, and do not place themselves at fixed distances in a quartet, waving their arms to express their emotions; that nowhere, except in theaters, do people walk about in such a manner, in pairs, with tinfoil halberds and in slippers; that no one ever gets angry in such a way, or is affected in such a way, or laughs in such a way, or cries in such a way; and that no one on earth can be moved by such performances — all this is beyond the possibility of doubt.

Instinctively the question presents itself: For whom is this being done? Whom *can* it please? If there are, occasionally, good melodies in the opera to which it is pleasant to listen, they could have been sung simply, without these stupid costumes and all the processions and recitatives and hand-wavings.

The ballet, in which half-naked women make voluptuous movements, twisting themselves into various sensual wreathings, is simply a lewd performance.

So one is quite at a loss as to whom these things are done for. The man of culture is heartily sick of them, while to a real workingman they are utterly incomprehensible. If anyone can be pleased by these things (which is doubtful), it can only be some young footman or depraved artisan who has contracted the spirit of the upper classes but is not satiated with their amusements and wishes to show his breeding.

And all this nasty folly is prepared, not simply, nor with kindly merriment, but with anger and brutal cruelty.

It is said that it is all done for the sake of art, and that art is a very important thing. But is it true that art is so important that such sacrifices should be made for its sake? This question is especially urgent because art, for the sake of which the labor of millions, the lives of men, and, above all, love between man and man, are being sacrificed — this very art is becoming something more and more vague and uncertain to human perception.

Criticism, in which the lovers of art used to find support for their opinions, has latterly become so self-contradictory that, if we exclude from the domain of art all that to which the critics of various schools themselves deny the title, there is scarcely any art left.

The artists of various sects, like the theologians of the various sects, mutually exclude and destroy themselves. Listen to the artists of the schools of our times, and you will find, in all branches, each set of artists disowning others. In poetry the old Romanticists deny the Parnassiens and the Decadents; the Parnassiens disown the Romanticists and the Decadents; the Decadents disown all their predecessors and the Symbolists; the Symbolists disown all their predecessors and *les mages*; and *les mages* disown all, all their predecessors. Among novelists we have naturalists, psychologists, and "nature-ists," all rejecting each other. And it is the same in dramatic art, in painting, and in music. So art, which demands such tremendous labor sacrifices from the people, which stunts human lives and transgresses against human love, is not only *not* a thing clearly and firmly defined, but it understood in such contradictory ways by its own devotees that it is difficult to say what is meant by art, and especially what is good, useful art — art for the sake of which we

might condone such sacrifices as are being offered at its shrine.

Chapter Two

For the production of every ballet, circus, opera, operetta, exhibition, picture, concert, or printed book, the intense and unwilling labor of thousands of people is needed at what is often harmful and humiliating work. It were well if artists made all they require for themselves, but, as it is, they all need the help of workmen, not only to produce art, but also for their own usually luxurious maintenance. And, one way or other, they get it, either through payments from rich people or through subsidies given by government (in Russia, for instance, in grants of millions of rubles to theaters, conservatories, and academies). This money is collected from the people, some of whom have to sell their only cow to pay the tax and who never get those aesthetic pleasures which art gives.

It was all very well for a Greek or Roman artist, or even for a Russian artist of the first half of our century (when there were still slaves and it was considered right that there should be), with a quiet mind to make people serve him and his art; but in our day, when in all men there is at least some dim perception of the equal rights of all, it is impossible to constrain people to labor unwillingly for art without first deciding the question whether it is true that art is so good and so important an affair as to redeem this evil.

If not, we have the terrible probability to consider that while fearful sacrifices of the labor and lives of men, and of morality itself, are being made to art, that same art may be not only useless but even harmful.

And therefore it is necessary for a society in which works of art arise and are supported, to find out whether all that professes to be art is really art, whether (as is presupposed in our society) all that which is art is good, and whether it is important and worth those sacrifices which it necessitates. It is still more necessary for every conscientious artist to know this, that he may be sure that all he does has a valid meaning; that it is not merely an infatuation of the small circle of people among whom he lives which excites in him the false assurance that he is doing a good work; and that what he takes from others for the support of his often very luxurious life will be compensated for by those productions at which he works. And that is why answers to the above questions are especially important in our time.

What is this art which is considered so important and necessary for humanity that for its sake these sacrifices of labor, of human life, and even of goodness may be made? . . .

Should Theater Be Subsidized?
A Ringing "Yes" Vote

Peter Hall

Sir Peter Hall is director of Britain's National Theater and
founder of the Royal Shakespeare Company. He is also artistic
director of the Glyndebourne Opera. Copyright © 1986 by The
New York Times Company. Reprinted by permission.

Theater is one of the main reasons why people come to Britain—1985 was the country's best year for tourism yet—but as hundreds of thousands of visitors from abroad packed our theaters, they might have been surprised to learn that there is a serious crisis in our performing arts. It is one that can now be expected to worsen, and which will inevitably weaken one of Britain's few remaining international success stories. For step by step the Thatcher government has been changing the pattern of subsidy for the performing arts, and thereby threatening our whole artistic endeavor.

Does this matter? Certainly it matters to Britons, and probably also it will matter to Americans who are likely to face similar problems in the near future.

Is British theater only subsidized theater? Of course not. We live in a mixed economy, and the commercial West End theater flourishes in London as well as the subsidized. We need both. But the West End flourishes chiefly because of the subsidized sector which feeds it and sustains it. A year ago the then Minister of Arts, Lord Gowrie, proudly declared in a speech that the West End theater was doing wonderfully well without a penny of public subsidy. His statement was spectacularly wrong. On the day he spoke, of 40 productions available to the London public over half had originated in subsidized theaters.

The annual British drama awards season has just ended. The prestigious Standard awards, and the equally important ones given by the Society of West End Theaters (the Laurence Olivier awards) cover, like the Broadway Tonys, the whole range of theater. In 1985 all these were won by performances either in or originating in the subsidized theater. The artistic strength of Britain's subsidized theater is clearly beyond question. What is not so well known is that it brings in huge financial returns, visible and invisible. In passing, it is worth noting too that the talents it produces nourish British television. The difference between the quality of performances in "Dynasty" and "Jewel in the Crown" is hundreds of years of theater experience shared collectively by the cast. Broadway has also benefited from British subsidized theater: "Nicholas Nickleby" and "Amadeus" are just two recent examples.

But if subsidized theater is such a success, why does it need subsidy? The answer is that with few exceptions, theater has always been subsidized—if not by the state, then by the church, the monarch or the rich patron. Shakespeare's company would have been less productive and less successful if it had not had money from royal patronage. Theater is labor intensive, handmade. It is for you on this very evening, not any other evening. The live experience is personal and, in an age of higher wages with shorter hours, increasingly expensive.

And because the actor remains the same size, and must be seen and heard, the buildings in which he performs cannot be made larger or he becomes ineffective.

On either side of the Atlantic, the only money-makers in the commercial theater are either plays with one set and not more than half a dozen actors, or spectacular events that can look to a four- or five-year run, and to exploitation all over the English-speaking world. Productions of Shakespeare or of big-cast classics are no longer economically possible without subsidy.

There is a further important consideration: subsidy keeps ticket prices at a reasonable level and so maintains the breadth of the audience. If we always charge what the market will bear, we cut out the young — the audience of tomorrow — and with them the plays of tomorrow.

Unfortunately the British Government of to-day appears to believe that everything can be measured in terms of financial worth. They regard subsidy for the performing arts as evidence that we are overmanned, antiquated industries, full of ancient work practices, consuming money instead of earning it. If fact, we in the performing arts are an excellent investment. We make money for the country. It comes from the tourism we attract, from foreign rights, from commercial exploitation, from taxes.

Yet over the last five years, the British Government has systematically eroded its subsidy to the arts by making the annual increase much less than inflation. Parallel with these reductions, theaters have been exhorted by government to fill the gap in their revenue by increasing commercial sponsorship. The American model has been held up as something the British theater should emulate. We should look to the private sector to provide us with money. Unfortunately, the spare cash is not there. More to the point, in Britain, unlike in America, there are no tax incentives for corporations or individual sponsors who support the arts.

So what as a consequence is happening to the performing arts? Up and down the country our subsidized theaters are producing much less than

in the past. Twenty years ago, a child in Birmingham, for instance, could see a representative range of British and foreign classics. Now the Birmingham Repertory Theater is often closed, and when it is open, is forced to play a much less adventurous program. The Royal Court Theater in London — the home of new British playwrights — used to do about 19 productions a year. Now it does six. True, our two big national companies, the Royal Shakespeare Company and the National Theater, are healthy. But both could do about 25 percent more work than at present, thus becoming even better value for money. And there is anxiety for where will our leading actors of tomorrow come from.

The Minister for the Arts used to represent the arts to government and fight our cause for us. Lately, it has been a case of the minister telling the arts that they are lucky to get subsidy at all, and can expect less. Yet Britain is at the bottom of the European league in per capita expenditure on the arts. The R.S.C. and the National Theater each earn about 50 percent of their income by their own efforts, and receive 50 percent in subsidy. In West Germany, comparable companies only earn about 15 percent, receiving no less than 85 percent from the state.

Our Prime Minister supports British sport, British design and the British heritage (protecting our countryside and historic buildings), and all these certainly help us internationally. But apparently she does not support the arts. Perhaps in this she accurately reflects the puritan streak of our country, the other side of the coin which makes us such uninhibited performers in the theater. Or is it that the new Tories are suspicious that the arts, in performance or education, are breeding grounds for radicalism? Yet it is curious for a Conservative government to have so little regard for the soul of the nation — our culture and education, qualities which cannot be measured by bread alone.

Within the next 10 years the Western world may well become one electronic community. Programs which appeal to the lowest common denominator are likely to be beamed into every country, making us all one plastic culture, unindividual and unexceptional. Britain has to safeguard its heritage and share it, if it is wanted. Fortunately, in the present crisis, public opinion in Britain is becoming increasingly aware. There may not be many votes in the arts, but there is concern about protecting our cultural heritage and about the quality of our lives. Why spend thousands of pounds teaching a child how to appreciate Shakespeare if he is unable to see a live performance of one of Shakespeare's plays?

from *The Democratic Muse*

Edward Banfield

But Is It Art?

. . . it is necessary for a society in which works of art arise and are supported, to find out whether all that professes to be art really is art, whether (as is presupposed in our society) all that which is art is good, and whether it is important and worth those sacrifices which it necessitates.

— *Tolstoy,* What Is Art?

Doubts filled the mind of Michael Straight, the deputy chairman of the NEA, as he confronted a pile of grant applications awaiting his signature. The chairman, Nancy Hanks, was home ill that day and he was acting chairman. The fifty or so applications he was facing that June in 1974 had been winnowed from among several thousand by one or another of several panels of consultants chosen by the staff for their professional competence and representativeness.

The panel's choices had then been approved by the National Council on the Arts, which met three or four times a year to advise the chairman. The acting chairman was now expected to "sign off" on the list of awards.

Straight had grown up with the arts. Born into a family of great wealth (his father was a banker, and his mother, Dorothy Whitney, was a philanthropist), famous works of art and famous artists had been a part of his everyday life since childhood. While still a youth he bought a Picasso. In later life, as editor and publisher of *The New Republic* (which his parents had founded), he was a vigorous advocate of "enlightened" and sometimes "advanced" opinions on political and cultural matters. He was a man who could be expected to make informed and sympathetic judgments about cultural matters.

Straight was perplexed by some of the applicants' brief accounts of what they proposed to do. He gives examples in *Twigs for an Eagle's Nest,* a small book that he published after leaving office:

— *My project is a series of paintings, ten to fifteen layers of paint deep, consisting entirely of extremely subtle gradations of grey.*
— *The project I propose will temporarily manipulate the Chicago skyline for the period of one year.*
— *My project is to introduce taxidermy as a sculpture media by using painted plywood construction, dirt, sand, gravel, and animals to create different environmental situations.*

After reflection, Straight signed these along with some other applications that he found puzzling. They were, after all, the choices of the professionals; besides, they "probably would not harm the Endowment." Certain other proposals, however, were "more questionable":

— *A loop tour of Western U.S. . . . dripping ink from Hayley, Idaho to Cody, Wyoming — an event commemorating the birthplace of Ezra Pound and Jackson Pollock.*
— *I will rent a ground level studio with high ceilings and a cement floor, adjacent to a lush meadow. And to this place I will bring*

Pigme, a full-grown sow (whom I have known since her ninth day), two female rabbits (who know each other and me), a buck (stranger), two ring-necked doves (strangers), a wooley monkey, Georgina (who knows me slightly). . . . We will all move together.

I will also bring those things necessary for a comfortable survival, including food and materials to use for building and maintaining nests. All of us will contribute to the creation, maintenance and change of such an environment. Once settled, we may discover that there are others who would like to join us even if just for a short time (birds, mice, people, etc.). I will record our activities so that those unable to visit and experience our situation directly will know something of what it is like. This will best be done by using portable video equipment.

Sometimes, we will leave our place and go together to another, or bring others to us. For these events, we will need a vehicle, preferably a motorbike with a large sidecar. Perhaps this communal way of life will be quite difficult. However, the educational value, for all of us will be extraordinary.

Straight refused to approve these grants, along with about twenty others. He was happy to concede that the artists were sincere, but he could not defend supporting these projects with public funds. Presumably, he believed that Congress, in giving the chairman sole authority to approve grants, intended that in cases of conflict the judgment of politically responsible officials should prevail over that of civil servants, representatives of the art world, and other advisers. He also believed that these grants would make the NEA appear ridiculous in the eyes of the press, the public, and Congress.

By refusing to sign all the applications approved by the staff, Straight created a crisis. The chairman was called from her sickbed. In a two-hour conference, the director of the Visual Arts Program defended the projects. They were, he explained, in styles much admired by the contemporary art world. Some of the applications that Straight was questioning reflected the influence of the great Marcel Duchamp, who, when he moved to New York, had brought with him a bottle labeled "Paris Air." Others were closer to the work of a well-known Italian painter, Piero Manzoni, who had bottled his own excrement and sold it as "Artist's Shit."

Straight, now speechless, steadfastly refused to sign. The grants were made, but over the signature of the chairman. And the rules were changed to circumvent similar crises in the future: hereafter, applicants were not to say what they intended to do with the fellowship. Thus there could be no public criticism of the NEA's choices, no matter how bizarre they might sometimes be.

DEFINING ART

Highly civilized people can define art in profoundly various ways. Here, art will be defined as that which has the capacity to engender in a receptive viewer an aesthetic experience. This definition, of course, is helpful only if it is possible to show that there is such an experience and to describe its nature.

The aesthetic experience is not universal as is, say, the experience of fear. Admittedly, it is probably impossible to point to a culture, past or present, in which people have not lavished effort far beyond what was needed for purely practical purposes on all sorts of things, especially objects connected with religious observances, but also on weapons, clothing, tools and utensils, and their own bodies. The marvelous drawings prehistoric men made on the walls of their caves tempt one to conclude that an impulse to create art has always and everywhere been a part of human nature. This, however, is a mistaken view. What we experience aesthetically could not be experienced in the same way by people whose culture — perceptions, thoughts, feelings — vastly differs from our own.

"Admiring as we do the art of the ancient Greeks," R. G. Collingwood writes, "we naturally suppose that they admired it in the same kind of spirit as ourselves. But we admire it as a kind of art, where the word 'art' carries with it all the subtle and elaborate implications of the modern European aesthetic consciousness. We can be perfectly certain that the Greeks did not admire it in any such way."

The point is elaborated by Johan Huizinga, who says that for the Greeks the visual arts belonged to a different and lower order of experience than did music, poetry, and dance — "play forms" that were closely related and that were presided over by Apollo and the Muses. The mechanical and plastic arts, if they were under divine guidance at all, were the concern of lesser gods and not of any Muse.

In most primitive societies, according to Richard L. Anderson, the concept "art" does not exist in native thought, and in those in which it does "... there is only an approximate correspondence between their notion of art and our own." Of the few hundred methodologically sound accounts of art in other societies, none, he says, contains systematically gathered information on the affective response to art.

Even within a culture — say, the western European since the Renaissance — there are from time to time and place to place very marked differences both in what is responded to as art and in the subjective state that constitutes the response. It is interesting that the word "aesthetic" did not appear until the early eighteenth century and that the concept itself is not much older. The word "art," used in its modern sense and without any qualifier, does not appear in any English dictionary before 1880.

In *Art as Experience* (1934), John Dewey maintains that art is making or doing something in a way that produces an aesthetic emotion, by which he means the feeling that one has when one perceives an intended action as running to its fulfillment by virtue of its internal integration:

> *Man whittles, carves, sings, dances, gestures, molds, draws and paints. The doing or making is artistic when the perceived result is of such a nature that its qualities as perceived have con-*

trolled the question of production. The act of producing that is directed by intent to produce something that is enjoyed in the immediate experience of perceiving has qualities that a spontaneous or uncontrolled activity does not have. The artist embodies in himself the attitude of the perceiver while he works.

The spectator also experiences art when he perceives that the action of the artist was directed in the appropriate way.

For Dewey the distinction between "fine" and other art is one of degree rather than of kind. Any conceivable activity is art if carried on (or perceived to have been carried on) in the right manner. "The intelligent mechanic," he writes, "engaged in his job, interested in doing well and finding a satisfaction in his handiwork, caring for his materials and tools with genuine affection, is artistically engaged."

A difficulty in Dewey's position — and in any that makes the intention a defining characteristic of art — is that one can rarely if ever know the intention of the maker of a work and therefore whether or not the result is a work of art. Suppose, Dewey writes, that a finely wrought object believed to be the product of some primitive people is proved to be an accidental product of nature: "As an external thing, it is now exactly what it was before. Yet at once it ceases to be a work of art and becomes a natural 'curiosity.' It now belongs in a museum of natural history, not in a museum of art."

Which museum should house a manmade object when the nature of its experience or intention is unknown? The object is not art unless it was the intention of the maker to produce something to be enjoyed in the immediate experience of perceiving. The fetishes of the Negro sculptor, Dewey remarks, were more useful to his tribal group than spears or clothing. They were not intended for enjoyment. But the fetishes, he says, are now "fine art," inspiring artists in the twentieth century "only because the anonymous artists lived and experienced so fully during the process of production." Presumably, if it were discovered that the sculptor was merely following a routine prescribed by tribal custom, the fetishes would cease to be fine art and would be exhibited in a museum of ethnology.

For the philosopher Eliseo Vivas the aesthetic experience consists essentially of perceiving things and events — and their symbols — in a way that engages the mind without referring to anything beyond them. An aesthetic object is interesting in itself because of meanings and values that pertain to it, not to something suggested by it. "I take the perception of aesthetic objects," he writes, "to be a rare kind of attention that is intensely directed to an object's imminent meanings as they present themselves immediately to the mind." As an example, Vivas tells of a moment when his attention was entirely absorbed at the sight of a panther pacing in a zoo. The value of the experience, he writes, cannot be compared to that of listening to Bach or Mozart or of seeing a canvas of Cézanne or Renoir:

> Held by the pacing animal, the affective rush that flooded me was not an object of direct awareness and a few moments later, when I turned away from the rail I could not have been able to tell, any more than I am now, what its components were: fear and wonder, admiration, joy, were present with other emotions, the nature of which I could not then have discriminated. I asked no questions when the beast held me, passed no judgment. I looked and saw, for a moment only; but for that brief moment it was a fascinating experience which in retrospect allows me to assert with confidence how little do I see ordinarily; what I usually do is look.

Vivas defines the artist as one who deliberately and successfully makes something that elicits this intense rapt attention. The majority of human beings, he says, do not see paintings as aesthetic objects; for them a painting "must be a painting of something and that something must be external to the painting and perceivable independently of it." There is a kind of mind, he adds, that is apparently incapable of aesthetic response; for such minds, experience is always cognitive.

Another influential theory is that of the philosopher George Dickie, who says that a thing is art if a member of the art world confers upon it "the status of a candidate for appreciation." Members of the art world include not only artists but museum directors, museum-goers, art historians, art theorists, and all others "who keep the machinery of the art world working." Dickie's view is that art is what people connected with arts institutions say it is. This is, of course, a circular definition, for what is an arts institution and what is an art world? The assumption is that there exist standards of some sort that define an arts institution or art world. But *are* there such standards? And if there are, why should it be assumed that what they define has anything in common with what is ordinarily called art? Vito Acconci is said to call the *New York Times* regularly to announce that his breathing is art. Ought his claim to be taken with greater seriousness now that he has been awarded a Guggenheim Fellowship, something that would not have happened had not members in good standing in the art world written letters endorsing his application?

Perhaps the most influential theorist of recent years is Nelson Goodman, whose *Languages of Art* — a development of ideas put forward by Cassier, Collingwood, Langer, and others — describes art as a "language," albeit nonverbal, of symbols. The real question, Goodman says, is not "What objects are (permanently) works of art? but "When is an object a work of art?" His point is that an object functions as a work of art only when viewed in the right context:

> Indeed, just by virtue of functioning as a symbol in a certain way does an object become, while so functioning, a work of art. The stone is normally no work of art while in the driveway but may be so when on display in an art museum. In the driveway it usually performs no symbolic function; in the art museum it exemplifies certain of its properties — e.g., shape, color, texture. The digging and filling of a hole functions as work insofar as our attention is directed to it as an exemplifying symbol. On the other hand, a Rembrandt painting

may cease to function as a work of art when used to replace a broken window or as a blanket.

This is not the place to attempt a critique of Goodman's very complicated theory. It is necessary to point out, however, that the visual art worlds do not agree on what objects are "exemplifying symbols." Claes Oldenberg, an artist mentioned by Goodman, thinks that digging and filling a hole in Central Park would be a work of art if done with artistic intent. But surely there are other eminent members of this same art world who would say that it would be a silly waste of time.

Recently, a skinned rabbit was hung in a gallery of the Art Institute of Chicago. Was it a work of art? Dewey would say yes if putting it there and seeing it produced aesthetic emotion. Vivas would agree if it elicited rapt attention. Dickie would say yes if, but only if, it were put there by a member of the art world who intended to offer it for appreciation, but not if it were put there as a prank. Goodman would say that it was art no matter who hung it there or why, provided that it functioned as an exemplifying symbol to at least some of those who viewed it.

It would be easy to multiply the number of these very different theories as to the nature of art. It is not surprising, then, to learn from the sociologist Howard S. Becker that "Art worlds typically devote considerable attention to trying to decide what is and isn't art, what is and isn't their kind of art, and who is and isn't an artist." Despite their doctrinal and other differences, Becker says, members of an art world characteristically produce "reliable judgments about which artists and works are serious and therefore worthy of attention." If by "reliable" he means that judgments tend to agree, then it is my impression that he considerably overstates the case as respects the world of contemporary visual art.

THE ROLE OF ART IN SOCIETY

As this brief sampling of views suggests, any conception of the nature of art has implications for policy making. A follower of Dewey, for example, would encourage ordinary people to do ordinary things — and to perceive them when done by others — in an artistic manner. It may be evidence of Dewey's influence on policymakers that in 1969 the authors of the first official publication of the "social indicators" movement wrote:

> *There is art not only in museums, theaters, opera houses, and books but in every aspect of life — in cooking, dress, and industrial design. Although this . . . concentrates on the conventionally most professional and "highbrow" forms of art, we must not forget that this is only a small part of the total and may not be the most important. (Emphasis added.)*

A follower of Vivas, by contrast, would see no artistic value in something made by an intelligent mechanic who was interested in doing his job, except in the unlikely event that it would elicit rapt attention without reference to its use or other associations. Although the Vivas-minded policy maker would attach great importance to art ("it is art that creates culture, that creates the values and meanings by which men in society fulfill their destiny"), he would not think it possible to universalize the art experience in its nontrivial forms.

A Goodmanite would keep the finely wrought object in the art museum, but only if it functioned as a significant symbol, which would be much more likely if it were made by an artist (i.e., one who uses a symbolic language that viewers can understand). Because the experience of art is cognitive as well as noncognitive, making and viewing art would be closely integrated into any educational process.

Whatever is taken to be its defining function, art obviously has other functions as well. Monroe C. Beardsley distinguishes between the *incidental* value of a work (he gives as an example the use of the *Winged Victory* as ballast) and its *inherent* value — its capacity to produce aesthetic enjoyment. Collingwood identifies seven forms of "pseudo-art" according to the purposes for which they are created. He renames them as follows:

Where an emotion is aroused for its own sake, as an enjoyable experience, the craft of arousing it is amusement; *where for the sake of its practical value,* magic. . . . *Where intellectual facilities are stimulated for the mere sake of their exercise, the work designed to stimulate them is a* puzzle; *where for the sake of knowing this or that thing, it is* instruction. *Where a certain practical activity is stimulated as expedient, that which stimulates it is* advertisement *or . . .* propaganda; *where it is stimulated as right,* exhortation (Emphasis added.)

Confusion arises, Collingwood says, because art may be combined with pseudo-art: for example, art and religion (magic) in which the artistic motive, although genuinely present, is subordinated to the religious. "What happens," he writes, "is that a combination of art and religion is elliptically called art, and then characteristics which it possesses not as art but as religion are mistakenly supposed to belong to it as art." He concludes, "The various kinds of pseudo-art are in reality various kinds of uses to which art may be put."

Vivas makes a similar point and lists some "non-residential" functions of art, that is, functions that are extrinsic or secondary in that they can be performed — some of them more efficiently — by other means (unlike those that he terms "residential," "intrinsic," or "primary"). Although less systematic, Vivas's list has elements in common with Collingwood's:

Socially, art has been conceived as a means of inculcating morality or the proper political beliefs and attitudes. Today it is widely held that its function is to impart knowledge. And sometimes it is thought to be capable of imparting so high, or so deep, a wisdom, that what it imparts is taken to be sacred and ineffable. At the individual level, art is held to offer us the healing illusion or escape, to be a means of exciting emotions, or of purging them, or of arousing vitality, or of saying yes to the terrible aspects of existence.

Art must be justified by its inherent (as opposed to incidental) values. Thus it is necessary to describe the nature of the aesthetic response: its worth, to the individual and to society, must be the basis for its justification. Aesthetic response, however, is rarely the same from time to time, place to place, and person to person. In an effort to deal with this complication, four principal modes of aesthetic experience are here outlined in ideal-typical form; that is, as logically improved-upon versions of reality, useful for analysis.*

The *ideational* mode of response engages the mind (and therefore in greater or lesser degree the feelings) by its subject matter and content. "Content," as opposed to the subject matter, Erwin Panofsky writes, "is the basic attitude of a nation, a class, a religious or philosophical persuasion — all this unconsciously qualified by one personality. . . ."

Consider the response of John Adams to a collection of paintings he viewed in London in 1786. There were, he writes in his diary, "the pleasure of imitation" in looking at pictures of landscapes, flowers, game; however, a million such pictures could be seen "with much indifference," for the things themselves were to be seen in nature at any time. "[T]here must," he says, "be action, passion, sentiment, and moral, to engage my attention very much. The story of the prince, who lost his own life in a bold attempt to save some of his subordinates from a flood of water, is worth all the paintings that have been exhibited this year."

In the eighteenth century this was a common response to art. Sir Joshua Reynolds in his *Discourses* comes close to making it orthodox, as does Diderot, who criticized Boucher for filling his pictures with nipples and buttocks. It was not the *only* mode then or later. "The greatest picture," John Ruskin declared in the nineteenth century, "is that which conveys to the minds of the spectators the greatest number of the greatest ideas." Although this is far from being the most common response to art today, some contemporary works are intended to — and do in fact —

---

*For expository convenience, references are made to historical figures. The reader should keep in mind, however, that the intention is to provide tools for analysis, not to say anything about art history. In the hope of avoiding confusion the types have been given names that do not suggest art-historical styles.

engage the attention with action, passion, sentiment, and moral.

The *romantic* mode of response differs in that subject matter is irrelevant; style or form produces the response, which is one of feeling. Historically, this mode can be traced to Edgar Allan Poe's essay "The Poetic Principle," in which he compares Beauty and Truth to oil and water. The contemplation of Beauty, he writes, produces "a pleasureable excitement of the soul," which is easily distinguishable both from the response to Truth (the satisfaction of the Reason) and from Passion (the excitement of the Heart).

As developed by Baudelaire and others in France and by Walter Pater and Oscar Wilde in England, the romantic concept holds that art exists solely to give pleasure, cannot be associated with moral or other meaning, and is transient by nature. A great picture, Pater writes, "has no more definite message for us than an accidental play of sunlight and shadow for a few moments on the wall or floor. . . ." Art comes to you "frankly proposing to give nothing but the highest quality to your moments as they pass, and simply for those moments' sake."

The *transcendental* mode is responded to with "disinterested intensity of contemplation." Art created to evoke this response is sometimes explained on the theory that there are two orders of experience: the ordinary experience of the real world, which is radically incapable of giving rise to aesthetic feelings, and the categorically different order of experience that does give rise to those feelings.

This mode is historically associated with "modern art," that is, art free of any representational elements (abstract) and art representing the internal world of feeling (expressionist) as opposed to the external or objective world. "This art," writes Wassily Kandinsky, whose abstract works consist of bright patches of color in asymmetrical arrangements, "creates alongside of the real world a new world which has nothing to do with *external reality*." Piet Mondrian, whose works consist of geometric lines and large, empty spaces, writes that the ultimate goal is the expression of "pure reality" by means of "pure plastics."

The *nihilist* mode is experienced as relief from boredom; it fills an "infinite emptiness of [the] soul" and affords an escape, however brief, from the "dreary length of . . . existence," according to the poet Friedrich von Schlegel, in whose late eighteenth-century work a recent writer has found a "theory of modernism." As Karsten Harries explains:

> The world assigns man a place: it tells him what to do. Nature, society, religion, and art fetter him by making demands. Defying these demands, the romantic nihilist posits freedom as his ideal. His conception of freedom is negative: to be free is to be free from the place which the individual has been assigned, to act other than one is expected to act, to enjoy what one is not expected to enjoy. The interesting serves this ideal. It dislocates man by presenting him with something unexpected or novel. Its appeal depends on certain expectations which are then disappointed. Thus the normal is boring, the abnormal interesting.

Although different in intent, art created for the nihilist response often resembles art created for the transcendental response. Both seek to confront or escape from the ordinary world in order to enter the aesthetic one—a world that *must* be strange, even unintelligible. Art in both of these modes must therefore continually jolt the viewer out of his accustomed ways of seeing and feeling. Taking a familiar thing out of context is one way of doing this. A can of Campbell's soup represented as a work of art, Harries remarks, is interesting: "To stress the unimportant, giving it great importance, can be interesting."

There are other strategies for inducing these modes of aesthetic experience. The work of art may shock ordinary sensibilities with something disgusting, loathsome, or obscene. ("Funk's lumpy, varicose limbs, droopy, deformed breasts and gargantuan genitals in sadistic fantasies and sexist fixation takes us beyond supposed vulgarity to matters of humanity and inhumanity.")

It may present a puzzle that is unsolvable by ordinary ways of seeing, thinking, or feeling. ("When the most ordinary, reliable materials of our experience—such as those reassuringly uniform brands found in supermarkets — are torn from their context to be strewn like boulders in the placid stream of our consciousness, the definitions both of art and of life become subject to doubt.")

The viewer may be bored to a state of vacuity that constitutes or produces a new kind of awareness. ("The knot of attention is untied [by Andy Warhol's six-hour movie of a man asleep], and its strands are laid out before us anew. . . . [T]he audience's participation in the image is never allowed to fall into the slot of that *other* temporal reality. . . .")

Finally, it may jolt the viewer by exhibiting the absurdity of things. ("He was literally crucified with nails driven through his palm, on the back of a Volkswagen . . . replacing the cross with a Volkswagen effectively transformed a religious cliché into a diabolically droll, nightmarish masque: Jesus indeed.")

Art and the Public Interest

. . . proponents of public support of art have tried to justify it on public-interest grounds. The arguments that were advanced in the hearings and debates that preceded passage of the 1965 National Foundation on the Arts and the Humanities Act are, allowing for minor variations, the same as those that have been made since.

Perhaps it is fair to say that the real reason for the passage of the act and for the making of appropriations year after year was, and is, to benefit special interests, especially the culture industry of New York City and the "humanist" professors who could not compete for grants with their colleagues in the sciences. It is significant, however, that these special interests could best be served — perhaps could *only* be served — from behind the protective cover of a barrage of arguments claiming an advantage to the public; for example, asserting the danger to its well-being from the cultural explosion and the no less frightening one resulting from the imbalance between scientific and humanistic studies.

Curiously, these public-interest claims rested on extra-aesthetic grounds. They asserted that the

public would benefit from values that are incidental to art, from values that could be served — doubtless sometimes better served — by altogether different means. The weight of such justifications would be no less if it were known to all concerned that no one would ever make or view a work of art for aesthetic satisfaction.

Probably, the argument that was most effective in getting "the arts" on the political agenda and then treated favorably was that support for the "culture industry" would contribute to prosperity. That it was the *culture* industry was incidental: the justification would have carried the same weight if it had been the widget industry. The essentials were that the industry employed a great many people directly and indirectly, attracted large numbers of tourists, enhanced real-estate values, and brought customers to hotels, restaurants, and expensive shops. All this was understood to give it a claim on public-interest grounds to be fostered by the government.

The argument is altogether without merit when the claim is made at the federal level. From the standpoint of the public it makes no difference where tourists spend their money; attracting them *to* some cities is attracting them *away* from others. If the federal government equally subsidized the efforts of all cities to attract tourists, then the competitive position of the cities would remain as it was. (Admittedly, the matter is somewhat complicated if the tourists are foreigners and certain assumptions are made about balance-of-payments problems.) The argument may have some merit when it proposes that local government provide the subsidies, especially in those instances where the local tax structure is such that the beneficiaries will pay the costs. But even local governments, as Dick Netzer points out, should not justify subsidy of art museums and symphony orchestras "by claiming that it promotes economic development more effectively than would the expenditure of the same amount of money on, say, raising the salaries of principal employees."

Some of the most frequently and earnestly made arguments rested on grounds that are, to put it generously, insubstantial. It was highly implausible (insofar as it had any meaning at all) that "giving official recognition," as by the establishment of an advisory council, would "give status and recognition to the importance of culture in the United States," increase "national prestige," contribute to international understanding and world peace by enabling other nations "to discover that America has a soul," and bring the ghettos of the cities into "the mainstream of American culture." What exactly is national prestige? How is it measured? Why should Americans want more of it? (After the Revolutionary War, according to historian Neil Harris, art was seen as a means of convincing skeptical foreigners of the existence of an American nation. By now, it is safe to say, they have been fully convinced.)

Nineteenth-century social reformers thought that art could be used, along with parks, playgrounds, and settlement houses, to prevent social unrest and alleviate social pathologies. "Whatever Central Park might cost," James Jackson Jarves asked in 1864, "is not so much saved from prisons, priests, police and physicians?" He understood art as something that "elevates and refines the popular mind by bringing it in contact with the true and the beautiful." A century later, however, when there was an accumulation of evidence to show that the popular mind was not affected by access to art and when art no longer had anything to do with truth and beauty or even, as many would say, with any aspect of ordinary experience, it was absurd to claim, as did Douglas Dillon, the chairman of both the Metropolitan Museum of Art and the Business Committee for the Arts, that ". . . artistic performances of one sort or another are essential in handling the crisis of our cities."

Another justification of public support (although one that was not used to help establish the NEA) is that the art experience contributes to the relief and rehabilitation of people confined to custodial institutions such as prisons, mental health centers, and homes for the aged. Art therapy usually consists not of viewing art but of carrying on activities that have some outward resemblance to what artists do.

Although art therapy is rapidly gaining the status of a profession (seven colleges give graduate degrees in it, two "professional" journals have been established to cover the field, and the NEA and the Department of Health and Human Services support artists who work as therapists), the evidence is sparse and shaky that it does more for patients than relieve boredom. "Before we tell people to spend a few million dollars on art instead of tranquilizers," Dr. John H. Knowles, the late president of the Rockefeller Foundation, told a conference on art therapy, "we had better do some serious research to see what the facts are."

Some psychologists hold that self-expression through art is a means of releasing inner tensions, which the American society urgently needs. Mihaly Csikszentmihalyi, chairman of the Committee on Human Development at the University of Chicago, writes that making symbolic information about existence more readily available to people is "one of the major survival tasks of our society." He envisions a federal Department of Symbolic Resources for this purpose.

But what of the justifications that *do* depend upon art being experienced aesthetically? These justifications, however, are also extra-aesthetic in that the values sought are not aesthetic experience as such but rather some change in the social state that is believed to result from it.

It is often taken for granted that the effect of the arts upon society is both profound and benign. This is surely unwarranted. Whatever may have been (or may be) the effect of the arts upon societies other than those of Western Europe, they were not (or are not) mediated by what in the past two centuries has been called aesthetic experience. As pointed out . . . even the Greeks did not experience what we call art in the manner that we do. Moreover, among those societies whose people do have what can properly be called aesthetic experience, there are striking differences in the manner and degree to which the societies appear to be affected by it. There are also striking differences in the kinds of social effects that seem to be produced by the various arts — say, music as opposed to painting.

Insofar as art, or the arts, has consequences for society, they may be beneficial, injurious, or both.

As Jacques Barzun has written, art "can dignify and exalt the civilization that gives it birth and also weaken and destroy it. It can transmit the ideals of a community. It can also detach the individual from the struggles of his age, making loyal citizenship appear to him as futile and perverse as revolutionary action."

The evidence here bearing on these matters is of course far from conclusive. But it strongly suggests that aesthetic experience of visual art has never greatly affected American society, and that the tendency has been, and is, for it to affect it less and less both because of changes in the nature of and the response to art and of the increasing democratization of American life that has caused arts institutions to subordinate aesthetic to other values. Modern art, Kenneth Clark remarks, "has become so hermetic, so removed from the average man's experience, as to be incomprehensible, even to a semi-professional like myself." Our hope lies, he says, in an expanding elite "drawn from every class, and with varying degrees of education, united in a belief that non-material values can be discovered in visible things."

It is possible that, although the size of the art-viewing public has increased substantially in absolute numbers in the past two or three decades, it has increased very little if at all as a proportion of the well-off and well-educated public from which most art viewers are drawn. In addition, art viewing is done more and more for nonaesthetic purposes, especially to learn about art and cultural history; moreover, insofar as art is responded to aesthetically, the response tends more and more to be a private one, having its effects mainly upon the viewer and little upon those he lives among and thus indirectly upon society. Finally, insofar as the experience of art does affect the society, it may sometimes be destructive of the values upon which social well-being depends.

It is arguable that from the standpoint of society art took a wrong turn with the acceptance of the doctrine "art for art's sake." Taken literally, the phrase is of course absurd. But it means that aesthetic values are not to be weighed against other values — moral ones, for example. The view

that aesthetic experience is "one of the ultimate values of human life," Harold Osborne tells us, is one of the "revolutionary changes of outlook" characteristic of present-day aesthetics. It is more revolutionary than may at first appear if the nature and variety of these experiences are fully taken into account.

If, as Aristotle and others believed, that which is distinctively human — reason above all, but love of the beautiful as well — is good, then whatever tends to exalt the distinctively human must also be good and whatever tends to debase it must be bad. By this ("prerevolutionary") standard, the aesthetic experience is good, bad, or indifferent as it raises man to his full potential or lowers him to the level of the brutes.

It may seem that if aesthetic experience has nothing to do with Truth or Beauty (the romantic mode) or, indeed, with any aspect of real or "ordinary" experience (the transcendental and nihilist modes) the worst that can be said from a moral standpoint is that it is irrelevant. If it sticks to its principles it cannot exalt or degrade man, attach or detach him from the struggles of his age, for it belongs to a world that is radically separated from the realm of real experience. This is presumably what Robert Rauschenberg means when he says, "It is extremely important that art be unjustifiable." To be justifiable, it would have to exist for some sake other than its own.

This view raises two problems. One is that much art in these modes does not stay within its aesthetic principle: under the pretense of having to jolt the viewer out of his ordinary perceptions, it comments on the real world. When it does so, its message is often that man is unlovely or deformed, that he is subrational, that he is garbage, that he is absurd.

The other problem concerns art in these modes that does stick to aesthetic principle. It implicitly conveys a message, whose tendency is to degrade human things. It says that man and all that concerns him, including art itself, do not matter. What else can be the message, for example, of the work *Abstract Painting*? Ad Reinhardt, who painted it, has described it as follows:

A square (neutral, shapeless) canvas, five feet wide, five feet high, as high as a man, as wide as a man's outstretched arms (not large, not small, sizeless), trisected (no composition) one horizontal form negating one vertical form (formless, no top, no bottom, directionless), three (more or less) dark (lightless), non-contrasting (colorless) colors, brushwork brushed out to remove brushwork, a mat, flat, free-hand painted surface (glossless, texture-less, non-linear, no hard edge, no soft edge) which does not reflect its surroundings — a pure, abstract, non-objective, timeless, spaceless, changeless, relationless, disinterested painting, an object that is self-conscious (no unconsciousness), ideal, transcendent, aware of nothing but art (absolutely no anti-art).

This book has argued that a justification for government support of art must rest on the inherent rather than the incidental values associated with it — aesthetic experience, that is, rather than values that could be as well or perhaps better secured by other means. If (to use Beardsley's *ad absurdum* example of an incidental use) sculpture were useful as ballast, this would not help to justify a program of support to the arts.

Most of the justifications that have been offered differ from the ballast example in an important way; that is, although sculptures would doubtless make good ballast, art is a quite unsuitable means of serving the public interest in the ways claimed. As mentioned earlier, attracting tourists to one city and away from another does not serve the public interest, and the effectiveness of art in increasing "national prestige," relieving psychic tensions, and so on is extremely dubious. But, to repeat, even if art were as well suited to these uses as sculpture is for use as ballast, these justifications would be irrelevant to the evaluation of a program for the support of art if its purpose is to engender aesthetic experience.

If aesthetic experience contributed significantly to the welfare (however defined) of large numbers of individuals, it would not necessarily follow that it would serve the public interest. Many activities contribute to welfare in this sense without being of concern from a public as opposed to a private standpoint. If, for example, the playing of chess afforded deep satisfaction to almost everyone, probably no one would claim that the playing of chess is therefore in the public interest.

Giving people pleasure has never been considered a proper function of the U.S. government, except as it may be supposed to affect, for good or for ill, aspects of life that are the proper concern of government. Only as an individual's enjoyment of art is correctly perceived by the public as affecting the well-being of the collectivity does it become a matter of public interest.

If it were clear that art significantly affects the quality of society, as opposed to the welfare of individuals, it would not follow that government might properly subsidize it or otherwise intervene in art matters. There are many things that affect society in ways that ennoble or debase men, ways that by common agreement are not the concern of government, either because it is incapable of managing them (e.g., enforcing rules of good manners) or because it is understood that government exists for other purposes.

It may be desirable for the Constitution to spell out in unambiguous detail the proper role of government, but it is impossible for it to do so because there is not, and never has been, general agreement on what that role should be. (If there were such a consensus, it would soon break down in a free society, for people are apt to use their freedom to renege upon their agreements when they think it advantageous, to themselves or to the public, to do so). The role of government in a free society must be a matter of continuous negotiation among members of its public. The American regime rests on the principle that the functions of government are to protect the individual in the exercise of certain inalienable rights and to establish the preconditions for the development of competent citizenry. Some think that the conditions of modern life have made this principle obsolete. It is, however, the principle that has made America what it is, and no one seems likely to propose an alternative that would be generally acceptable.

On Education

Leonard Bernstein

Testimony before the House Subcommittee on Select Education
regarding a bill calling for a White House Conference on the Arts
New York City, 17 December 1977

What I have to say at this aesthetic testimonial is of utmost urgency to me, and, I believe, to our nation. So many words have flowed over the years about the arts in America, the artist and his place in society, the built-in distrust of the arts for which America has long been famous — an aversion based on a long-standing Puritan concept of the artist as somehow unmanly. Congress roared with laughter in the thirties when bills for government support of the artist were introduced. A red-blooded American boy plays baseball, not the violin, and he certainly does not perform pirouettes. As for a red-blooded American girl, she was better off playing with dolls or sewing kits than with cameras or sculptures. In those days of Depression and fascism and antifascism, the arts seemed particularly pointless to our Congress; and it was only the WPA which saved the day and, ironically enough, gave the biggest boost to our artistic life in its entire history up to that point.

Today, almost half a century later, all that has changed. The arts are everywhere, booming and blooming. Anyone with any claim to being civilized *has* to have seen certain plays, heard certain concerts, at least sampled the opera, and contributed his quota of requisite *bravos* at the ballet. There are arts councils everywhere; grants flow in all directions, on federal, state and municipal levels; and there is, of course, this very meeting here today. But, I am sad to say, we are still an uncultured nation, and no amount of granting or funding is ever going to change that, unless — but

I anticipate. A White House conference? Of course. Money for artists? Naturally. I have fought all my life for it. Government subsidies? Again, I raise my voice in a loud Amen, as I have always done. But we are still victims of our ancient attitudes, regarding the arts as a light diversion, an evening out, a curious office building, a comforting blanket of background music, an occasional BBC play about Richard the Third on the educational TV channels — whatever superficially entertaining hour it may be; and we will always retain these attitudes until we become not only an art-producing people, but an art-consuming people; and that means a people *prepared* to receive the aesthetic product; and *that* means an *educated* people. Only a society prepared by education can ever be a truly cultured society. It is a simple case of supply and demand. Let me try to explain what I mean.

The word "education" is a turn-off; we all know that, to our sorrow. But that is only because education has been a forced activity, reluctantly endured because there is no alternative if we wish to succeed in our careers and at our cocktail parties. We tend to tolerate education, in the Victorian manner; to suffer it gladly for our own selfish interests, rather than to embrace it because we have been infused as children with the joy of learning. It is to this joy of learning that I propose the White House conference should address itself — not at the expense of encouraging the arts with financial aid, but in addition to it. In fact, I believe that this urgent need to take hold of and develop the innate curiosity and immense learning capacity which all children share must take precedence over all other considerations.

Let me focus down on the art of music — not only because it is my special field, but because it is the most natural, inborn aesthetic human experience, the most abstract and exalted of the arts. I note with pleasure that on page six of this Joint Resolution 600, the final paragraph lists music first among the arts. I quote: "The term 'arts' includes, but is not limited to, music (instrumental and vocal), dance, drama . . ." and then follows the long list of the other creative and performing arts. Bravo; *but*, though Music may lead the Muses, she is actually the stepchild, in terms of a public prepared for the musical experience. How many Americans can read music? How many Americans are even minimally capable of following the course of a Brahms symphony, to say nothing of a Mozart sonata, or even the fine points of a Gershwin tune? I would guess a fraction of one percent. Music desperately needs a prepared public, joyfully educated ears. After all, everyone learns to read words, to dance the Hustle, to act in school plays, to have some visual appreciation of graphic forms, to understand a poem by Keats or Robert Frost. But almost nobody is taught to read music, or to comprehend its basic principles. Music is an orphan; and will always be that orphan until we get a grip on a methodology of musical education of the young.

I propose that the reading and understanding of music be taught to our children from the very beginning of their school life; that they learn to participate with enthusiasm in the study of music from kindergarten through high school. No child is tone-deaf; every child has the natural ability and desire to assimilate musical ideas and comprehend their combinations into musical forms. Every child can be taught to read music as he or she is taught to read words; and there is no reason why both kinds of reading cannot be taught simultaneously. It is only a matter of presenting this material in a way that does not turn the student off; and I am deeply convinced that with time, intelligent funding, and proper assistance, one can find the ways in which this enormous project can be implemented on a national scale. I, for one, am willing to pledge my energy and time to this end. Children must receive musical instruction as naturally as food, and with as much pleasure as they derive from a ball game. And this must happen from the beginning of their school lives. Only then will we produce a generation of Americans prepared to receive the larger musical experience, and to have the passion to probe ever more deeply. Then we will have our true musical public, an alive, receptive, truly critical public which will demand the best that our artists can supply. That is what I mean by the simple law of demand and supply.

I addressed this problem, long ago, in an article entitled "The Muzak Muse: An Imaginary Conversation with George Washington," to be found in my book *The Infinite Variety of Music*. I respectfully ask that this article be entered into the record.

We *can* become a cultured nation; we have only to learn how first to apply our energies and public dollars in the right places. Let us be proud of America, and of our limitless resources and potential. And our children will be proud of us.

NEA
Financial Summary 1990

SUMMARY OF FUNDS AVAILABLE[1]	FISCAL YEAR 1989
Appropriation: Regular Program Funds[2]	$123,450,000
Appropriation: Treasury Funds (to match nonfederal gifts)	9,000,000
Appropriation: Challenge Grant Funds (to match nonfederal gifts)	18,200,000
Appropriation: Policy, Planning, and Research[1,3]	876,722
Total Federal Appropriations	$151,526,722
Nonfederal Gifts[1]	55,005
Interagency Transfers[1]	250,000
Unobligated Balance, Prior Year[1]	14,830,011
Total Funds Available	**$166,661,738**

[1]Excludes administrative operating funds.
[2]Not less than 20 percent for support of state arts agencies and regional arts groups.
[3]Administrative funds (see Office of Policy, Planning, and Research section).

FUNDS OBLIGATED	FISCAL YEAR 1989 OBLIGATIONS	CHALLENGE GRANT COMMITMENTS/OBLIGATIONS[5]
Dance	$9,513,800	$2,500,000
Design Arts	4,013,921	1,100,000
Expansion Arts	6,401,370	818,479
Folk Arts	3,135,200	700,000
Inter-Arts	4,540,314	2,525,000
Literature	5,061,093	200,000
Media Arts	12,739,200	3,700,000
Museum	12,651,604	7,300,000
Music	15,324,500	4,285,000
Opera-Musical Theater	6,187,005	2,310,000
Theater	10,732,500	3,840,000
Visual Arts	6,109,716	750,000
Arts in Education	5,904,445	224,230
Locals Program	2,606,642	100,000
States Program	25,547,182	1,250,000
Advancement	1,498,059	
Challenge	270,256[4]	
Policy, Planning, and Research[1,3]	876,722	
Total Funds Obligated	**$133,113,529**	**$31,602,709**

[4]Challenge Grants are shown in the column to the right.
[5]Of the $31,602,709 committed, $15,162,567 was obligated in Fiscal Year 1989.

Introduction to *Buying Time*

Ralph Ellison

Twenty years ago the Congress of the United States established the National Endowment for the Arts as an independent agency of the Federal government. Its mission was to encourage and support America's arts and its creative talent by fostering excellence, diversity and vitality in the realm of the imagination. In carrying out its mission the Endowment would stimulate an appreciation of the arts in all sectors of the land by making available the finest examples of artistic creativity. And it would pursue its mission by facilitating a creative collaboration between the Federal and local governments, private foundations, business corporations and the general public. The Act of Congress which created the National Foundation for the Arts was remarkable for the breadth and flexibility of its conception and is of broad historical significance.

For the Endowment came as a long-deferred answer to questions that had perplexed the nation's leaders for close to two hundred years: what role should the imaginative arts play in the official affairs of a democratic society, and what role should the Federal government play in relation to America's art and artists? In the case of literature this volume comes as an answer to such questions, and the variety and high quality of the literary works presented here celebrate the success of the Endowment's ongoing effort. Indeed, it has carried out its mission with such verve that one suspects that if it were possible for certain of the nation's Founding Fathers to read these writings they might well be amazed.

Amazed? Yes, and baffled — as much by the high quality of these examples of contemporary American literature as by the anthology's presentation of young along with well-established writers, the newly discovered along with those who preceded and inspired them. Also amazing would be the diversity of cultural and regional backgrounds from which the writers presented here have come, and the variety of their artistic styles and points of view. It is easy to speculate that the likes of John Adams and Benjamin Franklin would find in the very *idea* of such a collection a drastic reversal of their notions of the role the imaginative arts should (or shouldn't) play in the drama of American society. And that time-wrought reversal of their expectations might well be as startling — and as delightful — as that which occurs when, say, some drab and dejected creature of creepy obscure habit undergoes a metamorphosis through which it becomes before one's eyes a thing of brilliant color and soaring flight, stirring the mind with intimations of bomb-burst and rocket-flare.

In evaluating the role of the National Endowment for the Arts an historical perspective is instructive. For if being an American is, as Henry James put it, a "Complex fate," in the early days of our history being an American *artist* was perhaps the most complex and discouraging fate of all. And much of that complexity had to do with the Founding Fathers' uncertainty about the potential function of the arts in shaping American society. Not that they were unconcerned with the arts, but that, having achieved a successful revolution and mapped out the groundwork for the new nation, they were faced with a world of practical problems; problems which in their view called for military preparedness, statesmanship, a knowledge of law, and that variety of utilitarian skills today classified generally as "industrial arts and crafts." "First things first" was their guiding principle, and the fine arts seemed of a different order. For instance, George Washington believed that "only arts of a practical nature . . . would be esteemed" in the new republic, and suggested that because of the circumstance of its establishment the "genius" of the new society was "scientific rather than imaginative." Nevertheless the arts nagged him, and the first draft of his farewell address included a suggestion (later deleted at Alexander Hamilton's prompting) that the Federal government should promote literature and the arts.

So it wasn't that the Founding Fathers were unaware of the imaginative arts, but that they were baffled as to their proper role in the affairs of the new nation. As to the role of the arts in their *own* lives, they were less ambivalent. Washington was fond of theater, music and dancing; Jefferson was both an architect and a musician; Franklin was familiar with European arts, knew his way around the courts of Europe, and was the inventor of a musical instrument—the glass harmonica. He was also aware of the difficulties faced by America's imaginative artists, and in Constance Rourke's *The Roots of American Culture* he is quoted as having written Charles Wilson Peal (the struggling young painter who would become famous for his portraits of our Revolutionary leaders) that since "the arts have always traveled westward . . . there is no doubt of their flourishing hereafter on our side of the Atlantic."

It must be said, however, that this note of optimism was sounded in the spirit of exhilaration that followed the victorious Revolution, and that once the rigors attending the establishment of the new republic had set in Franklin consigned the role of the fine arts to a place in the nation's distant future. As Miss Rourke indicates, it was his opinion that:

> To America one school-master is worth a dozen poets, and the invention of a machine is of more importance than a masterpiece by Raphael. Nothing is good or beautiful but in the measure that it is useful: yet all things have a utility under particular circumstances. Thus poetry, painting, music (and the stage as their embodiment) are all necessary and proper gratifications of a refined state of society but objectionable at an earlier period, since their cultivation would make a taste for their enjoyment precede its means.

But while Franklin envisioned a possible role for the arts in the future, John Adams was strongly negative concerning their suitability in the life of a struggling democracy. Not only did he regard the imaginative arts as luxuries, but he viewed artists and writers with suspicion. Artists were, as he saw it, a lot of oddballs who "neglected their exercise" and destroyed their health for the sake of "reputation." It would seem that he saw artists as having nothing positive to contribute to the nation's welfare. But if artists—painters, sculptors and actors—were guilty of seeking "notoriety" and "celebration" above all else, those artists who identified themselves as men of letters were far worse. These were a type who demanded "a great deal of praise," a thing Adams saw as being in too short supply, even for statesmen. Nor was it simply a matter of writers being egotistical; they were by trait, as by trade, dishonest. Therefore if they were successful in arousing public interest in their creations it would be not because their work had inherent social value, but because they had managed to dupe "the people" into "bestowing their applause and adorations . . . on artifices and tricks."

The imaginative arts, as Adams saw them, were agencies of disorder—at least for a democratic republic—and as such they were a threat to be discouraged. For there was a possibility that the easily confused "people" would not only be seduced by such artistic ne'er-do-wells but would expect such distractions to be provided *gratis* by their hard-pressed government.

One hesitates to say it, and no disrespect is intended, but Adams' position regarding the arts and government seems to have counseled a position of "benign [if so mild a term applies] neglect." Nor is this said to saddle his illustrious shoulders with a mischievous oxymoron from our own contentious times. Nevertheless it *does* serve to describe Adams' sense of checkmate in the face of those questions now answered in the form of the National Endowment for the Arts. For in effect his attitude toward art and artists was as "discountenancing" as that held by Franklin and Noah Webster toward the slang and regional lingos that were taking root in the interaction between the English language and the diverse peoples and geography of the New World. Franklin and Webster took the vernacular as a threat to the proper English in which our documents of statehood were written — even though it had been transforming the mother tongue into an improvised catch-as-catch-can language long before the Revolution, and was becoming more distinctly and appallingly "American" than the nation in which it thrived. The conflict here was between the language in which the nation was conceived and that through which it would "improvise" its democratic identity — and that sportive, unruly action of language (more precisely of speech) was a clue to what was already happening, if at a much slower pace, to the imaginative arts, agriculture, architecture, engineering and the industrial techniques and processes.

Inspired by the principles of democracy, and adapting rapidly to the New World scene, both arts and crafts were becoming "Americanized" and were actively Americanizing the new society. The fine arts were less vulnerable to that process, though not entirely. The disruption brought by the Revolution made for new alignments, and divorced from their roots and roles in European societies the fine arts blended with the folk arts that had been transplanted from Europe — Yes, and from the artistic tendencies brought to Amer-

ica by the slaves — and were quietly providing modes of artistic communication which worked, ironically, to help bond the nation's diverse peoples ever closer to the ideas and ideals of the nation's founders. Democracy allowed more choices for the individual, and Americans were, if they chose to be, heirs of all the arts. Thus they chose, willy-nilly, those artistic modes and techniques which struck their fancy.

History has proved the Founding Fathers to have been wise statesmen who dealt brilliantly with the disrelationships and incongruities released by the Revolution, but it is useful to recall that they were children of the Old World and at once English Colonials *and* American Revolutionaries. Men of Old World culture, they thought of the arts in terms of European society and associated the fine arts with aristocracy. For them the imaginative arts were an enhancement of monarchic culture that required an educated elite for their proper appreciation. Thus their dilemma.

But art, like love, is where one finds it; a fact which artists know instinctively, no matter what statesmen might think about it. In the broader sense art emerges wherever there are human communities, for art is an extension of human character, an exploration of human creative potential that is not only irresistible but necessary, both for the individual and for the cohesion of society. Where men go the arts go, and where men mingle the arts arise to work their magic. And even when disregarded as inessential they persist in traveling, from east to west or north to south, across land, sea or mountain. They travel, sometimes in disguise, with forms of labor. They travel with forms of religious worship. They travel with secular rites and with the games of children. Most of all, they travel with itinerant and expatriate artists — who, contrary to John Adams' misconception, are a type who sacrifice themselves *not* for fame but through sheer necessity and pleasure of artistic creation.

In the nation's beginnings Americans were more "made" than born. Like their society they were products both of conscious thought and improvisation; the thought which shaped them arose from the Old World and embodied itself in the new. And so with the arts. Here the fine arts became a source of modes and motives for vernacular improvisation (as in our music, literature and dance) to give expression to the unfolding American experience. Its products were often crude and comically self-derisive, but they helped to shape the new society by helping to clarify and make bearable the endless contentions of democracy, and they were the unconscious underside of the conscious political efforts that were being asserted to incarnate democracy. Thus the vernacular mingling of the fine and folk arts occurred unnoticed in the process of nation-building.

As the creation of the National Endowment for the Arts bears witness, it was not a question of *when* the arts should be given official recognition in the new society, so much as *how*, and by what method. For as we say, art gives creative expression to a society's ideals by allowing its members an objective unofficial view of themselves and their culture, and it makes possible communication across the barriers of social hierarchy. And by projecting free-wheeling definitions of the diversity and complexity of American experience it allows for a more or less peaceful adjustment between the claims of "inferiors" and "superiors" — a function of inestimable value to a society based, as is ours, upon the abstract ideal of social equality.

Time has allowed us to recognize relationships which Franklin and Adams stood too close to the chaos of the Revolution to see: that the arts are not merely forms of expression that are of concern to artists, but forms of freedom which allow the American people to gauge their progress as they move toward and away from the fulfillment of their democractic ideals. As Congress recognized in granting the National Endowment for the Arts its broad measure of independence, even artistic dissent is conducive to our social health, and it is for the well-being of the nation that the arts' value as agencies of social order has been recognized. In this volume the National Endowment for the Arts demonstrates that ongoing process of Americanization as it finds expression in literature.

SUGGESTED EXERCISES

1. Are the arts irrelevant to competent citizenship? Write an essay explaining your answer.
2. Explore the assumptions Americans make about the use and value of the arts by investigating cases of the reception of public art. A good example to consider, in addition to Richard Serra's *Tilted Arc*, is the Vietnam War Memorial in Washington, D.C., which elicited a storm of controversy when it was first proposed and built, but which many members of the public have since come to accept warmly.

SUGGESTED ADDITIONAL READINGS

Alan Tormey, "Aesthetic Rights," *Journal of Aesthetics and Art Criticism* 31 (1973).

NOTES

1. Ernest Hauser, *Italy, A Cultural Guide* (New York: Antheum, 1981), pp. 182ff.
2. Vincent Cronin, *The Florentine Renaissance* (n.p.: Collins Fontana, 1967), p. 165. Compare what J. H. Plumb says about Florence, Milan, Rome, and Venice in the Renaissance: "Yet it was these four cities . . . in which the practice and patronage of art had become a civic virtue; it was these cities that witnessed the triumphs of painting and sculpture and the emergence

of the artist from the confine of a craft to the lonely pursuit of his genius." *The Italian Renaissance* (New York: Harper & Row, 1961), p. 31.

3. Morse Peckham, "Three Notions about Criticism," in *What is Criticism?* ed. Paul Hernadi (Bloomington: Indiana University Press, 1981), p. 50.

4. See Anthony Blunt, *Artistic Theory in Italy, 1400–1600* (Oxford: Oxford University Press, 1962), p. 55. Also see Cronin, *Florentine Renaissance*, Chapters 9–10.

5. This is a rough description of the Aspen (Colorado) Music Festival, whose budget is larger than many symphony orchestras.

6. A. B. Spellman, *Black Music: Four Lives* (New York: Schocken Books, 1970), p. 150.

7. T. S. Eliot, *The Use of Poetry and the Use of Criticism* (London: Faber & Faber, 1964), p. 154.

8. Richard Serra, "'Tilted Arc' Destroyed," *Art in America*, May 1989, p. 37.

9. To this day it is unclear whether the ground swell of support for the sculpture's removal was as large as the media claimed. Serra denies that there was a clear majority in favor of its removal. He claims that the controversy was manipulated by a few powerful people who hated the sculpture. See Serra, "'Tilted Arc' Destroyed," pp. 34–47.

10. Quoted in Serra, "'Tilted Arc' Destroyed," p. 35.

11. From the hearings on colorization of films held by the Senate Judiciary Subcommittee, broadcast on C-SPAN II, April 1987. All quotes in the paper are verbatim transcriptions from that hearing.

12. Eliot, *Use of Poetry*, p. 15.

CHAPTER 3

Pushpin or Poetry? — The Puzzle of Aesthetic Value

◀ Viewers of *Mona Lisa* at the Louvre. If the *Mona Lisa* is the most famous work of visual art, it may be because it was acclaimed even before it was finished. It inspired imitations while it was still in Leonardo's studio. By the nineteenth century it was the goal of pilgrimages. Is its fame based on aesthetic quality or on its compounding notoriety?

Why do folks go to museums, anyway?
All around us, treasures are heaped up
high.
Is that the sky
or a piece of bright-colored cloth?
If this is the work of our own hands,
what door will not open before us?
We are the architects of earths,
the decorators
of planets. We're miracle-makers.
We'll tie rays of light
into bundles and use them as brooms
to sweep the clouds from the sky
with electricity.

—Vladimir Mayakovsky, *Mystery-Bouffe*

THE CONCEPT OF AESTHETIC VALUE

What is art, and what is its value? Does art have the importance now customarily attributed to it? If so, why? In this chapter, I want to sharpen these fundamental questions and show how a skeptical line of thought brings a sense of urgency to them. Tolstoy questioned the value of individual works of art, but he never questioned the value of art itself. Some thinkers have gone much further and doubted that art has any special value. We will look at one such argument in this chapter, an argument based on a modern philosophy of value.

To some people it may seem almost incoherent to seriously question the value of art. One reason for this response has to do with language. The very words we use to describe art disguise the fact that there could be a genuine doubt that it is valuable. The special vocabulary reserved for art is heavily value laden. The word "art" itself is often used to express approval and positive value, as in, "The D-day invasion was a work of art!" or "There is an art to taking organized lecture notes." This use of the word "art" has *evaluative* implications; it commits the speaker to approving of the object or activity in question. Clearly, in this book we have been using "art" in a different sense, a *descriptive* sense in which it simply refers to the large body of artifacts that society conventionally labels "art" or "works of art."[1] In this sense, it is not self-contradictory to ask whether art has any value.

Other crucial words used in discourse about the arts are also value laden, for example, "masterpiece" and "genius." The great artists are geniuses, and their works are masterpieces. How can one question the value of such works? Why shouldn't such work be preserved in museums and performed in concert halls? Don't such works in fact constitute for us the very paradigm of cultural achievement? Yet, the use of such terms only reminds us again that art has a very high status and that some artworks are considered to be greater than other artworks. It does not explain what value art in general has.

Another reason why one could be puzzled by any attempt to question the value of art comes from the common failure to distinguish *historical* value from *aesthetic* value. "Historical" value derives from those properties that make an artifact important from a historical point of view, whereas by "aesthetic" value I mean the value — whatever it is — that artworks have in themselves. An artifact can be historically interesting for many reasons. Works of art can tell scholars much about the society in which they were produced. A painting, for example, can tell us what clothing people wore, how they played musical instruments, how they fought, what they believed, how servants related to their masters, and so forth. A work of art may also have historical interest from the point of view of the history of art. There are at least three different ways in which works can acquire art-historical interest. These ways correspond to three categories of artworks.

The first is work that achieved *fame* in its own time; that is, an artwork gains art-historical interest because it was very popular in its own time. An example is Leonardo's Mona Lisa (ca. 1503), a painting many people look at because it has always seemed important (see illustration opposite p. 1). A scholar of the painting tells us that when "it was still in Leonardo's Florence, and very probably not yet finished, it was already inspiring imitations. By the middle of the sixteenth century it was being pronounced divine rather than human in its perfection; by the middle of the nineteenth century it was a goal for pilgrimages. . . ."[2]

The second is work that has exerted *influence*; that is, a work may have art-historical interest because it had a discernible impact on subsequent artists. Examples are Beethoven's symphonies, the ninth and last completed in 1824, which dominated the thinking of most nineteenth-century composers. The third source of art-historical interest lies in the *originality* of work. The revolutionary verbal experiments of the early twentieth-century writers James Joyce and Gertrude Stein are examples. Each of these attributes of an artwork is a fact *about* it that gives it a scholarly interest and thus a historical importance that justifies preserving and studying such work.

Often these traits go together. Because work is famous or original, it is influential. Nonetheless, it is possible for a particular work of art to have any one of these attributes without having the others; and, although unlikely, for a work to have all of these attributes and not have what I am defining as aesthetic value. Art-historical value need not track with aesthetic value. It would be possible, that is, for artwork to be popular or influential for the wrong reasons. Much of the so-called academic painting of the nineteenth century, for example, which was both popular and influential, is now thought to be merely of historical interest. Confusing a work's historical popularity with its aesthetic value commonly leads to a false estimation of the work's value. Surely the Mona Lisa, for example, is no greater than hundreds of other paintings by Leonardo and his contemporaries, yet it is far more famous than any other visual artwork. Conversely, artwork that was not appreciated in its own time might now seem to have the highest possible aesthetic value. The same point obviously applies to influence, and even to originality. The composers at the Mannheim court in Germany literally invented the symphony in the 1760s. Yet although their symphonies are still played today, contemporary listeners do not consider them very significant. Similarly, the first true opera, *Dafne* (1597), is historically important only because it was the first of its kind. But the first *great* opera, the first opera that still speaks to audiences today, is Monteverdi's *Orfeo* (1607).[3]

The distinction between aesthetic value and historical value is particularly clear in the case of the composer Johann Sebastian Bach (1685–1750). Bach is usually considered one of the three greatest composers of all time, yet in his lifetime he worked in relative obscurity for a variety of church and court patrons. His work was thought old-fashioned even to his contemporaries and rapidly fell out of favor after his death. His work was neither popular nor influential. Nor was it particularly original; Bach pioneered no new musical forms, for example. All he had was incredible musical insight and genius—so much so that it took almost a century for audiences to begin to appreciate the depth, complexity, and beauty of his music.

I want to emphasize that I am using the expression "*aesthetic* value" in a special way:[4] aesthetic value is whatever value or values come from normal appreciation of a work of art, that is, from listening to music, reading a novel, looking at a painting, watching a play, and so forth. In contrast to historical importance, which derives from facts *about an artwork*, aesthetic value is founded on the *direct experience* of the work of art. Note that I have not tried to analyze appreciation, nor have I implied that one can properly respond to an artwork without having a great deal of historical knowledge about it. My aim has been limited to contrasting the value that fundamentally justifies art—what I have dubbed its aesthetic value—from a common reason for supposing that art is valuable, namely its historical importance.

It is especially important to avoid confusing aesthetic value with historical importance because the distinction is commonly blurred in the study of art history. Sometimes the two values are almost exquisitely intertwined, as in this praise of the poetry of Petrarch (1304–1374) and Boccaccio (1313–1375) by the great Renaissance scholar Jacob Burckhardt:

> . . . we shall find in them the earliest complete expression of modern European feeling. The question, be it remembered, is not to know whether eminent men of other nations did not feel so deeply and so nobly, but who were the first to give documentary proof of the widest knowledge of the movements of the human heart.[5]

Burckhardt seems to be praising the Italian poets for their originality, because they were the *first* to express a modern mentality. But closer reading suggests that he assumes that what they expressed—knowledge of the workings of the human heart—is profound and universally relevant.

To ask whether art has an important or unique type of value is to ask whether the aesthetic value of works of art is important or unique. There is no doubt that many works of art have great historical value, in the sense that they are important in the history of art in the ways delineated above. But such value must take second place to aesthetic value. The arts are not important because their history is important. Rather, their history is especially important because *they* are; artworks of the past are relevant and alive for spectators today just as they were for spectators in their own time. We are still deeply moved and enlightened by the plays, operas, poems, and so forth, of past centuries.

To be sure, historical value is value, but that alone cannot account for the importance placed on art, nor would it adequately answer Tolstoy's challenge (see Chapter 2).[6] Who can believe that Beethoven's symphonies are repeatedly performed because the audience is primarily interested in their historical importance, or that we could justify the great expense of so many live performances merely on historical grounds, given the great familiarity of the music and the availability of accurate recordings?

Our experience of art is largely an experience of art of the past. (This is true even if what we like are works of the more recent past, such as jazz records or Hitchcock movies.) This fact raises a host of further questions concerning what spectators today get out of art from the past. Do we get the same value? Do we even experience the art in the same way as its original audience did? A work of art may have been valued in its own time not for its aesthetic value but for other reasons. For instance, many art forms were thought of in their own times principally as having a practical, *functional* value. Their importance derived in large measure from the useful functions they served. Now that these works no longer fulfill their original function, we must ask, Do we correctly understand the works as they were intended, and have we really discovered an aesthetic value that replaces the lost functional value?

This functional value is exemplified in one of the greatest periods of painting, the middle Renaissance. (A noteworthy piece of this period, Giotto's *Kiss of Judas*, is illustrated in Plate 2.) As Michael Baxandall reminds us, "Most fifteenth-century pictures are religious pictures."[7] The religious function of these pictures was to excite and instruct spectators about the biblical stories. For the viewer, "it amounts to using pictures as respectively lucid, vivid and readily accessible stimuli to meditation on the Bible and the lives of the Saints."[8] The sense of sight was used as a powerful and precise replacement for the inadequate and often inaccessible medium of words. For a spectator of the period, the best paintings were those that most effectively heightened the ability to meditate on Christian themes. Today, most viewers of paintings by such great masters as Giotto, Fra Angelico, or Piero della Francesca do not have this aim at all. Are contemporary spectators able to find aesthetic value in works that were meant to be appreciated in a very different way?

It seems so. Indeed, the fact that a work of art has strongly and broadly appealed to spectators over a substantial period of time is evidence that a work has great *aesthetic* appeal. Consider, for example, Bach's *St. Matthew Passion* (1727). This work for chorus, solo voices, and orchestra has been aptly described as "one of the transcendent monuments of Christian musical art."[9] The content of Bach's *Passion* is, of course, the Gospel of St. Matthew. Yet the work appeals as strongly to nonreligious listeners as to religious listeners and as strongly to listeners today as to listeners in Bach's time. This suggests that the work's attraction comes not from its original liturgical function but from its powerful musical expression.

In sum, we have distinguished three broad sorts of value a work of art may be thought to have: historical, functional, and aesthetic value. But the *special value* that art is assumed to have can be neither historical value nor functional value. Functional value can in some cases explain why art was worth producing, historical value can account for why art is worth preserving, but only aesthetic value can account for why it is ultimately important. Fortunately, traditional theories of art have given accounts of aesthetic value. By investigating these theories, philosophy of art ought to be able to illuminate the nature of aesthetic value.

> The artistic value of a book is different from its economic value, and is differently determined, as is its weight in pounds, its utility as a doorstop, its elevating or edifying or life-enhancing properties, its gallery of truths: new truths, known truths, believed truths, important truths, alleged truths, trivial truths, absolute truths, coming truths, plain unvarnished truths.
>
> — William H. Gass[10]

SKEPTICISM ABOUT AESTHETIC VALUE

Can we identify the nature of aesthetic value? There is a skeptical position that claims that art has no special value, that in fact there is no special aesthetic value. Jeremy Bentham (1748–1832), the great English philosopher, is reputed to have put it this way:

> Prejudice aside, the game of pushpin is of equal value with the arts and sciences of music and poetry.[11]

Bentham's famous remark argues that the high status of such arts as poetry is based on sheer prejudice for which there is no objective basis. Poetry is no better than the children's game of pushpin; fundamentally, it is no different — it just appeals to a different group of participants. As the contemporary American philosopher Hilary Putnam comments,

> What makes this so shocking to the modern reader is how deeply it conflicts with our current cultural values. The arts have been exalted by us to a place higher than any they occupied in Plato's day or in the middle ages. . . . for a certain sort of educated person, art today is a religion, i.e. the closest thing to salvation available. (p. 84)

Bentham's position is important because it is founded on an influential theory of value. Bentham was one of the originators of *utilitarianism*, a moral theory that holds that that action is right which produces the greatest net sum of happiness. Since Bentham views happiness as compounded of pleasures, he holds that whatever gives pleasure is valuable to that extent. So there is a value to art beyond its historical and functional value, namely, the pleasure it gives members of the audience. But there is no *special* value that gives art more importance than other pleasurable activities. All one can say, objectively, is that one person enjoys reading a poem whereas another person enjoys reading the sports pages of a newspaper. Prejudice aside, one activity is as good (that is, as valuable) as the other; thus, the sports page is as valuable as any poem.

Many people think of the arts in terms that unintentionally support Bentham's shocking evaluation. Mary McCarthy's description of Venetian painting is quite typical:

> Venice's most wonderful invention — that of the easel painting — was designed solely for pleasure. Painting, up to Giorgione, had a utility basis: the glorification of God and the saints, the glorification of the state . . . the glorification of the individual (the portrait). Giorgione was the first to create canvases that had no purpose beyond sheer enjoyment, the production of agreeable moods, as Berenson puts it.[12]

(Giorgione's *Pastoral Concert*, one of the earliest easel paintings, is illustrated in Plate 1.) This is an insightful description of an important change in attitude toward painting that occurred during this period. But as an account of the aesthetic value of painting, from this or any other period, it falls right into Bentham's trap.

It is likely that no serious lover of painting would base the aesthetic value of painting on sheer pleasure, but what can be put in its place? Interestingly, Bernard Berenson, a famous connoisseur of Renaissance painting, gives an account of art different from that attributed to him by McCarthy:

> All the arts are compounded of ideated sensations, no matter through what medium conveyed, provided they are communicated in such wise as to produce a direct *effect of life-enhancement*. The question then is what, in a given art, produces life-enhancement; and the answer for each art will be as different as its medium.[13]

Unfortunately, Berenson never develops his vague concept of life-enhancement. It seems to be the pious hope that art *ought* to have an important positive value on the spectator.

Bentham's position, however, is not based simply on an oversight, or on an overstatement of the sort McCarthy makes, and it cannot be overturned by pious hopes. Bentham expresses the view that there is no life-enhancing effect except pleasure. Bentham's challenge can be formulated as the following inference:

1. If the value of the arts lies solely in the pleasure they give, then poetry is intrinsically no better than pushpin.
2. There is no value to the arts except pleasure.
3. Hence, poetry is intrinsically no better than pushpin.

Premise 2 follows from the hedonistic view that pleasure and pain are the only intrinsic values in the world. Bentham's eminent follower in the nineteenth century, John Stuart Mill, tried to develop a more sophisticated utilitarianism in which he distinguished "higher" from "lower" pleasures. (See the Readings.) By distinguishing among pleasures, one can hope to escape Bentham's reasoning. But it is essential to argue that some pleasures are intrinsically *better* than others. And this Mill does. He tries to argue that the higher pleasures of poetry count for more than the pleasure of pushpin. Thus Mill accepts premise 2 but rejects premise 1, and so Bentham's challenge collapses.

Mill's position is difficult to defend, however. It is far more common to reject premise 2 and thus to agree merely that *if* the value of art resided solely in pleasure, it would be difficult to elevate the arts above other enjoyments. In response to premise 2, many defenders of the arts would contend that the arts have meaning or truth that cannot be captured or expressed any other way. Hilary Putnam (see the Readings) claims,

> We *have* a reason for preferring poetry to pushpin, and that reason lies in the felt experience of great poetry, and of the after effects of great poetry — the enlargement of the imagination and the sensibility through the enlargement of our repertoire of images and metaphors, and the integration of poetic images and metaphors with mundane perceptions and attitudes that takes place when a poem has lived in us for a number of years. (p. 87)

This is an attractive suggestion. It replaces Bentham's premise that art only gives pleasure with the claim that art enlarges our capacity to experience the world. This claim is similar to the explanation that D. W. Griffith, the pioneering American film director, gave to his work: "The task I am trying to achieve is to make you see."[14]

Putnam's defense must assume both that there is some sort of truth in art and the way that it alters us and that it doesn't exist in other activities. Otherwise, Benthamites could reply that it is always possible to appeal to our prejudices about the value of the activities we prefer. Someone who preferred football to poetry, for example, could put his defense of football in exactly the same terms as Putnam's. He could appeal to the enlargement of perception and feeling caused by great football games, and his defense might seem plausible to those who enjoy football but find poetry meaningless. To evaluate defenses of art such as Putnam's adequately, we need to explore the plausibility of the claim that art does really "expand" the spectator and that it does so in ways that are unique and superior to non-art methods of "expanding" people.[15] To counter Bentham's skepticism, we must develop a plausible theory of art that identifies the unique and positive way in which art alters our experience.

Putnam's defense depends on a mimetic theory of art (see Chapter 9), which contends that the basic function of art is to represent the world. Presupposing such a view, Putnam is able to suggest that poetry represents the world in a way that is deep, unique, and truthful. He can argue that experience of the world through poetry, through the poet's sensibilities, increases and alters our perception. The mimetic theory of art, however, has an important weakness. It is hard-pressed to account for the existence of the nonrepresentational arts, such as instrumental music and abstract visual arts, yet these art forms are very highly regarded. Many of the greatest works of art of the last three centuries have been musical works (for example, the symphonies of Beethoven, the keyboard works of Bach). Without words or narrative, with nothing represented, what is the meaning or truth of such works? How could a defense like Putnam's be given for purely instrumental music?

Such works of art pose a general challenge to philosophy of art. Are we to fall back on a Bentham-like position in the case of music and abstract art, holding that such art has no value outside of the sensory pleasures it causes? For most people, this would be an outrageous partition of the arts. The usual view of the status of music, for example, is quite the opposite. The nineteenth-century aesthetician Walter Pater formulated this view in a famous saying: "All art aspires towards the condition of music." Music may indeed be the highest art of all! If this is right, we cannot ignore the need to find an account of the aesthetic value of music, as well as of the other nonrepresentational arts.

There appear to be three options. First, we can try to find a way to extend the mimetic theory to abstract art, showing how even such art has a representational content. Second, we can retain the mimetic theory for representational arts but develop a different theory for nonrepresentational art. Third, we can give up the mimetic theory, and with it defenses of art similar to Putnam's, and instead try to find an overarching theory of art that applies to all forms of art and accounts for its aesthetic value in a uniform way.

There is much to be said for each option. The first option appeals to those who feel that artworks must always represent something and that the mimetic theory of art is therefore the true account of art. The second option appeals to those who believe that the arts are a mixed bag and that more than one theory may be required to account for the nature and value of different arts. The third option is, of course, chosen by proponents of theories of art that compete with the mimetic theory, such as formalist and expression theories of art. We can make the final evaluation of these options only after we consider the major theories of art (see Part III).

Let's sum up this chapter. We have discovered that a central task of philosophy of art is to find a theory of art that accounts for its *aesthetic* value. We considered one simple but powerful skeptical view that denies the existence of a special aesthetic value over and above people's subjective preference. This skeptical challenge suggests that an adequate theory of art must be able to explain what is valuable about the arts, including nonrepresentational arts, beyond the pleasure they yield to the spectator. A successful theory of art must do even more: it must show not just that art has *some* aesthetic value, but that art is deep and profound, that its value is as high as anything that human culture produces.

READINGS FOR CHAPTER 3

John Stuart Mill, from *Utilitarianism*
Hilary Putnam, "Reason and History"

from *Utilitarianism*

John Stuart Mill

The creed which accepts as the foundation of morals Utility, or the Greatest-happiness Principle, holds that actions are right in proportion as they tend to promote happiness, wrong as they tend to produce the reverse of happiness. By happiness is intended pleasure and the absence of pain, by unhappiness, pain and the privation of pleasure. To give a clear view of the moral standard set up by the theory, much more requires to be said, in particular, what things it includes in the ideas of pain and pleasure, and to what extent this is left an open question. But these supplementary explanations do not affect the theory of life on which this theory of morality is grounded — namely, that pleasure and freedom from pain are the only things desirable as ends, and that all desirable things (which are as numerous in the utilitarian as in any other scheme) are desirable either for the pleasure inherent in themselves, or as means to the promotion of pleasure and the prevention of pain.

Now, such a theory of life excites in many minds, and among them in some of the most estimable in feeling and purpose, inveterate dislike. To suppose that life has (as they express it) no higher end than pleasure — no better and nobler object of desire and pursuit — they designate as utterly mean and groveling, as a doctrine worthy only of swine, to whom the followers of Epicurus were, at a very early period, contemptuously likened; and modern holders of the doctrine are occasionally made the subject of equally polite comparisons by its German, French, and English assailants.

When thus attacked, the Epicureans have always answered, that it is not they, but their accusers, who represent human nature in a degrading light, since the accusation supposes human beings to be capable of no pleasures except those of which swine are capable. If this supposition were true, the charge could not be gainsaid but would then be no longer an imputation; for, if the sources of pleasure were precisely the same to human beings and to swine, the rule of life which is good enough for the one would be good enough for the other. The comparison of the Epicurean life to that of beasts is felt as degrading, precisely because a beast's pleasures do not satisfy a human being's conceptions of happiness. Human beings have faculties more elevated than the animal appetites, and, when once made conscious of them, do not regard any thing as happiness which does not include their gratification. I do not, indeed, consider the Epicureans to have been by any means faultless in drawing out their scheme of consequences from the utilitarian principle. To do this in any sufficient manner, many Stoic as well as Christian elements require to be included. But there is no known Epicurean theory of life which does not assign to the pleasures of the intellect, of the feelings and imagination, and of the moral sentiments, a much higher value as pleasures than to those of mere sensation. It must be admitted, however, that utilitarian writers in general have placed the superiority of mental over bodily pleasures chiefly in the greater permanency, safety, uncostliness, etc., of the former — that is, in their circumstantial advantages rather than in their intrinsic nature. And, on all these points, utilitarians have fully proved their case, but they might have taken the other, and, as it may be called, higher ground, with entire consistency. It is quite compatible with the principle of utility to recognize the fact that some *kinds* of pleasure are more desirable and more valuable than others. It would be absurd that while, in estimating all other things, quality is considered as well as quantity, the estimation of pleasures should be supposed to depend on quantity alone.

If I am asked what I mean by difference of quality in pleasures, or what makes one pleasure more valuable than another, merely as a pleasure, except its being greater in amount, there is but one possible answer. Of two pleasures, if there be one to which all or almost all who have experience of both give a decided preference, irrespective of any feeling of moral obligation to prefer it, that is the most desirable pleasure. If one of the two is, by those who are competently acquainted with both, placed so far above the other that they prefer it, even though knowing it to be attended with a greater amount of discontent, and would not resign it for any quantity of the other pleasure which their nature is capable of, we are justified in ascribing to the preferred enjoyment a superiority in quality so far outweighing quantity, as to render it, in comparison, of small amount.

Now, it is an unquestionable fact, that those who are equally acquainted with and equally capable of appreciating and enjoying both do give a most marked preference to the manner of existence which employs their higher faculties. Few human creatures would consent to be changed into any of the lower animals for a promise of the fullest allowance of a beast's pleasures; no intelligent human being would consent to be a fool, no instructed person would be an ignoramus, no person of feeling and conscience would be selfish and base, even though they should be persuaded that the fool, the dunce, or the rascal is better satisfied with his lot than they are with theirs. They would not resign what they possess more than he for the most complete satisfaction of all the desires which they have in common with him. If they ever fancy they would, it is only in cases of unhappiness so extreme that, to escape from it, they would exchange their lot for almost any other, however undesirable in their own eyes. A being of higher faculties requires more to make him happy, is capable probably of more acute suffering, and certainly accessible to it at more points, than one of an inferior type, but, in spite

of these liabilities, he can never really wish to sink into what he feels to be a lower grade of existence. We may give what explanation we please of this unwillingness: we may attribute it to pride, a name which is given indiscriminately to some of the most and to some of the least estimable feelings of which mankind are capable; we may refer it to the love of liberty and personal independence—an appeal to which was with the Stoics one of the most effective means for the inculcation of it; to the love of power, or to the love of excitement, both of which do really enter into and contribute to it; but its most appropriate appellation is a sense of dignity, which all human beings possess in one form or other, and in some, though by no means in exact, proportion to their higher faculties, and which is so essential a part of the happiness of those in whom it is strong, that nothing which conflicts with it could be, otherwise than momentarily, an object of desire to them. Whoever supposes that this preference takes place at a sacrifice of happiness, that the superior being, in any thing like equal circumstances, is not happier than the inferior—confounds the two very different ideas of happiness and content. It is indisputable that the being whose capacities of enjoyment are low has the greatest chance of having them fully satisfied, and a highly endowed being will always feel that any happiness which he can look for, as the world is constituted, is imperfect. But he can learn to bear its imperfections, if they are at all bearable, and they will not make him envy the being who is indeed unconscious of the imperfections, but only because he feels not at all the good which those imperfections qualify. It is better to be a human being dissatisfied than a pig satisfied, better to be Socrates dissatisfied than a fool satisfied. And if the fool or the pig are of a different opinion, it is because they only know their own side of the question. The other party to the comparison knows both sides.

It may be objected that many who are capable of the higher pleasures occasionally, under the influence of temptation, postpone them to the lower. But this is quite compatible with a full appreciation of the intrinsic superiority of the higher. Men often, from infirmity of character, make their election for the nearer good, though they know it to be the less valuable, and this no less when the choice is between two bodily pleasures than when it is between bodily and mental. They pursue sensual indulgences to the injury of health, though perfectly aware that health is the greater good. It may be further objected, that many who begin with youthful enthusiasm for everything noble, as they advance in years sink into indolence and selfishness. But I do not believe that those who undergo this very common change voluntarily choose the lower description of pleasures in preference to the higher. I believe that, before they devote themselves exclusively to the one, they have already become incapable of the other. Capacity for the nobler feelings is in most natures a very tender plant, easily killed, not only by hostile influences but by mere want of sustenance, and, in the majority of young persons, it speedily dies away if the occupations to which their position in life has devoted them, and the society into which it has thrown them, are not favorable to keeping that higher capacity in exercise. Men lose their high aspirations as they lose their intellectual tastes, because they have not time or opportunity for indulging them, and they addict themselves to inferior pleasures, not because they deliberately prefer them, but because they are either the only ones to which they have access or the only ones which they are any longer capable of enjoying. It may be questioned whether any one who has remained equally susceptible to both classes of pleasures ever knowingly and calmly preferred the lower, though many in all ages have broken down in an ineffectual attempt to combine both.

From this verdict of the only competent judges, I apprehend there can be no appeal. On a question which is the best worth having of two pleasures, or which of two modes of existence is the most grateful to the feelings, apart from its moral attributes and from its consequences, the judgment of those who are qualified by knowledge of both, or, if they differ, that of the majority among them, must be admitted as final. And there needs be the less hesitation to accept this judgment respecting the quality of pleasures, since there is no other tribunal to be referred to even on the question of quantity. What means are there of determining which is the acutest of two pains, or the intensest of two pleasurable sensations, except the general suffrage of those who are familiar with both? Neither pains nor pleasures are homogeneous, and pain is always heterogeneous with pleasure. What is there to decide whether a particular pleasure is worth purchasing at the cost of a particular pain, except the feelings and judgment of the experienced? When, therefore, those feelings and judgment declare the pleasures derived from the higher faculties to be preferable *in kind*, apart from the question of intensity, to those of which the animal nature disjoined from the higher faculties is susceptible, they are entitled on this subject to the same regard.

Reason and History

Hilary Putnam

With the rise of science has come the realization that many questions cannot be settled by the methods of the exact sciences, ideological and ethical questions being the most obvious examples. And with the increase in our admiration and respect for the physicist, the cosmologist, the molecular biologist, has come a decrease in respect and trust for the political thinker, the moralist, the economist, the musician, the psychiatrist, etc.

In this situation some have gone with the cultural tide and argued that, indeed, there is no knowledge to be found outside of the exact sciences (and the social sciences to the extent that they succeed in aping the exact sciences, and only to this extent). This view may take the form of positivism or materialism, or some combination of these. Others have tried to argue that science too is "subjective" and arbitrary — this is the popular reading of Kuhn's immensely successful book *The Structure of Scientific Revolutions*, even if it is not the one Kuhn now says he intended. Others — e.g. the Marxist philosophers and the religious philosophers — adopt a sort of *double-entry* bookkeeping, leaving technical questions to the exact sciences and engineering and ideological or ethical questions to a different tribunal: the Party, the Utopian future, the church. But few can feel comfortable with any of these stances — with extreme scientism in either its positivist or materialist forms, with subjectivism and radical rela-

tivism, or with any of the species of double-entry bookkeeping. It is just because we feel uncomfortable that there is a real problem for us in this area.

To be sure, the problem is in one way *un*real. The same person who argues that ethical and political opinions are unverifiable argues with passion for *his* ethical and political opinions. Hume said that he left his scepticism whenever he left his study; and relativists are likely to do the same with their relativism. But this only shows that no one can consistently live by relativism; if this is all that can be said in response to relativism, then we are just pushed from relativism to 1945 style existentialism ("it's all absurd, but you have to choose"). And is *that* so different?

In order to fix our ideas, let us recall a remark by a philosopher of the last century whose Utilitarianism actually covered a good bit of relativism. I am thinking of Bentham, and of Bentham's challenging judgment that "prejudice aside, the game of pushpin is of equal value with the arts and sciences of music and of poetry." *Prejudice aside, pushpin is as good as poetry.*

What makes this so shocking to the modern reader is how deeply it conflicts with our current cultural values. The arts have been exalted by us to a place much higher than any they occupied in Plato's day or in the middle ages. As a number of authors have remarked, for a certain sort of educated person, art today is religion, i.e. the closest thing to salvation available.

Bentham is saying that a preference for "the arts and sciences of music and poetry" over the childish game of pushpin is merely subjective, like a preference for vanilla ice cream over chocolate ice cream. He does not wish to deny that music and poetry do have greater value than pushpin ("prejudice aside" is an important part of the sentence); in the context of his Utilitarianism, the very fact that a large majority *do* prefer music and poetry to pushpin *gives* music and poetry greater "utility" and hence greater value. But the value is, as it were, the *product* of "prejudice" (i.e. purely subjective interest); there is no fact of the matter about the relative value of pushpin and poetry apart from the fact that people prefer poetry to pushpin. We don't prefer poetry to pushpin *because* poetry has greater value than pushpin, Bentham is saying, rather, it's the other way around, and poetry has greater value than pushpin because people prefer poetry to pushpin. (For *no* reason apparently.)

Stating the position so baldly already makes it look implausible. Let us consider for the moment a really "subjective" preference.

One model that people sometimes seem to have in mind for subjective preference is this. There is something C which is the taste of chocolate ice cream; there is something V which is the taste of vanilla ice cream. There are two feelings L, D which are "liking" and "disliking." And what goes on and *all* that goes on, when Jones likes and Smith dislikes vanilla (and Smith likes and Jones dislikes chocolate), is that Jones experiences $V + L$ when he eats vanilla and $C + D$ when he eats chocolate whereas Smith experiences $V + D$ when he eats vanilla and $C + L$ when he eats chocolate.

Such an account is naive psychologically, however, as Köhler long ago argued. What vanilla taste like to Jones, who likes vanilla ice cream, is not what it tastes like to Smith, who can't stand vanilla ice cream. Rather it's like this: Call the quality vanilla has for Smith V_s. V_s is an "unpleas-

ant" taste; it may be imaginable that one could experience V_s and like it, but just barely, and, even if one did, there would be some kind of disassociation or repression. In short, psychologically if not metaphysically, V_s is "intrinsically" unpleasant. And Smith feels D (dislike for the taste) when he eats vanilla because vanilla has the taste quality V_s (for him). Similarly, V_j, the taste quality of vanilla for Jones is intrinsically "pleasant" (which is why Jones feels L, liking). In the language of G. E. Moore, the taste V_j and the positive value are an organic unity for Jones, and the taste V_s and the negative value are an organic unity for Smith. Phenomenologically, they cannot really ever be separated into two parts in the way the notation "$V_s + D$," "$V_j + L$" suggests. Almost certainly (barring special factors of repression or disassociation), Smith would like vanilla ice cream too if it evoked V_j in his mouth and not V_s, and Jones would dislike vanilla ice cream too if it evoked V_s in his mouth and not V_j.

Why do we regard the preference for vanilla over chocolate as "subjective" then? I mean, why do we regard it as subjective even when we don't think *all* value judgments are subjective or agree with Bentham that, prejudice aside, pushpin is as good as poetry? Obviously, if we think all preferences are subjective, we will think this one is too, but the interesting question is why this judgment doesn't even seem objective to us unless, perhaps, we *are* Smith or Jones, why it doesn't have the kind of objectivity that many value judgments do undeniably have.

It isn't just that there is disagreement. If we think there are objective (or warranted) value judgments at all, very likely we think some hotly disputed judgments are objectively right. The Nazis disputed the judgment that *wanton killing of Jews just because of their racial affiliation is wrong*, but anti-Nazis did not regard their disagreement with the Nazis over this judgment as "subjective." Those who think homosexuals should have full rights in our society violently disagree with those who think homosexual activity or civil rights of homosexuals should be legally proscribed; but neither side in this dispute regards its own position as "subjective." Indeed, disagreement frequently makes people more sure that their moral position is warranted. So it isn't just the fact that "some people prefer chocolate and some people prefer vanilla" that makes the Smith/Jones disagreement in preference subjective.

Part of the story may be that most people don't have strong preferences between vanilla and chocolate, but this cannot be decisive. If half of the population couldn't stand chocolate but liked vanilla, and the other half couldn't stand vanilla but liked chocolate, we would still (if we were reasonable about our preferences) regard this as a "matter of taste," i.e. as subjective. It isn't the existence of "neutrals" that is decisive.

What *is* decisive, in my opinion, is that whatever biological or psychological idiosyncrasies are responsible for Smith's and Jones' preferences are not correlated with important traits of mind and character. If we try the thought experiment of imagining the contrary, of imagining that there was a caste of character that we regarded as good, both for its own sake and because of its effects on feeling, judgment and action, and another caste of character that we regarded as bad, both in itself and for its effects, and that everyone knew that the good caste of mind and character always revealed itself in a preference for vanilla and the bad in a preference for chocolate, then I think we will find that the more vividly we can succeed in making this case real to ourselves, the more we will feel that in such a world the first preference would be seen as "normal" and "right" and the second as "perverse" or "monstrous" or something of that sort.

I don't mean to claim that *all* preferences are judged morally by the traits of character they are thought to express. Some "preferences" are terribly important in themselves: someone who thought it was just wonderful to torture small children for the fun of it would (if he was serious) be condemned on the basis of that one attitude. But if the matter preferred is not regarded as important in itself, then whether we make an

issue of the preference or take it to be "a matter of taste" will generally depend on *what*, if anything, we think the preference *shows*. Value judgments often come in clumps; and clumps of value judgments frequently express durable traits of mind, personality, and character. The *independence* of "I prefer vanilla to chocolate ice cream" from any interesting and significant "clump" of this kind is just what makes it "subjective" (along, of course, with the absence of any intrinsic importance to the choice itself).

Even if Smith's preference for vanilla is "subjective," that does not make it irrational or arbitrary. Smith has a reason—the best possible reason—for liking vanilla, namely *the way it tastes to him*. Values can be "subjective" in the sense of being relative and still be objective; it is objective that vanilla tastes *better* than chocolate *to* Smith. In *The Sovereignty of Good*, Iris Murdoch pointed out that philosophers as different as the French Existentialists and the logical positivists actually shared a common model of value judgment, the model of reason as supplying the mind with neutral "facts" on the basis of which the will must arbitrarily choose "values"—the choice of values must be arbitrary, precisely because "facts" are (by definition) neutral. But, since the will is given no clues by reason as to how to judge (reason only supplies "facts," on this picture) it has no *reason* for its arbitrary choice; which is why the French philosophers called it "absurd," and why more naturalistically inclined philosophers see instinct and emotion (the historic successors to Bentham's all-purpose category of pleasure) as the ultimate basis of moral choice.

In the case we have just examined, the Existentialist-Positivist model does not fit however. The "fact"—the *taste* itself—and the "value"—the goodness of the taste—are one, at least psychologically. Presented experiential qualities aren't, in general, neutral and they frequently seem to demand responses and attitudes. One may override these felt demands for good and sufficient reason, as when a child learns to bear the pain of an injection for the sake of the benefits conferred by the immunizing agent injected, but the *prima facie* goodness and badness of particular experiences can hardly be denied. (Interestingly enough, this point was recognized by Plato and the medievals — we are perhaps the first culture to conceive of experience as neutral).

The non-neutrality of experience also bears on the pushpin/poetry case. We find it virtually impossible to imagine that someone who really appreciates poetry, someone who is capable of distinguishing real poetry from mere verse, capable of responding to great poetry, *should* prefer a childish game to arts which enrich our lives as poetry and music do. We *have* a reason for preferring poetry to pushpin, and that reason lies in the felt experience of great poetry, and of the after effects of great poetry — the enlargement of the imagination and the sensibility through the enlargement of our repertoire of images and metaphors, and the integration of poetic images and metaphors with mundane perceptions and attitudes that takes place when a poem has lived in us for a number of years. These experiences too are *prima facie* good — and not just good, but enobling, to use an old fashioned word. . . .

NOTES

1. For further discussion of the claim that the expression "work of art" is often used to praise rather than describe see Morris Weitz, "The Role of Theory in Aesthetics," in the Readings for Chapter 1.

2. Roy McMullen, *Mona Lisa: The Picture and the Myth* (New York: Da Capo Press, 1975), p. 1.

3. See Gerald Abraham, *The Concise Oxford History of Music* (Oxford: Oxford University Press, 1979), p. 274.

4. In particular I wish to remain neutral about the validity of traditional aesthetic theories with their commitment to a special aesthetic attitude or aesthetic qualities. My use of the expression "aesthetic value" is meant to be neutral with respect to theories of art. See the Introduction.

5. Jacob Burckhardt, *The Civilization of the Renaissance* (New York: New American Library, 1960), p. 231.

6. This is not to deny that historical value can justify a certain amount of preservation of artworks. For example, it is arguably of great historical interest to preserve the deteriorating prints of movies of the first half of the twentieth century. This interest justifies the effort that has to be taken to make and preserve new copies of these movies. It is clear that even in this case aesthetic value plays a strong role. Because of the possibility that an unknown movie may turn out in retrospect to seem to be much better, i.e., to have great *aesthetic* value to future generations, the effort to preserve even less famous movies is especially imperative.

7. Michael Baxandall, *Painting and Experience in Fifteenth Century Italy* (Oxford: Oxford University Press, 1972), p. 40.

8. Baxandall, *Painting and Experience*, p. 41.

9. Abraham, *History of Music*, p. 535.

10. William H. Gass, "Goodness Knows Nothing of Beauty." (See the Readings for Chapter 4, pp. 108–115).

11. The original source of this quote is very obscure. It has become familiar through an article written about Bentham by J. S. Mill. Apparently, the original context was Bentham's discussion of the importance of art to the state. Although Bentham was making a point about art as a special public good (see Chapter 2), the remark is usually interpreted as a view about the value of art to the individual. Cf., Ross Harrison, *Bentham* (London: Routledge & Kegan Paul, 1983), p. 5.

12. Mary McCarthy, *Venice Observed* (New York: Penguin Books, 1972), p. 256.

13. Bernard Berenson, *Italian Painters of the Renaissance* (New York: Meridian Books, 1976), p. 329. Emphasis added.

14. Quoted in Ralph Stephenson and J. R. Debrix, *The Cinema as Art* (Middlesex, England: Penguin Books, 1965), p. 13.

15. Putnam's aim in the quoted passage may be much more limited than mine here. He may merely wish to show that *complete* relativism, such as Bentham espouses, is untenable. For such a purpose it is sufficient to show that poetry has more value than at least one other activity, in this case pushpin.

CHAPTER 4

Art and Morality

◄ This scene from *Triumph of the Will*, the documentary movie made by Leni Riefenstahl, shows Hitler addressing the 1934 Hitler rally in Nuremberg. Considered one of the most important films in the history of cinema, *Triumph of the Will* is above all visually beautiful. Nonetheless, it has been criticized as propaganda for an immoral cause because it associates Hitler and the Nazi Party with power, virility, and purity.

The Art inspired by God's laughter does not by nature
serve ideological certitudes, it contradicts them. Like
Penelope, it undoes each night the tapestry that the
theologians, philosophers, and learned men have woven
the day before.

— Milan Kundera, *The Art of the Novel*

Can a work of art be immoral? Can — and should — moral standards be applied to art? Some of the most interesting questions about art center on the relation of art to morality. Should art be governed by the moral values that apply to everyday life? Or is art so separated from the real world that we cannot apply values of fundamental importance in real life to art? The need to answer these questions indicates a further reason why we need to look at theories of the nature and value of art.

The history of the debate over art and morality goes back to *The Republic*, in which the Greek philosopher Plato (427–347 B.C.) attacks the arts of his day, most notably the epic poets and dramatists (see the Readings). He argues in favor of censorship of the arts, even maintaining that in an ideal society artists would be excluded. Several things about art bother Plato. First, he objects to the freedom with which artists can promote antisocial ideas and attitudes in their art. He disapproves, for example, of what he claims is an antireligious portrayal of the gods in the Greek epic poems. And he takes exception to the way poets can create a fear of death; Plato feels this will make citizens afraid to be warriors. Second, Plato objects to the way art appeals to the irrational side of our nature, to our emotions rather than to our reason. He feels that because of its inherent irrationality, art is not properly equipped to explore issues of right and wrong, good and evil. Yet it does in fact explore such issues, in such popular art forms of his day as the tragic drama.

In our society the arts have been given great freedom. Unlike Plato, who wants to control the arts, our legal system has allowed more and more freedom to artists. In the twentieth century, artists have frequently produced works containing sexual material unacceptable by ordinary social standards. In various cases of pornography and obscenity, the legal system has asked in effect whether the offensive piece in question is art or merely pornography. The case involving the banning of D. H. Lawrence's novel *Lady Chatterley's Lover*, is a noted example. Such an approach suggests that novels or pictures that are works of art should be judged by standards different from those by which other pieces are judged. Another noteworthy case involved the prosecution of the Cincinnati Arts Center and its director under local anti-obscenity statutes for mounting a show of Robert Mapplethorpe's homoerotic photographs (see Figure 4.1; this case and its implications are discussed further in Chapter 12).

Many issues are intertwined in the debate over art and morality. It will be useful to distinguish four: (a) censorship and freedom, (b) moral content, (c) the goal of art, and (d) quality and morality. There are also many positions on these issues, ranging from the suggestion that art (and artists) are above the law and morality (see Morrow's essay on Norman Mailer, in the Readings), through the claim that art is morally neutral (see Oscar Wilde's preface to *The Picture of Dorian Gray*, in the Readings), to the view that art has a special moral obligation.

FIGURE 4.1 Robert Mapplethorpe was an artist who offended many viewers with his explicit erotic photographs. An exhibition of his photographs in Cincinnati led to the trial of the Cincinnati Arts Center and its director on charges of obscenity in September 1990. This photograph shows marchers protesting censorship outside the courthouse during the trial.

Before we examine these four issues, a word should be said about ethical values. Ethics is one of the fundamental fields of philosophical study. While no one ethical theory is accepted by all thinkers, most thinkers accept that certain ethical values are real and fundamentally important. Surely most people, ethical theorists included, accept, for example, that it is bad, evil, or wrong to abuse, hurt, or murder persons for fun. But a few thinkers have denied even this and have held that there is no objective basis for our moral beliefs; thus, no actions are intrinsically wrong. Such a position can be called *nihilism*, and on a nihilist view it becomes trivially easy to conclude that art need not worry about morality. For morality is merely an illusion fostered by civilization; in reality nothing is right or wrong—anything goes! It is when we reject this view that the conflict between art and morality arises.

Confusion on this point can occur because important art has frequently rejected *conventional* values. Being aware of this history, we have a tendency to think that art often rejects *all* values. If we draw this invalid inference, we will likely think that art has shown the falseness of values, and we will reject the idea that morality ought to apply to art. But rejecting conventional values and rejecting all values are two very different things. D. H. Lawrence rejected conventional Victorian attitudes toward sex when he explicitly described sexual acts in his novels. But he did so in the belief that sex and physical love have a high spiritual value.

CENSORSHIP

The issue of censorship goes well beyond the question of whether art is or ought to be moral. In free societies, censorship is considered undesirable even for ideas that are repugnant and immoral to many people. In such societies it is often argued that more is gained than lost by allowing the free expression and exchange of conflicting ideas and attitudes. One might very well hold that art ought not to exemplify evil and offensive attitudes but nevertheless be very much against censoring art that does, on the general grounds of opposition to censorship in any form.

Indeed, in the twentieth century censorship has been practiced mainly by totalitarian societies. Works have been censored not because they were *morally* unacceptable but because they were *politically* unacceptable.[1] In Nazi Germany, in Stalinist Russia, and in Maoist China, for example, art was seen as an arm of propaganda and was constrained to follow the views of the political party in charge. This meant the suppression of abstract visual arts, atonal music, experimental theater, and so on — in short, of all so-called modern art — because such art failed to express the reigning political ideology.

Perhaps the most interesting question in a society that protects free speech (and extends this protection to the arts) but practices some censorship (for example, of pornography) is whether and why different standards should apply to genuine works of art and to other commercial projects. Why, for example, should an experimental noncommercial film be allowed to show scenes that a commercial film could not show? Should the arts be totally free from the restraints that govern other public pronouncements and performances? Are there no limits in terms of the offense an artwork might give to people (for example, suppose they take a work to be blasphemous) or the bad effects it might have on its audience (for example, suppose it extols really violent acts)? One justification for allotting a special freedom to the arts can be found in the traditional role that the arts have played in leading the way toward new values and attitudes. On this view, art ought to have freedom because it is on the cutting edge of progress. Tolstoy, who accepts something like this view of the role of art in history, thought that by the late nineteenth century art had actually abandoned this progressive role, and he objected to experimental art, which to him was art for art's sake and had little to do with real human issues.

A very different justification of freedom for art comes from insisting that art simply has no moral content. Let's look at this idea more closely.

MORAL CONTENT

Clearly, many forms of art have no content that could be considered either moral or immoral. What could be the moral content of a string quartet or a piano sonata? But some thinkers have claimed that even art forms that have representational narrative content are morally neutral. One of the most famous statements of such a position comes from Oscar Wilde (see the Readings): "There is no such thing as a moral or immoral book. Books are well written or badly written. That is all." Why does Wilde hold this? It could not be because he doubts that the subject matter of art involves morality. He says, "The moral and immoral life of man forms part of the subject matter of the artist, but the morality of art consists in the perfect use of an imperfect medium." He also states, "Vice and virtue are to the artist materials for an art" (p. 107). Although moral actions and character obviously constitute the writer's subject, the writing is not itself moral.

It is far from clear what model of art underlies these sentiments. It is obvious that to write about an immoral act is not to commit the same act; to write about betrayal is not to betray anyone. Perhaps we should adopt the analogy of photography. Photographs of events are not to be confused with those events; photographs are neutral. Paraphrasing Wilde, we might say, "Photographs are accurate or inaccurate. That is all." The trouble is that this analogy is questionable; besides, not even photography is always so neutral. Pictures have a way of influencing people, depending on how the photographers frame and emphasize their subjects. It may be that Wilde is merely offering an ideal to which artists *ought* to conform. He says, "An ethical sympathy in an artist is an unpardonable mannerism of style." The problem is that works of art, even photographs, always seem to have a point of view. And that point of view can promote or express attitudes and values. It is difficult to imagine a purely neutral work of art that has no particular point of view.

We could base a possible argument for the neutrality of art on a different analogy, that of art to works of technology. It is often claimed that technology is in itself neutral; morality only enters the picture when someone uses (or misuses) the technology. On this view, to build a weapon is an act of no moral consequence. The moral question enters when someone decides to use the weapon. Those who built the atom bomb are not responsible for its use. Analogously, no work of art is immoral, no matter what it says or what it promotes. The work of art does not tell the spectator how to respond; it merely expresses a point of view that everyone is free to interpret (accept or reject) in his or her own way.

Suppose, for example, that a movie glorifies violence and cruelty. According to this defense, the movie is not immoral (even assuming that violence is repugnant), because each spectator is responsible for his or her own response to the movie. However, a problem arises: It is one thing to argue about whether it is the artist or the spectators who are responsible for the response to the work; it is another thing to continue to claim that such art is morally neutral.

Some artists seem to have the even more extreme view that art is necessarily divorced from moral considerations because art is entirely divorced from the "real world." We might put this view this way: What is not acceptable in the real world becomes acceptable when transmuted into art. An example that seems to illustrate such an attitude is a videotape made and shown on an arts channel of cable television in New York in 1979. This art "piece" consists simply of a tape loop, played over and over again, showing the artist shooting and killing a pet dog.[2] A second example, also from New York from 1979, is a drawing show by a young white artist who called himself Donald. He titled his exhibit "Nigger Drawings."[3] This show caused a furor because of the title; the drawings themselves were obscure and not obviously racist. These artists may have thought that what would be offensive or wrong to do in real life becomes something else when it is part of a work of art.[4]

> All you moralists! It takes an amoral kid like me to make things move.
>
> —Donald[5]

The assertion that immoral content doesn't matter also springs from another, very different, belief: that art justifies all. This belief, which Plato didn't have to contend with, seems to be the result of the nineteenth-century cultural trends that have made art almost a religion. Norman Mailer expresses something like this in his defense of the writer Jack Abbott, a notorious murderer (see the Morrow essay in the Readings).

Certainly Mailer suggests that great art justifies an artist's evil life; he may also hold that literary merit is all that counts, even if the writer is saying how great it feels to cut people up with a chain saw. So a work of art can be great no matter how dubious its ideas and subject matter, and such greatness justifies or redeems not only the questionable subject matter but even the questionable actions of the artist in private life. The work of art and the artist are both exempt from the rules that govern the rest of society. This principle can also be used to answer Tolstoy's concern (see Chapter 2) about the exploitation of people in the making of a work of art.

Clearly, not many people are willing to go this far in embracing a doctrine of complete artistic freedom. But many people, especially those involved in the arts, are likely to think that there is a certain truth to Mailer's principle. It is essential for anyone who accepts this principle, however, to supply an account of the worth of art that explains how its value trumps questions of morality. What is art's value that would allow it to be immoral?

THE GOAL OF ART

Wilde adopts the extreme position that there are no immoral books in order to buttress his denial that artists have to accept a moral imperative. The view that art ought to be moral is frequently linked with the claim that art ought to make a so-called positive contribution to culture and society. During the nineteenth and twentieth centuries, many of the most sophisticated artists have strongly rejected this traditional function. In earlier times, it would have gone unquestioned that the point of art is to improve its audience, not with factual knowledge, but with moral edification.[6]

Modern artists tend to reject the idea that they have any such goal. But much of their hostility comes from making *conventional* values (which artists often question) into the goal of art. Even artists who merely try to develop the boundaries of their medium may be indirectly contributing, for example, to an advancement in the kinds of feelings that can be experienced by an audience. (Consider Shakespeare or Mozart.)

Many artists who reject conventional morality as a goal of art have embraced *political* morality as a valid aim, maintaining that an artist must have something to say about the injustices that go on in the real world. Picasso's famous painting of the bombing of the Spanish town Guernica during the Spanish civil war is an example, as is the work of many photographers (Walker Evans), filmmakers (Sergei Eisenstein), and painters (Goya and Millet). Although many contemporary artists are politically and morally engaged, many others hold that art cannot deal with such subject matter without becoming propaganda of one sort or another and thus inferior as art.[7]

QUALITY AND MORALITY

The subtlest question involving morality and art is this: Is criticism of the morality of a work of art legitimate art criticism? Is a work of art any better or worse *as a work of art* because of its moral (or political) attitudes? If we may suppose that a work of art can express an ideology — that is, a set of values — and if these values were repugnant, wouldn't this lessen the quality of that particular work? Put positively, can we think of *great* works of art that express repugnant moral ideals? If we can — it has been argued, for example, that the operas of Richard Wagner (1813–1883) express proto-Nazi ideas of racial superiority — does the repugnant morality weaken the work, or is it of no consequence? This is a fundamental question of art criticism.

William H. Gass denies that morality has anything to do with quality. He says, "Artistic quality depends upon a work's internal, formal, organic character, upon its inner system of relations, upon its structure and style, and not upon the morality it is presumed to recommend . . . "[8] (See Gass's "Goodness Knows Nothing of Beauty," in the Readings.)

There are two dubious ways to escape these questions. The first, which we have already mentioned, is to embrace some form of nihilism. No moral values are valid, so to criticize a work for having any particular values is quite irrelevant. The second is to reject the idea that works of art express moral attitudes or ideologies.

This strategy loses its plausibility if we come to see that many works of art without overt moral or political commitments do in fact promote certain underlying values. Much recent feminist criticism of the classical literary canon — Shakespeare, for example — is aimed at exposing a not very attractive ideology underlying the work. Susan Sontag has long practiced such a form of moral criticism. In "Fascinating Fascism," she discusses Leni Riefenstahl's movies and photographs.[9] Sontag easily exposes the Nazi sentiments in Riefenstahl's movie *Triumph of the Will* (see illustration on p. 90); moreover, Sontag argues that there is an underlying Nazi aesthetics both in Riefenstahl's early movies and in her more recent nonpolitical photos of the Nuba tribe. Sontag's analysis is persuasive if it can legitimately convince us that a work of art contains something that we might have naively accepted without noticing — in short, a hidden ideology.

But why should an ideology, hidden or not, affect the aesthetic quality of a work? Aren't Riefenstahl's movies still beautiful and powerful, independent of the values they express? (Recall Wilde's statement: "Books are well written or badly written. That is all.") But are they? Can we ignore the values and simply concentrate on the form? Great and powerful works of art should have a broad — some would insist universal — appeal. By this criterion, works that express repugnant values (brutality, sadism, racism, sexism) must be downgraded; many spectators will find it rightly impossible to embrace the artist's vision, and the power of the work will be undermined.

> Fascist art glorifies surrender, it exalts mindlessness, it glamorizes death.
>
> Such art is hardly confined to works labeled fascist or produced under fascist governments. (To cite films only: Walt Disney's *Fantasia*, Busby Berkeley's *The Gang's All Here*, and Kubrick's *2001* also strikingly exemplify certain formal structures and themes of fascist art.)
>
> —Susan Sontag, "Fascinating Fascism"[10]

READINGS FOR CHAPTER 4

Plato, from *The Republic*
Lance Morrow, "The Poetic License to Kill"
Oscar Wilde, Preface from *The Picture of Dorian Gray*
William H. Gass, "Goodness Knows Nothing of Beauty: On the Distance between Morality and Art"

from *The Republic*

Plato

In *The Republic*, Plato's most famous dialogue, Socrates and company discuss how to make the ideal state. This question soon focuses on how to make a state that is just and how to create the ideal just citizens for such a state. As Socrates puts it, "How do justice and injustice grow up in states?" In the following excerpt from Books II and III of *The Republic*, the question being discussed is the role of art in the ideal state and, in particular, in the education of the future ideal citizens. Socrates criticizes the great and influential poets of Greece—for example, Homer and Hesiod—for producing bad fiction, that is, false stories that have bad effects on their listeners. Socrates is thus one of the first to propose that the arts ought to improve or exert a positive influence on the audience. Since he doubts that the arts do have such an effect, he goes so far as to propose censorship of the arts. As we learn later in *The Republic*, Socrates believes that the arts are intrinsically flawed and that the problems mentioned in this part of the dialogue flow from the intrinsic nature of art. This nature, according to Socrates, requires that the artist represent only the appearance, not the underlying reality, of the world.

BOOK II

(Ed. note: Socrates speaks first.)

. . . And may we not say confidently of man also, that he who is likely to be gentle to his friends and acquaintances, must by nature be a lover of wisdom and knowledge?

That we may safely affirm.

Then he who is to be a really good and noble guardian of the State will require to unite in himself philosophy and spirit and swiftness and strength?

Undoubtedly.

Then we have found the desired natures; and now that we have found them, how are they to be reared and educated? Is not this an enquiry which may be expected to throw light on the greater enquiry which is our final end—How do justice and injustice grow up in States? for we do not want either to omit what is to the point or to draw out the argument to an inconvenient length.

Adeimantus thought that the enquiry would be of great service to us.

Then, I said, my dear friend, the task must not be given up, even if somewhat long.

Certainly not.

Come then, and let us pass a leisure hour in story-telling, and our story shall be the education of our heroes.

By all means.

And what shall be their education? Can we find a better than the traditional sort?—and this has two divisions, gymnastic for the body, and music for the soul.

True.

Shall we begin education with music, and go on to gymnastic afterwards?

By all means.

And when you speak of music, do you include literature or not?

I do.

And literature may be either true or false?

Yes.

And the young should be trained in both kinds, and we begin with the false?

I do not understand your meaning, he said.

You know, I said, that we begin by telling children stories which, though not wholly destitute of truth, are in the main fictitious; and these stories are told them when they are not of an age to learn gymnastics.

Very true.

That was my meaning when I said that we must teach music before gymnastics.

Quite right, he said.

You know also that the beginning is the most important part of any work, especially in the case of a young and tender thing; for that is the time at which the character is being formed and the desired impression is more readily taken.

Quite true.

And shall we just carelessly allow children to hear any casual tales which may be devised by casual persons, and to receive into their minds ideas for the most part the very opposite of those which we should wish them to have when they are grown up?

We cannot.

Then the first thing will be to establish a censorship of the writers of fiction, and let the censors receive any tale of fiction which is good, and reject the bad; and we will desire mothers and nurses to tell their children the authorised ones only. Let them fashion the mind with such tales, even more fondly than they mould the body with their hands; but most of those which are now in use must be discarded.

Of what tales are you speaking? he said.

You may find a model of the lesser in the greater, I said; for they are necessarily of the same type, and there is the same spirit in both of them.

Very likely, he replied; but I do not as yet know what you would term the greater.

Those, I said, which are narrated by Homer and Hesiod, and the rest of the poets, who have ever been the great story-tellers of mankind.

But which stories do you mean, he said; and what fault do you find with them?

A fault which is most serious, I said; the fault of telling a lie, and, what is more, a bad lie.

But when is this fault committed?

Whenever an erroneous representation is made of the nature of gods and heroes, — as when a painter paints a portrait not having the shadow of a likeness to the original.

Yes, he said, that sort of thing is certainly very blameable; but what are the stories which you mean?

First of all, I said, there was that greatest of all lies, in high places, which the poet told about Uranus, and which was a bad lie too, — I mean what Hesiod says that Uranus did, and how Cronus retaliated on him. The doings of Cronus, and the sufferings which in turn his son inflicted upon him, even if they were true, ought certainly not to be lightly told to young and thoughtless persons; if possible, they had better be buried in silence. But if there is an absolute necessity for their mention, a chosen few might hear them in a mystery, and they should sacrifice not a common [Eleusinian] pig, but some huge and unprocurable victim; and then the number of the hearers will be very few indeed.

Why, yes, said he, those stories are extremely objectionable.

Yes, Adeimantus, they are stories not to be repeated in our State; the young man should not be told that in committing the worst of crimes he is far from doing anything outrageous; and that even if he chastises his father when he does wrong, in whatever manner, he will only be following the example of the first and greatest among the gods.

I entirely agree with you, he said; in my opinion those stories are quite unfit to be repeated.

Neither, if we mean our future guardians to regard the habit of quarrelling among themselves as of all things the basest, should any word be said to them of the wars in heaven, and of the plots and fightings of the gods against one another, for they are not true. No, we shall never mention the battles of the giants, or let them be embroidered on garments; and we shall be silent about the innumerable other quarrels of gods and heroes with their friends and relatives. If they would only believe us we would tell them that quarrelling is unholy, and that never up to this time has there been any quarrel between citizens; this is what old men and old women should begin by telling children; and when they grow up, the poets also should be told to compose for them in a similar spirit. But the narrative of Hephaestus binding Here his mother, or how on another occasion Zeus sent him flying for taking her part when she was being beaten, and all the battles of the gods in Homer—these tales must not be admitted into our State, whether they are supposed to have an allegorical meaning or not. For a young person cannot judge what is allegorical and what is literal; anything that he receives into his mind at that age is likely to become indelible and unalterable; and therefore it is most important that the tales which the young first hear should be models of virtuous thoughts.

There you are right, he replied; but if any one asks where are such models to be found and of what tales are you speaking—how shall we answer him?

I said to him, You and I, Adeimantus, at this moment are not poets, but founders of a State: now the founders of a State ought to know the general forms in which poets should cast their tales, and the limits which must be observed by them, but to make the tales is not their business.

Very true, he said; but what are these forms of theology which you mean?

Something of this kind, I replied: — God is always to be represented as he truly is, whatever be the sort of poetry, epic, lyric or tragic, in which the representation is given.

Right.

And is he not truly good? and must he not be represented as such?

Certainly.

And no good thing is hurtful?

No, indeed.

And that which is not hurtful hurts not?

Certainly not.

And that which hurts not does no evil?

No.

And can that which does no evil be a cause of evil?

Impossible.

And the good is advantageous?

Yes.

And therefore the cause of well-being?

Yes.

It follows therefore that the good is not the cause of all things, but of the good only?

Assuredly.

Then God, if he be good, is not the author of all things, as the many assert, but he is the cause of a few things only, and not of most things that occur to men. For few are the goods of human life, and many are the evils, and the good is to be attributed to God alone; of the evils the causes are to be sought elsewhere, and not in him.

That appears to me to be most true, he said.

Then we must not listen to Homer or to any other poet who is guilty of the folly of saying that two casks

Lie at the threshold of Zeus, full of lots, one of good, the other of evil lots,

and that he to whom Zeus gives a mixture of the two

Sometimes meets with evil fortune, at other times with good;

but that he to whom is given the cup of unmingled ill,

Him wild hunger drives o'er the beauteous earth.

And again—

Zeus, who is the dispenser of good and evil to us.

And if any one asserts that the violation of oaths and treaties, which was really the work of Pandarus, was brought about by Athene and Zeus, or that the strife and contention of the gods was instigated by Themis and Zeus, he shall not have our approval; neither will we allow our young men to hear the words of Aeschylus, that

God plants guilt among men when he desires utterly to destroy a house.

And if a poet writes of the sufferings of Niobe — the subject of the tragedy in which these iambic verses occur — or of the house of Pelops, or of the Trojan war or on any similar theme, either we must not permit him to say that these are the works of God, or if they are of God, he must devise some explanation of them such as we are seeking; he must say that God did what was just and right, and they were the better for being punished; but that those who are punished are miserable, and that God is the author of their misery — the poet is not to be permitted to say; though he may say that the wicked are miserable because they require to be punished, and are benefited by receiving punishment from God; but that God being good is the author of evil to any one is to be strenuously denied, and not to be said or sung or heard in verse or prose by any one whether old or young in any well-ordered commonwealth. Such a fiction is suicidal, ruinous, impious.

I agree with you, he replied, and am ready to give my assent to the law.

Let this then be one of our rules and principles concerning the gods, to which our poets and reciters will be expected to conform — that God is not the author of all things, but of good only.

That will do, he said.

And what do you think of a second principle? Shall I ask you whether God is a magician, and of a nature to appear insidiously now in one shape, and now in another — sometimes himself changing and passing into many forms, sometimes deceiving us with the semblance of such transformations; or is he one and the same immutably fixed in his own proper image?

I cannot answer you, he said, without more thought.

Well, I said; but if we suppose a change in anything, that change must be effected either by the thing itself, or by some other thing?

Most certainly.

And things which are at their best are also least liable to be altered or discomposed; for example, when healthiest and strongest, the human frame is least liable to be affected by meats and drinks, and the plant which is in the fullest vigour also suffers least from winds or the heat of the sun or any similar causes.

Of course.

And will not the bravest and wisest soul be least confused or deranged by any external influence?

True.

And the same principle, as I should suppose, applies to all composite things — furniture, houses, garments: when good and well made, they are least altered by time and circumstances.

Very true.

Then everything which is good, whether made by art or nature, or both, is least liable to suffer change from without?

True.

But surely God and the things of God are in every way perfect?

Of course they are.

Then he can hardly be compelled by external influence to take many shapes?

He cannot.

But may he not change and transform himself?

Clearly, he said, that must be the case if he is changed at all.

And will he then change himself for the better and fairer, or for the worse and more unsightly?

If he change at all he can only change for the worse, for we cannot suppose him to be deficient either in virtue or beauty.

Very true, Adeimantus; but then, would any one, whether God or man, desire to make himself worse?

Impossible.

Then it is impossible that God should ever be willing to change; being, as is supposed, the fairest and best that is conceivable, every God remains absolutely and for ever in his own form.

That necessarily follows, he said, in my judgment.

Then, I said, my dear friend, let none of the poets tell us that

The gods, taking the disguise of strangers from other lands, walk up and down cities in all sorts of forms;

and let no one slander Proteus and Thetis, neither let any one, either in tragedy or in any other kind of poetry, introduce Here disguised in the likeness of a priestess asking an alms

For the life-giving daughters of Inachus the river of Argos;

—let us have no more lies of that sort. Neither must we have mothers under the influence of the poets scaring their children with a bad version of these myths—telling how certain gods, as they say, "Go about by night in the likeness of so many strangers and in diverse forms"; but let them take heed lest they make cowards of their children, and at the same time speak blasphemy against the gods.

Heaven forbid, he said.

But although the gods are themselves unchangeable, still by witchcraft and deception they may make us think that they appear in various forms?

Perhaps, he replied.

Well, but can you imagine that God will be willing to lie, whether in word or deed, or to put forth a phantom of himself?

I cannot say, he replied.

Do you not know, I said, that the true lie, if such an expression may be allowed, is hated of gods and men?

What do you mean? he said.

I mean that no one is willingly deceived in that which is the truest and highest part of himself, or about the truest and highest matters; there, above all, he is most afraid of a lie having possession of him.

Still, he said, I do not comprehend you.

The reason is, I replied, that you attribute some profound meaning to my words; but I am only saying that deception, or being deceived or uninformed about the highest realities in the highest part of themselves, which is the soul, and in that part of them to have and to hold the lie, is

what mankind least like;—that, I say, is what they utterly detest.

There is nothing more hateful to them.

And, as I was just now remarking, this ignorance in the soul of him who is deceived may be called the true lie; for the lie in words is only a kind of imitation and shadowy image of a previous affection of the soul, not pure unadulterated falsehood. Am I not right?

Perfectly right.

The true lie is hated not only by the gods, but also by men?

Yes.

Whereas the lie in words is in certain cases useful and not hateful; in dealing with enemies—that would be an instance; or again, when those whom we call our friends in a fit of madness or illusion are going to do some harm, then it is useful and is a sort of medicine or preventive; also in the tales of mythology, of which we were just now speaking—because we do not know the truth about ancient times, we make falsehood as much like truth as we can, and so turn it to account.

Very true, he said.

But can any of these reasons apply to God? Can we suppose that he is ignorant of antiquity, and therefore has recourse to invention?

That would be ridiculous, he said.

Then the lying poet has no place in our idea of God?

I should say not.

Or perhaps he may tell a lie because he is afraid of enemies?

That is inconceivable.

But he may have friends who are senseless or mad?

But no mad or senseless person can be a friend of God.

Then no motive can be imagined why God should lie?

None whatever.

Then the superhuman and divine is absolutely incapable of falsehood?

Yes.

Then is God perfectly simple and true both in word and deed; he changes not; he deceives not, either by sign or word, by dream or waking vision.

Your thoughts, he said, are the reflection of my own.

You agree with me then, I said, that this is the second type or form in which we should write and speak about divine things. The gods are not magicians who transform themselves, neither do they deceive mankind in any way.

I grant that.

Then, although we are admirers of Homer, we do not admire the lying dream which Zeus sends to Agamemnon; neither will we praise the verses of Aeschylus in which Thetis says that Apollo at her nuptials

Was celebrating in song her fair progeny whose days were to be long, and to know no sickness. And when he had spoken of my lot as in all things blessed of heaven he raised a note of triumph and cheered my soul. And I thought that the word of Phoebus, being divine and full of prophecy, would not fail. And now he himself who uttered the strain, he who was present at the banquet, and who said this — he it is who has slain my son.

These are the kind of sentiments about the gods which will arouse our anger; and he who utters them shall be refused a chorus; neither shall we allow teachers to make use of them in the instruction of the young, meaning, as we do, that our guardians, as far as men can be, should be true worshippers of the gods and like them.

I entirely agree, he said, in these principles, and promise to make them my laws.

BOOK III

Such then, I said, are our principles of theology — some tales are to be told, and others are not to be told to our disciples from their youth upwards, if we mean them to honour the gods and their parents, and to value friendship with one another.

Yes; and I think that our principles are right, he said.

But if they are to be courageous, must they not learn other lessons besides these, and lessons of such a kind as will take away the fear of death? Can any man be courageous who has the fear of death in him?

Certainly not, he said.

And can he be fearless of death, or will he choose death in battle rather than defeat and slavery, who believes the world below to be real and terrible?

Impossible.

Then we must assume a control over the narrators of this class of tales as well as over the others, and beg them not simply to revile, but rather to commend the world below, intimating to them that their descriptions are untrue, and will do harm to our future warriors.

That will be our duty, he said.

Then, I said, we shall have to obliterate many obnoxious passages, beginning with the verses,

I would rather be a serf on the land of a poor and portionless man than rule over all the dead who have come to nought.

We must also expunge the verse, which tells us how Pluto feared,

Lest the mansions grim and squalid which the gods abhor should be seen both of mortals and immortals.

And again: —

O heavens! verily in the house of Hades there is soul and ghostly form but no mind at all!

Again of Tiresias: —

[To him even after death did Persephone grant mind,] that he alone should be wise; but the other souls are flitting shades.

Again: —

The soul flying from the limbs had gone to Hades, lamenting her fate, leaving manhood and youth.

Again: —

And the soul, with shrilling cry, passed like smoke beneath the earth.

And, —

> *As bats in hollow of mystic cavern, whenever*
> *any of them has dropped out of the string and*
> *falls from the rock, fly shrilling and cling to*
> *one another, so did they with shrilling cry hold*
> *together as they moved.*

And we must beg Homer and the other poets not to be angry if we strike out these and similar passages, not because they are unpoetical, or unattractive to the popular ear, but because the greater the poetical charm of them, the less are they meet for the ears of boys and men who are meant to be free, and who should fear slavery more then death.

Undoubtedly.

Also we shall have to reject all the terrible and appalling names which describe the world below — Cocytus and Styx, ghosts under the earth, and sapless shades, and any similar words of which the very mention causes a shudder to pass through the inmost soul of him who hears them. I do not say that these horrible stories may not have a use of some kind; but there is a danger that the nerves of our guardians may be rendered too excitable and effeminate by them.

There is a real danger, he said.

Then we must have no more of them.

True.

Another and a nobler strain must be composed and sung by us.

Clearly.

And shall we proceed to get rid of the weepings and wailings of famous men?

They will go with the rest. . . .

The Poetic License to Kill

Lance Morrow

In E. B. White's lovely fable *Charlotte's Web*, the literate spider Charlotte saves a pig named Wilbur from execution by spinning blurbs about him in the barn doorway: SOME PIG, RADI-ANT, and so on. The astonished farm folk put away their thoughts of slaughter; they no longer regard Wilbur as pork, but as a tourist attraction, and even a celebrity who enjoys the favor of higher powers. Sweet Wilbur will survive to grow old in the barnyard. He gratefully sighs, "It is not often that someone comes along who is a true friend and a good writer."

Soak the story in reality, bad luck, stupidity and evil for a while, and it might marinate into the parable of Jack Abbott and Norman Mailer: the redemption of the distinctly uninnocent. In one sense, the tale is merely a particularly sensational item of literary gossip. But buried amid the blood and chic is an interesting question of princi-ple. Almost everything, as Thomas De Quincey noticed, has either a moral handle or an aesthetic handle. Which handle do you reach for in the Abbott-Mailer case?

In the beginning, Mailer spins publicity for convict and murderer Jack Abbott, helps get Ab-bott's prison book published and Abbott paroled. The con with the prose style of a Doberman (all speed and teeth) obeys his muse again. Six weeks after parole, Abbott kills a man in New York City's East Village. Mailer must concoct another redemption. He proposes a principle: "Culture is worth a little risk," Mailer tells reporters. Abbott should not be punished too harshly for this mur-der. It is true that he is not in any condition just now to walk around loose, but he is a talented writer. Being put away in prison for too long, says Mailer, might stifle Abbott's creativity.

Attempting to spook the bourgeois sensibility, of course, has been Mailer's vocation for a quar-ter of a century. He has rarely done it so effec-tively, perhaps because now the blood is real, for the first time since Mailer stabbed his second wife with a penknife in 1960 (and got off with a sus-pended sentence). A fierce outrage cascaded down on him last week. It was common to hear New Yorkers say that he should be tried as an accessory to murder. Mailer barged around giv-ing interviews and suing a newspaper for libel, looking truculent and stricken.

In one way it was unfair: Mailer had had the courage to sponsor a talented pariah, and then something in Abbott's transition from prison went disastrously wrong. Mailer was personally aggrieved and pained, not only for Abbott but for Abbott's victim. It is true that certain writers adopt convicts; criminals, sinister, romantic and stupid as sharks, become the executive arms of intellectuals' violent fantasies. For some reason, intellectuals rarely understand that they are being conned: convicts are geniuses of ingratiation. Still, Mailer after all was not promoting a killer but a prose stylist and what he judged to be a salvageable human being. He miscalculated: he overrated the writer in Abbott and underesti-mated the murderer.

It was not so much ideas as their loudmouthed idiot cousin — publicity — that helped soften the verdict. It began to seem that it was not Abbott and his admitted homicide that were on trial but, in a vague and sloppy way, the entire American criminal justice system. The jury decided that the system had just been too much for Abbott. So the verdict was manslaughter. Abbott had been acting, the jury decided, under "extreme emotional disturbance." Sentencing comes next month. A judge of Solomonic gifts might condemn Abbott and Mailer to be shackled together with molybdenum chains, inseparable ever after, like Tony Curtis and Sidney Poitier in *The Defiant Ones*, to clunk, snarling, from one literary dinner party to another.

Amid the travesty and pathos, however, Mailer had advanced an interesting proposition: the idea that a writer, or presumably any artist, deserves a special dispensation under the law. You can talk your way out of anything; Mailer suggested that a man ought to be able to write his way out of anything as well, including murder. Articulation leads to redemption; language can pick locks.

Mailer's principle—art should redeem or rather, more important, exculpate the artist—reached its full blossom as a tenet of Romanticism. The artist, for centuries regarded as merely a liveried servant of church and aristocracy, sprang up out of the bourgeoisie in the early 19th century as a dashing hierophant whose work connected him to the divine. It excused everything, from rudeness to homicide. "The fact of a man's being a poisoner," proclaimed Oscar Wilde, "is nothing against his prose."

It is a confused and essentially stupid doctrine. W. H. Auden's memorable lines about W. B. Yeats describe a sweet metaphysical arc: "Time that is intolerant/Of the brave and innocent/And indifferent in a week/To a beautiful physique/Worships language and forgives/Everyone by whom it lives." Yes: time grants pardon. But the law is not in the trade of metaphysics; the law's only hope of survival lies precisely in its struggle to be impartial. The Mailer doctrine suggests that somehow the law should set up separate standards for artists. There are grotesque possibilities here. Who judges the literary merit? What if a literary convict is really a terrible writer? String him up? Will we need a panel of literary judges to meet the first Monday of every month at Elaine's in Manhattan to hear its cases? If the perpetrator of the Texas chain-saw massacre shows a certain flair for the short story, do we let him off?

What distinguishes man from the animals is language, articulate consciousness. What distinguishes Jack Abbott from millions of other convicts is a prose style that was capable of catching a famous writer's attention. It is interesting that, as psychologists have noted, some hopelessly inarticulate teenagers have committed murder because they simply lacked the verbal skill to communicate their anger in any other way; Abbott has at his command both the sophisticated and the more primitive forms of communication.

If Mother Teresa of Calcutta should commit murder, any court might weigh her amazing life's labor against the evil of the one deed. The murder would be the exception in a life that otherwise displayed merit and extravagantly claimed mercy. But Jack Abbott's vividly ranting book, brutal and brutalized, should have made the jury wonder which was more characteristic of the man: literature or murder. In a long and essentially tragic perspective (in which all consequences are endured, all debts paid), literature performs its redemptions. Mailer's formula is a shallow little mechanism. "Culture is worth a little risk," he says. The world of that sentence is upside down: you defend culture, do you not, by locking up the people who try to kill it.

Preface from *The Picture of Dorian Gray*

Oscar Wilde

The artist is the creator of beautiful things.

To reveal art and conceal the artist is art's aim.

The critic is he who can translate into another manner or a new material his impression of beautiful things.

The highest, as the lowest, form of criticism is a mode of autobiography.

Those who find ugly meanings in beautiful things are corrupt without being charming. This is a fault.

Those who find beautiful meanings in beautiful things are the cultivated. For these there is hope.

They are the elect to whom beautiful things mean only Beauty.

There is no such thing as a moral or an immoral book. Books are well written or badly written. That is all.

The nineteenth-century dislike of Realism is the rage of Caliban* seeing his own face in a glass.

The nineteenth-century dislike of Romanticism is the rage of Caliban not seeing his own face in a glass.

The moral and immoral life of man forms part of the subject matter of the artist, but the morality of art consists in the perfect use of an imperfect medium.

*[Caliban is a subhuman slave of Prospero in Shakespeare's play *The Tempest*. He represents the brutish side of human nature.]

No artist desires to prove anything. Even things that are true can be proved.

No artist has ethical sympathies. An ethical sympathy in an artist is an unpardonable mannerism of style.

No artist is ever morbid. The artist can express everything.

Thought and language are to the artist instruments of an art.

Vice and virtue are to the artist materials for an art.

From the point of view of form, the type of all the arts is the art of the musician. From the point of view of feeling, the actor's craft is the type.

All art is at once surface and symbol.

Those who go beneath the surface do so at their peril.

Those who read the symbol do so at their peril.

It is the spectator, and not life, that art really mirrors.

Diversity of opinion about a work of art shows that the work is new, complex, and vital.

When critics disagree the artist is in accord with himself.

We can forgive a man for making a useful thing as long as he does not admire it. The only excuse for making a useless thing is that one admires it intensely.

All art is quite useless.

Goodness Knows Nothing of Beauty: On the Distance between Morality and Art

William H. Gass

William H. Gass is David May Distinguished University Professor
in the Humanities at Washington University in St. Louis.

We are to imagine a terrible storm like that which opens Verdi's *Otello*. The pavement of the *piazzetta* is awash. St. Mark's pigeons are flying about looking for land. The Venetian sun has gone down like a gondola in the lagoon. As we wade along in the dying light, a baby in a basket passes. It is being swept out to sea with the rest of the city's garbage. So is a large painting, beautifully framed, which floats its grand nude by us as if she were swimming. Then the question comes, bobbing like a bit of flotsam itself: Which one should we save, the tiny tot or the Tintoretto? the kid in the crib or the Canaletto?

It may be that during two thousand or more years of monsoons, tidal waves, and high water, this choice has not once actually presented itself, yet, undismayed, it is in this form that philosophers frequently represent the conflict between art and morality—a conflict, of course, they made up in the first place. Baby or Botticelli. What'll you have?

Not only is the dilemma an unlikely one; the choice it offers is peculiar. We are being asked to decide not between two different actions but between two different objects. And how different indeed these floating objects are. The baby is a vessel of human consciousness, if its basket isn't.

It is nearly pure potentiality. It must be any babe—no one babe but babe in general, babe in bulk—whose bunk is boating by. Never mind if it was born with the brain of an accountant, inflicted with a cleft palate, or given Mozartian talents: these are clearly irrelevant considerations, as are ones concerning the seaworthiness of the basket, or the prospect of more rain. One fist in this fight swings from the arm of an open future against the chest of a completed past. . . .

. . . A completed past because we have to know the pedigree of the painting or it's no contest. If it is the rosy nude who used to recline behind the bar in Harry's, or just another mislaid entrant in the latest Biennale, then the conditions of the case are fatally altered and there is no real conflict of interest, though the blank space behind the bar at Harry's will surely fill us with genuine sorrow each scotch-and-water hour. It is not between infant and image, then, that we are being asked to choose, but between some fully realized aesthetic quality and a vaguely generalized human nature, even though it is a specific baby who could drown.

It is the moralists, of course, who like to imagine these lunatic choices. It is the moralists who want to bully and beat up on the artists, not the other way around. The error of the artists is indifference. Not since Plato's day, when the politicians in their grab for public power defeated the priests, the poets, and the philosophers, have artists, except for an occasional Bronx cheer, molested a moralist. Authors do not gather to burn good deeds in public squares; laws are not passed by poets to put lying priests behind bars, nor do they usually suggest that the pursuit of goodness will lead you away from both beauty and truth, that it is the uphill road to ruin. Musicians do not hang moralizing lackeys from lampposts as though they were stringing their fiddles; moralizing lackeys do that.

On the other hand ... We know what the other hand is full of: slings and arrows, slanders and censorship, prisons, scaffolds, burnings and beatings. To what stake has Savonarola's piety been bound by the painters he disgraced? Throughout history, goodness has done more harm than good, and over the years moralists have managed to give morality a thoroughly bad name. Although lots of bad names have been loaned them by the poets, if the poets roast, they roast no one on the coals, while moralists, to their reward, have dispatched who knows how many thousands of souls.

The values which men prize have been variously classified. There may be said to be, crudely, five kinds. There are first of all those facts and theories we are inclined to call true, and which, we think, constitute our knowledge. Philosophy, history, science, presumably pursue them. Second, there are the values of duty and obligation — obedience and loyalty, righteousness and virtue — qualities which the state finds particularly desirable. Appreciative values of all kinds may be listed third, including the beauties of women, art, and nature, the various sublimes, and that pleasure which comes from the pure exercise of human faculties and skills. Fourth are the values of self-realization and its attendant pleasures — growth, well-being, and the like — frequently called happiness in deference to Aristotle. Finally, there are those which have to do with real or imagined redemption, with ultimate justice and immortality. Some would prefer to separate political values like justice or freedom from more narrowly moral ones, while others would do the same for social values like comfort, stability, security, conditions often labeled simply "peace." But a complete and accurate classification, assuming it could be accomplished, is not important here. Roughly, we might call our goals, as tradition has, Truth, Goodness, Beauty, Happiness, and Salvation. (We can reach port, sometimes, even with a bad map.)

If we allow our classificatory impulse to run on a little longer, it will encourage us to list at least four customary attitudes which can be taken toward the relationship of these value areas to one another. First, one can deny the legitimacy or reality of a particular value group. Reckless pragmatists and some sophists deny the objective existence of all values except utility, while positivists prefer to elevate empirical truth (which they don't capitalize, only underscore) to that eminence. It is, of course, truth thinned to the thickness of a wire, which is fine if you want to cut cheese. The values which remain are rejected as attitudes, moods, or emotions — subjective states of various sorts like wishing, hoping, willing, which suggest external objects without being able to establish them. I happen to regard salvation values as illusory or mythological, since I deny any significance to the assumptions on which they are grounded, but other people may pick out different victims.

Second, we might accept the values of a certain sphere as real enough, but argue that some or all of them are reducible to others, even eventually, to one. Reductionism is characteristic of Plato's famous argument that virtue is knowledge; of Keats's fatuous little motto, Beauty Is Truth; of materialists and idealists equally. Rather than reduce moral values to those of happiness, Aristotle simply ignored them.

Third, we can try to make some values subordinate to others. This is not the same as reduction. One might argue that artistic and moral values are mutually exclusive, or unique, and yet support the superiority of one over the other.

There are, however, two kinds of subordination. One asserts that X is more important than Y, so that when one has to choose between them (baby or Botticelli), one must always choose the baby. When designing buildings, for instance, beauty regularly runs afoul of function and economy. The other sort of subordination insists not only that X is more important, or "higher" in value, than Y, but that Y should serve or be a means to X: the baby is a model for the baby in the Botticelli. The slogan Form Follows Function is sometimes so understood. I take crude Marxism to require this kind of sacrifice from the artist.

Fourth, it is possible to argue, as I do, that these various value areas are significantly different. They are not only different; they are not reducible, but are independent of one another. Furthermore, no one value area is more important, abstractly considered, than any other. In short, these various values are different, independent, and equal.

This does not imply that in particular instances one would not choose one over the other and have good reasons for doing so; it is simply that what is chosen in any instance cannot be dictated in advance. Obviously, if one is starving, whether one's eventual food is served with grace and eaten with manners is less than essential. Should you skip dinner or lick the spilled beans from the floor? Should you choose to safeguard a painting or the well-being of its model? Should you bomb Monte Cassino?

That attachment to human life which demands that it be chosen over everything else is mostly humbug. It can be reasonably, if not decisively, argued that the world is already suffering from a surfeit of such animals; that most human beings rarely deserve the esteem some philosophers have for them; that historically humans have treated their pets better than they have treated one another; that no one is so essential he or she cannot be replaced a thousand times over; that death is inevitable anyhow; that it is our sense of community and our own identity which lead us to persist in our parochial overestimation;

that it is rather a wish of philosophers than a fact that man be more important than anything else that's mortal, since nature remains mum and scarcely supports the idea, nor do the actions of man himself. Man makes a worse God than God, and when God was alive, he knew it.

Baby or Botticelli is a clear enough if artificial choice, but it places the problem entirely in the moral sphere, where the differences involved can be conveniently overlooked. What differences?

The writing of a book (the painting of a painting, the creation of a score) is generally such an exacting and total process that it is not simply O.K. if it has many motives, it is essential. The difference between one of Flaubert's broken amatory promises to Louise Colet and his writing of *Madame Bovary* (both considered immoral acts in some circles) is greater even than Lenin's willingness to board a train and his intended overthrow of the czar. Most promises are kept by actions each one of which fall into a simple series; that is, I meet you at the Golden Toad by getting up from my desk, putting on my coat, and getting into my car: a set of actions each one of which can be serially performed and readily seen as part of "going to lunch." I may have many reasons for keeping our date, but having promised becomes the moral one.

However, when I create a work of art, I have entered into no contract of any kind with the public, unless the work has been commissioned. In this sense, most aesthetic acts are unbidden, uncalled-for, even unexpected. They are gratuitous. And unlike Lenin's intention to overthrow an empire (which can scarcely be an intention of the same kind as my meeting you for lunch, involving, as it does, several years, thousands of folks, and millions of dollars), my writing will, all along, be mine alone, and I will not normally parcel out the adjectives to subordinates and the sex scenes to specialists, or contract the punctuation.

I have many reasons for going to the Golden Toad, then: I am hungry; you are pretty; we have business; I need a change from the atmosphere of the office; you are paying, and I am broke — oh yes . . . and I promised. All these interests are easily satisfied by our having lunch. There is no need to order them; they are not unruly or at odds.

So why am I writing this book? Why to make money, to become famous, to earn the love of many women, to alter the world's perception of itself, to put my rivals' noses out of joint, to satisfy my narcissism, to display my talents, to justify my existence to my deceased father, to avoid cleaning the house; but if I wish to make money I shall have to write trash, and if I wish to be famous, I had better hit home runs, and if I wish to earn the love of many women, I shall have more luck going to work in a bank. In short, these intentions do conflict; they must be ordered; none of them is particularly "good" in the goodie sense; and none is aesthetic in any way.

But there is so much energy in the baser motives, and so little in the grander, that I need hate's heat to warm my art, I must have my malice to keep me going. For I must go, and go on, regardless. For making a work of art (writing a book, being Botticelli) requires an extended kind of action, an ordered group of actions. Yet these actions are not the sort which result, like a battle, in many effects, helter-skelter: in broken bodies, fugitive glories, lasting pains, conquered territories, power, ruins, ill will; rather, as a funnel forms the sand and sends it all in the same direction, the many acts of the artist aim at one end, one result.

We are fully aware, of course, that while I am meeting you for lunch, admiring your bodice, buying office equipment, I am not doing the laundry, keeping the books, dieting, or being faithful in my heart; and when I am painting, writing, singing scales, I am not cooking, cleaning house, fixing flats. So the hours, the days, the years of commitment to my work must necessarily withdraw me from other things, from my duties as a husband, a soldier, a citizen.

So the actions of the artist include both what he does and, therefore, what he doesn't do; what he does directly and on purpose, and what he

does incidentally and quite by the way. In addition, there are things done, or not done, or done incidentally, which are quite essential to the completion and character of the work, but whose effects do not show themselves in the ultimate object or performance. As necessary as any other element, they disappear in the conclusion like a middle term in an argument. A deleted scene, for instance, may nevertheless lead to the final one. Every line is therefore many lines: words rubbed out, thoughts turned aside, concepts canceled. The eventual sentence seems to lie there quietly, "kill the king," with no one knowing that it once read, "kiss the king," and before that, "kiss the queen." For moralists, only too often, writing a book is little different than robbing a bank, but actions of the latter sort are not readily subject to revisions.

The writer forms words on a page. This defaces the page, of course, and in this sense it is like throwing a brick through a window; but it is not like throwing a brick through a window in any other way. And if writing is an immense ruckus made of many minor noises, some shutting down as soon as they are voiced, reading is similarly a series of acts, better ordered than many, to be sure, but just as privately performed, and also open to choice, which may have many motives too, the way the writing had. Paintings and performances (buildings even more so) are public in a fashion that reading and writing never are, although the moralist likes to make lump sums of everything and look at each art as if it were nothing but a billboard or a sound truck in the street.

If we rather tepidly observe that a building stands on its street quite differently than a book in its rack, must we not also notice how infrequently architects are jailed for committing spatial hanky-panky or putting up obscene facades? Composers may have their compositions hooted from the hall, an outraged patron may assault a nude, a church burned to get at the God believed to be inside, but more often than not it is the littérateur who is shot or sent to Siberia. Moralists are not especially sensitive to form. It is the message that turns their noses blue. It is the message they will murder you for. And messages which are passed as secretly as books pass, from privacy to privacy, make them intensely suspicious. Yet work which refuses such interpretations will not be pardoned either. Music which is twelve-toned, paintings which are abstract, writing which seems indifferent to its referents in the world—these attacks on messages themselves—they really raise the watchdog's hackles.

In life, values do not sit in separate tents like harem wives; they mix and mingle rather like sunlight in a room, or pollution in the air. A dinner party, for example, will affect the diners' waists, delight or dismay their palates, put a piece of change in the grocer's pocket, bring a gleam to the vintner's eye. The guests may be entertained or stupefied by gossip, chat, debate, wit. I may lose a chance to make out, or happily see my seduction advance past hunt and peck. The host may get a leg up in the firm whose boss he's entertaining, serious arguments may break out, new acquaintances may be warmly made. And if I, Rabbi Ben Ezra, find myself seated next to Hermann Goering, it may put me quite off the quail—quail which the *Reichsminister* shot by machine gun from a plane. We should all be able to understand that. It would be a serious misjudgment, however, if I imagined that the quail was badly cooked on account of who shot it, or to believe that the field marshal's presence had soured the wine, although it may have ruined the taste in my mouth. It might be appropriate to complain of one who enjoyed the meal and laughed at the fat boy's jokes. Nevertheless, the meal will be well prepared or not quite independently of the guests' delightful or obnoxious presence, and it would be simple-minded to imagine that because these values were realized in such close proximity they therefore should be judged on other than their own terms—the terms, perhaps, of their pushier neighbors.

The detachment it is sometimes necessary to exercise in order to disentangle aesthetic qualities from others is often resented. It is frequently considered a good thing if moral outrage makes imbeciles of us. The aesthete who sees only the poppies blowing in Flanders fields is a sad joke, to be sure, but the politicized mind is too dense and too dangerous to be funny.

I have been mentioning some differences between moral acts as they are normally understood (keeping promises, saving the baby) and what might be called artistic ones (dancing the fandango, painting the Botticelli), and I have been drawing our attention to the public and private qualities of the several arts lest they be treated en bloc. Finally, I have suggested that values have to be judged by sharply different standards sometimes, though they come to the same table. However, my dinner party differs from Petronius' banquet in another essential: it is "thrown" only once. Even if the evening is repeated down to the last guest's happy gurgle, the initial party can be only vaguely imitated, since you can't swallow the same soup twice (as a famous philosopher is supposed to have said). The events of my party were like pebbles tossed into a pond. The stones appear to shower the surface of the water with rings, which then augment or interfere with one another as they widen, although eventually they will enlarge into thin air, the pond will become calm, and the stones' effects negligible.

Art operates at another level altogether. Petronius' story does not fling itself like a handful of stones at the public and then retire to contemplate the recession of its consequences, but occurs continually as readers reenact it. Of course these readings will not be identical (because no reading is written or a part of the text), but the text, unless it has been mutilated or reedited, will remain the same. I shall recognize each line as the line I knew, and each word as the word that was. The letter abides and is literal, though the spirit moves and strays. In short, the mouth may have an altered taste, but not the soup.

For this reason the powers of events are known to be brief, even when loud and unsettling, and unless they can reach the higher levels of historical accounts—unless they can reach language—

the events will be forgotten and their effects erased. Accounts, too, can be lost or neglected, so those texts which are truly strong are those whose qualities earn the love and loyalty of their readers, and enlist the support and stewardship of the organizations those readers are concerned with and control (schools, societies, academies, museums, archives), because the institutions encourage us to turn to these now canonical texts again and again, where their words will burn in each fresh consciousness as if they had just been lit.

Moralists are right to worry about works of art, then, because they belong to a higher level of reality than most things. Texts can be repeated; texts can be multiplied; texts can be preserved; texts beget commentaries, and their authors energize biographers; texts get quoted, praised, reviled, memorized; texts become sacred.

The effect of a text (as every failed commission on pornography has demonstrated) cannot be measured as you measure blows; the spread of a text cannot be followed like the course of an epidemic; there is no dye which can be spilled upon the ground to track the subtle seepages of its contamination. Texts are not acts of bodies but acts of minds; for the most part, then, they do not act on bodies as bodies act, but on minds as minds do.

So my position is not that literature has no relation to morality, or that reading and writing, or composing, or painting, aren't also moral, or possibly immoral, acts. Of course they can be. But they are economic acts as well. (They contribute to their author's health or illness, happiness or melancholy.) My position, however, is that the artistic value of a book is different from its economic value, and is differently determined, as is its weight in pounds, its utility as a doorstop, its elevating or edifying or life-enhancing properties, its gallery of truths: new truths, known truths, believed truths, important truths, alleged truths, trivial truths, absolute truths, coming truths, plain unvarnished truths. Artistic quality depends upon a work's internal, formal, organic character, upon its inner system of rela-

tions, upon its structure and its style, and not upon the morality it is presumed to recommend, or upon the benevolence of its author, or its emblematic character, when it is seen as especially representative of some situation or society.

As I have already suggested, values may reinforce one another, or interfere with their realization in some thing or person. The proximity of Herr Goering may put me off my feed. Perhaps I ought to be put off. Perhaps the chef should have poisoned the quail. Perhaps all of the guests should have left in a huff. And the housemaid and the butler grin as they quaff champagne in the kitchen, grin so little bones appear between their open teeth. How's the pâté no one would eat? Deelish.

Wagner's works are not wicked simply because he was; nor does even the inherent vulgarity deep within the music quite destroy it. Frost's poetry seems written by a better man than we've been told he was. In fact, we are frequently surprised when an author of genius (like Chekhov) appears to be a person of some decency of spirit. The moral points of view in works of art differ as enormously as Dante's do from Sophocles', or Shakespeare's from Milton's. Simply consider what we should have to say if the merit of these writers depended at all upon their being correct, even about anything. In any case, Balzac sees the world quite differently than Butor does; Goethe and Milton cannot both be right; so if being right mattered, we should be in a mess indeed, and most of our classics headed for the midden.

If author and art ought not to be confused, neither should art and audience. If we were to say, as I should prefer, that it is the moral world of the work which ought to matter to the moralist, not the genes of the author's grandfather, or the Jean who was a longtime lover, or a lean of the penholder toward the political right or left, we ought also to insist that the reactions of readers aren't adequate evidence either. If Wagner's anti-Semitism doesn't fatally bleed into his operas, and, like a bruise, discolor them, and if Balzac's insufferable bourgeois dreams don't irreparably damage his fictions, then why should we suppose the work itself, in so much less command of its readers than its author is of it, will communicate its immoral implications like a virus to the innocents who open its covers?

To be sure, authors often like to think of their works as explosive, as corrupting, as evil. It is such fun to play the small boy. Lautréamont asks Heaven to "grant the reader the boldness to become ferocious, momentarily, like what he is reading, to find, without being disoriented, his abrupt and savage path through the desolate swamps of these somber and poison-filled pages." Yet this is an operatic attitude; reading is never more than reading, and requires a wakeful understanding—that is all. Certainly we should like to think that we had written some "poison-filled" pages, but no luck. Even chewing them won't make you sick, not even queasy.

If the relation of morality to art were based simply on the demand that art be concerned with values, then almost every author should satisfy it even if they wrote with their pricks in their sleep. (Puritans will object to the language in that sentence, and feminists to the organ, and neither will admire or even notice how it was phrased.) Henry Miller's work has been condemned, but Henry Miller is obsessed with ethical issues, and his work has a very pronounced moral point of view. *Madame Bovary* was attacked; *Ulysses* was forbidden entry into the United States; *Lady Chatterley's Lover* was brought to court, where they worried about signs of sodomy in it; *Lolita*, of course, was condemned; and, as someone has said, who also has suffered such censorship, so it goes. How long the list would be, how tiresome and dismaying and absurd its recital, if we were to cite every work that has been banned, burned, or brought into the dock.

It is simply not possible to avoid ethical concerns; they are everywhere; one is scarcely able to move without violating someone's moral law. Nor are artists free of the desire to improve and instruct and chastise and bemoan their fellow creatures, whether they call themselves Dickens, D. H. Lawrence, or Hector Berlioz. Céline is so

intensely a moral writer that it warps his work. That is the worry. "There are still a few hatreds I'm missing," he wrote. "I am sure they exist." Hate, we mustn't forget, is a thoroughly moralized feeling.

It is the management of all these impulses, attitudes, ideas, and emotions (which the artist has as much as anyone) that is the real problem, for each of us is asked by our aims, as well as by our opportunities, to overcome our past, our personal aches and pains, our beloved prejudices, and to enlist them in the service of our skills, the art we say we're loyal to and live for. If a writer is in a rage, the rage must be made to energize the form, and if the writer is extended on the rack of love, let pain give the work purpose and disappointment its burnished point. So the artistic temperament is called cold because its grief becomes song instead of wailing. To be a preacher is to bring your sense of sin to the front of the church, but to be an artist is to give to every mean and ardent, petty and profound, feature of the soul a glorious godlike shape.

It is actually not the absence of the ethical that is complained of, when complaints are made, for the ethical is never absent. It is the absence of the *right* belief, the *right* act, which riles. Our pets have not been fed; repulsive enthusiasms have been encouraged; false gods pursued; obnoxious notions noised about; so damn these blank and wavy paintings and these hostile drums, these sentences which sound like one long scratch of chalk.

Goodness knows nothing of Beauty. They are quite disconnected. If I say *shit* in a sentence, it is irrelevant what else I say, whether it helps my sentence sing or not. What is relevant is the power of certain principles of decorum, how free to be offensive we are going to be allowed to be. When the Empress Dowager of China, Ci Xi, diverted funds intended for the navy to construct a large and beautiful marble boat, which thousands now visit at the Summer Palace in Beijing, she was guilty of expropriation. If her choice had been a free one, she would seem to have chosen to spend her money on a thing of peace rather than on things of war (a choice we might applaud); in fact, we know she simply spent the money on herself. She cannot have chosen the beauty she received because beauty is beyond choice. The elegant workmanship which went into the boat, the pleasure it has given to many, its rich and marvelous material, are serendipitous, and do not affect the morality of the case.

When a government bans nonobjective art, it is the threat of the very look it has, its veer from the upright, its deviationism, that is feared — a daub is just as dangerous. Finally, when the Soviet authorities decide to loosen their restrictions on the publication of books and the holding of performances, this is not suddenly a choice of art over politics on their part; it is politics, and has to do with issues such as the freedom of information, the quashing of the Stalin cults, not with art. They know what the novels in the drawers are about.

I do happen to feel, with Theodor Adorno, that writing a book is a very important moral act indeed, consuming so much of one's life, and that, in these disgusting times, a writer who does not pursue an alienating formalism, but rather tries to buck us up and tell us not to spit in the face of the present, this to serve a corrupt and debauched society in any way, is, if not a pawn of the system (a lackey, we used to say), then probably a liar and a hypocrite. It is a moral obligation to live in one's time, and to have a just and appropriate attitude toward it, not to live in the nineteenth century or to be heartless toward the less fortunate or to deny liberty and opportunity to others or to fall victim to nostalgia.

But good books have been written by bad people, by people who served immoral systems, who went to bed with snakes, by people who were frauds in various ways, by schemers and panderers. And beautiful books have been written by the fat and old and ugly, the lonely, the misbegotten (it is the same in all the arts), and some of these beautiful books are like Juan Goytisolo's, ferociously angry, and some of them are even somewhat sinister like Baudelaire's, and some are shakingly sensuous like those of Colette, and still others are dismayingly wise, or deal with terror tenderly, or are full of lamentable poppycock. (I am thinking most immediately of Pope's *Essay on Man*.)

I think it is one of the artist's obligations to create as perfectly as he or she can, not regardless of all other consequences, but in full awareness, nevertheless, that in pursuing other values — in championing Israel or fighting for women or defending the faith or exposing capitalism or speaking for your race — you may simply be putting a saving scientific, religious, political false face on your failure as an artist. Neither the world's truth nor a god's goodness will win you that race.

Finally, in a world which does not provide beauty for its own sake, but where the loveliness of flowers, landscapes, faces, trees, and sky are adventitious and accidental, it is the artist's task to add to the world objects and ideas — delineations, symphonies — which ought to be there, and whose end is contemplation and appreciation; things which deserve to become the focus of a truly disinterested affection.

There is perhaps a moral in that.

SUGGESTED EXERCISES

1. Write an analysis of a current movie to show whether it does or does not have a hidden ideology. List television programs or movies with *explicit* values, and list those values.
2. Write an essay on the attack on Salman Rushdie's *Satanic Verses*. Is it absurd to find a book of fiction blasphemous? Is it absurd to think that an artist should be sentenced to death for his published work of imagination? Why, or why not?

SUGGESTED ADDITIONAL READINGS

Simone de Beauvoir, "Must We Burn Sade?" in *The Marquis de Sade* (New York: Grove Press, 1953).

R. G. Collingwood, "Art as Magic," Chapter 4 of *The Principles of Art* (Oxford: Oxford University Press, 1958).

John Gardner, *On Moral Fiction* (New York: Basic Books, 1978).

Iris Murdoch, "Art and Eros: A Dialogue about Art," in *Acastos: Two Platonic Dialogues* (New York: Viking, 1987).

Leo Tolstoy, *What is Art?*, trans. Almyer Maude (New York: Macmillan, 1960).

NOTES

1. A striking exception is the recent banning in Muslim countries of *The Satanic Verses* by the Anglo-Indian writer Salman Rushdie. This work of imaginative fiction has been attacked as heretical and blasphemous by Islamic believers. See Gerald Marzorati, "Salman Rushdie: Fiction's Embattled Infidel," *New York Times Magazine*, 29 Jan. 1989.

2. The film, called "Shoot Dog Film," was made by sculptor Tom Otterneff. It shows a dog tied to a stake. Two shots are heard, and the dog falls twitching to the ground. This thirty-second loop is then repeated for half an hour. It was shown on a Manhattan cable public-access channel on Christmas Eve. The artist described the piece this way: "It was an execution." He would not discuss its purpose; he said, "It presents itself." See *Village Voice* 14 Jan. 1980, p. 26, and *New York Times* 14 Feb. 1980.

3. See *Village Voice* 2 Apr. 1979, p. 43.

4. Some of the most notorious examples are the works of Chris Burden (see Chapter 5). He has shot at an airplane, endangered himself and colleagues with high-voltage electricity, and taken a television show hostage at knife point—all as works of art.

5. Quoted in *Village Voice*, 2 Apr. 1979, p. 43.

6. See the selection from Edward Banfill in Chapter 2 readings.

7. R. G. Collingwood discusses this view in Chapter 12 of *The Principles of Art*.

8. William H. Gass, "Goodness Knows Nothing of Beauty." See the Readings, p. 108.

9. Susan Sontag, "Fascinating Fascism," in *Under the Sign of Saturn* (New York: Farrar, Straus & Giroux, 1980).

10. Sontag, "Fascinating Fascism," p. 91.

Plate 1. *Pastoral Concert* (c. 1510) by Giorgione (c. 1477–1510). Giorgione, an enigmatic Venetian master, is credited with being one of the originators of the modern sensibility in painting. This moody and poetic allegory, combining mythological with realistic figures, is an example of how in his work painting turned from religious and historical subjects. The writer Mary McCarthy has said that Giorgione was the first artist to make paintings that had no purpose beyond pleasure and the production of agreeable moods. Could such a goal explain the depth and power we attribute to paintings like this?

Plate 2. *Kiss of Judas* by Giotto (c. 1267–1337); frescoes painted c. 1305. This fresco is part of a series illustrating the life of Christ that Giotto painted in the Arena Chapel in Padua. Giotto is regarded as the most important artist to bring painting out of the Middle Ages. He was among the first to portray tangible figures in realistic poses. The *Kiss of Judas*, full of energy and even violence, illustrates Giotto's realism. But how differently it must have struck the devout viewers of Giotto's time from how it strikes a modern viewer! Are we misunderstanding artworks of other times and cultures if we approach them with modern aesthetic stances?

Plate 3. *Spiral Jetty* (Great Salt Lake, Utah, 1970) by Robert Smithson (1938–1973). Robert Smithson was one of the originators of earthworks, which are site-specific artworks that use natural geological features as their materials. When Smithson found this site on the Great Salt Lake, he was deeply struck: "As I looked at the site, it reverberated out to the horizons only to suggest an immobile cyclone while flickering light made the entire landscape appear to quake . . . This site was a rotary that enclosed itself in an immense roundness. From that gyrating space emerged the possibility of *Spiral Jetty*." [Robert Smithson, *The Writings of Robert Smithson: Essays with Illustrations* (New York: NYU Press, 1979) p. 111.]

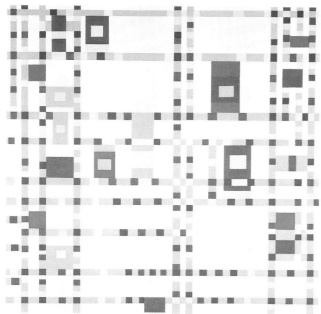

Plate 4. *Broadway Boogie-Woogie* (1942–1943) by Piet Mondrian (1872–1944). Mondrian developed an important school of abstract painting. In his art he practices a "dematerialization" of the natural world into its underlying abstract forms. In this painting Mondrian develops an image related to two subjects: New York City and jazz. The rhythmic patterns of the painting reflect the rhythms of jazz and the steps of jazz dancing; the geometry reflects the the right-angle grid characteristic of New York City's street layout and buildings.

Plate 5. *Innocent X* (1649–1650) by Diego Rodriguéz de Silva Velazquez (1599–1660). Because it seems to capture the psychology of Pope Innocent X—reputed to be cruel and suspicious—this painting is considered by many to be one of the great portraits of all time. In spite of its dazzling technique, one can ask what makes it true that it represents that particular individual, Innocent X. (The difficulty of accounting for visual representation is discussed in Chapter 9.) Is it because the pattern of paint actually resembles his visual appearance? But there are undoubtedly many people whom the painting equally resembles. Is it because the artist *intended* to represent that individual? Is it because Innocent played a crucial causal role as the model for the painting?

Plate 6. *Grainstacks* (1891?) by Claude Monet (1840–1926). Monet was the most influential of the impressionist painters. These paintings are two of a group of twenty-five paintings that Monet did to capture the fleeting appearances of the grainstacks at different times of day and in different seasons and weather. Monet's concern to capture the momentary impact of light on the eye gave impressionism its definition. In many of the grainstack paintings it would be nearly impossible to be certain what their subject is without being told; it could be a hut, a hat, a boulder, a billboard, a termite mound, a hill. It may be better to say that the paintings represent the subjective play of light waves on Monet's eyes at a given time, rather than a grainstack.

Plate 7. *Window or Wall Sign* (1967) by Bruce Nauman (1941–).The neon spiral says: "The true artist helps the world by revealing mystic truths." It blatantly asserts the mysticism that lies behind many formalist artworks. Nauman was influenced by the philosopher of language, Ludwig Wittgenstein, and he must have been aware that this piece is self-referential: If Nauman is a true artist, his saying must also reveal mystic truths. Wittgenstein might have said: It must reveal something that it cannot say.

Plate 8. *Who's Afraid of Red, Yellow, and Blue II* by Barnett Newman (1905–1970). Newman was one of the leaders of the New York school of painting. He rejected a decorative interpretation of abstract painting in favor of a religious art with symbolic associations. Critic Donald Kuspit notes that a color-field painting such as Newman's, when contemplated with full attention, "is functionally mystical—that is, it is not a vehicle of communication of religious dogma but of a certain kind of irreducible, nondiscursive experience." [Donald Kuspit, "Concerning the Spiritual in Contemporary Art" in *The Spiritual in Art: Abstract Painting 1890–1985* (New York: Abbeville Press and Los Angeles: Los Angeles County Museum of Art, 1987), p. 319]

Plate 9. *Orange and Red Streak* (1919) by Georgia O'Keeffe (1887–1986). O'Keeffe aimed to find visual equivalents for her emotional experience of nature. Often her paintings are almost wholly abstract as they focus on the form and feeling of what was often a concrete event for her. She commented: "It is surprising to me how many people separate the objective from the abstract. Objective painting is not good painting unless it is good in the abstract sense." [Georgia O'Keeffe, *Georgia O'Keeffe* (New York: Viking, 1976)]

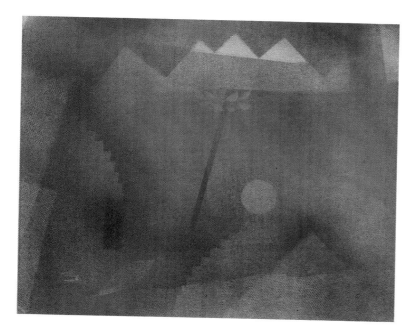

Plate 10. *Bird Wandering Off* (1926) by Paul Klee (1879–1940). This nearly abstract landscape captures a subtle mood. Klee's special sense of the atmospheric effects of color encourages us to experience the emotional essence of a transitory moment. Klee's stated goal was to make the invisible visible. "Formerly we used to represent things visible on earth, things we either liked to look at or would have liked to see. Today we reveal the reality that is behind visible things, thus expressing the belief that the visible world is merely an isolated case in relation to the universe and that there many other, latent realities."

Plate 11. *The Two Fridas* (1939) by Frida Kahlo (1907–1954). What is this picture really about, and can we understand it without taking it as the expression theory of art recommends, as an expression of the emotions of the artist? Frida Kahlo was a Mexican artist of mixed Indian and European heritage who led a troubled life married to the famous Mexican muralist Diego Rivera, who had abandoned Frida at the time of this painting. In this self-portrait she shows herself split into two women representing the two sides of her heritage. The painting is a striking expression of her pain, her fragmentation, and her isolation. She has only herself to depend on to stop her pain, as represented by the surgical pincers that the European Frida uses to slow the flow of her blood.

CHAPTER 5

The Challenge of the Avant-Garde

◀ Stelarc is a performance artist best known for performances in which he hangs by hooks piercing his skin. The photo shows a performance in 1984 in which he was suspended by eighteen fishhooks over 11th Street in New York. He described his performance as involving "the idea of the body as this projectile propelled by desire to transcend its evolutionary limitations."

All modern art is unpopular, and it is not so accidentally
and by chance, but essentially and by fate.

— José Ortega y Gasset, *The Dehumanization of Art*

Its whole *point* is to be gloriously pointless; its very
splendour is to exist entirely for its own sake. Like
humanity itself, art is entirely self-validating; and it can
come to function as a kind of negative politics, a mute,
lonely refutation of the remorseless instrumentalization of
powers it observes everywhere around it.

— Terry Eagleton, "The Ideology of the Aesthetic"

On the one hand specialization has become more and
more intense; on the other hand, the results of the pursuit
of specialized knowledge have become more and more
difficult to apply for the benefit of society as a whole. But
in art, as in science, this does not necessarily mean that
the laboratory discoveries are valueless.

— John Berger, "Problems of Socialist Art"

AVANT-GARDE ART

For over a hundred years, avant-garde artists in all areas of art have been challenging
conventional ideas about art. Their reward has seldom been popularity. Indeed, a very
common rhetorical strategy for attacking the role and importance of art in society
is to attack avant-garde art.[1] By making fun of what, to many people, are
incomprehensible and even repulsive artworks, critics of the arts can effectively
ground their case on the conservatism of the general public. Given this incom-
prehension and hostility, why does such radical and provocative art exist, and
what are its implications for the concept of art?

> [A Ready-Made]
> chooses you. If
> your choice en-
> ters into it, then
> taste is involved —
> bad taste, good
> taste, uninterest-
> ing taste. Taste is
> the enemy of art,
> A-R-T.
>
> — Marcel Duchamp[2]

By definition, avant-garde art is the most advanced art of its own time, but this
definition as it stands is inadequate. Mozart, for instance, was the most advanced
composer of his day, yet he was not an "avant-garde" artist. What, then, is the
distinction between an advanced artist, such as Mozart, and an avant-garde
artist? Although Mozart's work sometimes met with hostility and misunderstanding, it was probably not intended to confuse or offend his listeners' taste.
Nor is it likely that Mozart saw himself as a member of a self-conscious group of
artists who deliberately aimed to be socially or artistically revolutionary. By
contrast, twentieth-century composers such as Igor Stravinsky, Edgard Varèse, Arnold Schönberg, and Erik Satie have written music that consciously rejects conventional musical taste. A

great deal of art has been intentionally experimental since World War I, when many artists began to think that expanding the boundaries of art was the principal obligation of artists. Avant-garde artists in the twentieth century have ingeniously questioned traditional artistic values and concerns, such as beauty, originality, structure, and craft. This questioning of traditional artistic values has often gone hand in hand with questioning the more general values of the dominant social classes.3

Avant-garde artists see themselves as standing on the leading edge of a historical progression of art. They intentionally defy the values of both their culture and past art. For this reason, some people feel that avant-garde work strips art of any clear reason for being and any clear value to the society from which it comes. Paradoxically, avant-garde art is possible only because of the high status that art enjoys, yet it has relentlessly undermined the reasons commonly offered for that status.

The best way to appreciate the challenge that avant-garde art presents is to look at examples. Here is a brief catalogue of a few of the more prominent and intriguing artists and their works.

1. The father of twentieth-century experimentalism in visual art is the French artist Marcel Duchamp (1887–1968), who established himself as a major cubist painter between 1910 and 1915. Indeed, one of the real masterpieces of twentieth-century art is his *Nude Descending a Staircase, No. 2* (1912) (Figure 5.1), in which Duchamp explores the issue of representing the motion of an object over time — in this case a nude descending circular stairs — in painting. During and after World War I, he began to exhibit work that he called "Ready-Mades." These works, considered to be some of the most important of this century, are mass-produced objects that he purchased in stores. A piece called *Fountain*, for example, is a urinal (see illustration on p. 146); *In Advance of a Broken Arm* (Figure 5.2) is an ordinary snow shovel. The Ready-Mades are revolutionary in several obvious ways. Duchamp neither made the objects nor altered them; he simply exhibited them as he found them. Moreover, these objects are not unique or precious. They are the result of an industrial process that produces many identical copies. In fact, many of the original Ready-Mades have been lost, and for later retrospective shows of Duchamp's work authorized *copies* were made and exhibited!

Duchamp thus undermined many of the most fundamental assumptions underlying the visual arts: (1) that art is handmade, (2) that art is unique, (3) that art should look good or be beautiful, (4) that art should express a point of view, and (5) that art should require craft or technique.

Some of Duchamp's artworks are alterations of objects he found. His famous work *LHOOQ* (Figure 5.3) is simply a postcard of Leonardo's Mona Lisa with a mustache and goatee drawn on her face. By "appropriating" another artist's work, Duchamp thus questioned the necessity of originality and became one of the first artists to contend that art is really about ideas, not about physical objects or images. By taking a familiar object and exhibiting it in an art gallery, he could, as he put it, "place it under a different concept." Duchamp was therefore one of the first "conceptual" artists. During the 1960s and 1970s, conceptual, or concept, art was developed further by many hundreds of artists.

The fact that [Ready-Mades] are regarded with the same reverence as objects of art probably means I have failed to solve the problem of trying to do away entirely with art.

— Marcel Duchamp4

FIGURE 5.1 *Nude Descending a Staircase No. 2* (1912) by Marcel Duchamp. Now considered one of the masterpieces of twentieth-century art, this painting met with hostility in both Paris and New York. It is one of Duchamp's most sophisticated attempts to represent a moving object over time, and hence a temporal process, in a nontemporal painting. He analyzes the body into schematic anatomical subcomponents; using swirling lines and dots he creates almost a diagram of the motion of the body down the spiral stairs.

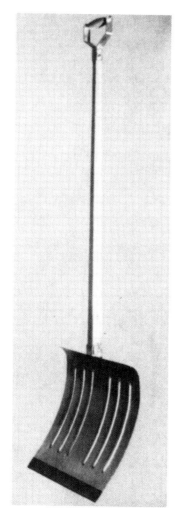

FIGURE 5.2 *In Advance of a Broken Arm* (1915) by Marcel Duchamp. This snow shovel is one of Duchamp's classic Ready-Mades. Duchamp bought it in a hardware store in New York City, signed it, and suspended it from the ceiling. His aim was to undermine our conventional ideas about common objects and art. Duchamp claimed it was not important that the artist makes something, but that he chooses something. He described his own art thus: "He took an ordinary article of life, placed it so that its useful significance disappeared under a new title and point of view — [he] created a new thought for that object."

2. Robert Barry, in the tradition of concept art, exhibited the following statement as an artwork: "All the things I know but of which I am not at the moment thinking — 1:36 P.M.; 15 June 1969, New York."[5] This piece suggests that a work of art can be not only a mere idea but also an unknown and unknowable idea.

3. The famous pop artist Robert Rauschenberg once sent a telegram stating, "This is a portrait of Iris Clert if I say it is."[6] This piece suggests that what a work represents is a function of what the artist intends. In claiming that this verbal message is a visual portrait, Rauschenberg also implies that the distinction between visual and literary arts is arbitrary.

FIGURE 5.3 *LHOOQ* (1919) by Marcel Duchamp. Duchamp added a mustache and a goatee to a reproduction of the *Mona Lisa*. This he called an "assisted Ready-Made." This piece, poking fun at a cultural icon, well represents the attitude of avant garde artists to the unthinking worship of famous artworks.

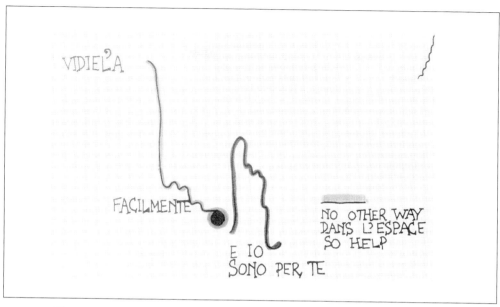

FIGURE 5.4 The American composer John Cage (b. 1912) has experimented with novel sounds and with novel ways to compose music. His most radical idea is to make music indeterminate with respect to performance. Each time a piece of Cage's music is performed, it can sound entirely different. He often leaves the choice of instruments, the order in which the music is played, and many other dimensions of the music up to the performers. This reproduction of page 4 of his work *Aria* illustrates the latitude for interpretation Cage leaves to the performer.

4. John Cage, a prominent and controversial experimentalist in contemporary music, is considered by many to be one of America's most important composers. He has developed a method of composing music that is *indeterminate* with respect to performance. He makes his compositional choices — for example, what notes to play — by random means (he flips coins, rolls dice, uses a random number generator), and he makes sure that each performance is also a function of variables beyond his control so that no two performances sound alike. For example, one of his pieces consists of instructions for several pairs of performers. Each pair has a radio tuned to frequencies determined without regard to what is being broadcast at that place and time. One of the performers randomly tunes the frequency of the radio while the other performer of the pair randomly adjusts the volume. As in this example, Cage's pieces often consist of sounds that are unpredictable and have not been specifically chosen. (Another of Cage's scores is shown in Figure 5.4.)

Perhaps Cage's most notorious piece is *4' 33"* for piano (first performed in 1952). The player comes out and sits at the piano for four minutes and thirty-three seconds, without playing anything, and then leaves the stage. Cage considers the sounds made by the audience and the ambient sounds that occur during the performance to be part of

> I try to deal with things that maybe other people haven't thought about, emptiness, making a painting that isn't a painting.
>
> — Robert Barry[7]

the piece. This example highlights another idea very important to Cage, namely, that when we listen to music there should be no conceptual barrier between the sounds of the music and the sounds around us.

> I have nothing
> to say and
> I am saying it
> and that is
> poetry as I need it.
>
> — John Cage[8]

5. Sherrie Levine is a photographer and painter who made a reputation in the 1980s by copying other artists' works. For example, she made exact copies of famous photographs by Walker Evans, Edward Weston, and Ansel Adams and exhibited these as her own photographs. (She has also made exact photographic copies of paintings, including those of Piet Mondrian.) She does not hide the fact that her works are copies; rather, she makes a point of appropriating familiar images. One critic suggests that her work threatens "the current reaffirmation of individual expressive creativity and its implicit reaffirmation of private property."[9] Her work also clearly undermines the institutions of the artworld that treat artworks — for example, photographs — as collectible, unique commodities. Her work thus questions the idea that artists own their own images. She explains her motivation this way: "I appropriate these images to express my own simultaneous longing for the passion of engagement and the sublimity of aloofness. I hope that in my photographs of photographs an uneasy piece will be made between my attraction to the ideals these pictures exemplify and my desire to have no ideals or fetters whatsoever."[10]

6. Carl André is a sculptor who in the 1960s exhibited a number of simple modular floor pieces made out of prefabricated or natural materials, such as bricks, metal plates, boulders, and bales of hay. This style of art has been dubbed "minimalism." One of André's most famous pieces, *Spill* (1968), in which eight hundred identical plastic blocks were thrown on a gallery floor, illustrates several themes in his work: a repudiation of artistic control and formal balance as well as a desire to take the artwork off its pedestal. He has said that "the ideal piece of sculpture is a road."[11] One of his earliest pieces, *Lever* (1966), was simply a row of unattached bricks on the floor. In 1976, the Tate Museum in England purchased one of André's pieces for a large sum of money, instigating a major controversy because he merely sent a box of bricks and directions for laying them on the floor. The Tate was severely criticized in the British newspapers because many people could not understand why his piece cost so much when the materials cost so little.[12] All of André's sculpture is simple and cheap to produce. Moreover, he does not usually build it himself. Some of his works are not even permanent; he has created artworks out of bales of hay placed in patterns on a field to rot and disintegrate with the seasons.

7. Robert Smithson (1938–1973) was, along with Walter De Maria and Michael Heizer, one of the founders of a movement of sculptors who made "earthworks." Earthworks are characterized by the use of dirt and other natural and geological features as sculptural material. Smithson's mature art pieces are situated in nature rather than in museums. In fact, his museum and gallery exhibitions often consisted only of documentation (photographs and materials) of the work he did elsewhere. His best known piece is *Spiral Jetty*, which is a semisubmerged spiral jetty built of local earth and rocks extending into the Great Salt Lake (see Plate 3). His works are barely discernible in their natural setting, especially after several years of weathering, erosion, and weed growth. They have been compared to Duchamp's Ready-Mades; just as Duchamp's works are found industrial objects, so Smithson's pieces are virtually found objects in nature.[13] Earthworks question the role of museums and the use of materials in the sculptural tradition; more generally, they question the boundary between nature and art.

8. Christo is another sculptor who builds pieces in nature. Unlike Smithson, however, Christo has not tried to make his work blend into nature. He began his career with artworks consisting of wrapped packages. Because the identity of the object wrapped is only suggested but not known, these pieces have a mysterious presence. He graduated to wrapping buildings and monuments. Finally, his interest in the packaging, or, more generally, in the framing of objects, led him to grandiose projects, in which Christo temporarily framed items in nature, such as hills, islands, and valleys. For example, *Valley Curtain* is a huge orange curtain strung across a valley in the Colorado mountains. Christo has also surrounded islands off the Florida coast with pink plastic sheets. His work is controversial because it seems to be an assault on nature that ignores the effects that even temporary barriers can have on wildlife. To environmentalists, who frequently oppose his projects, he seems much more concerned with art values than with ecological harmony.[14]

9. A great deal of revolutionary work has also occurred in both theater and dance. A theatrical group called the Living Theater became famous in the 1960s for confronting and interacting with the audience in various ways, thus breaking down the barrier between the play and the audience. The Living Theater rejected the illusion involved in traditional theater. What happened in a performance by the Living Theater really was happening:

> Even their name, the *Living*, was appropriate, signifying their commitment to abolishing the separation between what is happening on the stage and what is happening in life. . . . The Living provoked audiences into "acting" instead of only watching, and thus the theatrical event melded into a real one. . . . The Living . . . provoked the public's hostility, bombarded it with noise and chaos. . . . The actors' bizarre dress and gothic makeup, their unrestrained psychic and sexual energy . . . were thrust into the audiences faces — violently, aggressively, abrasively.[15]

The end of a performance by the Living Theater would often involve the audience participating in a riot or a "love pile," in which "everyone either groped or watched."[16]

Modern dance developed out of ballet by rejecting the conventions of beautiful movement that are basic to ballet. Experimental dance goes beyond even this. Some avant-garde choreographers have introduced an incredible range of actions, events, and movements, in particular, everyday and untutored movements. Some dances have been designed deliberately for people who don't know how to dance.

10. The sculptor Edward Keinholz has made a piece so challenging that it is banned in this country (it has been shown in Europe). The work, *Still Live* (1974), is a chair in which the spectator is invited to sit. The spectator faces a randomly activated gun that is supposed to go off once in several years. One critic claims that the work "places the viewer in a life-and-death situation not for the sake of risk but as a comment on the randomness and violence of terrorism."[17] This is only one of many pieces in which real physical danger is an integral part. Chris Burden's pieces (see below) involve danger to the artist. Keinholz's piece, along with many others, involves danger to the spectator.

FIGURE 5.5 *Shoot* (1971) by Chris Burden is a work documented by photography but not performed for an audience. In it Burden had himself shot by a friend. This is one of a group of works in which Burden used his body to explore themes of anxiety, risk, and fear.

11. Body art and performance art are genres that grew out of sculpture in the 1960s and 1970s. Chris Burden has performed many of the most famous works of this sort. His thesis show at Cal Arts consisted of his being confined in a small locker at art school for several days. His most famous piece, called *Shoot* (Figure 5.5), involved his being shot in the arm by a friend with a rifle. In another piece, *Trans-fixed* (Figure 5.6), Burden was crucified on a Volkswagen, which then briefly backed out of a garage and into an alley where he could be seen.

12. Stelarc is another body artist. In many of his pieces/performances he is suspended naked from large fishhooks stuck through the flesh of his back. He has performed these pieces in several places, once in 1984 over Eleventh Street in New York City until the police stopped him (see illustration on p. 118).

13. Tehching Hsieh is a conceptual artist who performs pieces that last for one year. He spent 1979 locked in a cell in his room. More recently, he spent a year entirely on the streets of New York, never allowing himself to go into a building. His most recent piece was performed with

FIGURE 5.6 *Trans-fixed* (1974) by Chris Burden. In this piece Burden was crucified on a Volkswagen by nails driven through his hands. The car was then briefly pushed into a public alley, its engine roaring, then pushed back into a garage. This piece has been interpreted as making a comment on our attachment to the automobile or to machinery in general.

another artist, Linda Montano (see C. Carr's "Roped," in the Readings). They were tied together by an eight-foot rope for a year. They did not touch, and they had to do everything together. They did not know each other before they began the year-long performance.

All of this performance and body art denies the customary expectation that the creative activity of a visual artist will result in a permanent object. Nothing is left after the performance, nor, often, is any skill or technique involved, except perhaps in the conceptualization of the piece. Such work cannot be associated with the traditions of the theater, either, for there is no illusion or story; the events are usually quite real.

This leaves us with several questions. If these examples are art, what, then, is art? And why is it valuable? If they are not art, why not? And why has such work been accepted by the artworld?

THE INSTITUTIONAL THEORY OF ART

Among the various challenges avant-garde art poses, one that has particularly fascinated philosophers of art is its challenge to any attempt to define art. What could such diverse work possibly have in common? Is there any feature or property that all of these works share?

As we saw in Chapter 1, by the 1950s many philosophers believed that to try to define art was a mistake. According to these philosophers, among them Morris Weitz (see the Readings for Chapter 1), traditional theories of art claim that we can define art by specifying its *essence*, that is, a set of necessary and sufficient conditions that make something an artwork. Weitz argues that art has no such essence; he insists that there are no conditions (or properties) such that something is a work of art *only if* it exemplifies these properties (a necessary condition of art) or such that it is a work of art *if* it exemplifies these properties (a sufficient condition of art). Weitz does not in fact base his argument on a consideration of the puzzling cases of avant-garde art such as we have just reviewed. Rather, Weitz, under the influence of the philosopher Ludwig Wittgenstein, is persuaded that there is simply nothing common to all the arts, that instead the arts share family resemblances that enable us to distinguish artworks from other sorts of artifacts. Nor does Weitz believe that there is anything common to all the items that make up any of the subcategories of "art," such as "novel," "painting," and so on. In addition, Weitz apparently thinks that because new sorts of art are always being produced, it is impossible to give a definition; he suggests that any definition would go against the "open" nature of the concept of art, which allows for novel and unpredictable artworks. Art cannot be pinned down to any rigid definition and still be art.

> One day the time will come when we shall be able to do without all the arts, as we know them now; beauty will be ripened into palpable reality. Humanity will not lose much by missing art.
>
> — Piet Mondrian[18]

Several philosophers have subsequently disagreed with this assessment. George Dickie (see the Readings) has argued that there is a complex property common to all works of art. To define this property is to define our concept of art. According to Dickie, those who argue that art cannot be defined make two mistakes. First, they conclude that the general concept of art cannot be defined because the various subconcepts of art cannot be defined. As Dickie points out, this doesn't really follow; there may be properties that all works of art have in common, even if there is no common property that makes something an example of a novel, for instance. One property that all works of art do have in common, Dickie argues, is that they are artifacts; that is, they are created by someone.

The second mistake made by those who deny that all works of art have something in common is that they look for that common property in the wrong place. Dickie points out that we are inclined to look for the essence of art *in* the work of art; we are inclined to expect that the property that makes something art will be an *exhibited* property of the artwork. But, Dickie maintains, what makes something art is a "nonexhibited" social property that pertains to the relation of the artifact to social institutions.

Dickie thus defines "work of art" as (1) an artifact (2) on which a society or one of its subgroups has conferred the status of candidate for appreciation (see p. 138). In other words, what makes something a work of art is that the institutions of art, dubbed by the philosopher Arthur Danto the "artworld," have granted it that status.[19] (Danto's own approach to the question of whether something is art tends to emphasize art-historical context, rather than art institutions. See the Readings.) Dickie's definition, therefore, constitutes an "institutional" theory of art. Anything, as Dickie points out, can be designated a work of art if it gains the status of candidate of appreciation. For Dickie, this definition takes away the mystery of how Duchamp's urinal can be a work of art. The acceptance of Duchamp's Ready-Mades in the artworld and the attention given them by museums, critics, and art historians have made them works of art. However, Dickie believes that to say *Fountain* is a work of art is to say nothing about its quality; it is not to imply that *Fountain* is a good work of art. To say that something is a work of art is merely to describe this social property.

What are the ways to confer this status? Dickie says, "An artifact's hanging in an art museum, a performance at a theater, and the like are sure signs that the status *has been conferred*" (p. 138). Dickie goes on to argue that because many works of art never make it to public display, artists themselves can confer the status on their own artifacts. But he seems to imply that the ability of artists to do this derives from their position within the artworld.

Many people find Dickie's institutional theory of art troubling.[20] It may seem to take away the point or value of art; on this view, there is nothing special about works of art, except that they are things that can be candidates for appreciation—and that could be just about anything! Indeed, one of the most criticized aspects of Dickie's theory is his account, or perhaps lack of an account, of appreciation.[21] Dickie's proposal explicitly rejects the notion that "appreciation" is unique to artworks: "many artifacts which are obviously not works of art are appreciated" (p. 139).

Much turns, then, on the question of which are the institutions that grant the status of art. One problem is whether we can give a noncircular definition of this set of institutions, the "artworld." Consider, for example, how this definition would apply to music. How will we define the institutions that determine which musical works are works of art? All music seems to be appreciated in the vague sense of Dickie's definition, so why not say that MTV or the Grand Ole Opry are institutions whose function is to confer the status of candidate for appreciation? It seems that all types of music should be considered "works of art," even pop and commercial music of all sorts. So either this definition would be too wide—that is, it would include too many cases of music as art—or we have to narrow the relevant class of "art institutions" to symphony orchestras, music schools, and so on. But the latter option seems arbitrary; after all, each type of music has its own set of institutions. Is there a way to define the right sort of institutions, a way to specify the general property that makes them *art* institutions, other than simply to make a list or point at them?

Since for Dickie there is nothing unique about either the inherent properties of artworks or our way of apprehending them, those who search for a special value in artworks must look for that value, on Dickie's theory, in the way artworks emphasize appreciation. Although appreciation is not unique to art, perhaps artworks provide a more concentrated occasion for the audience to exercise its propensity to appreciate objects. Even so, we need a fuller account of appreciation—what it is, why we do it, why we care about it—before we can accept Dickie's definition as a plausible explanation of our concept of art.

READINGS FOR CHAPTER 5

C. Carr, "Roped: A Saga of Art in Everyday Life"
George Dickie, "Defining Art"
Arthur C. Danto, "De Kooning's Three-Seater"

Roped: A Saga of Art in Everyday Life

C. Carr

Reprinted by permission of *The Village Voice* and the writer, © 1984.

Even as they came to the window to throw me a key, it was Art. Linda Montano and Tehching Hsieh have engaged in living every moment as Art since last July 4 when they were tied together at the waist with an eight-foot rope, declaring then that they would neither take the rope off nor touch each other for one year. When one of them had to get something, they both went to that something. When one went to the bathroom, they both were in the bathroom. When I saw Tehching at the window, I knew that Linda had to be there too. They both answered the door, the rope catching most of my attention. It was grayish, freakish, with a padlock at each waist. This July 4 at 6 P.M. in a ceremony suitably undramatic, the witness who hammered those locks onto the ropes last year will testify that they haven't been tampered with. Then Montano and Hsieh will each cut the rope at their waists to end "Art/Life One Year Performance 1983–84."

It's a piece no one's watched but in bits, with the performers often hiding from their audience, since they never set out to be spectacles of themselves. They have worked to keep their lives non-eventful, avoiding those colorful interactions that would interest a reporter, confining their activities on most days to Chinatown and their Tribeca neighborhood where people are used to seeing them. Daily life is as simple as Hsieh's Hudson Street loft where they've been living—two captain's beds at one end near the windows, two work tables down at the other.

They go out on jobs together. They must. They aren't funded. Often they work for other artists or art groups—to hang a show, put up a wall, do a mailing list, clean a loft, give a lecture. They split the money. Boredom, yes, it's just part of the piece. On a day without a job they may get up late, Montano often rising before Hsieh and exercising between the beds till he wakes. They take out the dog, they may run, they have tea, watch a lot of TV, spend hours at the work tables, sitting back to back. For pleasure, they see movies and ride their bikes around, one following behind the other. It's like Life, only harder. "We can't ask too much of each other," says Montano.

They rehearsed the piece for a week to determine the length and size of rope, how to tie it, make it comfortable at night, etc. Once during that week they had to cut themselves out of the rope when it began to shrink around them in a Chinese restaurant; they had showered before dinner. They both shaved their heads and began the piece. Hair length would measure the passage of time.

It's been difficult to see old friends or keep old habits. They must both agree to do something before they can do it. On jobs, they found they had totally different work styles. Committed together to this arduous piece, they found they didn't agree on what it meant to be doing it. I told them that when I pictured myself in the ropes, it felt like strangling in total dependency and lack of privacy.

Tehching said my reaction was just personal. Just emotional. Here, we were talking about Art.

Linda said Tehching thought the personal was subsumed by the Art. But she was interested in issues like claustrophobia and ego and power relationships—Life issues. They were as important as Art.

No, Tehching said, that was too personal. The piece was not about him with Linda. It was about all people.

See, Linda said, this is the way the man traditionally talks about his work. Most women traditionally talk about their personal feelings and the man says, "I am everybody."

Tehching said he hadn't finished. He wanted to say the piece was about individuals, all human beings. He had wanted to do the piece with a woman because he liked to spend time with women. But it didn't matter if it was two men or two women or a man and a woman tied together. Didn't matter if they were husband/wife or total strangers before it started, or planned to ever see each other once it ended. These things were personal and not important.

Linda said the piece was more than just a visible work of Art. It was a chance for the mind to practice paying attention, a way to stay in the moment. If they didn't do that, they had accidents. One would get into an elevator, the other wouldn't, and the door would close.

One or the other wears a Walkman at all times to record whatever they say. She sees this as a way to be conscious that she's talking. He says it symbolizes communication, that they're conceptual art tapes. (Indeed, they will never be listened to.)

Montano thinks of art as ascetic training. Hsieh thinks his art is often misunderstood to be ascetic training.

This is his fourth year-long performance. In 1978–79 he lived in an eight-by-nine-by-twelve-foot cage in his loft, without speaking, reading, watching TV, etc. In 1980–81, he punched a time clock every hour on the hour every day, every night. In 1981–82, he lived on the street, never entering a building, subway, tent, or other shelter. Hsieh communicates in English with a limited but direct vocabulary about what motivates him.

Though he painted in Taiwan, he says he's working now from his experience of this country and what he does is "New York Art."

Montano shares his capacity for self-discipline and his attraction to ordeals. An ex-nun, her performances have included drumming for six hours a day for six days, handcuffing herself to another artist for three days, and living in a sealed room for five days as five different people she found in her personality. Over a 15-year career, she has lived in galleries for days at a time, calling it Art. She has lived in the desert for 10 days, calling it Art. She has danced blindfolded in a trance, done astral travel events and once, dressed as a nun, "danced, screamed, and heard confessions."

Montano's attraction to Hsieh's work led her to call him, just as he had conceived of the rope piece and was looking for someone to collaborate with. They had never met before. "We feel strong to do work together," says Hsieh. "When we're feeling good, we're like soulmates," says Montano.

But they do not touch. As Hsieh says, the piece is "not about couple." Montano says the fact that they're male/female can make them look like a couple, but the fact that they're different races, different ages (he's 33, she's 42), and different sizes "throws everything into some strange balance."

Hsieh talks of how they're "married to Art," that they are sacrificing sex, not denying it. They could, in theory, have sex with other people, but, says Hsieh, that would just be a way to try escaping the piece. And, says Montano, it would be kinky, an impossible thing to do to someone else. She says it's a vacation not to have the choice, that not having sex is as interesting as having it, and allows her to see where else she can relate from on the astral or imaginative or visual level.

They ate and dreamt a lot when the piece began, says Montano, because "we were doing something very difficult and repressive. Food was our only pleasure and dreaming was the way the mind processed the new information and brought some ease." Dreaming was the one privacy, Hsieh said, and for him food was important because while living on the street last year, he was never able to eat well.

Montano made a sound, barely audible, when the Walkman ran out of tape, and they both got up to get a new one. She said they were communicating with sounds now — "it's regressed in a beautiful way" — for they had started with talking and yanking the rope, then moved to gestures, now to noises. They were down to about an hour of talking a day.

By the time the piece ends, they will have something like 700 of the 90-minute tapes, each dated on the red and white label that reads: "TALKING." If they have a show of their documentation, the tapes will be displayed along with the photographs they've made, one-a-day, since the performance began. Most show them engaged in some daily activity. For a few days — days when they were fighting or thought of nothing to photograph — there are only gray-green blanks. On several days they photographed the word "FIGHT."

"Eighty percent of the year was an incredible struggle," says Montano.

"A lot of ego issues to struggle about," says Hsieh.

They spent most of the winter in the loft, taking away each other's permission. They simply said NO to anything the other one wanted to do outside of the jobs they had to do for money. At one point, the fight went on for three weeks, till they finally just quit, they said, from boredom. In the spring it began to get more physical, pushing and pulling on the rope without touching each other, until Montano insisted they get help from friends. Hsieh still insists this wasn't necessary, because if they fought, it was just part of the piece. They never considered "divorce," since as Hsieh says, they are not like a marriage, more like a business. Montano says, "It's being done for Art, so the emotions are withstood, no matter what they are."

Eight days before the piece was to end, I met them to go to the park and sensed that they were fighting. The didn't say so, but it was in the air. They were straining at each other, not walking easily — one would start off before the other had noticed, and pull. Weeks earlier, Linda had described how the piece accentuated the negative

and "brought it up to the rim of Art . . . the frustration, the claustrophobia, the lack of privacy . . . to surrender to the chosen and call it Art — I've always had that as an ideal."

Tehching said the cage piece had been easier. He could focus on Art. This was too much Life. Once, in a better mood, he had said there was little difference for him between these pieces: Linda was his cage. Now, as we sat on the grass, he said Linda was his mirror, and he could see his "weakness part." He couldn't hide. It was "much struggle."

After a year of constant exposure to each other, they're obviously tuned in on a nonverbal level. On a day when we were going out for dinner, I'd been sitting with them at the kitchen table when suddenly they were both walking around getting things, putting chairs on the bed to keep the dog off, and I began to figure out that we were leaving now. They hadn't said a word.

This would be my chance to see how people reacted to them on the street. We stood on the sidewalk discussing restaurants. Tehching asked if Chinese food would be okay. Then I realized I'd already forgotten that they were wearing a rope. As we crossed West Broadway, a woman approached and said, "I must ask why I always see you attached." Linda answered, "It's an experiment." That's become their standard response to the question, Linda said, because calling it Art "plays with that definition too much for a lot of people and then they get angry." It may also play with their definition of Life.

I was most surprised by the Oblivious Ones who passed us. And by the Frightened Ones, with the seen-a-ghost look about them. The Perplexed Ones I expected. In Philadelphia, where they'd gone to teach a performance art class, they found it much more difficult and abrasive to be public. In New York, the heightened level of strangeness absorbs some of the attention they don't want. On a recent visit to Area, people stared at them, Linda thought, not because of the rope but because they weren't dressed right.

I asked if we could visit the art world together sometime. No, they mostly avoided those places. Just recently in Soho, they could hear everyone talking about them as they walked down the street, snatches of "tied together for one year" floating by, and it made them feel like they were giving a show. They didn't want to give a show. "Too sensationalize," [*sic*] Hsieh says. They've turned down *That's Incredible, Entertainment Tonight*, and *Ripley's Believe It or Not*.

Dinner and a kung fu movie was more like what they normally did. The ushers at the kung fu theater looked worried when they saw us, while I was forgetting more and more that the rope existed. I made myself look at it and thought, God, they have guts to walk down the street like this. We watched something astonishing whose title Hsieh couldn't translate: a grandmother fighting five villains, men jumping magic distances, girls twirling swords, pairs and groups testing each other to the death. The ritualized fighting looked as powerful, perfect, and hard to choreograph as a wave crashing off a rock. Then we sat through the next movie on the bill, *Boat People* without subtitles. Watching was a little hint of Endurance Art. A chance to think: I've chosen this and I'll just have to wait till it's over.

It helped immensely to know I was with them, was now part of the piece, and that sitting there was Art.

Defining Art

George Dickie

American Philosophical Quarterly, Volume 6, Number 3, July 1969. Reprinted by permission of the publisher.

In recent years it has been argued that the expression "work of art" cannot be defined and Morris Weitz has even argued that *being an artifact* is not a necessary condition for being a work of art.[1] More recently, however, Joseph Margolis has offered a definition[2] and Maurice Mandelbaum has made tentative suggestions about defining "art."[3]

I shall not repeat the well-known argument of Weitz, whose views I take to be representative of those who maintain that "art" cannot be defined, but shall state his main conclusion and comment on one of his arguments. Neither shall I repeat the arguments of Margolis or Mandelbaum, but I do want to note (1) that they agree that artifactuality is a necessary condition of art, and (2) that Mandelbaum points out the significance of the *nonexhibited* characteristics of art for the definition of "art."

Weitz's main conclusion is that there are no necessary and sufficient conditions for the definition of "art" or for any of the subconcepts of art, such as "novel," "tragedy," "painting," and so on. All of these notions are open concepts and their instances have "family resemblances."

Weitz rejects artifactuality as a necessary condition of art because we sometimes make statements such as "This driftwood is a lovely piece of sculpture."[4] We do sometimes speak this way of natural objects, but nothing follows from this fact. Weitz is confused because he takes the driftwood remark to be a descriptive statement and it is not. Weitz himself, quite correctly, distinguishes between an evaluative use and a descriptive use of "work of art,"[5] and once this distinction is understood it can be seen that the driftwood remark is an evaluation of the driftwood. But it is, of course, the descriptive sense of "work of art" which is at issue when the question of whether "art" can be defined is raised. I maintain that the descriptive use of "work of art" is used to indicate that a thing belongs to a certain category of artifacts. By the way, the evaluative sense can be applied to artifacts as well as nonartifacts, as when we say, "That painting is a work of art." Such remarks are not intended as tautologies.

Before going on to discuss the second condition of the definition of the descriptive sense of "art," it will be helpful to distinguish the generic concept of art from the various subconcepts which fall under it. It may very well be the case that all or some of the subconcepts of art, such as

---

[1] Morris Weitz, "The Role of Theory in Aesthetics," *The Journal of Aesthetics and Art Criticism*, vol. 15 (1956), pp. 27–35; reprinted in *Philosophy Looks at the Arts*, ed. by Joseph Margolis (New York, 1962); Paul Ziff, "The Task of Defining a Work of Art," reprinted in *Aesthetics and the Philosophy of Criticism*, ed. by Marvin Levich (New York, 1963); William Kennick, "Does Traditional Aesthetics Rest on a Mistake?" *Mind*, vol. 66 (1958), pp. 317–334.

[2] *The Language of Art and Art Criticism* (Detroit, 1965), pp. 37–47. Margolis' definition is not satisfactory, however; see Andrew Harrison's review in *Philosophical Books*, vol. 7 (1966), p. 19.

[3] "Family Resemblances and Generalization Concerning the Arts," *American Philosophical Quarterly*, vol. 2 (1965), pp. 219–228.

[4] *Op. cit.*, p. 57.

[5] *Ibid.*, p. 56.

novel, tragedy, ceramics, sculpture, painting, and so on, may lack necessary and sufficient conditions for their application as subconcepts and it still be the case that "work of art," which is the genus of all these subconcepts, can be defined. For example, there may not be any characteristics which all tragedies have which would distinguish them from comedies, satyr plays, happenings, and the like within the domain of art. Even if this were the case, in the light of the foregoing, tragedies and all other works of art would have at least one characteristic in common, namely, artifactuality. Perhaps artifactuality and some one or more other features of works of art distinguish them from nonart. If all or some of the subconcepts of art cannot be defined and, as I think is the case, "art" can be, then Weitz is right in part.

Assuming that artifactuality is the genus of art, the differentia is still lacking. This second condition will be a social property of art. Furthermore, this social property will, in Mandelbaum's terminology, be a nonexhibited, relational property.

W. E. Kennick contends that such an approach to the definition of "art" is futile. He argues from such facts as that the ancient Egyptians sealed up paintings and sculptures in tombs to the conclusion that "the attempt to define Art in terms of what we do with certain objects is as doomed as any other."[6] There are several difficulties with Kennick's argument. First, the fact that the Egyptians sealed up paintings and sculptures in tombs does not entail that they generally regarded them differently from the way in which we regard them. Indeed, they might have put them there for the dead to appreciate, or simply because they belonged to the dead person, or for some other reason. The Egyptian practice does not prove a radical difference between their conception of art and ours such that a definition which subsumes both is impossible. Secondly, there is no need to assume that we and the ancient Egyptians (or any other group) share a common conception of art. I would be happy to be able to specify the necessary and sufficient conditions for the concept of art which we have (we present-day Americans, we

present-day Westerners, we Westerners since the organization of the system of the arts in or about the 18th century — I am not sure of the exact limits of the "we"). Kennick notwithstanding, we are most likely to discover the differentia of art by considering "what we do with certain objects," that is, "works of art." But, of course, there is no guarantee that any given thing we or an ancient Egyptian might possibly do with a work of art will throw light on the concept of art. Not every *doing* will reveal what is required.

Arthur Danto's stimulating article, "The Artworld,"[7] is helpful here. In speaking of Warhol's Brillo Carton and Rauschenberg's Bed, he writes, "To see something as art requires something the eye cannot de[s]cry — an atmosphere of artistic theory, a knowledge of history of art: an artworld."[8] What the eye cannot descry is a complicated nonexhibited characteristic of the artifacts in question. The "atmosphere" of which Danto speaks is elusive, but it has a substantial content. Perhaps this content can be captured in a definition. I shall first state the definition and then go on to defend it. *A work of art in the descriptive sense is (1) an artifact (2) upon which some society or some sub-group of a society has conferred the status of candidate for appreciation.*

The definition speaks of the conferring of the status of *candidate* for appreciation: nothing is said about actual appreciation and this leaves open the possibility of works of art which, for whatever reason, are not appreciated. Also, not every aspect of a work is included in the candidacy for appreciation, for example, the color of the back of a painting is not ordinarily an object of appreciation. The problem of *which* aspects of a work of art are to be included within the candidacy for appreciation is a question which I have pursued elsewhere.[9]

Just how is the status of candidate for appreciation conferred? An artifact's hanging in an art

[6]Kennick, *op. cit.*, p. 330.

[7]*The Journal of Philosophy*, vol. 61 (1964), pp. 571–584.
[8]*Ibid.*, p. 580.
[9]In my "Art Narrowly and Broadly Speaking," *American Philosophical Quarterly*, vol. 5 (1968), pp. 71–77, where I analyze the notion of *aesthetic object*. The subject of the present essay is the concept of *art* which, although related to the notion of aesthetic object, is distinct from it.

museum, a performance at a theater, and the like are sure signs that the status *has been conferred*. But many works of art never reach museum walls and some are never seen by anyone but the artist himself. The status, therefore, must be conferrable by a single person's treating an artifact as a candidate for appreciation, usually the artist himself, although not always, because someone might create an artifact without ever considering it as a candidate for appreciation and the status be conferred by some other person or persons. But can status be conferred so easily? We associate status with ceremony — the wedding ceremony and the status of being married, for example. However, ceremony is not the only way of getting married, in some jurisdictions common-law marriage is possible — a status acquired without ceremony. What I want to suggest is that, just as two persons can acquire the status of common-law marriage within a legal system, an artifact can acquire the status of a candidate for appreciation within the system which Danto has called "the artworld."

A number of questions arise about this notion of status of candidate for appreciation and perhaps the whole matter can best be clarified by stating them and trying to answer them. Probably the first question is: what *kind* of appreciation? Surely the definition does seem to suggest that there is a special kind of "aesthetic" appreciation. Appreciation is not crucial, but something should be said about it to prepare the way for the crucial point. The kind of appreciation I have in mind is simply the kind characteristic of our experiences of paintings, poetry, novels, and the like. This remark seems to collapse the definition into circularity, but it does not because "work of art" (the term defined) does not appear in the explanation of appreciation, only subconcept terms appear. Another apparent problem is that works of art differ so much from one another — for example, comedies are very different from tragedies — that it seems unlikely that the appreciation characteristic of our experience of one kind of work has something in common with the appreciation characteristic of our experience of another kind of work. But paintings, poems, and plays are the *objects* of our appreciation and the fact that the objects differ considerably does not mean that the various appreciations differ. Indeed, if we mean by "appreciation" something like "in experiencing the qualities of a thing one finds them worthy or valuable," then there is no problem about the similarity of the various appreciations.

It can now be seen that appreciation will not serve to pick out the subclass of works of art from the class of artifacts — it is too broad: many artifacts which are obviously not works of art are appreciated. To pick out the class of works of art one must stress the conferring of the status of candidate rather than appreciation. When, for example, a salesman of plumbing supplies spreads his wares before us, he presents them for our appreciation all right, but the presenting is not a conferring of status of candidate, it is simply a placing before us. But what is the difference between "placing before" and "conferring the status of candidate?" The difference is analogous to the difference between my uttering "I declare this man to be a candidate for alderman" and the head of the election board uttering the same sentence while acting in his official capacity. When I utter the sentence it has no effect because I have not been vested with any authority in this regard. Of course the analogy is not a complete one — lines of authority in the politico-legal world are by and large explicitly defined and incorporated into law, while lines of authority (or something like authority) in the artworld are nowhere codified. The artworld carries on its business at the level of customary practice. Still there *is* a practice and this defines a social institution. To return to the plumbing line, the salesman's presentation is different from Duchamp's superficially similar act of placing a urinal which he christened "Fountain" in that now famous art show. The point is that Duchamp's act took place within a certain institutional setting and that makes all the difference. Our salesman of plumbing supplies could do what Duchamp did, that is, convert a urinal into a work of art, but he probably would not — such weird ideas seem to occur only to artists with bizarre senses of humor. Please remember that when I say "Fountain" is a work of art, I am not saying it is a good one. And in making this last remark I am not insinuating that it is a bad one either.

Duchamp's "ready-mades" raise the question—"If urinals, snowshovels, and hatracks can become works of art, why can't natural objects such as driftwood become works of art?" and, of course, driftwood and other natural objects can become works of art if any one of a number of things is done to them. One thing which would do the trick would be to pick it up, take it home, and hang it on the wall. Another thing which would do the trick would be to pick it up and enter it in an exhibition. (I was, by the way, assuming that Weitz's sentence about driftwood referred to a piece of driftwood in its ordinary situation on a beach and untouched by human hand.) This means that natural objects which become works of art acquire their artifactuality (are artifactualized) at the same time that the status of candidate for appreciation is conferred on them. But perhaps a similar thing ordinarily happens with paintings, poems, and such; they come to exist as artifacts at the same time that they have conferred on them the status of candidate for appreciation. (Of course, being an artifact and being a candidate for appreciation are not the same thing—they are two properties of a single thing which may be acquired at the same time.) A somewhat more complicated case would be an artifact from a primitive culture which played a role in a religious system and which had no artistic function in the sense developed here. Such an artifact might become a work of art in our culture in a way similar to that in which driftwood might become a work of art. However, such a religious object which becomes a work of art would be an artifact in two senses, but the driftwood in only one. (I am not suggesting that something cannot be a religious object and work of art at the same time—there are many counter-instances to this in our own culture.)

A question which frequently arises in connection with discussions of the concept of art is "How are we to conceive of paintings done by individuals such as Betsy the chimpanzee from the Baltimore Zoo?" It all depends on what is done with the paintings. (Note that I unhesitatingly call the objects paintings, although I am uncertain about their status as works of art.) For example, The Field Natural History Museum in Chicago recently exhibited some chimpanzee paintings. In the case of these paintings we must say that they are not works of art. However, if they had been exhibited a few miles away at the Chicago Art Institute they would have been works of art. (If, so to speak, the director of the Art Institute had gone out on a limb.) It all depends on the institutional setting.

In concluding, it may be worthwhile to consider in what ways the definition offered here differs from some traditional definitions. (1) It does not attempt to smuggle a conception of good art into the definition of "art." (2) It is not, to use Margolis' term, "overloaded," as is the one Margolis cites as a horrible example: "Art is a human activity which explores, and hereby creates, new reality in a suprarational, visional manner and presents it symbolically or metaphorically as a microcosmic whole signifying a macrocosmic whole."[10] (3) It does not contain any commitment to any metaphysical or unempirical theory, as contrasted with, for example, the view that art is unreal. (4) It is broad enough so that those things generally recognized as art can be brought under it without undue strain, as contrasted with, for example, the imitation definition which involves enormous strain in trying to show that every work of art is an imitation of something or other. (5) It takes into account (or at least attempts to) the actual practices of the artworld of the past and of the present day.

Now what I have been saying may sound like saying, "a work of art is an object of which someone has said, 'I christen this object a work of art'." And I think it is rather like that. So one *can* make a work of art out of a sow's ear, but of course that does not mean that it is a silk purse.

---

[10]*Op. cit.*, p. 44. The passage is quoted from Erick Kahler's "What is Art?," in *Problems in Aesthetics*, ed. by Morris Weitz (New York, 1959).

De Kooning's Three-Seater

Arthur C. Danto

From *The Nation*, March 9, 1985 © 1985 The Nation Co., Inc.
Reprinted by permission of the publisher.

Charles Vanderveer 3d, the legendary auctioneer of the South Fork of Long Island, is a resourceful and in many ways an idealistic man. Given his relentless curiosity about the archeology of his region, it was inevitable that odds and ends from the kitchen middens of the Abstract Expressionist tribe, which settled in the area in the late 1940s, should turn up as collectibles in one or another of his auctions. Recently, however, he has acquired an object that puts enough pressure on the borderline between art works and curiosities to raise a question about the firmness of that borderline. Since the object is "by" Willem de Kooning, it seems somewhat urgent that the matter be resolved.

The philosophical question of separating art from everything else is given a certain comic turn in the present instance since the object at issue is a three-hole toilet seat from the period before Abstract Expressionists were in command of sufficient resources to afford running water. De Kooning did not so much paint the seat, in the way that a handyman might, as put paint on it, in a way that raises issues of connoisseurship. Yeats assures us through Crazy Jane that love has pitched his mansion in the place of excrement. If love has such a locus, why not art?

The question posed in the headline of *The New York Times* article that reported this find — "But Is it Art?" — has been raised at every stage of modern art since Impressionism, and doubtless it is made inevitable by the fact that the concept of art allows for revolution from within. Still, certain objects very like this one have made it across the border into museum space, and it was to be expected that someone would instantly draw an analogy between the de Kooning three-seater and one of the most controverted objects in the history of art, that urinal Duchamp titled "Fountain." "Fountain" was signed with the pseudonym R. Mutt and dated 1917, and was rejected by the hanging committee in the jury-free Independents Exhibition of that year, though it is unclear whether the grounds were that it was bad art or just not art at all. Certainly it has been enfranchised as art since, and though the "original" has been lost — it exists only in a photograph by Alfred Stieglitz — it may even today be kicking around someone's barn. Were Charles Vanderveer 3d to stumble upon it, he need have few worries about his children's tuition payments or, for that matter, his old age. Esthetically, however, the urinal's loss is not as important as it might seem, since the relationship between the work and the object is tenuous. Duchamp's work dates from 1917, but who knows when the urinal was made or by whom? De Kooning put paint on the privy seat in 1954, but the seat must have preceded the work — if it is a work — by a good many years. It was crafted by an itinerant carpenter, perhaps, a contemporary of Walt Whitman for all anyone knows.

Not far from the site of the seat stands the structure where, in the first warm days of 1947, Jackson Pollock, in de Kooning's own words, "broke the ice." This was one of the epochal gestures of modern art: flinging skeins of house paint across canvas placed on the floor. Like Duchamp's work, Pollock's was vindicated not

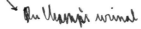

141

only as art but as great art, but in 1947 Pollock himself was far from sure of its status. Barbara Rose cites a very moving memory of Lee Krasner's: "You know, Jackson used to grab me by the arm, shaking, and ask 'Is this a painting?' Not a good or bad painting—just was it a painting at all.' By 1954 that question had been massively resolved, though problems might have been created if Pollock's dropcloths resembled his paintings drip for drip, or if he had flung paint at a field mouse because of his well-known irascibility. Pollock's style spread to the outer bounds of artistic consciousness with the speed of light, and even in nursery schools, children were soon flinging paint "to express themselves."

In painting the toilet seat, de Kooning used what *The Times* speaks of as "angry blobs of black paint reminiscent of the style used by Jackson Pollock, who frequently visited the de Koonings." It is plain that an art-historical reference and an in-joke is being transacted across the punctuated boards: de Kooning put the paint on in just a few minutes, according to Elaine de Kooning, who "authenticated" the object, for the further gaiety of a croquet party. Art-historical allusions on toilet seats by master painters must be exceedingly rare, so we are dealing with something beyond mere artifact. But, as the question goes, Is it art? And if it isn't, where is the line to be drawn between it and "Fountain," or any of those Pollockian arabesques?

Let me complicate the matter with an example that has some claim to kinship with "Fountain" and with the de Kooning privy. In my student days in Paris, I used to enjoy philosophical conversation with Alberto Giacometti, whose studio I got to know quite well. One part of it I remember vividly: Giacometti's water closet was outside, in the courtyard. It was of an old-fashioned sort known as a *vespasienne*, two footrests on either side of a hole. It was a lonely place, it now occurs to me, in comparison with the convivial three-holer of Long Island. In any case, Alberto used to draw while squatting, and the closet was covered with sketches as precious and precise as those in the caves at Altamira. At the time I wondered whether, in the event of Giacometti's death,

it should be transported intact to the Musée d'Art Moderne. I was in New York when he died and I have no idea what happened to it, but even if I had been in Montparnasse, I doubt my first or even last thought would have been to ask what was to become of the water closet. Yet I am certain that the walls did bear works of art—if Giacometti drawings are works of art at all. They were products of a restless artistic consciousness coping with the inconveniences of the body. Their being there, in that private space, is perhaps an unintended comment on Yeats's beautiful line. Needless to say, were drawings done by Michelangelo under similar circumstances, there would be little question of their status.

The first thing to note, it seems to me, is that "But is it art?" cannot be asked of isolated objects. There is an implicit generalization in the question, which asks: is a thing of this *kind* a work of art? "Fountain," for example, was one of a class of ready-mades, commonplace objects transfigured into works of art through the acceptance of a theory. There would be questions about the scope and limitations of the theory, as well as questions about whether a given ready-made was good in its kind or bad, but the question of art had to be settled for the entire class. One may ask: What of the first ready-made? Well, even though there was only the single instance, the question of its kind was already settled, and the kind had a natural location in what Duchamp had already achieved as an artist. Also, "Fountain" made it possible for him to go on to the next kind of thing. Artistic kinds are like species, where the possibility of generation is a serious criterion. Much the same thing may be said of Pollock's paintings. They were enfranchised by a theory which evolved as the works evolved, and they fit in Pollock's corpus with what preceded them and what came next. As for Giacometti's water-closet drawings, there is no problem at all: they were examples of his mature style, placed on an unusual surface.

None of this applies to de Kooning's three-seater. The mock Pollockian marbling is isolated from everything that went before and came after; it has no place in the de Kooning corpus. Objects similar to it were to become accepted in the next generation of artists. Rauschenberg could easily have made a combine out of a paint-streaked privy stool. There are well-known works of his with which this could have fitted: bedclothes, for example, streaked and smeared with house paint and hung on the wall. Critics and curators adore the language of anticipation, but it would be as inane as the principle that generates major exhibitions at the Museum of Modern Art to say that de Kooning was ahead of his time, that his privy anticipated the kind of works that were to supersede Abstract Expressionism, or that there was an affinity between Vanderveer's acquisition and — excuse me — a Johns. Perhaps de Kooning could have evolved in this direction, but he did not, and there is no space in his corpus for an object of 1954 like this. The great art historian Heinrich Wölfflin said, "Not everything is possible at every time." I incline to the view that Johns and Rauschenberg were not possible in 1954, and it would not be possible for this to have been a de Kooning at any time. The corpus is closed.

So here is my thought: this particular object can be a work of art only if it is a de Kooning, and there is no way it can be that; so it's not a work of art. Neither, in compensation, is a sheet of drawings done for an illiterate servant by Michelangelo, illustrating what he wanted for a meal: two rolls, some fish, etc. Nobody is going to throw that illuminated menu away, as there are more reasons for keeping things than that they are works of art. And this, I dare say, will be the case with the three-seater. It has some archeological interest as a reminder of *la vie de bohème* led by artists near Amagansett before they all became famous. Not even de Kooning has the Midas touch, turning everything his brush comes in contact with into the gold of art. It is not just that the intention is lacking here; the requisite intention could not have been formed, because of historical circumstance. Of course I am not saying what it is worth. I imagine it will go for a pretty price, just because collectors will be afraid not to purchase it.

SUGGESTED ADDITIONAL READINGS

Ted Cohen, "The Possibility of Art: Remarks on a Proposal by Dickie," *The Philosophical Review* 82, no. 1 (Jan. 1973): 69–82.

Arthur C. Danto, *The Transfiguration of the Commonplace* (Cambridge, Mass.: Harvard University Press, 1981).

George Dickie, *The Art Circle* (New York, 1984).

Lucy R. Lippard, *Six Years: The Dematerialization of the Art Object* (New York: Praeger, 1973).

Renato Poggioli, *The Theory of the Avant-Garde* (Cambridge, Mass.: Harvard University Press, 1968).

Robert Stecker, "The End of an Institutional Definition of Art," *British Journal of Aesthetics* 26, no. 2 (Spring 1986): 124–32.

NOTES

1. For an example of such an attack, see the discussion of Edward Banfield's position, in Chapter 2.
2. Marcel Duchamp, from a 1963 interview quoted in Richard Kostelanetz, ed., *John Cage* (New York, Praeger, 1974), p. xvii.
3. For a much deeper analysis of the avant-garde, see Renato Poggioli, *The Theory of the Avant-Garde* (Cambridge, Mass.: Harvard University Press, 1968).
4. Duchamp, quoted in Kostelanetz, *John Cage*, p. xvii.
5. Robert Barry, quoted in Lucy P. Lippard, *Six Years: The Dematerialization of the Art Object* (New York: Praeger, 1973), p. 112.

6. Robert Rauschenberg, quoted in Lippard, *Six Years*, p. 27.

7. Barry, quoted in Lippard, *Six Years*, p. 40.

8. John Cage, "Lecture on Nothing," in *Silence: Lectures and Writings by John Cage* (Middletown, Conn.: Wesleyan University Press, 1973), p. 109.

9. Benjamin H. D. Buchloh, "Allegorical Procedures: Appropriation and Montage in Contemporary Art," *Art Forum*, Sept. 1982, p. 52.

10. Quoted in Buchloh, "Allegorical Procedures," pp. 52–53.

11. See the entry on Carl André in Colin Naylor, ed., *Contemporary Artists*, 3d ed. (Chicago: St. James Press, 1989).

12. Eventually the piece was removed from public exhibition when a man sprayed blue food coloring over it. See the *New York Times*, 20 Feb. 1976 and 25 Feb. 1976.

13. See the entry on Robert Smithson in Naylor, *Contemporary Artists*.

14. A recent piece by Christo illustrates the potential conflict between Christo's artistic concerns and the nature and needs of the sites he uses. His piece, *The Umbrellas*, consisting of 1,340 giant blue umbrellas (twenty feet high, twenty-eight feet wide) placed along a river valley in Japan and 1,760 yellow umbrellas along Tejon Pass in California had to be dismantled after a gust of wind picked up one of the umbrellas and blew it against a spectator, killing her and injuring a child. (See *Newsweek*, 21 Oct. 1991 and *USA Today*, 28 Oct. 1991.)

15. Margaret Croyden, *Lunatics, Lovers and Poets: The Contemporary Experimental Theater* (New York: McGraw-Hill, 1974), pp. 95–96.

16. Croyden, *Lunatics*, p. 120.

17. Ron Glowen, entry on Edward Keinholz, in Naylor, *Contemporary Artists*.

18. Quoted in T. J. Clark, "On the Social History of Art," in *Image of the People* (London: Thames & Hudson, 1973), p. 20.

19. It is in fact difficult to know what Dickie thinks the "artworld" is and whether his concept is the same as Danto's. See the Suggested Additional Readings for this chapter.

20. For an influential analysis of Dickie's position, see Ted Cohen, "The Possibility of Art: Remarks on a Proposal by Dickie," *The Philosophical Review* 82, no. 1 (Jan. 1973): 69–82.

21. For criticism of Dickie's views about appreciation, see Arthur Danto, *The Transfiguration of the Commonplace* (Cambridge, Mass.: Harvard University Press, 1981), and Cohen, "The Possibility of Art."

Part II   Art and Non-Art

THE EASY ANSWERS   Part I raised a number of questions that we hope an adequate philosophy of art will be able to answer. Part II examines answers to those questions that are implicit in our unreflective attitudes. These attitudes are ways of thinking of the arts that are very common, if seldom explicitly articulated. Three of the most prevalent are (*a*) thinking of the arts as a set of art forms (Chapter 6), (*b*) thinking of the arts as a group of crafts (Chapter 7), and (*c*) thinking of the arts as a group of amusements (Chapter 8).

I call these the "easy" answers because they are not the result of careful thought; rather, they reflect the way the arts are often treated and discussed in our society. They might be the quick answers given by the proverbial man-in-the street when asked what art is. Each of these answers, however, falls short of providing a satisfying conception of art. Thus, it can be argued that these ways of thinking of art represent widespread misconceptions about the nature of art. None of these views of art provides a positive account of aesthetic value or the high status of the arts, and one of them (art as entertainment) seems to confirm the worst fears of the critics we studied in Part I (Plato, Banfield, Bentham, and Tolstoy). Moreover, on each of these views, avant-garde art becomes unintelligible. Indeed, adherence to one or more of these views is what no doubt largely accounts for the hostility new art regularly meets. For this reason, it is a matter of some urgency to rescue our notion of art from these inadequate conceptions. These easy answers either disguise or render unanswerable some important questions about art.

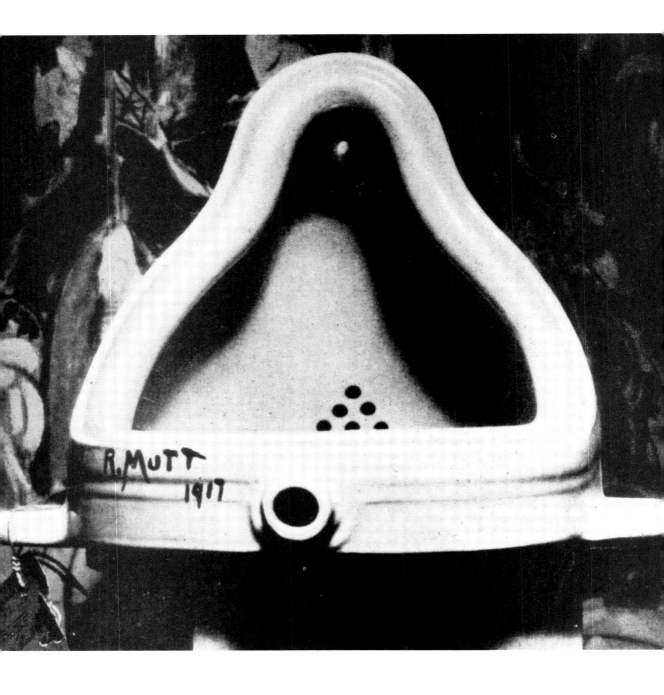

CHAPTER 6

The Very Idea of an Art Form

Fountain (1917) by Marcel Duchamp. Duchamp was a member of an art group that sponsored a show supposedly open to all artists. Duchamp tested this premise by submitting a urinal he purchased at a plumbing supply company and which he signed with the pseudonym "R. Mutt" and titled Fountain. The art group refused to exhibit it. No doubt it failed to correspond to their idea of sculpture. Whether or not it is sculpture, it is now one of the most famous works of twentieth-century art.

ARTIFACTS

What sort of thing is a work of art? As we have seen, this can be a puzzling question. Just in virtue of being art, an entity may have a greater value, a special meaning, a status that obliges us to preserve it, and a certain degree of freedom from the constraints of morality. Consider Duchamp's *Fountain*; just in virtue of being chosen as a work of art by Duchamp, this mass-produced urinal gained a value and a meaning that it otherwise did not have.

Let's start with the following minimal claim: The "things" that are art can all be subsumed under the more general classification "artifact."[1] Art is what is made by artists. So, all art has the characteristic that it is *made or created*. All works of art are artifacts, although it is obviously not true that all artifacts are works of art.

What is an artifact? Since a paradigm case of an artifact is a tool, we tend to think of artifacts as physical objects that have been made by someone. But although this may be the most common application for the term "artifact," to limit the term to such cases seems unnecessary. We can reasonably define artifacts as anything made or created by a human being; on this definition, ideas, theories, and laws can be artifacts even though they are not physical objects. Similarly, poems, symphonies, and novels are not physical objects, but they are made by someone. Hence, they are artifacts. Even when a physical object is created — such as a painting or a sculpture — it isn't universally accepted that the object itself can be equated with the artwork. For example, the philosopher R. G. Collingwood claims that the work of art is not the physical object an artist makes but an imaginary object associated with it, namely, the spectator's imaginary experience.[2]

Some works of art hardly seem to be objects of any sort. Agreeing that art is an artifact does not settle what an artifact is, nor does it limit the sorts of entities that can be artifacts.[3] One interesting feature of experimental art is that it constantly stretches the boundaries of the artifact category. Consider an example: the American artist Walter De Maria has created an artwork in New Mexico that he calls *Lightning Field* (Figure 6.1). This is a large array of lightning rods spread over several acres. The piece is open to the public; the best time to see it is, of course, during an electrical storm. But what exactly is "the piece"? One artifact that De Maria created is the array of lightning rods. But is the piece the array of lightning rods? (Including the land? Can the piece be moved?) Or is it the events constituting the lightning displays (the rods being a mere means to make this happen)? Or is it the idea of the lightning display? As a second example, consider the art piece that comprised the artist Tehching Hsieh spending a year on the streets of New York (see Chapter 5). This is something the artist did, but is it any sort of object?

Even traditional cases can appear puzzling if we ask just what sorts of things they are. Consider the performance arts, such as music, theater, and dance. A performance of a piece of

FIGURE 6.1 *Lightning Field* by Walter De Maria is a one-mile by one-kilometer rectangular grid array of 400 twenty-foot-high stainless steel poles completed in New Mexico in 1977. De Maria intends the work to be seen by the spectator alone or in a small group over a period of at least twenty-four hours. In describing the work he has said that "the land is not the setting for the work but a part of the work" and "the light is as important as the lightning."

music is certainly an object of auditory attention. But is the piece of music to be equated with that performance? That seems wrong; for example, that performance can be canceled in the middle, but the music cannot be canceled in the middle. If the piece of music is an object, what sort of object is it? And how is it related to its performances?

One way to object to the thesis that every work of art must be an artifact is to consider cases of found art. Suppose that an artist finds and displays unaltered objects from nature, such as driftwood, as works of art. (For example, several years ago two graduate students at the University of Colorado had an art show consisting of various samples of dried cow dung found on the western prairie.) These objects are not artifacts in the usual sense. Therefore, we must conclude either (a) that the thesis that a work of art must be an artifact cannot be correct[4] or (b) that we must not equate the artwork with the natural object the artist displays.[5] We can spell out this latter idea by supposing that in finding and displaying natural objects, the artist has made something over and above, and different from, the natural object itself. It might be thought that the artist's intentions give meaning to the object and transform it into something more than its identity as a natural object. (This may not seem entirely plausible, but consider Duchamp's Ready-Mades. Isn't it naive to equate Duchamp's *In Advance of a Broken Arm* (Figure 5.2) with the snow shovel Duchamp purchased in a hardware store?) If this is right, it seems plausible to think that even if the artist merely displays a natural object, he or she has *created* a piece which has that object as a constituent; hence the work of art (that is, the piece) is an artifact.

ONTOLOGICAL AND DEFINITIONAL QUESTIONS

It should now be clear that when we ask, "What is art?" we may be raising a number of different questions. I will distinguish three questions in particular. The issue we have just been exploring can be called the "ontological question":

What type of entity is a work of art?[6]

This question is not the same as the "definitional question" we have looked at in both Chapters 1 and 5:

What criteria or conditions define something as a work of art?

This question is closely related to, but distinguishable from, the "nature question":

What is the nature of art?

This question is the guiding question of this text. Taking "nature" as "the special character of art," this question calls for a philosophical analysis or a theory of art. The answer need not be in terms of necessary and sufficient conditions for something to be art; witness Weitz's position on the concept of art, which claims that the nature of art, in this sense, refutes the idea that art can be defined by such conditions. The traditional theories examined in Part III are all theories about the nature of art. Some attempt to answer the definitional question; some do not.

Clearly, these questions are very closely related to each other, and an answer to one may determine an answer to the others. Dickie's institutional theory of art answers not only the definitional question, but also the nature question. As we have just seen, however, an answer to either or both of these questions doesn't necessarily solve the ontological question. For instance, consider the formalist theory of art (see Chapter 10). It says that the nature of art is to have significant form. But what sort of thing is a significant form?

Having distinguished these three related—and easily confused—questions, lets leave ontological questions and return once more to the definitional and nature questions. There is a very common answer to both questions that needs to be discussed.

ART MEDIA AND ART FORMS

Many people assume that artworks are just those artifacts that fall into special subcategories, such as "novels," "paintings," "symphonies," and so forth. Even the philosopher George Dickie seems to think of works of art in this way. According to his famous institutional theory of art (see Chapter 5) "A work of art in the descriptive sense is (1) an artifact (2) upon which society or some subgroup of a society has conferred the status of candidate for appreciation" (p. 138). But having defined "work of art" in terms of "candidate for appreciation," we need to know what appreciation is. Dickie tells us, "The kind of appreciation I have in mind is simply the kind characteristic of our experiences of paintings, poetry, novels, and the like" (p. 139). This explanation suggests that these familiar categories of artworks are central to the the very definition of art, because they elicit from us a characteristic kind of response. This also suggests that being a work in one of these forms or media is a *sufficient* condition for being a work of art.

It is common to assume that certain media or forms of artifact making are art media and that other media are non-art media. (This seems to be the way the National Endowment for the Arts (NEA) functions. It funds the arts on the basis of medium or art form: painting, sculpture, dance, and so on.) This position is even stronger than Dickie's; it supposes that any work in one of these media is automatically art (though not necessarily good art) and that any work not in one of these media is automatically not art. This carries with it the supposition that anyone who produces work in one of these media is an artist, and anyone who does not produce work in a recognizable medium is not an artist.

In the twentieth century, the idea that art is inherently related to certain art forms has been elevated into a major movement called "modernism." Modernism gained its most explicit articulation in mid-twentieth-century theoretical writings, but as one of the chief modernists, Clement Greenberg, asserts, modernism can be traced back much farther:

I identify Modernism with the intensification, almost the exacerbation of this self-critical tendency that began with the philosopher Kant. Because he was the first to criticize the means itself of criticism, I conceive of Kant as the first real Modernist. (p. 155)

For Greenberg, this self-criticism means that each art

had to determine, through the operations peculiar to itself, the effects peculiar and exclusive to itself. . . . It quickly emerged that the unique and proper area of competence of each art coincided with all that was *unique to the nature of its medium*. . . . Thereby each art would be rendered "pure," and in its "purity" find the guarantee of its standards of quality as well as of its independence. (p. 155)

The notion of a pure exploration of an art medium has been used to explain the various trends in twentieth-century art — for example, the increasing abstraction in all the arts — as well as to provide a critical definition of which artists and artworks seriously advance the art form and which ones are backward-looking. Thus Greenberg judges that "Manet's paintings became the first Modernist ones by virtue of the frankness with which they declared the surfaces on which they were painted" (p. 156).

Because modernism is very powerful as a way of explaining and understanding art, it is important to distinguish modernism from the media definition of art. Modernism, in Greenberg's formulation, says that the best art is the most self-conscious art. In this context, "Self-consciousness" is the desire to explore the nature of an art medium. This presupposes (*a*) that there are art media (or forms) and (*b*) that they have a nature to be explored.[7] It also presupposes that the artist *ought* to be engaged in that exploration. These are interesting but controversial assumptions. They are weaker and less controversial, however, than the assumptions required to say that art in general can be defined by a list of media. Greenberg's position requires only that art be self-critical; it does not limit art to a list of traditional media. Anything that discovers and explores its medium, whatever that might be, can be art. Moreover, modernism tends to be a critical tool, a way of assessing the artistic quality of artworks rather than a way of dealing with the question of how to define art descriptively. Nevertheless, modernism — as both an art movement and a critical theory — is in many ways a consequence of the complacent assumption that art is to be defined by particular art forms. This assumption may reflect the way "art" and "artist" are commonly used, but the media view of art leads to several significant difficulties.

THE CASE AGAINST ART MEDIA

The attempt to define art in terms of certain media poses a serious problem. We are in danger of giving a circular definition of art. We wish to say that something is art if it is in an art medium or art form. Yet it is not clear that the definition of an art medium or art form is logically independent of the assumption that it is art. For instance, when we call a collection of materials "sculpture," it may be that we must have already categorized it as art. Think of the piles of bricks and bales of hay that Carl André (see Chapter 5) has offered as works of art. Whether these are sculptures depends on whether they are artworks. Hence, if we want to know whether a physical object is a work of art, it won't be possible to decide this by determining that it is in the medium of sculpture. We have to know *first* that the object is a work of art before we can determine that it is a sculpture.

> The artistic activity does not "use" a "ready-made language," it "creates" language as it goes along.
> — R. G. Collingwood[9]

Take another example: poetry. Is poetry necessarily an art medium;[8] that is, is every poem a work of art? The answer depends on how we define poetry. We might define poetry in terms of properties, such as rhyme and verse. But then a problem arises: If rhyming or versified language isn't put to an artistic use — for example, if it is used in an advertisement — it isn't *real* poetry. Hence, not every bit of rhyming or versified language would be poetry; only those examples that have real artistic merit would be counted as poetry. Thus poetry, like sculpture, could be counted an art medium, but only by a circular definition, such that if a rhyme isn't art, it isn't poetry.

It is natural to suggest that the intentions of the person who makes the piece determines whether an artifact is an artwork. If the writer's intention is to write a poem rather than a rhymed advertisement, for example, then the work is a work of art. However, the danger of circularity is still present, because we don't yet know what it is to intend to write a poem. If the intentions of the artist are the more general intentions associated with art generally, then these are what makes the artifact art, not its being a poem. If the intention is merely to write something that conforms to some precise definition of a poem (as a school assignment, for example), then we are still left with a question: Is this poem an artwork or just some sort of exercise?

We are thus faced with a general dilemma. If an artifact must already be a work of art for it to be a work in the medium, then we can define art in terms of art media. But then our definition is circular. Moreover it is misleading, for we will easily fall into the tendency to

define a medium more objectively, according to its formal features and materials and methods of construction. For example, we can define the following "media" more objectively in such ways: photography, television, sonata, sonnet, and so on. But if we define media in terms of objective characteristics, then not all instances of work in a medium appear to be works of art; therefore, what makes an object a work of art is something over and above its being in one of these media objectively defined.

MORE ON THE NOTION OF ART MEDIA

The media approach to art offers a "disjunctive" definition of "art"; that is, what makes an artifact a work of art is that it is a novel *or* a painting *or* a symphony, and so on. The problem is that this definition is either circular and thus uninformative or just wrong.

The case against a media definition of art becomes even more compelling when we consider media that are not automatically counted as art, for example, photography. There are dozens of different uses of photography: scientific, journalistic, military, mercantile, educational, artistic, and so on. It's clear that we cannot suppose that every photograph is art. What we can do is ask why some photographs are considered art. Because so much photography has been involved with practical uses, many photographs — for example, most nineteenth-century photographs — were not considered art when they were first made. Yet, they are now considered part of the history of visual art. Even in the twentieth century, photographs taken for journalistic purposes are sometimes retrospectively treated as works of art.

If photographs that were not intended to be works of art nonetheless can be, then we have to admit that the class of artworks can overlap with the class of functional objects. An object can both have a functional use and also be a work of art. This is far from the idea that art is strictly defined by special and distinct art media.

There are further questions about the notion that art is to be found in and only in certain forms or media. How did those media gain this status? What about them makes them *art* media? Could they lose this status? Why are other media unable to attain it? These questions highlight the problem of whether works in new media can be accepted as art. The difficulty that photography, film, and video have met with in being accepted as art is based on the equation of art with certain media. The media definition of art not only overlooks new forms of art but also pays too much honor to all of the members of accepted media. For example, to consider every novel a work of art would force us to count supermarket novels as works of art, yet they may have less quality artistically and aesthetically than a good photograph, movie, or rock song.

READINGS FOR CHAPTER 6

Clement Greenberg, "Modernist Painting"

Modernist Painting

Clement Greenberg

From *Art and Literature*, Spring 1963.

Modernism includes more than just art and literature. By now it includes almost the whole of what is truly alive in our culture. It happens, also, to be very much of a historical novelty. Western civilization is not the first to turn around and question its own foundations, but it is the civilization that has gone furthest in doing so. I identify Modernism with the intensification, almost the exacerbation of this self-critical tendency that began with the philosopher Kant. Because he was the first to criticize the means itself of criticism, I conceive of Kant as the first real Modernist.

The essence of Modernism lies, as I see it, in the use of the characteristic methods of a discipline to criticize the discipline itself — not in order to subvert it, but to entrench it more firmly in its area of competence. Kant used logic to establish the limits of logic, and while he withdrew much from its old jurisdiction, logic was left in all the more secure possession of what remained to it.

The self-criticism of Modernism grows out of but is not the same thing as the criticism of the Enlightenment. The Enlightenment criticized from the outside, the way criticism in its more accepted sense does; Modernism criticizes from the inside, through the procedures themselves of that which is being criticized. It seems natural that this new kind of criticism should have appeared first in philosophy, which is critical by definition, but as the nineteenth century wore on it made itself felt in many other fields. A more rational justification had begun to be demanded of every formal social activity, and "Kantian" self-criticism was called on eventually to meet and interpret this demand in areas that lay far from philosophy.

We know what has happened to an activity like religion that has not been able to avail itself of "Kantian" immanent criticism in order to justify itself. At first glance the arts might seem to have been in a situation like religion's. Having been denied by the Enlightenment all tasks they could take seriously, they looked as though they were going to be assimilated to entertainment pure and simple, and entertainment itself looked as though it were going to be assimilated, like religion, to therapy. The arts could save themselves from this leveling down only by demonstrating that the kind of experience they provided was valuable in its own right and not to be obtained from any other kind of activity.

Each art, it turned out, had to effect this demonstration on its own account. What had to be exhibited and made explicit was that which was unique and irreducible not only in art in general, but also in each particular art. Each art had to determine, through the operations peculiar to itself, the effects peculiar and exclusive to itself. By doing this each art would, to be sure, narrow its area of competence, but at the same time it would make its possession of this area all the more secure.

It quickly emerged that the unique and proper area of competence of each art coincided with all that was unique to the nature of its medium. The task of self-criticism became to eliminate from the effects of each art any and every effect that might conceivably be borrowed from or by the medium of any other art. Thereby each art would be rendered "pure," and in its "purity" find the guarantee of its standards of quality as well as of its independence. "Purity" meant self-definition, and the enterprise of self-criticism in the arts became one of self-definition with a vengeance.

Realistic, illusionist art had dissembled the medium, using art to conceal art. Modernism used art to call attention to art. The limitations that constitute the medium of painting—the flat surface, the shape of the support, the properties of pigment—were treated by the Old Masters as negative factors that could be acknowledged only implicitly or indirectly. Modernist painting has come to regard these same limitations as positive factors that are to be acknowledged openly. Manet's paintings became the first Modernist ones by virtue of the frankness with which they declared the surfaces on which they were painted. The Impressionists, in Manet's wake, abjured underpainting and glazing, to leave the eye under no doubt as to the fact that the colors used were made of real paint that came from pots or tubes. Cézanne sacrificed verisimilitude, or correctness, in order to fit drawing and design more explicitly to the rectangular shape of the canvas.

It was the stressing, however, of the ineluctable flatness of the support that remained most fundamental in the processes by which pictorial art criticized and defined itself under Modernism. Flatness alone was unique and exclusive to that art. The inclosing shape of the support was a limiting condition, or norm, that was shared with the art of the theater; color was a norm or means shared with sculpture as well as the theater. Flatness, two-dimensionality, was the only condition painting shared with no other art, and so Modernist painting oriented itself to flatness as it did to nothing else.

The Old Masters had sensed that it was necessary to preserve what is called the integrity of the picture plane: that is, to signify the enduring presence of flatness under the most vivid illusion of three-dimensional space. The apparent contradiction involved—the dialectical tension, to use a fashionable but apt phrase—was essential to the success of their art, as it is indeed to the success of all pictorial art. The Modernists have neither avoided nor resolved this contradiction; rather, they have reversed its terms. One is made aware of the flatness of their pictures before, instead of after, being made aware of what the flatness contains. Whereas one tends to see what is *in* an Old Master before seeing it as a picture, one sees a Modernist painting as a picture first. This is, of course, the best way of seeing any kind of picture, Old Master or Modernist, but Modernism imposes it as the only and necessary way, and Modernism's success in doing so is a success of self-criticism.

It is not in principle that Modernist painting in its latest phase has abandoned the representation of recognizable objects. What it has abandoned in principle is the representation of the kind of space that recognizable, three-dimensional objects can inhabit. Abstractness, or the nonfigurative, has in itself still not proved to be an altogether necessary moment in the self-criticism of pictorial art, even though artists as eminent as Kandinsky and Mondrian have thought so. Representation, or illustration, as such does not abate the uniqueness of pictorial art; what does do so are the associations of the things represented. All recognizable entities (including pictures themselves) exist in three-dimensional space, and the barest suggestion of a recognizable entity suffices to call up associations of that kind of space. The fragmentary silhouette of a human figure, or of a teacup, will do so, and by doing so alienate pictorial space from the two-dimensionality which is the guarantee of painting's independence as an art. Three-dimensionality is the province of sculpture, and for the sake of its own autonomy painting has had above all to divest itself of everything it might share with sculpture. And it is in the course of its effort to do this, and not so much—I repeat—to exclude the representational or the "literary," that painting has made itself abstract.

At the same time Modernist painting demonstrates precisely in its resistance to the sculptural, that it continues tradition and the themes of tradition, despite all appearances to the contrary. For the resistance to the sculptural begins long before the advent of Modernism. Western painting, insofar as it strives for realistic illusion, owes an enormous debt to sculpture, which taught it in the beginning how to shade and model towards an illusion of relief, and even how to dispose that illusion in a complementary illusion of deep space. Yet some of the greatest feats of Western painting came as part of the effort it has made in the last four centuries to suppress and dispel the sculptural. Starting in Venice in the sixteenth century and continuing in Spain, Belgium, and Holland in the seventeenth, that effort was carried on at first in the name of color. When David, in the eighteenth century, sought to revive sculptural painting, it was in part to save pictorial art from the decorative flattening-out that the emphasis on color seemed to induce. Nevertheless, the strength of David's own best pictures (which are predominantly portraits) often lies as much in their color as in anything else. And Ingres, his pupil, though subordinating color far more consistently, executed pictures that were among the flattest, least sculptural done in the West by a sophisticated artist since the fourteenth century. Thus by the middle of the nineteenth century all ambitious tendencies in painting were converging (beneath their differences) in an anti-sculptural direction.

Modernism, in continuing this direction, made it more conscious of itself. With Manet and the Impressionists, the question ceased to be defined as one of color versus drawing, and became instead a question of purely optical experience as against optical experience modified or revised by tactile associations. It was in the name of the purely and literally optical, not in that of color, that the Impressionists set themselves to undermining shading and modeling and everything else that seemed to connote the sculptural. And in a way like that in which David had reacted against Fragonard in the name of the sculptural, Cézanne, and the Cubists after him, reacted against Impressionism. But once again, just as David's and Ingres' reaction had culminated in a kind of painting even less sculptural than before, so the Cubist counter-revolution eventuated in a kind of painting flatter than anything Western art had seen since before Cimabue — so flat indeed that it could hardly contain recognizable images.

In the meantime the other cardinal norms of the art of painting were undergoing an equally searching inquiry, though the results may not have been equally conspicuous. It would take me more space than is at my disposal to tell how the norm of the picture's inclosing shape or frame was loosened, then tightened, then loosened once again, and then isolated and tightened once more by successive generations of Modernist painters; or how the norms of finish, of paint texture, and of value and color contrast, were tested and retested. Risks have been taken with all these, not only for the sake of new expression, but also in order to exhibit them more clearly as norms. By being exhibited and made explicit they are tested for their indispensability. This testing is by no means finished, and the fact that it becomes more searching as it proceeds accounts for the radical simplifications, as well as radical complications, in which the very latest abstract art abounds.

Neither the simplifications nor the complications are matters of license. On the contrary, the more closely and essentially the norms of a discipline become defined the less apt they are to permit liberties (*liberation* has become a much abused word in connection with avant-garde and Modernist art). The essential norms or conventions of painting are also the limiting conditions with which a marked-up surface must comply in order to be experienced as a picture. Modernism has found that these limiting conditions can be pushed back indefinitely before a picture stops being a picture and turns into an arbitrary object; but it has also found that the further back these limits are pushed the more explicitly they have to be observed. The intersecting black lines and colored rectangles of a Mondrian may seem hardly enough to make a picture out of, yet by echoing the picture's inclosing shape so self-evidently they impose that shape as a regulating norm with a new force and a new completeness. Far from incurring the danger of arbitrariness in the absence of a model in nature, Mondrian's art proves, with the passing of time, almost too disciplined, too convention-bound in certain respects; once we have gotten used to its utter abstractness we realize that it is more traditional in its color, as well as in its subservience to the frame, than the last paintings of Monet are.

It is understood, I hope, that in plotting the rationale of Modernist art I have had to simplify and exaggerate. The flatness towards which Modernist painting orients itself can never be an utter flatness. The heightened sensitivity of the picture plane may no longer permit sculptural illusion, or *trompe-l'oeil*, but it does and must permit optical illusion. The first mark made on a surface destroys its virtual flatness, and the configurations of a Mondrian still suggest a kind of illusion of a kind of third dimension. Only now it is a strictly pictorial, strictly optical third dimension. Where the Old Masters created an illusion of space into which one could imagine oneself walking, the illusion created by a Modernist is one into which one can only look, can travel through only with the eye.

One begins to realize that the Neo-Impressionists were not altogether misguided when they flirted with science. Kantian self-criticism finds its perfect expression in science rather than in philosophy, and when this kind of self-criticism was applied in art the latter was brought closer in spirit to scientific method than ever before — closer than in the early Renaissance. That visual art should confine itself exclusively to what is given in visual experience, and make no reference to anything given in other orders of experience, is a notion whose only justification lies, notionally, in scientific consistency. Scientific method alone asks that a situation be resolved in exactly the same kind of terms as that in which it is presented — a problem in physiology is solved in terms of physiology, not in those of psychology; to be solved in terms of psychology, it has to be presented in, or translated into, these terms first. Analogously, Modernist painting asks that a literary theme be translated into strictly optical, two-dimensional terms before becoming the subject of pictorial art — which means its being translated in such a way that it entirely loses its literary character. Actually, such consistency promises nothing in the way of esthetic quality or esthetic results, and the fact that the best art of the past seventy or eighty years increasingly approaches such consistency does not change this; now as before, the only consistency that counts in art is esthetic consistency, which shows itself only in results and never in methods or means. From the point of view of art itself its convergence of spirit with science happens to be a mere accident, and neither art nor science gives or assures the other of anything more than it ever did. What their convergence does show, however, is the degree to which Modernist art belongs to the same historical and cultural tendency as modern science.

It should also be understood that the self-criticism of Modernist art has never been carried on in any but a spontaneous and subliminal way. It has been altogether a question of practice, immanent to practice and never a topic of theory. Much has been heard about programs in connection with Modernist art, but there has really been far less of the programmatic in Modernist art than in Renaissance or Academic art. With a few untypical exceptions, the masters of Modernism have betrayed no more of an appetite for fixed ideas about art than Corot did. Certain inclinations and emphases, certain refusals and abstinences seem to become necessary simply because the way to stronger, more expressive art seems to lie through them. The immediate aims of Modernist artists remain individual before anything else, and the truth and success of their work is individual before it is anything else. To the extent that it succeeds as art Modernist art partakes in no way of the character of a demonstration. It has needed the accumulation over decades of a good deal of individual achievement to reveal the self-critical tendency of Modernist painting. No one artist was, or is yet, consciously aware of this tendency, nor could any artist work successfully in conscious awareness of it. To this extent — which is by far the largest — art gets carried on under Modernism in the same way as before.

And I cannot insist enough that Modernism has never meant anything like a break with the past. It may mean a devolution, an unraveling of anterior tradition, but it also means its continuation. Modernist art develops out of the past without gap or break, and wherever it ends up it will never stop being intelligible in terms of the continuity of art. The making of pictures has been governed, since pictures first began to be made, by all the norms I have mentioned. The Paleolithic painter or engraver could disregard the norm of the frame and treat the surface in both a literally and a virtually sculptural way because he made images rather than pictures, and worked on a support whose limits could be disregarded because (except in the case of small objects like a bone or horn) nature gave them to the artist in an unmanageable way. But the making of pictures, as against images in the flat, means the deliberate choice and creation of limits. This deliberateness is what Modernism harps on: that is, spells out the fact that the limiting conditions of art have to be made altogether human limits.

I repeat that Modernist art does not offer theoretical demonstrations. It could be said, rather, that it converts all theoretical possibilities into empirical ones, and in doing so tests, inadvertently, all theories about art for their relevance to the actual practice and experience of art. Modernism is subversive in this respect alone. Ever so many factors thought to be essential to the making and experiencing of art have been shown not to be so by the fact that Modernist art has been able to dispense with them and yet continue to provide the experience of art in all its essentials. That this "demonstration" has left most of our old *value* judgments intact only makes it the more conclusive. Modernism may have had something to do with the revival of the reputations of Uccello, Piero, El Greco, Georges de la Tour, and even Vermeer, and it certainly confirmed if it did not start other revivals like that of Giotto; but Modernism has not lowered thereby the standing of Leonardo, Raphael, Titian, Rubens, Rembrandt or Watteau. What Modernism has made clear is that, though the past did appreciate masters like these justly, it often gave wrong or irrelevant reasons for doing so.

Still, in some ways this situation has hardly changed. Art criticism lags behind Modernist as it lagged behind pre-Modernist art. Most of the things that get written about contemporary art belong to journalism rather than criticism properly speaking. It belongs to journalism — and to the millennial complex from which so many journalists suffer in our day — that each new phase of Modernism should be hailed as the start of a whole new epoch of art making a decisive break with all the customs and conventions of the past. Each time, a kind of art is expected that will be unlike previous kinds of art, and so "liberated" from norms of practice or taste, that everybody, regardless of how informed or uninformed, will be able to have his say about it. And each time, this expectation is disappointed, as the phase of Modernism in question takes its place, finally, in the intelligible continuity of taste and tradition, and as it becomes clear that the same demands as before are made on artist and spectator.

Nothing could be further from the authentic art of our times than the idea of a rupture of continuity. Art is, among many other things, continuity. Without the past of art, and without the need and compulsion to maintain past standards of excellence, such a thing as Modernist art would be impossible.

SUGGESTED EXERCISES

1. Consider uses of nature in the "earthworks" by the American artist Robert Smithson (1938–1973). What is "the piece" in the works of Smithson such as his Non-Site Sights?
2. How would you define a medium? Further, how would you try to pick out the *art* media? Formulate some objective definitions of "art media."

SUGGESTED ADDITIONAL READINGS

Tim Binkley, "Piece: Contra Aesthetics," in *Philosophy Looks at the Arts*, ed. Joseph Margolis (Philadelphia: Temple University Press, 1987).

Arthur C. Danto, *The Transfiguration of the Commonplace* (Cambridge, Mass.: Harvard University Press, 1981).

Nicolas Wolterstorff, "Towards an Ontology of Artworks," *Nous* 9 (1975): 115–42.

NOTES

1. We must note that even this claim has been denied. As we saw in Chapters 1 and 5, Morris Weitz denies it, whereas George Dickie affirms it.

2. The chief problem with this view lies in preserving the objectivity of critical assessments against the charge that each person will have his or her own different experience of the piece and thus that the artwork becomes whatever people think it is.

3. For an extensive discussion of the ontological status of various types of artwork, see Nicolas Wolterstorff, "Towards an Ontology of Artworks," *Nous* 9 (1975): 115–42.

4. Thus, some thinkers prefer to argue that when artists display natural objects (wood, rocks, dung), they are presenting these very objects for our *aesthetic appreciation*. It might be said that (visual) art is about looking, thinking, and feeling, and we don't need to talk about "the piece" — the artists who display driftwood are merely setting up a situation for aesthetic responses.

5. Or we can follow George Dickie, who claims that to display a found object is to "artifactualize" it, that is, make it into an artifact (see Chapter 5). Going even farther along this line, maybe Duchamp was making the point that he could make an object *his* artifact by merely displaying it as an artwork.

6. For the answer that different kinds of art are different types of entity, see Wolterstorff, "Towards an Ontology of Artworks."

7. In addition, it appears to presuppose that that nature is specific, unique, and knowable, in some sense, by the artist and the critic, so that the critic can praise or condemn works in a medium because they define or fail to define that nature.

8. There are two important senses of "medium" for our discussion: (1) A medium is a type of communication channel that conveys information from A to B. (2) A medium is a type of material that is worked into a finished artifact (the medium can be words, dance movements, musical sounds, and so on). When we speak of media in the arts, we loosely combine these two ideas, depending on the medium in question. The arguments of this chapter apply to either sense of the term "art medium" and to the term "art form" as well.

9. R. G. Collingwood, *The Principles of Art* (Oxford: Oxford University Press, 1958), p. 275.

CHAPTER 7

The Relation of Art to Craft

◀ This T'ang era ceramic bowl has straight sides and engraved phoenixes inside. It is made of light gray stoneware with a thin, middle-green glaze; it was made in the first half of the tenth century. It is sophisticated, formally beautiful, and an example of extremely subtle craft, for example, in the production of the glaze. Does that make it an artwork? What is the relation of art to craft?

Skill without imagination is craftsmanship and gives us
many useful objects, such as wickerwork picnic baskets.
Imagination without skill gives us modern art.

— a character in the Tom Stoppard play *Artist Descending a Staircase*

One of the most subtle and important distinctions that needs to be made in an investigation of art is the distinction between technical skill and artistry. As R. G. Collingwood observes, modern society tends to equate art with craft. This is a serious misunderstanding.

To investigate the relation of art to craft, we need to spell out an adequate definition of craft. In *The Principles of Art*, Collingwood lists six conditions that characterize paradigm cases of craft (see p. 167). In his view, craft is a type of *process* for producing results. Collingwood's aim is not to define "the crafts," but rather to define a way in which many kinds of artifacts are produced.

The six features that Collingwood associates with craft deal mainly with the distinction between means and ends. In his view, a craft has a particular means for achieving its end, the end is specified before the activity begins, the end can be achieved through a process of planning and technical execution, and the craft is applied to raw material to alter its form. The craft of tailoring well illustrates these points. A tailor has the knowledge and skill to make a suit that fits a given individual (the predetermined goal), knows how to alter and assemble the fabric to achieve the right result, and so forth. The first of Collingwood's claims is that his analysis is a good analysis of craft in general.

His six conditions are not separately necessary or sufficient for something to be craft, but, Collingwood holds, a process that has *most* of them is craft. His defense of this position is simply that most clear cases of craft (for example, tailoring) have these features. Collingwood then argues that works of art can and occasionally do lack most of these features. Hence, there is a distinction between art and craft.

Collingwood is arguing against the common view that *an artifact is art only if it is a work of craft*, that is, that craft or technique is *necessary* for art; Collingwood calls this the technical theory of art. Proponents of the technical theory do not hold that every display of craft is art; rather, they hold that craft of a certain sort — for example, craft in the arts of representation — is both necessary and sufficient for art. Collingwood's argument thus opposes the view that art just is craft of certain sorts.

In analyzing craft, Collingwood attempts to define a process that is learnable, a process that, although not purely mechanical, is much more mechanical than the processes that go into creating a work of art. The processes that go into the making of art are frequently *creative* in a way that craft is not. In historical terms, Collingwood articulates a shift in the way art has been viewed over the last two centuries. Formerly, it was held that art involves a high degree of certain technical abilities — an idea that goes back to Greek philosophy — whereas now creative inspiration is considered essential to art.

The essence of Collingwood's notion of craft is this: An artifact is a work of craft if and only if the following points are true of it.

a. It is a result produced by a learnable technique or method for producing prespecified results from a range of outcomes governed by the technique. (This captures his first three points.)

b. It takes some skill to apply the method or learn the techniques. (Collingwood presupposes this.)

c. The craftsperson alters raw material into finished product. (This captures his fourth and fifth points. Collingwood's sixth point — that there is a hierarchy of crafts — is peripheral to his main insights about craft.)

d. Retrospectively, we can always evaluate the work with respect to a preestablished paradigm, that is, a clearly conceived model or example of what the finished product should be. We can always judge that the finished product is well or poorly done with respect to the paradigm that the work is intended to approximate. (This is an additional important point not included in Collingwood's six characteristics.)

Collingwood points out that many artworks do not consist of raw material that the artist has transformed. Nor in creating art can the result be specified ahead of time; if it could, the process would not much resemble a creative process, which typically produces original results. Collingwood has to admit that artists usually do have a vague plan when they start to work, but this is not the sort of planning that involves a known method for getting a known result. Could one, for example, have a method for producing a poem on the death of someone? There is nothing wrong with having a method for producing a prespecified result, but that is craft. Insofar as artists have such a method, that aspect of what they do is craft, and as craft it can be well or poorly done.

Collingwood does not deny that works of art generally involve a lot of craft, but they also involve something more. Craft is a learnable and teachable technique, whereas making art is not a technical skill. To be sure, many skills are taught in art schools, but these are skills necessary for making the kinds of artifacts common in the arts, such as how to carve in marble, how to write counterpoint, or how to play a piano. They are not the skills for creating art itself.

Looking back at (d), we can see that one obvious attraction of equating art and craft is that it gives us a measure of quality in the otherwise subjective area of art. We may praise or criticize an artwork because it has or lacks craft and technical accomplishment. Undoubtedly, this is how people frequently evaluate the arts. But if art is not craft, this simple answer to the problem of how to evaluate art is incorrect. Art cannot be evaluated in the same way as craft. In craft there is a preestablished and well-understood goal. Art is different. To evaluate art requires art *criticism* and *interpretation*, matters in which disagreement can and does exist. All of this is absent from the evaluation of true craft.

A further reason to question the equation of art and craft is that it cannot explain new and experimental art. Many works of art explore new forms and new subject matter. Those that do necessarily go beyond the notion of being a well-made X (where "X" is some familiar kind of art object, for example, a portrait or overture). Hence, treating art as a sort of craft makes it difficult to explain the historical development of art. Perhaps in the Middle Ages art and craft were not to be distinguished, but in recent centuries artists have continually and self-consciously done and made things that are new and original. Any view that fuses art with craft and technique cannot account for this development without stretching the notion of craft so far as to make it rather meaningless.

Does the distinction between art and craft have anything to do with appreciating art? Yes, for it seems to imply that those who look only for craft in art are responding not to the art but to the craft. Such a typical approach to art turns out to be misguided if the distinction is right. Moreover, if the distinction is correct, it would not be valid to criticize a work just because it did not involve a high degree of craft or technique. Here we must be careful, however; it all depends on what the artist is trying to do. Most works of art are also works of craft; they are attempts to produce a well-defined type of artifact. If a musician (here considered a potential artist) is trying to perform a piece of music by Bach, for example, then he or she must have the technique to play the music correctly. There is more to an artistic performance than this, but no less is required.

Another welcome consequence of this distinction between art and craft is that it removes a traditional barrier to counting the crafts as art. Whether an artifact ought to be treated as an artwork, on this view, does not depend on whether it is a "high" art craft, such as oil painting or string quartet composition, as opposed to a traditional craft, such as ceramics or furniture making. Rather, it depends on whether the artifact goes beyond the craftlike elements of its medium. This is a requirement as much for the crafts of painting or poetry as it is for the traditional crafts. Some crafts, such as tailoring, might have additional limitations that prevent them from meeting the positive requirements that would make them art, for example, that the craft must be a medium for expression of feeling (see Chapter 11) or a medium that enables development of significant form (see Chapter 10). But that is a separate question. The mere fact that an artifact is a work of traditional craft does not mean it cannot be considered a work of art, once we accept Collingwood's conception of craft as defined by a type of process rather than by a subject matter or type of material.

Let's conclude with a puzzle for those who accept the distinction between art and craft. Can something be produced by craft that is appreciated as if it were not craft? Consider, for example, the possibility of copying. It is not just that someone may copy or replicate another artist's work (as in forgeries, which are clearly paradigm cases of craft), for in such a case the craft of copying is distinct from the original artwork. A more difficult case is the artists who copy from themselves, using motifs that they have developed in previous work. Let us suppose that at first a certain style is imaginative and original but then is incorporated into later work. This style may be unknown to the casual spectator, who takes the later work to be entirely novel. Thus, much of what goes into an artwork might actually amount to routine craft for the artist. Andy Warhol's lithographs of the 1960s, for example, were at first shocking and novel in the way they combined photography and abstract expressionist paint gestures. But Warhol continued to make the same type of image into the 1980s. Is the result craft or art? This is an interesting problem for Collingwood's argument, because many artists develop their work by borrowing from their own past work.

READINGS FOR CHAPTER 7

R. G. Collingwood, from *The Principles of Art*

from *The Principles of Art*

R. G. Collingwood

Reprinted by permission of Oxford University Press. This reading is from the 1938 edition.

Art and Craft

§ 1. THE MEANING OF CRAFT

The first sense of the word "art" to be distinguished from art proper is the obsolete sense in which it means what in this book I shall call craft. This is what *ars* means in ancient Latin, and what τέχνη* means in Greek: the power to produce a preconceived result by means of consciously controlled and directed action. In order to take the first step towards a sound aesthetic, it is necessary to disentangle the notion of craft from that of art proper. In order to do this, again, we must first enumerate the chief characteristics of craft.

1. Craft always involves a distinction between means and end, each clearly conceived as something distinct from the other but related to it. The term "means" is loosely applied to things that are used in order to reach the end, such as tools, machines, or fuel. Strictly, it applies not to the things but to the actions concerned with them: manipulating the tools, tending the machines, or burning the fuel. These actions (as implied by the literal sense of the word means) are passed through or traversed in order to reach the end, and are left behind when the end is reached. This may serve to distinguish the idea of means from two other ideas with which it is sometimes confused: that of part, and that of material. The relation of part to whole is like that of means to

end, in that the part is indispensable to the whole, is what it is because of its relation to the whole, and may exist by itself before the whole comes into existence; but when the whole exists the part exists too, whereas, when the end exists, the means have ceased to exist. As for the idea of material, we shall return to that in (4) below.

2. It involves a distinction between planning and execution. The result to be obtained is preconceived or thought out before being arrived at. The craftsman knows what he wants to make before he makes it. This foreknowledge is absolutely indispensable to craft: if something, for example stainless steel, is made without such foreknowledge, the making of it is not a case of craft but an accident. Moreover, this foreknowledge is not vague but precise. If a person sets out to make a table, but conceives the table only vaguely, as somewhere between two by four feet and three by six, and between two and three feet high, and so forth, he is no craftsman.

3. Means and end are related in one way in the process of planning; in the opposite way in the process of execution. In planning the end is prior to the means. The end is thought out first, and afterwards the means are thought out. In execution the means come first, and the end is reached through them.

4. There is a distinction between raw material and finished product or artifact. A craft is always exercised upon something, and aims at the transformation of this into something different. That

[techne]

upon which it works begins as raw material and ends as finished product. The raw material is found ready made before the special work of the craft begins.

5. There is a distinction between form and matter. The matter is what is identical in the raw material and the finished product; the form is what is different, what the exercise of the craft changes. To describe the raw material as raw is not to imply that it is formless, but only that it has not yet the form which it is to acquire through "transformation" into finished product.

6. There is a hierarchical relation between various crafts, one supplying what another needs, one using what another provides. There are three kinds of hierarchy: of materials, of means, and of parts. (*a*) The raw material of one craft is the finished product of another. Thus the silviculturist propagates trees and looks after them as they grow, in order to provide raw material for the felling-men who transform them into logs; these are raw material for the saw-mill which transforms them into planks; and these, after a further process of selection and seasoning, become raw material for a joiner. (*b*) In the hierarchy of means, one craft supplies another with tools. Thus the timber-merchant supplies pit-props to the miner; the miner supplies coal to the blacksmith; the blacksmith supplies horseshoes to the farmer; and so on. (*c*) In the hierarchy of parts, a complex operation like the manufacture of a motor-car is parcelled out among a number of trades: one firm makes the engine, another the gears, another the chassis, another the tyres, another the electrical equipment, and so on; the final assembling is not strictly the manufacture of the car but only the bringing together of these parts. In one or more of these ways every craft has a hierarchical character; either as hierarchically related to other crafts, or as itself consisting of various heterogeneous operations hierarchically related among themselves.

Without claiming that these features together exhaust the notion of craft, or that each of them separately is peculiar to it, we may claim with tolerable confidence that where most of them are absent from a certain activity that activity is not a craft, and, if it is called by that name, is so called either by mistake or in a vague and inaccurate way.

§2. THE TECHNICAL THEORY OF ART

It was the Greek philosophers who worked out the idea of craft, and it is in their writings that the above distinctions have been expounded once for all. The philosophy of craft, in fact, was one of the greatest and most solid achievements of the Greek mind, or at any rate of that school, from Socrates to Aristotle, whose work happens to have been most completely preserved.

Great discoveries seem to their makers even greater than they are. A person who has solved one problem is inevitably led to apply that solution to others. Once the Socratic school has laid down the main lines of a theory of craft, they were bound to look for instances of craft in all sorts of likely and unlikely places. To show how they met this temptation, here yielding to it and there resisting it, or first yielding to it and then laboriously correcting their error, would need a long essay. Two brilliant cases of successful resistance may, however, be mentioned: Plato's demonstration (*Republic*, 330 D–336 A) that justice is not a craft, with the pendant (336 E–354 A) that injustice is not one either; and Aristotle's rejection (*Metaphysics*, Λ) of the view stated in Plato's *Timaeus*, that the relation between God and the world is a case of the relation between craftsman and artifact.

When they came to deal with aesthetic problems, however, both Plato and Aristotle yielded to the temptation. They took it for granted that poetry, the only art which they discussed in detail, was a kind of craft, and spoke of this craft as . . . poet-craft. What kind of craft was this?

There are some crafts, like cobbling, carpentering, or weaving, whose end is to produce a certain type of artifact; others, like agriculture or stock-breeding or horse-breaking, whose end is to produce or improve certain non-human types of organism; others again, like medicine or education or warfare, whose end is to bring certain human beings into certain states of body or mind.

But we need not ask which of these is the genus of which poet-craft is a species, because they are not mutually exclusive. The cobbler or carpenter or weaver is not simply trying to produce shoes or carts or cloth. He produces these because there is a demand for them; that is, they are not ends to him, but means to the end of satisfying a specific demand. What he is really aiming at is the production of a certain state of mind in his customers, the state of having these demands satisfied. The same analysis applies to the second group. Thus in the end these three kinds of craft reduce to one. They are all ways of bringing human beings into certain desired conditions.

The same description is true of poet-craft. The poet is a kind of skilled producer; he produces for consumers; and the effect of his skill is to bring about in them certain states of mind, which are conceived in advance as desirable states. The poet, like any other kind of craftsman, must know what effect he is aiming at, and must learn by experience and precept, which is only the imparted experience of others, how to produce it. This is poet-craft, as conceived by Plato and Aristotle and, following them, such writers as Horace in his *Ars Poetica*. There will be analogous crafts of painting, sculpture, and so forth; music, at least for Plato, is not a separate art but is a constituent part of poetry.

I have gone back to the ancients, because their thought, in this matter as in so many others, has left permanent traces on our own, both for good and for ill. There are suggestions in some of them, especially in Plato, of a quite different view; but this is the one which they have made familiar, and upon which both the theory and the practice of the arts has for the most part rested down to the present time. Present-day fashions of thought have in some ways even tended to reinforce it. We are apt nowadays to think about most problems, including those of art, in terms either of economics or of psychology; and both ways of thinking tend to subsume the philosophy of art under the philosophy of craft. To the economist, art presents the appearance of a specialized group of industries; the artist is a producer, his audience consumers who pay him for benefits ultimately definable in terms of the states of mind which his productivity enables them to enjoy. To the psychologist, the audience consists of persons reacting in certain ways to stimuli provided by the artist; and the artist's business is to know what reactions are desired or desirable, and to provide the stimuli which will elicit them.

The technical theory of art is thus by no means a matter of merely antiquarian interest. It is actually the way in which most people nowadays think of art; and especially economists and psychologists, the people to whom we look (sometimes in vain) for special guidance in the problems of modern life.

But this theory is simply a vulgar error, as anybody can see who looks at it with a critical eye. It does not matter what kind of craft in particular is identified with art. It does not matter what the benefits are which the artist is regarded as conferring on his audience, or what the reactions are which he is supposed to elicit. Irrespectively of such details, our question is whether art is any kind of craft at all. It is easily answered by keeping in mind the half-dozen characteristics of craft enumerated in the preceding section, and asking whether they fit the case of art. And there must be no chopping of toes or squeezing of heels; the fit must be immediate and convincing. It is better to have no theory of art at all, than to have one which irks us from the first.

§3. BREAK-DOWN OF THE THEORY

1. The first characteristic of craft is the distinction between means and end. Is this present in works of art? According to the technical theory, yes. A poem is means to the production of a certain state of mind in the audience, as a horseshoe is means to the production of a certain state of mind in the man whose horse is shod. And the poem in its turn will be an end to which other things are means. In the case of the horseshoe, this stage of the analysis is easy: we can enumerate lighting the forge, cutting a piece of iron off a bar, heating it, and so on. What is there analogous to these processes in the case of a poem? The

poet may get paper and pen, fill the pen, sit down and square his elbows; but these actions are preparatory not to composition (which may go on in the poet's head) but to writing. Suppose the poem is a short one, and composed without the use of any writing materials; what are the means by which the poet composes it? I can think of no answer, unless comic answers are wanted, such as "using a rhyming dictionary," "pounding his foot on the floor or wagging his head or hand to mark the metre," or "getting drunk." If one looks at the matter seriously, one sees that the only factors in the situation are the poet, the poetic labour of his mind, and the poem. And if any supporter of the technical theory says "Right: then the poetic labour is the means, the poem the end," we shall ask him to find a blacksmith who can make a horseshoe by sheer labour, without forge, anvil, hammer, or tongs. It is because nothing corresponding to these exists in the case of the poem that the poem is not an end to which there are means.

Conversely, is a poem means to the production of a certain state of mind in an audience? Suppose a poet had read his verses to an audience, hoping that they would produce a certain result; and suppose the result were different; would that in itself prove the poem a bad one? It is a difficult question; some would say yes, others no. But if poetry were obviously a craft, the answer would be a prompt and unhesitating yes. The advocate of the technical theory must do a good deal of toe-chopping before he can get his facts to fit his theory at this point.

So far, the prospects of the technical theory are not too bright. Let us proceed.

2. The distinction between planning and executing certainly exists in some works of art, namely those which are also works of craft or artifacts; for there is, of course, an overlap between these two things, as may be seen by the example of a building or a jar, which is made to order for the satisfaction of a specific demand, to serve a useful purpose, but may none the less be a work of art. But suppose a poet were making up verses as he walked; suddenly finding a line in his head, and then another, and then dissatisfied with them and altering them until he had got them to his liking: what is the plan which he is executing? He may have had a vague idea that if he went for a walk he would be able to compose poetry; but what were, so to speak, the measurements and specifications of the poem he planned to compose? He may, no doubt, have been hoping to compose a sonnet on a particular subject specified by the editor of a review; but the point is that he may not, and that he is none the less a poet for composing without having any definite plan in his head. Or suppose a sculptor were not making a Madonna and child, three feet high, in Hoptonwood stone, guaranteed to placate the chancellor of the diocese and obtain a faculty for placing it in the vacant niche over a certain church door; but were simply playing about with clay, and found the clay under his fingers turning into a little dancing man: is this not a work of art because it was done without being planned in advance?

All this is very familiar. There would be no need to insist upon it, but that the technical theory of art relies on our forgetting it. While we are thinking of it, let us note the importance of not over-emphasizing it. Art as such does not imply the distinction between planning and execution. But (a) this is a merely negative characteristic, not a positive one. We must not erect the absence of plan into a positive force and call it inspiration, or the unconscious, or the like. (b) It is a permissible characteristic of art, not a compulsory one. If unplanned works of art are possible, it does not follow that no planned work is a work of art. That is the logical fallacy[1] that underlies one, or some, of the various things called romanticism. It may very well be true that the only works of art

---

[1]It is an example of what I have elsewhere called the fallacy of precarious margins. Because art and craft overlap, the essence of art is sought not in the positive characteristics of all art, but in the characteristics of those works of art which are not works of craft. Thus the only things which are allowed to be works of art are those marginal examples which lie outside the overlap of art and craft. This is a precarious margin because further study may at any moment reveal the characteristics of craft in some of these examples. See *Essay on Philosophical Method*.

which can be made altogether without a plan are trifling ones, and that the greatest and most serious ones always contain an element of planning and therefore an element of craft. But that would not justify the technical theory of art.

3. If neither means and end nor planning and execution can be distinguished in art proper, there obviously can be no reversal of order as between means and end, in planning and execution respectively.

4. We next come to the distinction between raw material and finished product. Does this exist in art proper? If so, a poem is made out of certain raw material. What is the raw material out of which Ben Jonson made *Queene and Huntresse, chaste, and faire*? Words, perhaps. Well, what words? A smith makes a horseshoe not out of all the iron there is, but out of a certain piece of iron, cut off a certain bar that he keeps in the corner of the smithy. If Ben Jonson did anything at all like that, he said: "I want to make a nice little hymn to open Act v, Scene vi of *Cynthia's Revels*. Here is the English language, or as much of it as I know; I will use *thy* five times, *to* four times, *and, bright, excellently*, and *goddesse* three times each, and so on." He did nothing like this. The words which occur in the poem were never before his mind as a whole in an order different from that of the poem, out of which he shuffled them till the poem, as we have it, appeared. I do not deny that by sorting out the words, or the vowel sounds, or the consonant sounds, in a poem like this, we can make interesting and (I believe) important discoveries about the way in which Ben Jonson's mind worked when he made the poem; and I am willing to allow that the technical theory of art is doing good service if it leads people to explore these matters; but if it can only express what it is trying to do by calling these words or sounds the materials out of which the poem is made, it is talking nonsense.

But perhaps there is a raw material of another kind: a feeling or emotion, for example, which is present to the poet's mind at the commencement of his labour, and which that labour converts into the poem. "Aus meinem grossen Schmerzen mach' ich die kleinen Lieder,"* said Heine; and he was doubtless right; the poet's labour can be justly described as converting emotions into poems. But this conversion is a very different kind of thing from the conversion of iron into horseshoes. If the two kinds of conversion were the same, a blacksmith could make horseshoes out of his desire to pay the rent. The something more, over and above that desire, which he must have in order to make horseshoes out of it, is the iron which is their raw material. In the poet's case that something more does not exist.

5. In every work of art there is something which, in some sense of the word, may be called form. There is, to be rather more precise, something in the nature of rhythm, pattern, organization, design, or structure. But it does not follow that there is a distinction between form and matter. Where that distinction does exist, namely, in artifacts, the matter was there in the shape of raw material before the form was imposed upon it, and the form was there in the shape of a preconceived plan before being imposed upon the matter; and as the two coexist in the finished product we can see how the matter might have accepted a different form, or the form have been imposed upon a different matter. None of these statements applies to a work of art. Something was no doubt there before a poem came into being; there was, for example, a confused excitement in the poet's mind; but, as we have seen, this was not the raw material of the poem. There was also, no doubt, the impulse to write; but this impulse was not the form of the unwritten poem. And when the poem is written, there is nothing in it of which we can say, "this is a matter which might have taken on a different form," or "this is a form which might have been realized in a different matter."

When people have spoken of matter and form in connexion with art, or of that strange hybrid distinction, form and content, they have in fact been doing one of two things, or both confusedly

---

*[Out of my great pain I make small songs.]

at once. Either they have been assimilating a work of art to an artifact, and the artist's work to the craftsman's; or else they have been using these terms in a vaguely metaphorical way as means of referring to distinctions which really do exist in art, but are of a different kind. There is always in art a distinction between what is expressed and that which expresses it; there is a distinction between the initial impulse to write or paint or compose and the finished poem or picture or music; there is a distinction between an emotional element in the artist's experience and what may be called an intellectual element. All these deserve investigation; but none of them is a case of the distinction between form and matter.

6. Finally, there is in art nothing which resembles the hierarchy of crafts, each dictating ends to the one below it, and providing either means or raw materials or parts to the one above. When a poet writes verses for a musician to set, these verses are not means to the musician's end, for they are incorporated in the song which is the musician's finished product, and it is characteristic of means, as we saw, to be left behind. But neither are they raw materials. The musician does not transform them into music; he sets them to music; and if the music which he writes for them had a raw material (which it has not), that raw material could not consist of verses. What happens is rather that the poet and musician collaborate to produce a work of art which owes something to each of them; and this is true even if in the poet's case there was no intention of collaborating.

Aristotle extracted from the notion of a hierarchy of crafts the notion of a supreme craft, upon which all hierarchical series converged, so that the various "goods" which all crafts produce played their part, in one way or another, in preparing for the work of this supreme craft, whose product could, therefore, be called the "supreme good."[2] At first sight, one might fancy an echo of this in Wagner's theory of opera as the supreme art, supreme because it combines the beauties of

music and poetry and drama, the arts of time and the arts of space, into a single whole. But, quite apart from the question whether Wagner's opinion of opera as the greatest of the arts is justified, this opinion does not really rest on the idea of a hierarchy of arts. Words, gestures, music, scenery are not means to opera, nor yet raw materials of it, but parts of it; the hierarchies of means and materials may therefore be ruled out, and only that of parts remains. But even this does not apply. Wagner thought himself a supremely great artist because he wrote not only his music but his words, designed his scenery, and acted as his own producer. This is the exact opposite of a system like that by which motorcars are made, which owes its hierarchical character to the fact that the various parts are all made by different firms, each specializing in work of one kind.

§ 4. TECHNIQUE

As soon as we take the notion of craft seriously, it is perfectly obvious that art proper cannot be any kind of craft. Most people who write about art to-day seem to think that it is some kind of craft; and this is the main error against which a modern aesthetic theory must fight. Even those who do not openly embrace the error itself, embrace doctrines implying it. One such doctrine is that of artistic technique.

The doctrine may be stated as follows. The artist must have a certain specialized form of skill, which is called technique. He acquires his skill just as a craftsman does, partly through personal experience and partly through sharing in the experience of others who thus become his teachers. The technical skill which he thus acquires does not by itself make him an artist; for a technician is made, but an artist is born. Great artistic powers may produce fine works of art even though technique is defective; and even the most finished technique will not produce the finest sort of work in their absence; but all the same, no work of art whatever can be produced without some degree of technical skill, and, other things being equal, the better the technique the better will be the

---

[2]*Nicomachean Ethics*, beginning: 1094 a 1–b 10.

work of art. The greatest artistic powers, for their due and proper display, demand a technique as good in its kind as they are in their own.

All this, properly understood, is very true; and, as a criticism of the sentimental notion that works of art can be produced by any one, however little trouble he has taken to learn his job, provided his heart is in the right place, very salutary. And since a writer on art is for the most part addressing himself not to artists, but to amateurs of art, he does well to insist on what every artist knows, but most amateurs do not: the vast amount of intelligent and purposeful labour, the painful and conscientious self-discipline, that has gone to the making of a man who can write a line as Pope writes it, or knock a single chip off a single stone like Michelangelo. It is no less true, and no less important, that the skill here displayed (allowing the word skill to pass for the moment unchallenged), though a necessary condition of the best art, is not by itself sufficient to produce it. A high degree of such skill is shown in Ben Jonson's poem; and a critic might, not unfruitfully, display this skill by analysing the intricate and ingenious patterns of rhythm and rhyme, alliteration, assonance, and dissonance, which the poem contains. But what makes Ben Jonson a poet, and a great one, is not his skill to construct such patterns but his imaginative vision of the goddess and her attendants, for whose expression it was worth his while to use that skill, and for whose enjoyment it is worth our while to study the patterns he has constructed. Miss Edith Sitwell, whose distinction both as poet and critic needs no commendation, and whose analyses of sound-pattern in poetry are as brilliant as her own verse, has analysed in this way the patterns constructed by Mr. T. S. Eliot, and has written warmly of the skill they exemplify; but when she wishes conclusively to compare his greatness with the littleness of certain other poets who are sometimes ridiculously fancied his equals, she ceases to praise his technique, and writes, "here we have a man who has talked with fiery angels, and with angels of a clear light and holy peace, and who

has 'walked amongst the lowest of the dead.'"[3] It is this experience, she would have us understand, that is the heart of his poetry; it is the "enlargement of our experience" by his own (a favourite phrase of hers, and one never used without illumination to her readers) that tells us he is a true poet; and however necessary it may be that a poet should have technical skill, he is a poet only in so far as this skill is not identified with art, but with something used in the service of art.

This is not the old Greco-Roman theory of poet-craft, but a modified and restricted version of it. When we examine it, however, we shall find that although it has moved away from the old poet-craft theory in order to avoid its errors, it has not moved far enough.

When the poet is described as possessing technical skill, this means that he possesses something of the same nature as what goes by that name in the case of a technician proper or craftsman. It implies that the thing so called in the case of a poet stands to the production of his poem as the skill of a joiner stands to the production of a table. If it does not mean this, the words are being used in some obscure sense; either an esoteric sense which people who use them are deliberately concealing from their readers, or (more probably) a sense which remains obscure even to themselves. We will assume that the people who use this language take it seriously, and wish to abide by its implications.

The craftsman's skill is his knowledge of the means necessary to realize a given end, and his mastery of these means. A joiner making a table shows his skill by knowing what materials and what tools are needed to make it, and being able to use these in such a way as to produce the table exactly as specified.

The theory of poetic technique implies that in the first place a poet has certain experiences which demand expression; then he conceives the possibility of a poem in which they might be expressed; then this poem, as an unachieved end,

[3]*Aspects of Modern Poetry*, ch. v and p. 251.

demands for its realization the exercise of certain powers or forms of skill, and these constitute the poet's technique. There is an element of truth in this. It is true that the making of a poem begins in the poet's having an experience which demands expression in the form of a poem. But the description of the unwritten poem as an end to which his technique is means is false; it implies that before he has written his poem he knows, and could state, the specification of it in the kind of way in which a joiner knows the specification of a table he is about to make. This is always true of a craftsman; it is therefore true of an artist in those cases where the work of art is also a work of craft. But it is wholly untrue of the artist in those cases where the work of art is not a work of craft; the poet extemporizing his verses, the sculptor playing with his clay, and so forth. In these cases (which after all are cases of art, even though possibly of art at a relatively humble level) the artist has no idea what the experience is which demands expression until he has expressed it. What he wants to say is not present to him as an end towards which means have to be devised; it becomes clear to him only as the poem takes shape in his mind, or the clay in his fingers.

Some relic of this condition survives even in the most elaborate, most reflective, most highly planned works of art. That is a problem to which we must return in another chapter: the problem of reconciling the unreflective spontaneity of art in its simplest forms with the massive intellectual burden that is carried by great works of art such as the *Agamemnon* or the *Divina Commedia*. For the present, we are dealing with a simpler problem. We are confronted with what professes to be a theory of art in general. To prove it false we need only show that there are admitted examples of art to which it does not apply.

In describing the power by which an artist constructs patterns in words or notes or brush-marks by the name of technique, therefore, this theory is misdescribing it by assimilating it to the skill by which a craftsman constructs appropriate means to a preconceived end. The patterns are no doubt real; the power by which the artist con-

structs them is no doubt a thing worthy of our attention; but we are only frustrating our study of it in advance if we approach it in the determination to treat it as if it were the conscious working-out of means to the achievement of a conscious purpose, or in other words technique.

§ 5. ART AS A PSYCHOLOGICAL STIMULUS

The modern conception of artistic technique, as stated or implied in the writings of critics, may be unsuccessful; but it is a serious attempt to overcome the weaknesses of the old poet-craft theory, by admitting that a work of art as such is not an artifact, because its creation involves elements which cannot be subsumed under the conception of craft; while yet maintaining that there is a grain of truth in that theory, because among the elements involved in the creation of a work of art there is one which can be thus subsumed, namely, the artist's technique. We have seen that this will not do; but at least the people who put it forward have been working at the subject.

The same cannot be said about another attempt to rehabilitate the technical theory of art, namely, that of a very large school of modern psychologists, and of critics who adopt their way of speaking. Here the entire work of art is conceived as an artifact, designed (when a sufficient degree of skill is present to justify the word) as means to the realization of an end beyond it, namely, a state of mind in the artist's audience. In order to affect his audience in a certain way, the artist addresses them in a certain manner, by placing before them a certain work of art. In so far as he is a competent artist, one condition at least is fulfilled: the work of art does affect them as he intends it should. There is a second condition which may be fulfilled: the state of mind thus aroused in them may be in one way or another a valuable state of mind; one that enriches their lives, and thus gives him a claim not only on their admiration but also on their gratitude.

The first thing to notice about this stimulus-and-reaction theory of art is that it is not new. It is the theory of the tenth book of Plato's *Republic*, of Aristotle's *Poetics*, and of Horace's *Ars Poetica*. The psychologists who make use of it have, knowingly or unknowingly, taken over the poet-craft doctrine bodily, with no suspicion of the devastating criticism it has received at the hands of aestheticians in the last few centuries.

This is not because their views have been based on a study of Plato and Aristotle, to the neglect of more modern authors. It is because, like good inductive scientists, they have kept their eye on the facts, but (a disaster against which inductive methods afford no protection) the wrong facts. Their theory of art is based on a study of art falsely so called.

There are numerous cases in which somebody claiming the title of artist deliberately sets himself to arouse certain states of mind in his audience. The funny man who lays himself out to get a laugh has at his command a number of well-tried methods for getting it; the purveyor of sob-stuff is in a similar case; the political or religious orator has a definite end before him and adopts definite means for achieving it, and so on. We might even attempt a rough classification of these ends.[4] First, the "artist's" purpose may be to arouse a certain kind of emotion. The emotion may be of almost any kind; a more important distinction emerges according as it is aroused simply for its own sake, as an enjoyable experience, or for the sake of its value in the affairs of practical life. The funny man and the sob-stuff monger fall on one side in this division, the political and religious orator on the other. Secondly, the purpose may be to stimulate certain intellectual activities. These again may be of very various kinds, but they may be stimulated with either of two motives: either because the objects upon which they are directed are thought of as worth understanding, or because the activities themselves are thought of as

worth pursuing, even though they lead to nothing in the way of knowledge that is of importance. Thirdly, the purpose may be to stimulate a certain kind of action; here again with two kinds of motive: either because the action is conceived as expedient, or because it is conceived as right.

Here are six kinds of art falsely so called; called by that name because they are kinds of craft in which the practitioner can by the use of his skill evoke a desired psychological reaction in his audience, and hence they come under the obsolete, but not yet dead and buried, conception of poet-craft, painter-craft, and so forth; falsely so called, because the distinction of means and end, upon which every one of them rests, does not belong to art proper.

Let us give the six their right names. Where an emotion is aroused for its own sake, as an enjoyable experience, the craft of arousing it is amusement; where for the sake of its practical value, magic. Where intellectual faculties are stimulated for the mere sake of their exercise, the work designed to stimulate them is a puzzle; where for the sake of knowing this or that thing, it is instruction. Where a certain practical activity is stimulated as expedient, that which stimulates it is advertisement or (in the current modern sense, not the old sense) propaganda; where it is stimulated as right, exhortation.

These six between them, singly or in combination, pretty well exhaust the function of whatever in the modern world wrongfully usurps the name of art. None of them has anything to do with art proper. This is not because (as Oscar Wilde said, with his curious talent for just missing a truth and then giving himself a prize for hitting it) "all art is quite useless," for it is not; a work of art may very well amuse, instruct, puzzle, exhort, and so forth, without ceasing to be art, and in these ways it may be very useful indeed. It is because, as Oscar Wilde perhaps meant to say, what makes it art is not the same as what makes it useful. Deciding what psychological reaction a so-called work of art produces (for example, asking yourself how a certain poem "makes you feel") has nothing whatever to do with deciding whether it is a real

---

[4]The reason why I call it a rough classification is because you cannot really 'stimulate intellectual activities', or 'stimulate certain kinds of action', in a man. Anybody who says you can, has not thought about the conditions under which alone these things can arise. Foremost among these conditions is this: that they must be absolutely spontaneous. Consequently they cannot be responses to stimulus.

work of art or not. Equally irrelevant is the question what psychological reaction it is meant to produce.

The classification of psychological reactions produced by poems, pictures, music, or the like is thus not a classification of kinds of art. It is a classification of kinds of pseudo-art. But the term "pseudo-art" means something that is not art but is mistaken for art; and something that is not art can be mistaken for it only if there is some ground for the mistake: if the thing mistaken for art is akin to art in such a way that the mistake easily arises. What must this kinship be? We have already seen . . . that there may be a combination of, for example, art with religion, of such a kind that the artistic motive, though genuinely present, is subordinated to the religious. To call the result of such a combination art, *tout court*, would be to invite the reply, "it is not art but religion"; that is, the accusation that what is simply religion is being mistaken for art. But such a mistake could never in fact be made. What happens is that a combination of art and religion is elliptically called art, and then characteristics which it possesses not as art but as religion are mistakenly supposed to belong to it as art.

So here. These various kinds of pseudo-art are in reality various kinds of use to which art may be put. In order that any of these purposes may be realized, there must first be art, and then a subordination of art to some utilitarian end. Unless a man can write, he cannot write propaganda. Unless he can draw, he cannot become a comic draughtsman or an advertisement artist. These activities have in every case developed through a process having two phases. First, there is writing or drawing or whatever it may be, pursued as an art for its own sake, going its own way and developing its own proper nature, caring for none of these things. Then this independent and self-sufficient art is broken, as it were, to the plough, forced aside from its own original nature and enslaved to the service of an end not its own. Here lies the peculiar tragedy of the artist's position in the modern world. He is heir to a tradition from which he has learnt what art should be; or at least, what it cannot be. He has heard its call and

devoted himself to its service. And then, when the time comes for him to demand of society that it should support him in return for his devotion to a purpose which, after all, is not his private purpose but one among the purposes of modern civilization, he finds that his living is guaranteed only on condition that he renounces his calling and uses the art which he has acquired in a way which negates its fundamental nature, by turning journalist or advertisement artist or the like; a degradation far more frightful than the prostitution or enslavement of the mere body.

Even in this denatured condition the arts are never mere means to the ends imposed upon them. For means rightly so called are devised in relation to the end aimed at; but here, there must first be literature, drawing, and so forth, before they can be turned to the purposes described. Hence it is a fundamental and fatal error to conceive art itself as a means to any of these ends, even when it is broken to their service. It is an error much encouraged by modern tendencies in psychology, and influentially taught at the present day by persons in a position of academic authority; but after all, it is only a new version, tricked out in the borrowed plumage of modern science, of the ancient fallacy that the arts are kinds of craft.

If it can deceive even its own advocates, that is only because they waver from one horn of a dilemma to the other. Their theory admits of two alternatives. Either the stimulation of certain reactions in its audience is the essence of art, or it is a consequence arising out of its essence in certain circumstances. Take the first alternative. If art is art only so far as it stimulates certain reactions, the artist as such is simply a purveyor of drugs, noxious or wholesome; what we call works of art are nothing but a section of the Pharmacopoeia.[5] If we ask on what principle that branch can be distinguished from others, there can be no answer.

This is not a theory of art. It is not an aesthetic but an anti-aesthetic. If it is presented as a true account of its advocates' experience, we must

[5]Cf. D. G. James, *Scepticism and Poetry* (1937).

accept it as such; but with the implication that its advocates have no aesthetic experience whatever, or at least none so robust as to leave a mark on their minds deep enough to be discernible when they turn their eyes inward and try to recognize its main features.[6] It is, of course, quite possible to look at pictures, listen to music, and read poetry without getting any aesthetic experience from these things; and the exposition of this psychological theory of art may be illustrated by a great deal of talk about particular works of art; but if this is really connected with the theory, it is no more to be called art-criticism or aesthetic theory than the annual strictures in *The Tailor and Cutter* on the ways in which Academy portrait-painters represent coats and trousers. If it attempts to develop itself as a method of art-criticism, it can only (except when it forgets its own principles) rely on anti-aesthetic standards, as when it tries to estimate the objective merits of a given poem by tabulating the "reactions" to it of persons from whom the poet's name has been concealed, irrespective of their skill or experience in the difficult business of criticizing poetry; or by the number of emotions, separately capable of

[6]Dr. I. A. Richards is at present the most distinguished advocate of the theory I am attacking. I should never say of him that he has no aesthetic experience. But in his writings he does not discuss it; he only reveals it from time to time by things he lets slip.

being recorded by the psychologist and severally regarded by him as valuable, which it evokes in a single hearer.

On this horn of the dilemma art disappears altogether. The alternative possibility is that the stimulating of certain reactions should be regarded not as the essence of art but as a consequence arising in certain conditions out of the nature of that essence. In that case, art survives the analysis, but only at the cost of making it irrelevant, as a pharmacologist's account of the effect of a hitherto unanalysed drug would be irrelevant to the question of its chemical composition. Granted that works of art in certain conditions do stimulate certain reactions in their audience, which is a fact; and granted that they do so not because of something other than their nature as works of art, but because of that nature itself, which is an error; it will even so not follow that light is thrown on the nature itself by the study of these reactions.

Psychological science has in fact done nothing towards explaining the nature of art, however much it has done towards explaining the nature of certain elements of human experience with which it may from time to time be associated or confused. The contribution of psychology to pseudo-aesthetic is enormous; to aesthetic proper it is nil. . . .

CHAPTER 8

Art and Entertainment

◀ A still from *Once Upon a Time in the West*, the longest and most grandiose "spaghetti" western. Like the other westerns of Sergio Leone (most of which starred Clint Eastwood), it uses the conventions of an entertainment genre to incorporate grander visual and dramatic themes. Such movies are perhaps comparable to nineteenth-century operas; in their time they, too, were considered somewhat vulgar entertainment; in retrospect we rank them as high art.

We who write and read this book are persons interested
in art. We live in a world where most of what goes by that
name is amusement. Here is our garden. It seems to need
cultivating.

— R. G. Collingwood

A common attitude in our society is to consider art just another form of entertainment. There are two problems with this idea. First, it implies that the initial challenges concerning the value of art (discussed in Chapters 2 through 5) are not likely to be answered in art's favor. Second, there are reasons to believe that it is simply incorrect. One reason is that entertainment is plausibly thought of as a form of craft. Thus, supposing that art is not a craft (see Chapter 7), entertainment and art should be distinguished. I will explain these two points in turn.

Whatever entertainment is, its reason for being lies in the enjoyment or pleasure of the audience. *As entertainment*, this is its primary value; its value to its audience depends on how well it pleases them. Circuses entertain children; drive-in movies entertain teenagers. Perhaps that is all there is to art; perhaps art is a form of entertainment for the elite in a society.[1]

If this is true, then the questions raised in earlier chapters would have no answer favorable to art. There would be no justification for a society to provide special support for art, nor would there be any justification for artists to create works that society largely disapproves of. Nor would there be any question of a deeper meaning to art; a Beethoven symphony would merely be an entertaining musical event for a certain group of people. It would have no more or better value than the latest heavy-metal rock and roll; indeed, it might have less value, because it is less purely entertaining (as judged by the audience's visible excitement) and entertains many fewer people.

These points motivate us to consider Collingwood's argument that entertainment is a craft. Since art is not craft, according to Collingwood, the assumption that art is a form of entertainment is misguided; we can hope to discover more in art than we can find in mere entertainment (see the Collingwood readings in this chapter and in Chapter 7).

What, then, is entertainment? Collingwood argues that it is a form of deliberate and controlled action whose goal is to manipulate the emotions of the audience in a make-believe way. Entertainment is thus a psychological craft. The audience gains pleasure from having the make-believe emotions aroused and then discharged, according to Collingwood. If the entertainer knows how to produce this effect, it follows that he or she is a competent craftsman. If the entertainer doesn't know how to do this, does not know how to achieve this preestablished goal, he or she is a poor craftsman.

Collingwood distinguishes entertainment from more serious psychological crafts that attempt to cause emotion in an audience, such as propaganda, politics, religious ritual, and advertising, by pointing out that the audience does not really take seriously the content of the entertainment. The emotions that entertainment elicits are connected to a make-believe situation, not to the reality of the audience members' actual lives. The intention, understood by both entertainer and audience alike, is that the emotions elicited by the amusement are not to be taken away from the entertainment or directly related to our actual lives. When, as at a rock-and-roll concert, an audience gets very involved and takes the make-believe seriously, the performance is no longer entertainment but is more akin to other sorts of genuinely affecting experiences, such as the political rally or a revivalist church service.

One significant difficulty with Collingwood's notion of entertainment is that it requires us to distinguish *make-believe* in entertainment from imagination in genuine art. We can view make-believe as a kind of escapist fantasy that is irrelevant to the actual conditions of our lives. There are two main features of this sort of escapism. First, the fantasy is created to satisfy desires (an extreme example is pornography). Second, the situation depicted is personally uninvolving to the spectator. Collingwood's idea is that entertainment amuses, and somehow involves emotions, but it does not really affect or change the spectator in any way beyond the entertaining experience.[2] Whether Collingwood's conception of make-believe is correct or not, his idea that entertainment is primarily a psychological craft designed to provide pleasure in a predictable way seems quite plausible. It appears reasonable to conclude that the intention to entertain is very different from the intentions involved in creating art.

The topic of amusement illuminates an important way in which Collingwood, and other thinkers inclined to an expression theory of art, differ from thinkers who view the goal of art as the production of beauty. Expression theories maintain that art has a real emotional impact on people, whereas the other view traditionally treats art as if it were something that we contemplated without any effect other than experiencing pleasure (maybe a special sort of pleasure). Collingwood, like Tolstoy, is aware that much that passes for art makes no real difference to its audience, whose members neither expect nor want any more than enjoyment from the work. Yet to treat art this way is paradoxical when we think both about the high cultural status of the arts and about the sacrifices many famous artists have made for art. One explanation, the one favored by Tolstoy and Collingwood, is that art that makes no difference to people is not really art. Collingwood hypothesizes that such work is often some form of entertainment.

To see how emotions are engaged in amusement, consider horror movies. Their goal is to make the viewer afraid—the scarier the better—yet the viewer is not *really* afraid and in a sense does not really care what happens to the characters, provided that the result is entertaining. Clearly, all sorts of craft are applied to make a film scary. For example, filmmakers have used 3-D to heighten the "realism" and scariness of these films. Still, if spectators were really afraid, they would leave the theater. Sometimes, as in Alfred Hitchcock's film *Psycho*, the fear spills over into one's real feelings and therefore one's life. After seeing *Psycho*, taking a shower doesn't seem the same. One might argue that this film has partially failed *as entertainment* because of this. By genuinely affecting us, it has gone beyond the constraints of entertainment and either seriously manipulated our feelings (what Collingwood calls magic) or has perhaps genuinely managed to *express* horror (what Collingwood calls art).[3]

The example of *Psycho*, as well as other Hitchcock movies, illustrates that the same work can involve both craft and art; it can aim both to be entertainment and also to do more. Although the intentions and goals of art and entertainment are different, it is possible, if not easy, for an artist to combine both in one creation. Mozart certainly tried to make his operas entertaining—and we think today that he succeeded—while also making them deep and ground-breaking musical works. Unfortunately for him, his contemporaries found his music too difficult, and he often met with commercial failure. (Recall the emperor's famous response to Mozart's opera *The Abduction from the Seraglio*: "Far too many notes, Mozart!")

It is obviously important to distinguish true art from entertainment if, like Collingwood, we believe that entertainment is actually a bad influence. But we must make this distinction even if we find entertainment merely innocuous. Clearly, much confusion is caused if an audience expects art to be entertaining. Works of genuine art can be difficult and unpleasant as well as ground-breaking. If the distinction between art and entertainment is correct, then artists, insofar as they are creating art, will not accept the audience's attitudes, values, and desires as constraints on their expression. But insofar as they aim to entertain and please the audience, they *must* take these things into consideration. This is not to say that artists can ignore the attitudes of their audiences but, rather, that the main aim of artists is not to offer emotional titillation.

Mozart provides us with many examples of the difficulty of trying to combine art and entertainment. Consider the end of the slow (adagio) movement of his great String Quintet in G Minor, K. 516. The adagio movement is hauntingly sad and becomes, toward the end, a lament expressive of tragic longing, only to break suddenly into a lighthearted final movement (rondo). Many have questioned the appropriateness of this abrupt contrast between some of the most tragic music ever written and a conventionally happy conclusion. Interpreters and critics have tried to show how these two movements really fit together, but isn't it possible that they simply do not? Isn't it possible that Mozart drew back from the personal expression of the adagio and decided that he had better conclude with a conventionally happy and light ending *to please his audience*? Composers in more recent times have felt able to ignore such considerations in favor of the structure and emotional logic of the music they are composing. Thus Stravinsky's *Rite of Spring* (1913), in its portrayal of primitive rites, made no concessions to the audience's expectations of music and ballet. Not coincidentally, the first performance of the ballet caused a riot.

Does the distinction between art and entertainment carry with it a sharp distinction between "high" art and pop culture? Are artifacts of pop culture, such as movies, television programs, and pop music excluded from the realm of art by this distinction? Pop culture artifacts are certainly dominated by the commercial need to pay for themselves, and they pay for themselves, sometimes very handsomely, by achieving popularity with a mass audience. It is relatively clear, then, that these artifacts are severely constrained by the audience's desire to be amused and to have its beliefs and values reinforced. A primary intention of those who make pop artifacts, therefore, must be to please the audience.

Earlier we saw that such an intention is completely different from the intentions (whatever they may be) involved in making art. This is a more serious difference than the difference between the intention to make a work of craft and a work of art. The latter intentions, although they are different, are perfectly compatible with each other, whereas, as we saw in the case of the Mozart string quintet, the intention to amuse the audience seems *incompatible* with the aims of art. Must we agree, then, with the traditionalist who thinks that pop artifacts cannot possibly be art? I think not, but it depends on one's theory of art.

If one's view of art requires that an artwork originate from purely noncommercial intentions, then pop artifacts cannot be art. But no major theory of art necessitates such a requirement. Moreover, such a requirement would be so stringent that it would exclude much high art throughout history in addition to present-day popular culture.[4] One of the strongest reasons to reject a purist distinction between real art and pop culture artifacts is that some of the most interesting artworks of the twentieth century may well turn out to have been produced within the constraints of commercial art forms. For example, both movies and jazz are art forms that have entered the realm of art, if we judge by the amount of serious criticism they have elicited and by the status that individual works produced in these media have already attained. Jazz composers and performers, such as Duke Ellington, Charlie Parker, and Louis Armstrong, have been the subject of analytical books and articles that treat their music very seriously even though the music was produced for commercial success.

The same can be said of movies, perhaps the most characteristic art form of the twentieth century. Although many movies are mere entertainment, some movies are considered to be among the most important works of art of the twentieth century. And some directors are considered artistic geniuses, for example, D. W. Griffith, Charles Chaplin, Buster Keaton, Alfred Hitchcock, Sergei Eisenstein, and Orson Welles. Not all of these film artists produced work for commercial success, but all worked under comparable constraints. Nonetheless, they and their co-workers were able to produce works of deep interest from almost any point of view.

Even crassly commercial artifacts can be discovered retrospectively to have embodied important artistic values. Take the much maligned genre of moviemaking derogatively called "spaghetti Westerns." These films, the most famous of which are the "Dollar Trilogy" of Sergio Leone (see illustration on p. 178), were treated at the time of their original release as mere commercial exploitations of the violence inherent in an already commercial type of moviemaking. But more recently, critics have argued that these movies were ground-breaking in many respects, especially in their use of symbolic sound, with musical scores dominating the visual images in a way clearly parallel to opera and Greek tragedy. If this is right, the attempt to appeal to a broad and unsophisticated audience did not prevent the makers of these films from exploring dimensions that make their films potentially important as art. As the authors of a recent book on the Italian Western say about the early innovators of the original Western movies,

> They were working in an essentially commercial concern in which success was measured by whether or not films broke even at the box office. Like Leone much later, they judged their success as directors on general appeal to an audience, not to a minority of critics . . . ; they too had their share of adverse criticism. It was not until a much later time that their interests in the field of the Western were thoroughly understood. Who can claim that the same thing will not happen with the Italian Western?[5]

READINGS FOR CHAPTER 8
R. G. Collingwood, from *The Principles of Art*

from *The Principles of Art*

R. G. Collingwood

Reprinted by permission of Oxford University Press.
This reading is from the 1938 edition.

Art As Amusement

§ 1. AMUSEMENT ART

If an artifact is designed to stimulate a certain emotion, and if this emotion is intended not for discharge into the occupations of ordinary life, but for enjoyment as something of value in itself, the function of the artifact is to amuse or entertain. Magic is useful, in the sense that the emotions it excites have a practical function in the affairs of every day; amusement is not useful but only enjoyable, because there is a watertight bulkhead between its world and the world of common affairs. The emotions generated by amusement run their course within this watertight compartment.

Every emotion, dynamically considered, has two phases in its existence: charge or excitation, and discharge. The discharge of an emotion is some act done at the prompting of that emotion, by doing which we work the emotion off and relieve ourselves of the tension which, until thus discharged, it imposes upon us. The emotions generated by an amusement must be discharged, like any others; but they are discharged within the amusement itself. This is in fact the peculiarity of amusement. An amusement is a device for the discharge of emotions in such a way that they shall not interfere with the concerns of practical life. But since practical life is only definable as that part of life which is not amusement, this statement, if meant for a definition, would be circular. We must therefore say: to establish a distinction between amusement and practical life[1] is to divide experience into two parts, so related that the emotions generated in the one are not allowed to discharge themselves in the other. In the one, emotions are treated as ends in themselves; in the other, as forces whose operation achieves certain ends beyond them. The first part is now called amusement, the second part practical life.

In order that emotion may be discharged without affecting practical life, a make-believe situation must be created in which to discharge it. This situation will of course be one which "represents" the real situation in which the emotion would discharge itself practically. The difference between the two, which has been indicated by calling them respectively real and make-believe, is simply this: the so-called make-believe situation is one in which it is understood that the emotion discharged shall be "earthed," that is, shall not involve the consequences which it would involve under the conditions of practical life. Thus, if one man expresses hatred for another by shaking his fist at him, threatening him, and so forth, he will ordinarily be regarded as a dangerous character, dangerous in particular to the man he has threatened, who will therefore take steps of one kind or another to protect himself: perhaps by appeasing the first, perhaps by attacking him and overpowering him, perhaps by obtaining police protection. If it is understood that nothing of this sort is

[1]Aestheticians who discuss the relation between two mutually exclusive things called "Art" and "Life" are really discussing this distinction.

to be done, that life is to go on exactly as if nothing had happened, then the situation in which the anger was expressed is called a make-believe situation.

Situations of this kind resemble those created by magic in being representative, that is, in evoking emotions like those evoked by the situations they are said to represent. They differ in being "unreal" or "make-believe"; that is, in that the emotions they evoke are intended to be earthed instead of overflowing into the situations represented. This element of make-believe is what is known as (theatrical) "illusion," an element peculiar to amusement art, and never found either in magic or in art proper. If in a magical ritual one says of a painting "this is a bison," or of a wax figure "this is my enemy," there is no illusion. One knows perfectly well the difference between the two things. The make-believe of amusement art differs radically, again, from the so-called make-believe of childish games, which is not amusement but a very serious kind of work, which we call make-believe by way of assimilating it to something that occurs in our adult experience. Calling it by that misdescriptive name, we patronizingly license the child to go on with it; so that the child can work at the really urgent problems of its own life unhampered by the interference which would certainly be forthcoming if adults knew what it was doing.

Comparisons have often been made, sometimes amounting to identification, between art and play. They have never thrown much light on the nature of art, because those who have made them have not troubled to think what they meant by play. If playing means amusing oneself, as it often does, there is no important resemblance between play and art proper; and none between play and representative art in its magical form; but there is more than a mere resemblance between play and amusement art. The two things are the same. If playing means taking part in ritual games, art proper bears little resemblance to that, and amusement art even less; but such games, as we have already seen, not only resemble

magic, they are magic. But there is another thing we call play: that mysterious activity which occupies the waking and working lives of children. It is not amusement, though we adults may amuse ourselves by imitating it, and even on privileged occasions taking part in it. It is not magic, though in some ways rather like it. Perhaps it is a good deal like art proper. Giambattista Vico, who knew a lot both about poetry and about children, said that children were "sublime poets," and he may have been right. But no one knows what children are doing when they play; it is far easier to find out what poets are doing when they write, difficult though that is; and even if art proper and children's play are the same thing, no light is thrown for most of us on art proper by saying so.[2]

There is a hedonistic theory of art: open, like all forms of hedonism, to the objection that even if the function of art is to give "delight" (as many good artists have said), still this delight is not pleasure in general but pleasure of a particular kind. When this objection has been met, the theory is a fair enough account of amusement art. The artist as purveyor of amusement makes it his business to please his audience by arousing certain emotions in them and providing them with a make-believe situation in which these emotions can be harmlessly discharged.

The experience of being amused is sought not for the sake of anything to which it stands as means, but for its own sake. Hence, while magic is utilitarian, amusement is not utilitarian but hedonistic. The work of art, so called, which provides the amusement, is, on the contrary, strictly utilitarian. Unlike a work of art proper, it has no value in itself; it is simply means to an end. It is as skilfully constructed as a work of engineering, as skilfully compounded as a bottle of medicine, to produce a determinate and preconceived

[2]Dr. Margaret Lowenfeld (*Play in Childhood*, 1935) has devised a method for exploring the unknown world of children's play, and has made strange discoveries about the relation of this play to the child's health. My own interpretation of her discoveries may be expressed by saying that they suggest an identity between "play" in children and art proper. . . .

effect, the evocation of a certain kind of emotion in a certain kind of audience; and to discharge this emotion within the limits of a make-believe situation. When the arts are described in terms implying that they are essentially forms of skill, the reference, as the terms are ordinarily used nowadays, is to this utilitarian character of amusement art. When the spectator's reception of them is described in psychological terms as a reaction to stimulus, the reference is the same. Theoretically, in both cases, the reference might be to the magical type of representation; but in the modern world that is generally ignored. For the student of modern aesthetic, it is a good rule, whenever he hears or reads statements about art which seem odd or perverse or untrue, to ask whether their oddity (or apparent oddity) may not be due to a confusion between art proper and amusement; a confusion either in the mind of their authors, or in his own. . . .

§ 3. EXAMPLES OF AMUSEMENT ART

The emotions which admit of being thus played upon for purposes of amusement are infinitely various; we shall take a few examples only. Sexual desire is highly adaptable to these purposes; easily titillated, and easily put off with make-believe objects. Hence the kind of amusement art which at its crudest and most brutal is called pornography is very common and very popular. Not only the representation of nudity which reappeared in European painting and sculpture at the Renaissance, when art as magic was replaced by art as amusement, but the novel, or story based on a sexual motive, which dates from the same period, is essentially an appeal to the sexual emotions of the audience, not in order to stimulate these emotions for actual commerce between the sexes, but in order to provide them with make-believe objects and thus divert them from their practical goal in the interests of amusement. The extent to which this make-believe sexuality has affected modern life can hardly be believed until the fact has been tested by appeal to the circulating libraries, with their flood of love-stories; the

cinema, where it is said to be a principle accepted by almost every manager that no film can succeed without a love-interest; and above all the magazine and newspaper, where cover-designs, news-items, fiction, and advertisement are steeped in materials of the same kind: erotic stories, pictures of pretty girls variously dressed and undressed, or (for the female reader) of attractive young men: pornography homoeopathically administered in doses too small to shock the desire for respectability, but quite large enough to produce the intended effect. Small wonder that Monsieur Bergson has called ours an "aphrodisiac civilization." But the epithet is not quite just. It is not that we worship Aphrodite. If we did, we should fear these make-believes as a too probable cause of her wrath. An aphrodisiac is taken with a view to action: photographs of bathing girls are taken as a substitute for it. The truth may rather be that these things reveal a society in which sexual passion has so far decayed as to have become no longer a god, as for the Greeks, or a devil, as for the early Christians, but a toy: a society where the instinctive desire to propagate has been weakened by a sense that life, as we have made it, is not worth living, and where our deepest wish is to have no posterity.

The case of sexual fantasy is peculiar, because it seems in this way to have got out of hand, and thus to betray something amiss with our civilization as a whole. There are plenty of other cases where this complication is absent. For example, much pleasure may be derived from the emotion of fear; and to-day this is provided by a galaxy of talent devoted to writing stories of terrible adventure. The "thriller," to give the thing its current name, is not new. We find it on the Elizabethan stage, in the charnel-house sculpture of seventeenth-century tombs (the Last Judgements of medieval art were aimed not at making flesh creep but at reforming sinful lives), in the novels of Mrs. Radcliffe and "Monk" Lewis, in the engravings of Doré, and, raised to the level of art proper, in the first movement of Beethoven's Fifth Symphony and the Finale of Mozart's *Don Giovanni*.

Among ourselves, the spread of literacy has begotten upon the old penny dreadful a monstrous progeny of hair-raising fiction concerned with arch-criminals, gunmen, and sinister foreigners. Why the ghost story, once so valuable for this purpose, has lost its efficacy, although heathenish rites, with much explicit bloodshed and even more hinted obscenity, are still in lively demand, is a curious problem for the historian of ideas.

The detective story, the most popular form of amusement offered by the profession of letters to the modern public, is based partly on appeal to the reader's fear, but partly on a rich medley of other emotions. In Poe the element of fear was exceedingly strong, and either because of his influence, or because of something ingrained in the civilization of the United States, the present-day American detective story shows a stronger inclination towards that type than those of any other nation. American corpses are the bloodiest and most horribly mangled; American police the most savage in their treatment of suspects.[3] Another emotion of great importance in such stories is the delight in power. In what may be called the Raffles period, this was gratified by inviting the reader to identify himself with a gallant and successful criminal; nowadays the identification is with the detective. A third is the intellectual excitement of solving a puzzle; a fourth, the desire for adventure, that is to say, the desire to take part in events as unlike as possible to the dreary business of actual everyday life. Members of the scholastic and clerical professions from time to time express a belief that young people who read these stories, and see films resembling them, are thereby incited to a career of crime. This is bad psychology. There is no evidence that stories of crime are the favourite readings of habitual criminals. In point of fact, those who constantly read them are on the whole thoroughly law-abiding folk; and this is only natural, for the constant earthing

of certain emotions, by arousing and discharging them in make-believe situations, makes it less likely that they will discharge themselves in practical life.

No one has yet taken up the detective story and raised it to the level of genuine art. Miss Sayers, indeed, has given reasons why this cannot be done. Perhaps one reason is the mixture of motives which this *genre* has traditionally accepted as inevitable. A mixture of motives is, on the whole, favourable to good amusement, but it can never produce art proper.

Malice, the desire that others, especially those better than ourselves, should suffer, is a perpetual source of pleasure to man; but it takes different shapes. In Shakespeare and his contemporaries, bullying in its most violent form is so common that we can only suppose the average playgoer to have conceived it as the salt of life. There are extreme cases like *Titus Andronicus* and *The Duchess of Malfi*, where torture and insult form the chief subject-matter; cases like *Volpone* or *The Merchant of Venice*, where the same motive is veiled by a decent pretence that the suffering is deserved; and cases like *The Taming of the Shrew*, where it is rationalized as a necessary step to domestic happiness. The same motive crops out so repeatedly in passages like the baiting of Malvolio or the beating of Pistol, passages wholly unconnected with the plot of the play, so far as these plays have a plot, that it has obviously been dragged in to meet a constant popular demand. The theme is raised to the level of art proper here and there in Webster, in a few of Shakespeare's tragedies, and above all in Cervantes.

In a society which has lost the habit of overt bullying, the literature of violence is replaced by the literature of cattishness. Our own circulating libraries are full of what is grandiloquently called satire on the social life of our time; books whose popularity rests on the fact that they give the reader an excuse for ridiculing the folly of youth and the futility of age, despising the frivolity of the educated and the grossness of the uneducated, gloating over the unhappiness of an ill-assorted

[3]Cf. Superintendent Kirk: ". . . I couldn't rightly call them a mellering influence to a man in my line. I read an American story once, and the way the police carried on — well, it didn't seem right to me." Dorothy L. Sayers, *Busman's Honeymoon*, p. 161.

couple, or triumphing over the feebleness of a henpecked merchant prince. To the same class of pseudo-art (they are certainly not history) belong the biographies of cattishness, whose aim is to release the reader from the irksome reverence he has been brought up to feel for persons who were important in their day.

If the Elizabethan was by temperament a bully, the Victorian was by temperament a snob. Literature dealing with high life at once excites and in fancy gratifies the social ambition of readers who feel themselves excluded from it; and a great part of the Victorian novelist's work was devoted to making the middle classes feel as if they were sharing in the life of the upper. Nowadays, when "society" has lost its glamour, a similar place is taken by novels and films dealing with millionaires, criminals, film-stars, and other envied persons. There is even a literature catering for the snobbery of culture: books and films about Beethoven, Shelley, or, combining two forms of snobbery in one, a lady in high station who wins fame as a painter.

There are cases in which we find, not a mixture of amusement and magic, but a wavering between the two. A considerable literature exists devoted to sentimental topography: books about the charm of Sussex, the magic of Oxford, picturesque Tyrol, or the glamour of old Spain. Are these intended merely to recall the emotions of returned travellers and to make others feel as if they had travelled, or are they meant as an invocation—I had almost said, to call fools into a circle? Partly the one and partly the other; if the choice had been decisively made, literature of this kind would be better than it is. Similar cases are the sentimental literature of the sea, addressed to landsmen, and of the country, addressed to town-dwellers; folk-songs as sung not in pubs and cottages but in drawing-rooms; pictures of horses and dogs, deer and pheasants, hung in billiard-rooms partly as charms to excite the sportsman, partly as substitutes for sport. There is no reason why works of this kind should not be raised to the level of art, though cases in which that has hap-

pened are exceedingly rare. If it is to happen, there is one indispensable condition: the ambiguity of motive must first be cleared up. . . .

§ 5. AMUSEMENT IN THE MODERN WORLD

We have already seen that amusement implies a bifurcation of experience into a "real" part and a "make-believe" part, and that the make-believe part is called amusement in so far as the emotions aroused in it are also discharged in it and are not allowed to overflow into the affairs of "real" life.

This bifurcation is no doubt as ancient as man himself; but in a healthy society it is so slight as to be negligible. Danger sets in when by discharging their emotions upon make-believe situations people come to think of emotion as something that can be excited and enjoyed for its own sake, without any necessity to pay for it in practical consequences. Amusement is not the same thing as enjoyment; it is enjoyment which is had without paying for it. Or rather, without paying for it in cash. It is put down in the bill and has to be paid for later on. For example, I get a certain amount of fun out of writing this book. But I pay for it as I get it, in wretched drudgery when the book goes badly, in seeing the long summer days vanish one by one past my window unused, in knowing that there will be proofs to correct and index to make, and at the end black looks from the people whose toes I am treading on. If I knock off and lie in the garden for a day and read Dorothy Sayers, I get fun out of that too; but there is nothing to pay. There is only a bill run up, which is handed in next day when I get back to my book with that Monday-morning feeling. Of course, there may be no Monday-morning feeling: I may get back to the book feeling fresh and energetic, with my staleness gone. In that case my day off turned out to be not amusement but recreation. The difference between them consists in the debit or credit effect they produce on the emotional energy available for practical life.

Amusement becomes a danger to practical life when the debt it imposes on these stores of energy is too great to be paid off in the ordinary course of living. When this reaches a point of crisis, practical life, or "real" life, becomes emotionally bankrupt; a state of things which we describe by speaking of its intolerable dullness or calling it a drudgery. A moral disease has set in, whose symptoms are a constant craving for amusement and an inability to take any interest in the affairs of ordinary life, the necessary work of livelihood and social routine. A person in whom the disease has become chronic is a person with a more or less settled conviction that amusement is the only thing that makes life worth living. A society in which the disease is endemic is one in which most people feel some such conviction most of the time.

A moral (or in modern jargon a psychological) disease may or may not be fatal to the person suffering from it; he may be driven to suicide, as the only release from *taedium vitae*, or he may try to escape it by going in for crime or revolution or some other exciting business, or he may take to drink or drugs, or simply allow himself to be engulfed in a slough of dullness, a dumbly accepted life in which nothing interesting ever happens, tolerable only when he does not think how intolerable it is. But moral diseases have this peculiarity, that they may be fatal to a society in which they are endemic without being fatal to any of its members. A society consists in the common way of life which its members practise; if they become so bored with this way of life that they begin to practise a different one, the old society is dead even if no one noticed its death.

This is perhaps not the only disease from which societies may die, but it is certainly one of them. It is certainly, for example, the disease from which Greco-Roman society died. Societies may die a violent death, like the Inca and Aztec societies which the Spaniards destroyed with gunpowder in the sixteenth century; and it is sometimes thought by people who have been reading historical thrillers that the Roman Empire died in the same way, at the hands of barbarian invaders. That theory is amusing but untrue.

It died of disease, not of violence, and the disease was a long-growing and deep-seated conviction that its own way of life was not worth preserving.

The same disease is notoriously endemic among ourselves. Among its symptoms are the unprecedented growth of the amusement trade, to meet what has become an insatiable craving; an almost universal agreement that the kinds of work on which the existence of a civilization like ours most obviously depends (notably the work of industrial operatives and the clerical staff in business of every kind, and even that of the agriculture labourers and other food-winners who are the prime agents in the maintenance of every civilization hitherto existing) is an intolerable drudgery; the discovery that what makes this intolerable is not the pinch of poverty or bad housing or disease but the nature of the work itself in the conditions our civilization has created; the demand arising out of this discovery, and universally accepted as reasonable, for an increased provision of leisure, which means opportunity for amusement, and of amusements to fill it; the use of alcohol, tobacco, and many other drugs, not for ritual purposes, but to deaden the nerves and distract the mind from the tedious and irritating concerns of ordinary life; the almost universal confession that boredom, or lack of interest in life, is felt as a constant or constantly recurring state of mind; the feverish attempts to dispel this boredom either by more amusement or by dangerous or criminal occupations; and finally (to cut the catalogue short) the discovery . . . that customary remedies have lost their bite and that the dose must be increased.

These symptoms are enough to alarm any one who thinks about the future of the world in which he is living; enough to alarm even those whose thought for the future goes no farther than their own lifetime. They suggest that our civilization has been caught in a vortex, somehow connected with its attitude towards amusement, and that some disaster is impending which, unless we prefer to shut our eyes to it and perish, if we are to perish, in the dark, it concerns us to understand. . . .

SUGGESTED ADDITIONAL READINGS

Lawrence W. Levine, *Highbrow/Lowbrow: The Emergence of Cultural Hierarchy in America* (Cambridge, Mass.: Harvard University Press, 1988).

NOTES

1. See the discussions of relativism in Chapter 1 and Bentham's challenge in Chapter 3.
2. Music presents an interesting difficulty for this account of entertainment. On the one hand, music is one of the most common forms of entertainment, very frequently used to amuse and distract people. On the other hand, such uses of music do not always involve, as far as one can see, make-believe.
3. On the difference between arousing feelings and expressing feelings, see Chapter 11 and the excerpt from R. G. Collingwood's *Principles of Art*, in the Readings for that chapter.
4. See Lawrence Levine, *Highbrow/Lowbrow: The Emergence of Cultural Hierarchy in America* (Cambridge, Mass.: Harvard University Press, 1988).
5. Laurance Staig and Tony Williams, *Italian Western: The Opera of Violence* (London: Lorrimer Publishing, 1975), p. 46.

Part III Major Theories of Art

WHAT ARE THEORIES OF ART? We have seen that the study of philosophy of art is motivated by a number of deep puzzles about art. It has been suggested that a theory of art is needed to explain the social worth of art (Tolstoy's challenge), to explain the unique aesthetic value of art, to settle the question of the relation of art to morality, and finally to tell us whether there is a rationale for avant-garde art. A theory of art will not necessarily draw conclusions that favor all aspects of art, nor will it show that Tolstoy, Bentham, and Plato are wrong. But theoretical discussion seems the only way rationally to carry forward the discussion of these issues. And the most important benefit of such discussion is that it enlivens our appreciation of the artworks themselves.

The word "theory" seems to have no established meaning in art discourse. What are sometimes called art theories or theories of individual arts (for example, "literary theory," "film theory") are often no more than expressions of current fashions in the art world. By contrast, we have been using "theory of art" to refer to an account of the nature of art that answers the question "What is art?" A theory of art in this sense attempts to explain what makes an artifact a work of art and what makes an activity the act of creating art.

How are we to determine whether a theory does this successfully? We have seen in Part I that we ought to ask how a theory of art defines art and accounts for its aesthetic value. An adequate definition of art must first be sufficiently general to cover all the arts over a time span of centuries. But is such a definition too permissive? Does it make everything art? These questions must be addressed for any theory of art.

Although present-day theories of art often ignore the value questions, traditional theories such as those to be considered in Part III (mimetic, formalist, expression) take such questions as central. In Part I we saw the relevance of such questions. Any theory of art that does not include a believable account of the importance and value of art is incomplete. If no such account can be developed from a given theory of art, then we can argue that the theory fails to explicate our concept of art. Remember, we want a theory of art to solve the puzzles inherent in our thinking about art.

Because theories of art do not aim to capture all the various uses of the term "art," we can evaluate them only by three factors: their internal coherence, their ability to explain works of art, and their ability to answer the value questions. Even if each of the following theories is wrong in claiming that it has the *essential* feature of art, each does emphasize an absolutely central feature of artworks. A combination of these accounts may be as close as we get to an adequate account of art. But before we can combine them, we need to understand much more clearly the main concepts of each account: representation, form, and expression. Each concept embodies a dimension of art worth understanding for its own sake.

CHAPTER 9

Mimetic Theory

◀ A production of *Oedipus the King* by Sophocles (c. 497–406 B.C.). Sophocles'
tragedies are widely regarded as the most perfect Greek dramas and the high
point of the early tragedy as an art form. In *Oedipus* (429 B.C.), Sophocles
delineates the tragic destiny that befalls Oedipus because of his moral blindness
and pride. The tragedy as an art form was first codified by Aristotle, who found
great value in its effects. Plato, on the other hand, expressed criticism of the
effects of theater on audiences. In Plato's time these effects were certainly
dramatic; it was said, for example, that "boys fainted and women miscarried"
at the appearance of the furies in Aeschylus' *Eumenides*.

Something decisive happened in the history of art around Manet which set painting and the other arts upon a new course. Perhaps the change can be described as a kind of scepticism, or at least unsureness, as to the nature of representation in art.

— T. J. Clark, *The Painting of Modern Life*

Humankind lingers unregenerately in Plato's cave, still reveling, its age-old habit, in mere images of the truth.

— Susan Sontag, *On Photography*

Undoubtedly, the oldest, most influential, and most deeply entrenched way of understanding art has to do with the fact that artworks — pieces of sculpture, tragic plays, poems, movies, short stories, novels, operas — are representations. They represent something outside themselves, something in the world. Plato and Aristotle were the first to codify this idea as a sort of theory or general account of the arts, which we may call the *mimetic theory*. Plato used this idea to attack the arts, Aristotle to defend them. Both philosophers used the central metaphor of "imitation" in their accounts of the arts, a metaphor that Plato goes to some length to try to spell out in Book X of *The Republic*. The central thought is that artworks imitate or (for Plato) participate in the appearance of the external things that are represented in them. Imitation explains not only the nature of artworks but also *how* artworks manage to represent objects and events.

This emphasis on art as representation is not just the invention of intellectuals. When ordinary people encounter an artwork, they often seem to think first about what it represents and about whether it provides a good likeness of what it represents. For many people, the whole point of experiencing an artwork — a movie, play, novel, painting — is to experience the illusory representation of its subject matter. At its most naive, such an approach to art means thinking of representations of beautiful objects as beautiful representations, and conversely, representations of ugly or offensive objects as ugly or offensive representations.

There is more than one way to think about what it means for a work to represent something external to it: it may be thought that the work *stands for* the external item or that it *re-presents* the external item. If people respond to an artwork *as if* it were the real thing, then it looks as though they take the artwork to *re*-present that thing. But since an artwork literally cannot do this, we encounter the first of many puzzles about how to understand the notion of representation. The mimetic theory in fact raises a host of questions: Must artworks *always* represent something? Are all artworks and all arts representational? What differentiates art representations from ordinary, non-art representations, for example, non-art uses of pictures and language? What is representation, and what makes an artwork, say, a picture, a representation of its subject and not of something else? What is the value of representation in the arts? These questions boil down to three fundamental ones: (*a*) Is representation (or, more narrowly, imitation) adequate to define the essence of art? (*b*) What would be an adequate explanation of representation? (For example, is Plato's concept of imitation adequate?) (*c*) What value would the arts have if the mimetic theory were correct?

Ever since Plato and Aristotle, arguments for and against the arts have typically assumed that art is representational. From the time of the Greeks through the eighteenth century, this was the fundamental way of thinking about the nature and value of the arts. Only with the rise of romanticism, with its emphasis on expression, and modernism, with its emphasis on form and abstraction, did the terms of such discussions change. The influence of the assumption that artworks are primarily representations can be seen in the idea of progress in the arts, especially in the visual arts. The constant "progress" that painting in the West made from the Byzantine middle ages through the Renaissance invention of perspective to later forms of realism, such as Dutch still lifes, is surely often understood as a progress in the competence of visual artists to represent their subjects more and more realistically or accurately. (A similar progress can be seen in parts of this larger history, for example, the development of Greek sculpture from "archaic" to "classical," or movies from silent to sound, black-and-white to color.) It isn't just that different and competing styles developed over time, but, rather, that the capacity of artworks to fulfill their function supposedly improved. This view presupposes that an important goal of visual art is perfect representation and that this is what artists aim at and viewers look for. This supposition accounts for the nineteenth-century notion that painting was dead because photography had been invented. For a brief period, photography appeared to make painting outmoded and superfluous by doing better the job a painting tries to do.

Representation is also important for art criticism. Criticism has always emphasized questions about the representational content of artworks, questions that go back to Aristotle's *Poetics*: Is a story unified? Does it end appropriately? Is it believable? Indeed, the whole issue of realism in artworks, a question as old as mimetic theory, makes sense only within the context of representational art. With the recent demise of modernism, many critics, theorists, and artists seem once again to be focusing their attention on representational content rather than form or expression. The questions raised by Plato and Aristotle concerning the nature and value of art as representation turn out to be of current as well as perennial interest.

> Poesy therefore is an arte of imitation, for so Aristotle termeth it in his word *Mimesis*, that is to say, a representing, counterfetting, or figuring foorth: to speake metaphorically, a speaking picture. . . .
>
> — Sir Philip Sidney, "An Apology for Poetrie" (1581)[1]

PLATO'S MIMETIC THEORY OF ART

Plato's *Republic* is undoubtedly his most famous dialogue. In Book X, Plato's teacher, Socrates, presents an elaborate attack on the arts (see the Readings). Socrates' argument against the arts concludes by proposing that poetry be banned from the ideal republic that Socrates and his friends are designing. Careful reading reveals that the argument is meant to count against all the "imitative arts"; none is a desirable element in an ideal society.[2] It would be somewhat anachronistic, however, to ascribe to Plato the claim that all art is imitative — that all art imitates the appearances of things. For one thing, Greek thinkers, including Plato, no doubt lacked our modern conception of art in general (see Chapter 1). Nonetheless, Socrates does generalize back and forth between poetry and visual arts quite freely; he seems to assume that the arts he is concerned with form a natural grouping and that what they all have in common is imitation of nature.

This is why Socrates' attack on the arts is complex. His attack is founded on a theory about art's nature. He is not critical of the arts just because they do not appeal to him; on the contrary, it is because they are so enjoyable and alluring that they are potentially dangerous and must be subjected to critical scrutiny.[3] It is only because Socrates attributes a certain nature or essence to art that he is led to reject it. As Arthur Danto reminds us, "Plato did not precisely propose that art was mimesis, but that mimetic art was pernicious."[4] We thus have two questions to answer: What is the nature of mimetic art, and why is such art "pernicious"?

To understand Plato's view of mimesis, we need some understanding of his metaphysics. (It is surprising, then, that his criticism of art as mimesis is quite relevant to our thinking about art even when divorced from his metaphysical views, which are largely out of intellectual fashion today.) Plato views an artwork as a sort of illusory object to be contrasted with real objects and events. He illustrates this thesis with the striking analogy of art to a mirror. He implies that just as a mirror creates a reflection of real things, an artwork (for example, a painting or sculpture) creates an imitation of the appearance of things. Later Plato extends this analysis to poetry: "And the tragic poet is an imitator, and therefore, like all other imitators, he is thrice removed from . . . the truth" (p. 217).

> The only perfect act of representation would be a duplicate, a pointless copy.
>
> — Daniel Albright, *Representation and the Imagination*[5]

But can we view poetry and, more generally, literature as mimetic? Doubtless, we can view painting and sculpture as imitating the appearances of things. And tragedies and other plays may seem to be mimetic arts par excellence, for in them people and events can be imitated almost perfectly. But literature does not *look* (or sound or feel) like what it represents. In the *Odyssey*, Odysseus vividly describes the moment when he and his companions put out the eye of the giant Cyclops holding them captive: "So with our brand we bored that great eye-socket while blood ran out around the red-hot bar. Eyelid and lash were seared; the pierced ball hissed broiling, and the roots popped."[6] This is incredibly graphic, but does it *imitate* the appearance of such events? William Gass emphatically denies that it even could: "Neither the name nor its arrangements, the propriety of its prepositions, the sweet taste *of* the cake, for instance, has the faintest resemblance, or any other reasonable relation, to the light coat of chocolate on my tongue."[7]

> A novel is a mirror that strolls along a highway. Now it reflects the blue of the skies, now the mud puddles underfoot.
>
> — Stendhal, *The Red and the Black*

Words, whether spoken or written, do not resemble the appearance of such an event. Yet both Plato and Aristotle speak of poetry as mimetic. What can we make of this?[8] One possibility that might have appealed to the Greeks is to view poetry as if it were spoken by characters (as in the example from the *Odyssey*), thereby making it analogous to dramatic characterization. As a general solution, however, this is unsatisfactory. For one thing, not all literary works have an identified character as speaker. Even if we suppose that poetry is always spoken, by the writer or a reader, the question remains whether the language produced by that speaker — the sounds, words, or sentences — imitate appearances. When Odysseus refers to the "red-hot bar," do his words, which certainly conjure up an image of a red-hot bar, *imitate* the appearance of a red-hot bar? It is difficult to see how they do.[9] If imitation can't explain literary representation, then it can't explain representation in general, for literature is clearly representational.

Even if Plato had to relinquish the idea that verbal arts *imitate* appearances, he would still wish to maintain that what poetry describes or represents is *appearances*, for that point is essential to his objection to all mimetic art, as we will see.

Plato postulates that art is remote from reality and truth. We can understand this in two related ways. On a metaphysical level, Socrates contrasts individual beds with what they all have in common that makes them beds — we might call this "bedhood" or the form of bed. This form, Socrates says, was made not by any person, but by God or the maker of nature. When a carpenter makes a bed, he imitates this ideal form of a bed in the particular bed he constructs. And when a painter makes a painting of the bed the carpenter has constructed, he imitates the appearance of this particular bed on the surface of his painting. From Socrates' assumption that paintings imitate the appearance of things, it follows that the painting is an imitation of an imitation. If we accord full reality only to the form of a bed, as Plato does, then the artwork of a bed is several levels removed from that true reality. For Plato, ultimate reality consists of the pure unchanging forms, best exemplified by mathematical forms such as triangularity, and moral concepts, such as justice. All actual triangles only approximate to perfect triangularity, the form which they participate in and which makes them triangles. In comparison with pure forms, the physical objects that we experience in the perceptual world are less real, according to Plato, because they are constantly changing. What is real, for Plato, are properties, such as triangularity or justice, which cannot change, rather than ordinary entities that are constantly subject to change. Even if we reject Plato's views about forms, we still seem forced to accept that a painting *as a representation* is much less real than the perceptual objects of which it is a painting.

The fact that the (mimetic) arts produce imitations of appearances leads to the second, *epistemological*, objection to them: To what extent can images be considered embodiments or objects of knowledge? For Plato, the unchanging reality of the forms allows us to have true knowledge of them — witness mathematics — whereas our "knowledge" of ordinary, changeable objects is merely correct opinion. Imagine, then, whether imitations of the appearances of physical objects amount to knowledge! Thus, the worry that Socrates puts forth has to do with taking artworks as sources of knowledge. Against the view that Homer and the tragedians have knowledge of "all the arts and all things human, virtue as well as vice, and divine things too" — subjects of fundamental importance — Socrates tries to argue that in fact Homer and the other poets lack knowledge of their subject matter; otherwise, why did they not act to do important things in the world? "Do you suppose that if a person were able to make the original as well as the image, he would seriously devote himself to the image-making branch?" (p. 218). To this Socrates adds that we are not likely to ask Homer for answers to real questions about medicine, military tactics, education, or politics — all subjects of his poems; moreover: "Can you imagine, Glaucon, that if Homer had really been able to educate and improve mankind — if he had possessed knowledge and not been a mere imitator — can you imagine . . . that he would not have had many followers, and been honoured and loved by them?" (p. 219).

This argument is not entirely convincing. But a stronger one is readily available: What knowledge does an imitator *need* to have to produce imitations? Socrates points out that mimetic works "could easily be made without any knowledge of the truth, because they are appearances only and not realities" (p. 218). Imitation per se does not need to be based on any real knowledge. In the example of a horse's bit and reins, Socrates distinguishes the horseman, who knows their right form because he knows how to use them, from the workers in brass

Will it not seem entirely natural that our speech as we proceed . . . should be shaped, even if from nothing more substantial than a system of fixed sounds, into a hollow in which we try to hold our world like water in leaking hands?
— William Gass, "Representation and the War for Reality"[10]

and leather, who have less knowledge; they know only how to make them. The painter, by contrast, is relegated to a third level: all he needs to know is what they look like. This goes back to the point that appearances are far removed from real things and their natures.

Things are even worse than this, for an imitator needs to know only what the audience *believes* the appearances of things are like. "The poet is like a painter who . . . will make a likeness of a cobbler though he understands nothing of cobbling; and his picture is good enough for those who know no more than he does, and judge only by colours and figures" (p. 219). This leads to another aspect of an art of appearances. What enables the audience to understand imitations of appearances? Socrates postulates that art—that is, imitation— appeals to an "inferior" principle or part of the mind, opposed to the rational understanding. Basically he means that appearances are deceiving (he mentions the straight stick that looks bent in water and other visual illusions) and that the way to gain knowledge of things is not through the use of sensation and emotion—the very principles the arts appeal to—but through the use of reason, logic, calculation, and measurement. To gain true knowledge, we need to go beyond appearances, to analyze appearances using reason. Art is constitutionally unable to do this.

> Courbet is said to have been able to paint an object without even knowing what it was. . . .
>
> — Linda Nochlin, *Realism*[11]

Plato worries not only that visual or auditory images do not yield knowledge but also that many of the other representations in the arts, such as the actions of characters in plays, are not subject to the dictates of reason. It is, as Socrates points out, much easier to imitate irrational actions than rational behavior, which tends to be undemonstrative. All in all, Socrates holds that art not only appeals to irrationality, but also positively encourages us to be irrational. It reinforces behavior that reason tells us is inconsistent with our being good citizens and good people: "Poetry feeds and waters the passions instead of drying them up; she lets them rule, although they ought to be controlled, if mankind are ever to increase in happiness and virtue" (p. 223).

Thus, Socrates adds a third dimension to his metaphysical and epistemological concerns. From the metaphysical perspective, artworks are inferior kinds of entities. From the epistemological perspective, they do not convey any real knowledge or truth. And now, from a moral perspective, they turn out to be deceptive guides to right action.

In Plato's society, Homer and the tragedians undoubtedly were considered sources of important knowledge concerning life, death, and the gods; and their plays, performed as elements of religious festivals, were probably respected above the results gained from mere reasoning—they were certainly more widely accessible. For this reason, it is easy to understand why Plato attacked the poets, for he was trying to demonstrate that they were being foolishly venerated and that their influence was entirely inappropriate given the real value of their works.

Here we come to a fundamental disagreement about values. Plato accuses the arts of appealing to our irrational side, of being far removed from truth, and of actually encouraging our irrational beliefs and tendencies. Many modern thinkers seem to be in unthinking agreement with Plato. We now generally accept that the arts do not produce truth, at least the sort of truth that the sciences and scholarship produce. The connection between the arts and the unconscious, or at least nonrational mental processes, is also widely supposed. Yet, whereas for Plato all of this constitutes a decisive objection to the arts, for many modern thinkers these points merely illustrate the distinctive nature and function of the arts. But Plato's concerns are not dismissed easily. He thinks he has discovered a way to get at the truth—through the sort of dialectical reasoning process exemplified in his dialogues—and he notices that the results of his and other philosophers' investigations are often at variance with the implicit recommendations emanating from artworks. This raises many questions: What *is* the best way to gain knowledge of important subjects, such as virtue and vice? Is it through a play, for example, or is it through reasoning? How could a play contain the truth, except by accident? What is a play based on that will make it necessarily reflect the truth? Yet if we agree that morality or ethics is best explored through other means, then are not the arts rather dangerous? For, as Plato is clearly aware, the audience for mimetic arts seems to be taken in by them; spectators revel in the story and often take away a "moral" that may not be valid. Consider, for instance, the reaction of Vietnam veteran Henry Allen to praise for movies about the Vietnam War. He raises objections very similar to Plato's: "I'd try to explain that it was just a movie, it was colored light moving around on a screen. It wasn't that these folks couldn't tell the difference between a war and a movie; they didn't want to. . . . War is too wildly stupid, glorious, hideous, huge and human for us to think that art can tell us what it really is."[12]

It is worth noting that Plato's objections to the arts do not appear to depend essentially on his views about the reality of the pure Forms, nor on his assumption that representation is to be understood as mimesis. Merely accepting that artworks are representations, that they represent appearances, and that representations are in some sense less real than what they represent is enough to state these objections with some urgency. Of course, there is an important case where we will hesitate to count a representation as less real than what it represents, and that is the case of fiction. Is the representation of Anna Karenina in the novel *Anna Karenina* less real than Anna Karenina? We certainly cannot say that it is, since Anna is a fictional character — she isn't real at all! But this leads to another issue that, as we saw earlier (Chapter 4), also causes Plato to be suspicious of art. Artworks are often fictional; artists can just make up their stories; none of it need be true! This is a new objection, but one that would have been very manifest to Plato. In Book III of *The Republic*, Socrates objects to stories about the gods that cannot be correct, and a particular episode in his life would have brought this point home. In his comedy *The Clouds* (423 B.C.) Aristophanes makes fun of Socrates by portraying him as an unscrupulous Sophist running a school to teach people how to win arguments no matter which side they take. In reality, Socrates was no Sophist; indeed, he opposed the Sophists and many of their ideas. By ignoring the actual facts, Aristophanes is able to attack and ridicule Socrates without taking into account truth or reason. *The Clouds* is still great fun, but is it any way to learn about Socrates, about his ideas, or even about the Sophists? Surely not; yet, no doubt, the audience in Socrates' Athens, not knowing any better, took from this play beliefs and attitudes that were based on fiction. (Alan Sommerstein suggests that "the Athenians who sat on the jury in 399," which convicted Socrates of corrupting the young, "would have been superhuman if twenty-five years of this had not prejudiced them."[13]) What value, then, does fiction have? How can teaching falsehoods — for that is how Plato views many fictions — be a positive value to society? That surely is a question that Plato insists on.

The idea that art involves falsehoods and does not represent knowledge was widely accepted among medieval thinkers as well as the ancients. The Italian philosopher Umberto Eco tells us that medieval Scholasticism, the main philosophical movement of the Middle Ages, "unlike modern theories, could not envisage the possibility that poetry might reveal the nature of things with an intensity and breadth lacking in rational thought."[14] For example, Thomas Aquinas (1225–1274) holds that "poetic matters cannot be grasped by the human reason because they are deficient in the truth,"[15] and Conrad of Hirsau (ca. 1070–1150) says that a poet is called a *fictor* "because he either speaks falsehood instead of truth or mingles the true with the false."[16] Of course, to think this does not commit the Medievals to Plato's negative position. Alan of Lille (1128–1202) actually praises painting for the very features that worry Plato: "Oh painting with your new wonders! What can have no real existence comes into being and painting, aping reality and diverting itself with a strange art, turns the shadows of things into things and changes every lie into truth."[17]

MIMESIS AS AN ACCOUNT OF REPRESENTATION

We have seen that mimesis (imitation) does not seem adequate to account for verbal representation. But can imitation even explain pictorial representation? It is very natural to think that it can. Recent philosophical debate about the nature of pictorial representation, however, suggests that representation in the visual (and other) arts is a very difficult phenomenon to explain by any theory, including an imitation theory.[18] We form an interpretation of what pictures represent so automatically that we fail to notice how we do it; it seems almost like looking at the objects represented. Like language, pictures can seem so *transparent* that we fail to notice the interesting questions about how they get their reference to the world and how we learn to understand them.

We ought to differentiate two related questions concerning pictorial representation: (*a*) How (on what basis) do we interpret pictures? (Is is just "natural," or is it an operation similar to reading a language?) (*b*) What makes it true that a picture is *about* a certain subject matter? A skeptic might argue that pictures are not in reality about anything, that there is nothing but our various interpretations of them—hence, the only real question is about how we interpret pictorial representations. I will assume this is wrong; I will assume that we can interpret incorrectly what a picture is about and that often, without further information, we may fail to know what a picture is about or what it refers to. Thus there is a distinction between our immediate interpretation of a picture and what the picture is (truly) about. In briefly considering theories of representation, I will focus on what makes it true that a picture is about a certain subject. The answer to that question ought to tell us a lot about how we do in fact interpret pictures.

What makes Velázquez's renowned portrait of Pope Innocent X (Plate 5) a portrait of that exact individual, Innocent X, and not some other person? What makes Monet's paintings of grainstacks (Plate 6) paintings of grainstacks and not of trees, hills, or goose bumps? What makes Mantegna's *Dead Christ* (Figure 9.1), with its famous extreme foreshortening, a representation of the dead Christ and not of the actual model who posed for Mantegna's painting?[19]

There are two tempting answers that, together, capture what Plato seems to have had in mind by "mimesis" and show what he fears about it. The first answer, or theory of representation, illustrates what he fears about mimesis, for it emphasizes *illusion*. The illusion theory hypothesizes that what makes a picture (or other visual object) a representation of Y is that it causes spectators to believe that Y is before them. This might seem to be an especially plausible account of theatrical (and film) representation. The main problem with this theory is that either it seems false or it seems to require a very peculiar sense of "belief." Even in the theater, we know very well that the play we are seeing is not real; we do not believe that

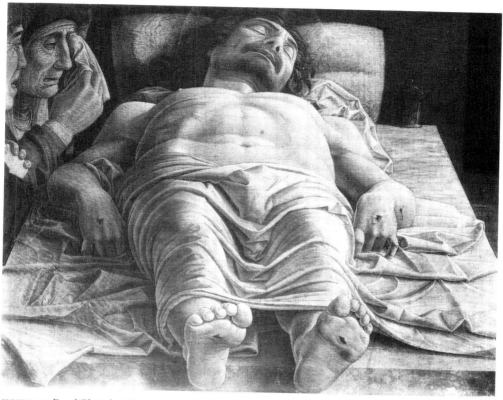

FIGURE 9.1 *Dead Christ* by Mantegna. Mantegna (1431–1506) was famous for his experimental use of daring perspectives. In this painting he uses dramatic foreshortening to substantially heighten the drama of the dead Christ. Since Mantegna certainly did not observe the subject, why does it not represent what he did observe (a dead body, for example) rather than Christ?

Hamlet is literally before us. To produce a true illusion would in fact completely transform, if not destroy, our experience of the play as the experience *of an artwork*. And when it comes to paintings, nothing could be more obvious than that the items represented are not literally before us; we are seeing pictures, not haystacks, on the wall. Even photographs are not convincing illusions. We see what the photo is a photo of, but we do not think the photo *is* what it is a photo of.

The second theory of mimesis, the one that may seem more obvious, is that each of the paintings mentioned above simply *looks like* its subject; each *resembles* what it represents. This account of representation is now called the *resemblance theory*: What makes a picture (or other visual object) a representation of Y is that it resembles Y. Unfortunately, because everything resembles everything else in some aspects and to some degree, this crude definition would make everything represent everything else! We need to spell out the respects or degrees of resemblance required for representation, and this is very hard to do. Unfortunately, however we try to spell out the resemblance required for representation, the theory runs into serious trouble.

One problem is this: Is resemblance a sufficient condition of representation? If X resembles Y, does X represent Y? The answer must be no, for if X resembles Y, then Y resembles X. Thus, if a portrait resembles its subject, then the subject also resembles the portrait. Therefore if resemblance were a sufficient condition, we should be forced to hold that the subject represents the portrait![20] Another counterexample comes from the fact that, except in the cases of portraits, pictures do not represent the models who sat for them, even though they are the persons the pictures most resemble: Mantegna's painting represents Christ, not the model; Caravaggio's painting of Saint John the Baptist (Figure 9.2) represents John the Baptist, not the Roman lad who sat for it, and so on. In each of these cases, resemblance does not guarantee representation.

In fact, most visual representations resemble objects they do *not* represent more than they resemble what they are supposed to represent. For instance, Velázquez's portrait resembles other paintings, especially other portraits, much more than it resembles the appearance of Innocent X. Yet if resemblance explained representation, we should have to say that it also represents these other paintings — but of course it does not. (Another example: An ancient Greek bas-relief sculpture of, say, a man carrying on his shoulders a sheep for sacrifice resembles other rough rock surfaces — in scale, color, texture, and form — much more than it resembles a man and a sheep. Yet the piece represents a man, not those other things that it much more closely resembles.) To be sure, the man *in* the Velázquez portrait resembles or looks like Innocent X more than he looks like, for example, the woman, Mrs. Cézanne, *in* Cézanne's famous portrait of his wife (Figure 9.3). But to say this is already to talk about figures represented *in* paintings, and such talk assumes the very phenomenon to be explained: Why is one darkish blob of color a man and the other a woman?

Rather than positing natural resemblance as the foundation of representation, it looks more plausible to suppose that we have learned to "read" pictures within particular sets of conventions, and when we see a picture we automatically interpret it within those conventions. This position has been vigorously supported by the art historian E. H. Gombrich, who claims, "All art is 'image-making' and all image making is rooted in the creation of substitutes. Even the artist of an 'illusionist' persuasion must make the manmade, the 'conceptual' image of convention his starting point."[21] The conventions Gombrich is thinking of are created by pictorial traditions rather than an object's external form. He goes on to suggest that perhaps "the reason is that contrary to the hopeful belief of many artists the 'innocent eye' which should see the world afresh would not see it at all. It would smart under the painful impact of a chaotic medley of forms and colors. In this sense the conventional vocabulary of basic forms [generated by visual art traditions] is indispensable to the artist. . . ."[22]

Is significant resemblance even a *necessary* condition of representation? We know that it is not because of all of the examples of representation that depend entirely on convention. For instance, a weather front is represented on the weather map by a line with semicircles and wedges, but this obviously does not resemble a change in air

* The "reality-is-formless" theory.

FIGURE 9.2 *St. John the Baptist* (ca. 1602–1603) by Caravaggio. Caravaggio (1573–1610) became famous for portraying sacred subjects in a naturalistic manner. He sets his biblical subjects among the Roman lower classes of his own time. This painting portrays St. John the Baptist as a sensual, street-wise boy. The question naturally arises, what makes it true that the painting is really a representation of St. John the Baptist?

FIGURE 9.3 *Madame Cézanne* (ca. 1877) by Paul Cézanne (1839–1906). The garish, unrealistic colors and the crude forms make this painting of Madame Cézanne almost abstract. The paint pattern that represents her skirt more closely resembles a fence or an awning. It seems that only by knowing conventions of dress and hairstyle can we tell that this painting represents a woman. Nonetheless, it is a particular woman, Madame Cézanne, in a red armchair and a striped skirt.

pressure. Moreover, cartoons and caricatures do not significantly resemble what they represent, and they appear to be interpretable only on the basis of an elaborate set of conventions. Peter Kivy points out that a cartoon of a dog running (think of Daisy, the dog in *Blondie*, running with speed lines behind her) does not "in any obvious way 'look like' a dog in motion. When a dog runs, he does not leave a string of lines visible behind." As Kivy points out, we are so used to such conventions that "we are hardly aware how little like a running dog this drawing really is."[24] R. A. Sharpe notes that "it would be easy to misidentify a caricature [of Churchill] as a representation of a bulldog (which it more nearly resembles in the relevant (?) ways) than Churchill, whom it actually represents."[25]

The most attractive remaining theory of representation posits that representation depends on the artist's intentions.[26] This theory claims that what makes a picture (or other visual object) a representation of Y is that the artist *intended* it to represent Y. Surely this highlights an important element. What so many of our examples appear to have in common is that they depend on the artist's intentions for their subject. If Cézanne looked at his wife while producing a painting whose subject was, according to him, a mythological woman, then his painting would not be a portrait of his wife. If we did not know the title of Caravaggio's *Saint John the Baptist*, we would have no way of knowing or even guessing that the naked teenager reclining with his arm around a ram was Saint John. When we move to paintings that are much less realistic, such as Munch's famous painting *The Scream* (Figure 9.4), intention seems to give us a much better account of representational content than does resemblance. *The Scream* does not significantly resemble a human or a bridge (much less a human screaming). Moreover, we can assume that Munch painted it from his imagination rather than using a bridge and a screaming person as causal models. We can understand why this painting depicts what we suppose it does by hypothesizing that from its appearance and its title, we understand what Munch *intended* it to represent.

Like the other theories we have examined, however, the intention theory also has problems. One objection is that the intention theory does not seem to account for the *experience* of seeing spaces and objects in paintings, sometimes even in very abstract paintings. The intention theory makes pictures more like language; representation in both is a matter of deciphering the artist's meaning. But a visual artwork, unlike a verbal text, seems to encompass a visual experience of the subject matter. A second problem involves the validity of using artists' intentions to determine the interpretation of artworks. A prominent tradition in twentieth-century aesthetics rejects the appeal to the artist's intentions as support for an interpretation.[28] The anti-intentionalist's concerns are twofold: (*a*) How can we know the artist's intentions? (*b*) Can intentions by themselves determine representation? Can artists arbitrarily determine what their works mean or represent? The intention theory implies that they can, that, for example, Caravaggio could have intended his image of Saint John to represent the Virgin Mary or a haystack. Many thinkers regard this as an exaggeration of the power of intention to determine meaning or representation.[29]

No theory that adequately explains what determines representation has yet been proposed. Each theory we have examined has some problems. Yet it seems reasonable to draw two conclusions. One is that imitation is not a good theory, even of pictorial representation.

> It must be admitted that if imitation is the sole purpose of the graphic arts, it is surprising that the works of such arts are ever looked upon as more than curiosities, or ingenious toys, are ever taken seriously by grown-up people.
>
> — Roger Fry, "An Essay in Aesthetics"[27]

FIGURE 9.4 *The Scream* (1893) by Edvard Munch. In this familiar painting, visual resemblance has given way to emotional equivalence. The whole picture is strikingly permeated by the scream. Munch (1863–1944) has found a visual equivalent for the character of fear, the way feeling simultaneously overpowers the inner world and penetrates the outer world.

The second is that several factors determine what a picture represents; most prominent among these factors are both the artist's intentions and also pictorial conventions about how to interpret visual images. Neither intention nor convention by themselves can account for our examples, but together they make a good beginning.

REPRESENTATION AS A DEFINITION OF ART?

Mimesis cannot account for representation. Can representation, however it is explained, account for art? Can we define art and its value by means of the concept of representation? Although representation is a central property of most artworks, it appears that the class of artworks and the class of representations overlap:

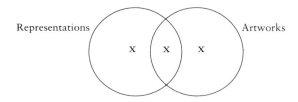

The X's indicate that there are representations that are not artworks and artworks that are not representations. Let's examine these two claims.

There are countless representations that no one considers works of art: reconnaissance photographs, newspapers, history books, maps, newsreels, catalogues and advertisements, highway signs, and so forth. Representational media, such as language and pictures, are for the most part used for non-art purposes. Therefore, we cannot claim that being a representation is a sufficient condition of being art. The only way to evade this conclusion would be to find a special type or mode of representation that could uniquely define art.[30]

There are indeed many important differences between art representations and other sorts of representations. Perhaps the most conspicuous is that artworks are commonly fictions; thus, they are false representations. But, of course, this difference does not uniquely mark artworks. There are hoaxes, falsehoods, and lies that are not artworks. Even the prevalent characteristic of representing nonexistent beings, for example, mythological beings, could not by itself mark art. Anthropologists and other scholars also talk about mythological beings, thereby representing them without producing artworks. Besides, even if representing nonexistent things were a sufficient condition of being an artwork, it would be far from necessary, because many art representations are of real, existing objects and events (for instance, Velázquez's portrait of Innocent X).

Another significant trait of art representations is that often they are intentionally ambiguous. For example, Arthur Miller's play *The Crucible* (1953) can be viewed as representation on two very different levels. On the obvious level, it is about the Salem witch trials in colonial America. On a subtler level, we can take it to be about the witch hunts in Miller's own time, those instigated by Senator Joseph McCarthy in the 1950s, in which many theater and movie artists, as well as academics, were accused of being communists and hounded out of their professions. The multiplication of levels of representation is a widespread phenomenon in the arts. Another vivid example comes from the operas of Giuseppe Verdi (1813–1901). Many were putatively about distant historical events, but Verdi intended them and the Italian audiences took them to be also about the Italian risorgimento, the Italian nationalist movement to overthrow Austrian control of Italy. His opera *Nabucco*, for instance, recounts the biblical story of the Babylonian captivity of the Hebrews. Yet its chorus of the Hebrew slaves, "Oh, my country, so beautiful and so lost," became a patriotic song of Italian nationalism.

The suggestion that artworks are uniquely ambiguous representations is attractive, but to be satisfactory it needs to answer further questions. Can it be applied to all works of art, or is it a characteristic of only some? If it cannot, it would be a strange trait, one that makes something art but is not necessary to art. Moreover, the suggestion needs to be refined. Simple ambiguity, even intentional ambiguity, is not a trait just of artworks. (Consider diplomatic communiqués.) But if what makes something an artwork is multiple representation put to other ends—for example, expressive purposes—then the simple fact that the work is a multiple representation is not what makes it art.

Another intriguing trait of representation in the arts has to do with the self-consciousness of the image, by which I mean that what is important in art representations is *how* the subject is represented, not *that* it is represented. In most non-art representations the reverse holds. Fidelity to the facts is always primary for non-art representations, whereas it is almost never primary in art. The image in art has a life of its own; it is put together differently and is judged differently from ordinary representations. The unity that is so important in art is a unity dependent on the inner relation of the elements of the image to themselves; unity in art does not refer to the relation of the image to what it represents. The art image is judged, not by its fidelity to external elements, but by its overall cohesion and internal meaning.

We can amplify this suggestion by considering the process of constructing a representation in the arts. A painter, for example, is concerned first and foremost about the relation of the colors on the canvas to each other, not to the colors of the objects in the world. It might even be argued that the painter who is primarily concerned with getting the colors of the objects right is producing factual documentation and not art. (This would explain why we might not want to count Audubon's bird pictures as art. It also explains what ultimately defeats the notion that there could be a *perfect* realism in the arts. Works that are created to be art never have as their *central* purpose simply to represent the world accurately.[31]) Philosophers, including Benedetto Croce and Collingwood, who have emphasized that the artwork is a mental process of constructing a representation have touched on this special characteristic of representation in the arts. Collingwood says that "a good painter . . . paints things because until he has painted them he doesn't know what they are like."[32] Yet since we all know in an obvious sort of way what things look like, this implies that in its internal logic the image develops its own meanings, which go beyond a mere accurate report of what things look like. The aesthetican W. Charlton remarks that the painter may "have before his eyes in reality the scene he wishes to represent; but until he has started to think how he is going to colour the canvas, he has no image in his mind of the represented scene."[33] We might simplify this point by saying that all art representations have an "aesthetic" component. This weakens the importance of representation but does not eliminate it, since the subject that is being represented surely plays a role in our understanding of the image and our appreciation of its values.

Even if we can make out a case that artworks do exhibit a special type of representation, we still have a major objection to any attempt to define art in terms of representation or even to make representation a *necessary condition* for art. The objection is that many types of art are not representational, most obviously abstract paintings, abstract sculpture, and instrumental music. Though less common, there are also many examples of abstract and self-referential writings and abstract films and photographs. And we haven't yet mentioned works of architecture, most of which are not usually representations of something else. Because of a commitment to the mimetic theory, thinkers have sometimes been inclined to deny that there are nonrepresentational artworks; they either find some represented subject in everything we call art, or they deny the status of art to supposed artworks that are not representational. The latter sort of maneuver is a familiar response to abstract art, both historically and in our everyday experience. Instead of allowing that paintings and sculpture could be art even when they do not represent any discernible subject, many people respond negatively to abstract paintings and sculptures (see Chapter 10). When people ask in regard to an abstract painting, "What does that painting *mean*?" they often seem to mean, "What does that painting *represent*?"

On the other hand, freedom *from* representation has attracted many thinkers. Romantic theorists in the early 1800s considered the greatest instrumental masterpieces of Haydn, Mozart, and Beethoven to be nonrepresentational. For this very reason, the musicologist Joseph Kerman suggests, these thinkers came to regard music as the highest of all arts: "Music became the paradigmatic art for the Romantics because it was the freest, the least tied down to earthly manifestations such as representation in painting and denotation in literature. When Pater said that all art aspires towards the condition of music, he meant the condition of symphonies, not the condition of hymns or waltzes or cantatas."[34]

Those who insist that every artwork must represent something or otherwise be meaningless are equating meaning or content with representational content. This equation appears to be mistaken. As Arthur Danto has persuasively argued,[35] abstract artworks — indeed, he claims, absolutely *all* artworks — have a *content*, that is, they are *about* something; they have an interpretation. But that does not mean that all works are representational. As we saw in Chapter 2, for example, Ad Reinhardt's black-on-black paintings are about many ideas, most of which are based on his repudiation of representation: timelessness, self-consciousness, purity, and so on. But if there is nothing represented, can there be anything to experience and think about? I think this is the reason why many people are puzzled by abstract arts. Art ought to involve experience and the imagination, yet if a work is not a representation of anything, how can the imagination work? What is there to think about? The answer is that artworks always *present* something, and that something provides the material for experience and thought, *if* the spectator knows how to react to the artwork appropriately. The striking characteristic of many representations is that the spectator who understands the conventions usually can immediately, if superficially, interpret the work: "That represents a Y." Many people are satisfied to stop at this point in their understanding of an artwork; indeed, they may habitually require artworks to be this simple and obvious. However, two problems arise. First, there is another level of interpretation for even the simplest image: "What is the representation of Y *about*?" This prompts interesting interpretative questions. Second, some representations also require much more knowledge to interpret what they represent. For example, Duchamp's *Large Glass* (*The Bride*) (see illustration on p. 392) tells a very complicated story; what it represents (a bride and a groom) can be deciphered only by those who have access to a great deal of independent information, such as the many pages of explanatory material that Duchamp wrote over the course of the eight years that he worked on this piece. So, representation may not always be direct and may require background knowledge, just as some nonrepresentational works require. That nonrepresentational work can present much to think about is demonstrated simply by Duchamp's *Fountain* (see illustration on p. 146). That such art can present much to experience is demonstrated by many avant-garde works, especially abstract or environmental sculpture (see Chapter 5). Both Christo's *Running Fence* and John Cage's *4'33"* are (in)famous works that emphasize experience without grounding that experience in any representation. But, of course, these are just the sorts of works that the mimetic theorist might be inclined to deny are art.

Such a denial would be a bit desperate. If we were to affirm the universality of representation in art, every nonrepresentational work would have to be rejected as art. Even a few examples show the possibility that art can be nonrepresentational. Who would deny the status of art to the greatest examples of instrumental music, for example, the symphonies, sonatas, and string quartets of Mozart, Haydn, and Beethoven? These are certainly among the best-respected artworks in human history. These works are examples of what has been called "absolute" music, that is, music that is to be understood purely in terms of its sounds and sound structures without any appeal to words, stories, or other sorts of represented content.[36] Some people may assume that because most music is vocal music with a verbal text, music in general is representational. But absolute music, which began with instrumental pieces of Bach, Haydn, and Mozart, is intended to be listened to without a verbal text or story associated with it. Since the early 1800s it has been a dogma of classical music that instrumental music should always be approached without representational content in mind, even when, as in the many tone poems of Richard Strauss, the composer intended the sounds to illustrate a story, and even when, as in Vivaldi's *The Four Seasons*, there seem to be musical passages that clearly imitate various sounds (birds in the spring, stamping feet in the snow, and so forth).

It may be too strong to say, as most music theorists have, that it is impossible for nonverbal music to represent.[37] But it is equally wrong to claim that such music must represent. After all, countless musicians, composers, and music critics claim to listen to music without associating any represented scene — indeed they claim this is the only proper way to appreciate music. So it is clearly possible for music to function, and function well, without having representational content.

Perhaps the only general rebuttal to this argument is to claim that music always represents emotions.[38] Aristotle, for instance, asserts in his *Politics* that music imitates emotions and states of character: "Rhythm and melody supply imitations of anger and gentleness, and also of courage and temperance, and of all the qualities contrary to these, and of the other qualities of character, which hardly fall short of actual affections."[39] As an extension of this assertion, it might further be urged that abstract art generally represents emotional (or perhaps spiritual) states. This is too large a claim to be thoroughly investigated here. Part of the difficulty is that the claim that music *represents* emotions must be sharply distinguished from the claim that music *expresses* emotions. The latter claim has quite a distinguished history and will be examined in Chapter 11. It does not follow from the fact that music expresses an emotion that it represents that emotion. Moreover, if music represents emotions it cannot do so, Aristotle to the contrary, by imitating them. As Thomas Twining, the eighteenth-century commentator on Aristotle, noted, "between *sounds themselves*, and *natural affections*" — by which he means emotions — "there can be no resemblance."[40] An emotion does not have a sound, so how can a sound *sound like* an emotion? One might add that this is just as true for character traits—what does courage sound like?

I do not mean to imply that music is disconnected from feelings—far from it—nor that terms that describe feelings, such as "angry" or "gentle," cannot be applied to music. I merely question whether we can adequately understand these facts by hypothesizing that the function of music is to "represent" emotions. I will assume that we cannot. Hence, while some music, both vocal and instrumental, can and does represent a variety of things (events, sounds, objects, stories), not all instrumental music can be understood in this way. And in this latter group I count some of the greatest works by Bach, Mozart, and the rest. The inescapable conclusion is that we cannot explain all art as representational. To that extent, representational theories are inadequate as general theories of art.

A REALISTIC ART MEDIUM?

If it is not the nature of all art to represent, perhaps nonetheless it is the nature of particular art media to represent. If this is so, may we conclude that producing nonrepresentational works in such media is a misuse of those media? And may we also infer that the best or most appropriate use of such media is to produce representations that are the most realistic?

Just such arguments have been made for photographic media. It has been argued that because of the mechanical processes that define it, photography is intrinsically representational. Hence, abstract photographs or photographs that are manipulated in various ways in the developing and printing processes are a misuse of the medium. An influential school of film theorists, headed by Siegfried Kracauer and André Bazin, have gone even further, arguing that movies are not merely representational, but essentially realistic. According to this school of thought, many styles of moviemaking, such as the montage[41] style of Soviet silent films or the heavily edited style of Hollywood movies, violate the distinctive nature of the medium. As the film theorist Noel Carroll notes, even American silent-film comedy violates this nature, "for its central structural gambit—the sight gag . . . —denies that film is a simple recording insofar as its basic donnée is always that reality can be seen in more than one way. In *The Gold Rush*, for example, a boot can be a turkey; a nail, a bone; and a shoelace, spaghetti."[42]

All such approaches to filmmaking are criticized by Kracauer. He asserts that "films may claim aesthetic validity if they build from their basic properties; like photographs, that is, they must record and reveal physical reality."[43] (Ironically, the very same consideration—that photography is a mechanical reproduction of physical reality—has been used many times to argue that it is not an art at all! One letter printed in the *New York Times*, for example, argues that because a photograph is formed mechanically and chemically, it "is not a work of art, properly speaking, because it fails to satisfy this essential requirement: total creative control by its maker."[44]) Aware that many genres of moviemaking do not show the world as it really is, Kracauer argues that only those movies that reproduce the real physical world are true to the medium; they alone "afford insight and enjoyment otherwise unattainable."[45] His idea seems to be that the only aesthetically "valid" films are those that bring out the unique feature of the cinematic medium: its ability to reproduce physical reality. (For related arguments, see Chapter 10.)

André Bazin arrives at a similar position from a different direction. In "The Myth of Total Cinema" (see the Readings), Bazin contends that the nineteenth-century originators of photographic cinema were aiming at a total reproduction of reality: "In their imaginations they saw the cinema as a total and complete representation of reality; they saw in a trice the reconstruction of a perfect illusion of the outside world in sound, color, and relief" (p. 235). He goes on to argue that what these "founding fathers" dreamed is pertinent to what film ought to be: "If the origins of an art reveal something of its nature, then one may legitimately consider the silent and the sound film as stages of a technical development that little by little made reality out of the original 'myth'" (p. 236). Bazin's thought is that if the inherent goal of film is perfect reproduction of our experience of the world, then those techniques that diverge from such reproduction will be inferior and those that highlight realistic reproduction will be superior.[46] Thus, for Bazin, sound films are superior to silent films, because they give us not only the visual image of a scene but also its sounds. And he championed camera techniques that give a more palpable sense of physical reality, for example, the use of a single unedited shot, a style often called spatial realism.

One difficulty with positions like those of Kracauer and Bazin is that although they make claims about the essential nature of a medium, in this case film, they cannot deny that many examples of work in the medium do not conform or even try to conform to this nature. Thus, at best, they are expressing an insight into some underlying feature of the medium: the feature that they feel *ought* to be brought out. They seem reduced to arguing that realism *ought* to be practiced and that films that practice these forms of realistic representation are better, deeper, more profound, and so on. This position is hard to defend, given the other possibilities of film. Noel Carroll argues that recognizable images are an *achievement* of a movie camera used in a certain way, not the essence of photographing: "Distortion and abstraction are possibilities, as well. The point here is that representation is a decision about how to use cinema."[47] Carroll is saying that photography no more has a realistic or even representational essence than does painting.

ARISTOTLE'S DEFENSE OF ART

Having argued that there is a significant amount of art that is nonrepresentational, what can we make of the great amount that is? In particular, what are we to make of Plato's powerful attack on representational art? I will conclude this chapter by sketching the theory that Aristotle expounds in his *Poetics* (ca. 330 B.C.) (see the Readings). Aristotle was probably not aiming to refute Plato's objections to art; nonetheless, his account of mimetic art provides a significant rejoinder to Plato's arguments. No doubt this is why Aristotle's theory strongly influenced the arts for the next two thousand years, far more so than Plato's denunciation.

Aristotle puts forth a version of the mimetic theory of the arts that is more complex than Plato's. The complexity appears right at the beginning of the *Poetics*, when Aristotle suggests a way to use mimesis to create a taxonomy of the arts.

> Epic poetry and Tragedy, as also Comedy, Dithyrambic poetry, and most flute-playing and lyre-playing, are all, viewed as a whole, modes of imitation. But at the same time they differ from one another in three ways, either by a difference of kind in their means or by a difference in the objects, or in the manner of their imitations. (p. 225).

Not only can we differentiate the various arts through distinguishing the means, the objects, and the manners of imitation, but we can also use this scheme to differentiate subgenres of art. Aristotle does this in comparing and contrasting epic poetry, comedy, and tragedy.

Aristotle has a favorable view of poetry in general and tragedy in particular. He differs from Plato in part by taking a different view of human nature and of our relation to the natural world. Aristotle does not share Plato's dim view of the possibility of gaining knowledge of the world through sensation. Nor does he view human nature as a battle between the rational intellect on the one hand and the senses and emotions on the other. Thus he begins his general discussion of poetry by noting with approval that imitation is natural to humans (and not therefore a bad thing), that we *learn* by viewing imitations, and that it is natural for us to gain *pleasure* from viewing them because we are learning. He thus views imitation as natural to our biological species, and poetry as merely a sophisticated outgrowth of this useful capacity.

Aristotle's theory of tragedy, on which the *Poetics* focuses, provides answers to Plato's most serious charges against art. Recall Plato's objections: Art does not produce knowledge and is not based on knowledge, and it is socially dangerous because its emotional appeal "waters the passions." (The ontological objection—that images are inferior to their subjects—does not concern Aristotle.) Aristotle proposes two very famous ideas in his explication of tragedy that beautifully counter Plato's charges.

The first has to do with what poetry represents or imitates. Whereas Socrates speaks as if mimetic arts imitate the appearance of particular objects and events, Aristotle holds that different mimetic arts imitate different things. He says the object of imitation in most poetry, for example, is human action. Although this may seem like a minor divergence from Plato's assumptions, it has major consequences. Action is a deeper or more abstract concept than the concept of behavior, which functions on the level of mere appearance. If someone waves his arm at you (behavior), he may be doing (action) a variety of different things. He may be asking you to come nearer; he may be insulting you; he may be signaling a turn, and so on. To understand the action, we must know what the behavior *means*. Aristotle repudiates the idea that tragedy imitates spectacle (what things look like) or all the events that befall the characters. Instead, the object imitated is one particular, if abstract, kind of thing: "Tragedy is essentially an imitation not of persons but of action and life, of happiness and misery." The particular object of imitation is an action which necessarily involves agents and their characters and thoughts: "Character is what makes us ascribe certain moral qualities to the agents; and Thought is shown in all they say." These two, character and thought, are the causes of the agent's actions, "and consequently of their success or failure in their lives" (p. 227).

Thus Aristotle repudiates Plato's fundamental assumption that mimesis can only imitate appearances. He goes even further. By propounding the view that what really counts in tragedy is the plot and that the plot must imitate one unified action, "with its several incidents so closely connected that the transposal or withdrawal of any one of them will disjoin and dislocate the whole," Aristotle proposes a theory so far removed from the blank, mirrorlike reflective realism assumed by Plato that he is able to conclude that "poetry is something more philosophic and of graver import than history, since its statements are of the nature rather of universals, whereas those of history are singulars." Poetry describes "not the thing that has happened"—as Aristotle imagines history does—"but a kind of thing that might happen, i.e. what is possible as being probable or necessary" (p. 229). The poet does *not* simply report what has happened or could possibly happen; in a well-constructed plot, the poet tells us what must happen or will probably happen. Clearly this requires a knowledge of the causal and moral laws of the world, as well as a deep knowledge of human nature. Thus poetry, for Aristotle, is based on knowledge and gives us knowledge of how the world works.

Aristotle's idea that the statements of poetry are of the nature of universals can be related to our earlier proposal of ambiguous reference for artworks. I have suggested that *The Crucible* intentionally represented both seventeenth-century colonial Salem and the United

States of the 1950s. But, in truth, it could be taken to represent *any* situation in which mass hysteria is fostered by demagogic leaders who create and focus a mob's fear on the task of repressing dissenters or heretics. Thus multiple reference becomes universal reference, for the poem or play turns out to about every situation of the type described in it. An appealing feature of Aristotle's influential idea is that it accounts for the continued life and importance of artworks of the past. If they are universal in the sense just suggested, then later audiences can find truths in them that apply to other times and contexts, especially to their own time. As Kenneth Dover suggests, "If we generalise tragic predicaments, we recognize our own experience in tragedy: the obstinate adherence to a choice made in doubt and haste, or the destruction of something we love (our own lives, among other things) for the sake of good repute and in fear of humiliation."[48]

Aristotle's second famous idea has to do with how he accounts for emotions in art. From what we have said so far, it might seem that Aristotle has an excessively intellectual view of the arts; Plato, at least, acknowledged that artworks appeal to the emotions as much as to the intellect. However, Aristotle does hypothesize a major role for the emotions in tragedy.

Representations, I have said, are things possessing the social function of serving as props in games of make-believe, although they also prompt imaginings, and are sometimes objects of them as well.

— Kendall Walton, *Mimesis as Make-Believe*[50]

Emotional arousal of a special sort is essential to his definition of tragedy: A tragedy, he says, must contain "incidents arousing pity and fear, wherewith to accomplish its catharsis of such emotions" (p. 226). With the claim that the very goal of tragedy is emotional catharsis, Aristotle has turned Plato's objection on its head. But Plato's objection will not have been adequately answered until we have a clear account of why catharsis is a valuable process. Plato never doubts that poetry arouses emotions; rather, his view of this emotional arousal is negative. He asks, What good is this arousal? To answer this, we have to determine what Aristotle thinks catharsis is and also decide whether Aristotle is more correct than Socrates, who claims that "poetry feeds and waters the passions instead of drying them up; she lets them rule, although they ought to be controlled" (p. 223). (There is a third problem. Even if Aristotle's hypothesis of catharsis is successful, it applies only to tragedy, leaving the emotional appeal of the other arts unexplained and unjustified.)

Unfortunately, we do not have enough evidence of Aristotle's thinking to determine his theory of catharsis with any certainty.[49] There are almost as many views about what he had in mind as there are commentators on the relevant texts. It is natural to read "catharsis" as the purification and purgation of the aroused emotions, pity and fear. To emphasize purgation would be to claim that the function of tragedy is to get rid of the emotions of pity and fear, as if they build up to the point where they need to be drained away. One might call this the "emotional release" theory. A different way to read the text is to note Aristotle's frequent mention of pleasure; a catharsis of pity and fear gives pleasure, according to Aristotle. If this is the purpose of the arousal, we could call this the "horror movie" model. People go to horror movies to be frightened, and this (surprisingly) gives them much pleasure. Finally, other views emphasize the notion that the aroused emotions are *purified* in some way, not purged, possibly through a restructuring or reaffirming of the relation of the emotions to beliefs and other cognitive states. For example, through understanding the universal statements concerning happiness and misery that underpin the tragedy, the audience may see the mistakes made by the tragic hero and relate that to their own feelings about what is the right thing to do in situations like those portrayed in the tragedy.

Whichever position Aristotle means to put forth, the question is whether any of these theories provide an adequate answer to a critic like Plato. Clearly an answer emphasizing pleasure, such as the horror movie model, would be a weak rejoinder to Plato's concerns. And in terms of the larger issues of this book, such as Tolstoy's challenge, such an answer would be problematic. The other interpretations, by contrast, postulate a socially useful function for catharsis. Thus they provide a significant rejoinder to Plato. The question is whether they are true.

However we interpret Aristotle's theory of catharsis, the most important point is that with it he provides a necessary addition to any theory that bases art on representation. Aristotle clearly sees the need for some account of emotions and art. Representation by itself seems to leave out an essential dimension of all art: the fact that art addresses not just our intellect but also our emotions.

READINGS FOR CHAPTER 9

Plato, from *The Republic*
Aristotle, from *Poetics*
André Bazin, ''The Myth of Total Cinema''

from *The Republic*

Plato

BOOK X
The participants in the dialogue are Socrates and Glaucon.

Of the many excellences which I perceive in the order of our State, there is none which upon reflection pleases me better than the rule about poetry.

To what do you refer?

To the rejection of imitative poetry, which certainly ought not to be received; as I see far more clearly now that the parts of the soul have been distinguished.

What do you mean?

Speaking in confidence, for I should not like to have my words repeated to the tragedians and the rest of the imitative tribe—but I do not mind saying to you, that all poetical imitations are ruinous to the understanding of the hearers, and that the knowledge of their true nature is the only antidote to them.

Explain the purport of your remark.

Well, I will tell you, although I have always from my earliest youth had an awe and love of Homer, which even now makes the words falter on my lips, for he is the great captain and teacher of the whole of that charming tragic company; but a man is not to be reverenced more than the truth, and therefore I will speak out.

Very good, he said.

Listen to me then, or rather, answer me.

Put your question.

Can you tell me what imitation is? for I really do not know.

A likely thing, then, that I should know.

Why not? for the duller eye may often see a thing sooner than the keener.

Very true, he said; but in your presence, even if I had any faint notion, I could not muster courage to utter it. Will you enquire yourself?

Well then, shall we begin the enquiry in our usual manner: Whenever a number of individuals have a common name, we assume them to have a corresponding idea or form. Do you understand me?

I do.

Let us take any common instance; there are beds and tables in the world—plenty of them, are there not?

Yes.

But there are only two ideas or forms of them—one the idea of a bed, the other of a table.

True.

And the maker of either of them makes a bed or he makes a table for our use, in accordance with the idea—that is our way of speaking in this and similar instances—but no artificer makes the ideas themselves: how could he?

Impossible.

And there is another artist,—I should like to know what you would say of him.

Who is he?

One who is the maker of all the works of all other workmen.

What an extraordinary man!

Wait a little, and there will be more reason for your saying so. For this is he who is able to make not only vessels of every kind, but plants and animals, himself and all other things—the earth and heaven, and the things which are in heaven or under the earth; he makes the gods also.

He must be a wizard and no mistake.

Oh! you are incredulous, are you? Do you mean that there is no such maker or creator, or that in one sense there might be a maker of all these things but in another not? Do you see that there is a way in which you could make them all yourself?

What way?

An easy way enough; or rather, there are many ways in which the feat might be quickly and easily accomplished, none quicker than that of turning a mirror round and round — you would soon enough make the sun and the heavens, and the earth and yourself, and other animals and plants, and all the other things of which we were just now speaking, in the mirror.

Yes, he said; but they would be appearances only.

Very good, I said, you are coming to the point now. And the painter too is, as I conceive, just such another — a creator of appearances, is he not?

Of course.

But then I suppose you will say that what he creates is untrue. And yet there is a sense in which the painter also creates a bed?

Yes, he said, but not a real bed.

And what of the maker of the bed? Were you not saying that he too makes, not the idea which, according to our view, is the essence of the bed, but only a particular bed?

Yes, I did.

Then if he does not make that which exists he cannot make true existence, but only some semblance of existence; and if any one were to say that the work of the maker of the bed, or of any other workman, has real existence, he could hardly be supposed to be speaking the truth.

At any rate, he replied, philosophers would say that he was not speaking the truth.

No wonder, then, that his work too is an indistinct expression of truth.

No wonder.

Suppose now that by the light of the examples just offered we enquire who this imitator is?

If you please.

Well then, here are three beds: one existing in nature, which is made by God, as I think that we may say — for no one else can be the maker?

No.

There is another which is the work of the carpenter?

Yes.

And the work of the painter is a third?

Yes.

Beds, then, are of three kinds, and there are three artists who superintend them: God, the maker of the bed, and the painter?

Yes, there are three of them.

God, whether from choice or from necessity, made one bed in nature and one only; two or more such ideal beds neither ever have been nor ever will be made by God.

Why is that?

Because even if He had made but two, a third would still appear behind them which both of them would have for their idea, and that would be the ideal bed and not the two others.

Very true, he said.

God knew this, and He desired to be the real maker of a real bed, not a particular maker of a particular bed, and therefore He created a bed which is essentially and by nature one only.

So we believe.

Shall we, then, speak of Him as the natural author or maker of the bed?

Yes, he replied; inasmuch as by the natural process of creation He is the author of this and of all other things.

And what shall we say of the carpenter — is not he also the maker of the bed?

Yes.

But would you call the painter a creator and maker?

Certainly not.

Yet if he is not the maker, what is he in relation to the bed?

I think, he said, that we may fairly designate him as the imitator of that which the others make.

Good, I said; then you call him who is third in the descent from nature an imitator?

Certainly, he said.

And the tragic poet is an imitator, and therefore, like all other imitators, he is thrice removed from the king and from the truth?

That appears to be so.

Then about the imitator we are agreed. And what about the painter? — I would like to know whether he may be thought to imitate that which originally exists in nature, or only the creations of artists?

The latter.

As they are or as they appear? You have still to determine this.

What do you mean?

I mean, that you may look at a bed from different points of view, obliquely or directly or from any other point of view, and the bed will appear different, but there is no difference in reality. And the same of all things.

Yes, he said, the difference is only apparent.

Now let me ask you another question: Which is the art of painting designed to be — an imitation of things as they are, or as they appear — of appearance or of reality?

Of appearance.

Then the imitator, I said, is a long way off the truth, and can do all things because he lightly touches on a small part of them, and that part an image. For example: A painter will paint a cobbler, carpenter, or any other artist, though he knows nothing of their arts; and, if he is a good artist, he may deceive children or simple persons, when he shows them his picture of a carpenter from a distance, and they will fancy that they are looking at a real carpenter.

Certainly.

And whenever any one informs us that he has found a man who knows all the arts, and all things else that anybody knows, and every single thing with a higher degree of accuracy than any other man — whoever tells us this, I think that we can only imagine him to be a simple creature who is likely to have been deceived by some wizard or actor whom he met, and whom he thought all-knowing, because he himself was unable to analyse the nature of knowledge and ignorance and imitation.

Most true.

And so, when we hear persons saying that the tragedians, and Homer, who is at their head, know all the arts and all things human, virtue as well as vice, and divine things too, for that the good poet cannot compose well unless he knows his subject, and that he who has not this knowledge can never be a poet, we ought to consider whether here also there may not be a similar illusion. Perhaps they may have come across imitators and been deceived by them; they may not

have remembered when they saw their works that these were but imitations thrice removed from the truth, and could easily be made without any knowledge of the truth, because they are appearances only and not realities? Or, after all, they may be in the right, and poets do really know the things about which they seem to the many to speak so well?

The question, he said, should by all means be considered.

Now do you suppose that if a person were able to make the original as well as the image, he would seriously devote himself to the image-making branch? Would he allow imitation to be the ruling principle of his life, as if he had nothing higher in him?

I should say not.

The real artist, who knew what he was imitating, would be interested in realities and not in imitations; and would desire to leave as memorials of himself works many and fair; and, instead of being the author of encomiums, he would prefer to be the theme of them.

Yes, he said, that would be to him a source of much greater honour and profit.

Then, I said, we must put a question to Homer; not about medicine, or any of the arts to which his poems only incidentally refer: we are not going to ask him, or any other poet, whether he has cured patients like Asclepius, or left behind him a school of medicine such as the Asclepiads were, or whether he only talks about medicine and other arts at second hand; but we have a right to know respecting military tactics, politics, education, which are the chiefest and noblest subjects of his poems, and we may fairly ask him about them. "Friend Homer," then we say to him, "if you are only in the second remove from truth in what you say of virtue, and not in the third — not an image maker or imitator — and if you are able to discern what pursuits make men better or worse in private or public life, tell us what State was ever better governed by your help? The good order of Lacedaemon is due to Lycurgus, and many other cities great and small have been similarly benefited by others; but who says that you have been a good legislator to them and have done them any good? Italy and Sicily boast of Charondas, and there is Solon who is renowned among us; but what city has anything to say about you?" Is there any city which he might name?

I think not, said Glaucon; not even the Homerids themselves pretend that he was a legislator.

Well, but is there any war on record which was carried on successfully by him, or aided by his counsels, when he was alive?

There is not.

Or is there any invention of his, applicable to the arts or to human life, such as Thales the Milesian or Anacharsis the Scythian, and other ingenious men have conceived, which is attributed to him?

There is absolutely nothing of the kind.

But, if Homer never did any public service, was he privately a guide or teacher of any? Had he in his lifetime friends who loved to associate with him, and who handed down to posterity an Homeric way of life, such as was established by Pythagoras who was so greatly beloved for his wisdom, and whose followers are to this day quite celebrated for the order which was named after him?

Nothing of the kind is recorded of him. For surely, Socrates, Creophylus, the companion of Homer, that child of flesh, whose name always makes us laugh, might be more justly ridiculed for his stupidity, if, as is said, Homer was greatly neglected by him and others in his own day when he was alive?

Yes, I replied, that is the tradition. But can you imagine, Glaucon, that if Homer had really been able to educate and improve mankind — if he had possessed knowledge and not been a mere imitator — can you imagine, I say, that he would not have had many followers, and been honoured and loved by them? Protagoras of Abdera, and Prodicus of Ceos, and a host of others, have only to whisper to their contemporaries: "You will never be able to manage either your own house or your own State until you appoint us to be your ministers of education" — and this ingenious device of theirs has such an effect in making men love them that their companions all but carry them about on

their shoulders. And is it conceivable that the contemporaries of Homer, or again of Hesiod, would have allowed either of them to go about as rhapsodists, if they had really been able to make mankind virtuous? Would they not have been as unwilling to part with them as with gold, and have compelled them to stay at home with them? Or, if the master would not stay, then the disciples would have followed him about everywhere, until they had got education enough?

Yes, Socrates, that, I think, is quite true.

Then must we not infer that all these poetical individuals, beginning with Homer, are only imitators; they copy images of virtue and the like, but the truth they never reach? The poet is like a painter who, as we have already observed, will make a likeness of a cobbler though he understands nothing of cobbling; and his picture is good enough for those who know no more than he does, and judge only by colours and figures.

Quite so.

In like manner the poet with his words and phrases may be said to lay on the colours of the several arts, himself understanding their nature only enough to imitate them; and other people, who are as ignorant as he is, and judge only from his words, imagine that if he speaks of cobbling, or of military tactics, or of anything else, in metre and harmony and rhythm, he speaks very well — such is the sweet influence which melody and rhythm by nature have. And I think that you must have observed again and again what a poor appearance the tales of poets make when stripped of the colours which music puts upon them, and recited in simple prose.

Yes, he said.

They are like faces which were never really beautiful, but only blooming; and now the bloom of youth has passed away from them?

Exactly.

Here is another point: The imitator or maker of the image knows nothing of true existence; he knows appearances only. Am I not right?

Yes.

Then let us have a clear understanding, and not be satisfied with half an explanation.

Proceed.

Of the painter we say that he will paint reins, and he will paint a bit?

Yes.

And the worker in leather and brass will make them?

Certainly.

But does the painter know the right form of the bit and reins? Nay, hardly even the workers in brass and leather who make them; only the horseman who knows how to use them—he knows their right form.

Most true.

And may we not say the same of all things?

What?

That there are three arts which are concerned with all things: one which uses, another which makes, a third which imitates them?

Yes.

And the excellence or beauty or truth of every structure, animate or inanimate, and of every action of man, is relative to the use for which nature or the artist has intended them.

True.

Then the user of them must have the greatest experience of them, and he must indicate to the maker the good or bad qualities which develop themselves in use; for example, the flute-player will tell the flute-maker which of his flutes is satisfactory to the performer; he will tell him how he ought to make them, and the other will attend to his instructions?

Of course.

The one knows and therefore speaks with authority about the goodness and badness of flutes, while the other, confiding in him, will do what he is told by him?

True.

The instrument is the same, but about the excellence or badness of it the maker will only attain to a correct belief; and this he will gain from him who knows, by talking to him and being compelled to hear what he has to say, whereas the user will have knowledge?

True.

But will the imitator have either? Will he know from use whether or no his drawing is correct or beautiful? Or will he have right opinion from

being compelled to associate with another who knows and gives him instructions about what he should draw?

Neither.

Then he will no more have true opinion than he will have knowledge about the goodness or badness of his imitations?

I suppose not.

The imitative artist will be in a brilliant state of intelligence about his own creations?

Nay, very much the reverse.

And still he will go on imitating without knowing what makes a thing good or bad, and may be expected therefore to imitate only that which appears to be good to the ignorant multitude?

Just so.

Thus far then we are pretty well agreed that the imitator has no knowledge worth mentioning of what he imitates. Imitation is only a kind of play or sport, and the tragic poets, whether they write in Iambic or in Heroic verse, are imitators in the highest degree?

Very true.

And now tell me, I conjure you, has not imitation been shown by us to be concerned with that which is thrice removed from the truth?

Certainly.

And what is the faculty in man to which imitation is addressed?

What do you mean?

I will explain: The body which is large when seen near, appears small when seen at a distance?

True.

And the same object appears straight when looked at out of the water, and crooked when in the water; and the concave becomes convex, owing to the illusion about colours to which the sight is liable. Thus every sort of confusion is revealed within us; and this is that weakness of the human mind on which the art of conjuring and of deceiving by light and shadow and other ingenious devices imposes, having an effect upon us like magic.

True.

And the arts of measuring and numbering and weighing come to the rescue of the human understanding—there is the beauty of them—and the apparent greater or less, or more or heavier, no longer have the mastery over us, but give way before calculation and measure and weight?

Most true.

And this, surely, must be the work of the calculating and rational principle in the soul?

To be sure.

And when this principle measures and certifies that some things are equal, or that some are greater or less than others, there occurs an apparent contradiction?

True.

But were we not saying that such a contradiction is impossible—the same faculty cannot have contrary opinions at the same time about the same thing?

Very true.

Then that part of the soul which has an opinion contrary to measure is not the same with that which has an opinion in accordance with measure?

True.

And the better part of the soul is likely to be that which trusts to measure and calculation?

Certainly.

And that which is opposed to them is one of the inferior principles of the soul?

No doubt.

This was the conclusion at which I was seeking to arrive when I said that painting or drawing, and imitation in general, when doing their own proper work, are far removed from truth, and the companions and friends and associates of a principle within us which is equally removed from reason, and that they have no true or healthy aim.

Exactly.

The imitative art is an inferior who marries an inferior, and has inferior offspring.

Very true.

And is this confined to the sight only, or does it extend to the hearing also, relating in fact to what we term poetry?

Probably the same would be true of poetry.

Do not rely, I said, on a probability derived from the analogy of painting; but let us examine further and see whether the faculty with which poetical imitation is concerned is good or bad.

By all means.

We may state the question thus:—Imitation imitates the actions of men, whether voluntary or involuntary, on which, as they imagine, a good or bad result has ensued, and they rejoice or sorrow accordingly. Is there anything more?

No, there is nothing else.

But in all this variety of circumstances is the man at unity with himself—or rather, as in the instance of sight there was confusion and opposition in his opinions about the same things, so here also is there not strife and inconsistency in his life? Though I need hardly raise the question again, for I remember that all this has been already admitted; and the soul has been acknowledged by us to be full of these and ten thousand similar oppositions occurring at the same moment?

And we were right, he said.

Yes, I said, thus far we were right; but there was an omission which must now be supplied.

What was the omission?

Were we not saying that a good man, who has the misfortune to lose his son or anything else which is most dear to him, will bear the loss with more equanimity than another?

Yes.

But will he have no sorrow, or shall we say that although he cannot help sorrowing, he will moderate his sorrow?

The latter, he said, is the truer statement.

Tell me: will he be more likely to struggle and hold out against his sorrow when he is seen by his equals, or when he is alone?

It will make a great difference whether he is seen or not.

When he is by himself he will not mind saying or doing many things which he would be ashamed of any one hearing or seeing him do?

True.

There is a principle of law and reason in him which bids him resist, as well as a feeling of his misfortune which is forcing him to indulge his sorrow?

True.

But when a man is drawn in two opposite directions, to and from the same object, this, as we affirm, necessarily implies two distinct principles in him?

Certainly.

One of them is ready to follow the guidance of the law?

How do you mean?

The law would say that to be patient under suffering is best, and that we should not give way to impatience, as there is no knowing whether such things are good or evil; and nothing is gained by impatience; also, because no human thing is of serious importance, and grief stands in the way of that which at the moment is most required.

What is most required? he asked.

That we should take counsel about what has happened, and when the dice have been thrown order our affairs in the way which reason deems best; not, like children who have had a fall, keeping hold of the part struck and wasting time in setting up a howl, but always accustoming the soul forthwith to apply a remedy, raising up that which is sickly and fallen, banishing the cry of sorrow by the healing art.

Yes, he said, that is the true way of meeting the attacks of fortune.

Yes, I said; and the higher principle is ready to follow this suggestion of reason?

Clearly.

And the other principle, which inclines us to recollection of our troubles and to lamentation, and can never have enough of them, we may call irrational, useless, and cowardly?

Indeed, we may.

And does not the latter — I mean the rebellious principle — furnish a great variety of materials for imitation? Whereas the wise and calm temperament, being always nearly equable, is not easy to imitate or to appreciate when imitated, especially at a public festival when a promiscuous crowd is assembled in a theatre. For the feeling represented is one to which they are strangers.

Certainly.

Then the imitative poet who aims at being popular is not by nature made, nor is his art intended, to please or to affect the rational principle in the soul; but he will prefer the passionate and fitful temper, which is easily imitated?

Clearly.

And now we may fairly take him and place him by the side of the painter, for he is like him in two ways: first, inasmuch as his creations have an inferior degree of truth — in this, I say, he is like him; and he is also like him in being concerned with an inferior part of the soul; and therefore we shall be right in refusing to admit him into a well-ordered State, because he awakens and nourishes and strengthens the feelings and impairs the reason. As in a city when the evil are permitted to have authority and the good are put out of the way, so in the soul of man, as we maintain, the imitative poet implants an evil constitution, for he indulges the irrational nature which has no discernment of greater and less, but thinks the same thing at one time great and at another small — he is a manufacturer of images and is very far removed from the truth.

Exactly.

But we have not yet brought forward the heaviest count in our accusation: — the power which poetry has of harming even the good (and there are very few who are not harmed), is surely an awful thing?

Yes, certainly, if the effect is what you say.

Hear and judge: The best of us, as I conceive, when we listen to a passage of Homer, or one of the tragedians, in which he represents some pitiful hero who is drawling out his sorrows in a long oration, or weeping, and smiting his breast — the best of us, you know, delight in giving way to sympathy, and are in raptures at the excellence of the poet who stirs our feelings most.

Yes, of course I know.

But when any sorrow of our own happens to us, then you may observe that we pride ourselves on the opposite quality — we would fain be quiet and patient; this is the manly part, and the other which delighted us in the recitation is now deemed to be the part of a woman.

Very true, he said.

Now can we be right in praising and admiring another who is doing that which any one of us would abominate and be ashamed of in his own person?

No, he said, that is certainly not reasonable.

Nay, I said, quite reasonable from one point of view.

What point of view?

If you consider, I said, that when in misfortune we feel a natural hunger and desire to relieve our sorrow by weeping and lamentation, and that this feeling which is kept under control in our own calamities is satisfied and delighted by the poets;—the better nature in each of us, not having been sufficiently trained by reason or habit, allows the sympathetic element to break loose because the sorrow is another's; and the spectator fancies that there can be no disgrace to himself in praising and pitying any one who comes telling him what a good man he is, and making a fuss about his troubles; he thinks that the pleasure is a gain, and why should he be supercilious and lose this and the poem too? Few persons ever reflect, as I should imagine, that from the evil of other men something of evil is communicated to themselves. And so the feeling of sorrow which has gathered strength at the sight of the misfortunes of others is with difficulty repressed in our own.

How very true!

And does not the same hold also of the ridiculous? There are jests which you would be ashamed to make yourself, and yet on the comic stage, or indeed in private, when you hear them, you are greatly amused by them, and are not at all disgusted at their unseemliness;—the case of pity is repeated;—there is a principle in human nature which is disposed to raise a laugh, and this which you once restrained by reason, because you were afraid of being thought a buffoon, is now let out again; and having stimulated the risible faculty at the theatre, you are betrayed unconsciously to yourself into playing the comic poet at home.

Quite true, he said.

And the same may be said of lust and anger and all the other affections, of desire and pain and pleasure, which are held to be inseparable from every action—in all of them poetry feeds and waters the passions instead of drying them up;

she lets them rule, although they ought to be controlled, if mankind are ever to increase in happiness and virtue.

I cannot deny it.

Therefore, Glaucon, I said, whenever you meet with any of the eulogists of Homer declaring that he has been the educator of Hellas, and that he is profitable for education and for the ordering of human things, and that you should take him up again and again and get to know him and regulate your whole life according to him, we may love and honour those who say these things—they are excellent people, as far as their lights extend; and we are ready to acknowledge that Homer is the greatest of poets and first of tragedy writers; but we must remain firm in our conviction that hymns to the gods and praises of famous men are the only poetry which ought to be admitted into our State. For if you go beyond this and allow the honeyed muse to enter, either in epic or lyric verse, not law and the reason of mankind, which by common consent have ever been deemed best, but pleasure and pain will be the rulers in our State.

That is most true, he said.

And now since we have reverted to the subject of poetry, let this our defence serve to show the reasonableness of our former judgment in sending away out of our State an art having the tendencies which we have described; for reason constrained us. But that she may not impute to us any harshness or want of politeness, let us tell her that there is an ancient quarrel between philosophy and poetry; of which there are many proofs, such as the saying of "the yelping hound howling at her lord," or of one "mighty in the vain talk of fools," and "the mob of sages circumventing Zeus," and the "subtle thinkers who are beggars after all"; and there are innumerable other signs of ancient enmity between them. Notwithstanding this, let us assure our sweet friend and the sister arts of imitation that if she will only prove her title to exist in a well-ordered State we shall be delighted to receive her—we are very conscious of her charms; but we may not on that account betray the truth. I dare say, Glaucon, that you are as much charmed by her as I am, especially when she appears in Homer?

Yes, indeed, I am greatly charmed.

Shall I propose, then, that she be allowed to return from exile, but upon this condition only — that she make a defence of herself in lyrical or some other metre?

Certainly.

And we may further grant to those of her defenders who are lovers of poetry and yet not poets the permission to speak in prose on her behalf: let them show not only that she is pleasant but also useful to States and to human life, and we will listen in a kindly spirit; for if this can be proved we shall surely be the gainers — I mean, if there is a use in poetry as well as a delight?

Certainly, he said, we shall be the gainers.

If her defence fails, then, my dear friend, like other persons who are enamoured of something, but put a restraint upon themselves when they think their desires are opposed to their interests, so too must we after the manner of lovers give her up, though not without a struggle. We too are inspired by that love of poetry which the educa-tion of noble States has implanted in us, and therefore we would have her appear at her best and truest; but so long as she is unable to make good her defence, this argument of ours shall be a charm to us, which we will repeat to ourselves while we listen to her strains; that we may not fall away into the childish love of her which capti-vates the many. At all events we are well aware that poetry being such as we have described is not to be regarded seriously as attaining to the truth; and he who listens to her, fearing for the safety of the city which is within him, should be on his guard against her seductions and make our words his law.

Yes, he said, I quite agree with you.

Yes, I said, my dear Glaucon, for great is the issue at stake, greater than appears, whether a man is to be good or bad. And what will any one be profited if under the influence of honour or money or power, aye, or under the excitement of poetry, he neglect justice and virtue?

Yes, he said; I have been convinced by the argument, as I believe that any one else would have been.

from *Poetics*

Aristotle

1

Our subject being Poetry, I propose to speak not only of the art in general but also of its species and their respective capacities; of the structure of plot required for a good poem; of the number and nature of the constituent parts of a poem; and likewise of any other matters in the same line of inquiry. Let us follow the natural order and begin with the primary facts.

Epic poetry and Tragedy, as also Comedy, Dithyrambic poetry, and most flute-playing and lyre-playing, are all, viewed as a whole, modes of imitation. But at the same time they differ from one another in three ways, either by a difference of kind in their means, or by differences in the objects, or in the manner of their imitations.

I. Just as colour and form are used as means by some, who (whether by art or constant practice) imitate and portray many things by their aid, and the voice is used by others; so also in the above-mentioned group of arts, the means with them as a whole are rhythm, language, and harmony — used, however, either singly or in certain combinations. A combination of harmony and rhythm alone is the means in flute-playing and lyre-playing, and any other arts there may be of the same description, e.g. imitative piping. Rhythm alone, without harmony, is the means in the dancer's imitations; for even he, by the rhythms of his attitudes, may represent men's characters, as well as what they do and suffer. There is further an art which imitates by language alone, without harmony, in prose or in verse, and if in verse, either in some one or in a plurality of metres. This form of imitation is to this day without a name. . . .

2

II. The objects the imitator represents are actions, with agents who are necessarily either good men or bad — the diversities of human character being nearly always derivative from this primary distinction, since the line between virtue and vice is one dividing the whole of mankind. It follows, therefore, that the agents represented must be either above our own level of goodness, or beneath it, or just such as we are; in the same way as, with the painters, the personages of Polygnotus are better than we are, those of Pauson worse, and those of Dionysius just like ourselves. It is clear that each of the above-mentioned arts will admit of these differences, and that it will become a separate art by representing objects with this point of difference. Even in dancing, flute-playing, and lyre-playing such diversities are possible; and they are also possible in the nameless art that uses language, prose or verse without harmony, as its means; Homer's personages, for instance, are better than we are; Cleophon's are on our own level; and those of Hegemon of Thasos, the first writer of parodies, and Nicochares, the author of the *Diliad*, are beneath it. . . . This difference it is that distinguishes Tragedy and Comedy also; the one would make its personages worse, and the other better, than the men of the present day.

3

III. A third difference in these arts is in the manner in which each kind of object is represented. Given both the same means and the same kind of object for imitation, one may either (1) speak at one moment in narrative and at another in an assumed character, as Homer does; or (2) one may remain the same throughout, without any such change; or (3) the imitators may represent the whole story dramatically, as though they were actually doing the things described.

As we said at the beginning, therefore, the differences in the imitation of these arts come under three heads, their means, their objects, and their manner.

So that as an imitator Sophocles will be on one side akin to Homer, both portraying good men; and on another to Aristophanes, since both present their personages as acting and doing. . . .

4

It is clear that the general origin of poetry was due to two causes, each of them part of human nature. Imitation is natural to man from childhood, one of his advantages over the lower animals being this, that he is the most imitative creature in the world, and learns at first by imitation. And it is also natural for all to delight in works of imitation. The truth of this second point is shown by experience: though the objects themselves may be painful to see, we delight to view the most realistic representations of them in art, the forms for example of the lowest animals and of dead bodies. The explanation is to be found in a further fact: to be learning something is the greatest of pleasures not only to the philosopher but also to the rest of mankind, however small their capacity for it; the reason of the delight in seeing the picture is that one is at the same time learning — gathering the meaning of things, e.g. that the man there is so-and-so; for if one has not seen the thing before, one's pleasure will not be in the picture as an imitation of it, but will be due to the execution or colouring or some similar cause. Imitation, then, being natural to us — as also the sense of harmony and rhythm, the metres being obviously species of rhythms — it was through their original aptitude, and by a series of improvements for the most part gradual on their first efforts, that they created poetry out of their improvisations.

Poetry, however, soon broke up into two kinds according to the differences of character in the individual poets; for the graver among them would represent noble actions, and those of noble personages; and the meaner sort the actions of the ignoble. . . .

5

. . . Epic poetry, then, has been seen to agree with Tragedy to this extent, that of being an imitation of serious subjects in a grand kind of verse. It differs from it, however, (1) in that it is in one kind of verse and in narrative form; and (2) in its length — which is due to its action having no fixed limit of time, whereas Tragedy endeavours to keep as far as possible within a single circuit of the sun, or something near that. This, I say, is another point of difference between them, though at first the practice in this respect was just the same in tragedies as in epic poems. They differ also (3) in their constituents, some being common to both and others peculiar to Tragedy — hence a judge of good and bad in Tragedy is a judge of that in epic poetry also. All the parts of an epic are included in Tragedy; but those of Tragedy are not all of them to be found in the Epic.

6

Reserving hexameter poetry and Comedy for consideration hereafter, let us proceed now to the discussion of Tragedy; before doing so, however, we must gather up the definition resulting from what has been said. A tragedy, then, is the imitation of an action that is serious and also, as having magnitude, complete in itself; in language with pleasurable accessories, each kind brought in separately in the parts of the work; in a dramatic, not in a narrative form; with incidents arousing pity and fear, wherewith to accomplish its catharsis of such emotions. Here by "language with pleasurable accessories" I mean that with rhythm and harmony or song superadded; and by "the kinds separately" I mean that some portions are worked out with verse only, and others in turn with song.

I. As they act the stories, it follows that in the first place the Spectacle (or stage-appearance of the actors) must be some part of the whole; and in the second Melody and Diction, these two being the means of their imitation. Here by "Diction" I mean merely this, the composition of the verses; and by "Melody," what is too completely understood to require explanation. But further: the subject represented also is an action; and the action involves agents, who must necessarily have their distinctive qualities both of character and thought, since it is from these that we ascribe certain qualities to their actions. There are in the natural order of things, therefore, two causes, Thought and Character, of their actions, and consequently of their success or failure in their lives. Now the action (that which was done) is represented in the play by the Fable or Plot. The Fable, in our present sense of the term, is simply this, the combination of the incidents, or things done in the story; whereas Character is what makes us ascribe certain moral qualities to the agents; and Thought is shown in all they say when proving a particular point or, it may be, enunciating a general truth. There are six parts consequently of every tragedy, as a whole (that is) of such or such quality, viz. a Fable or Plot, Characters, Diction, Thought, Spectacle, and Melody; two of them arising from the means, one from the manner, and three from the objects of the dramatic imitation; and there is nothing else besides these six. Of these, its formative elements, then, not a few of the dramatists have made due use, as every play, one may say, admits of Spectacle, Character, Fable, Diction, Melody, and Thought.

II. The most important of the six is the combination of the incidents of the story. Tragedy is essentially an imitation not of persons but of action and life, of happiness and misery. All human happiness or misery takes the form of action; the end for which we live is a certain kind of activity, not a quality. Character gives us qualities, but it is in our actions — what we do — that we are happy or the reverse. In a play accordingly they do not act in order to portray the Characters; they include the Characters for the sake of the action. So that it is the action in it, i.e. its Fable or Plot, that is the end and purpose of the tragedy; and the end is everywhere the chief thing. Besides this, a tragedy is impossible without action, but there may be one without Character. The tragedies of most of the moderns are characterless — a defect common among poets of all kinds, and with its counterpart in painting in Zeuxis as compared with Polygnotus; for whereas the latter is strong in character, the work of Zeuxis is devoid of it. And again: one may string together a series of characteristic speeches of the utmost finish as regards Diction and Thought, and yet fail to produce the true tragic effect; but one will have much better success with a tragedy which, however inferior in these respects, has a Plot, a combination of incidents, in it. And again: the most powerful elements of attraction in Tragedy, the Peripeties and Discoveries, are parts of the Plot. A further proof is in the fact that beginners succeed earlier with the Diction and Characters than with the construction of a story; and the same may be said of nearly all the early dramatists. We maintain, therefore, that the first essential, the life and soul, so to speak, of Tragedy is the Plot; and that the Characters come second — compare the parallel in painting, where the most beautiful colours laid on without order will not give one the same pleasure as a simple black-and-white sketch of a portrait. We maintain that Tragedy is primarily an imitation of action, and that it is mainly for the sake of the action that it imitates the personal agents. Third comes the element of Thought, i.e. the power of saying whatever can be said, or what is appropriate to the occasion. This is what, in the speeches in Tragedy, falls under the arts of Politics and Rhetoric; for the older poets make their personages discourse like statesmen, and the moderns like rhetoricians. One must not confuse it with Character. Character in a play is that which reveals the moral purpose of the agents, i.e. the sort of thing they seek or avoid, where that is not obvious — hence there is no room for Character in a speech on a purely indifferent subject. Thought, on the other hand, is shown in all they say when proving or disproving some particular point, or enunciating some universal proposition. Fourth among the literary elements is the Diction of the personages, i.e., as before explained, the expression of their thoughts in words, which is practically the same thing with verse as with prose. As for the two remaining parts, the Melody is the greatest of the pleasurable accessories of Tragedy. The Spectacle, though an attraction, is the least artistic of all the parts, and has least to do with the art of poetry. The tragic effect is quite possible without a public performance and actors; and besides, the getting-up of the Spectacle is more a matter for the costumier than the poet.

7

Having thus distinguished the parts, let us now consider the proper construction of the Fable or Plot, as that is at once the first and the most important thing in Tragedy. We have laid it down that a tragedy is an imitation of an action that is complete in itself, as a whole of some magnitude; for a whole may be of no magnitude to speak of. Now a whole is that which has beginning, middle, and end. A beginning is that which is not itself necessarily after anything else, and which has naturally something else after it; an end is that which is naturally after something itself, either as its necessary or usual consequent, and with nothing else after it; and a middle, that which is by nature after one thing and has also another after it. A well-constructed Plot, therefore, cannot either begin or end at any point one likes; beginning and end in it must be of the forms just described. Again: to be beautiful, a living creature, and every whole made up of parts, must not only present a certain order in its arrangement of parts, but also be of a certain definite magnitude. Beauty is a matter of size and order, and therefore impossible either (1) in a very minute creature, since our perception becomes indistinct as it approaches instantaneity; or (2) in a creature of vast size — one, say, 1,000 miles long — as in that case, instead of the object being seen all at once, the unity and wholeness of it is lost to the beholder. Just in the same way, then, as a beautiful whole made up of parts, or a beautiful living creature, must be of some size, but a size to be taken in by

the eye, so a story or Plot must be of some length, but of a length to be taken in by the memory. As for the limit of its length, so far as that is relative to public performances and spectators, it does not fall within the theory of poetry. If they had to perform a hundred tragedies, they would be timed by water-clocks, as they are said to have been at one period. The limit, however, set by the actual nature of the thing is this: the longer the story, consistently with its being comprehensible as a whole, the finer it is by reason of its magnitude. As a rough general formula, "a length which allows of the hero passing by a series of probable or necessary stages from misfortune to happiness, or from happiness to misfortune," may suffice as a limit for the magnitude of the story.

8

The Unity of a Plot does not consist, as some suppose, in its having one man as its subject. An infinity of things befall that one man, some of which it is impossible to reduce to unity; and in like manner there are many actions of one man which cannot be made to form one action. One sees, therefore, the mistake of all the poets who have written a *Heracleid*, a *Theseid*, or similar poems; they suppose that, because Heracles was one man, the story also of Heracles must be one story. Homer, however, evidently understood this point quite well, whether by art or instinct, just in the same way as he excels the rest in every other respect. In writing an *Odyssey*, he did not make the poem cover all that ever befell his hero — it befell him, for instance, to get wounded on Parnassus and also to feign madness at the time of the call to arms, but the two incidents had no necessary or probable connexion with one another — instead of doing that, he took as the subject of the *Odyssey*, as also of the *Iliad*, an action with a Unity of the kind we are describing. The truth is that, just as in the other imitative arts one imitation is always of one thing, so in poetry the story, as an imitation of action, must represent one action, a complete whole, with its several incidents so closely connected that the transposal or withdrawal of any one of them will disjoin and dislocate the whole. For that which makes no perceptible difference by its presence or absence is no real part of the whole.

9

From what we have said it will be seen that the poet's function is to describe, not the thing that has happened, but a kind of thing that might happen, i.e. what is possible as being probable or necessary. The distinction between historian and poet is not in the one writing prose and the other verse — you might put the work of Herodotus into verse, and it would still be a species of history; it consists really in this, that the one describes the thing that has been, and the other a kind of thing that might be. Hence poetry is something more philosophic and of graver import than history, since its statements are of the nature rather of universals, whereas those of history are singulars. By a universal statement I mean one as to what such or such a kind of man will probably or necessarily say or do — which is the aim of poetry, though it affixes proper names to the characters; by a singular statement, one as to what, say, Alcibiades did or had done to him. In Comedy this has become clear by this time; it is only when their plot is already made up of probable incidents that they give it a basis of proper names, choosing for the purpose any names that may occur to them, instead of writing like the old iambic poets about particular persons. In Tragedy, however, they still adhere to the historic names; and for this reason: what convinces is the possible; now whereas we are not yet sure as to the possibility of that which has not happened, that which has happened is manifestly possible, else it would not have come to pass. . . .

It is evident from the above that the poet must be more the poet of his stories or Plots than of his verses, inasmuch as he is a poet by virtue of the imitative element in his work, and it is actions that he imitates. And if he should come to take a subject from actual history, he is none the less a poet for that; since some historic occurrences may very well be in the probable and possible order of things; and it is in that aspect of them that he is their poet.

Of simple Plots and actions the episodic are the worst. I call a Plot episodic when there is neither probability nor necessity in the sequence of its episodes. Actions of this sort bad poets construct through their own fault, and good ones on account of the players. His work being for public performance, a good poet often stretches out a Plot beyond its capabilities, and is thus obliged to twist the sequence of the incident.

Tragedy, however, is an imitation not only of a complete action, but also of incidents arousing pity and fear. Such incidents have the very greatest effect on the mind when they occur unexpectedly and at the same time in consequence of one another; there is more of the marvellous in them then than if they happened of themselves or by mere chance. Even matters of chance seem most marvellous if there is an appearance of design as it were in them; as for instance the statue of Mitys at Argos killed the author of Mitys' death by falling down on him when a looker-on at a public spectacle; for incidents like that we think to be not without a meaning. A Plot, therefore, of this sort is necessarily finer than others.

10

Plots are either simple or complex, since the actions they represent are naturally of this twofold description. The action, proceeding in the way defined, as one continuous whole, I call simple, when the change in the hero's fortunes takes place without Peripety or Discovery; and complex, when it involves one or the other, or both. These should each of them arise out of the structure of the Plot itself, so as to be the consequence, necessary or probable, of the antecedents. There is a great difference between a thing happening *propter hoc* and *post hoc*.

11

A Peripety is the change of the kind described from one state of things within the play to its opposite, and that too in the way we are saying, in the probable or necessary sequence of events; as it is for instance in *Oedipus*: here the opposite state of things is produced by the Messenger, who, coming to gladden Oedipus and to remove his fears as to his mother, reveals the secret of his birth. And in *Lynceus*: just as he is being led off for execution, with Danaus at his side to put him to death, the incidents preceding this bring it about that he is saved and Danaus put to death. A Discovery is, as the very word implies, a change from ignorance to knowledge, and thus to either love or hate, in the personages marked for good or evil fortune. The finest form of Discovery is one attended by Peripeties, like that which goes with the Discovery in *Oedipus*. There are no doubt other forms of it; what we have said may happen in a way in reference to inanimate things, even things of a very casual kind; and it is also possible to discover whether some one has done or not done something. But the form most directly connected with the Plot and the action of the piece is the first-mentioned. This, with a Peripety, will arouse either pity or fear — actions of that nature being what Tragedy is assumed to represent; and it will also serve to bring about the happy or unhappy ending. The Discovery, then, being of persons, it may be that of one party only to the other, the latter being already known; or both the parties may have to discover themselves. Iphigenia, for instance, was discovered to Orestes by sending the letter; and another Discovery was required to reveal him to Iphigenia.

Two parts of the Plot, then, Peripety and Discovery, are on matters of this sort. A third part is Suffering; which we may define as an action of a destructive or painful nature, such as murders on the stage, tortures, woundings, and the like. The other two have been already explained.

12

The parts of Tragedy to be treated as formative elements in the whole were mentioned in a previous Chapter. From the point of view, however, of its quantity, i.e. the separate sections into which it is divided, a tragedy has the following parts: Prologue, Episode, Exode, and a choral portion, distinguished into Parode and Stasimon; these two are common to all tragedies, whereas songs from the stage and *Commoe* are only found in some. The Prologue is all that precedes the Parode of the chorus; an Episode all that comes in between two whole choral songs; the Exode all that follows after the last choral song. In the choral portion the Parode is the whole first statement of the chorus; a Stasimon, a song of the chorus without anapaests or trochees; a *Commos*, a lamentation sung by chorus and actor in concert. The parts of Tragedy to be used as formative elements in the whole we have already mentioned; the above are its parts from the point of view of its quantity, or the separate sections into which it is divided.

13

The next points after what we have said above will be these: (1) What is the poet to aim at, and what is he to avoid, in constructing his Plots? and (2) What are the conditions on which the tragic effect depends?

We assume that, for the finest form of Tragedy, the Plot must be not simple but complex; and further, that it must imitate actions arousing fear and pity, since that is the distinctive function of this kind of imitation. It follows, therefore, that there are three forms of Plot to be avoided. (1) A good man must not be seen passing from happiness to misery, or (2) a bad man from misery to happiness. The first situation is not fear-inspiring or piteous, but simply odious to us. The second is the most untragic that can be; it has no one of the requisites of Tragedy; it does not appeal either to the human feeling in us, or to our pity, or to our fears. Nor, on the other hand, should (3) an extremely bad man be seen falling from happiness into misery. Such a story may arouse the human feeling in us, but it will not move us to either pity or fear; pity is occasioned by undeserved misfortune, and fear by that of one like ourselves; so that there will be nothing either piteous or fear-inspiring in the situation. There remains, then, the intermediate kind of personage, a man not pre-eminently virtuous and just, whose misfortune, however, is brought upon him not by vice and depravity but by some error of judgement, of the number of those in the enjoyment of great reputation and prosperity; e.g. Oedipus, Thy-estes, and the men of note of similar families. The perfect Plot, accordingly, must have a single, and not (as some tell us) a double issue; the change in the hero's fortunes must be not from misery to happiness, but on the contrary from happiness to misery; and the cause of it must lie not in any depravity, but in some great error on his part; the man himself being either such as we have de-scribed, or better, not worse, than that. Fact also confirms our theory. Though the poets began by accepting any tragic story that came to hand, in these days the finest tragedies are always on the story of some few houses, on that of Alcmeon, Oedipus, Orestes, Meleager, Thyestes, Telephus, or any others that may have been involved, as either agents or sufferers, in some deed of horror. The theoretically best tragedy, then, has a Plot of this description. The critics, therefore, are wrong who blame Euripides for taking this line in his tragedies, and giving many of them an unhappy ending. It is, as we have said, the right line to take. The best proof is this: on the stage, and in the public performances, such plays, properly worked out, are seen to be the most truly tragic; and Euripides, even if his execution be faulty in every other point, is seen to be nevertheless the most tragic certainly of the dramatists. After this comes the construction of Plot which some rank first, one with a double story (like the *Odyssey*) and an opposite issue for the good and the bad per-sonages. It is ranked as first only through the weakness of the audiences; the poets merely fol-low their public, writing as its wishes dictate. But the pleasure here is not that of Tragedy. It belongs rather to Comedy, where the bitterest enemies in the piece (e.g. Orestes and Aegisthus) walk off good friends at the end, with no slaying of any one by any one.

14

The tragic fear and pity may be aroused by the Spectacle; but they may also be aroused by the very structure and incidents of the play — which is the better way and shows the better poet. The Plot in fact should be so framed that, even without seeing the things take place, he who simply hears

the account of them shall be filled with horror and pity at the incidents; which is just the effect that the mere recital of the story in *Oedipus* would have on one. To produce this same effect by means of the Spectacle is less artistic, and requires extraneous aid. Those, however, who make use of the Spectacle to put before us that which is merely monstrous and not productive of fear, are wholly out of touch with Tragedy; not every kind of pleasure should be required of a tragedy, but only its own proper pleasure.

The tragic pleasure is that of pity and fear, and the poet has to produce it by a work of imitation; it is clear, therefore, that the causes should be included in the incidents of his story. Let us see, then, what kinds of incident strike one as horri-ble, or rather as piteous. In a deed of this descrip-tion the parties must necessarily be either friends, or enemies, or indifferent to one another. Now when enemy does it on enemy, there is nothing to move us to pity either in his doing or in his medi-tating the deed, except so far as the actual pain of the sufferer is concerned; and the same is true when the parties are indifferent to one another. Whenever the tragic deed, however, is done within the family — when murder or the like is done or meditated by brother on brother, by son on father, by mother on son, or son on mother — these are the situations the poet should seek after. The traditional stories, accordingly, must be kept as they are, e.g. the murder of Clytaemnestra by Orestes and of Eriphyle by Alcmeon. At the same time even with these there is something left to the poet himself; it is for him to devise the right way of treating them. Let us explain more clearly what we mean by "the right way." The deed of horror may be done by the doer knowingly and con-sciously, as in the old poets, and in Medea's mur-der of her children in Euripides. Or he may do it, but in ignorance of his relationship, and discover that afterwards, as does the Oedipus in Sopho-cles. Here the deed is outside the play; but it may be within it, like the act of the Alcmeon in As-tydamas, or that of the Telegonus in *Ulysses Wounded*. A third possibility is for one meditat-ing some deadly injury to another, in ignorance of his relationship, to make the discovery in time to draw back. These exhaust the possibilities, since the deed must necessarily be either done or not done, and either knowingly or unknowingly.

The worst situation is when the personage is with full knowledge on the point of doing the deed, and leaves it undone. It is odious and also (through the absence of suffering) untragic; hence it is that no one is made to act thus except in some few instances, e.g. Haemon and Creon in *Antigone*. Next after this comes the actual perpetration of the deed meditated. A better situation than that, however, is for the deed to be done in ignorance, and the relationship discovered afterwards, since there is nothing odious in it, and the Discovery will serve to astound us. But the best of all is the last; what we have in *Cresphontes*, for example, where Merope, on the point of slaying her son, recognizes him in time; in *Iphigenia*, where sister and brother are in a like position; and in *Helle*, where the son recognizes his mother, when on the point of giving her up to her enemy.

This will explain why our tragedies are restricted (as we said just now) to such a small number of families. It was accident rather than art that led the poets in quest of subjects to embody this kind of incident in their Plots. They are still obliged, accordingly, to have recourse to the families in which such horrors have occurred.

On the construction of the Plot and the kind of Plot required for Tragedy, enough has now been said. . . .

26

The question may be raised whether the epic or the tragic is the higher form of imitation. It may be argued that, if the less vulgar is the higher, and the less vulgar is always that which addresses the better public, an art addressing any and every one is of a very vulgar order. It is a belief that their public cannot see the meaning, unless they add something themselves, that causes the perpetual movements of the performers — bad flute-players, for instance, rolling about, if quoit-throwing is to be represented, and pulling at the conductor, if Scylla is the subject of the piece. Tragedy, then, is

said to be an art of this order — to be in fact just what the later actors were in the eyes of their predecessors; for Mynniscus used to call Callippides "the ape," because he thought he so overacted his parts; and a similar view was taken of Pindarus also. All Tragedy, however, is said to stand to the Epic as the newer to the older school of actors. The one, accordingly, is said to address a cultivated audience, which does not need the accompaniment of gesture; the other, an uncultivated one. If, therefore, Tragedy is a vulgar art, it must clearly be lower than the Epic.

The answer to this is twofold. In the first place, one may urge (1) that the censure does not touch the art of the dramatic poet, but only that of his interpreter; for it is quite possible to overdo the gesturing even in an epic recital, as did Sosistratus, and in a singing contest, as did Mnasitheus of Opus. (2) That one should not condemn all movement, unless one means to condemn even the dance, but only that of ignoble people — which is the point of the criticism passed on Callippides and in the present day on others, that their women are not like gentlewomen. (3) That Tragedy may produce its effect even without movement or action in just the same way as Epic poetry; for from the mere reading of a play its quality may be seen. So that, if it be superior in all other respects, this element of inferiority is no necessary part of it.

In the second place, one must remember (1) that Tragedy has everything that the Epic has (even the epic metre being admissible), together with a not inconsiderable addition in the shape of the Music (a very real factor in the pleasure of the drama) and the Spectacle. (2) That its reality of presentation is felt in the play as read, as well as in the play as acted. (3) That the tragic imitation requires less space for the attainment of its end; which is a great advantage, since the more concentrated effect is more pleasurable than one with a large admixture of time to dilute it — consider the *Oedipus* of Sophocles, for instance, and the effect of expanding it into the number of lines of the *Iliad*. (4) That there is less unity in the imitation of the epic poets, as is proved by the fact that any one work of theirs supplies matter for several tragedies; the result being that, if they take what is really a single story, it seems curt when briefly told, and thin and waterish when on the scale of length usual with their verse. In saying that there is less unity in an epic, I mean an epic made up of a plurality of actions, in the same way as the *Iliad* and *Odyssey* have many such parts, each one of them in itself of some magnitude; yet the structure of the two Homeric poems is as perfect as can be, and the action in them is as nearly as possible one action. If, then, Tragedy is superior in these respects, and also, besides these, in its poetic effect (since the two forms of poetry should give us, not any or every pleasure, but the very special kind we have mentioned), it is clear that, as attaining the poetic effect better than the Epic, it will be the higher form of art.

So much for Tragedy and Epic poetry — for these two arts in general and their species; the number and nature of their constituent parts; the causes of success and failure in them; the Objections of the critics, and the Solutions in answer to them.

The Myth of Total Cinema

André Bazin

Paradoxically enough, the impression left on
the reader by Georges Sadoul's admirable book
on the origins of the cinema is of a reversal, in
spite of the author's Marxist views, of the relations between an economic and technical evolution and the imagination of those carrying on the
search. The way things happened seems to call for
a reversal of the historical order of causality,
which goes from the economic infrastructure to
the ideological superstructure, and for us to consider the basic technical discoveries as fortunate
accidents but essentially second in importance to
the preconceived ideas of the inventors. The cinema is an idealistic phenomenon. The concept
men had of it existed so to speak fully armed in
their minds, as if in some platonic heaven, and
what strikes us most of all is the obstinate resistance of matter to ideas rather than of any help
offered by techniques to the imagination of the
researchers.

Furthermore, the cinema owes virtually nothing to the scientific spirit. Its begetters are in no
sense savants, except for Marey, but it is significant that he was only interested in analyzing
movement and not in reconstructing it. Even Edison is basically only a do-it-yourself man of genius, a giant of the *concours Lépine*. Niepce,
Muybridge, Leroy, Joly, Demeny, even Louis Lumière himself, are all monomaniacs, men driven
by an impulse, do-it-yourself men or at best inge-

nious industrialists. As for the wonderful, the
sublime E. Reynaud, who can deny that his animated drawings are the result of an unremitting
pursuit of an *idée fixe*? Any account of the cinema
that was drawn merely from the technical inventions that made it possible would be a poor one
indeed. On the contrary, an approximate and
complicated visualization of an idea invariably
precedes the industrial discovery which alone can
open the way to its practical use. Thus if it is
evident to us today that the cinema even at its
most elementary stage needed a transparent, flexible, and resistant base and a dry sensitive emulsion capable of receiving an image instantly —
everything else being a matter of setting in order a
mechanism far less complicated than an eighteenth-century clock — it is clear that all the definitive stages of the invention of the cinema had
been reached before the requisite conditions had
been fulfilled. In 1877 and 1880, Muybridge,
thanks to the imaginative generosity of a horse-
lover, managed to construct a large complex device which enabled him to make from the image
of a galloping horse the first series of cine-
matographic pictures. However to get this result
he had to be satisfied with wet collodion on a
glass plate, that is to say, with just one of the three
necessary elements — namely instantaneity, dry
emulsion, flexible base. After the discovery of
gelatino-bromide of silver but before the appear-

ance on the market of the first celluloid reels, Marey had made a genuine camera which used glass plates. Even after the appearance of celluloid strips Lumière tried to use paper film.

Once more let us consider here only the final and complete form of the photographic cinema. The synthesis of simple movements studied scientifically by Plateau had no need to wait upon the industrial and economic developments of the nineteenth century. As Sadoul correctly points out, nothing had stood in the way, from antiquity, of the manufacture of a phenakistoscope or a zootrope. It is true that here the labors of that genuine savant Plateau were at the origin of the many inventions that made the popular use of his discovery possible. But while, with the photographic cinema, we have cause for some astonishment that the discovery somehow precedes the technical conditions necessary to its existence, we must here explain, on the other hand, how it was that the invention took so long to emerge, since all the prerequisites had been assembled and the persistence of the image on the retina had been known for a long time. It might be of some use to point out that although the two were not necessarily connected scientifically, the efforts of Plateau are pretty well contemporary with those of Nicéphore Niepce, as if the attention of researchers had waited to concern itself with synthesizing movement until chemistry quite independently of optics had become concerned, on its part, with the automatic fixing of the image.

I emphasize the fact that this historical coincidence can apparently in no way be explained on grounds of scientific, economic, or industrial evolution. The photographic cinema could just as well have grafted itself onto a phenakistoscope foreseen as long ago as the sixteenth century. The delay in the invention of the latter is as disturbing a phenomenon as the existence of the precursors of the former.

But if we examine their work more closely, the direction of their research is manifest in the instruments themselves, and, even more undeniably, in their writings and commentaries we see

that these precursors were indeed more like prophets. Hurrying past the various stopping places, the very first of which materially speaking should have halted them, it was at the very height and summit that most of them were aiming. In their imaginations they saw the cinema as a total and complete representation of reality; they saw in a trice the reconstruction of a perfect illusion of the outside world in sound, color, and relief.

As for the latter, the film historian P. Potoniée has even felt justified in maintaining that it was not the discovery of photography but of stereoscopy, which came onto the market just slightly before the first attempts at animated photography in 1851, that opened the eyes of the researchers. Seeing people immobile in space, the photographers realized that what they needed was movement if their photographs were to become a picture of life and a faithful copy of nature. In any case, there was not a single inventor who did not try to combine sound and relief with animation of the image—whether it be Edison with his kinetoscope made to be attached to a phonograph, or Demenay and his talking portraits, or even Nadar who shortly before producing the first photographic interview, on Chevreul, had written, "My dream is to see the photograph register the bodily movements and the facial expressions of a speaker while the phonograph is recording his speech" (February, 1887). If color had not yet appeared it was because the first experiments with the three-color process were slower in coming. But E. Reynaud had been painting his little figurines for some time and the first films of Méliès are colored by stencilling. There are numberless writings, all of them more or less wildly enthusiastic, in which inventors conjure up nothing less than a total cinema that is to provide that complete illusion of life which is still a long way away. Many are familiar with that passage from L'Éve Future in which Villiers de l'Isle-Adam, two years before Edison had begun his researches on animated photography, puts into the inventor's mouth the following description of a fantastic achievement: ". . . the vision, its transparent flesh miraculously photographed in color and wearing a spangled costume, danced a kind of popular Mexican dance. Her movements had the flow of life itself, thanks to the process of successive photography which can retain six minutes of movement on microscopic glass, which is subsequently reflected by means of a powerful lampascope. Suddenly was heard a flat and unnatural voice, dull-sounding and harsh. The dancer was singing the *alza* and the *olé* that went with her *fandango*."

The guiding myth, then, inspiring the invention of cinema, is the accomplishment of that which dominated in a more or less vague fashion all the techniques of the mechanical reproduction of reality in the nineteenth century, from photography to the phonograph, namely an integral realism, a recreation of the world in its own image, an image unburdened by the freedom of interpretation of the artist or the irreversibility of time. If cinema in its cradle lacked all the attributes of the cinema to come, it was with reluctance and because its fairy guardians were unable to provide them however much they would have liked to.

If the origins of an art reveal something of its nature, then one may legitimately consider the silent and the sound film as stages of a technical development that little by little made a reality out of the original "myth." It is understandable from this point of view that it would be absurd to take the silent film as a state of primal perfection which has gradually been forsaken by the realism of sound and color. The primacy of the image is both historically and technically accidental. The nostalgia that some still feel for the silent screen does not go far enough back into the childhood of the seventh art. The real primitives of the cinema, existing only in the imaginations of a few men of the nineteenth century, are in complete imitation of nature. Every new development added to the cinema must, paradoxically, take it nearer and nearer to its origins. In short, cinema has not yet been invented!

It would be a reversal then of the concrete order of causality, at least psychologically, to place the scientific discoveries or the industrial techniques that have loomed so large in its development at the source of the cinema's invention. Those who had the least confidence in the future of the cinema were precisely the two industrialists Edison and Lumière. Edison was satisfied with just his kinetoscope and if Lumière judiciously refused to sell his patent to Méliès it was undoubtedly because he hoped to make a large profit out of it for himself, but only as a plaything of which the public would soon tire. As for the real savants such as Marey, they were only of indirect assistance to the cinema. They had a specific purpose in mind and were satisfied when they had accomplished it. The fanatics, the madmen, the disinterested pioneers, capable, as was Berard Palissy, of burning their furniture for a few seconds of shaky images, are neither industrialists nor savants, just men obsessed by their own imaginings. The cinema was born from the converging of these various obsessions, that is to say, out of a myth, the myth of total cinema. This likewise adequately explains the delay of Plateau in applying the optical principle of the persistence of the image on the retina, as also the continuous progress of the syntheses of movement as compared with the state of photographic techniques. The fact is that each alike was dominated by the imagination of the century. Undoubtedly there are other examples in the history of techniques and inventions of the convergence of research, but one must distinguish between those which come as a result precisely of scientific evolution and industrial or military requirements and those which quite clearly precede them. Thus, the myth of Icarus had to wait on the internal combustion engine before descending from the platonic heavens. But it had dwelt in the soul of everyman since he first thought about birds. To some extent, one could say the same thing about the myth of cinema, but its forerunners prior to the nineteenth century have only a remote connection with the myth which we share today and which has prompted the appearance of the mechanical arts that characterize today's world.

SUGGESTED ADDITIONAL READINGS

Jonas Barish, *The Antitheatrical Prejudice* (Berkeley: University of California Press, 1981).

H. Gene Blocker, *Philosophy of Art* (New York: Charles Scribner's Sons, 1979). See especially chapter 2, "Representation."

Noel Carroll, *Philosophical Problems of Classical Film Theory* (Princeton: Princeton University Press, 1988).

R. G. Collingwood, *The Principles of Art* (Oxford: Oxford University Press, 1958). See especially chapter 3, "Art and Representation."

William Gass, "Representation and the War for Reality," in *Habituations of the Word* (New York: Simon & Schuster, 1986).

E. H. Gombrich, "Meditations on a Hobby Horse." This article has been reprinted in many anthologies, including *Aesthetics Today*, ed. Philipson and Gudel (New York: Meridian Books, 1980).

Nelson Goodman, *The Languages of Art* (Indianapolis: Bobbs-Merrill, 1968).

Peter Kivy, *Sound and Semblance: Reflections on Musical Representation* (Princeton: Princeton University Press, 1984).

Linda Nochlin, *Realism* (Baltimore: Penguin Books, 1971).

R. A. Sharpe, *Contemporary Aesthetics: A Philosophical Analysis* (New York: St. Martin's Press, 1983). See especially chapter 3, pp. 49–92.

Susan Sontag, *On Photography* (New York: Dell, 1977).

Kendall Walton, *Mimesis as Make-Believe: On the Foundations of the Representational Arts* (Cambridge, Mass.: Harvard University Press, 1990).

Richard Wollheim, *Art and Its Objects*, 2d ed. (Cambridge: Cambridge University Press, 1980).

NOTES

1. Quoted in Ernest Rhys, ed., *The Prelude to Poetry: The English Poets in Defense and Praise of their own Art* (New York: Dutton, 1970), p. 16.

2. I am simplifying a complex interpretative question. Some philosophers may wish to argue that the ban on the arts applies strictly only to most forms of poetry. But clearly Socrates' arguments are equally telling against all forms of imitative art. For a different opinion, see chapter 3 of R. G. Collingwood's *Principles of Art* (Oxford: Oxford University Press, 1958).

3. A similar concern about the hypnotizing effect of theater led the twentieth-century German playwright Bertold Brecht to make special efforts to call attention to the illusionism of his plays. Jonas Barish describes them thus: "Through devices of distancing like sudden songs and jingles, the use of narrators or placards or didactic captions flashed on screens . . . he calls our attention to the element of artifice in his fables. We are gazing not at a slice of life but at an artfully composed fiction, designed to teach us momentous truths about our lives." *The Antitheatrical Prejudice* (Berkeley: University of California Press, 1981), pp. 455ff.

4. Arthur C. Danto, *The Transfiguration of the Commonplace* (Cambridge, Mass.: Harvard University Press, 1981), p. 11.

5. Daniel Albright, *Representation and the Imagination: Beckett, Kafka, Nabokov and Schönberg* (Chicago: University of Chicago Press, 1981), p. 11.

6. Homer, *Odyssey*, trans. Robert S. Fitzgerald (New York: Doubleday, 1963), Book 9, lines 375–85.

7. William Gass, "Representation and the War for Reality," in *Habitations of the Word* (New York: Simon & Schuster, 1986), p. 74.

8. As Peter Kivy points out, although the traditional translation of "mimesis" is "imitation,"

some recent translations have offered the more general term "representation." *Sound and Semblance: Reflections on Musical Representation* (Princeton: Princeton University Press, 1984), p. 17. Such a translation avoids the puzzle about how literature could be mimetic.

9. It is worth considering whether we might save the imitation theory as a general explanation of representation by positing that we form mental images when we experience artworks and that these images are the entities which really imitate the appearances of things. This would allow us to give a unified account of both linguistic and visual artworks: both cause the spectator to form a mental image, and that image is an imitation of things. One problem with this proposal is that it gives up on the idea that the artwork itself, for example a physical sculpture, resembles what it represents.

10. Gass, "Representation," p. 73.

11. Linda Nochlin, *Realism* (Baltimore: Penguin Books, 1971), p. 39.

12. Henry Allen, "Just a Movie?" *Washington Post*, rpt. in *Boulder Daily Camera*, 7 Feb. 1987.

13. Alan H. Sommerstein, trans., Aristophanes' *Lysistrata, The Acharnians, The Clouds* (New York: Penguin Books, 1973), p. 108.

14. Umberto Eco, *Art and Beauty in the Middle Ages* (New Haven: Yale University Press, 1986), p. 106. Ironically, the followers of Plato in Hellenistic times turned his theory in favor of art: "In Classical aesthetics, Plato's theory of ideas, had undergone a change. It was used initially for denigrating art, but became instead an explanation of the artists' interior phantasm. Hellenistic thought achieved a revaluation of artistic endeavour, and came to accept the view that art involved an idea or image of beauty not found in nature" (p. 108).

15. Quoted in Eco, *Art and Beauty*, p. 105.

16. Quoted in Eco, *Art and Beauty*, p. 106.

17. Quoted in Eco, *Art and Beauty*, p. 101.

18. See the books by Goodman, Wollheim, Sharpe, Walton, Kivy, and Carroll in the Suggested Additional Readings for this chapter.

19. For analyses of the positions sketched in this section, see the books by Carroll and Sharpe in the Suggested Additional Readings.

20. As Nelson Goodman has pointed out (*The Languages of Art* [Indianapolis: Bobbs-Merrill, 1968], chapter 4) resemblance is a *symmetric* relation; X resembles Y if and only if Y resembles X. By contrast, representation is not symmetric but one-way: it does not follow that if X represents Y, Y represents X—indeed, it is almost never the case that the objects represented themselves represent the representation.

21. E. H. Gombrich, "Meditations on a Hobby Horse," in *Aesthetics Today*, ed. Philipson and Gudel (New York: Meridian Books, 1980), p. 181.

22. Gombrich, "Meditations," p. 181.

23. Linda Nochlin, "The Realist Criminal and the Abstract Law," in Richard Hertz, ed., *Theories of Contemporary Art* (Englewood Cliffs, N.J.: Prentice Hall, 1985), p. 25 (Originally published in *Art in America*, Sept. 1973.)

24. Kivy, *Sound and Semblance*, p. 9.

25. R. A. Sharpe, *Contemporary Aesthetics: A Philosophical Analysis* (New York: St. Martin's Press, 1983), p. 58.

26. Sometimes a causal theory is proposed: What makes a picture (or other visual object) a representation of Y is that Y was the proximate object that caused the artist to draw a certain pattern of marks or that caused the camera to record certain light patterns on a film. The difficulties with this causal theory are similar to those with the resemblance theory. Is the causal link *sufficient* to determine representation? Plainly not, for the model is *not* who is represented in Mantegna's *Dead Christ* or Caravaggio's *Saint John the Baptist*. Is the causal link *necessary* for representation? How could it be? Consider the same two paintings: they

represent individuals who were *not* causal elements in the production of the paintings. Again, being the causal object cannot be necessary, because of all the representations of nonexistent, fictional, or mythological entities or of entities that have no visual appearance.

27. Roger Fry, "An Essay in Aesthetics," in *Modern Art and Modernism: A Critical Anthology*, ed. Francis Frascina and Charles Harrison (New York: Harper & Row, 1982), p. 79.

28. These concerns were first and most forcefully presented in the context of literary interpretation. See Wimsatt and Beardsley, "The Intentional Fallacy," which is reprinted in many anthologies, including Joseph Margolis, ed., *Philosophy Looks at the Arts*, 3d ed. (Philadelphia: Temple University Press, 1987).

29. Some have also objected that the intention theory is logically circular, since it presupposes representation in its definition ("the artist intends X to *represent* Y"). This is not a real problem; to say that X represents Y is to say that the shapes and colors of X stand for and characterize Y. The point of the intention theory, like that of the other theories, is not to define what representation *is*, but rather to give an explanation of what determines just what a picture represents. This the intention theory does in terms of what the artist means the shapes and colors to represent.

30. In *The Transfiguration of the Commonplace* (Cambridge, Mass.: Harvard University Press, 1981), Arthur Danto presents one of the most significant recent theories of art. In the last chapter, he tries to differentiate art, which for Danto has a certain special "aboutness," from what he calls "mere representations" in terms of the artwork's dependence on metaphor and style. Nowhere, unfortunately, does Danto succeed in giving a summary account of what the difference is between art and other representations.

31. See John Andrew Fisher, "The Very Idea of Perfect Realism," *The Philosophical Forum* 22, no. 1 (Fall 1990): 49–64.

32. Collingwood, *Principles of Art*, p. 304.

33. W. Charlton, *Aesthetics* (London: Hutchinson & Co., 1970), p. 74.

34. Joseph Kerman, *Contemplating Music: Challenges to Musicology* (Cambridge, Mass.: Harvard University Press, 1985), p. 65.

35. Danto, "Content and Causation," chapter 3 of *Transfiguration of the Commonplace*.

36. The most influential proponent of this concept was the nineteenth-century music critic Eduard Hanslick. See Chapter 10.

37. Peter Kivy has shown, in *Sound and Semblance*, that music is often representational. But even he does not claim that it is always representational. He says, "Nor, I think, would anyone wish to argue today that music is primarily a representational or pictorial art" (p. 19).

38. Proponents of absolute music deny this, as well as any other representation. See Hanslick, *On the Beautiful in Music*, in the Readings for Chapter 10.

39. Aristotle, *Politics*, trans. Benjamin Jowett, in *The Basic Works of Aristotle*, ed. Richard McKeon (New York: Random House, 1941), p. 1311.

40. Thomas Twining, trans., *Aristotle's Treatise on Poetry* (London 1789), quoted in Kivy, *Sound and Semblance*, p. 4.

41. "Montage means joining together shots of situations that occur at different times and places." Rudolf Arnheim, *Film as Art* (Berkeley: University of California Press, 1957), p. 87.

42. Noel Carroll, *Philosophical Problems of Classical Film Theory* (Princeton: Princeton University Press, 1988), p. 29.

43. Siegfried Kracauer, *Theory of Film*, excerpted in Gerald Mast and Marshall Cohen, *Film Theory and Criticism* (New York: Oxford University Press, 1979), p. 19.

44. Letter by Louis Torres, *New York Times*, 13 Aug. 1989.

45. Kracauer, *Theory of Film*, pp. 19–20.

46. Also see Bazin's *What is Cinema?*, vol. 1, trans. Hugh Gray (Berkeley: University of California

Press, 1967). Bazin's position is thoroughly analyzed by Noel Carroll in chapter 2 of *Philosophical Problems of Classical Film Theory*.

47. Carroll, *Philosophical Problems*, p. 135.

48. Kenneth Dover, *The Greeks* (Austin: University of Texas Press, 1980), p. 97.

49. For example, the second book of the *Poetics* has been lost. Aristotle's *Politics*, Book VIII, chapter 7, contains the other important discussion of catharsis, there in relation to music.

50. Kendall Walton, *Mimesis as Make-Believe: On the Foundations of the Representational Arts* (Cambridge, Mass.: Harvard University Press, 1990), p. 69.

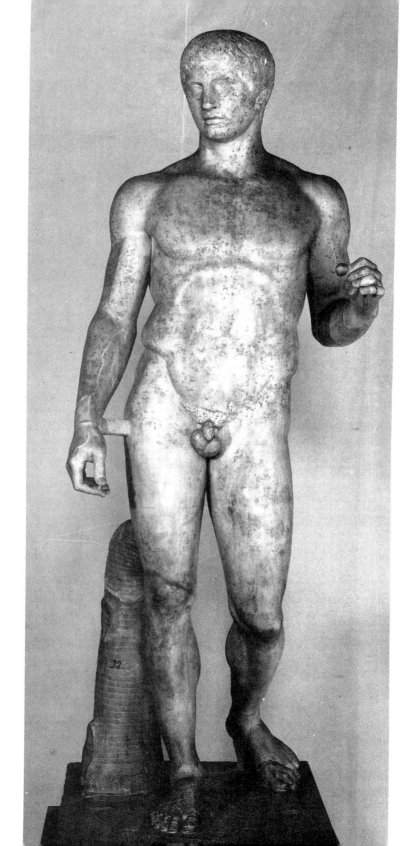

CHAPTER 10

The Varieties of Formalism

◄ *Doryphorus* (Roman copy after original, ca. 450–440 B.C.). The *Doryphorus* (Spear Bearer) was the most renowned statue of its time. Its harmonious proportions were taken to be the standard for ideal human beauty. This standard involved the relation of the parts of the body to each other so as to make a beautiful whole. Thus the Greeks saw form and rationality as central to sculpture.

No one has yet been able to demonstrate that the
representational as such either adds or takes away from
the merit of a picture or a statue.
— Clement Greenberg, *Art and Culture*

At a certain point we begin to be told that there is only one
thing, one thing alone, to be looked for in art.
— Leo Steinberg, *Other Criteria: Confrontations with Twentieth-Century Art*

It is necessary, therefore, for me to put up a preliminary
hypothesis of the existence of pure and impure works of
art. . . .
— Roger Fry, "Some Questions on Esthetics"

AUTONOMY AND ART FOR ART'S SAKE

What is art? How is it to be judged? Why is it valuable? The mimetic tradition answers
these questions by reference to the subject matter the artworks represent. According to this
theory, artworks are to be judged by the accuracy and propriety with which they represent
their external subject matter; thus, artworks are *subordinate* to truth and morality. But in the
nineteenth century, a directly opposing view gained wide acceptance among art theorists:
the idea that art is an *autonomous* realm, sufficient unto itself. This view is expressed in the
familiar slogan "art for art's sake," already common in the nineteenth century. The aesthetician Monroe Beardsley explains this slogan as "the recognition of a work of art as an object in
its own right, intelligible and valuable as such, with intrinsic properties independent of its
relation to other things and to its creator and perceiver."[1]

Autonomy for art is the freedom from having to conform to external rules or community
standards. And just as freedom craves to be absolute, autonomy for art tends toward *absolute*
autonomy; art is to be judged in its own terms, absolutely, and not by external standards of
any sort.

But if art is to be judged totally in its own terms, by values inherent in the artwork, what
are these? It is clear what they are *not*: not representational qualities, not moral values, not
the pleasure the audience derives from the work. As we saw in Chapter 4, Oscar Wilde, in his
famous preface from *The Picture of Dorian Gray* (1891), denies that art is to be judged by
standards of realism or morality: "Books are well written or badly written. That is all." And
he denies that art has any useful function: "The only excuse for making a useless thing is that
one admires it intensely. All art is quite useless" (p. 107). But how is one to judge whether a
book is well written, if not in terms of its traditional narrative and descriptive properties, or
that a painting is well painted, if not in terms of how well it depicts the likeness of things? And
which features of the "useless" artwork is one to admire intensely?

The idea that art is autonomous was also a logical development of one of the fundamental
ideas of eighteenth-century aesthetics. In *The Critique of Judgment* (1790), Immanuel Kant
asserts that aesthetic judgments — represented paradigmatically by judgments of beauty — are

logically independent of judgments of morality, utility, and truth. When William Gass claims, as we saw in Chapter 4, that "goodness knows nothing of beauty," he is just making the traditional Kantian claim that beauty is independent of utility and morality. Writing in 1912, Roger Fry, one of the pioneering formalists, echoes Kant's theory: "All art depends upon cutting off the practical responses to sensations of ordinary life, thereby setting free a pure and as it were disembodied functioning of the spirit."[2] This describes just the sort of impersonal response that Kant argues is the hallmark of an aesthetic response. Fry's theory of art (1909) as an "expression of the imaginative life" also emphasizes freedom, and therefore autonomy, since an imaginative life "is separated from actual life by the absence of responsive action. Now this responsive action implies in actual life moral responsibility. In art we have no such moral responsibility — it presents a life freed from the binding necessities of our actual existence."[3] Kant, too, emphasizes that aesthetic response and aesthetic pleasure are functions of the operation of the imagination, free from considerations that are external to the object being experienced, such as the utility or perfection of the object. For Kant, the pure aesthetic judgment is one which he calls "nonconceptual," by which he means that it is not made by reference to any concepts of what the object being judged ought to be like. This is the artwork's absolute freedom from having to correspond to anything external to itself.

There are two aspects to the idea that art is autonomous. One aspect is that art is free from external considerations, that is, free from being judged by its relation to things outside the artwork. The other aspect, the corollary of this freedom, is that artworks must have an internal subject matter that is sufficient unto itself. The idea that art is autonomous thus naturally leads to the concept of form, for the form of an artwork is the central feature it has that is independent of external considerations. Thus, the quest for autonomy naturally leads to formalist theories of art.

> The fundamental principle of aesthetics *before the modern era* was that art imitates life, and is therefore in the last analysis answerable to it: art must tell the truth about life, and contribute to making it better, or at least more bearable.
>
> — David Lodge, "Modernism, Anti-modernism and Postmodernism"[4]

FORM AND CONTENT

The term "form" is generally used to identify what individual members of a given class of objects have in common, as when we think of the form of an elm tree, a bicycle, or a triangle. But in the context of the discussion of art, "form" stands for the organization of an artwork, where each artwork has its own unique form. The unique form of each artwork, however, is made up of formal properties that more than one work can share. Consider some examples of shared formal properties: two lines of verse in two different poems can both be in iambic pentameter; many pieces of music have the same sonata form (exposition, development, and recapitulation); several pieces of sculpture can have circular forms. The formal properties of art must be universal properties (that is, they must be found in many works), but each work's overall form must be unique, just as each snowflake has a unique shape, even though all snowflakes share the property of having a six-sided symmetrical figure. In the case of a piece of pure instrumental music, its form is often identified with its rhythmic, tonal, and harmonic structures; in the case of architecture, form might be identified with the relations of the visual elements (the geometric relations, patterns, and proportions) of the designed building.

One way to understand form is to contrast it with content. We can think of form as the bottle and content as the wine that is poured into it. If these are independent of each other, then the same form could contain two different contents, and two works with different forms could contain the same content. For example, the story of Oedipus (the content) could be contained in very different forms: a tragedy, a ballet, a movie. If we claim that each of these works has the same content, we would be saying that the content is determined by what is represented; thus, many different works can represent the same thing. But content also must include what those works say *about* the represented subjects, and that makes it more difficult to maintain that content is independent of form. Do we want to claim that, for example, Shakespeare's play *Othello* and Verdi's opera *Otello*, or Shakespeare's play *Romeo and Juliet* and Prokofiev's ballet *Romeo and Juliet*, have the same content — that they say even roughly the same thing, only in very different forms? To maintain this, we would have to ignore the overwhelming differences between song, dance, and drama.

Clearly, the distinction between form and content is even more difficult to draw in nonrepresentational media, such as music or architecture; in both, it is often claimed that the form *is* the content. Yet even in literature it is difficult to make any clear distinction between form and content. Contrast a literary work with an ordinary letter. In a letter, the same content, that is, message, can be stated in different forms. In such cases, "content" is a concept like that of the shared "proposition" or "meaning" that is expressed by two different sentences. For example, "A kissed B" and "B was kissed by A" are two different sentences that have the same meaning or express the same proposition; they have the same content. Could we, in a similar way, view two different poems that have the same subject and that make the same point about that subject as having the same content but differing in form? It is difficult to think of any examples, because each artwork seems to say something different. This very fact seems significant. By contrast, we can easily imagine letters that have identical content even though they have different forms. Why, then, are there no two artworks whose content is identical even though their forms are different? Why do there seem to be as many "messages" as there are works of art? The explanation may be that each artwork has a unique form. But if this uniqueness of form accounts for the work's uniqueness of message, then form seems to generate content rather than to be separable from it.

The view that content can be separated from form is problematic for other reasons as well. Consider two: (*a*) The distinction between poetry and prose is surely a formal distinction, based on such features of poetry as rhythmic sound patterns and rhyming sounds. We cannot explain the very different qualities of poetry and prose, however, by reference to the differences between poets and prose writers or between their topics. Instead, the formal differences between poetry and prose seem to change the kind of message. An artist cannot do the same sort of thing in different art media; different art forms are not like different but intertranslatable languages. (*b*) Even within poetry it doesn't seem possible to separate form from content. The poet e. e. cummings experimented with syntax, sound, and punctuation to achieve a unique type of result that does not seem duplicatable by any other formal poetic strategy. Consider, for instance, the first stanza of his poem "anyone lived in a pretty how town":

> anyone lived in a pretty how town
> (with up so floating many bells down)
> spring summer autumn winter
> he sang his didn't he danced his did

However we interpret the meaning and impact of this poem, how can we even begin to separate it from the exact way it is expressed? The content of the line "he sang his didn't he danced his did" can no more be separated from its form — its word order and punctuation — than the content of a musical theme can be separated from the theme.[5]

Another way to understand form is to view it strictly as the organization of the "elements" of a work. Beardsley characterizes form in music and visual arts this way by distinguishing "(1) those statements that describe the local qualities of elements, and the regional qualities of complexes, within a visual design or a musical composition, and (2) those statements that describe internal *relations* among the elements and among the complexes within the object. These latter statements we may call 'form-statements'."[6] Form is any relation between elements that figures in our appreciation of the work.

This definition does not tell us at what *level* of analysis to look for the distinction between form and the elements (or constituents) of the work. But at least this definition guarantees that there is a sensible notion of form to apply to every work, provided that we can also pick out the *elements* of the work. Since the elements of the work can be picked out at more than one level of experience of the work, formal properties can occur at various levels as well. In poetry, for example, there is the aspect of sound; there is also the visual aspect of how the words are arranged on the page; and there is the complex aspect of meaning. We can thus make formal statements about (*a*) the relations of the sounds and (*b*) the visual structure of the words on the page, as well as (*c*) patterns and structures of meaning, considering not only the relation of words to each other but also relations among larger structures, such as verses and stanzas.

Beardsley even considers the author's method to be an aspect of form: "the point of view he chooses, or the manner of transition from scene to scene, or the proportion of description to dialogue."[7] With such a broad definition of form, we can deal more effectively with the formal experiments of twentieth-century artists, such as this one from Samuel Beckett's novel *Watt*: "As for his feet, sometimes he wore on each a sock, or on the one a sock and on the other a stocking, or a boot, or a shoe, or a slipper, or a sock and boot, or a sock and shoe, or a sock and slipper, or a stocking and boot, or a stocking and shoe. . . .' and so on for a page and a half.[8] As David Lodge points out, this is a page and a half of permutations,[9] but not so much of sounds or even of words as of ideas and possibilities; formal structures of possibilities can be built up, too.

To summarize, "form" in the arts is defined as one half of a contrast, but more than one contrast can be made: form versus content and form versus elements. The form/content contrast can be further subdivided: "content" can refer to a common message, meaning, or proposition that can be expressed by more than one formal vehicle. In this sense, it is hard to defend the distinction, because form seems to determine content. "Content" can also refer to the represented subject, and in this sense a form/content distinction *can* be maintained, but only for representational arts. In the other arts, this sense of "form" could not apply. The other way to understand "form" in the arts is to contrast it with the matter or elements that the work organizes. This definition of form applies to every type of artwork and probably best captures what formalism is all about.

WHEN DID FORM BEGIN?

Although the desire for autonomy led to an intense exploration of form in the early twentieth century, this doesn't mean that form had never before been a prominent concern. What was new was the explicit idea that form is what art is about. Artworks have always had some form or other, and artworks from the past have often been very intricately and self-consciously organized. From Greek sculpture to Renaissance polyphonic music to Renaissance experiments with perspective, proportion, organization, and form were important considerations for artists. But such form was often considered subservient to mimetic goals. Sometimes, too, form was subservient to beauty, but this was mimetic beauty, that is, a beauty of what is represented. An example of this is Polykleitos' "canon"—allegedly derived from his sculpture *Doryphorus* (The Spear Bearer) (450 B.C.)—which dictated the proportional sizes of fingers, arms, legs, and other body structures to yield an ideally beautiful harmonious human figure (see illustration on p. 242).

In contrast to mimetic beauty, purely formal beauty is beauty of form that does not represent anything. Examples of this began to appear with Baroque music. Bach's extremely complex and profound *Art of Fugue* (1750) is a prime example. Although such music is attractive, it must have been a bit puzzling before the emergence of explicit formalist doctrines. The Bach scholar Denis Arnold remarks that "these abstract works of Bach's old age [such as the *Art of Fugue*] have puzzled musicians and scholars."[10] In Bach's time, the mimetic theory's only serious competitor for explaining the arts, especially music, was the new idea that music is an expression of emotion (see Chapter 11). Bach's "abstract works" were puzzling because they neither had a representational function, as did his religious music, nor struck listeners as emotionally expressive. Arnold goes on to recall that "before the Renaissance the idea of music as patterns of sound was quite common. The Netherlands composers of the later fifteenth century were as intrigued with canons as polyphonic device as Bach was."[11] However, this does not explain what Bach's contemporaries or earlier musicians thought the point of purely formal music was.

Thus, although the arts had been concerned with form before the first formalists began to work out their ideas at the turn of the century, it is safe to say that before then no doctrine of the arts that locates the very nature and meaning of artworks in form had been put forth. And it is also safe to say that the appearance of formalist doctrines authorized artists to create purely formal, nonrepresentational artworks, first in music, then in visual arts and literature.

The desire to treat the arts as autonomous has led to two distinguishable formalist philosophies of art, which I call *formalism proper* and *media formalism*. Before investigating these theories of art, I will turn to a brief discussion of the related idea of modernism.

MODERNISM

When many people in the arts think of formalism, they think of modernism. Formal concerns have been very important to modern art, so it is not surprising that the difference between the two is blurred in the writings of many thinkers. For instance, the art writer Kim

> It is necessary to be absolutely modern.
> — Rimbaud, "Adieu"

Levin claims, "Modernism, toward the end of its reign, came to be seen as reductive and austere. Its purity came to seem puritanical. It was in the terminology—in a word, formalism—which implied not only the logical structures of modernist invention but also the strictures of rigid adherence to established forms."[12] Although the claim that "formalism" means adherence to established forms is unquestionably mistaken, it is clear that Levin, like many others, makes no clear distinction between modernism and formalism. Since we are going to use the term "formalism" for something very different from a trend in recent art, we need to pause and briefly examine the term "modernism."

"Modernism" is a vague and ambiguous term. In an illuminating survey of the history and meaning of the term, Malcolm Bradbury and James McFarlane (see the Readings) point out an initial problem: The word "modern" is an unfortunate term to use for a historical movement because it tends to refer to whatever is currently thought to be up-to-date:

> Modernity is a crucial word for us, but it is tied up with definitions of our situation which are subject to change. The notion of the "modern" undergoes semantic shift much faster than similar terms of comparable function, like "romantic" or "neo-classical"; indeed, as Lionel Trilling says, it can swing round in meaning until it is facing in the opposite direction. We use the term historically to locate a distinct stylistic phase which is ceasing or has ceased (hence the current circulation of counters like . . . Post-Modernism). We also use it to sum up a permanent modernising state of affairs and the state of mind and view of man it engenders—that "type of consciousness frequent in the modern world, obsessed by a compulsion to keep up." (p. 299)

No doubt, as Bradbury and McFarlane insist, "Modernism does indeed exist; acknowledgement can no longer sensibly be withheld. . . . But on what scale, at what time, and with what character?" (p. 299). Part of the trouble is that "modernism" as a concept stands for an extremely complex historical movement covering roughly the last century and literally dozens of submovements in literature, painting, architecture, and the other arts. We can appreciate some sense of the multiplicity of traits that people associate with modernism by comparing the words of Richard Hertz, who regards modernism as "ahistorical, scientific, self-referential, reductionistic" as well as being committed to "exclusivity, purity and removal from societal and cultural concerns,"[13] with the suggestion of Bradbury and McFarlane that "the movement towards sophistication and mannerism, towards introversion, technical display, internal self-scepticism, has often been taken as a common base for a *definition* of Modernism" (p. 301).[14]

The idea that the arts have now rejected modernism and entered the postmodernist phase is therefore obscure as long as "postmodernism" depends for its definition on the multiple and even conflicting meanings of "modernism." As Bradbury and McFarlane point out, "if there is an argument about when Modernism began, and hence, implicitly, about what its causes and character are, then there is also one about whether it has yet ended" (p. 305). It may well be that "postmodernism" is a misleading term invented by critics and artists to impart a spurious suggestion that art trends in recent years, especially those in architecture, visual arts, and literature, are of revolutionary importance relative to the last century of modern art. Ironically, the suggestion of such revolutionary importance is exactly what modernist art has claimed for itself throughout its history. As Bradbury and McFarlane note, many thinkers associate modernism with "the idea of a Great Divide between past and present, art before and art now" (p. 298)—a seismic shift in artistic sensibilities that is currently being claimed for postmodernism. It is thus arguable that so-called postmodernism is just a subphase of modernism!

The basic distinction between modernism and formalism is that modernism (like romanticism) is a historical movement, whereas formalism, as I construe it, is a philosophy of art in general. The modern movement may have been the occasion when

> The art that makes life, the drama of the artist's consciousness, the structure that lies beyond time, history, character or visible reality, the moral imperative of technique; are not these the basis of a great aesthetic revolution into literary possibilities greater than ever dreamt of?
>
> —Malcolm Bradbury and James McFarlane, "The Name and Nature of Modernism"[15]

formalism was first articulated — as a part of what "modernist" artists were aiming for — but formalism, as a theory of art, applies to all art, including art of the past. Just as democratic theory can be abstracted from the events and rhetoric of the French and American revolutions, so can formalism as a philosophy of art be extracted from the various art movements that we label modern art or modernism. And once abstracted, democratic theory is a general way of assessing types of government of the past and of the future, just as formalism is a general way of thinking about art of the past and of the future.

FORMALISM PROPER

Formal relations and properties can be considered *important* in an artwork, or, more extremely, they can be considered *primary*. Most people who care about artworks would support the former view. Strong and intriguing form is one of the first things critical viewers look for in an artwork. Awareness and control of form is the mark of a mature artist; failure to be aware of form or know how to control it is the mark of a student learning about an art form. It is more radical to hold that the formal properties of a work are primary, and that other concerns — for instance, its subject matter — are secondary. Formalists typically take a position even more extreme than either of these. They hold that form is not just the most important consideration, but the *only relevant consideration*. Other considerations, especially those concerning representation and expression, are quite irrelevant to a work as a work of *art*.

Formalists commonly claim that formal properties — and nothing else — are what makes artifacts of the past *art*. This is the position of Clive Bell, one of the most articulate proponents of formalism. In his book *Art* (1914), he argues that what he calls "significant form" is the defining quality of art (see the Readings).

Surprisingly, he begins his argument from a subjective standpoint: "The starting point for all systems of aesthetics must be the personal experience of a peculiar emotion. The objects that provoke this emotion we call works of art" (p. 269). Among the many emotions provoked by artworks (and here he is addressing only *visual* artworks) Bell claims that there is a particular *kind* of emotion, which he calls "the aesthetic emotion," that is "provoked by every kind of visual art, by pictures, sculptures, buildings, pots, carvings, textiles, etc." (p. 269). Each artwork provokes its own particular emotion, but each particular emotion is of this special type. Everyone who has felt it will agree, he contends. He also argues that "either all works of visual art have some common quality, or when we speak of 'works of art' we gibber" (p. 269). He grounds this claim on the need to justify the classification of certain objects as art. This classification is justified, he thinks, only if there is some essential quality that all artworks share that we refer to when we use the term "art." (See the readings by Weitz and Dickie, in Chapters 1 and 5, for debate about this assumption.) To Bell, this common quality is what causes the aesthetic emotion by which we know and experience objects as works of art. The question, then, is, What is this common quality that makes something art? His answer is to hypothesize that what he calls the significant form of the object is what causes our aesthetic emotion toward the object and thus causes us to label it "art."

Bell is a very clear writer, but he does not make explicit why he thinks that significant form is the answer. One thing is clear: Bell is not claiming to be able to deduce this hypothesis from an a priori intuition (that is, from the sort of an intuition appealed to in pure mathematics) of the concept of art. He clearly regards his proposal as an empirical hypothesis based on, and intended to account for, observations. In this case, the relevant observations are simply our collective experience of artworks. As such, if his hypothesis can survive refutation by counterexamples — works of art without significant form — and can explain relevant phenomena concerning art, then it can be considered a plausible theory of the nature of art.

We can surmise how Bell arrived at this hypothesis. He is struck by the range of objects we consider art and the range of historical periods and cultures they come from. What *could* all these things have in common, given the diversity of their subject matter? he seems to say. The emotional associations dependent on specific cultural contexts, as well as the specific meanings of subject matter, will be lost on observers from other times and cultures. Yet as such observers, we count many such items as works of art. To explain the powerful aesthetic emotions we feel in the presence of objects from other times and cultures whose specific meanings we don't understand, we seem driven to the hypothesis that it is the formal properties of such works that move us aesthetically.

To Bell, it is better that observers not understand artworks; this makes their responses purer. It is difficult to ignore subject matter when we understand it. Not surprisingly, Bell praises so-called primitive art: "In primitive art you will find no accurate representation; you will only find significant form" (p. 273). It isn't that "representation is bad in itself. . . . The representative element in a work of art may or may not be harmful; always it is irrelevant" (p. 274). Bell would clearly disagree with the common art-historical view, alluded to in Chapter 9, that progress in art, in terms of greater power and accuracy of representation, has been made over the course of history. On the contrary, he views primitive art as a more sophisticated expression of the essential quality of art, and he finds the intense focus on details of representation, which is so characteristic of European art, to be a distraction for both the artist and the viewer.

One of the things that makes a theory credible is its ability to explain otherwise unexplainable facts. It can be argued that Bell's formalism provides an explanation of great art's appeal to viewers of widely divergent cultures and times. These familiar facts are hard to explain on either mimetic or expression theories of art (see Chapters 9 and 11); on either theory, the represented subject needs to be understood, yet such artworks are immediately appealing to many viewers who do not properly understand the represented subject or, indeed, even the conventions of representation so essential to any mimetic tradition. The explanation offered by formalism — that it is form to which viewers are responding — seems plausible.

Bell does not deny that art can be representational, nor does he claim that representation is in itself bad. Indeed, he does not even mention purely abstract visual art, which at the time of his writing was just beginning to be produced by the Parisian cubists, the Italian futurists, and such painters as Wassily Kandinsky, Kazimir Malevich, and Frantisek Kupka. Nor does he deny that art is usually associated with emotion. But he does draw a distinction among the emotions elicited by artworks. He contrasts "aesthetic emotion" with the "emotions of life": "A painter too feeble to create forms that provoke more than a little aesthetic emotion will try to eke that little out by suggesting the emotions of life. To evoke the emotions of life he must use representation. Thus a man will paint an execution, and fearing to miss with his first barrel of significant form, will try to hit with his second by raising an emotion of fear or pity" (p. 275). (Notice Bell's implication that tragedy, as explained by Aristotle's theory [Chapter 9], would not be art, because it aims to elicit pity and fear.) Objects like this are inferior art, or not art at all. While such items may be interesting or valuable for historical reasons, they miss what is valuable about art: "A good work of visual art carries a person who is capable of appreciating it out of life into ecstasy: to use art as a means to the emotions of life is to use a telescope for reading the news" (p. 275). Those who can properly appreciate artworks "win an emotion more profound and far more sublime than any that can be given by the description of facts and ideas" (p. 275). Bell's thought is that in a representation the represented subject becomes the object of emotional associations, whereas aesthetic emotion makes the form of the artwork the object of emotion: "We are all familiar with pictures that interest us and excite our admiration, but do not move us as works of art. To this class belongs what I call 'Descriptive Painting' — that is, painting in which forms are used not as objects of emotion, but as a means suggesting emotion or conveying information" (p. 271).

Although Bell does not explicitly generalize his theory to all art, his comments on music make clear that he thinks the same account applies to music, and presumably it applies as well to the other arts in so far as they are art. Such an extension we could call the *general theory of formalism*. Bell admits that although his understanding of music is too weak to enable him to discern form in music, he does at times "appreciate music as pure musical form, as sounds combined according to the laws of a mysterious necessity, as pure art with a tremendous significance of its own and no relation whatever to the significance of life" (p. 275). Failure to understand art in this way is not necessarily worthless, and "provided that there be some fraction of pure aesthetic emotion, even a mixed and minor appreciation of art is, I am sure, one of the most valuable things in the world" (p. 276).

Like any interesting theory, Bell's formalist theory of art contains a number of difficult and controversial points. One is the reason why we are so moved and enriched by aesthetic emotion; I address this later, in the discussion of Bell's so-called metaphysical hypothesis. Here I will concentrate on two related issues: What is meant by "significant form," and is it true that "to appreciate a work of art we need bring with us nothing but a sense of form and colour and a knowledge of three-dimensional space" (p. 274)? Is it true that we do not need to understand the representational elements of artworks to appreciate them properly?

Bell does not fully explain his concept of "significant form." Roger Fry, another important formalist theorist, admits that attempting to explain the concept adequately would take one to "the depths of mysticism."[16] This does not in itself make the concept invalid or fruitless. However, if we have no idea what Bell means by "significant form," his theory is quite useless. Naturally, we do have some idea. The puzzle comes when we try to accommodate three facts about significant form: (*a*) that apparently some art-like artifacts — Bell mentions the painting *Paddington Station* as an example — lack significant form, even though they surely have many formal properties; (*b*) that some genuine artworks seem to have a *more* significant form than others, although each artwork has plenty of formal qualities; and (*c*) that to appreciate a work's significant form we do not need any knowledge of what the work represents.

Because every visual work has both form and formal properties but not every work has *significant* form, we must suppose that in addition to significant form there is *in*significant form. Bell says he will not disagree with those "who judge it more exact to call these combinations and arrangements of form that provoke our aesthetic emotions, not 'significant form,' but 'significant relations of form'" (p. 271). So, equally, we can say that there must also be insignificant relations of form. In the general theory of formalism, this would apply to all of the arts; only some relations of elements of artworks would be significant or have significance. This raises a question: Which relations are "significant," and why?

One answer is obvious but unhelpful. Bell often implies (as he does above) that forms are "significant," by definition, if and only if they provoke aesthetic emotion. So, those forms that do not provoke an aesthetic emotion are not significant. This creates a problem for Bell's aesthetic hypothesis. For this to be a genuine hypothesis, it must be able to explain; and indeed, significant form is supposed to explain what provokes our aesthetic emotions. Thus, Bell's theory must give an account of "significant form" that is *logically independent* of its ability to cause aesthetic emotion. Otherwise, Bell's theory would be no more explanatory than the theory that sleeping potions cause sleepiness because they possess a dormative virtue. ("Dormative virtue" simply means the power to cause sleep; thus, the alleged explanation simply repeats the fact that the potion causes sleepiness because it causes sleepiness.) Unless Bell can produce some independent explanation of "significant form," his hypothesis collapses into a similar circularity.

Unfortunately, the best Bell does is to locate significant form in the lines and colors of the artwork — but he always specifies it as those forms that cause aesthetic emotion: "When I speak of significant form, I mean a combination of lines and colours (counting white and black as colours) that moves me aesthetically" (p. 270). Bell's subjectivism prevents him from given any objective characterization of which combinations these are.[17] Can we even accept that significant form in pictures could be just arrangements of lines and colors? Of course it might be in *some* pictures, especially purely abstract paintings. But could the stronger claim also be true: that significant form is nothing but such arrangements in *all* pictures? This is connected to Bell's claim that we need apply no knowledge except that of three-dimensional space. Bell claims that visual form does not depend on the visual relations of the figures considered as representations of particular objects; what is represented is irrelevant to the visual forms that move us aesthetically.

This claim seems extreme if it is applied to representational paintings. In some paintings, for example, impressionist paintings, we would not even be able to pick out the objects in the three-dimensional space of the representation if we did not know what was being represented. Bell might reply that this is a weakness in such paintings and that if their form does not move us unless we know what is represented in the painting, then such paintings lack significant form. But the same criticisms of Bell's theory can be raised considering paintings that must surely have significant form. Consider, for example, the great and mysterious *Flagellation* (Figure 10.1) by a favorite painter of formalist critics, Piero della Francesca (ca. 1420–1492).

This painting, as well as countless others from the Renaissance, raises questions about the extreme claim that viewers can appreciate the form without considering what is represented. This panel makes a very strong formal impact; it seems fair to assume that it has very significant relations of form. But are these just a product of geometry? Is the effect due solely to the prominent architectural framework developed in perspective and the objects and their colors arrayed within that framework? It seems absurd to say it is. The powerful impact of this work is a function of the fact, to begin with, that the objects represented are *people*; this helps us to see the right-hand cluster of objects as much nearer than the left-hand cluster of objects. More than that, we see the left-hand figures as two men in the process of beating a third while two other men look on; thus, the relations we see are between moving objects in three-dimensional space. There is more, for the powerful impact of the painting has to do with the fact that it is Christ who is being flagellated and there are three men much nearer to us (on the right) who are apparently ignoring this important event. It is true that *part* of the effect of this juxtaposition is created by the use of colors and perspective. But another reason why we focus on this juxtaposition, why we feel there is an almost metaphysical distance between the two groups and thus accord a "significance" to the relation of distance, is that

FIGURE 10.1 *Flagellation of Christ* (ca. 1455–60), by Piero della Francesca (1415–92). This dramatic painting is also very mysterious; dozens of scholars have tried to interpret the meaning of the three figures on the right and their relationship to the scene on the left in which Christ is whipped. Do the right-hand figures occupy the same space and time as the flagellation, or are they from another time, and is there some relation between them and the flagellation? Are they remembering the flagellation? Are they planning to do something that in some way relates to the flagellation? Formalists find such questions aesthetically beside the point, but must not even formalists admit that the formal power of the painting partly resides in what it represents?

Christ is being flagellated and the three men and their gazes are directed elsewhere. As the historian Carlo Ginzburg points out, "Between the two planes is a distance which . . . is not only physical but ontological."[18] There are other relations of objects in this picture that we do not feel have the same "significance" in part because the objects themselves are not significant (for example, the stairs in the distance and the columns in the upper right).

Even a cursory examination of this painting tends to support two assertions that run counter to Bell's more extreme formulations: (*a*) Sometimes, at least, the visual relations that seem significant gain their significance from the objects represented; and (*b*) without a knowledge of the object represented, the viewer cannot perceive certain visual relations.

Remarks Bell makes elsewhere about Cézanne[19] tend to support these assertions and to go against Bell's official position. He praises Cézanne for coming to understand landscape, "not as a mode of light, nor yet as a player in the game of human life, but as an end in itself — as pure form that is to say. . . . Everything can be seen as pure form, and behind pure form lurks the mysterious significance that thrills to ecstasy."[20] Bell further explains the significance of pure form in a way that brings back represented content:

> What is a tree, a dog, a wall, a boat? What is the particular significance of anything? . . . Imagine a boat in complete isolation, detach it from man and his urgent activities and fabulous history, what is it that remains, what is it to which we still react emotionally? What but pure form, and that which, lying behind pure form, gives it its significance. It was for this Cézanne felt the emotion he spent his life in expressing."[21]

Bell is claiming that Cézanne discovered how to paint the *essence* of things, such as a boat or a landscape; that is, he discovered how to bring out the significance of the landscape as a philosophical thing-in-itself. This explanation, which is part of Bell's metaphysical hypothesis about the value of form, seems to require that we look at Cézanne's landscapes as about landscape, not just lines and patches of color. The explanation appeals not just to the value of forms per se but to forms as the essence *of* something (a landscape, apples, a boat). To create a painting that captures the essential form of something would seem to be quite a deep artistic achievement, and this would explain the felt "significance" of the forms. But this explanation seems clearly inconsistent with Bell's more radical claim that "significant form" can be separated from what the artwork represents.

OBJECTIVITY AND FORMALISM

Formalism in music has had to challenge different opponents than those Clive Bell confronts. Whereas Bell fights against the customary emphasis in visual art on representation, Eduard Hanslick (1825–1904) vehemently argues against the customary emphasis in music on emotions. Both thinkers seek to replace traditional ways of thinking about the arts with a new emphasis on form.

In stark contrast to Bell, who claims that any aesthetics must be founded on subjectivity, Hanslick, the most influential formalist theorist of music, insists that his theory of music derives from a purely objective approach. The argument of Hanslick's *On the Beautiful in Music* (1854) (see the Readings) in fact depends on the conceptual connections between autonomy, objectivity, and form. Hanslick devotes much of *On the Beautiful in Music* to refuting the idea that music is to be evaluated on the basis of the emotional response it elicits. This is a key feature of most theories of music that were prevalent in Hanslick's time. Hanslick rejects two ideas: (*a*) that the point of music—its meaning—is ultimately to be understood in terms of its emotional *effects* and (*b*) that the meaning of music is to be understood in terms of its alleged ability to *represent* emotional states. Hanslick's rejection of these positions is predicated on his desire to develop an objective musical aesthetics that deals with music in its own terms, that is, as an *autonomous* phenomenon.

Hanslick begins by rejecting the notion of "aesthetics as founded on feelings." He notes that in the aesthetics of every other art form "the rule has already been laid down that aesthetic investigations must above all consider the beautiful object, and not the perceiving subject. Music alone is unable, apparently, to adopt this objective mode of procedure" (p. 281). Hanslick aims to bring the aesthetics of music in line with objective and scientific approaches: "The beautiful is and remains beautiful though it arouse no emotion whatever, and although there be no one to look at it. In

> Modern musi-
> cians — compo-
> sers, scholars and
> performers
> of every stripe —
> are essentially
> formalists at
> heart. And so are
> modern listeners.
>
> — Richard Taruskin,
> "Facing Up, Finally, to
> Bach's Dark Vision"[22]

other words, although the beautiful exists for the gratification of an observer, it is independent of him" (p. 281).

Hanslick points out that emotional responses to music differ as time goes on. For example, Mozart's music at first struck listeners as full of violent expressions of passion, a start contrast to the Olympian classicism of Haydn. But after the symphonies of Beethoven became familiar, Mozart was heard as a classical master, much like Haydn, to be contrasted with the romantic excesses and violence of Beethoven. And so it goes. A more recent example is Strávinsky's *Rite of Spring*. Once considered outrageously brutal — a cause for rioting in the concert hall — the work is now a familiar crowd pleaser. According to Hanslick, our emotional estimate of a piece of music varies too much, from context to context and person to person, to be a valid basis for detecting and analyzing what is beautiful in music: "It is manifest, therefore, that the effect of music on the emotions does not possess the attributes of inevitableness, exclusiveness, and uniformity that a phenomenon from which aesthetic principles are to be deduced ought to have." Hanslick does not deny that music provokes strong emotions: "It is only the unscientific procedure of deducing aesthetic principles from such facts against which we protest" (p. 284).

Hanslick is occupied with a notion of "pure" music, that is, music without words or any associated program that the musical sounds are supposed to illustrate. For example, most listeners suppose Vivaldi's *Four Seasons* (his violin concertos, op. 8, nos. 1–4) illustrates events associated with spring, summer, fall, and winter; to such listeners, the music is not pure music, but rather a mechanism for telling a story. Pure instrumental music, commonly called "absolute music" in music theory, is championed by Hanslick and other nineteenth- and twentieth-century theorists as the highest form of music. The result is a virtual canonization of purely instrumental music and the formalist analysis of it in musical education and theory. (One of the most interesting problems for proponents of absolute music is to explain the relation of the words to the instrumental part in vocal music. If the instrumental music has no determinate expressive or referential function, why does some music go better with some verbal content?) According to Hanslick, to confuse pure music with its effects upon us is a logical mistake: "In the pure act of listening we enjoy the music alone and do not think of importing into it any extraneous matter. But the tendency to allow our feelings to be aroused implies something extraneous to the music" (p. 282). What defines musical beauty, as opposed to visual or literary beauty, has to be *in* the music, not in whatever emotions or associations we may connect to the music.

Like many thinkers after Kant, Hanslick thinks of the imagination as an active organ of the mind; the imagination performs the function of constructing experience to enable us to mentally grasp external perceptual objects. This is the organ that we use in perceiving and assessing music: "An art aims, above all, at producing something beautiful which affects not our feelings but the organ of pure contemplation, our *imagination*" (p. 282). What is it to hear sounds as music? Is it to feel emotions or to think of distant scenes while hearing the sounds? Hanslick asserts that it is not either of these; rather, it is our capacity to hear the sounds with our imagination, which can represent the sounds as pure music: "Our imagination, it is true, does not merely contemplate the beautiful, but contemplates it with intelligence — the object being, as it were, mentally inspected and criticized" (p. 282).

Instrumental music is intended to be an object experienced by this organ, or capacity. Hanslick distinguishes the *direct* effect of music on our imaginations from music's undoubted *indirect* effects on our emotions: "For we have already seen that the excitation of feelings by the beautiful in music is but one of its indirect effects, our imagination only being directly affected" (p. 283). It is clear to Hanslick that the only valid analysis of the beauty of music must focus on the music itself, on what is *in* the music, not on the music's variable and indirect effects. Hanslick's argument thus shows that a demand for complete autonomy for artworks implies a rejection of mimetic theories (see Chapter 9) and expression theories of art (see Chapter 11) in favor of the formal relation of elements within the artwork.

We have learned what beauty in music is *not*. What, then, is the beautiful in music? What remains after we put aside the emotional and representational content? What is left is the musical content, the musical properties of sounds:

> The primordial element of music is euphony, and rhythm is its soul. . . . The crude material which the composer has to fashion . . . is the entire scale of musical notes and their inherent adaptability to an endless variety of melodies, harmonies, and rhythms. Melody . . . is preeminently the source of musical beauty." (p. 284)

Although formalism in music is concerned with the sounds and their properties, it does not focus on sounds just as sounds:

> The "specifically musical" must not, however, be understood only in the sense of acoustic beauty or symmetry of parts. . . . But, by laying stress on musical beauty, we do not exclude the intellectual principle; on the contrary, we imply it as essential, for we would not apply the term "beautiful" to anything wanting in intellectual beauty; and in tracing the essential nature of beauty to a morphological source, we wish it to be understood that the intellectual element is most intimately connected with the sonorific forms. (p. 286)

Hanslick admits there is much that is mysterious about musical form and its hold on us. He says, "It is extremely difficult to define this self-subsistent and specifically musical beauty." He makes an analogy to a language "we speak and understand, but which we are unable to translate" (p. 286).

In contending that musical beauty is created by musical form and that musical form is a function of rhythm, melody, and harmonic development, Hanslick appears to embrace the view that musical form, and thus beauty, is a *temporal* phenomenon. In "On Rehearing Music," Leonard Meyer, a contemporary formalist theorist of music, usefully distinguishes two different formal approaches to music (see the Readings), a temporal and a nontemporal approach.[23] The nontemporal approach, according to Meyer, holds that a musical event "must be complete, or virtually so, before its formal design can be comprehended"; thus, "for such theorists, music is mobile architecture" (p. 289). Such thinkers maintain that music is to be contemplated as a completed whole. By contrast, those who adopt what he calls "the kinetic-syntactic" approach contend that music "is a dynamic process. Understanding and enjoyment depend upon the perception of and response to attributes such as tension and repose. . . . music is seen as a developing process" (p. 289). The primary example of music to be experienced in this way is Western music from 1600–1900, which is characterized by a kind of harmonic development that requires modulation between keys and resolution of harmonic tensions. This harmonic development, in conjunction with manipulation of thematic material, gives such music a prospective and dramatic air, as Meyer notes, a sense that the music is always progressing forward.[24]

Meyer summarizes the kinetic position: "The significance of a musical event — be it a tone, a motive, a phrase, or a section — lies in the fact that it leads a practiced listener to expect, consciously or unconsciously, the arrival of a subsequent event or one of a number of alternative subsequent events'' (p. 290). The degree of the probability of subsequent events contributes to the sense of significance or meaning we feel when the actual musical events happen. If a piece of music is very predictable (for example, ''Twinkle, Twinkle, Little Star''), it has little meaning; if, however, our expectations are much more complex and the fulfillment is much less probable (as in a Beethoven symphony), then the music has much more significance, because the musical notes are surprising. This analysis of music is clearly formalist.

For Meyer, meaning depends on syntactic or structural complexity, which in turn is connected to enjoyment. He seems to understand this enjoyment as a psychological process to be explained some day by a more advanced cognitive science. Ultimately, then, for Meyer the value of this sort of music lies in the enjoyment it gives us.[25] By comparison, Hanslick grounds his account on the more traditional concepts of beauty as well as what pleases us:

> The beauty of an independent and simple theme appeals to our aesthetic feeling with that directness which tolerates no explanation except, perhaps, that of its inherent fitness and the harmony of its parts, to the exclusion of any alien factor. It pleases for its own sake, like an arabesque, a column, or some spontaneous product of nature — a leaf or a flower.'' (p. 287)

We shall see in the next section, however, that Hanslick does not just rest his account on the notions of beauty and pleasure; at times he hints that form furnishes music with even more profound values.

ABSTRACT ART AND THE VALUE OF FORM

Formalism typically involves an interplay between positive and negative claims. On the negative side, formalists claim that art is *not* about what it might appear to be about — rather, it is about form. On the positive side, they claim that form is to be understood in a given way and that, so understood, form is important for given reasons. Why do we need the positive account? If we suppose that what makes artifacts art is their form and that formal concerns are primary to all art worthy of the name, we are clearly left with the fundamental questions: What is form? What is the value of form? What is the value of art if formalist theories of art are correct? These questions call for a positive account of form and its value. This account must spell out this value so that it can address the guiding questions of this text, such as Tolstoy's challenge to justify the status and costs of the arts.

Fortunately, theorists of art have until recently felt that the demand for such an account is legitimate, and even formalist theorists have tried to provide answers. Nonetheless, there is no widely accepted account of the positive value of form, and this is one of the weaknesses of formalism as a philosophy of art. Formalism's greatest strength is its universal applicability to both abstract and representational arts, to contemporary as well as to ancient art, and to every type of art. Its great weakness as a theory is that it gives perhaps the most esoteric account of the value of art. In this section we will look at Bell's and Hanslick's attempts to provide a positive account of the value of form, as well as an attempt to explain abstract art by reintroducing mimetic values.

Let's begin by thinking about abstract visual art. Here is a type of art whose value must depend on the value of form, or so it seems. Why do we call some paintings and sculpture ''abstract''? Simply because there is no apparent representational content, so that ''abstract'' means "nonrepresentational." We could just as well call absolute music "abstract" music. Why, then, does abstract visual art present greater hurdles to appreciation for many people and meet with much greater resistance than does instrumental music? Why do many of us expect and, indeed, even demand that a painting represent? We do not demand that all, or even most, music be vocal or illustrate a program of events, yet many spectators seem to make such a demand of visual arts. Is it due to the nature of visual art? Is it due to the way the visual systems of our brains work? Or is it merely a culturally bound expectation that many people have learned? I do not know of any systematic attempt to answer this crucial question. The French artist Francis Picabia draws the parallel between visual art and music and suggests that we need to *learn* how to experience nonrepresentational visual art:

> The laws of this new convention have as yet been hardly formulated but they will become gradually more defined, just as musical laws have become more defined, and they will very rapidly become as understandable as were the objective representations of nature.[26]

A diametrically opposed approach is to insist on the necessity of representation in visual art and thus to maintain either that abstract art is meaningless or that it necessarily represents something after all. This "mimetic dilemma" is vividly proposed by Maurice Tuchman, senior curator of twentieth-century art at the Los Angeles County Museum of Art, who in 1986 organized a large and important show of abstract art for museums in Los Angeles, Chicago, and the Netherlands called "The Spiritual in Art: Abstract Painting 1890–1985." Tuchman begins with a provocative claim:

> Abstract art remains misunderstood by the majority of the viewing public. Most people, in fact, consider it quite meaningless. Yet around 1910, when groups of artists moved away from representational art toward abstraction, preferring symbolic color to natural color, signs to perceived reality, ideas to direct observation, there was never an outright dismissal of meaning.

Tuchman goes on to ascribe meaning to abstract arts based on spiritual ideas:

> Instead, artists made an effort to draw upon deeper and more varied levels of meaning, the most pervasive of which was that of the spiritual. . . . the genesis and development of abstract art were inextricably tied to spiritual ideas current in Europe in the late nineteenth and early twentieth centuries. . . . their art reflects a desire to express spiritual, utopian, or metaphysical ideas that cannot be expressed in traditional pictorial terms.[27]

This suggests that Tuchman holds something like a mimetic theory of visual art: that abstract art has meaning if and only if it represents some ideas, experiences, objects, or scenes. The difference between traditional representational art and abstract art would only involve the subject matter. In traditional art, the subject matter is the natural world; in abstract art, the subject matter is (often at least) the spiritual world, or esoteric experiences. This implies that abstract art lacking such esoteric subject matter would be meaningless.

Tuchman embraces this consequence. He criticizes formalist interpretations of the history of abstract art—for example, those of such famous critics and curators as Alfred Barr, Clement Greenberg, and Harold Rosenberg—as merely "aesthetic." The result, Tuchman charges, is that these interpretations have made the art meaningless:

Just as the history of early abstract art, as written by many critics and historians of the 1930s through the 1960s, disregarded the presence of any meaning in these works, so too was Cubism stripped of its content. The process facilitated an easy formalist reading of abstract art, but it is now widely acknowledged that Cubist works do have content, that they are about something.[28]

These claims are very controversial. Why should we equate having meaning, or having content, or being about something, with having some sort of representational imagery? Tuchman holds the position that abstract art would be meaningless, would have no content, and would not be about anything if it didn't illustrate the various spiritual ideas and interests of the artists. There are several objections to this position:

a. If we were to maintain this position, we would have to say that abstract artists who reject spiritualism produce paintings that are literally meaningless and have no content. Why say this about paintings but not about instrumental music? No one thinks that music can be understood or justified only if it illustrates either natural or supernatural imagery.

b. Tuchman's position also places a disproportionate weight on artists' intentions and even on their amateur interests, for example, theosophy and so-called sacred geometry. Many critics and theorists consider such an approach to interpretation naive. (It is in fact an approach that was until recently widely rejected by art theorists as committing the "intentional fallacy.")

c. If the point is not really to insist that abstract images must be some sort of representation, but only to require that there be some ideas "behind" the visual appearance — for example, occult ideas — then Tuchman's objection to formalist understandings of this work collapses. No one, least of all any formalist, has ever proposed that there are no ideas behind abstract artworks and that such artworks are literally without meaning and point. Formalists would only insist, as does Hanslick for music, that the meaning or content is contained within the formal properties, or at any rate that the viewer can understand the meaning of the work without attributing referents to the images in the work.

d. Finally, Tuchman's insistence on a mimetic reading of abstract art ignores two obvious traditional answers to the question of what meaning abstract works have. The first is simply the familiar attribution of *beauty* to the elements and their relations in visual artworks. Beauty may not explain everything about the paintings of Fra Angelico and Titian or the sculptures of Michelangelo and Bernini, but it surely accounts for a lot of their meaning and value to us. And the same can be said of abstract paintings and sculptures; the paintings of Kazimir Malevich, Georgia O'Keeffe, and Mark Rothko are certainly beautiful!

The second and equally obvious alternative to the need for mimetic content is to take abstract works as emotionally expressive, that is, as expressions of emotional states and attitudes. This is an extremely common way to appreciate and interpret abstract artworks. Admittedly, formalists do not interpret visual art this way any more than Hanslick allows this sort of interpretation of music. But it is an attractive and coherent alternative to the claim that work is meaningless if it does not represent.

The paintings of Georgia O'Keeffe (1887–1986) illustrate this possibility. Although many of her famous works are abstract but recognizable representations of objects (skulls, bones, flowers, shells) and landscapes, some are so abstract that they are unrecognizable as representations (see Plate 9). Nevertheless, in all cases she thinks of her works as expressions of her inner experience of nature: "A hill or tree cannot make a good painting just because it is a hill or tree. It is lines and color put together so they say something. . . . The abstraction is often the most definite form of the intangible thing in myself that I can only clarify in paint."[29] What is important in painting, for O'Keeffe, is not representation per se but getting at the emotional essence of form: "I had to create an equivalent for what I felt about what I was looking at — not copy it."[30]

We may conclude that Tuchman does not justify the mimetic dilemma. He does not provide any adequate argument to support his contention that abstract art must either represent something or be meaningless. Tuchman does have a valid point: to those who think that abstract art *must* be understood along formal lines or emotional lines, he shows that there is another way to approach a lot of abstract art. Tuchman demonstrates that many of the most influential early abstract artists tried to illustrate spiritual ideas, and this current of thought has characterized the tradition of abstract art. To ignore the ideas of these artists would be to distort the history of abstraction.

The most prominent case is Wassily Kandinsky (1866–1944), perhaps the most influential early abstract painter, who was known for his interest in occult subjects, such as theosophy and anthroposophy. He even write a famous book, *The Spiritual in Art*. But what did he mean by "spiritual"? He seems to have had in mind a combination of the occult and the mental. Kandinsky believed in mental "vibrations" caused by musical tones as well as colors. Kandinsky's goal, as Sixten Ringbom describes it, was "to produce vibrations in the beholder, and the work of art is the vehicle through which this purpose is served. . . . The formative factor in the creation of the work is the artist's same vibration."[31] This is a recipe for art that an expression theorist could live with (or even a formalist like Bell!). It does not say that the painting is meant to *illustrate* the theosophical theory of vibrations; rather, Kandinsky *used* that theory to understand and perhaps direct the emotional power of the abstractions he was beginning to paint.

Many other abstract artists had ideas about the meaning of their works that were not strictly formalist. Piet Mondrian (1872–1944) arrived at his famous abstract paintings consisting of rectangles and primary colors by a process of "dematerialization." Mondrian was one of a Dutch school of artists, "De Stijl," who were influenced by Dutch theosophists who, as Ringbom remarks, held the Platonic belief in "an immutable, ordered, and mathematically defined reality behind appearances."[32] Ringbom argues that "Mondrian's increasingly geometricized designs became a reflection of his idea that 'one passes through a world of forms ascending from reality to abstraction.'"[34] (See his abstract rendering of Broadway in New York, *Broadway Boogie-Woogie*, Plate 4). Mondrian clearly expressed an interest in representing the timeless truths about the reality behind appearances: "Hence as matter becomes redundant, the representation of matter becomes redundant. We arrive at the representation of other things such as the laws which hold matter together. These are the great generalities, which do not change."[35]

A later generation of abstract painters, the New York school of the 1940s and 1950s, which included Barnett Newman, Mark Rothko, and Ad Reinhardt, were also interested in

> The cultivated man of today is gradually turning away from natural things, and his life is becoming more and more abstract.
>
> — Piet Mondrian, "Natural Reality and Abstract Reality"[33]

religion and mystical ideas. Newman rejected what he called the objective approach to painting: "The present feeling seems to be that the artist is concerned with form, color and spatial arrangement. This objective approach to art reduces it to a kind of ornament." Instead, Newman held that the painter was concerned "with the penetration into the world mystery. His imagination is therefore attempting to dig into metaphysical secrets. . . . It is a religious art which through symbols will catch the basic truth of life."[36] (See Plate 8.)

Donald Kuspit notes, "For Reinhardt the 'square, cruciform, unified absolutely clean' mandala shape he utilized in his famous 'black,' or negative paintings serves the same purpose as Rothko's 'disembodied chromatic sensations,' namely to preserve the spiritual atmosphere."[37] Reinhardt explicitly connected his paintings with "a long tradition of negative theology in which the essence of religion, and in my case the essence of art, is protected . . . from being pinned down or vulgarized or exploited."[38]

Whereas the paintings of Newman, Rothko, and Reinhardt were based on the assumption that the artist is trying to articulate mystical truths, an artwork that makes a direct assertion of the connection between art and mysticism is Bruce Nauman's *Window or Wall Sign* (1967), which says in neon words: "The true artist helps the world by revealing mystic truths" (see Plate 7). The lack of visual illusion, the use of light as a medium, the use of geometric form (the spiral — recalling Duchamp's fascination with spirals in his art), the self-referential nature of its message, all work to give this piece a mysterious sense of exemplifying what it asserts.

It is clear that all these artists in fact meant their work to concern "spiritual" ideas of one sort or another. Even though some of them repudiated what they understood as "formalist" interpretations of their work, it does not follow that formalism, if properly characterized, cannot give meaning and substance to their works. Nor does it follow that mimetic theories must be brought in to interpret such work; much that concerned many of these artists seems to be related to what the expression theory of art tries to explain: namely, the externalization of our inner lives.

What would a formalist say about the meaning and value of abstract art? Undoubtedly, a formalist would claim that abstract images are merely purified versions of the formal values found in representational art. Clive Bell is sure that form is the thrilling aspect of art and what makes something truly art. He is less sure just why form is important, less sure what the meaning of form is. Thus, in addition to his aesthetic hypothesis he also proposes a metaphysical hypothesis, which he presents with much less assurance than he does his aesthetic hypothesis. The metaphysical hypothesis, which we have already seen prefigured in his remarks on Cézanne, is an attempt to address the meaning or importance of form.

As we saw, Bell agrees that the significance of some forms (the "significant" forms) and the ecstasy they cause needs to be explained. His metaphysical hypothesis involves several speculations: (*a*) It appeals to the communication of emotion between artist and viewer; viewers are moved not because the work is beautiful but because they feel the emotion the artist feels. (*b*) The emotion the artist feels is for the pure forms of reality. (*c*) This emotion is for things seen not as means but as ends in themselves. Bell says, "If this suggestion were accepted it would follow that 'significant form' was form behind which we catch a sense of ultimate reality" (p. 279).

It is striking that this explanation is in the same spirit as the thinking of many early abstract artists. They, too, often concerned themselves with the artwork as a communication of inner feelings, and many of them viewed their ascent to abstraction as an attempt to portray the metaphysical structure underlying material reality. But here Bell's explanation runs into trouble: it seems to work only for images that are not completely abstract. If a work makes no reference to material reality, how can it portray the essence of that reality? Or must abstract works always relate to things in the real world? Bell cannot resolve this problem, for he is aware that visual art does *not* always relate to things in the real world: "Those who incline to believe that the artist's emotion is felt for reality will admit that visual artists . . . come at reality generally through material form. But don't they come at it sometimes through imagined form? And ought we not to add that sometimes the sense of reality comes we know not whence?" (p. 279). The problem is that Bell cannot generalize the explanation that he gives in Cézanne's case—that Cézanne portrays the essence of a landscape—for forms that do not derive from observation.

Nevertheless, the value of *significant* form, Bell feels, is that it gives us an experience of metaphysical truth. An interesting point about this explanation, other than its avowedly speculative nature, is that Bell does not wish to base formalism on any foundation as shallow as mere pleasure or enjoyment. Hanslick, too, is eager to link the beautiful in music with themes more profound than pleasure. Hanslick also seems to agree with Bell's contention that there is a communication of emotion between artist and audience. Hanslick toys with the theory, which he never makes clear, that our strong reaction to purely musical beauty springs from our realization that the sounds which stimulate our imaginations are produced in the composer's imagination. He draws a contrast between music and "the ever-changing tints and forms of a kaleidoscope." The difference between a kaleidoscope and music, he claims, is "that the musical kaleidoscope is the direct product of a creative mind, whereas the optic one is but a cleverly constructed mechanical toy" (p. 285).

The idea that when we listen to music we are in communion with another mind figures prominently in Hanslick's explanations of the value of musical beauty. Because he rejects the idea that music can represent reality, he certainly would reject Bell's belief that the forms in music reveal a metaphysical truth about reality. In Bell's view, the best artists are inspired by insights into the nature of external reality. In Hanslick's view, the composer is inspired by the structures of musical reality and the free play of the imagination.

> It is . . . both ennobling and elevating to follow the creative mind as it unlocks with magic keys a new world of elements, and to observe how at its bidding they enter into all conceivable combinations; how it builds up and casts down, creates and destroys. . . . (p. 287)

In the grip of "musical contemplation" (rather than emotion), the listener experiences the "sublime indifference of Beauty" (p. 287). Hanslick is saying both that absolute music has value and also that listening to music in this special way, that is, contemplating it, is valuable. When these two, the proper object and the proper way of listening, come together, the result is a refined form of experience and an exercise of our highest imaginative and intellectual faculties.

MEDIA FORMALISM

The most important recent formalist theory is associated with the influential critic Clement Greenberg. Although Greenberg is commonly identified as one of the chief theoreticians of modernism, and although we have sharply differentiated modernism as an *art movement*

What was new was [the Romantics'] conviction that autonomous instrumental music, exemplified first and foremost by the symphonies of Beethoven, could penetrate into what Hoffman called "the spirit realm," the sphere of the highest human signification.

—Joseph Kerman, *Contemplating Music*[39]

from formalist *theories of art*, we can nonetheless extract from Greenberg's advocacy of modernism a brand of formalism different from the classical formalist positions we have examined; I call it "media formalism," for reasons that will soon become apparent.

In "Modernist Painting" (see the Readings for Chapter 6), Greenberg proposes an interpretation of the history of the last 150 years of art, according to which modernism is a natural response to the intellectual and cultural currents of the times. Characteristically, he praises modernism as being both inevitable and "almost the whole of what is truly alive in our culture." Greenberg submits that the crucial tendency of this period in all fields has been the drive toward self-criticism: "The essence of Modernism lies, as I see it, in the use of the characteristic methods of a discipline to criticize the discipline itself—not in order to subvert it, but to entrench it more firmly in its area of competence" (p. 155). One might also add that the intent is not to create artworks that are superior in traditional aesthetic terms (for instance, beauty or mimetic accuracy) but, rather, self-criticism for its own sake. Greenberg sees the history of painting in this period as a process of experimentation in the service of modernism. By using the methods of painting, artists bring out what is unique and essential to painting, removing whatever factors are accidental to painting, such as—according to Greenberg—representation and illusion. The end result is often abstract paintings that are about the conventions and limitations of painting. Greenberg is aware that this process of trying to create "pure" paintings has taken a great deal of time and has been approached only incrementally and unconsciously. Modernist art, for Greenberg, has the status of a historical inevitability; understanding the forces of modernism both explains and provides the basis for appreciating what Greenberg calls the "advanced" painting of our time.

What Greenberg appreciates in painting is its exploration of its own limitations, such as two-dimensionality and the shape of the frame. These qualities are very different from the sublimity, beauty, or significance that classical formalists find in the formal qualities of artworks. Greenberg does not appear to emphasize either beautiful or meaningful form. In what sense, then, is he a formalist? On one level, his approach is formalist just by virtue of his view that representation and illusion are irrelevant to painting. But more deeply, Greenberg's formalism shares a fundamental principle with the classical formalism we have examined: *autonomy*. Greenberg lays primary emphasis on the independence and uniqueness of each art. The goal of autonomy dictates an imperative to each art. If the art meets the imperative, it is automatically successful: "Each art had to determine, through the operations peculiar to itself, the effects peculiar and exclusive to itself. By doing this each art would, to be sure, narrow its area of competence, but at the same time it would make its possession of this area all the more secure" (p. 155). This conception of a self-validating autonomy is in many ways the most strict or "pure" form of formalism, because it appears to be based on absolutely no values external to the artwork. Greenberg's vision amounts to the purist form of art for art's sake.

We can understand how media formalism differs from ordinary formalism by considering an analogy from the study of language. Linguists and philosophers of language have for a long time distinguished *using* words from *mentioning* them. The distinction is often marked by the use of quotation marks. If we say, "Symphonies have a complex harmonic development," we are using the word "symphonies" to refer to symphonies. But if we say, "'Symphonies' has ten letters," or "'Symphonies' is a plural noun," we are *mentioning* the word "symphonies" in order to talk about that word, not about symphonies. The distinction is between first-order (or ordinary) use of language to talk about the world and second-order use of language to talk about language rather than the world. In second-order study of language, the language itself is the object of study. This is analogous to art itself becoming the object of study by art.

This is exactly the kind of formalism that Greenberg endorses: second-order art about art. Not art about being an artist, however, or art about the values of the art world or about the history of art—rather, art about the *nature* of art. The specific appropriate object of investigation is what he calls the limiting conditions or norms of an art; these are *conventions* that govern the making of artworks in the various media. Greenberg accepts the idea that investigating the conventions of an art is the same as investigating the medium: "It quickly emerged that the unique and proper area of competence of each art coincided with all that was unique to the nature of its medium" (p. 155). The limiting conditions or norms of painting include flatness (two-dimensionality), the enclosing frame shape, and "norms of finish, of paint texture, and of value and color contrast" (p. 157). Instead of using the conventions or norms of a medium to create significant forms, artists who follow this vision create artworks that examine the conventions and nature of the medium—that is, they *mention* forms instead of *using* them.

Does media formalism qualify as a theory art? Is it a general account of the nature of art? This is a difficult question. It is easy to see that Greenberg's position is meant to explain recent art history, but can it be interpreted in a more general way? Although Greenberg does not formulate his approach in the same abstract and universal way that Hanslick and Bell do, we can construct a general theory of art from various remarks he makes. Four propositions seem particularly central:

1. Every art has a nature, which it has uniquely. This nature is determined by the norms governing the art.[40]

2. The nature of an art is identical to the nature of its medium.

3. Those elements of artworks that concern the nature of the medium are critical for appreciation and criticism of artworks.

4. The best artworks are those that explore their nature (within the constraints of their art-historical context.)

Propositions (1) and (2) are implied throughout "Modernist Painting." Propositions (3) and (4) are obvious critical principles suggested by Greenberg's various remarks about the history of art. He makes it clear that the arts have always had to deal with "norms" and "limitations": "The making of pictures has been governed, since pictures first began to be made, by all the norms I have mentioned" (p. 159). Greenberg says the least about the critical evaluation expressed in proposition 4. Still, some remarks are suggestive. For example, "What Modernism has made clear is that, though the past did appreciate masters like these [Leonardo, Raphael, Titian, Rubens, Rembrandt, and Watteau] justly, it often gave wrong or irrelevant reasons for doing so" (p. 159). Presumably the relevant or correct reasons for appreciating these masters has to do with the way they explored and displayed the norms of painting.[41]

We can derive a general, if as yet sketchy, theory of art from these four propositions if we add a fifth proposition defining what art is:

5. A necessary and sufficient condition for X to be a work of art is that X be a work in some art medium.

Having specified media formalism in this way, can we consider it a plausible theory of art? The idea that some artworks are concerned, partly or mainly, with investigating the limitations and norms of their media is clearly insightful. There are many artworks like this, and not all were created in the twentieth century. Revolutionary artworks of the past all to some extent explored limitations that had appeared to govern previous works. But media formalism, as it has been spelled out here, makes much stronger claims. Each of propositions (1) through (4) is questionable. And in Chapter 6 we encountered objections to proposition 5: It is both circular and difficult to apply to works that go beyond any medium at all, such as many works of conceptual art. But if the media formalist surrenders proposition 5, a question arises: Why are art media so important? Are they as essential to art as the media formalist claims?

Let's examine proposition (1) more closely. Do art media have an essence? Not if, as seems plausible, there is no one quality that all works in a particular art medium, such as painting, have in common. And if there is a quality common to all works in the medium, is that common nature made up of properties *unique* to the art medium? Are not some arts, such as opera, jazz, and movies, a unique *combination* of qualities none of which is unique to that art? And even if there is an essence to an art, how are we to determine what it is? Greenberg's argument, for example, that the essence of painting is flatness seems unjustified. On the one hand, are not drawings flat as well? But if so, flatness is not unique to painting. On the other hand, what if a mimetic theorist claimed that the essence of painting was not just two-dimensionality but, rather, the representation of space and objects on a two-dimensional surface? Greenberg claims that representation of three dimensions is not unique to painting and hence not a feature of its essence: "Three-dimensionality is the province of sculpture, and for the sake of its own autonomy painting has had above all to divest itself of everything it might share with sculpture" (p. 156). This is a fallacious inference. Only paintings (and drawings) *represent* three-dimensionality on a two-dimensional surface; so, paintings do not share three-dimensionality per se with sculpture. There are *two* properties: (*a*) flatness and (*b*) flatness that is illusionistic or representational, that are properties of painting, not sculpture. Greenberg's exclusion of representation (the second property) from the potentially unique properties of painting seems merely arbitrary. Moreover, two-dimensionality is itself a feature of every sculptural surface, so by itself it is not unique to painting. In short, the whole idea that there are natures in the sense required by the theory of media formalism seems questionable.

Even if there are no essences to art forms, certainly there are conventions in operation at any given time in each art form. And certainly some works more directly explore those conventions than others. Even so, what support is there for the evaluative claims, (3) and (4), which say that we ought to look for this exploration in every artwork and that those artworks that most plainly and consistently explore such issues are the best artworks? What grounds do we even have for defending such a principle of evaluation restricted to art in the modernist era? Greenberg admits that the justification for this position is weak: "That visual art should confine itself exclusively to what is given in visual experience, and make no reference to anything given in other orders of experience, is a notion whose only justification lies, notionally, in scientific consistency" (p. 158). Undoubtedly, many practices can be construed as consistent in their own way. That does not make them necessarily valuable. The real argument here seems to be a version of historical inevitability. If we view the "progress" of art historically as aiming toward the goal of pure painting, painting with all irrelevant features removed, then those artists who have been and are now contributing to this goal may seem to be producing art that is in accord with their historical task and therefore more valuable. But here we are assuming that there is a historical process inevitably leading toward this goal — a picture of history rejected by many thinkers — and also that the value of art is to be found only in contributions to this "progress." Even Greenberg concedes this is a dubious position. He recognizes that the consistency of modernism "promises nothing in the way of esthetic quality or esthetic results" (p. 158).

To summarize: For the media formalist, form has to do with the relation of a work to the limitations and norms of its medium. Media formalism thus has difficulty accounting for work in mixed media or in no salient medium. This theory ignores the first-order sensory, emotional, or mimetic responses to a work almost entirely in favor of a second-order response to a work as art about the nature of art. Clive Bell wants to ignore what a work represents, but the consistent media formalist wants to ignore even the forms of what is represented asking only how the forms and physical properties are related to the limitations of the medium. Finally, if media formalism has any account of the value of this dimension of artworks, it seems to lie with the value of purity and consistency of method and with the relation of the artwork to the history of its art form. If media formalism is the best theory of art, art would have to be valued as a process of investigation for its own sake, analogous to basic knowledge in science. Unlike basic scientific knowledge, however, it would not be useful in any way outside itself.

READINGS FOR CHAPTER 10

Clive Bell, from *Art*
Eduard Hanslick, from *On the Beautiful in Music*
Leonard B. Meyer, "On Rehearing Music"
Malcolm Bradbury and James McFarlane, "The Name and Nature of Modernism"

from *Art*
Clive Bell

1. *The Aesthetic Hypothesis*

It is improbable that more nonsense has been written about aesthetics than about anything else: the literature of the subject is not large enough for that. It is certain, however, that about no subject with which I am acquainted has so little been said that is at all to the purpose. The explanation is discoverable. He who would elaborate a plausible theory of aesthetics must possess two qualities — artistic sensibility and a turn for clear thinking. Without sensibility a man can have no aesthetic experience, and, obviously, theories not based on broad and deep aesthetic experience are worthless. Only those for whom art is a constant source of passionate emotion can possess the data from which profitable theories may be deduced; but to deduce profitable theories even from accurate data involves a certain amount of brain-work, and, unfortunately, robust intellects and delicate sensibilities are not inseparable. As often as not, the hardest thinkers have had no aesthetic experience whatever. I have a friend blessed with an intellect as keen as a drill, who, though he takes an interest in aesthetics, has never during a life of almost forty years been guilty of an aesthetic emotion. So, having no faculty for distinguishing a work of art from a handsaw, he is apt to rear up a pyramid of irrefragable argument on the hypothesis that a handsaw is a work of art. This defect robs his perspicuous and subtle reasoning of much of its value; for it has ever been a maxim that faultless logic can win but little credit for conclusions that are based on premises notoriously false. Every cloud, however, has its silver lining, and this insensibility, though unlucky in that it makes my friend incapable of choosing a sound basis for his argument, mercifully blinds him to the absurdity of his conclusions while leaving him in full enjoyment of his masterly dialectic. People who set out from the hypothesis that Sir Edwin Landseer was the finest painter that ever lived will feel no uneasiness about an aesthetic which proves that Giotto was the worst. So, my friend, when he arrives very logically at the conclusion that a work of art should be small or round or smooth, or that to appreciate fully a picture you should pace smartly before it or set it spinning like a top, cannot guess why I ask him whether he has lately been to Cambridge, a place he sometimes visits.

On the other hand, people who respond immediately and surely to works of art, though, in my judgment, more enviable than men of massive intellect but slight sensibility, are often quite as incapable of talking sense about aesthetics. Their heads are not always very clear. They possess the data on which any system must be based; but, generally, they want the power that draws correct inferences from true data. Having received aesthetic emotions from works of art, they are in a position to seek out the quality common to all that have moved them, but, in fact, they do nothing of the sort. I do not blame them. Why should they bother to examine their feelings when for them to feel is enough? Why should they stop to think when they are not very good at thinking? Why should they hunt for a common quality in all objects that move them in a particular way when they can linger over the many delicious and peculiar charms of each as it comes? So, if they write criticism and call it aesthetics, if they imagine that they are talking about Art when they are talking about particular works of art or even about the technique of painting, if loving particular works they find tedious the consideration of art in general, perhaps they have chosen the better part. If they are not curious about the nature of their emotion, nor about the quality common to all objects that provoke it, they have my sympathy, and, as what they say is often charming and suggestive, my admiration too. Only let no one suppose that what they write and talk is aesthetics; it is criticism, or just "shop."

The starting-point for all systems of aesthetics must be the personal experience of a peculiar emotion. The objects that provoke this emotion we call works of art. All sensitive people agree that there is a peculiar emotion provoked by works of art. I do not mean, of course, that all works provoke the same emotion. On the contrary, every work produces a different emotion. But all these emotions are recognisably the same in kind; so far, at any rate, the best opinion is on my side. That there is a particular kind of emotion provoked by works of visual art, and that this emotion is provoked by every kind of visual art, by pictures, sculptures, buildings, pots, carvings, textiles, &c., &c., is not disputed, I think, by anyone capable of feeling it. This emotion is called the aesthetic emotion; and if we can discover some quality common and peculiar to all the objects that provoke it, we shall have solved what I take to be the central problem of aesthetics. We shall have discovered the essential quality in a work of art, the quality that distinguishes works of art from all other classes of objects.

For either all works of visual art have some common quality, or when we speak of "works of art" we gibber. Everyone speaks of "art," making a mental classification by which he distinguishes the class "works of art" from all other classes. What is the justification of this classification? What is the quality common and peculiar to all members of this class? Whatever it be, no doubt it is often found in company with other qualities; but they are adventitious—it is essential. There must be some one quality without which a work of art cannot exist; possessing which, in the least

degree, no work is altogether worthless. What is this quality? What quality is shared by all objects that provoke our aesthetic emotions? What quality is common to Sta. Sophia and the windows at Chartres, Mexican sculpture, a Persian bowl, Chinese carpets, Giotto's frescoes at Padua, and the masterpieces of Poussin, Piero della Francesca, and Cézanne? Only one answer seems possible—significant form. In each, lines and colours combined in a particular way, certain forms and relations of forms, stir our aesthetic emotions. These relations and combinations of lines and colours, these aesthetically moving forms, I call "Significant Form"; and "Significant Form" is the one quality common to all works of visual art.

At this point it may be objected that I am making aesthetics a purely subjective business, since my only data are personal experiences of a particular emotion. It will be said that the objects that provoke this emotion vary with each individual, and that therefore a system of aesthetics can have no objective validity. It must be replied that any system of aesthetics which pretends to be based on some objective truth is so palpably ridiculous as not to be worth discussing. We have no other means of recognising a work of art than our feeling for it. The objects that provoke aesthetic emotion vary with each individual. Aesthetic judgments are, as the saying goes, matters of taste; and about tastes, as everyone is proud to admit, there is no disputing. A good critic may be able to make me see in a picture that had left me cold things that I had overlooked, till at last, receiving the aesthetic emotion, I recognise it as a work of art. To be continually pointing out those parts, the sum, or rather the combination, of which unite to produce significant form, is the function of criticism. But it is useless for a critic to tell me that something is a work of art; he must make me feel it for myself. This he can do only by making me see; he must get at my emotions through my eyes. Unless he can make me see something that moves me, he cannot force my emotions. I have no right to consider anything a work of art to which I cannot react emotionally;

and I have no right to look for the essential quality in anything that I have not *felt* to be a work of art. The critic can affect my aesthetic theories only by affecting my aesthetic experience. All systems of aesthetics must be based on personal experience — that is to say, they must be subjective.

Yet, though all aesthetic theories must be based on aesthetic judgments, and ultimately all aesthetic judgments must be matters of personal taste, it would be rash to assert that no theory of aesthetics can have general validity. For, though A, B, C, D are the works that move me, and A, D, E, F the works that move you, it may well be that *x* is the only quality believed by either of us to be common to all the works in his list. We may all agree about aesthetics, and yet differ about particular works of art. We may differ as to the presence or absence of the quality *x*. My immediate object will be to show that significant form is the only quality common and peculiar to all the works of visual art that move me; and I will ask those whose aesthetic experience does not tally with mine to see whether this quality is not also, in their judgment, common to all works that move them, and whether they can discover any other quality of which the same can be said.

Also at this point a query arises, irrelevant indeed, but hardly to be suppressed: "Why are we so profoundly moved by forms related in a particular way?" The question is extremely interesting, but irrelevant to aesthetics. In pure aesthetics we have only to consider our emotion and its object: for the purposes of aesthetics we have no right, neither is there any necessity, to pry behind the object into the state of mind of him who made it. Later, I shall attempt to answer the question; for by so doing I may be able to develop my theory of the relation of art to life. I shall not, however, be under the delusion that I am rounding off my theory of aesthetics. For a discussion of aesthetics, it need be agreed only that forms arranged and combined according to certain unknown and mysterious laws do move us in a particular way, and that it is the business of an artist so to combine and arrange them that they shall move us. These moving combinations and arrangements I

have called, for the sake of convenience and for a reason that will appear later, "Significant Form."

A third interruption has to be met.

"Are you forgetting about colour?" someone inquires. Certainly not; my term "significant form" included combinations of lines and of colours. The distinction between form and colour is an unreal one; you cannot conceive a colourless line or a colourless space; neither can you conceive a formless relation of colours. In a black and white drawing the spaces are all white and all are bounded by black lines; in most oil paintings the spaces are multi-coloured and so are the boundaries; you cannot imagine a boundary line without any content, or a content without a boundary line. Therefore, when I speak of significant form, I mean a combination of lines and colours (counting white and black as colours) that moves me aesthetically.

Some people may be surprised at my not having called this "beauty." Of course, to those who define beauty as "combinations of lines and colours that provoke aesthetic emotion," I willingly concede the right of substituting their word for mine. But most of us, however strict we may be, are apt to apply the epithet "beautiful" to objects that do not provoke that peculiar emotion produced by works of art. Everyone, I suspect, has called a butterfly or a flower beautiful. Does anyone feel the same kind of emotion for a butterfly or a flower that he feels for a cathedral or a picture? Surely, it is not what I call an aesthetic emotion that most of us feel, generally, for natural beauty. I shall suggest, later, that some people may, occasionally, see in nature what we see in art, and feel for her an aesthetic emotion; but I am satisfied that, as a rule, most people feel a very different kind of emotion for birds and flowers and the wings of butterflies from that which they feel for pictures, pots, temples and statues. Why these beautiful things do not move us as works of art move is another, and not an aesthetic, question. For our immediate purpose we have to discover only what quality is common to objects that do move us as works of art. In the last part of this chapter, when I try to answer the question —

"Why are we so profoundly moved by some combinations of lines and colours?" I shall hope to offer an acceptable explanation of why we are less profoundly moved by others.

Since we call a quality that does not raise the characteristic aesthetic emotion "Beauty," it would be misleading to call by the same name the quality that does. To make "beauty" the object of the aesthetic emotion, we must give to the word an over-strict and unfamiliar definition. Everyone sometimes uses "beauty" in an unaesthetic sense; most people habitually do so. To everyone, except perhaps here and there an occasional aesthete, the commonest sense of the word is unaesthetic. Of its grosser abuse, patent in our chatter about "beautiful huntin'" and "beautiful shootin'," I need not take account; it would be open to the precious to reply that they never do so abuse it. Besides, here there is no danger of confusion between the aesthetic and the non-aesthetic use; but when we speak of a beautiful woman there is. When an ordinary man speaks of a beautiful woman he certainly does not mean only that she moves him aesthetically; but when an artist calls a withered old hag beautiful he may sometimes mean what he means when he calls a battered torso beautiful. The ordinary man, if he be also a man of taste, will call the battered torso beautiful, but he will not call a withered hag beautiful because, in the matter of women, it is not to the aesthetic quality that the hag may possess, but to some other quality that he assigns the epithet. Indeed, most of us never dream of going for aesthetic emotions to human beings, from whom we ask something very different. This "something," when we find it in a young woman, we are apt to call "beauty." We live in a nice age. With the man-in-the-street "beautiful" is more often than not synonymous with "desirable"; the word does not necessarily connote any aesthetic reaction whatever, and I am tempted to believe that in the minds of many the sexual flavour of the word is stronger than the aesthetic. I have noticed a consistency in those to whom the most beautiful thing in the world is a beautiful woman, and the next most beautiful thing a picture of one. The confusion between aesthetic and sensual beauty is not in their case so great as might be supposed. Perhaps there is none; for perhaps they have never had an aesthetic emotion to confuse with their other emotions. The art that they call "beautiful" is generally closely related to the women. A beautiful picture is a photograph of a pretty girl; beautiful music, the music that provokes emotions similar to those provoked by young ladies in musical farces; and beautiful poetry, the poetry that recalls the same emotions felt, twenty years earlier, for the rector's daughter. Clearly the word "beauty" is used to connote the objects of quite distinguishable emotions, and that is a reason for not employing a term which would land me inevitably in confusions and misunderstandings with my readers.

On the other hand, with those who judge it more exact to call these combinations and arrangements of form that provoke our aesthetic emotions, not "significant form," but "significant relations of form," and then try to make the best of two worlds, the aesthetic and the metaphysical, by calling these relations "rhythm," I have no quarrel whatever. Having made it clear that by "significant form" I mean arrangements and combinations that move us in a particular way, I willingly join hands with those who prefer to give a different name to the same thing.

The hypothesis that significant form is the essential quality in a work of art has at least one merit denied to many more famous and more striking—it does help to explain things. We are all familiar with pictures that interest us and excite our admiration, but do not move us as works of art. To this class belongs what I call "Descriptive Painting"—that is, painting in which forms are used not as objects of emotion, but as means of suggesting emotion or conveying information. Portraits of psychological and historical value, topographical works, pictures that tell stories and suggest situations, illustrations of all sorts, belong to this class. That we all recognize the distinction is clear, for who has not said that such and such a drawing was excellent as illustration, but as a work of art worthless? Of course many descriptive pictures possess, amongst other qualities, formal significance, and are therefore works of art: but many more do not. They interest us; they may move us too in a hundred different ways, but they do not move us aesthetically. According to my hypothesis they are not works of art. They leave untouched our aesthetic emotions because it is not their forms but the ideas or information suggested or conveyed by their forms that affect us.

Few pictures are better known or liked than Frith's "Paddington Station"; certainly I should be the last to grudge it its popularity. Many a weary forty minutes have I whiled away disentangling its fascinating incidents and forging for each an imaginary past and an improbable future. But certain though it is that Frith's masterpiece, or engravings of it, have provided thousands with half-hours of curious and fanciful pleasure, it is not less certain that no one has experienced before it one half-second of aesthetic rapture — and this although the picture contains several pretty passages of colour, and is by no means badly painted. "Paddington Station" is not a work of art; it is an interesting and amusing document. In it line and colour are used to recount anecdotes, suggest ideas, and indicate the manners and customs of an age: they are not used to provoke aesthetic emotion. Forms and the relations of forms were for Frith not objects of emotion, but means of suggesting emotion and conveying ideas.

The ideas and information conveyed by "Paddington Station" are so amusing and so well presented that the picture has considerable value and is well worth preserving. But, with the perfection of photographic processes and of the cinematograph, pictures of this sort are becoming otiose. Who doubts that one of those *Daily Mirror* photographers in collaboration with a *Daily Mail* reporter can tell us far more about "London day by day" than any Royal Academician? For an account of manners and fashions we shall go, in future, to photographs, supported by a little bright journalism, rather than to descriptive painting. Had the imperial academicians of Nero, instead of manufacturing incredibly loathsome imitations of the antique, recorded in fresco and mosaic the manners and fashions of their day, their stuff, though artistic rubbish, would now be an historical gold-mine. If only they had been Friths instead of being Alma Tademas! But photography has made impossible any such transmutation of modern rubbish. Therefore it must be confessed that pictures in the Frith tradition are grown superfluous; they merely waste the hours of able men who might be more profitably employed in works of a wider beneficence. Still, they are not unpleasant, which is more than can be said for that kind of descriptive painting of which "The Doctor" is the most flagrant example. Of course "The Doctor" is not a work of art. In it form is not used as an object of emotion, but as a means of suggesting emotions. This alone suffices to make it nugatory; it is worse then nugatory because the emotion it suggests is false. What it suggests is not pity and admiration but a sense of complacency in our own pitifulness and generosity. It is sentimental. Art is above morals, or, rather, all art is moral because, as I hope to show presently, works of art are immediate means to good. Once we have judged a thing a work of art, we have judged it ethically of the first importance and put it beyond the reach of the moralist. But descriptive pictures which are not works of art, and, therefore, are not necessarily means to good states of mind, are proper objects of the ethical philosopher's attention. Not being a work of art, "The Doctor" has none of the immense ethical value possessed by all objects that provoke aesthetic ecstasy; and the state of mind to which it is a means, as illustration, appears to me undesirable.

The works of those enterprising young men, the Italian Futurists, are notable examples of descriptive painting. Like the Royal Academicians, they use form, not to provoke aesthetic emotions, but to convey information and ideas. Indeed, the published theories of the Futurists prove that their pictures ought to have nothing whatever to do with art. Their social and political theories are respectable, but I would suggest to young Italian painters that it is possible to become a Futurist in thought and action and yet remain an artist, if one has the luck to be born one. To associate art with politics is always a mistake. Futurist pictures are descriptive because they aim at presenting in line and colour the chaos of the mind at a particular moment; their forms are not intended to promote aesthetic emotion but to convey information. These forms, by the way, whatever may be the nature of the ideas they suggest, are themselves anything but revolutionary. In such Futurist pictures as I have seen—perhaps I should except some by Severini—the drawing, whenever it becomes representative as it frequently does, is found to be in that soft and common convention brought into fashion by Besnard some thirty years ago, and much affected by Beaux-Art students ever since. As works of art, the Futurist pictures are negligible; but they are not to be judged as works of art. A good Futurist picture would succeed as a good piece of psychology succeeds; it would reveal, through line and colour, the complexities of an interesting state of mind. If Futurist pictures seem to fail, we must seek an explanation, not in a lack of artistic qualities that they never were intended to possess, but rather in the minds the states of which they are intended to reveal.

Most people who care much about art find that of the work that moves them most the greater part is what scholars call "Primitive." Of course there are bad primitives. For instance, I remember going, full of enthusiasm, to see one of the earliest Romanesque churches in Poitiers (Notre-Dame-la-Grande), and finding it as ill-proportioned, over-decorated, coarse, fat and heavy as any better class building by one of those highly civilised architects who flourished a thousand years earlier or eight hundred later. But such exceptions are rare. As a rule primitive art is good—and here again my hypothesis is helpful—for, as a rule, it is also free from descriptive qualities. In primitive art you will find no accurate representation; you will find only significant form. Yet no other art moves us so profoundly. Whether we consider Sumerian sculpture or pre-dynastic Egyptian art, or archaic Greek, or the Wei and T'ang master-

pieces,[1] or those early Japanese works of which I had the luck to see a few superb examples (especially two wooden Bodhisattvas) at the Shepherd's Bush Exhibition in 1910, or whether, coming nearer home, we consider the primitive Byzantine art of the sixth century and its primitive developments amongst the Western barbarians, or, turning far afield, we consider that mysterious and majestic art that flourished in Central and South America before the coming of the white men, in every case we observe three common characteristics—absence of representation, absence of technical swagger, sublimely impressive form. Nor is it hard to discover the connection between these three. Formal significance loses itself in preoccupation with exact representation and ostentatious cunning.[2]

Naturally, it is said that if there is little representation and less saltimbancery in primitive art, that is because the primitives were unable to catch a likeness or cut intellectual capers. The contention is beside the point. There is truth in it, no doubt, though, were I a critic whose reputation depended on a power of impressing the public with a semblance of knowledge, I should be more

[1] The existence of the Ku K'ai-chih makes it clear that the art of this period (fifth to eighth centuries), was a typical primitive movement. To call the great vital art of the Liang, Chen, Wei, and Tang dynasties a development out of the exquisitely refined and exhausted art of the Han decadence—from which Ku K'ai-chih is a delicate straggler—is to call Romanesque sculpture a development out of Praxiteles. Between the two something has happened to refill the stream of art. What had happened in China was the spiritual and emotional revolution that followed the onset of Buddhism.

[2] This is not to say that exact representation is bad in itself. It is indifferent. A perfectly represented form may be significant, only it is fatal to sacrifice significance to representation. The quarrel between significance and illusion seems to be as old as art itself, and I have little doubt that what makes most palaeolithic art so bad is a preoccupation with exact representation. Evidently palaeolithic draughtsmen had no sense of the significance of form. Their art resembles that of the more capable and sincere Royal Academicians: it is a little higher than that of Sir Edward Poynter and a little lower than that of the late Lord Leighton. That this is no paradox let the cave-drawings of Altamira, or such works as the sketches of horses found at Bruniquel and now in the British Museum, bear witness. If the ivory head of a girl from the Grotte du Pape, Brassempouy (*Musée St. Germain*) and the ivory torso found at the same place (*Collection St. Cric*), be, indeed, palaeolithic, then there were good palaeolithic artists who created and did not imitate form. Neolithic art is, of course, a very different matter.

cautious about urging it than such people generally are. For to suppose that the Byzantine masters wanted skill, or could not have created an illusion had they wished to do so, seems to imply ignorance of the amazingly dexterous realism of the notoriously bad works of that age. Very often, I fear, the misrepresentation of the primitives must be attributed to what the critics call, "wilful distortion." Be that as it may, the point is that, either from want of skill or want of will, primitives neither create illusions, nor make display of extravagant accomplishment, but concentrate their energies on the one thing needful — the creation of form. Thus have they created the finest works of art that we possess.

Let no one imagine that representation is bad in itself; a realistic form may be as significant, in its place as part of the design, as an abstract. But if a representative form has value, it is as form, not as representation. The representative element in a work of art may or may not be harmful; always it is irrelevant. For, to appreciate a work of art we need bring with us nothing from life, no knowledge of its ideas and affairs, no familiarity with its emotions. Art transports us from the world of man's activity to a world of aesthetic exaltation. For a moment we are shut off from human interests; our anticipations and memories are arrested; we are lifted above the stream of life. The pure mathematician rapt in his studies knows a state of mind which I take to be similar, if not identical. He feels an emotion for his speculations which arises from no perceived relation between them and the lives of men, but springs, in human or super-human, from the heart of an abstract science. I wonder, sometimes, whether the appreciators of art and of mathematical solutions are not even more closely allied. Before we feel an aesthetic emotion for a combination of forms, do we not perceive intellectually the rightness and necessity of the combination? If we do, it would explain the fact that passing rapidly through a room we recognise a picture to be good, although we cannot say that it has provoked much emotion. We seem to have recognised intellectually the rightness of its forms without staying to fix our attention, and collect, as it were, their emo-

tional significance. If this were so, it would be permissible to inquire whether it was the forms themselves or our perception of their rightness and necessity that caused aesthetic emotion. But I do not think I need linger to discuss the matter here. I have been inquiring why certain combinations of forms move us; I should not have travelled by other roads had I enquired, instead, why certain combinations are perceived to be right and necessary, and why our perception of their rightness and necessity is moving. What I have to say is this: the rapt philosopher, and he who contemplates a work of art, inhabit a world with an intense and peculiar significance of its own; that significance is unrelated to the significance of life. In this world the emotions of life find no place. It is a world with emotions of its own.

To appreciate a work of art we need bring with us nothing but a sense of form and colour and a knowledge of three-dimensional space. That bit of knowledge, I admit, is essential to the appreciation of many great works, since many of the most moving forms ever created are in three dimensions. To see a cube or a rhomboid as a flat pattern is to lower its significance, and a sense of three-dimensional space is essential to the full appreciation of most architectural forms. Pictures which would be insignificant if we saw them as flat patterns are profoundly moving because, in fact, we see them as related planes. If the representation of three-dimensional space is to be called "representation," then I agree that there is one kind of representation which is not irrelevant. Also, I agree that along with our feeling for line and colour we must bring with us our knowledge of space if we are to make the most of every kind of form. Nevertheless, there are magnificent designs to an appreciation of which this knowledge is not necessary: so, though it is not irrelevant to the appreciation of some works of art it is not essential to the appreciation of all. What we must say is that the representation of three-dimensional space is neither irrelevant nor essential to all art, and that every other sort of representation is irrelevant.

That there is an irrelevant representative or descriptive element in many great works of art is not in the least surprising. Why it is not surprising I shall try to show elsewhere. Representation is not of necessity baneful, and highly realistic forms may be extremely significant. Very often, however, representation is a sign of weakness in an artist. A painter too feeble to create forms that provoke more than a little aesthetic emotion will try to eke that little out by suggesting the emotions of life. To evoke the emotions of life he must use representation. Thus a man will paint an execution, and, fearing to miss with his first barrel of significant form, will try to hit with his second by raising an emotion of fear or pity. But if in the artist an inclination to play upon the emotions of life is often the sign of a flickering inspiration, in the spectator a tendency to seek, behind form, the emotions of life is a sign of defective sensibility always. It means that his aesthetic emotions are weak or, at any rate, imperfect. Before a work of art people who feel little or no emotion for pure form find themselves at a loss. They are deaf men at a concert. They know that they are in the presence of something great, but they lack the power of apprehending it. They know that they ought to feel for it a tremendous emotion, but it happens that the particular kind of emotion it can raise is one that they can feel hardly or not at all. And so they read into the forms of the work those facts and ideas for which they are capable of feeling emotion, and feel for them the emotions that they can feel — the ordinary emotions of life. When confronted by a picture, instinctively they refer back its forms to the world from which they came. They treat created form as though it were imitated form, a picture as though it were a photograph. Instead of going out on the stream of art into a new world of aesthetic experience, they turn a sharp corner and come straight home to the world of human interests. For them the significance of a work of art depends on what they bring to it; no new thing is added to their lives, only the old material is stirred. A good work of visual art carries a person who is capable of appreciating it out of life into ecstasy: to use art as a means to the emotions of life is to use a telescope for reading the news. You will notice that people who cannot feel pure aesthetic emotions remember pictures by their subjects; whereas people who can, as often as not, have no idea what the subject of a picture is. They have never noticed the representative element, and so when they discuss pictures they talk about the shapes of forms and the relations and quantities of colours. Often they can tell by the quality of a single line whether or no a man is a good artist. They are concerned only with lines and colours, their relations and quantities and qualities; but from these they win an emotion more profound and far more sublime than any that can be given by the description of facts and ideas.

This last sentence has a very confident ring — over-confident, some may think. Perhaps I shall be able to justify it, and make my meaning clearer too, if I give an account of my own feelings about music. I am not really musical. I do not understand music well. I find musical form exceedingly difficult to apprehend, and I am sure that the profounder subtleties of harmony and rhythm more often than not escape me. The form of a musical composition must be simple indeed if I am to grasp it honestly. My opinion about music is not worth having. Yet, sometimes, at a concert, though my appreciation of the music is limited and humble, it is pure. Sometimes, though I have a poor understanding, I have a clean palate. Consequently, when I am feeling bright and clear and intent, at the beginning of a concert for instance, when something that I can grasp is being played, I get from music that pure aesthetic emotion that I get from visual art. It is less intense, and the rapture is evanescent; I understand music too ill for music to transport me far into the world of pure aesthetic ecstasy. But at moments I do appreciate music as pure musical form, as sounds combined according to the laws of a mysterious necessity, as pure art with a tremendous significance of its own and no relation whatever to the significance of life; and in those moments I lose myself in that infinitely sublime state of mind to which pure visual form transports me. How inferior is my normal state of mind at a concert. Tired or perplexed, I let slip my sense of form, my aesthetic emotion collapses, and I begin weaving into the harmonies, that I cannot grasp, the ideas of life. Incapable of feeling the austere emotions of art, I begin to read into the musical forms human emotions of terror and mystery, love and hate, and spend the minutes, pleasantly enough, in a world of turbid and inferior feeling. At such times, were the grossest pieces of onomatopoeic representation — the song of a bird, the galloping of horses, the cries of children, or the laughing of demons — to be introduced into the symphony, I should not be offended. Very likely I should be pleased; they would afford new points of departure for new trains of romantic feeling or heroic thought. I know very well what has happened. I have been using art as a means to the emotions of life and reading into it the ideas of life. I have been cutting blocks with a razor. I have tumbled from the superb peaks of aesthetic exaltation to the snug foothills of warm humanity. It is a jolly country. No one need be ashamed of enjoying himself there. Only no one who has ever been on the heights can help feeling a little crestfallen in the cosy valleys. And let no one imagine, because he has made merry in the warm tilth and quaint nooks of romance, that he can even guess at the austere and thrilling raptures of those who have climbed the cold, white peaks of art.

About music most people are as willing to be humble as I am. If they cannot grasp musical form and win from it a pure aesthetic emotion, they confess that they understand music imperfectly or not at all. They recognise quite clearly that there is a difference between the feeling of the musician for pure music and that of the cheerful concertgoer for what music suggests. The latter enjoys his own emotions, as he has every right to do, and recognises their inferiority. Unfortunately, people are apt to be less modest about their powers of appreciating visual art. Everyone is inclined to believe that out of pictures, at any rate, he can get all that there is to be got; everyone is ready to cry "humbug" and "impostor" at those who say that more can be had. The good faith of people who feel pure aesthetic emotions is called in question by those who have never felt anything of the sort. It is the prevalence of the representative element, I suppose, that makes the man in the street so sure

that he knows a good picture when he sees one. For I have noticed that in matters of architecture, pottery, textiles, &c., ignorance and ineptitude are more willing to defer to the opinions of those who have been blest with peculiar sensibility. It is a pity that cultivated and intelligent men and women cannot be induced to believe that a great gift of aesthetic appreciation is at least as rare in visual as in musical art. A comparison of my own experience in both has enabled me to discriminate very clearly between pure and impure appreciation. Is it too much to ask that others should be as honest about their feelings for pictures as I have been about mine for music? For I am certain that most of those who visit galleries do feel very much what I feel at concerts. They have their moments of pure ecstasy; but the moments are short and unsure. Soon they fall back into the world of human interests and feel emotions, good no doubt, but inferior. I do not dream of saying that what they get from art is bad or nugatory; I say that they do not get the best that art can give. I do not say that they cannot understand art; rather I say that they cannot understand the state of mind of those who understand it best. I do not say that art means nothing or little to them; I say they miss its full significance. I do not suggest for one moment that their appreciation of art is a thing to be ashamed of; the majority of the charming and intelligent people with whom I am acquainted appreciate visual art impurely; and, by the way, the appreciation of almost all great writers has been impure. But provided that there be some fraction of pure aesthetic emotion, even a mixed and minor appreciation of art is, I am sure, one of the most valuable things in the world — so valuable, indeed, that in my giddier moments I have been tempted to believe that art might prove the world's salvation.

Yet, though the echoes and shadows of art enrich the life of the plains, her spirit dwells on the mountains. To him who woos, but woos impurely, she returns enriched what is brought. Like the sun, she warms the good seed in good soil and causes it to bring forth good fruit. But only to the perfect lover does she give a new strange gift — a gift beyond all price. Imperfect lovers bring to art and take away the ideas and emotions of their own age and civilisation. In twelfth-century Europe a man might have been greatly moved by a Romanesque church and found nothing in a T'ang picture. To a man of a later age, Greek sculpture meant much and Mexican nothing, for only to the former could he bring a crowd of associated ideas to be the objects of familiar emotions. But the perfect lover, he who can feel the profound significance of form, is raised above the accidents of time and place. To him the problems of archaeology, history, and hagiography are impertinent. If the forms of a work are significant its provenance is irrelevant. Before the grandeur of those Sumerian figures in the Louvre he is carried on the same flood of emotion to the same aesthetic ecstasy as, more than four thousand years ago, the Chaldean lover was carried. It is the mark of great art that its appeal is universal and eternal.[3] Significant form stands charged with the power to provoke aesthetic emotion in anyone capable of feeling it. The ideas of men go buzz and die like gnats; men change their institutions and their customs as they change their coats; the intellectual triumphs of one age are the follies of another; only great art remains stable and unobscure. Great art remains stable and unobscure because the feelings that it awakens are independent of time and place, because its kingdom is not

of this world. To those who have and hold a sense of the significance of form what does it matter whether the forms that move them were created in Paris the day before yesterday or in Babylon fifty centuries ago? The forms of art are inexhaustible; but all lead by the same road of aesthetic emotion to the same world of aesthetic ecstasy.

3. The Metaphysical Hypothesis

. . . I want now to consider that metaphysical question—"Why do certain arrangements and combinations of form move us so strangely?" For aesthetics it suffices that they do move us; to all further inquisition of the tedious and stupid it can be replied that, however queer these things may be, they are no queerer than anything else in this incredibly queer universe. But to those for whom my theory seems to open a vista of possibilities I willingly offer, for what they are worth, my fancies.

It seems to me possible, though by no means certain, that created form moves us so profoundly because it expresses the emotion of its creator. Perhaps the lines and colours of a work of art convey to us something that the artist felt. If this be so, it will explain that curious but undeniable fact, to which I have already referred, that what I call material beauty (*e.g.* the wing of a butterfly) does not move most of us in at all the same way as a work of art moves us. It is beautiful form, but it is not significant form. It moves us, but it does not move us aesthetically. It is tempting to explain the difference between "significant form" and "beauty"—that is to say, the difference between form that provokes our aesthetic emotions and form that does not—by saying that significant form conveys to us an emotion felt by its creator and that beauty conveys nothing.

For what, then, does the artist feel the emotion that he is supposed to express? Sometimes it certainly comes to him through material beauty. The contemplation of natural objects is often the immediate cause of the artist's emotion. Are we to suppose, then, that the artist feels, or sometimes

---

[3]Mr. Roger Fry permits me to make use of an interesting story that will illustrate my view. When Mr. Okakura, the Government editor of *The Temple Treasures of Japan*, first came to Europe, he found no difficulty in appreciating the pictures of those who from want of will or want of skill did not create illusions but concentrated their energies on the creation of form. He understood immediately the Byzantine masters and the French and Italian Primitives. In the Renaissance painters, on the other hand, with their descriptive preoccupations, their literary and anecdotic interests, he could see nothing but vulgarity and muddle. The universal and essential quality of art, significant form, was missing, or rather had dwindled to a shallow stream, overlaid and hidden beneath weeds, so the universal response, aesthetic emotion, was not evoked. It was not till he came on to Henri-Matisse that he again found himself in the familiar world of pure art. Similarly, sensitive Europeans who respond immediately to the significant forms of great Oriental art, are left cold by the trivial pieces of anecdote and social criticism so lovingly cherished by Chinese dilettanti. It would be easy to multiply instances did not decency forbid the labouring of so obvious a truth.

feels, for material beauty what we feel for a work of art? Can it be that sometimes for the artist material beauty is somehow significant—that is, capable of provoking aesthetic emotion? And if the form that provokes aesthetic emotion be form that expresses something, can it be that material beauty is to him expressive? Does he feel something behind it as we imagine that we feel something behind the forms of a work of art? Are we to suppose that the emotion which the artist expresses is an aesthetic emotion felt for something the significance of which commonly escapes our coarser sensibilities? All these are questions about which I had sooner speculate than dogmatise.

Let us hear what the artists have got to say for themselves. We readily believe them when they tell us that, in fact, they do not create works of art in order to provoke our aesthetic emotions, but because only thus can they materialise a particular kind of feeling. What, precisely, this feeling is they find it hard to say. One account of the matter, given me by a very good artist, is that what he tries to express in a picture is "a passionate apprehension of form." I have set myself to discover what is meant by "a passionate apprehension form," and, after much talking and more listening, I have arrived at the following result. Occasionally when an artist—a real artist—looks at objects (the contents of a room, for instance) he perceives them as pure forms in certain relations to each other, and feels emotion for them as such. These are his moments of inspiration: follows the desire to express what has been felt. The emotion that the artist felt in his moment of inspiration he did not feel for objects seen as means, but for objects seen as pure forms—that is, as ends in themselves. He did not feel emotion for a chair as a means to physical well-being, nor as an object associated with the intimate life of a family, nor as the place where someone sat saying things unforgettable, nor yet as a thing bound to the lives of hundreds of men and women, dead or alive, by a hundred subtle ties; doubtless an artist does often feel emotions such as these for the things that he sees, but in the moment of aesthetic vision he sees objects, not as means shrouded in associations, but as pure forms. It is for, or at any rate through, pure form that he feels his inspired emotion.

Now to see objects as pure forms is to see them as ends in themselves. For though, of course, forms are related to each other as parts of a whole, they are related on terms of equality; they are not a means to anything except emotion. But for objects seen as ends in themselves, do we not feel a profounder and a more thrilling emotion than ever we felt for them as means? All of us, I imagine, do, from time to time, get a vision of material objects as pure forms. We see things as ends in themselves, that is to say; and at such moments it seems possible, and even probable, that we see them with the eye of an artist. Who has not, once at least in his life, had a sudden vision of landscape as pure form? For once, instead of seeing it as fields and cottages, he has felt it as lines and colours. In that moment has he not won from material beauty a thrill indistinguishable from that which art gives? And, if this be so, is it not clear that he has won from material beauty the thrill that, generally, art alone can give, because he has contrived to see it as a pure formal combination of lines and colours? May we go on to say that, having seen it as pure form, having freed it from all casual and adventitious interest, from all that it may have acquired from its commerce with human beings, from all its significance as a means, he has felt its significance as an end in itself?

What is the significance of anything as an end in itself? What is that which is left when we have stripped a thing of all its associations, of all its significance as a means? What is left to provoke our emotion? What but that which philosophers used to call "the thing in itself" and now call "ultimate reality"? Shall I be altogether fantastic in suggesting, what some of the profoundest thinkers have believed, that the significance of the thing in itself is the significance of Reality? Is it possible that the answer to my question, "Why are we so profoundly moved by certain combinations of lines and colours?" should be, "Because artists can express in combinations of lines and colours an emotion felt for reality which reveals itself through line and colour"?

If this suggestion were accepted it would follow that "significant form" was form behind which we catch a sense of ultimate reality. There would be good reason for supposing that the emotions which artists feel in their moments of inspiration, that others feel in the rare moments when they see objects artistically, and that many of us feel when we contemplate works of art, are the same in kind. All would be emotions felt for reality revealing itself through pure form. It is certain that this emotion can be expressed only in pure form. It is certain that most of us can come at it only through pure form. But is pure form the only channel through which anyone can come at this mysterious emotion? That is a disturbing and a most distasteful question, for at this point I thought I saw my way to cancelling out the word "reality," and saying that all are emotions felt for pure form which may or may not have something behind it. To me it would be most satisfactory to say that the reason why some forms move us aesthetically, and others do not, is that some have been so purified that we can feel them aesthetically and that others are so clogged with unaesthetic matter (*e.g.* associations) that only the sensibility of an artist can perceive their pure, formal significance. I should be charmed to believe that it is as certain that everyone must come at reality through form as that everyone must express his sense of it in form. But is that so? What kind of form is that from which the musician draws the emotion that he expresses in abstract harmonies? Whence come the emotions of the architect and the potter? I know that the artist's emotion can be expressed only in form; I know that only by form can my aesthetic emotions be called into play; but can I be sure that it is always by form that an artist's emotion is provoked? Back to reality.

Those who incline to believe that the artist's emotion is felt for reality will readily admit that visual artists — with whom alone we are concerned — come at reality generally through material form. But don't they come at it sometimes through imagined form? And ought we not to add that sometimes the sense of reality comes we know not whence?

from *On the Beautiful in Music*

Eduard Hanslick

Aesthetics as Founded on Feelings

The course hitherto pursued in musical aesthetics
has nearly always been hampered by the false
assumption that the object was not so much to
inquire into what is beautiful in music as to describe the feelings which music awakens. This
view entirely coincides with that of the older systems of aesthetics, which considered the beautiful
solely in reference to the sensations aroused and
the philosophy of beauty as the offspring of
sensation.

Such systems of aesthetics are not only un-
philosophical, but they assume an almost sentimental character when applied to the most
ethereal of all arts; and though no doubt pleasing
to a certain class of enthusiasts, they afford but
little enlightenment to a thoughtful student who,
in order to learn something about the real nature
of music, will, above all, remain deaf to the fitful
promptings of passion and not, as most manuals
on music direct, turn to the emotions as a source
of knowledge.

The tendency in science to study as far as
possible the objective aspect of things could not
but affect researches into the nature of beauty. A
satisfactory result, however, is only to be attained
by relinquishing a method which starts from subjective sensation only to bring us face to face with
it once more after taking us for a poetic ramble
over the surface of the subject. Any such investigation will prove utterly futile unless the method
obtaining in natural science be followed, at least
in the sense of dealing with the things themselves,
in order to determine what is permanent and
objective in them when dissociated from the ever-
varying impressions which they produce.

Poetry, sculpture, and painting are, in point of
well-grounded aesthetic treatment, far in advance
of music. Few writers on these subjects still labor
under the delusion that from a general metaphysical conception of beauty (a conception which
necessarily varies with the art) the aesthetic principles of any specific art can be deduced. Formerly, the aesthetic principles of the various arts
were supposed to be governed by some supreme
metaphysical principle of general aesthetics.
Now, however, the conviction is daily growing
that each individual art can be understood only
by studying its technical limits and its inherent
nature. "Systems" are gradually being sup-
planted by "researches" founded on the thesis
that the laws of beauty for each art are insepara-
bly associated with the individuality of the art
and the nature of its medium.[1]

[1]Robert Schumann has done a great deal of mischief by his proposition (*Collected Works*, I, 43): "The aesthetic principles of one art
are those of the others, the material alone being different."
Grillparzer expresses a very different opinion and takes the right
view when he says (*Complete Works*, IX, 142): "Probably no worse
service has ever been rendered to the arts than when German
writers included them all in the collective name of art. Many points
they undoubtedly have in common, yet they diverge widely not only

In the aesthetics of rhetoric, sculpture, and painting, no less than in art criticism — the practical application of the foregoing sciences — the rule has already been laid down that aesthetic investigations must above all consider the beautiful object, and not the perceiving subject.

Music alone is unable, apparently, to adopt this objective mode of procedure. Rigidly distinguishing between its theoretico-grammatical rules and its aesthetic researches, men generally state the former in extremely dry and prosaic language, while they wrap the latter in a cloud of high-flown sentimentality. The task of clearly realizing music as a self-subsistent form of the beautiful has hitherto presented insurmountable difficulties to musical aesthetics, and the dictates of "emotion" still haunt their domain in broad daylight. Beauty in music is still as much as ever viewed only in connection with its subjective impressions, and books, critiques, and conversations continually remind us that the emotions are the only aesthetic foundations of music, and that they alone are warranted in defining its scope.

Music, we are told, cannot, like poetry, entertain the mind with definite conceptions; nor yet the eye, like sculpture and painting, with visible forms. Hence, it is argued, its object must be to work on the feelings. "Music has to do with feelings." This expression, "has to do," is highly characteristic of all works on musical aesthetics. But what the nature of the link is that connects music with the emotions, or certain pieces of music with certain emotions; by what laws of nature it is governed; what the canons of art are that determine its form — all these questions are left in complete darkness by the very people who have "to do" with them. Only when one's eyes have become somewhat accustomed to this ob-

scurity does it become manifest that the emotions play a double part in music, as currently understood.

On the one hand it is said that the aim and object of music is to excite emotions, i.e., pleasurable emotions; on the other hand, the emotions are said to be the subject matter which musical works are intended to illustrate.

Both propositions are alike in this, that one is as false as the other.

The refutation of the first of these propositions, which forms the introduction to most manuals of music, must not detain us long. The beautiful, strictly speaking, aims at nothing, since it is nothing but a form which, though available for many purposes according to its nature, has, as such, no aim beyond itself. If the contemplation of something beautiful arouses pleasurable feelings, this effect is distinct from the beautiful as such. I may, indeed, place a beautiful object before an observer with the avowed purpose of giving him pleasure, but this purpose in no way affects the beauty of the object. The beautiful is and remains beautiful though it arouse no emotion whatever, and though there be no one to look at it. In other words, although the beautiful exists for the gratification of an observer, it is independent of him.

In this sense music, too, has no aim (object), and the mere fact that this particular art is so closely bound up with our feelings by no means justifies the assumption that its aesthetic principles depend on this union.

In order to examine this relation critically we must, in the first place, scrupulously distinguish between the terms "feeling" and "sensation," although in ordinary parlance no objection need be raised to their indiscriminate use.

"Sensation" is the act of perceiving some sensible quality such as a sound or a color, whereas "feeling" is the consciousness of some psychical activity, i.e., a state of satisfaction or discomfort.

If I note (perceive) with my senses the odor or taste of some object, or its form, color, or sound, I call this state of consciousness "my sensation" of these qualities; but if sadness, hope, cheerfulness, or hatred appreciably raise me above or depress

---

in the means they employ, but also in their fundamental principles. The essential difference between music and poetry might be brought into strong relief by showing that music primarily affects the senses and, after rousing the emotions, reaches the intellect last of all. Poetry, on the other hand, first raises up an idea which in its turn excites the emotions, while it affects the senses only as an extreme result of its highest or lowest form. They, therefore, pursue an exactly opposite course, for one spiritualizes the material, whereas the other materializes the spiritual."

me below the habitual level of mental activity, I am said to "feel."[2]

The beautiful, first of all, affects our senses. This, however, is not peculiar to the beautiful alone, but is common to all phenomena whatsoever. Sensation, the beginning and condition of all aesthetic enjoyment, is the source of feeling in its widest sense, and this fact presupposes some relation, and often a highly complex one, between the two. No art is required to produce a sensation; a single sound or color may suffice. As previously stated, the two terms are generally employed promiscuously; but older writers speak of "sensation" where we should use the term "feeling." What those writers intend to convey, therefore, is that the object of music is to arouse our feelings, and to fill our hearts with piety, love, joy, or sadness.

In point of fact, however, this is the aim neither of music nor of any other art. An art aims, above all, at producing something beautiful which affects not our feelings but the organ of pure contemplation, our *imagination*.[3]

It is rather curious that musicians and the older writers on aesthetics take into account only the contrast of "feeling" and "intellect," quite oblivious of the fact that the main point at issue lies halfway between the horns of this supposed dilemma. A musical composition originates in the composer's imagination and is intended for the imagination of the listener. Our imagination, it is true, does not merely contemplate the beautiful, but contemplates it with intelligence — the object being, as it were, mentally inspected and criticized. Our judgment, however, is formed so rapidly that we are unconscious of the separate acts involved in the process, whence the delusion arises that what in reality depends upon a complex train of reasoning is merely an act of intuition.

The word *Anschauung* (viewing, contemplating) is no longer applied to visual processes only but also to the functions of the other senses. It is, in fact, eminently suited to describe the act of attentive hearing, which is nothing but a mental inspection of a succession of musical images. Our imagination, withal, is not an isolated faculty, for though the vital spark originates in the senses, it forthwith kindles the flame of the intellect and the emotions. A true conception of the beautiful is, nevertheless, independent of this aspect of the question.

In the pure act of listening we enjoy the music alone and do not think of importing into it any extraneous matter. But the tendency to allow our feelings to be aroused implies something extraneous to the music. An exclusive activity of the intellect, resulting from the contemplation of the beautiful, involves not an aesthetic but a *logical* relation, while a predominant action of the feelings brings us onto still more slippery ground, implying, as it does, a *pathological* relationship.

These inferences, drawn long ago from principles of general aesthetics, apply with equal force to the beautiful in every art. If music, therefore, is to be treated as an art, it is not our feelings but our imagination which must supply the aesthetic tests. It is as well to make this premise hypothetical, seeing that the soothing effect of music on the human passions is always affirmed with such emphasis that we are often in doubt whether music is a police regulation, an educational rule, or a medical prescription.

Yet musicians are less prone to believe that all arts must be uniformly gauged by our feelings than that this principle is true of music alone. It is this very power and tendency of music to arouse in the listener any given emotion which, they think, distinguishes this art from all the others.[4]

---

[2]Older philosophers agree with modern physiologists in the definition of these terms, and I unhesitatingly prefer this definition to the terminology of Hegel's school of philosophy, which, as is well known, distinguishes between internal and external sensations.

[3]Hegel has shown that the method of examining into the "sensations" (i.e., "feelings" according to our terminology) which a work of art awakens proceeds on indefinite lines and ignores the truly concrete element altogether. "What we are sensible of," he says, "is indissolubly connected with the most abstract and individual subjectivity. The several kinds of sensations produced are, therefore, different in a subjective sense only and not distinct modes of the thing itself." (*Aesthetik*, I, 142.)

[4]At a time when no distinction was made even between "feeling" and "sensation," a more critical examination into the varieties of the former was, of course, out of the question. Sensuous and intellectual feelings, the enduring state known as "frame of mind,"

As on a previous occasion we were unable to accept the doctrine that it is the aim of art in general to produce any such effect, we are now equally unable to regard it as the specific aim of music to do so. Grant that the true organ with which the beautiful is apprehended is the imagination, and it follows that all arts are likely to affect the feelings indirectly. Are we not moved by a great historical picture with the vividness of actual experience? Do not Raphael's Madonnas fill us with piety, and do not Poussin's landscapes awaken in us an irresistible desire to roam about in the world? Do our feelings remain callous to a sight such as the Strasbourg Cathedral? All these questions admit of but one reply, which is equally true of poetry and of many extra-aesthetic states of mind such as religious fervor, eloquence, etc. We thus see that all other arts, too, affect us with considerable force. The inherent peculiarities assumed to distinguish music from the other arts would depend, therefore, upon the degree of intensity of this force. The attempt, however, thus to solve the problem is not only highly unscientific but is, moreover, of no avail, because the decision whether one is more deeply affected by a symphony by Mozart, a tragedy by Shakespeare, a poem by Uhland, or a rondo by Hummel must depend, after all, on the individual himself. Those again who hold that music affects our feelings "directly," whereas the other arts do so only through the medium of ideas, express the same error in other words. For we have already seen that the excitation of feelings by the beautiful in music is but one of its indirect effects, our imagination only being directly affected. Musical dissertations constantly recall the analogy which undoubtedly exists between music and architecture, but what architect in his senses ever conceived the *aim* of architecture to be the excitation of feelings, or the feelings the subject matter of his art?

Every real work of art appeals to our emotional faculty in some way, but none in any exclu-

sive way. No canon peculiar to musical aesthetics only can be deduced from the fact that there is a certain connection between music and the emotions. We might as well study the properties of wine by getting drunk. The crux of the question is the specific mode in which music affects our feelings. Hence, instead of enlarging on the vague and secondary effects of musical phenomena, we ought to endeavor to penetrate deeply into the spirit of the works themselves and to explain their effects by the laws of their inherent nature. A poet or painter would hardly persuade himself that when he has ascertained the "feelings" his landscape or drama awakens, he has obtained a rationale of the beauties contained in it. He will seek to discover the source of the irresistible power which makes us enjoy the work in this particular form and in no other. Writers on this subject are by no means justified in confusing emotional impressions and musical beauty (instead of adopting the scientific method of keeping these two factors apart as much as possible) simply because an inquiry of this kind offers in respect of music, as we shall presently see, far greater difficulties than any other art, and because such an inquiry cannot go below a certain depth.

Independently of the fact that our feelings can never become the basis of aesthetic laws, there are many cogent reasons why we should not trust to the feelings aroused by music. As a consequence of our mental constitution, words, titles, and other conventional associations (in sacred, military, and operatic music more especially) give to our feelings and thoughts a direction which we often falsely ascribe to the character of the music itself. For, in reality, there is no causal nexus between a musical composition and the feelings it may excite, as the latter vary with our experience and impressibility. The present generation often wonder how their forefathers could imagine that just this arrangement of sounds adequately represented just this feeling. We need but instance the effects which works by Mozart, Beethoven, and Weber produced when they were new as compared with their effects on us. How many compositions by Mozart were thought by his contemporaries to be the most perfect expressions of

the acute or emotional state, inclination and passion, no less than the gradations peculiar to the latter, the *pathos* of the Greeks and the *passio* of the more modern Romans, were all confounded in one inextricable jumble, while of music nothing was predicated except that it was the art of exciting emotions.

passion, warmth, and vigor of which music is capable! The placidity and moral sunshine of Haydn's symphonies were placed in contrast with the violent bursts of passion, the internal strife, the bitter and acute grief embodied in Mozart's music.[5] Twenty or thirty years later, precisely the same comparison was made between Beethoven and Mozart. Mozart, the emblem of supreme and transcendent passion, was replaced by Beethoven, while he himself was promoted to the Olympic classicality of Haydn. Every observant musician will, in the course of his own life, experience analogous changes of taste. The musical merit of the many compositions which at one time made so deep an impression, and the aesthetic enjoyment which their originality and beauty still yield, are not altered in the least by this dissimilar effect on the feelings at different periods. Thus, there is no invariable and inevitable nexus between musical works and certain states of mind; the connection being, on the contrary, of a far more transient kind than in any other art.

It is manifest, therefore, that the effect of music on the emotions does not possess the attributes of inevitableness, exclusiveness, and uniformity that a phenomenon from which aesthetic principles are to be deduced ought to have.

Far be it from us to underrate the deep emotions which music awakens from their slumber, or the feelings of joy or sadness which our minds dreamily experience. It is one of the most precious and inestimable secrets of nature that an art should have the power of evoking feelings entirely free from worldly associations and kindled, as it were, by the spark divine. It is only the unscientific procedure of deducing aesthetic principles from such facts against which we protest. Music may, undoubtedly, awaken feelings of great joy or intense sorrow; but might not the same or a still

greater effect be produced by the news that we have won the first prize in the lottery, or by the dangerous illness of a friend? So long as we refuse to include lottery tickets among the symphonies, or medical bulletins among the overtures, we must refrain from treating the emotions as an aesthetic monopoly of music in general or a certain piece of music in particular. Everything depends upon the specific *modus operandi* by means of which music evokes such feelings. . . .

The Beautiful in Music

So far we have considered only the negative aspect of the question, and have sought to expose the fallacy that the beautiful in music depends upon the accurate expression of feelings.

We must now, by way of completing the exposition, bring to light also its positive aspect, and endeavor to determine the nature of the beautiful in music.

Its nature is specifically musical. By this we mean that the beautiful is not contingent upon nor in need of any subject introduced from without, but that it consists wholly of sounds artistically combined. The ingenious co-ordination of intrinsically pleasing sounds, their consonance and contrast, their flight and reapproach, their increasing and diminishing strength—this it is which, in free and unimpeded forms, presents itself to our mental vision.

The primordial element of music is euphony, and rhythm is its soul: rhythm in general, or the harmony of a symmetrical structure, and rhythm in particular, or the systematically reciprocal motion of its several parts within a given measure. The crude material which the composer has to fashion, the vast profusion of which it is impossible to estimate fully, is the entire scale of musical notes and their inherent adaptability to an endless variety of melodies, harmonies, and rhythms. Melody, unexhausted, nay, inexhaustible, is pre-eminently the source of musical beauty. Harmony, with its countless modes of transforming, inverting, and intensifying, offers the material for constantly new developments; while rhythm, the

---

[5]Of Rochlitz in particular there are sayings on record about Mozart's instrumental music which sound rather strange to our ears. This same Rochlitz describes the graceful *minuet-capriccio* in Weber's "Sonata in A flat" as "the copious, incessant effusion of a passionate and fiercely agitated mind, controlled, withal, by a marvelous steadiness of purpose."

main artery of the musical organism, is the regulator of both, and enhances the charms of the timbre in its rich variety.

To the question: What is to be expressed with all this material? the answer will be: Musical ideas. Now, a musical idea reproduced in its entirety is not only an object of intrinsic beauty but also an end in itself, and not a means for representing feelings and thoughts.

The essence of music is sound and motion.

The arabesque, a branch of the art of ornamentation, dimly betokens in what manner music may exhibit forms of beauty though no definite emotion be involved. We see a plexus of flourishes, now bending into graceful curves, now rising in bold sweeps; moving now toward, and now away from each other; correspondingly matched in small and large arcs; apparently incommensurable, yet duly proportioned throughout; with a duplicate or counterpart to every segment; in fine, a compound of oddments, and yet a perfect whole. Imagine now an arabesque, not still and motionless, but rising before our eyes in constantly changing forms. Behold the broad and delicate lines, how they pursue one another; how from a gentle curve they rise up into lofty heights, presently to descend again; how they widen and contract, surprising the eye with a marvelous alternation of quiescence and mobility. The image thus becomes nobler and more exalted. If, moreover, we conceive this living arabesque as the active emanation of inventive genius, the artistic fullness of whose imagination is incessantly flowing into the heart of these moving forms, the effect, we think, will be not unlike that of music.

When young, we have probably all been delighted with the ever-changing tints and forms of a kaleidoscope. Now, music is a kind of kaleidoscope, though its forms can be appreciated only by an infinitely higher ideation. It brings forth a profusion of beautiful tints and forms, now sharply contrasted and now almost imperceptibly graduated; all logically connected with each other, yet all novel in their effect; forming, as it were, a complete and self-subsistent whole, free from any alien admixture. The main difference

consists in the fact that the musical kaleidoscope is the direct product of a creative mind, whereas the optic one is but a cleverly constructed mechanical toy. If, however, we stepped beyond the bounds of analogy, and in real earnest attempted to raise mere color to the rank of music by foisting on one art the means of another, we should be landed in the region of such puerile contrivances as the "color piano" or the "ocular organ," though these contrivances significantly prove both phenomena to have, morphologically, a common root.

If any sentimental lover of music thinks that analogies such as the one mentioned are degrading to the art, we reply that the only question is whether they are relevant or not. A subject is not degraded by being studied. If we wish to disregard the attributes of motion and successive formation, which render a comparison with the kaleidoscope particularly applicable, we may, forsooth, find a more dignified parallel for beautiful music in architecture, the human body, or a landscape, because these all possess original beauty of outline and color quite irrespective of the intellectual substratum, the soul.

The reason why people have failed to discover the beauties in which pure music abounds is, in great measure, to be found in the underrating by the older systems of aesthetics of the sensuous element and in its subordination to morality and feeling — in Hegel, to the "idea." Every art sets out from the sensuous and operates within its limits. The theory relating to the expression of feelings ignores this fact and, disdainfully pushing aside the act of hearing, it passes on immediately to the feelings. Music, say they, is food for the soul, and the organ of hearing is beneath their notice.

True, it is not for the organ of hearing as such, for the "labyrinth" or the "tympanum," that a Beethoven composes. But our imagination, which is so constituted as to be affected by auditory impressions (and in relation to which the term "organ" means something very different from a channel directed toward the world of physical phenomena), delights in the sounding forms and musical structures and, conscious of their sensuous nature, lives in the immediate and free contemplation of the beautiful.

It is extremely difficult to define this self-subsistent and specifically musical beauty. As music has no prototype in nature, and expresses no definite conceptions, we are compelled to speak of it either in dry, technical terms, or in the language of poetic fiction. Its kingdom is, indeed, "not of this world." All the fantastic descriptions, characterizations, and periphrases are either metaphorical or false. What in any other art is still descriptive is in music already figurative. Of music it is impossible to form any but a musical conception, and it can be comprehended and enjoyed only in and for itself.

The "specifically musical" must not, however, be understood only in the sense of acoustic beauty or symmetry of parts — both of which elements it embraces as of secondary importance — and still less can we speak of "a display of sounds to tickle the ear," or use similar phraseology which is generally intended to emphasize the absence of an intellectual principle. But, by laying stress on musical beauty, we do not exclude the intellectual principle; on the contrary, we imply it as essential, for we would not apply the term "beautiful" to anything wanting in intellectual beauty; and in tracing the essential nature of beauty to a morphological source, we wish it to be understood that the intellectual element is most intimately connected with these sonorific forms. The term "form" in musical language is peculiarly significant. The forms created by sound are not empty; not the envelope enclosing a vacuum, but a well, replete with the living creation of inventive genius. Music, then, as compared with the arabesque, is a picture, yet a picture the subject of which we cannot define in words, or include in any one category of thought. In music there is both meaning and logical sequence, but in a musical sense; it is a language we speak and understand, but which we are unable to translate. It is a highly suggestive fact that, in speaking of musical compositions, we likewise employ the term "thought," and a critical mind easily distinguishes real thoughts from hollow phrases, precisely as in speech. The Germans significantly use the term *Satz* ("sentence") for the logical consummation of a part of a composition, for we know exactly when it is finished, just as in the case of a written or spoken sentence, though each has a logic of its own.

The logic in music, which produces in us a feeling of satisfaction, rests on certain elementary laws of nature which govern both the human organism and the phenomena of sound. It is, above all, the primordial law of "harmonic progression" which, like the curve lines in painting and sculpture, contains the germ of development in its main forms, and the (unfortunately almost unexplained) cause of the link which connects the various musical phenomena.

All musical elements are in some occult manner connected with each other by certain natural affinities, and since rhythm, melody, and harmony are under their invisible sway, the music created by man must conform to them — any combination conflicting with them bearing the impress of caprice and ugliness. Though not demonstrable with scientific precision, these affinities are instinctively felt by every experienced ear, and the organic completeness and logic, or the absurdity and unnaturalness of a group of sounds, are intuitively known without the intervention of a definite conception as the standard of measure, the *tertium comparationis*.[1]

From this negative rationalness, inherent in music and founded on laws of nature, springs the possibility of its becoming invested also with positive forms of beauty.

The act of composing is a mental working on material capable of receiving the forms which the

---

[1] "Poetry may utilize the ugly (the unbeautiful) even in a fairly liberal measure, for, as it affects the feelings only through the medium of the ideas which it directly suggests, the knowledge that it is a means adapted to an end will, from the outset, soften its impression, even to the extent of creating a most profound sensation by force of contrast and by stimulating the imagination. The effect of music, however, is perceived and assimilated directly by the senses, and the verdict of the intellect comes too late to correct the disturbing factor of ugliness. It is for this reason that Shakespeare was justified in making use of the horrible, while Mozart was obliged to remain within the limits of the beautiful." (Grillparzer, IX, 142.)

mind intends to give. The musical material in the hands of creative genius is as plastic and pliable as it is profuse. Unlike the architect, who has to mold the coarse and unwieldy rock, the composer reckons with the ulterior effect of past sounds. More ethereal and subtle than the material of any other art, sound adapts itself with great facility to any idea the composer may have in his mind. Now, as the union of sounds (from the interdependence of which the beautiful in music flows) is not effected by mechanically stringing them together but by acts of a free imagination, the intellectual force and idiosyncrasy of the particular mind will give to every composition its individual character. A musical composition, as the creation of a thinking and feeling mind, may, therefore, itself possess intellectuality and pathos in a high degree. Every musical work ought to bear this stamp of intellectuality, but the music itself must furnish evidence of its existence. Our opinion regarding the seat of the intellectual and emotional elements of a musical composition stands in the same relation to the popular way of thinking as the idea of immanence does to that of transcendence. The object of every art is to clothe in some material form an idea which has originated in the artist's imagination. In music this idea is an acoustic one; it cannot be expressed in words and subsequently translated into sounds. The initial force of a composition is the invention of some definite theme, and not the desire to describe a given emotion by musical means. Thanks to that primitive and mysterious power whose mode of action will forever be hidden from us, a theme, a melody, flashes on the composer's mind. The origin of this first germ cannot be explained, but must simply be accepted as a fact. When once it has taken root in the composer's imagination, it forthwith begins to grow and develop, the principal theme being the center round which the branches group themselves in all conceivable ways, though always unmistakably related to it. The beauty of an independent and simple theme appeals to our aesthetic feeling with that directness which tolerates no explanation except, perhaps, that of its inherent fitness and the harmony of parts, to the exclusion of any alien factor. It pleases for its own sake, like an arabesque, a column, or some spontaneous product of nature — a leaf or a flower. . . .

Musical Contemplation

This morbid sensitivity, in our opinion, is in direct opposition to the voluntary and pure act of contemplation which alone is the true and artistic method of listening. Compared to it the ecstasies of the musical enthusiast sink to the level of the crude emotion of the savage. The beautiful is not suffered but enjoyed, and the term "aesthetic enjoyment" clearly confirms this fact. Sentimentalists regard it, of course, as heresy against the omnipotence of music to take exception to the emotional revolutions and conflicts which they discover in every musical composition, and of which they never fail to experience the full force. Those who cannot agree with them are "callous," "apathetic," "cold reasoners." No matter. It is, nevertheless, both ennobling and elevating to follow the creative mind as it unlocks with magic keys a new world of elements, and to observe how at its bidding they enter into all conceivable combinations; how it builds up and casts down, creates and destroys, controlling the whole wealth of an art which exalts the ear to an organ of sense of the greatest delicacy and perfection. That which calls forth from us a sympathetic response is not in the least the passion professed to be described. With a willing mind, calm but acutely sensitive, we enjoy the work of art as it passes before us, and thoroughly realize the meaning of what Schelling so felicitously terms "the sublime indifference of Beauty." Thus to enjoy with a keenly observant mind is the most dignified and salutary mode, and by no means the easiest one, of listening to music.

The most important factor in the mental process which accompanies the act of listening to music, and which converts it into a source of pleasure, is frequently overlooked. We here refer to the intellectual satisfaction which the listener derives from continually following and anticipating the composer's intentions — now to see his expectations fulfilled, and now to find himself agreeably mistaken. It is a matter of course that this intellectual flux and reflux, this perpetual giving and receiving, takes place unconsciously and with the rapidity of lightning flashes. Only that music can yield truly aesthetic enjoyment which prompts and rewards the act of thus closely following the composer's thoughts and which with perfect justice may be called a pondering of the imagination. Indeed, without men-

tal activity no aesthetic enjoyment is possible. But the kind of mental activity alluded to is quite peculiar to music, because its products, instead of being fixed and presented to the mind at once in their completeness, develop gradually and thus do not permit the listener to linger at any point or to interrupt his train of thought. It demands, in fact, the keenest watching and the most untiring attention. In the case of intricate compositions, this may even become a mental exertion.

On Rehearing Music

Leonard B. Meyer

From *Music, The Arts, and Ideas: Patterns and Predictions in Twentieth-Century Culture* by Leonard B. Meyer © 1967 The University of Chicago Press. Reprinted by permission.

Few musicians, listeners, or aestheticians have doubted that music is meaningful communication. But there have been frequent and sometimes heated disagreements as to the means, substance, and logical status of such communication. Depending upon what are viewed as the essential characteristics of musical signification, three basic positions may be distinguished: (1) the formal, (2) the kinetic-syntactic, and (3) the referential.

1. The heirs of the time-honored Pythagorean mysteries have emphasized the central importance of the formal relationships existing among the structural units that constitute a musical event — whether that event be a phrase, a section, or a whole work. For them, musical understanding and enjoyment depend upon the comprehension of such factors as symmetry, balance, and perfection of proportion. Since a structural unit (a musical event) must be complete, or virtually so, before its formal design can be comprehended, this view of music tends to be retrospective, contemplative, and somewhat static. For such theorists, music is mobile architecture.

2. Those who adopt the kinetic-syntactic position contend that the cardinal characteristics of a musical event are functional rather than formal. Music is a dynamic process. Understanding and enjoyment depend upon the perception of and response to attributes such as tension and repose, instability and stability, and ambiguity and clarity. Because music is seen as a developing process, this viewpoint tends to be prospective, dramatic, and Faustian.

There are, however, differences of opinion within this group. Some, Hanslick[1] for instance, argue that the kinetic-syntactic process is purely and exclusively intra-musical. Others believe that the shape and form of the musical process symbolize the life of feeling[2] or directly evoke affective responses.

3. Though not generally esteemed by music theorists and academic critics, popular opinion — as well as a good number of practicing musicians and composers — has favored the referential position, which holds that music depicts or evokes the concepts, actions, and passions of "real," extra-musical experience. Because of their seeming similarities, this position must be distinguished from the one described above, in which kinetic-syntactic processes were said to symbolize or evoke feelings similar to those occurring in non-musical experience. The referential mode focuses attention not primarily upon the evolving, changing aspect of music, but upon the more or less constant, enduring moods and connotations delineated by tempo, timbre, dynamics, accentuation, and the other attributes of music that themselves tend to be relatively stable for considerable periods of time.

[1]Eduard Hanslick, *The Beautiful in Music*; see particularly p. 135.

[2]Susanne K. Langer, *Philosophy in a New Key*.

Whatever the relative merits of these different viewpoints may be, it seems safe to say that any account of musical communication that pretends to completeness must find a place for all three.[3] For the aspects of musical experience designated by these positions are inextricably linked. Thus the apprehension of the kinetic-syntactic process presupposes and is qualified by the inferences that listeners necessarily make about the kind of musical event that the process will probably produce when it is completed. Conversely, comprehension of a completed event necessarily includes and is qualified by the listener's awareness of the particular process by which the event came into being. In like manner, the referential character of an event influences our judgments (inferences) of how an event will progress kinetically. Conversely, the kinetic development of the music—whether it is continuous or interrupted, expected or surprising—performs an important function in characterizing gesture, mood, and connotation.

Musical communication, like that of literature and the plastic arts, depends upon the simultaneous interaction of all three modes of signification. This does not, however, mean that the modes play equally important roles in such communication.[4] And though the kinetic-syntactic position has always had champions, asserting that this mode is the central and crucial one for musical communication, their number and influence has been steadily growing since the end of the nineteenth century.[5]

As long as the kinetic position was stated in more or less general, philosophical terms it seems unobjectionable. But in recent years there has been an increasing tendency for music theorists and aestheticians, using psychological concepts or those of information theory, to specify as precisely as possible the particular way in which the kinetic processes of music become significant communication. These specifications of the kinetic position have important implications for the problem of rehearing music.

The kinetic position, thus specified, can be crudely summarized as follows: the significance of a musical event—be it a tone, a motive, a phrase, or a section—lies in the fact that it leads the practiced listener to expect, consciously or unconsciously, the arrival of a subsequent event or one of a number of alternative subsequent events. Such expectations (or "subjective predictions") are entertained with varying degrees of certainty, depending upon what is *felt* to be the probability of any particular event in a specific set of musical circumstances.[6] Or, viewed objectively, because of the way the human mind perceives patterns and because of the listener's learned stylistic habits, one musical event implies subsequent musical events with particular degrees of probability.

Musical significance is a function of the degree of probability that a particular musical event is felt to have; such probability depends not only upon the character of the event itself, but also upon the nature and probability of all the events that have gone before. Looked at in another way, the significance of an event is inseparable from the means employed in reaching it. The greater the probability of the relationship between an event

---

[3]Perhaps those who would point out the importance of the sensuous enjoyment of music should be included in a separate category. However, while admitting that this aspect of music contributes to our pleasure, few theorists or aestheticians have seriously contended that it is of primary importance.

[4]Nor is the relative importance of the three modes of signification the same for all the arts. Moreover, within the stylistic history of one of the arts the amount of *relative* dependence upon any one of the modes may change. Debussy's style, for instance, places more emphasis upon referential significance and less upon syntactic process than does the style of the earlier Romantic composers.

[5]This is, of course, in part a reflection of the growing influence of this viewpoint in other disciplines. In philosophy, it is apparent in Whitehead's emphasis upon "process" and in Dewey's insistence upon the "dynamic" character of experience. In psychology, it appears in the Freudian notion of psychic "drives" and in the

Gestalt analysis of perception in terms of "forces and tension." In literature, it has been implicit in the studies of Empson. In music theory, the work of Heinrich Schenker has perhaps been the most important single influence fostering the growth of the kinetic viewpoint.

[6]In part the listener's sense of *felt* probability is a product of the frequency with which a particular musical relationship has been experienced. In part, however, it is the result of the nature of human mental processes.

and the means employed in reaching it, the less the significance of the event. Thus less expected routes toward "probable" events and less probable events reached in a more or less expected fashion (or some combination of these) will be more meaningful than predictable events that arrive in probable ways. Total probability of both means and ends amounts to tautology. Also, the more ambiguous the antecedent event (and hence the less certain our expectations as to what will follow), the greater the significance of the particular consequent that does arrive.

Stated in terms of information theory, which many of these writers have employed in their analyses: "It is the flux of information created by progression from event to event in a pattern of events that constitutes the reality of experience."[7] "The informedness of each new event in a pattern depends upon the predictions that the pattern of events has led us to formulate to the moment. The new event may confirm these predictions or it may fail to confirm them. . . . Information will be a measure of the degree to which a single prediction or an array of predictions is 'nonconfirmed' by the present event."[8]

A theory of communication in which the unexpected, the ambiguous, and the less probable are of crucial importance for the understanding of, and response to, music is apparently in direct conflict with the belief that good music can be reheard and re-enjoyed countless times. For if a work has been heard already, we will *know* what is going to happen and, in later hearings, the improbable will become probable, the unexpected will be expected, and all predictions will be confirmed. According to the kinetic-syntactic view, later hearings of a work should, therefore, yield less information — and consequently less enjoyment — than earlier ones.

But is not precisely the opposite the case? The better we know a work — the more often we have heard it — the more we enjoy it and the more meaningful it is. If this is so, then those who contend that the kinetic mode of signification is the crucial one for musical communication must be mistaken.

The matter is not, however, so simple. For without weakening the logical position of these theorists, cogent reasons can be advanced explaining not only why it is possible to enjoy a piece of music after repeated hearings, but also why later hearings of a work often yield more enjoyment than earlier ones.

1. Understanding music is not merely a matter of perceiving separate sounds. It involves relating sounds to one another in such a way that they form patterns (musical events). Furthermore, smaller patterns combine with one another to form larger, more extensive ones — patterns on higher architectonic levels. These in turn influence the further development of patterns on both lower and higher levels. Thus the implications of patterns on the several architectonic levels exist simultaneously and interact with one another.

Because listening to music is a complex art involving sensitivity of apprehension, intellect, and memory, many of the implications of an event are missed on first hearing. For to comprehend the implications of a musical event fully, it is necessary to understand the event itself clearly and to remember it accurately. Hence it is only *after* we come to know and remember the basic, axiomatic events of a work — its motives, themes, and so on — that we begin to appreciate the richness of their implications. It is partly for these reasons that a good piece of music can be reheard and that, at least at first, enjoyment increases with familiarity.

2. Memory is not a mechanical device for the immutable registration of stimuli. It is an active force which, obeying the psychological "law of good shape," organizes, modifies, and adjusts the impressions left by perception. In so doing, it

---

[7]Edgar Coons and David Kraehenbuehl, "Information as a Measure of Structure in Music," p. 145.

[8]*Ibid.*, p. 129. Also see Fred Attneave, "Stochastic Composition Processes"; Lejaren A. Hiller and Leonard M. Isaacson, *Experimental Music*; David Kraehenbuehl and Edgar Coons, "Information as a Measure of the Experience of Music"; A. Moles, "Informationstheorie der Musik"; and Joseph E. Youngblood, "Style as Information."

tends either to "improve" (regularize) irregular but well-structured patterns or to "forget" poorly structured ones.[9] For instance, themes or parts of themes, which are strongly structured, are generally remembered quite accurately and easily, while transition sections and developments, which are weakly structured (less expected and predictable), are often forgotten, or are remembered as being more highly structured (more predictable) than they actually are. Because they tend to be forgotten or regularized in memory, the less well-structured parts of a work often remain unpredicted and unexpected through a number of hearings.[10] Consequently musical experience maintains its vitality longer than would otherwise be the case.

3. Though not wholly determined by the frequency with which a particular syntactic relationship has previously been heard,[11] prediction (expectation) is nonetheless significantly dependent upon the listener's learned habit responses, which are a product of his past musical experience. Hence each musical experience — whether of a work heard before or not — modifies, though perhaps only slightly, the internalized probability system (the habit responses) upon which prediction depends.[12]

As T. S. Eliot has pointed out, this process of modification is ahistorical.[13] Not only does hearing or rehearing a work, say, by Schubert, by modifying our internalized probability system, change our experience of the work of later composers (say, Stravinsky); it also changes our experience of the music of earlier composers — for instance, Bach.

The extent to which habit responses are altered by hearing a particular work depends both upon the breadth of the listener's musical experience and upon the stylistic novelty of the work. Generally speaking, the greater the number of works already experienced by a listener and the greater the number of styles with which he is familiar, the less hearing any particular work will modify his internalized probability system. Works in an unfamiliar style will effect more substantial modifications in habit responses than works in a familiar idiom. Works already heard will influence internalized probability even less.

Insofar as a listener's internalized probability system and consequently his expectations have been modified by subsequent musical experiences, a work will tend to retain its interest and vitality upon rehearing. However, it is clear that the more music we know, the less our predictive habits will be changed by any particular musical experience.

4. A piece of music is more than a series of symbols in a score. It is their specific realization in sound or imagined sound. The performer, guided by traditional practice, interprets and articulates the composer's symbols, and in so doing both actualizes and particularizes the potential information contained in the score. He shapes and confirms (or non-confirms) our expectations not about *what* events will take place (these have been more or less stipulated by the composer), but about *how* the events will take place — the manner and timing of their arrival. Insofar as each performance of a piece of music creates a unique work of art, to that extent the information contained in the performance is new. And by creating new information, the performer helps to make the rehearing of music rewarding and enjoyable.

5. Finally, the act of listening to a piece of music — whether for the first or the tenth time — tends to bring into play culturally conditioned beliefs and attitudes which facilitate and sustain

---

[9]See Kurt Koffka, *Principles of Gestalt Psychology*, pp. 499–500, 507–8. The words "weak" or "strong," as used here, are terms of description, not valuation. Weak shapes perform an important function in molding kinetic process.

[10]The distinction between "recognition" and "recall" is important here. One may *recognize* that an unexpected consequent event is one experienced in a previous hearing without being able to *recall* (predict) it when one hears the antecedent event. In the former case, one frequently says, "Ah, now I remember."

[11]See n. 6, above.

[12]The formation of internalized probability systems is discussed in Meyer, *Emotion and Meaning in Music*, pp. 56–59.

[13]T. S. Eliot, *Selected Essays*, p. 15. Also see Max J. Friedländer, *On Art and Connoisseurship*, pp. 155–56.

aesthetic experience. Just as we are able to believe in—take seriously—the reality of a dramatic action, knowing at the same time that it is "make believe,"[14] and are able to believe in that action (following its unfolding and responding to its surprises as if it were being revealed for the first time) even though we have seen it before and know what will take place, so too we are able to believe in the reality of a piece of music—to become involved in its syntactic structure—even though it has been heard before.

But our ability to enter into the aesthetic illusion is not constant. Rather it seems that the better we know a work, the more difficult it is to believe in, to be enchanted by, its action. Thus, although readiness to become vitally involved in a work of art always depends to some extent upon the charismatic power of the performance, the better the work is known the more difficult it is to be enthralled by it, and, consequently, the more crucial becomes the power of the performance to make us believe again.

It may, at this point, be objected that while perhaps good reasons have been suggested for why it is possible to rehear music with enjoyment, it has not really been shown that a piece of music can be continually fresh and vital. The theoretical question has basically been begged. For suppose that a listener knows a work thoroughly, remembering the unexpected and the improbable as accurately as the expected and probable; suppose too that the listener's musical experience is so extensive that the modifications of his internalized probability system wrought by new experiences are so small as to be inconsequential; assume further that the work in question is recorded so that the performer's deviations have been learned and are predictable, and that the power of the particular performance has been attenuated by repeated listening. (And such a situation is not impossible.) Under these circumstances, will the listener find rehearing the work a rewarding experience?

The question put here is not one of theory. It is one of fact. If the answer is, "Yes, other things

being equal, he will be able to enjoy the work as much as he ever did," then a theory asserting that kinetic process is the central and crucial fact of musical communication must be mistaken. For it is incompatible with experience.

The facts are not, however, as easily ascertained as one might suppose. Because they have generally had to depend upon the questionable reliability of introspection, empirical studies of musical enjoyment have been able to tell us very little about the nature and basis of musical experience. In addition to the reasons given above, rehearing may often be tolerated precisely because *listening* is not taking place—even though physiological responses are recorded and "something" is felt introspectively. In such a case, music might merely constitute a fortuitous stimulus to pleasurable daydreams of which each of us evidently has an inexhaustible supply.

Perhaps some day, when psychology has learned how to deal satisfactorily with higher mental and affective processes, we shall have empirically validated answers to our questions. For the present, however, we must turn to everyday experience. And ordinary observation indicates that composers, performers, and listeners do in fact tend to tire of music with which they become very familiar.

In the case of composers, the evidence is not direct. We know little about their listening habits. The evidence comes rather from a consideration of the nature of stylistic development.

It is frequently suggested that stylistic innovations are, directly or indirectly, the result of changes in the social, economic, and intellectual milieu in which the composer works. While such changes have undoubtedly influenced the development of musical styles, a view that attempts to trace all stylistic changes directly to social, economic, and intellectual forces is not tenable.[15] Even within a stable social-cultural continuum, composers develop and transform the tradition they inherit from the past, modifying modes of organization and enriching the syntax of style

---

[14]See Ernst Kris, *Psychoanalytic Explorations in Art*, p. 42.

[15]At times, of course, social-cultural developments play a major role in shaping style changes. The emergence of monody at the end of the Renaissance seems a case in point.

with innovation. The degree to which a particular composer transforms tradition depends both upon his particular personality and upon the cultural conditions of his time. Some composers make only modest modifications, others change style radically. But even a relatively "conservative" composer, such as Bach, transforms and develops the stylistic norms he inherits.

Why should such intra-musical changes occur? Let us look at a relatively simple instance of this process. It is frequently said that by the end of the classical period the dominant-tonic cadence had become a worn-out "formula." What does this mean? Does it imply that an emotion, a gesture, or a connotation became tiresome or that a beautiful proportion lost its perfection? Not at all. It asserts, as the word "formula" indicates, that the relationship became obvious and tautological — that the progression became so probable (predictable) that it furnished only minimal musical information.[16] The composer of the nineteenth century searched for and discovered new cadential progressions, not because new moods or emotions were better or more desirable than the old or because new proportions were more pleasing, but because the dominant-tonic cadence had become a cliché. The information potential of the style needed to be renewed.

The performer's behavior, too, indicates a need for novelty or, negatively, a distaste for rigid repetition.[17] He not only seeks new works to play (though his choice is limited by his own stylistic taste and that of his audience) but also tends to change his interpretation of works he already

knows well. In part such changes may be traced to maturation and artistic growth. But the mature artist — perhaps even more than the less experienced one — tends to vary his performance of familiar works. He does so partly because he is forever seeking the "ideal" performance of his imagination, which can never be realized because as his experience grows and changes, so does his imagined ideal. Partly, however, interpretations are changed because the performer delights in the challenge of creating — of making something new and fresh, not alone for the sake of the audience, but for himself. He reinterprets a work not because he could not play it as before but because through his discovery of new possibilities and implications in it, the work becomes revitalized for him.

Again it seems implausible to ascribe these changes primarily to a desire to depict different moods or connotations, though these will necessarily be somewhat modified by reinterpretation. And ordinary language corroborates this point. For we generally compare interpretations in terms of articulation and phrasing, which are syntactic, rather than in terms of moods or connotations.

It is even more difficult to see how the formalist position can explain changes in interpretation: does one performance create more perfect proportion than another? If so, why would the great performer, whose excellence presumably depends upon his having discovered such perfection, change his interpretation of a work?

Even allowing for the influence of economic factors, the preferences of performers, and passing musical fashions, the growth in the repertory of both live and recorded music seems to indicate that, within the limits of his particular taste and stylistic understanding, the listener too seeks new works to hear and new interpretations of familiar ones. But since the data available can be interpreted in a number of ways, a more theoretical approach must be sought.

Assuming that two works are generally of the same quality of excellence, it is, I think, clear that the more complex can be reheard with enjoyment

---

[16]Though a growing emphasis upon artistic freedom and personal expression, nurtured by social revolution, undoubtedly quickened the rate of change, it did not determine or "cause" the change.

[17]The importance of the need for patterned novelty as a basic human requirement is implicit or explicit in a large number of recent studies of creativity, developmental psychology, and stimulus privation. To cite but a few: Frank Barron, "The Psychology of Imagination"; D. W. Fiske and S. R. Maddi, *Functions of Varied Experience* (contains an extensive bibliography); J. W. Getzels and P. W. Jackson, "The Highly Intelligent and Highly Creative Adolescent"; Woodburn Heron, "The Pathology of Boredom"; John R. Platt, "The Fifth Need of Man"; and D. E. Berlyne, "Curiosity and Exploration."

more often than the simpler. But if the cardinal characteristic of musical experience lies in the ability of tones to depict moods or extra-musical associations, how is this to be explained? Why should one mood or association be more viable than another? Indeed, granting that a period of "psychic recovery" may be necessary between similar mood or connotative experiences, it is difficult, if one adopts the referential position, to see why enjoyment should be influenced by re-hearing at all.

Similarly, if musical enjoyment arises out of the contemplation of ideal proportion and inevitable order, why should a complex work survive rehearing better than a simple one? Does a formal relationship increase in elegance when perceived for the second time and lose it when perceived for the fiftieth time?[18]

There are, however, two significant and instructive exceptions to the proposition that music cannot be reheard indefinitely. The first is the example of primitive music. Here apparently repetition is not only enjoyed, it is prescribed. The difference lies in the cultural situation. In primitive cultures music is not separated from other aspects of living—it is not placed in a special, "aesthetic" category. It is one with ritual and religion; and perhaps their inherent conservatism—particularly when their existence is threatened by alien cultures—accounts for the tendency toward exact repetition. Moreover, different cultures may have different attitudes toward repetition. In the West, for instance, exact repetition is felt to be wasteful and pointless, while, according to Whorf, the Hopi consider it efficacious and productive.[19]

The second exception is found in the tendencies of some recent experimental music. This music—whether employing chance operations in composition or in performance (e.g., requiring that the order of parts shall be decided by the capricious choice of the performer or even of the page turner)—is often purposefully and avowedly *anti*-kinetic. The music is without tendency or direction. Tones do not imply other tones; they simply exist. As Edward T. Cone has written: "The connections are mechanistic rather than teleological: no event has any purpose—each is there only because it has to be there."[20] Such music seems timeless not only in the sense that one experiences no awareness of motion through time in hearing it and in the sense that its temporal order is not fixed but also in the sense that our response to it is probably not affected by the number of times we hear it. The twentieth hearing is as meaningful (or meaningless) as the first.

Looked at from the standpoint of information theory, the situation might be stated thus: the more "purely" random music is, the higher its information content, *but* the lower its utility as communication. For if communication is to take place, the symbols used must have the same significance (the same implications) for both the sender (composer) and the receiver (listener)—that is, they must evoke similar expectations. There must be a common universe of discourse. Randomness (the less- or un-predictable) must, if it is to play a part in human communication, arise within those finite and ordered systems of probability relationship that we call "style."

Since whatever order is heard in non-stylistic random works (and the human mind is such that it will discover patterns, if it can) is the order of the listener *only*, the question of rehearing such works is not a generic one, but is purely subjective and will vary from individual to individual.

Whatever the future of non-teleological music may be, the kinetic-syntactic mode has been the

---

[18]I do not intend to minimize the importance of the formal and referential modes of signification in shaping musical experience. But . . . these do not form the essential basis for musical judgment. Scriabin delineates moods and evokes connotations just as readily as—if not more readily than—Brahms; the phrase structure of Stamitz' music is more regular (perfectly proportioned?) than that of Haydn.

[19]Benjamin Lee Whorf, *Collected Papers on Metalinguistics*, p. 29. In Oriental music the kinetic process is evidenced in the changes that occur in quasi-improvised performance rather than in permanent changes in the style itself.

[20]"Analysis Today," p. 176.

dominant one in the tradition of Western music, at least since the Renaissance. And it is at first disturbing and disheartening to face the fact that treasured masterpieces can, with repeated hearings, become exhausted and lose their savor. But two considerations may save us from despair. We can forget. And by forgetting we can, enchanted by a great performance, again experience the vitality which a familiar work once had for us. Such rediscovery of the beauty of, say, a Beethoven symphony once cherished and then too well known is not an uncommon experience. Second, and more important, it is partly because familiar works and accustomed styles become exhausted that new compositions are needed and new styles are developed. And these, by changing us — our ears, our minds, and our habit responses — are paradoxically able to redeem and revitalize the very works and styles they were created to replace.

The Name and Nature of Modernism

Malcolm Bradbury and James McFarlane

From *Modernism*, by Malcolm Bradbury and James McFarlane,
© 1978, Humanities Press International, Inc.

Unlike dates, periods are not facts. They are retrospective conceptions that we form about past events, useful to focus discussion, but very often leading historical thought astray.
G. M. Trevelyan

1

Cultural seismology—the attempt to record the shifts and displacements of sensibility that regularly occur in the history of art and literature and thought—habitually distinguishes three separate orders of magnitude. At one end of the scale are those tremors of fashion that seem to come and go in rhythm with the changing generations, the decade being the right unit for measuring the curves that run from first shock to peak activity and on to the dying rumbles of derivative *Epigonentum*. To a second order of magnitude belong those larger displacements whose effects go deeper and last longer, forming those extended periods of style and sensibility which are usefully measured in centuries. This leaves a third category for those overwhelming dislocations, those cataclysmic upheavals of culture, those fundamental convulsions of the creative human spirit that seem to topple even the most solid and substantial of our beliefs and assumptions, leave great areas of the past in ruins (noble ruins, we tell ourselves for reassurance), question an entire civilization or culture, and stimulate frenzied rebuilding. That the twentieth century brought us a new art is undeniable, and it is the purpose of this volume to explore some of its crucial manifestations. But we have also increasingly come to believe that this new art comes from, or is, an upheaval of the third and cataclysmic order.

This view is not surprising; one of the features of the age we are talking about is that it is remarkably historicist, disposed to apocalyptic, crisis-centred views of history. So familiar is the view that it needs only brief exemplification. Herbert Read, for instance, writing in 1933, puts the point succinctly:

> There have been revolutions in the history of art before today. There is a revolution with every new generation, and periodically, every century or so, we get a wider or deeper change of sensibility which is recognized as a period — the Trecento, the Quattro Cento, the Baroque, the Rococo, the Romantic, the Impressionist and so on. But I do think we can already discern a difference in kind in the contemporary revolution: it is not so much a revolution, which implies a turning over, even a turning back, but rather a break-up, a devolution, some would say a dissolution. Its character is catastrophic.

Contemplating the impact first of Gauguin and Van Gogh, then of Picasso, Read claimed that "we are now concerned, not with a logical development of the art of painting in Europe, not even

with a development for which there is any historical parallel, but with an abrupt break with all
tradition . . . The aim of five centuries of European effort is openly abandoned."[1] The late C. S.
Lewis constructed his inaugural lecture at Cambridge in 1954, *De Descriptione Temporum*, on a
similar notion. In his view, the greatest of all
divisions in the entire history of western man —
greater than that which divides Antiquity from
the Dark Ages, or the Dark from the Middle
Ages — is that separating the present from the age
of Jane Austen and Walter Scott. In politics, religion, social values, art and literature, a chasm lies
between:

> *I do not think that any previous age produced
> work which was, in its own time, as shat-
> teringly and bewilderingly new as that of the
> Cubists, the Dadaists, the Surrealists, and Pi-
> casso has been in ours. And I am quite sure this
> is true . . . of poetry . . . I do not see how
> anyone can doubt that modern poetry is not
> only a greater novelty than any other "new
> poetry" but new in a new way, almost in a new
> dimension.*[2]

Latterly there have been attempts to locate the
Great Divide even more precisely: the French
critic Roland Barthes identifies it with the plural-
ization of world-views deriving from the evolution of new classes and communications and puts
it at mid-century: "Around 1850 . . . classical
writing therefore disintegrated, and the whole of
literature, from Flaubert to the present day, became the problematics of language."[3]

As a general article of belief — before the fret-
ful details are reached and the character and
causes analysed — the idea of a Great Divide between past and present, art before and art now,
has drawn much allegiance. But it is also a fact
that about the nature of the modern situation,
and the consequences for that situation on the
form and character of art, there is less than unanimity. "*Il faut être absolument moderne*" ("It is
necessary to be absolutely modern"): Rimbaud's
exhortation has a particular appeal to our temper, but it is subject to many interpretations. And
the stylistic plurality of twentieth-century art — a

plurality so great that André Malraux speaks, in
Les voix du silence (The Voices of Silence), of the
"imaginary museum" of stylistic heterodoxy that
marks our age — reminds us how variously it has
been interpreted, by writers and artists themselves, and of course by the critics and commentators. There is an abundance of accounts of the
condition of modern art, and a wealth of explanation of its character and causes. Most of these
views are apocalyptic; though one is that our art
is not totally divorced from tradition and humanism, and that there is nothing especially singular
and novel about our art and situation at all. In the
present state of artistic and critical opinion — a
highly fluid state marked by sharp differences of
view — then perhaps the most any account can
offer is a personal or at least partial version of an
overwhelmingly complex phenomenon, an individual selection from the infinity of detail, which
may in time compost down with other views into
that sifted and resolved thing, a critical concept.

But if about the phenomenon there is much
variety and conflict of opinion, there is, alas,
growing agreement about its name. Clearly the
world of criticism has settled for some variant or
collocation of the word "modern" to identify the
arts of its time, or if not all of them, then some
part of them. So the Modern Movement; the
Modern Tradition; the Modern Age; the Modern
Century; the Modern Temper; Modernism; or —
to all appearances a Germanic neologism, though
presumably by analogy with labels like the Renaissance and the Enlightenment — simply The
Modern, *tout court*. One's regret at the choice is
not only that it predetermines the nature of our
view of modern literature; it also comes from the
inappropriateness of applying so semantically
mobile and indeed febrile a term to a historical
phenomenon we now wish to root in time. Modernity, in normal usage, is something that pro-
gresses in company with and at the speed of the
years, like the bow-wave of a ship; last year's
modern is not this year's. Apt as it is to the sensibility of the age to prefer such terms, to insist on
the association with time and history, matters
have now reached the point where we wish to fix

and stabilize the modern. When an extra-historical dimension is admitted, when — following G. S. Fraser or the editors of *The Modern Tradition*[4] — one claims as "modern" Catullus (but not Virgil), Villon (but not Ronsard), Donne (but not Spenser), Clough (but not Tennyson), and when one does the same for one's own time (Conrad, but not Galsworthy), the semantic instability of the term becomes obvious. Modernity is a crucial word for us, but it is tied up with definitions of our situation which are subject to change. The notion of the "modern" undergoes semantic shift much faster than similar terms of comparable function, like "romantic" or "neo-classical"; indeed, as Lionel Trilling says, it can swing round in meaning until it is facing in the opposite direction.[5] We use the term historically to locate a distinct stylistic phase which is ceasing or has ceased (hence the current circulation of counters like Proto-Modernism, Palaeo-Modernism, Neo-Modernism and Post-Modernism). We also use it to sum up a permanent modernising state of affairs and the state of mind and view of man it engenders — that "type of consciousness frequent in the modern world, obsessed by a compulsion to keep up, reduced to despair by the steadily increasing speed of the total movement."[6] Yet the word retains its force because of its association with a characteristic contemporary feeling: the historicist feeling that we live in totally novel times, that contemporary history is the source of our significance, that we are derivatives not of the past but of the surrounding and enfolding environment or scenario, that modernity is a new consciousness, a fresh condition of the human mind — a condition which modern art has explored, felt through, sometimes reacted against.

The name, then, is clear; the nature of the movement or movements — the where, when, why and what of it — is much less so. And equally unclear is the status of the stylistic claim we are making. We have noted that few ages have been more multiple, more promiscuous in artistic style; to distil from the multiplicity an overall style or mannerism is a difficult, perhaps even an impossible, task. We can describe eighteenth-century literature in western countries as "Neo-Classical," nineteenth-century literature in even more countries as "Romantic"; though the labels paper over innumerable cracks, we can suggest a general drift in most of the significant arts among most of the significant artists we are dealing with in those periods. A. O. Lovejoy has pointed out that we use the term "romanticism" to mean not only a wide variety of different things but a wide variety of contradictory things.[7] So we do; and the quest for definition is now raging again. But Romanticism has a recognizable general meaning and serves as a broad stylistic description of a whole era. What, though, is so striking about the modern period is that there is no word we can use in quite that same way. Modernism has been used, from time to time, analogously to Romanticism, to suggest the general temper of the twentieth-century arts; it has equally been appropriated by those who wish to distinguish and isolate *one* current at one particular time . . . a powerful movement, certainly, and an international one, reaching, like Romanticism, through the western cultures. It has been urged that Modernism is our inevitable art — as Gertrude Stein put it, the only "composition" appropriate to the new composition in which we live, the new dispositions of space and time. But it has also been seen as a form of late bourgeois aestheticism, especially by Marxist critics like Lukács who see the characteristic, the truly self-realizing modern art as a species of Realism.[8] The term has been used to cover a wide variety of movements subversive of the realist or the romantic impulse and disposed towards abstraction (Impressionism, Post-Impressionism, Expressionism, Cubism, Futurism, Symbolism, Imagism, Vorticism, Dadaism, Surrealism); but even these are not, as we shall see, all movements of one kind, and some are radical reactions against others. In some nations Modernism has seemed central to the evolution of the literary and artistic tradition; in others it has seemed simply to visit and then go away again. Modernism does indeed exist; acknowledgement can no longer sensibly be withheld; the movements and experiments of modern writers have come right to the forefront of artistic attention. But on what scale, at what time, and with what character?

2

When we speak of the style of an age, we can mean two very different things. We can mean that "general form of the forms of thought," of which Alfred North Whitehead spoke, which affects all a period's writing and is "so translucent . . . that only by extreme effort can we become aware of it."[9] But we can also mean a conscious mannerism, elected by some writers and artists though not by all, which expresses "a prevailing, dominant, or authentically contemporary view of the world by those artists who have most successfully intuited the quality of the human experience peculiar to their day and who are able to phrase this experience in a form deeply congenial to the thought, science, and technology which are part of that experience."[10] The term "Modernism" can hardly be taken in the former sense; for in any working definition of it we shall have to see in it a quality of abstraction and highly conscious artifice, taking us behind familiar reality, breaking away from familiar functions of language and conventions of form. It could be said that this is simply its initial shock, stage one of movement that leads us all into Modernism. And one can argue, to a point, that in graphics, architecture, design, and especially in the conventions of media like film and television, Modernism has become an invisibly communal style. Yet in some ways this is to defeat Modernism's presumptions; the shock, the violation of expected continuities, the element of de-creation and crisis, is a crucial element *of* the style. It has more commonly been urged that Modernism is our style in the second sense; these are the artistic forms consequent on modern thought, modern experience, and hence the Modernist writers and artists express the highest distillation of twentieth-century artistic potential. But many twentieth-century artists have rejected the label and the associated aesthetics, the modes of abstraction, discontinuity, and shock. And it can be well argued that the twentieth-century artist tradition is made up, not of one essential strand, but of two—roughly antithetical, though meeting from time to time. This, for instance, is the view of Stephen Spender, who, in his book *The Struggle of the Modern*, sees two streams: the "moderns" and the "contemporaries."[11]

The case for Modernism's total dominance has often been put and is easy to see. One of the word's associations is with the coming of a new era of high aesthetic self-consciousness and nonrepresentationalism, in which art turns from realism and humanistic representation towards style, technique, and spatial form in pursuit of a deeper penetration of life. "No artist tolerates reality," Nietzsche tells us; the task of art is its own self-realization, outside and beyond established orders, in a world of abnormally drawn perspectives. "What strikes me as beautiful, what I should like to do, is a book about nothing, a book without external attachments, which would hold itself together by itself through the internal force of its style"—this Flaubertian dream of an order in art independent of or else transcending the humanistic, the material, the *real*, has been crucially important to a whole segment of the modern arts. And what such artists have achieved can be considered—has been considered—the ultimate achievement of artistic possibility in the twentieth century, part of the progress and evolution of the arts towards sophistication and completion. The art that makes life, the drama of the artist's consciousness, the structure that lies beyond time, history, character or visible reality, the moral imperative of technique; are not these the basis of a great aesthetic revolution into literary possibilities greater than ever dreamt of? Hence Virginia Woolf, holding that the modern stylistic revolution came from the historical opportunity for change in human relationships and human character, and that modern art therefore had a social and epistemological *cause*, nonetheless believed in the aesthetic nature of the opportunity; it set the artist free to be more himself, let him move beyond the kingdom of necessity to the kingdom of light. Now human consciousness and

[handwritten marginal note: This is not the Flaubertian dream.]

especially *artistic* consciousness could become more intuitive, more poetic; art could now fulfil *itself*. It was free to catch at the manifold — the atoms as they fall — and create significant harmony not in the universe but within itself (like the painting which Lily Briscoe completes at the end of *To the Lighthouse*). The world, reality, is discontinuous till art comes along, which may be a modern crisis for the world; but within art all becomes vital, discontinuous, yes, but within an aesthetic system of positioning. Or, as Wallace Stevens puts it, the poet must be able to abstract reality "which he does by placing it in his imagination," by giving it the substance or meaning of a fiction. There may be a poverty in the universe and a trauma in man, but the artist has the means to transcend both history and reality by the dispositions of his technique, creating Joyce's "luminous silent stasis of aesthetic pleasure."

The movement towards sophistication and mannerism, towards introversion, technical display, internal self-scepticism, has often been taken as a common base for a *definition* of Modernism. Certainly, a number of technical features do reappear from movement to movement, even when these are radically at odds in other ways: anti-representationalism in painting, atonalism in music, *vers libre* in poetry, stream-of-consciousness narrative in the novel. And certainly, as Ortega y Gasset has said, the aesthetic refinement involves a dehumanization of art, the "progressive elimination of the human, all too human, elements predominant in romantic and naturalist production."[12] This has meant, though, not only radical remaking of form, but also, as Frank Kermode says, the tendency to bring it closer to chaos, so producing a sense of "formal desperation."[13] This, in turn, suggests that Modernism might mean not only a new mode or mannerism in the arts, but a certain magnificent disaster for them. In short, experimentalism does not simply suggest the presence of sophistication, difficulty and novelty in art; it also suggests bleakness, darkness, alienation, disintegration. Indeed Modernism would seem to be the point at which the idea of the radical and innovating arts, the experi-

mental, technical, aesthetic ideal that had been growing forward from Romanticism, reaches formal crisis — in which myth, structure and organization in a traditional sense collapse, and not only for formal reasons. The crisis is a crisis of culture; it often involves an unhappy view of history — so that the Modernist writer is not simply the artist set free, but the artist under specific, apparently historical strain. If Modernism is the imaginative power in the chamber of consciousness that, as James puts it, "converts the very pulses of the air into revelations," it is also often an awareness of contingency as a disaster in the world of time: Yeats's "Things fall apart; the centre cannot hold." If it is an art of metamorphosis, a Daedalus voyage into unknown arts,[14] it is also a sense of disorientation and nightmare, feeling the dangerous, deathly magic in the creative impulse explored by Thomas Mann. If it takes the modern as a release from old dependencies, it also sees the "immense panorama of futility and anarchy" that Eliot saw in *Ulysses*.[15] And if an aesthetic devotion runs deep in it, it is capable of dispensing with that abruptly and outrageously, as in the auto-destructive dimension of Dada or Surrealism.

This leads us toward another kind of account as to why Modernism is our art; it is the one art that responds to the scenario of our chaos. It is the art consequent on Heisenberg's "Uncertainty principle," of the destruction of civilization and reason in the First World War, of the world changed and reinterpreted by Marx, Freud and Darwin, of capitalism and constant industrial acceleration, of existential exposure to meaninglessness or absurdity. It is the literature of technology. It is the art consequent on the disestablishing of communal reality and conventional notions of causality, on the destruction of traditional notions of the wholeness of individual character, on the linguistic chaos that ensues when public notions of language have been discredited and when all realities have become subjective fictions. Modernism is then the art of modernization — however stark the separation of the artist from society may have been, however oblique the artistic gesture he has made. Thus, to the Expressionist or the Surrealist for instance, it is the anti-art which decomposes old frames of reference and carries the anarchy of men's evolving desire, the expressive form of human evolution in energetic release. By this view, Modernism is not art's freedom, but art's necessity. The communal universe of reality and culture on which nineteenth-century art had depended was over; and the explosively lyrical, or else the ironic and fictive modes, modes which included large elements not only of creation but of de-creation, were inevitable. The assumption that the age demands a certain kind of art, and that Modernism is the art that it demands, has been fervently held by those who see in the modern human condition a crisis of reality, an apocalypse of cultural community. What, though, is clear is that not all artists have believed this to be so — that, indeed, ours has been a century not only of de-realization but of realism, not only of ironic but of expansive modes.

The paradox of Modernism lies in the relationship between these two very different explanations of and justifications for it; indeed one can distinguish, in the difference between (say) Symbolism and Surrealism, *two* Modernisms. On the one hand, modernism has been an arcane and a private art: as Ortega y Gasset says in *The Dehumanization of Art*, it tends to divide its audience aristocratically into two groups — those who understand it and those who do not, those trained in and acquiescent to its techniques and premises, and those who find it not only incomprehensible but hostile. Thus its main qualities — which Ortega sees as a view of art as "play" or "delightful fraud"; an aversion to the traditional; a tendency towards self-hate or irony; a self-diminishing quality, or belief that art has few consequences other than that of being itself — are not simply *avant-garde* but represent a privation and a hoarding of the artistic powers against the populace and the claims of time and history. On the other hand, specialism and experimentalism can be held to have great social meaning; the arts are *avant-garde* because they are revolutionary probes into future human consciousness. Then

we could indeed say that the Modernist tendency is that which saw most deeply and truthfully into the situation of the arts and of man in our time, securing us a worthy art in an age which seemed not to grant us one; that most of our important writers have been of its tendency, and that its implications are inescapable for all other artists. By this view, Modernism, while not our total style, becomes the movement which has expressed our modern consciousness, created in its works the nature of modern experience at its fullest. It may not be the only stream, but it is the *main* stream. Like Romanticism, it originated with historical neatness about the beginning of a century, in a period of deep intellectual reappraisal and social and intellectual change, and has come increasingly to dominate the sensibility, aesthetics and mind of the hard core of our greatest writers, and to become the essential and appropriate vision to our most sensitive readers. Like Romanticism, it is a revolutionary movement, capitalizing on a vast intellectual readjustment and radical dissatisfaction with the artistic past — a movement that is international in character and marked by a flow of major ideas, forms and values that spread from country to country and developed into the main line of the western tradition.

Today it must surely seem to us that the truth lies somewhere between the view that Modernism is the supreme modern expression and the view that it is of marginal importance. Modernism is, clearly, more than an aesthetic event, and some of the conditions that lie behind it are discernible and clear. Yet it contains a highly aesthetic response, one which turns on the assumption that the registering of modern consciousness or experience was not a problem in representation but a profound cultural and aesthetic crux . . . a problem in the making of structures, the employment of language, the uniting of form, finally in the social meaning of the artist himself. The search for a style and a typology becomes a self-conscious element in the Modernist's literary production; he is perpetually engaged in a profound and ceaseless journey through the means and integrity of art. In this sense, Modernism is less a style than a search for a style in a highly individualistic sense; and indeed the style of one work is no guarantee for the next. This, perhaps, is what Irving Howe means when he remarks that "modernism does not establish a prevalent style of its own; or if it does, it denies itself, thereby ceasing to be modern."[16] The qualities which we associate with painters like Matisse, Picasso and Braque, with musicians like Stravinsky and Schoenberg, novelists like Henry James, Mann, Conrad, Proust, Svevo, Joyce, Gide, Kafka, Musil, Hesse and Faulkner, poets like Mallarmé, Valéry, Eliot, Pound, Rilke, Lorca, Apollinaire, Breton and Stevens, with dramatists like Strindberg, Pirandello and Wedekind, are indeed their remarkably high degree of self-signature, their quality of sustaining each work with a structure appropriate only to that work. The condition for the style of the work is a presumed absence of style for the age; and each work is a once-and-for-all creation, subsisting less for its referential than its autotelic constituents, the order and rhythm made for itself and submerged by itself. Modernism in this sense is indeed an international tendency, and we can predicate origins and causes for it and reflect on its significance. But it is hard to convert it into a universal style or tradition, despite the fact that its environment is not simply the work of individuals but of broader movements and tendencies. It is indeed a *part* of our modern art, not all of it. Yet there seems to be a discernible centre to it: a certain loose but distinguishable group of assumptions, founded on a broadly symbolist aesthetic, an *avant-garde* view of the artist, and a notion of a relationship of crisis between art and history. To this extent, one would also want to argue that there is an historical "peak," where impulses from many varied sources begin to coalesce, and come through in a particular core of moments, out from which run many variant and diverse versions of the primary impulse.

3

Perhaps the oblique nature of Modernism explains why critics have found it so hard a movement to find a clear place or date for. For the potential of Modernism was long present in the development of literature; it is possible to discern its origins long before we see its fruition. If Modernism is movements, then movements had been coming in increasing waves right through the nineteenth century. If the movements have to be bohemian or *avant-garde*, then bohemia was active in Paris from the 1830s; and the theory of the artist as a futurist, an agent free and loose in the realm of dangerous knowledge, was active throughout romantic thought. If an explicit aesthetic of experimentalism is required, then Émile Zola published *Le Roman expérimental* in 1880 (though he used the word in a scientific or laboratory sense). The crucial idea of the modern as a special imperative and a special state of exposure exists in Nietzsche. If Modernism means the ruffling of the hard naturalistic surface by a state of multiplicity of consciousness, then Walter Pater in the 1870s in England and other thinkers in Europe were talking of "quickened, multiplied consciousness." If Modernism means a response of the imagination to an urbanized, *Gesellschaft* world, then Baudelaire spoke of the unreal city and the need for the imagination to produce "the sensation of newness." As for other aspects of Modernism — its use of anti-form or desecration of established conventions; its use of the hard, resonant and "witty" image and its dependence on "associated sensibility"; its sense of anguish and its dependence on what Lionel Trilling calls an "adversary culture" — then we can trace these back through the western tradition, to Sterne, or Donne, or Villon. Modernism was indeed an international movement and a focus of many varied forces which reached their peak in various countries at various times. In some it seemed to stay for a long period; in others, to function as a temporary disturbance and then go away again. In some it seemed to do great violence to the received tradition — of Romanticism or Victorianism, Realism or Impressionism — and in others it seems a logical development of it. Indeed Modernism can look surprisingly different depending on where one finds the centre, in which capital (or province) one happens to stand. Just as "modern" in the England of today can mean something very different from what it meant a century ago for Matthew Arnold, so it can also be observed varying significantly from country to country, from language to language. Because the essence of Modernism is its international character—one critic, indeed, has argued that "Modernism, in short, is synonymous with internationalism"[17]—and because lexically, the term "modern" is itself internationally recognizable at sight and without translation, it is prudent to look briefly at these international connotations first.

Let us begin with one familiar version of the tendency. The title and sub-title of Cyril Connolly's 1965 book provide a usefully laconic definition: *The Modern Movement: One Hundred Key Books from England, France and America, 1880–1950*. Here, France is clearly identified as the source from which Anglo-American Modernism drew strength: "The French fathered the Modern Movement, which slowly moved beyond the Channel and then across the Irish Sea until the Americans finally took it over, bringing to it their own demonic energy, extremism and taste for the colossal."[18] Although, as Connolly is very ready to admit, it is impossible to fix on any one particular time as the start of the Modern movement, 1880 is taken as the point where the Enlightenment's "critical intelligence" had combined with Romanticism's "exploring sensibility" to stimulate the work of the first generation of truly modern writers, all owing something to Flaubert and Baudelaire—James, Mallarmé, Villiers de l'Isle-Adam, Huysmans, and "the mysterious Lautréamont." Thereafter followed wave after wave of writers, artists and musicians contributing to a very modern sensibility—Debussy, Yeats, Gide, Proust and Valéry; followed by Eliot, Pound, Lawrence and Joyce; Virginia Woolf, Edith Sitwell and Marianne Moore; Hemingway, Cummings, Faulkner, Malraux, Huxley and Graves; and thus to the present day. Within the outside limits of 1880 and 1950, it is clear that as Connolly sees it the high season was somewhere between 1910 and 1925. Somewhat similar views are to be found in Edmund Wilson's seminal book *Axel's Castle*, which relates the English and American modern movement to Symbolism, and

in Maurice Bowra, who includes a great part of modern literature as a Symbolist heritage.[19] And though Graham Hough believes that English literature never really had a Symbolist movement proper, that what happened about the time of the First World War was at most "symbolism without the magic," and that the nativist line predominated in England even if not in America, his basic interpretation of events is close to Connolly's.[20]

A more catholic Anglo-American view informed another book published in the same year as Connolly's: *The Modern Tradition*, the anthology of Modernist items edited by Richard Ellmann and Charles Feidelson. Not only do the editors acknowledge by their choice of items that there were key books in languages other than French and English, which Connolly, for stated (and honourable) reasons, does not; they extend their inquiry beyond the confines of literature as it is narrowly understood and into the wider realms of the imagination and the intellect; and they also embody in their book an awareness of "a modern tradition that reaches well back into the romantic era and beyond."[21] The outside limits, the envelope of their Modernism, assume a much more expansive shape; and their items range in kind and time, from Vico to Sartre, from Goethe and Wordsworth to Camus and Robbe-Grillet, from Blake to Picasso. Nevertheless, when they begin to focus upon the period of high intensity, they too give their closest attention to what is roughly the first quarter of the twentieth century, to Yeats and Joyce and Eliot and Lawrence and to their Continental coevals, Proust, Valéry and Gide, Mann, Rilke and Kafka. And if to other Anglo-American critics one turns with the two blunt interrogatives—who? and when?—to get a rough outline of their sense of Modernism, similar pictures emerge. Who is to be included in our identification parade of the Modernist spirit? Which are seen as the years of gathering force, of breakthrough, of concentrated change? A. Alvarez thinks that he who goes looking for Modernism must seek it in the first thirty years or so of this century, and that at the epicentre of the change will be found Pound and Eliot, Joyce and Kafka. For Frank Kermode the nineties are certainly forerunners of Modernism, but he claims that nevertheless "anybody who thinks about what modernism now means will rightly look more closely at the period between 1907 and, say, 1925." Neither Stephen Spender nor Graham Hough would seriously disagree with these chronological limits, though they further detect within them a period of enhanced intensity between about 1910 and the beginning of the First World War—years which, in Graham Hough's view, witnessed "a revolution in the literature of the English language as momentous as the Romantic one." As for personalities, because he recognizes that the Anglo-American developments were part of a larger European affair, he would set beside the names of Yeats, Joyce, Eliot and Pound also those of Gide, Valéry, and Thomas Mann, and perhaps also of Proust and Rilke.[22]

As the focus narrows and there is pressure to identify the really crucial event, the wholly significant work, the *annus mirabilis*, so the phrases grow in audacity. Tamping down an enormous cultural change into a brief moment in time, Virginia Woolf saw a quite explosive event: "On or about December 1910 human nature changed . . . All human relations shifted — those between masters and servants, husbands and wives, parents and children. And when human relations change there is at the same time a change in religion, conduct, politics, and literature."[23] The year of the death of King Edward and the first Post-Impressionist Exhibition was doubtless crucial, though D. H. Lawrence used an equally apocalyptic assumption for a different year and with a different interpretation: "It was in 1915 the old world ended," he wrote in *Kangaroo*. Such comments confirm the contemporary sense of participating in a profound transition; and the Anglo-American focus on these years just before the war is utterly understandable, since — as later essays in this volume suggest — there is a sharpening of the claims of the new, manifest in literary texts and literary groupings, over this period. But there have been efforts to push things earlier; Richard Ellmann, for example, says that if a moment must be found for human character to have changed, "I should suggest that 1900 is both more convenient

and more accurate than Virginia Woolf's 1910," since the modernist theme sounds through the Edwardian period.[24] Other critics have transferred this point of intensity to the years after the First World War; Harry Levin, for instance, if pressed to identify *the* Modernist year, would rather want to point to the miraculous yield of 1922: the year of *Ulysses* and *The Waste Land*, of Rilke's *Duineser Elegien* (*Duino Elegies*) and *Die Sonette an Orpheus* (*Sonnets to Orpheus*), of Brecht's first play *Baal*, of Lawrence's *Aaron's Rod* and Virginia Woolf's *Jacob's Room*, of Proust's *Sodome et Gomorrhe* (*Sodom and Gomorrah*) and Eugene O'Neill's *Anna Christie*. Nor, he adds, would it be difficult to compile a list of comparable quality for the year 1924, and thus discover a peak of intensity in the early twenties[25] — a period which certain other critics would however regard as one in which the Modernist impulse was reaching a point of exhaustion. An even later emphasis may be found among those critics who would argue that Modernism, far from being exhausted, has continued as our essential art right to the present, and who see the entire inter-war period as the main phase of Modernist evolution — like Harold Rosenberg, who focuses particularly on the Paris of this period, "the only spot where . . . it was possible to shake up such "modern" doses as Viennese psychology, African sculpture, American detective stories, Russian music, neo-Catholicism, German technique, Italian desperation."[26] The argument depends, in part, upon essential definitions about what characterizes Modernism, and also about whether the tendency has sustained itself, particularly via the surrealistic line, through into post-war art.

For if there is an argument about when Modernism began, and hence, implicitly, about what its causes and character are, then there is also one about whether it has yet ended. We have now amassed, on the basis of the art or anti-art of the post-war period — which at first appeared to be moving away from Modernism in the direction of realism and linearity — a new entity, called Post-Modernism. The term is acquiring high currency now to talk about a compound of that art of chance or minimalization, that "literature of silence," in which, as in Beckett or Borges, the idea of absurd creation, random method, parody or self-exhausting fictionality is paramount; of the new *chosisme*, which expands to include not only the *nouveau roman* in France but the non-fiction novel in Germany and the States, where facts, objects or historical events are placed in the context of questioning narrative; of multi-media forms, like the happening or the street theatre; and of the anti-rationalistic anti-art of psychedelics, pornography, and revolutionary outrage.[27] Various aspects of this can be seen as continuous with the logic and the modes of Modernism — especially that part of it concerned with evolutionary psychic exploration, like Dada and Surrealism, or with romantic self-immersion, like Hermann Hesse, or with the revolution of the word, like Gertrude Stein or the later Joyce. The overall case for continuity has been forcibly put in the essay "Modernisms" by Frank Kermode, which has appeared in several places, including the volume *Innovations*, where it is set against opposite views. Kermode holds that the contemporary art of the random — the squaring out of a piece of space or time, the specifying and signing of an environment, as in Cage or Burroughs — is blood-cousin to the earlier tendencies, though he draws a line across to distinguish early Modernism, which was much more formalist, or devoted to the paradoxes of form, from later or Neo-Modernism, which is anti-formalist, though compelled to use form to subvert it. The use of loose structure or aleatory art (i.e. art based on chance), as in Cage or Tinguely or the happening, or the art of conscious fictiveness, as in Nabokov, Borges, or Barthelme, is not outrightly at odds with its predecessors; it is a new disposition of old forces. Thus what Kermode calls Neo-Modernism and others have chosen to call Post-Modernism involves a change in what Harold Rosenberg calls the "tradition of the new" — a change falling perhaps around Dada — but it is still that same tradition. But other critics in *Innovations* dissent; if there is now a new *avant-garde* and a new aesthetic or group of aesthetics — based, say, on

Cage, Burroughs, Beckett and Borges, concrete poetry and the *nouveau roman*, but also on the happening, drugs, the counter-culture, and *négritude* — this is no longer simply a style; it is a form of post-cultural *action*, a politics.[28] The *avant-garde* has entered the streets, and become instinctive or radical behaviour; and we are in a new stylistic age, in which that enterprise of humanism and civilization Modernism attempted desperately to reinstate by its subversions of form is over. Anarchism and revolutionary subjectivism predominate; the uniqueness of the work vanishes; the cults of impersonality and pure form are done; art is either action, outrage, or play. In a spectacular essay called "POSTmodernISM," Ihab Hassan has explored some of the continuities and the discontinuities, stressing that the new mood assumes a totally technological and dehumanized universe; and he argues that the newer developments must at least force us to reconsider Modernism and distinguish the obviously continuous elements in it.[29] Something of the same revisionism inhabits the new stress being put on the surrealistic wing of Modernism, and Modernism's affiliations with Romanticism. In short, the argument around Post-Modernism now adds to the abundance of versions of Modernism.

4

But what is clear is that there is in nearly all of these versions a sense of Modernism as an historical evolution coupled with a notion of crisis and a notion of a point of culmination. And, for most Anglo-American critics, that culmination falls in the first part of the twentieth century. Although the reports vary increasingly in their detail, as the lore begins to shift, they have in common an emphasis on the Anglo-American achievement following on from the innovations of French symbolism, behind which again stand two prime initiators, Flaubert and Baudelaire. The stress may then fall on the new classicism, or else on the continuation of Romanticism. But the period of highest intensity is seen by and large as the first quarter of the twentieth century, within which are two peaks: the years immediately preceding, and the years immediately following the First World War. Such is the concept of Modernism as it is commonly viewed from a New York–London–Paris axis. But what is not always adequately acknowledged is that Modernism or the Modern, when viewed, say, from Berlin, or Vienna, or Copenhagen, or Prague, or St. Petersburg, is a thing with a quite different chronological profile, with a rather different set of representative figures and influential precursors, with a very different group of origins. Even if our task is less to make Modernism fit into line with contemporary experimentalism and radical attitudes than to straighten and clarify the record, which is the primary aim of this volume, this is something that deserves our best attention. This is not only because any account of Modernism that seeks to be genuinely synoptic and international must accommodate this sort of awareness, but also because these other manifestations of Modernism provide a broader, a thicker base for the generalizations to which all investigations like the present one are prone.

Let us try, then, to illuminate the conventional history of the tendency from the standpoint of Germanic Modernism. It would be convenient if Germanic Modernism could stand for the combined and conflated literature of Germany, Austria, and Scandinavia over these years; unfortunately, here too, such tidy simplifications will not quite fit. Berlin as it was in the nineties, especially the early nineties, may by its cultural and intellectual clamour draw attention to itself; but it would be a great mistake to allow Berlin to represent Germany in its totality at a time when Munich and Darmstadt and other provincial German cities were important and lively centres of literary activity. There is also the complex and ambiguous role of Vienna in these late-Hapsburg years, a multifarious role appropriate to a capital so influentially placed by history, geography and ethnic mix between north and south, east and west, past and present. In Vienna the modern ferment was strong; indeed, George Steiner tells us, "from the eighteen-nineties until its enthusias-

tic swoon into Hitler's arms in 1938, Vienna was the foremost generator of our current sensibility."[30] And there can be no doubt that the city of Karl Kraus, Freud, the Vienna Circle, Schoenberg and Wittgenstein was alive with Modernist perspectives. And then Scandinavia, with Ibsen, the age's most European figure of all, and Strindberg, whose influence was growing fast, made its own striking and peculiar contribution, had its own distinctive if Nietzschean passions of desperation and joy. Still, if from this complicated scene some identifiable range of phenomena that might approximately be designated as Germanic Modernism can be separated out, then the first and most striking thing is that it is—in its most significant manifestations—a good generation *earlier* than the Anglo-American Modernist upswing located by Connolly, Kermode and Hough. In Scandinavia, in Germany, and to a substantial extent in Austria, it was the eighties, nineties and early 1900s that witnessed a debate about the nature and name of Modernism of quite unparalleled passion and vehemence—years with, for the Germanic north, a much higher degree of self-consciousness, of articulateness, of documentation than perhaps any other part of Europe.

In trying to pin Modernism down—tentatively and crudely—in terms of men, books and years, attention is first drawn to Scandinavia: to the publication in 1883 of a series of critical essays by the Danish critic Georg Brandes with the significant title of *Men of the Modern Breakthrough (Det moderne Gjennembruds Mænd)*. In no time at all—conceivably by virtue of the stature Brandes had achieved throughout the Germanic world—the epithet "modern" became a rallying slogan of quite irresistible drawing power. One is, incidentally, struck by the contrast between this near-obsessive concern for the term "modern" and the comparative disregard of it during these same years in England, where between Meredith's *Modern Love* of 1862 and Michael Roberts's anthology *The Faber Book of Modern Verse* in 1936, the term is rarely used in any programmatic way. Though one might argue that its function, in English, is served by the word "new": "The range of the adjective [new] spread," notes Holbrook Jackson, "until it embraced the ideas of the whole period [the eighteen nineties], and we find innumerable references to the 'New Spirit,' the 'New Humour,' the 'New Hedonism,' the 'New Drama,' the 'New Unionism,' the 'New Party,' and the 'New Woman.'"[31]

In Germany, the anthology with which the new generation of iconoclastic poets announced their *credo* in 1885 was given the title *Moderne Dichtercharaktere (Modern Poet Characters)*.[32] The introductions to it, written by Conradi and Henckell, constituted a manifesto in which were defined the objectives for what was proudly called the "modern" lyric — a manifesto, the programmatic urgency of which carried over into the poems themselves. Conspicuous is that poem by Arno Holz, one of the chief theorists of this Germanic age, which insisted:

> *"Modern sei der Poet,*
> *modern vom Scheitel bis zur Sohle."**

From this moment on, and over the following decade, there were few writers in German who did not take some opportunity to discuss with rare vehemence the aims and ideals of so-called "modern" literature. One of the most influential periodicals of the day, *Die Gesellschaft*, which began publication in 1885, was defined by its editor as "*ein Organ der modernen Bewegung in der Literatur*" ("an organ of the modern movement in literature"). In 1886 came the invention of that bewildering and disturbing term "The Modern"; Eugen Wolff, in an address to the Berlin literary circle known as *Durch* ("Through") — in which there might well be an echo of Brandes's concept of "The Modern Breakthrough" — invented and launched the term "*Die Moderne*," "the Modern," later elaborated and more widely disseminated in his article of 1888 entitled "Die jüngste deutsche Literaturströmung und das Prinzip der Moderne" ("The most recent German literary currents and the principle of the Modern").[33] Articles with titles that announced their

interest in "Charles Darwin and the modern aesthetic," "Truth in the modern novel," "The significance of literature for the modern world," and so on, are conspicuous in these years.

The years 1890 and 1891 in Germany, as in Vienna, Oslo and to a lesser extent Zürich, witnessed a preoccupation with the concept of Modernism that approached the dimensions of a fever. There was a whole new range of "moderne" periodicals: *Freie Bühne für modernes Leben, Moderne Blätter* or even quite simply *Die Moderne*. Their pages were full of "modern" contributions: "Die Sozialdemokratie und die Modern") ("Social democracy and the Modern") (1891); "Moderne Wahrheitsdichtung" ("Modern poetry of truth") (1891); "Moderne Bestrebungen" ("Modern aspirations") (1892); "Der moderne Roman" ("The modern novel") or, more than once, "Die Moderne." Any bibliography of nineties literature in German would reveal an extraordinarily high concentration of titles making explicit reference to Modernism and the concept of the Modern, many of them crucial for an understanding of this decade: Hermann Bahr's *Zur Kritik der Moderne (On the Criticism of the Modern)* (Zürich 1890), Leo Berg's *Das sexuelle Problem in der modernen Literatur (The Sexual Problem in Modern Literature)* (Berlin 1891) and *Der Übermensch in der modernen Literatur) (The Superman in Modern Literature)* (Leipzig 1897), and Eugen Dühring's *Die Grossen der modernen Literatur (The Great of Modern Literature)* (Leipzig 1893).

The flame of controversy burned bright, consuming a large part of the intellectual fuel of the writers and critics of these years. But it took its toll. By the time Samuel Lublinski drew up the pros and cons of these developments in his *Die Bilanz der Moderne (Balance Sheet of the Modern)* (Berlin 1904), the issue had become a spent force; having run its turbulent course for well over twenty years, it finally lost impetus. Five years later, its "exit" was announced by the title of Lublinski's follow-up study, *Der Ausgang der Moderne (The Exit of the Modern)* (Dresden 1909); the literary world of Germany was surfeited and sickened by the term. "The Modern,"

---

*"Let the poet be modern,
Modern from head to toe."

even the adjective "modern," had become the sign of all that was old-fashioned and bourgeois, a term the connotations of which suggested nothing so much as exhaustion and decay. For the brave new generation of First World War writers in Germany, the term was something positively to be repudiated. The Expressionists went out of their way to declare how "unmodern" they were—an irony surely not lost upon those whose view of Modernism is largely Anglo-French. The very moment of the Germanic repudiation of the Modern as a valid term marks the start of Anglo-American Modernism as it is currently understood; any comprehensive account of European Modernism must have as one of its major tasks the resolution of this discrepancy.

5

But it would not do to leave the impression that this Germanic "Modern" was a simple, undifferentiated thing which grew predictably from its origins in the 1880s through to maturity and thence to inevitable decline in the early years of this century. For somewhere along the line of the semantic development of the term there was, not a break, not a rupture, not a reversal or revolution, but an abrupt change of direction, a realignment of thought. Something in its nature is not unlike the notion of the *Wendepunkt* (turning point), familiar to those acquainted with Tieck's theory of the *Novelle*—a point at which there is an unexpected yet in retrospect not unmotivated turn of events, a reorientation which one can see now is not only wholly consistent but logical and possibly even inevitable. It might be argued that it is precisely this same phenomenon, which, in the French–English–American line, constitutes that element of distinctiveness that the critics have sought for. But what is striking about this development in the Germanic Modern—and to place it somewhere about the year 1890 would not be far wrong—is that, because the moment was so unusually self-conscious and articulate, it is particularly well-documented and therefore accessible to investigation, like some *dy* by *dx* of a much larger configuration of change within which is contained the larger meaning of Modernism.

Some sense of the nature of this event is perhaps possible if we return to Lionel Trilling's comments on the modern. Trilling entitles his essay of 1961 "On the Modern Element in Modern Literature"; his title alludes to an event of over a century before—Matthew Arnold's lecture of 1857, called "On the Modern Element in Literature." Arnold was among those Victorians who had an active sense of modernity and change, and felt this generated new claims upon mind and art. The connotations of the term "modern" were central to him; but they are connotations totally different from those of our day. They were substantially classical: the modern element was repose, confidence, tolerance, the free activity of the mind winning new ideas in conditions of material well-being; it involved the willingness to judge by reason and search for the laws of things. If Arnold felt, as we know he did, the power of unreason, chaos, deep personal depression, a strong sense of social anarchy, he did not see these as the essential characteristics of the modern element. Yet, as Trilling says, the modern element to our mind is almost the opposite of what Arnold sees—it is nihilism, a "bitter line of hostility to civilization," a "disenchantment with culture itself."[34] Somewhere in the sequence—Trilling notes the importance here of Nietzsche, Freud, Conrad, and Sir James Frazer's anthropology—a radical alteration takes place to give us the intellectual conventions of Plight, Alienation, and Nihilism; the idea of the modern is bound up with consciousness of disorder, despair, and anarchy. So words like "modern" can alter suddenly in content; a body of sensibility can recede and another grow without the terms changing. Imagine then such a cycle of development focused and concentrated into a brief span of time—a few months, at most a year or two—and one begins to sense the nature of our *Wendepunkt*.

Suffusing the entire 1880s sense of the modern was a confident faith in social advance, a readiness to believe that to expose abuses was to invite their annihilation, that to repudiate the conventional past was to clear the way for a healthy moral growth, for welcome ideals. Hard work, clear vision, courage, purposefulness—these were the keys to the future, to the evolution of new types of men, of society, of art. In Eugen Wolff's article of 1888 in which he first enunciated and defined the concept of the modern—a concept the detail of which one can find expressed in the Anglo-American line, too—he invents a spokesman who explains how that concept might be expressed in plastic, sculptural terms:

> *As a woman, a* modern *woman, filled with the modern spirit, and at the same time a typical figure, a* working *woman, who is nevertheless saturated with beauty, and full of ideals, returning from her material work to the service of goodness and nobility, as though returning home to her beloved child—for she is no young virgin, silly and ignorant of her destiny; she is an experienced but pure woman, in rapid movement like the spirit of the age, with fluttering garments and streaming hair, striding forward . . . That is our new divine image: the Modern.*[35]

But this salutary ikon was not to remain such for long. A few brief years, and the modern was associated with a very different set of images. An earlier ally of Wolff's, M. G. Conrad, writing in 1892, could not repress the scorn and bitterness he felt for the spirit of transformation that was coming over the Modern and its representatives; and in a welter of mixed metaphors he abused the new literary leaders:

> *The only true poetry now is the virtuoso art of the nerves, that which feeds us with the most outrageous sensations, which titillates us with techniques gathered from literary clinics all over the world, all tested for refinement; and it is with these that we are to march at the head of the cultural movement in Europe, we immoralists by the grace of Nietzsche, we magicians of the hypererotic sporting world, we mystics of the international passing show, we raging Rolands blessed by impotence and foolishness . . . For the healthy-minded man of today it is a matter of complete indifference what alien cuckoo's eggs the more extreme specialists of the Modern hatch out in their little* fin-de-siècle *chapels and brothels, wagging their little "isms" like tails behind them:*

> *symbolism, satanism, neo-idealism, hallucinism . . . Give things a few years, and no cocks will crow for any of this ultra-modern charlatanism practised by these comic turns of literature and art.*[36]

Conrad's statement, despite its own comic aspects, thus confronts a spectacle that was to complicate the revolt of the 1890s and is much more familiar to us in the observations of Max Nordau: the crossing of the "modern" spirit with the spirit of Decadence and Aestheticism.

To get at the quality of this change, it is useful once again to take a roll-call. When, in the early 1880s, Georg Brandes wrote of the "modern minds," as he called them, of the men of the Modern Breakthrough, of whom did he speak? Of Ibsen and Bjørnson, of Jacobsen and Drachman, of Flaubert, Renan, John Stuart Mill. But particularly of Ibsen. When the German writers of the late 1880s thought of "modern" literature, of whom did *they* think? Of Ibsen, of Zola and Tolstoy, Daudet, Bret Harte, and Whitman. But particularly, again, of Ibsen. When, however, the 1890s generation of critics—often the same men as before—looked for specifically "modern" qualities, to whom did *they* turn? To Strindberg and Nietzsche, Büchner and Kierkegaard, Bourget and Hamsun and Maeterlinck. But especially to Strindberg. This is a sharp change, and nowhere is it more dramatically revealed than in two successive articles by the Viennese critic, Hermann Bahr—one of 1890, in the first of his series of studies called *Zur Kritik der Moderne* (*In Criticism of the Modern*), and the other of 1891, in the second series.[37] In the former he defined the task of 'modern' literature as that of achieving a synthesis of naturalism and romanticism, and urged the example of Ibsen as the supreme exponent. Within a year he speaks of "the wild frenzy of the galloping development" that had so exceeded expectation that things half-anticipated for the end of the century had arrived after no more than six months; he points to Strindberg and the group of Scandinavians gathered about him—Ola Hansson and Arne Garborg, for example—as the most modernistic literature of the day. And here, in this brief time-span, one gets a sense both of the displacement and of the nonetheless essential *continuity* of events. The Ibsen vogue and the Strindberg vogue in Germany — and indeed throughout Europe — might be traced to one chief source, Georg Brandes: the Ibsen vogue to Brandes' elaboration of the concept of the Modern Breakthrough, and the Strindberg vogue to the seminal lectures given by Brandes in Copenhagen in 1888, which stimulated not only Strindberg but the whole German nation (which had hitherto virtually ignored him) to discovery of Nietzsche, and spread his importance right through Europe and into England and the United States.

This same crossover point, which (in crude terms) comes when something happens to the fortunes of realism and naturalism, themselves modern but not quite Modernist movements, can be seen elsewhere. In 1891, when the Parisian journalist Jules Huret enlisted from Paul Alexis, the novelist and Zola-disciple, what must be the classic literary telegram — "Naturalism not dead," it said, "letter follows" — he stirred the hornets' nest; out of its buzz Modernism derives. Alexis, in the letter that did indeed follow, defended the claims of the naturalists to be *the* movement of the modern: it was not a school but a mode of knowledge, and its scientizing, rationalizing, democratizing tendency would bring into the domain of literature for the twentieth century "the broad general current which carries our age toward more science, more truth, and no doubt more happiness." As for the tendencies toward symbolism, decadence and psychology in art, he found these out of date and "merely comical." Yet it is precisely in the breaking up of the naturalistic surface and its spirit of positivism that one senses the growth of Modernism; as H. Stuart Hughes points out, "nearly all students of the last years of the nineteenth century have sensed in some form or another a profound psychological change"[38] — a reaction against positivism, toward a fascination with irrational or unconscious forces. But, looking at the two Germanic Modernisms, early (before 1890) and late

(after 1890), one can see clearly in this context — something that the more confused events elsewhere perhaps disguise — the one *growing out* of the other. That one might then, with some expectation of reward, polarize Modernism along an Ibsen–Strindberg axis is a natural consequence; especially since during the years about 1890 Scandinavian leadership in European drama coincided so provocatively with such ferment in German cultural life, and reached elsewhere as well — to, for instance, those very different modern talents Shaw and Joyce. It is almost symbolic that scarcely had Ibsen left Germany in 1891, after long years of residence there, to return to his native Norway than Strindberg himself arrived at Berlin to shock and provoke its cultural world with his and his associates' goings-on at the Black Boar tavern. It is equally appropriate that in the closing years of a century which had been gradually accumulating a body of apocalyptic, historicist, Nietzschean and indeed Dionysian aesthetic theories and presumptions, increasing in proportion as the modern age was seen as historically novel and distinct, one should sense, right across the European countries, not simply an extension but a *bifurcation* of the impulse to be modern.

6

The reader who has followed our exercise in Modernist revisionism thus far is now likely to ask the obvious question: what follows from such recognitions? Perhaps what follows first is that the suspicion, already strong, of current nomenclature as a guide to events is further reinforced. It is clear that many of the standard labels — Naturalism, Impressionism, Symbolism, Imagism, Futurism, Expressionism, to go no further — were forbiddingly intertwined and overlapped, producing a doubtful synthesis of many movements radically different in kind and degree. What is clear is that Modernism, whether used as a term within the sequence or a term to describe the sequence, is no exception, and is subject to extreme semantic confusion. But what is equally clear is that the terminological confusion should not be used as an excuse to disguise some of our difficulties. It is tempting to suppose that Anglo-American Modernism and the Germanic Modernisms were two quite different things, happening at different times, which just happened to acquire cognate labels. And so, if we are looking for significant similarities, we might cast our eyes across and try to equate Anglo-American Modernism of the early twentieth century with the contemporary movement in the German tradition, which would be Expressionism. In fact the notion that the common factor among Modernisms is, precisely, Expressionism has been advanced by R. P. Blackmur.[39] However, Graham Hough has pointed up some of the dangers of this generalization and comparison:

> Mr. Blackmur has referred to the whole European movement, with which the English one belongs, as Expressionism. I should not be very happy with this as far as our domestic affair is concerned. Expressionism in art has Germanic connotations, and the literature we are considering is Anglo-American profoundly influenced by France. And Expressionism is a name for a kind of critical doctrine, a doctrine of personality and self-expression, that is precisely the one not held by our twentieth-century school.[40]

Hough, therefore, is talking about one obvious bifurcation within Modernism, and he is referring, of course, to the doctrines of impersonality and classicism that mark much Anglo-American Modernist thought, and especially that vein in it that concentrates into Imagism, which becomes in every sense the hard core of the Anglo-American tendency.

What this shows us is that there are severe difficulties within any standard chronology of events (which sees the same things as happening at the same time in different countries), and that many of the basic ideas and motifs of Modernism were distilled over an extended time-span in a variety of different circumstances. But there is a further complication: divergence between Expressionism and Imagism is not the whole story either. Briefly looking at it from the Anglo-American end for a moment, we can now see that there are links between various Germanic developments and various phases of Anglo-American experiment. The impact of Ibsen and Nietzsche has long been known in both England and America. But there is also growing evidence of links between D. H. Lawrence and the early phases of Expressionism, through his wife Frieda; of strong Expressionist elements in John Dos Passos and Eugene O'Neill; and so on. Similarly Futurist developments, which tended to share with Expressionism a buoyant *acceptance* of the modern city, the modern machine, the sense of contingency, clearly pass on into English-language experimentalism. The Anglo-American line is not single, as becomes clear when we look at the differences between a Lawrence poem and a Pound poem in an Imagist anthology, or note the way in which poets like William Carlos Williams and Hart Crane could, while respecting *The Waste Land*, believe that it had, by virtue of its nihilism and despair, set poetry *back* twenty years.[41] In short, Modernism was in most countries an extraordinary compound of the futuristic and the nihilistic, the revolutionary and the conservative, the naturalistic and the symbolistic, the romantic and the classical. It was a celebration of a technological age and a condemnation of it; an excited acceptance of the belief that the old régimes of culture were over, and a deep despairing in the face of that fear; a mixture of convictions that the new forms were escapes from historicism and the pressures of the time with convictions that they were precisely the living expressions of these things. And in most of these countries the fermenting decade was the eighteen nineties.

Modernism does have, then, its distinct phases and its distinct lines and traditions, but there is great profit in trying to relate and reconcile them. And, of the many reassessments and realignments that this salutary exercise brings in its train, we might note one of especially large order. For the earlier and the wider we push in our attempts to get at the roots of Modernism, the more we are likely to ask questions about the relationship between Modernism and two of the essential mental and artistic movements of the nineteenth century: Romanticism, and positivistic Naturalism. A number of critics have been tempted to see Modernism as a resurgence of Romanticism, though conceivably in a more extreme and strained form of pure irrationalism. Thus Frank Kermode and A. Alvarez, while taking the tendency as a whole, and recognizing the "classical" elements within it, both suggest that the intense subjectivity of the Romantic spirit remains central to the modern arts.[42] And an even more elaborate case has been put by recent scholars of Romanticism like Geoffrey Hartman, Harold Bloom, Robert Langbaum, Morse Peckham and, with more qualifications, Hillis Miller, who in various ways propose a continuity into Modernism of the primary Romantic concerns with consciousness, with self—object relationships, and with intensified experience.[43] But most of these arguments do have to recognize an element of discontinuity hidden somewhere in the sequence; as Hillis Miller puts it, "a new kind of poetry has appeared in our day, a poetry which grows out of romanticism, but goes beyond it."[44] And an examination of the period between 1880 and the turn of the century, both in the Germanic and the Anglo-American line, should bring home the fact that we are concerned with more than a swing back to the spirit of Romanticism. For if anything distinguishes these decades and gives them their intellectual and historical character it is a fascination with evolving consciousness: consciousness aesthetic, psychological, and historical. And the preoccupation arises under the pressure of history, the push of modern times, that carry with them new evolutionary hopes and desires, and new underlying forces, psychic and social. The new registers of consciousness alter our sense of history, and our sense of the stability of consciousness itself, taking us into new concepts of mental and emotional association. "Since they are modern characters," says Strindberg of his people in *Miss Julie* (1888), "living in an age of transition more urgently hysterical at any rate than the age that preceded it, I have drawn them

as split and vacillating . . . conglomerations of past and present . . . scraps from books and newspapers . . ."[45] This is much the sort of comment that might have been made by any Modernist writer between the 1880s and the 1930s; and, in its consonance between fragmentation, discontinuity, and the modern age of transition, it is itself modern.

It is one of the larger commonplaces of cultural history that we can distinguish a kind of oscillation in style over periods of time, an ebb and flow between a predominantly rational world-view (Neo-Classicism, Enlightenment, Realism) and alternate spasms of irrational or subjective endeavor (Baroque, *Sturm und Drang*, Romanticism). The resultant temptation is to regard ages as being identifiably one or the other: head or heart is in command, reason or emotion dominates, the cultural pattern is "*naïv*" or "*sentimentalisch*," Apollo or Dionysus claims allegiance. It may help us to understand Modernism if we recognize that these spirits can cross and interfuse. They are, arguably, not fixed poles between which the spirit oscillates, but are subject to the dynamism of change, moving on convergent paths. Suppose, then, that the period we are calling the Modern shows us not the mere rehabilitation of the irrational after a period of ordered Realism, or for that matter the reverse, a period of Classicism after a phase of Romanticism, but rather a compounding of all these potentials: the interpenetration, the reconciliation, the coalescence, the fusion—perhaps an appallingly explosive fusion—of reason and unreason, intellect and emotion, subjective and objective. Let us recall one of the central tenets of the Anglo-American Modern, the Imagist definition of Image, in the words of Ezra Pound: "An image is that which presents an intellectual and emotional complex in an instant of time."[46] Pound is here talking about the juxtaposing of contradictions for resolution, and we may extend that notion of fusion into other areas of experience. Or consider Paul Klee, speaking of painting: "Formerly we used to represent things visible on earth, things we either liked to look at or would have liked to see. Today . . . things appear to assume a broader and more diversified meaning, often seemingly contradicting the rational experience of yesterday. There is a striving to emphasize the essential character of the accidental." Immediately, again, we recognize the quality common to many of the most characteristic events, discoveries and products of this modern age: in the concern to objectify the subjective, to make audible or perceptible the mind's inaudible conversations, to halt the flow, to irrationalize the rational, to defamiliarize and dehumanize the expected, to conventionalize the extraordinary and the eccentric, to define the psychopathology of *everyday* life, to intellectualize the emotional, to secularize the spiritual, to see space as a function of time, mass as a form of energy, and uncertainty as the only certain thing.

An explosive fusion, one might suppose, that destroyed the tidy categories of thought, that toppled linguistic systems, that disrupted formal grammar and the traditional links between words and words, words and things, inaugurating the power of ellipsis and parataxis and bringing in its train the task — to use Eliot's phrase — of making new juxtapositions, new wholes; or, in Hofmannsthal's words, of creating "from man and beast and dream and thing" an infinity of new relationships. And if, finally, one were to seek the precisely defining event, the supremely symbolical point, one would surely turn back to the nineties; and to, for instance, Strindberg's complete, desperate and protracted attention to alchemy, that unique fusion of reason and unreason, science and magic; or to Yeats's evolutionary cosmology, with its search for unity between time and the timeless, the dancer and the dance. One would turn to the intensifying discovery that the thrust of modern consciousness raised issues that were more than representational, were crucially aesthetic, problems in the making of structures and the employment of language and the social role of the artist himself. One would need to contemplate the uneasy awareness that the spirit of naturalism, with its implied optimistic scien-

tific temper, its sense of political emancipation, must find some way of comprehending the strange pressures of unconscious forces and answer to those luminous, unpositivistic metamorphoses that art uniquely could produce. The great works of Modernism live amidst the tools of modern relativism, scepticism, and hope for secular change; but they balance on the sensibility of transition, often holding in suspension the forces that persist from the past and those that grow from the novel present. They turn on ambiguous images: the city as a new possibility and an unreal fragmentation; the machine, a novel vortex of energy, and a destructive implement; the apocalyptic moment itself, the blast or explosion which purges and destroys — images, like Forster's Marabar Caves, which are potentially a synthesis of all possible experience, globally conceived, or of the empty multiplicity and anarchy of the world. It is the image of art holding transition and chaos, creation and de-creation, in suspension which gives the peculiar concentration and sensibility of Modernist art — gives it what one of the contributors in this volume calls its "Janus-faced" quality.

It is perhaps, then, characteristic that Modernist writers tend to suppress certain features of modern sensibility — some of its optimism in history, science, evolution and progressive reason — while choosing to release others. The sequence of Modernism, we have said, is a very various sequence running through different subversions of the realist impulse: Impressionism, Post-Impressionism, Cubism, Vorticism, Futurism, Expressionism, Dada and Surrealism. They are not all movements of the same kind and some are little more than coterie names; and writers tended to move in and out of them. But one feature that links the movements at the centre of sensibility we are discerning is that they tend to see history or human life not as a sequence, or history not as an evolving logic; art and the urgent now strike obliquely across. Modernist works frequently tend to be ordered, then, not on the sequence of historical time or the evolving sequence of character, from history or story, as in realism and naturalism; they tend to work spatially or through layers of consciousness, working towards a logic of metaphor or form. The symbol or image itself, whether romantic or classic, whether it be the translucent symbol with its epiphany beyond the veil, or the hard objective centre of energy, which is distilled from multiplicity, and impersonally and linguistically integrates it — helps to impose that synchronicity which is one of the staples of Modernist style. By such means can occur that compacting, that sense of generative distillation which can — to borrow Eliot's phrase about compacting contemporaneity and antiquity in *Ulysses* — "make the modern world possible for art." Hence there is a preservative element in Modernism, and a sense of primary epistemological difficulty; the task of art is to redeem, essentially or existentially, the formless universe of contingency. Reality is not a material given, and nor is it a positivistic historical sequence. The act of fictionality thus becomes the crucial act of imagining; and Modernism thus tends to have to do with the intersection of an apocalyptic and modern time, and a timeless and transcendent symbol or a node of pure linguistic energy.

Now if these propositions about the complexity and nature of Modernism do have any validity, we can find nearly all the significant manifestations at dates much earlier than those points in the 1920s which some of our critics have seen as the heyday of it all. The significance of de-creating the given surface of reality; intersecting historical time with time according with the movement and rhythm of the subjective mind; the pursuit of the luminous image, or else of fictional order sustained against consecutive story; the belief in perception as plural, life as multiple, reality as insubstantial; these crucial notions form into a creative compound long before the First World War and are there in the last century, as symbolism and naturalism cross and interfuse. One reason why the post-war period has seemed so crucial is that the war itself can be recognized as the apocalyptic moment of transition into the new. But in this matter we might better look at the significance of the turn of the century itself, a topic on which Frank Kermode writes brilliantly

in *The Sense of an Ending*, a book which does much to distil the character of modern theories of fictionality and also the apocalyptic and historiographic features of Modernist sensibility.[47] Kermode suggests that the turning of a century has a strongly chiliastic effect; it helps distil men's millenarian disposition to think about crisis, to reflect on history as revolution or cycle, to consider, as so many *fin-de-siècle* and *aube-de-siècle* minds did consider, the question of endings and beginnings, the going and coming of the world. The sensibility itself has, of course, an extended history, going deep into the Judaic tradition and the kind of importance we attach to secular time. What Modernism does is to raise in ferment the notion not only of form but also of significant time, and this is one reason why audacious attempts to discern a moment of transition (Henry Adams's 1900; Virginia Woolf's 1910; D. H. Lawrence's 1915) are themselves a feature of Modernist sensibility. The consequences of this apocalyptic ferment of order help explain much of Modernism. It illuminates the symbolist effort to transcend historical sequence by intersecting with it the timelessness of artistic revelation: the artist, like Scott Fitzgerald's Gatsby, tips back the clock on the mantelpiece and sees beauty, form, dream. It illuminates the desire to reappraise the structure and operation of mind: "To appreciate the pagan manner of thought," D. H. Lawrence tells us, "we have to drop our own manner of on-and-on-and-on, from a start to a finish, and allow the mind to move in cycles, or to flit here and there over a cluster of images. Our idea of time as a continuity in an eternal, straight line has crippled our consciousness cruelly."[48] It illuminates, too, that passion in Modernism to see the universe as contingent, poverty-stricken, denuded until it has been reimagined, its local virilities apprehended through the planes and conjunctions available to the fictionalizing mind.

This crucial compound persists until after the war, and certainly up to 1930. After that it seems that certain elements of Modernism seem to be reallocated, as history increasingly came back in for intellectuals, as, with the loss of purpose and social cohesion, and the accelerating pace of technological change, modernity was a visible scene open to simple report, and as the world depression tends increasingly to bring back political and economic determinism into the intellectual ideologies. Our own concentration in this book is therefore on the period before 1930, even though the lines of demarcation here cannot be clear, for the broader view of Modernism we have offered must suggest an extraordinary range of continuities through into present art. There is a further reason for this concentration; for perhaps one of the most remarkable features of this period between 1890 and 1930 is the extraordinary galaxy of talent that we find there. Few historical phases contain such an extraordinary wealth of major writers — European, English, American — whose complexity of aesthetic inquiry, whose generative sense of style, whose sustaining and self-risking intelligence offers so much work worthy of detailed consideration. Modernism may be a stylistic abstraction, one exceptionally difficult to formulate. But it does catch under its loose but invigorating label a large number of writers who manifest art for us in a major way. It does not, as we have said, catch *all* the important writers of the twentieth century. But enough to make a volume devoted to Modernist experimentalism an exploration of some of the most interesting and essential literary creation to be found in our difficult century.

Notes to the Reading

1. Herbert Read, *Art Now* (London, 1933; revised edition 1960).
2. C. S. Lewis, *De Descriptione Temporum: An Inaugural Lecture* (Cambridge 1955). The lecture is reprinted in his *They Asked for a Paper* (London 1962), pp. 9–25.
3. Roland Barthes, *Writing Degree Zero* (*Le Degré zero de l'écriture*), translated by Annette Lavers and Colin Smith (London 1967), p. 9.
4. G. S. Fraser, *The Modern Writer and His World* (London 1953); Richard Ellmann and Charles Feidelson (eds.), *The Modern Tradition: Backgrounds of Modern Literature* (New York and London 1965).
5. Lionel Trilling, "On the Modern Element in Modern Literature," in *Beyond Culture: Essays in Literature and Learning* (London 1966).
6. Northrop Frye, *The Modern Century* (New York and London 1967), p. 23.
7. A. O. Lovejoy, "On the Discrimination of Romanticisms" (1924), reprinted in M. H. Abrams (ed.), *English Romantic Poets: Modern Essays in Criticism* (New York 1960).
8. See especially Georg Lukács, *The Meaning of Contemporary Realism*, translated by John and Necke Mander (London 1962).
9. Alfred North Whitehead, *Science and the Modern World* (London 1927); quoted in Wylie Sypher, *From Rococo to Cubism in Art and Literature* (New York 1960).
10. Wylie Sypher, *From Rococo to Cubism in Art and Literature* (New York 1960), p. xix.
11. Stephen Spender, *The Struggle of the Modern* (London 1963).
12. Jose Ortega Y Gasset, "The Dehumanization of Art," in *The Dehumanization of Art, and Other Writings on Art and Culture* (Garden City, N.Y. 1956).
13. Frank Kermode, "Modernisms," in *Modern Essays* (London 1971).
14. This is Harry Levin's interpretation of a primary characteristic of modernism in "What Was Modernism?," in *Refractions: Essays in Comparative Literature* (New York and London 1966).
15. T. S. Eliot, "*Ulysses*, Order, and Myth," *Dial*, no. 75 (New York 1923), pp. 480–83, reprinted in Richard Ellmann and Charles Feidelson (eds.), *The Modern Tradition: Backgrounds of Modern Literature* (New York and London 1965).
16. Irving Howe, "Introduction to the Idea of the Modern," in Irving Howe (ed.), *Literary Modernism* (Greenwich, Conn. 1967), p. 13.
17. A. Alvarez, *Beyond All This Fiddle: Essays, 1955–1967* (London 1968).

18. Cyril Connolly, *The Modern Movement: One Hundred Key Books from England, France, and America, 1880–1950* (London 1965), p. 4.

19. Edmund Wilson, *Axel's Castle: A Study in the Imaginative Literature of 1870–1930* (New York 1931); C. M. Bowra, *Heritage of Symbolism* (London 1943).

20. Graham Hough, *Image and Experience: Studies in a Literary Revolution* (London 1960).

21. Richard Ellmann and Charles Feidelson (eds.), *The Modern Tradition: Backgrounds of Modern Literature* (New York and London 1965), p. vi.

22. A. Alvarez, *Beyond All This Fiddle: Essays, 1955–1967* (London 1968); Frank Kermode, "Modernisms," in *Modern Essays* (London 1971); Stephen Spender, *The Struggle of the Modern* (London 1963); Graham Hough, *Image and Experience: Studies in a Literary Revolution* (London 1960).

23. Virginia Woolf, "Mr Bennett and Mrs Brown" (1924), reprinted in *Collected Essays, volume 1* (London 1966), p. 321.

24. Richard Ellmann, "The Two Faces of Edward," in R. Ellmann (introd.), *Edwardians and Late Victorians* (New York 1960); reprinted in his *Golden Codgers: Biographical Speculations* (New York and London 1973).

25. Harry Levin, "What Was Modernism?," in *Refractions: Essays in Comparative Literature* (New York and London 1966).

26. Harold Rosenberg, *The Tradition of the New* (New York 1959, London 1962).

27. For useful comments on Post-Modernism, see Ihab Hassan, *The Literature of Silence: Henry Miller and Samuel Beckett* (New York 1967), and his *The Dismemberment of Orpheus: Toward a Postmodern Literature* (New York 1971). Also see George Steiner, *Language and Silence: Essays 1958–1966* (London 1967), and Susan Sontag, *Against Interpretation and other Essays* (New York 1966).

28. Bernard Bergonzi (ed.), *Innovations: Essays on Art and Ideas* (London 1968). In addition to Kermode's essay, see that by Leslie Fiedler on "The New Mutants" and that by Leonard B. Mayer on "The End of the Renaissance?".

29. Ihab Hassan, "POSTmodernISM," *New Literary History*, vol. III, no. 1 (Autumn 1971), pp. 5–30; reprinted in I. Hassan, *Paracriticisms: Seven Speculations of the Times* (Urbana and London 1975). Other essays on the same topic are to be found in this issue. For a more critical view, see Gerald Graff, "The Myth of the Postmodernist Breakthrough," *Tri-Quarterly*, no. 26 (Winter 1973), pp. 383–417. Other essays in this same special issue — especially that by Philip Stevick — are relevant.

30. George Steiner, "From the Vienna Woods," *New Yorker* (23 July 1973), pp. 73–7.

31. Holbrook Jackson, *The Eighteen-Nineties* (London 1913; reprinted in Pelican Books, 1939). The quotation comes from p. 19 in the Pelican edition.

32. Wilhelm Arendt (ed.), *Moderne Dichtercharaktere* (Leipzig 1885).

33. In *Literarische Volkshefte*, vol. III (1888).

34. Lionel Trilling, "On the Modern Element in Modern Literature," in *Beyond Culture: Essays in Literature and Learning* (London 1966).

35. Eugen Wolff, "Die Moderne," reprinted in Erich Ruprecht (ed.), *Literarische Manifeste des Naturalismus, 1880–1892* (Stuttgart 1962), pp. 138–41.

36. M. G. Conrad, "Moderne Bestrebungen," reprinted in Erich Ruprecht (ed.), *Literarische Manifeste des Naturalismus, 1880–1892* (Stuttgart 1962), pp. 254–6.

37. Hermann Bahr, *Zur Kritik der Moderne* (Zürich 1890); second series (Dresden 1891).

38. H. Stuart Hughes, *Consciousness and Society: The Reorientation of European Social Thought, 1890–1930* (London 1959), p. 34.

39. R. P. Blackmur, *Anni Mirabiles, 1921–1925: Reason in the Madness of Letters* (Washington D. C. 1956).

40. Graham Hough, *Image and Experience: Studies in a Literary Revolution* (London 1960), p. 8.

41. Thus William Carlos Williams comments: "I'd felt at once that it [*The Waste Land*] had set me back twenty years, and I'm sure it did. Critically Eliot returned us to the classroom just at the moment when I felt that we were on the point of an escape much closer to the essence of a new art form itself — rooted in the locality which should give it fruit . . ." (William Carlos Williams, *Autobiography* (London 1968), p. 174).

42. Frank Kermode, *Romantic Image* (London

1957) and A. Alvarez, *Beyond All This Fiddle: Essays, 1955–1967* (London 1968).

43. Geoffrey Hartman, *Beyond Formalism: Literary Essays, 1958–1970* (New Haven 1970); Harold Bloom, *Yeats* (New York 1970); Harold Bloom (ed.), *Romanticism and Consciousness: Essays in Criticism* (New York 1970); Robert Langbaum, *The Poetry of Experience* (New York 1963); and Morse Peckham, *Beyond the Tragic Vision: The Quest for Identity in the Nineteenth Century* (New York 1962). Also see the essays in David Thorburn and Geoffrey Hartman (eds.), *Romanticism: Vistas, In-stances, Continuities* (Ithaca and London 1973).

44. J. Hillis Miller, *Poets of Reality* (Cambridge, Mass. 1965).

45. August Strindberg, "Preface" to *Lady Julie* (1888).

46. Ezra Pound, "A Retrospect" (1918), reprinted in T. S. Eliot (ed.), *Literary Essays of Ezra Pound* (London 1954), p. 4.

47. Frank Kermode, *The Sense of an Ending* (London and New York 1966).

48. D. H. Lawrence, *Apocalypse* (London 1932), pp. 97–8.

SUGGESTED ADDITIONAL READINGS

Malcolm Bradbury and James McFarlane, eds., *Modernism, 1890–1930* (Atlantic Highlands, N.J.: Humanities Press, 1978).

Francis Frascina and Charles Harrison, eds., *Modern Art and Modernism: A Critical Anthology* (New York: Harper & Row, 1982).

Immanuel Kant, *Critique of Judgment*.

Frederick R. Karl, *Modern and Modernism: The Sovereignty of the Artist 1885–1925* (New York: Antheum, 1985).

Leonard B. Meyer, *Music, the Arts and Ideas: Patterns and Predictions in Twentieth-Century Culture* (Chicago: University of Chicago Press, 1967).

The Spiritual in Art: Abstract Painting 1890–1985, exhibition catalogue (Los Angeles: Los Angeles County Museum of Art and Abbeville Press, 1986). Various essays promoting an antiformalist interpretation of abstract art.

NOTES

1. Monroe Beardsley, *Aesthetics from Classical Greece to the Present* (New York: Macmillan, 1966), pp. 363–64.
2. Roger Fry, "The French Post-Impressionists," in *Modern Art and Modernism: A Critical Anthology*, ed. Francis Frascina and Charles Harrison (New York: Harper & Row, 1982), p. 91.
3. Roger Fry, "An Essay in Aesthetics," in Frascina and Harrison, *Modern Art and Modernism*, p. 81.
4. David Lodge, "Modernism, Antimodernism, and Postmodernism," in *Working with Structuralism* (London: Routledge & Kegan Paul, 1981), p. 5. Emphasis added.
5. A counterargument to this should be considered. The common practice of translating literature, even poetry, into other languages seems to presuppose that there is a content that can be transferred to another linguistic vehicle — that is, if we assume that the translated poem is the *same poem* as the original.
6. Beardsley, *Aesthetics*, p. 167.
7. Beardsley, *Aesthetics*, p. 220.
8. Samuel Beckett, *Watt* (New York: Grove Press, 1959), pp. 200–201.
9. Lodge makes this observation in *Working with Structuralism*, p. 13.
10. Denis Arnold, *Bach* (Oxford: Oxford University Press, 1984), pp. 80–81.

11. Arnold, *Bach*, pp. 81–82.

12. Kim Levin, "Farewell to Modernism," in *Theories of Contemporary Art*, ed. Richard Hertz (Englewood Cliffs, N.J.: Prentice-Hall, 1985), p. 3. (Originally published in the October 1979 issue of *Arts* magazine.)

13. Richard Hertz, Introduction to *Theories of Contemporary Art*, p. 1.

14. Whereas most thinkers view these traits as features of modernism, Marxist-Leninist art theorists associate these characteristics with what *they* call "formalism." These thinkers use the term "formalism" to stand for those movements in the arts characterized by artists' indifference to the social and political context in which they make art and by their replacement of representational and didactic goals for art with the pursuit of art for art's sake — in short, Marxist-Leninists view formalism as a repudiation of the artist's social responsibility. In the USSR during the Stalinist era, artists who were accused of "formalism" were being accused of creating art that was not in the officially approved style of "socialist realism" and thus did not further the communist revolution.

15. Malcolm Bradbury and James McFarlane, "The Name and Nature of Modernism." See the Readings for this chapter, page 300.

16. Roger Fry, *Vision and Design* (London: William Clowes & Sons, 1920), p. 199.

17. Kant, in his *Critique of Judgment*, develops a subjectivist account of beauty that is similar to Bell's theory in that it is based on our private inner responses. Philosophers often adopt a double standard with respect to Bell, rejecting his theory out of hand while attempting to sympathetically interpret and justify Kant's comparable account. For an analysis of Kant's theory, see J. Fisher and J. Maitland, "The Subjectivist Turn in Aesthetics: A Critical Analysis of Kant's Theory of Appreciation," *The Review of Metaphysics* 27, no. 4 (June 1974): 726–51. For a criticism of Bell's theory, see Beryl Lake Steele, "A Study of the Irrefutability of Two Aesthetic Theories," in *Aesthetics and Language*, ed. W. Elton (Oxford: Oxford University Press, 1954), reprinted in many other anthologies on aesthetics, as well.

18. Carlo Ginzburg, *The Enigma of Piero: Piero della Francesca: The Baptism, The Arezzo Cycle, The Flagellation* (London: Verso, 1985), p. 126.

19. Clive Bell, "The Debt to Cézanne," in *Art* (New York: Capricorn Books, 1958), pp. 135–43.

20. Bell, "Debt to Cézanne," p. 140.

21. Bell, "Debt to Cézanne," pp. 142–43.

22. Richard Taruskin, "Facing Up, Finally, to Bach's Dark Vision," *The New York Times*, 27 Jan. 1991.

23. He, unfortunately, calls the nontemporal approach the "formal" position. But according to the prevailing terminology in aesthetics, the other position, the "kinetic-syntactic" position is also a formalist position, as long as the dynamic development of the music is not held to be a reflection of processes external to the music, such as emotional responses in the listener.

24. Meyer also notes that in addition to these positions, as well as a mimetic position, there are theories that account for music in terms of pure "sensuous enjoyment." He rejects this as a serious account of music: "While admitting that this aspect of music contributes to our pleasure, few theorists or aestheticians have seriously contended that it is of primary importance" (p. 290).

25. Meyer is aware of the limitations of his syntactic theory when it comes to giving a convincing explanation of the value of music to us. He discusses these limitations in "Value and Greatness in Music," chapter 2 of *Music, the Arts, and Ideas: Patterns and Predictions in Twentieth-Century Culture* (Chicago: University of Chicago Press, 1967).

26. Quoted in Maurice Tuchman, "Hidden Meanings in Abstract Art," in *The Spiritual in Art: Abstract Painting 1890–1985*, exhibition catalogue (Los Angeles: Los Angeles County Museum of Art and Abbeville Press, 1986), p. 32.

27. Tuchman, "Hidden Meanings," p. 17.

28. Tuchman, "Hidden Meanings," p. 37.

29. Georgia O'Keeffe, *Georgia O'Keeffe* (New York: Viking Press, 1976), illustration no. 88.

30. O'Keeffe, *Georgia O'Keeffe*, illustration no. 63.

31. Quoted in Tuchman, "Hidden Meanings," p. 35.

32. Sixten Ringbom, "Transcending the Visible: The Generation of the Abstract Pioneers," in *The Spiritual in Art*, p. 146.

33. Piet Mondrian, "Natural Reality and Abstract Reality," in Herschel B. Chipp, ed., *Theories of Modern Art* (Berkeley: University of California Press, 1971), p. 321.

34. Ringbom, "Transcending the Visible," Ringbom is quoting Mondrian, from *Mondrian Sketchbooks*.

35. Piet Mondrian, *Mondrian Sketchbooks*, quoted in Ringbom, "Transcending the Visible," p. 146.

36. Barnett Newman, quoted in Tuchman, "Hidden Meanings," p. 49.

37. Donald Kuspit, "Concerning the Spiritual in Contemporary Art," in *The Spiritual in Art*, p. 319.

38. Quoted in Kuspit, "Concerning the Spiritual," pp. 317–18.

39. Joseph Kerman, *Contemplating Music: Challenges to Musicology* (Cambridge, Mass.: Harvard University Press, 1985), p. 65.

40. Among the many problems with such a claim is the question of whether an art's nature or its norms are timeless or whether they change and develop historically. Greenberg treats both nature and norm as timeless Platonic entities that underlie and explain the historical development of each art.

41. In fairness to Greenberg, he also suggests different critical values. He explicitly separates modernist goals from what he views as aesthetic considerations: "Actually, such [modernist] consistency promises nothing in the way of aesthetic quality or aesthetic results. . . . now, as before, the only consistency which counts in art is aesthetic consistency, which shows itself only in results and never in methods or means" (p. 158). These remarks might merely mean that being a consistent modernist is not sufficient for success. But if they also mean that aesthetic success has nothing to do with the media formalist goals I have specified, it becomes questionable whether it is accurate to attribute the media formalist position to Greenberg.

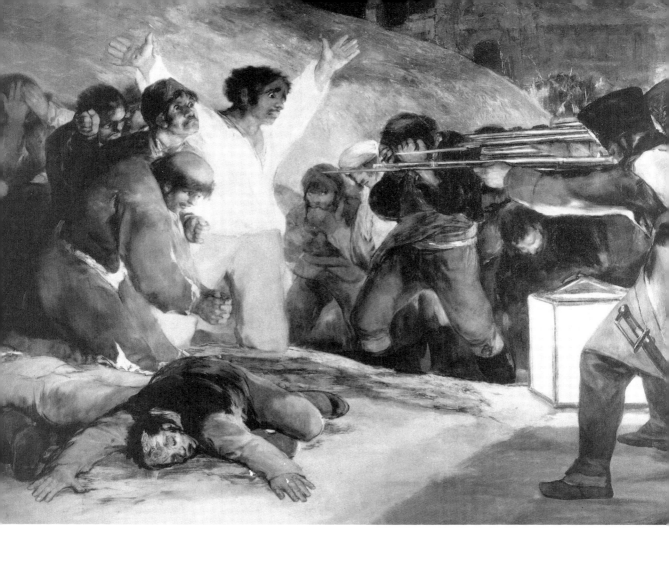

Expression
Theory

◀ *Third of May, 1808* (1814–15), Francisco Goya (1746–1828). This painting shows an execution of Spanish citizens by occupying French troops. Instead of bringing reform, Napoleon's armies brought savage tyranny. Goya made modern martyrs out of the resistance fighters as he showed them pitilessly gunned down by the faceless, mechanical troops. Undoubtedly this is an emotional painting—but where is the emotion? In the painting, in the artist, in the viewer, or in all three?

Art does not render the visible but renders visible.

— Paul Klee, "Creative Credo"

TRADITIONAL EXPRESSION THEORY

Four concepts dominate traditional aesthetics: beauty, representation, expression, and form. Of these, expression is probably the most complex and difficult to understand. Expression is also potentially the most important for an understanding of the arts. If we ask *why* art is created, many people would respond that its function as expression better answers that question than do any of the other traditional aesthetic concepts.

Expression is a concept with many aspects. People express; words express; actions express; pictures, sounds, and objects are said to express. And each of these subjects can express ideas, thoughts, facts, feelings, attitudes, moods, and so forth. In short, different types of subjects and different types of objects can fit into the grammatical structure "X expresses Y." Here are some examples: "George expressed his intentions"; "His obscene gesture expressed his frustration"; "That the team punted expressed the fact that the game was lost"; "Goya's painting *The Third of May, 1808* (see illustration on p. 322) expresses outrage at the brutality of war"; "Goya's painting expressed his bitter feelings toward political tyranny"; and so on.

Of all these possibilities for what can do the expressing and what can be expressed, theorists have focused on the idea that artists and/or their works do the expressing and that what they express is emotion or feeling (including, perhaps, moods and attitudes). Undoubtedly, artworks also often express ideas, beliefs, arguments, and so forth, but so does ordinary discourse. Nor does all art express ideas, beliefs, and so forth; it would be hard to contend that any idea or belief was expressed, for instance, by a piano sonata. Therefore, in seeking a characteristic that is unique and applicable to all art, expression theorists have naturally been led to assert that it is the expression of *emotion* that is the hallmark of art.

Although expression of emotion is quite familiar, it is in fact a difficult phenomenon to conceptualize properly — especially when applied to artworks. This partly explains the impatience which some philosophers have displayed toward expression theories of art. To such philosophers, expression theories seem like attempts to explain the enigmatic by the incomprehensible. To many thinkers, expression of emotion seems to be too simple and primitive a phenomenon to account for the subtleties and sophistication of art — if we think of expression of emotion on the model of an angry person ranting and raving. On the other hand, suggesting that expression of emotion might be analyzed as something far more complex is to appeal to a phenomenon too obscure and unfamiliar to provide a satisfactory explanation of art. The difficulty of understanding expression also explains why expression theorists do not agree among themselves about the nature of artistic expression.

Nonetheless, expression theories of art became very popular in the nineteenth and early twentieth centuries, falling out of favor only with the rise of analytic trends in philosophy of art, which in the 1950s, 1960s, and 1970s yielded many searching criticisms of the notion of art as expression. Alan Tormey, in *The Concept of Expression* (1971) notes that "it would only be a slight exaggeration to claim that from the close of the eighteenth century to the present 'expression' and its cognates have dominated both aesthetic theorizing and the critical appraisal of the arts."[2] The philosopher John Hospers adds, "The expression theory of art, in one form or another, has dominated the aesthetic scene for the past two centuries as much, perhaps, as the imitation theory had done previously."[3]

Expression theory has been especially dominant in nonrepresentational arts, such as abstract visual arts and music. As we saw in Chapter 10, this dominance incited Eduard Hanslick in the nineteenth century to formulate one of the first formalist theories of art. He was motivated by his opposition to the romantic idea that the function of music is to express the composer's emotions or to evoke an emotional response in the listener. Yet today, in spite of the influence of formalism on music theory, the idea that absolute music (music without a vocal text or program) is to be understood in terms of its relation to emotions is, for most of us, still the most common way of thinking about the import of instrumental music.

Before examining expression theories more closely, we should contrast "expression" with two other terms commonly used in art history and criticism: "expressionistic" and "expressionism." "Expressionistic" refers to a style of art, whereas "expressionism" refers to a particular art movement. Expression*istic* art is art with a high level of extreme emotions as its content. Expression*ism* refers to the great proliferation of expressionistic art in the early decades of the twentieth century. Expressionistic art, whether literature, painting, music, or cinema, often involves intense psychic disturbance and distortion in the perspective adopted by the artwork. It is remote from objective or realistic portrayals of the world, as well as from the happier emotions. By contrast to these two terms, "expression," as it is used in aesthetics, refers to something that artists supposedly *always* do in the act of creating art: expressing themselves or their feelings in or through the artwork. Whereas only a small percentage of artworks throughout the history of art is "expressionistic" and only a certain group of artworks belongs to the movement called "expressionism," the expression theory of art claims that *all* art—even artworks that were created well before the rise of expressionism as a movement—are a function of expression.

Many thinkers over the last century have put forth expression theories of art. We will concentrate on two such thinkers: the nineteenth-century Russian novelist Leo Tolstoy (1828–1910) and the twentieth-century English philosopher R. G. Collingwood (1889–1943). The theories of Tolstoy and Collingwood are two of the best known and most influential expositions of expression theory, and they sharply contrast with each other.

Tolstoy and Collingwood do not disagree over whether art is expression of emotion. They both hold that it is, and this is why we are right to say that both thinkers put forth an expression theory of art. But every expression theory claims not only that art is expression but also that expression is to be analyzed in certain ways. It is here that expression theories diverge significantly from each other. Tolstoy and Collingwood have entirely different views about what it means to express an emotion, although both agree that certain other accounts of expression are definitely wrong.

Both Tolstoy and Collingwood develop their ideas about expression and art as part of a general theory of art; that is, they try to say what the nature of art is, why we make and appreciate art, and why the arts are valuable. This leads both Tolstoy and Collingwood to deny the status of art to works that, even though they may be created in a traditional art medium, are not attempts by the artist to express emotion. Tolstoy, for example, contrasts real with counterfeit art, while Collingwood contrasts "art proper" with "art falsely so called." Expression theories of art typically make expression of emotion by the artist both a necessary and a sufficient condition for an object to be art; that is, they define art this way:

> X is a work of art if and only if X is an expression of the emotions of the person who fabricated or created X.

It is clear that no matter what our definition of "expression" is, this definition of art will be both too wide (because it counts non-art as art) and too narrow (because it does not count some genuine artworks as art), unless we reject the claim that all and only those items called art by the artworld are to be counted as art. The institutional theory of art (see Chapter 5), by contrast, accepts as art all examples validated by the artworld—for example, everything shown in a gallery or performed in a theater or studied in a literature class—and then it attempts to formulate a theory of art that explains why all of those examples really are

What is considered the definition of art is no definition at all, but only a shuffle to justify existing art.

— Leo Tolstoy[4]

artworks. If we do accept as genuine art everything the artworld deems art, then expression theories will come up short, because they will not count all such works as genuine expression. Both Tolstoy and Collingwood argue that being conferred status in the artworld is not sufficient for a work to be counted as art. Nor is it necessary: both of their theories are broader than the institutional theory in that they count any genuine expression of emotion (if it meets their special definitions of expression) as art, whether the expression has been recognized by the artworld or not.

In contrast to the institutional theory, which attempts to explain what concept underlies the linguistic usage of the word "art," both Tolstoy and Collingwood regard art as a real phenomenon in the world existing independently of how we use the word. Both theorists feel free to argue that what contemporary society counts as art may not really be art, and they accordingly imply that a society could develop a mistaken view about the phenomena of art.

The Causal-Communication Theory of Expression

Arguably the most famous statement of an expression theory of art is given by Tolstoy in his book *What is Art?* (see the Readings for this chapter):

> To evoke in oneself a feeling one has once experienced, and having evoked it in oneself, then, by means of movements, lines, colors, sounds, or forms expressed in words, so to transmit that feeling that others may experience the same feeling—this is the activity of art.
>
> Art is a human activity consisting in this, that one man consciously, by means of certain external signs, hands on to others feelings he has lived through, and that other people are infected by these feelings and also experience them. (p. 353)

A theory of this type is what most thinkers associate with the idea of an expression theory of art. For Tolstoy, to say that artists produce real as opposed to counterfeit art is to say that they express their emotions by means of their artworks; and to say that they express themselves through their artworks is to say that they produce their artworks in conformity with the process Tolstoy delineates. Note that Tolstoy's model requires several distinct elements:

a. The artist must have a genuine feeling or emotion.

b. The artist must intentionally produce an external artwork that will transmit his or her feeling to others; that is, the artist intentionally aims to evoke that feeling in members of the audience.

c. If the artwork is successful, members of the audience will experience the same emotions as the artist did.

If conditions (a) or (b) are not met, then what has been produced is not art at all. If condition (c) is not met, then what is produced is not good, or successful, art. So, if artists do not set out to transmit their own genuine feelings to others, then they have not made real art. If those who experience the work are not infected with the artist's feelings, then the work is at best unsuccessful art.

Condition (b) reflects an obvious but important feature of art making: it is intentional. Thus, unintentionally exhibiting the *symptoms* of emotion does not count as expressing them, not even if others are affected. Tolstoy argues:

> If a man infects another or others directly, immediately, by his appearance or by the sounds he gives vent to at the very time he experiences the feeling; if he causes another man to yawn when he himself cannot help yawning, or to laugh or cry when he himself is obliged to laugh or cry . . . that does not amount to art. (p. 352)

> Your freedom as a writer is not freedom of expression in the sense of wild blurting; you may not let rip.
>
> — Annie Dillard, *The Writing Life*[5]

Collingwood calls the unintentional venting or exhibiting of marks of emotion "betraying emotion" (see the Readings). Like Tolstoy, he sharply distinguishes betraying emotion from expressing emotion, and only works that do the latter are art:

> A person who writes or paints and the like in order to blow off steam, using the traditional materials of art as a means for exhibiting the symptoms of emotion, may deserve praise as an exhibitionist, but loses for the moment all claim to the title of artist. (p. 364)[6]

Tolstoy cites an example from everyday experience as a paradigm of art:

> . . . a boy, having experienced, let us say, fear on encountering a wolf, relates that encounter; and, in order to evoke in others the feelings he has experienced, describes himself, his condition before the encounter, the surroundings, the wood, his own lightheartedness, and then the wolf's appearance, . . . etc. All this, if only the boy, when telling the story, again experiences the feelings he had lived through and infects the hearers and compels them to feel what the narrator had experienced, is art. (p. 352)

This is an extremely egalitarian theory; there is no talk of "genius"[7] or of special inspiration that only a select class of artists possesses. We can all be artists, even in everyday life and without any special training, if only we tell stories or paint pictures or play music in order to get others to feel our emotions. Like other expression theorists, Tolstoy is thus radically anti-elitist. Tolstoy makes clear throughout *What is Art?*, as well as in his essay "Shakespeare and the Drama," that he prefers literary works like Harriet Beecher Stowe's *Uncle Tom's Cabin* to the tragedies of Shakespeare. He lists *Uncle Tom's Cabin* and Charles Dickens's *A Christmas Carol* as modern examples of the highest type of art,[8] whereas he rejects much of the canon of masterpieces of art history as counterfeit art: "Sophocles, Euripides, Aeschylus . . . Dante . . . Milton, Shakespeare; in painting, all of Raphael, all of Michael Angelo . . . ; in music the whole of Bach and the whole of Beethoven."⁹ By labeling all these works as false art, Tolstoy is claiming that the works of these artists are not inspired by real feeling. The fact that we continue to consider them art — in the face of direct experience that must tell us otherwise — is a result of the malign influence of art criticism and schools of art, according to Tolstoy.

Clearly, Tolstoy's theory is radical; it turns many of our usual assumptions about art upside down. What makes it plausible is that expression theories in general can explain a number of features about art: they explain why we customarily attach great importance to the artist and why artists are motivated to make art; they explain why we care about art and why artworks so frequently move us (according to expression theories, that is the very function of art). These theories also provide an explanation of the meaning of nonrepresentational arts, such as music and abstract painting, that many thinkers and artists have found highly attractive. As we saw in Chapters 9 and 10, one of the vexing problems for art theory is to account for nonrepresentational arts; the mimetic theory flounders at this point, and even formalism ends up appealing to emotions to explain the import of significant form in abstract art.

Tolstoy's objective, of course, is not to explain abstract art. On the contrary, he wishes to explain how *representations* can be meaningful as art; for Tolstoy, what counts in art representations, as in the example of the boy and the wolf, is our feelings *about* the represented subject matter. This notion can be illustrated by Frida Kahlo's striking painting *The Two Fridas* (1939) (see Plate 11). Frida Kahlo (1907–1954) was one of the most distinctive painters of the twentieth century. She suffered many severe medical problems and underwent many operations as a result of an accident that left her handicapped; she also endured two tumultuous marriages to the famous Mexican mural painter Diego Rivera. She was obsessed by the folklore of her native Mexico and by her mixed Mexican Indian and European heritage. In *The Two Fridas*, she represents herself as split into two women tied to together by a bleeding vein. The concentration on the two women isolated against a dramatically moody sky helps to express Kahlo's anguish at Rivera's insistence that she divorce him, the event that led her to create this painting. It vividly expresses not only Kahlo's mixed ethnic heritage (note that the right-hand Frida has slightly darker skin and is dressed in an Indian skirt and blouse, whereas the left-hand Frida is lighter and is dressed in a Victorian dress) but also the painful experience of being loved and rejected at the same time.¹⁰ The unloved Frida on the left — as the biographer Hayden Herrera interprets this figure — tries to stop the flow of blood with surgical pincers, but the drips persist. The blood on the white cloth evokes associations with Kahlo's accident, her operations, and her miscarriages. As the example of *The Two Fridas* illustrates, expression theory gives an extremely plausible account of at least some art; it almost amounts to common sense about how we think about such works.

Expression theory can also give an account of nonrepresentational art. Consider the case of Mozart's last three symphonies: nos. 39, 40 (in G Minor), and 41 (*Jupiter*). The composition of these three symphonies in the summer of 1788 is remarkable in two ways. First, although these complex masterpieces are perhaps the three greatest Mozart symphonies, they were composed in the space of two months. Second, they were not, as far as we know, commissioned or composed for any specific performance dates or concerts — in fact, they were not even performed in Mozart's lifetime. Mozart's fortunes had fallen to a new low during this period, which Edward Tatnall Canby describes as "the most dismal in the dreary succession of bad times for the Mozart family"[11] and biographer Michael Levey describes as a "period of experiences blacker than any [Mozart] had known before."[12]

At that time, it was extremely unusual for composers to compose music just for its own sake. Thus, many people have concluded that Mozart composed these works out of some inner necessity to express himself. And the symphonies themselves run a rich gamut of emotional expression. The Fortieth Symphony in particular, written in the "sad" key of G minor, seems to express all sorts of dark or negative emotions and moods. A Tolstoyan explanation of this symphony is that Mozart needed to express and thus evoke his feelings in listeners. This explanation also accounts for the meaning and power of the Fortieth Symphony; it is not just a work of pleasant sounds, diverting melodies or rhythms, or unusual formal beauty—although the symphony certainly has all of these. It is more than this; it causes us to experience certain *feelings* when we listen to the music. Michael Levey notes that the equation of this symphony's dark moods with Mozart's "black thoughts" "has perturbed some critics who fear too pat a correlation between an artist's life and his art." He concludes, however, that "it cannot be denied that [Mozart] had undergone these sensations. It would be a strange obtuseness to refuse them any part whatsoever in the most starkly despairing of his symphonies."[13]

Some thinkers resist interpreting artworks as the literal expression of artists' feelings and therefore doubt Tolstoy's version of expression theory. Another concern is this: given that art, in Tolstoy's view, is a universal and everyday phenomenon and is not a matter of special genius or of exceptional craft, does his theory of art forfeit the possibility of attributing a high value to art? Such a result would certainly be ironic; as we saw in Chapter 2, Tolstoy argues that it is essential for theories of art to explain the value of art. Not surprisingly, Tolstoy has an answer to his own challenge. The value of art, which justifies its prestige and the sacrifices made for it—assuming such sacrifices are being made for real rather than counterfeit art—does not reside in flashy craft or technique, nor does it reside in the genius of a special class of superior artists. Rather, the value of art comes from the function art serves in society and in human historical development:

> Speech, transmitting the thoughts and experiences of men, serves as a means of union among them, and art acts in a similar manner. The peculiarity of this latter means of intercourse, distinguishing it from intercourse by means of words, consists in this, that whereas by words a man transmits his thoughts to another, by means of art he transmits his feelings. (p. 352)

Art, for Tolstoy, is of parallel importance to language. (By "speech" Tolstoy clearly means the factual or scientific uses of language, as opposed to uses of language to produce art, for example, poetry, fiction, or drama.) Art is the essential means of transmitting and therefore sharing our emotional lives. Tolstoy thinks such a function is of obvious importance:

> And if men lacked this other capacity of being infected by art, people might be almost more savage still, and, above all, more separated from, and more hostile to, one another.
>
> And therefore the activity of art is a most important one, as important as the activity of speech itself and as generally diffused. (p. 353)

Some critics charge that Tolstoy's theory invalidly broadens the conception of art to include all sorts of ordinary everyday phenomena. Tolstoy cheerfully accepts this result:

All human life is filled with works of art of every kind — from cradlesong, jest, mimicry, the ornamentation of houses, dress, and utensils, up to church services, buildings, monuments, and triumphal processions. It is all artistic activity. (p. 353)

Many other objections have been made to Tolstoy's expression theory. Some argue that Tolstoy's theory is not an adequate account of art, whereas others argue that Tolstoy's theory is not an adequate account of expression as it occurs in art. This distinction is important because it might be that Tolstoy is not wrong to think that art is expression of feelings even though he misunderstands the mechanism of expression.

Among the objections to Tolstoy's account as a theory of art we can include the following:

1. Tolstoy's theory seems to ignore the art medium. For Tolstoy, the medium, whether words, paint, or music, is incidental to the emotion conveyed. Apparently, the same feelings could be conveyed by many different media. Indeed, the external work of art becomes merely a causal agent functioning to elicit an emotional response in the audience, rather than an object important in itself with independent aesthetic properties.

2. The emphasis on emotion in the arts threatens to lower the status of art. This concern may stem from the low status that emotion has customarily had in the European intellectual tradition. It is important here to distinguish those who hold that emotion is not fundamentally important to art from those who hold that emotion is not the *only* important dimension of art. The latter would object that Tolstoy's theory overstates the case, whereas the former would assert that he is altogether wrong to contend that emotional communication is essential to art.

3. If we maintain that expression theory offers an account of why art is made, another problem arises: it is factually untrue that artists are always motivated by strong and clear emotions that they intentionally want to share.[14] As John Hospers puts it, "I doubt whether Shakespeare was always expressing feelings; sometimes he probably wrote, although he did not feel like it, to meet a deadline, or to have money coming in for the next month, or because the plot he borrowed from somewhere else intrigued him."[15] In response to this criticism, expression theorists ask, Why must we always count as art the productions of famous artists? Tolstoy would vigorously argue that when Shakespeare was not consciously emotionally motivated, he did not produce art, however diverting, interesting, and complex his dramas.

If we find this answer a bit unconvincing, it may be because of a difficulty in Tolstoy's account of emotional expression. The model of strong, perhaps even crude, emotions clearly understood by the artist and then intentionally aroused in an audience would seem to fit only a small percentage of cases of art. On this point Collingwood sharply diverges from Tolstoy. Collingwood claims that art can be emotional expression even when the artist is operating with no simple clear emotion analogous to the boy's fear of the wolf.

This last point leads into an entirely different set of difficulties raised by Tolstoy's account. These problems do not necessarily question whether art is expression; rather, they question whether Tolstoy's analysis of expression is plausible. An immediately obvious difficulty is that often when we express our emotions, we do not cause those to whom we express them to have the *same* emotions. If, for example, I express my fear to an unsympathetic audience, this may elicit feelings of contempt or disdain in the audience members; even if I express fear to a sympathetic audience, they may feel pity or a desire to comfort me rather than sharing my feeling of fear. To take Tolstoy's example, they may know that the boy was never really threatened by the wolf and therefore feel sympathy for him but not literally share his fear of the wolf. These considerations suggest that it is not correct to claim that the artist has successfully expressed his or her feelings only if he or she has elicited the *same* emotions in the audience. Depending on their respective psychologies, the audience and artist may experience opposite emotions or emotions that are only related in complicated ways. Or the audience may experience an emotion that the artist could not have felt. Suppose the boy in Tolstoy's example told his story to parents of young boys; we can readily imagine that their emotions would be different from the boy's. It does not follow that because the audience does not share the same emotions, the artist has not truly expressed his or her emotions.

Negative Emotions

Many thinkers have questioned whether we feel *real* emotions at all as a result of experiencing art. As Jerrold Levinson points out in "Music and Negative Emotions" (see the Readings for this chapter), there is a paradox in supposing that we experience real emotions when we experience artworks. Many of the emotions identified with artworks are unpleasant. Why would we seek out these emotions in art if we avoid them in real life? Yet we do seek out artworks that involve negative emotions. This paradox constitutes an objection to Tolstoy's version of expression theory since Tolstoy does propose that genuine art actually moves the audience to feel the emotions that the artist attempts to convey.

Levinson finds this paradox particularly obvious in the case of music. Many of the greatest works of classical composers involve distressing feelings. Levinson describes an imaginary but perfectly familiar case in which a listener happily listens to a sequence of pieces of instrumental music that involve "intense grief, unrequited passion, sobbing melancholy, tragic resolve, and angry despair" (p. 374). The question is why people would find such experiences not only enjoyable but also rewarding, even though in real life having such feelings is neither enjoyable nor rewarding.

The answer frequently given by music theorists and philosophers is that listeners do *not* feel the emotions embodied in music. If the music does evoke a real emotional response in a listener, according to this school of thought, this response should be considered inappropriate. For example, if I *associate* a particular piece of music with a tragic event in my life, this association is coincidental and has nothing to do with the essential aesthetic properties of the music. Levinson notes that there is a "virtual consensus of these writers that negative emotion is not actually evoked in the attuned listener by even the most intense of musical works" (p. 375). Levinson, however, rejects this solution to the paradox: "It seems to me that there are indeed compositions that can, when listened to in certain appreciatively admissible frames of mind, produce in one real feelings of both the positive and negative variety" (p. 375).

Levinson's solution requires a philosophical analysis of emotions. He identifies two primary components of emotion: a cognitive component and an affective component. The cognitive component is "a belief, attitude, desire, or evaluation, focused on and identifying the *object* of emotion" (p. 378). Tolstoy's boy, for example, had a *belief* that a wolf was stalking him and he *evaluated* the wolf as a dangerous threat to him; this is part of what fear of the wolf consisted in. Levinson conceives of the affective component—how the emotion *feels*—as involving both a phenomenological aspect (a certain pleasant or painful quality of inner feeling) and a sensational aspect (internal bodily sensations—goose bumps, for example, or lump in the throat).

If this is a correct analysis of what emotions are, it raises an immediate problem for any view of music as properly involving evocation of emotion. The problem was discovered by the great music critic and formalist Eduard Hanslick in the nineteenth century (see Chapter 10). Hanslick rejects the usual attempts to explain the meaning of music in terms of its emotional content or its emotional effects because, as he notes, emotions require an object as well as cognitive mental states toward that object. For example, "The feeling of love cannot be conceived apart from the image of the beloved being, or apart from the desire and the longing for the possession of the object of our affections."[16] Hanslick argues that pure instrumental music—music without words or program—is incapable of representing objects and situations toward which the listener could adopt appropriate cognitive states. He generalizes, not implausibly, that all emotions require objects and cognitive states toward those objects and that because music is incapable of representing any objects, music therefore can neither represent true emotions nor properly invoke emotions in listeners. To Levinson's example mentioned above, Hanslick would reply, "Grief about *what*? Passion toward *whom*? Resolve to do *what*? Despair about *what*?" To Hanslick, music cannot possibly give rise to such feelings, except perhaps in the minds of suggestible listeners who have been programmed to think of the music that way.

In response to this criticism, Levinson claims that although the cognitive component of emotion is necessarily lacking in music, the affective component is "retained in something like full force. If music inevitably fails to induce by itself a proper, contextually embedded *emotion* of sadness, still, some music appears fully capable of inducing at least the characteristic *feeling* of sadness" (p. 378). Levinson claims, in short, that we experience something like objectless feelings in response to music; presumably, this would also be a possible response to abstract visual art.[17] Levinson offers a number of interesting speculations about why experiencing the affective component of emotion without the cognitive components can be both enjoyable and positively rewarding; these speculations, if correct, would solve the paradox of music and negative emotions.

Is Emotion the Criterion of Art?

Skepticism about expression theory can come from still another direction. If we understand expression as Tolstoy suggests, i.e., if we conceive of artworks as emotional communications along the lines of Tolstoy's model, then epistemological concerns can arise. How do the viewers or listeners *know* that the emotions they experience when they look at or listen to the art are the same as those the artist felt when he or she created the work? How can we infer with any reliability the inner states of artists just on the basis of their works? How could such a communication system ever get started?

If we look back at the Frida Kahlo example, for instance, we have to admit that we used a great deal of collateral information to understand her painting; she wrote and spoke to many people about her art. Even so, isn't it possible that she did not tell the truth or did not recognize the truth about her own feelings? And how is a naive viewer to know on the basis of her paintings alone what they are about emotionally? Some people might respond that we can just tell, perhaps in a vague way without the specific details, what the moods and emotions of an artwork are, even if we do not yet have the knowledge to interpret the representational content precisely.

For his part, Tolstoy is very optimistic about the possibility of knowing the artist's emotions. He claims that observers directly intuit the artist's emotions when they experience an artwork. He even asserts that this intuition is a decisive criterion indicating that something is art:

> If a man, without exercising effort and without altering his standpoint on reading, hearing, or seeing another man's work, experiences a mental condition which unites him with that man and with other people who also partake of that work of art, then the object evoking that condition is a work of art. (p. 354)

Tolstoy offers an intriguing analogy to the observer's intuition of the emotions of the artist, namely, the ability to see color. We have a mental capacity to experience color directly in observing the external world. Tolstoy suggests that we also have the mental capacity to experience each other's emotions through the mechanism of artworks. This claim is compatible with the fact that there are people who, unfortunately, lack this capacity. The existence of color-blind persons does not undermine the reality of color nor the capacity of those who can perceive color to distinguish and agree upon shades of color. This is Tolstoy's way of dealing with the fact that what he wants to count as real art — and, correlatively, what he wants to count as counterfeit art — is not necessarily congruent with what many people count as real art in modern societies. He proposes that many of us have become deadened to the feeling of real art. He suggests that the ability to feel that an artwork expresses our own emotions has atrophied in many of us and we longer even expect this experience in the arts.

A feeling of unity between audience and artist is a common theme among expression theorists. The chief peculiarity of the inner feeling that tells us something is art, Tolstoy claims, "is that the receiver of a true artistic impression is so united to the artist that he feels as if the work were his own and not someone else's — as if what it expresses were just what he had long been wishing to express" (p. 354). Although he holds a very different account of expression, Collingwood also speaks of a sort of identification: when someone reads a poem "he is not merely understanding the poet's expression of his, the poet's, emotions, he is expressing emotions of his own in the poet's words, which have thus become his own words" (p. 362).

Our empathetic identification with the artist seems real enough subjectively. At the least, we identify with the voice that speaks the poem or the eye and hand that paint the picture, the musician who plays the music. But in Tolstoy's account of art, we experience an objective reality beyond our subjective experience. That objective reality is the inner feelings of the artist who actually made the art. But how could we verify that what we experience is in fact the artist's true feelings? The analogy to color perception is not very helpful. Tolstoy suggests that we identify with the artist's feelings directly, just as we experience color directly. But how can we claim to have a *direct* experience of the artist's inner feelings? Thus we have an epistemological quandary: we have direct knowledge of something of which we cannot have direct knowledge. It must be that although we seem to have an immediate knowledge of the artist's feelings, we in fact know them only by *inference*. A proponent of the communication model will have to explain how we gain this inferential knowledge.

We have now canvassed many interesting problems concerning the communication model. Because the most serious problems center on Tolstoy's theory of expression rather than on his claim that art is expression, we will turn next to two other approaches to understanding expression and emotion in the arts.

It is far from clear why Tolstoy is so convinced that art is the infectious communication of feeling. Is it that he realizes that art *must* have an important function in order to account for its existence and importance? Is he thus committed to his theory as a hypothesis that answers his own challenge to find such an important function? Or is it that as a great writer and reader he had direct experience of the transmission of feeling, direct experience that convinced him of the validity of the theory he proposes, in spite of its problems? Or is it, rather, that the emotional side of art is just plain obvious—as even Plato observes—and that Tolstoy's hypothesis is designed to explain how works of art could have emotional properties and emotional meaning? That question leads to another question: What is the undeniable phenomenon concerning emotions and expression in art that any plausible theory of art must account for? The answer, many philosophers argue, is that artworks have expressive *properties*, such as gaiety, melancholy, anxiousness, forcefulness, serenity, or sadness. Let's examine this idea more closely.

RECENT EXPRESSION THEORY

Expressive Properties

To avoid what they see as blatant inadequacies in the expression theory, many philosophers have tried to account for the core phenomenon of emotional expression while jettisoning the theory itself. It is not so clear, however, what this core is. What is it about art, expression, and emotion that needs to be accounted for by a theory of art? Surely feeling is involved in the arts in a special way that it is not in other cultural artifacts, such as scientific hypotheses, technological inventions, interoffice memos, or city ordinances. These and other such items are, of course, discovered, made, or promulgated in part because of our real feelings, and they also frequently give rise to real emotions in us. But in themselves they seldom express anything, whereas artworks are expressive *of* feeling, not just caused by feelings. But does this mean, as Tolstoy assumes, that artworks are caused by the artist's feelings and that their function is to arouse similar feelings in the observer? Or is the indisputable phenomenon simply that artworks considered in themselves seem to possess expressive properties?[18]

Consider Claude Debussy's famous orchestral work, *Prelude to the Afternoon of a Faun* (1894). Instead of thinking of its languid sensuality and its delicate, halting peacefulness as qualities that somehow emanate from the feelings of the composer or performer, or from our own inner feelings as the musical sounds work on us, some propose that we think of these features as properties of the musical sounds themselves. These properties are part of the music in just the same way as are the prominence of the flute and the French horn, the number of measures the piece contains, and Debussy's use of woodwind and brass to achieve, in the words of the conductor Pierre Boulez, "a miracle of proportion, balance and transparency."[19] Transparency is clearly a property of the sounds; similarly, those who consider expressive properties to be fundamental would argue that the musical sounds of the *Prelude* also possess the property of languid sensuality.

Many thinkers accordingly claim that it is what *the work* expresses, and only what the work expresses, that must be accounted for. According to many of these thinkers, to say that an artwork is expressive is equivalent to saying that it has qualities or properties that can be designated by expressive terms, such as "joyous," "sad," "solemn," and "serene." These thinkers contend that the emotionality of art is to be explained purely in terms of properties of artworks and not at all by reference to the emotions of the artist or the audience. Monroe Beardsley, writing in 1980, asserts: "I think it is fair to say that in the past two decades this general view of the arts — that what was true and important in the Expression Theory can be stated in terms of (let us say) aesthetic qualities — has come to be the prevailing view."[20] On this position we can say either that the artwork expresses joy or that it is a joyous artwork.

If we say that artworks have expressive properties, we cannot mean that they are literally sad or joyous. Only people are sad or joyous. So, those who hold that aesthetic attention ought to be focused only on the properties of artworks, and that expression is thus to be located within the work and not the artist, must explain what it means to attribute expressive qualities to art and what makes it true that artworks have specific expressive qualities.[21] This problem is only slightly lessened by Nelson Goodman's suggestion that artworks are only *metaphorically* joyous or sad. He suggests that "what is metaphorically sad is actually sad but not literally sad."[22] This still leaves the problem of understanding how a painting or sequence of sounds can be even metaphorically sad.

Note that theories of expressive properties are much less general and much less ambitious than traditional expression theories. Philosophers who try to give accounts of expressive properties of artworks do not necessarily seek to explain what art is in general. They aim instead to give an account of one dimension of art. And this is a particularly puzzling dimension compared to the formal and representational elements of art. Expressive properties are really, as Guy Sircello points out, *anthropomorphic* predicates applied to artworks:

> That is, we may often properly characterize works of art as, for example, gay, sad, witty, pompous, aloof, impersonal, sentimental, etc. A "theory" of art as expression . . . can say no more than that artworks have properties designated by the same words which designate feelings, emotions, attitudes, moods, and personal characteristics of human beings.[23]

As we have seen, this view creates an immediate puzzle that does not exist when we consider form or representation in art. It is admittedly a difficult theoretical challenge to explain *how* representation works (see Chapter 9), but there is no literal incompatibility between being a painting and representing some item. Yet that is not the case for expressive properties; there seems to be a literal incompatibility between being a painting and being aloof.

Another problem with expressive properties is that they do not comfortably or naturally apply to all art. It is more usual to apply such terms to paintings, poems, and musical works than to more segmented and narrative works, such as movies, plays, operas, or novels. Nevertheless, it is possible to assign expressive properties to *some* narrative works. In the spirit of Tolstoy, we might even propose this as a measure of artistic merit: Does a movie (or scene in a movie), for example, have expressive properties? If it does not, perhaps it is not art, or at any rate not good art. Great movies, such as *Citizen Kane*, seem to be so consistently put together, from the writing and acting to the lighting and photography, that there is an overall unity to scenes and sequences that gives them atmospheric and emotional qualities that compare with poems or movements in musical works. (Consider some of the famous scenes in Sergei Eisenstein's movies, for example, the violent sequence on the Odessa steps in *Potemkin*.) By contrast, it is often difficult and unnatural to try to apply expressive predicates to movies that are merely entertaining, such as Kevin Costner's *Dances With Wolves*, no matter how successful such movies may be in other respects. We could use this fact, if it is a fact, to argue that accounts of expressive properties are limited to only certain artworks; or, we could assert that having expressive properties is a necessary condition of art and that therefore works lacking expressive properties are not art at all.

Theorists who propose accounts of expressive properties above all wish to account for these qualities *without* appealing to the emotional states of the artist; they wish to treat these properties as "objectively" as possible. Can they do this without also considering the subjective states, the feelings, of members of the audience? For surely it is clear that the anthropomorphic terms we assign to artworks must be based on how the works strike observers. Is there an objective way to assign such qualities? Can we say that because the sounds or the paint daubs have certain clearly objective properties—a certain sequence of tonal intervals, a certain pattern of colors—that the music or the painting has certain expressive properties? Can we say that the work is happy because it has certain sounds or sad because it has certain colors? This seems far too mechanical to be plausible, and it ignores the fact that each artwork achieves its expressive capacities through a unique combination of features.[24] Moreover, how would we establish the required connections between the clearly objective properties of a work—those features we can all agree that it has—and the expressive properties?

From an "objectivist" viewpoint, such epistemological problems have always seemed insurmountable. The music theorist Benjamin Boretz, for example, dismisses expressive qualities: "The only problem with 'sad' is that we simply have nothing observational to tie it to in either music or painting, and so it makes no difference to the music or painting. . . ."[25]

Theorists who favor expressive qualities have not advanced very far in dealing with this problem. They commonly note that we regard facial expressions and other behavior as expressive ("a sad smile," "an aloof countenance") and that we can readily agree about the validity of such attributions of emotional terms. This is one familiar sort of case where expressive terms are applied objectively. Some theorists try to extend this paradigm to art. One influential theory of expressive properties claims that we assign them to artworks on the basis of a perceived *similarity* between the features of the artworks and features of human behavior and facial expression.[26] The idea is *not* that we infer how the artist felt on the basis of the similarity, but rather that we use the obvious similarity between human expressive behavior and artworks to explain why we agree on assigning a certain expressive term to an artwork. The proposed theory might even explain why we respond in emotional ways to the artwork. After all, we respond to another person's display of emotion in just such ways.

There is doubtless some truth to the similarity theory. Take for example, the second movement of Beethoven's Third Symphony (*Eroica*). Its strong emotional effect—mournful, agonized, gloomy—is due in part to its slow, dirgelike tempo; the movement of the music is similar in its slow tempo, restrained low notes, and repetitive structure to the behavior of mourners at a funeral. The music plods along for much of the movement, with occasional plaintive high notes from the oboes and flutes that mimic the crying of mourners expressing their grief.

Nonetheless, the similarity theory has severe limitations.[27] Fundamentally, it seems that no matter how much we stretch them, natural similarities between human behavior and artworks explain only a small portion of the expressive properties we attribute to artworks. First, music is uniquely qualified to mimic human behavior; for example, the tempo of music can mimic the tempo of human action, which in turn typically reflects our emotional states: fast (happy) music is similar to sprightly (happy) people. But other art forms could not be explained that way. What similarity is there between gloomy human behavior (or facial expressions) and color schemes that strike us as gloomy? There is no question, of course, that every art form can represent a *character* who sings, acts, looks, or dances in a gloomy way;

the issue is whether *the artwork*, not a character *in* the artwork, has expressive properties. Second, even in music there are many expressive properties that cannot be explained by the similiarity theory. For instance, the extreme tension in the second movement of the *Eroica*, which contributes to the mood of bereavement, is created partly by harmonic developments in the movement. Yet there seems no natural similarity between these tonal relationships and human behavior. Third, the expressive qualities of artworks are so subtle and complex that they defy verbal description. Crude words such as "sad" and "gay" hardly differentiate the unique and complex sort of sadness or gaiety that an individual artwork has. Yet, is human behavior, which is the alleged basis for our attributions of expressive qualities, rich and complex enough to provide us with a basis for our experience of expressive qualities in artworks? This account seems questionable; the similarities it appeals to give us too little to go on to explain how we experience and assign expressive properties to each artwork.

Guy Sircello has argued that the theory just criticized, which he labels the "canonical position" on expression in art, makes another mistake. By maintaining that expressive properties of artworks are based on objective similarities between artworks and human behavior, the canonical position, in effect, implies that those qualities of artworks are the same as expressive qualities of natural objects. He gives these examples: "An ocean may be angry in virtue of its sound and the force and size of its waves; a tree may be sad in virtue of the droop and shape of its branches."[28] Sircello, however, wants to criticize the idea that artworks are happy or sad in the same ways as things in nature are happy or sad. According to the canonical position, a weeping willow tree is sad only in an extended sense—it resembles a sad person—whereas a person is sad in a clearly literal sense. In this regard no contrast is drawn between artworks and nature. The fact that artworks are created by artists does not enter into the explanation; when one says that the second movement of Beethoven's Third Symphony is sad, according to the canonical position, one means exactly the same thing as when one says that the weeping willow tree is sad. The sadness in Beethoven's symphony comes to no more than the sadness of a tree. Although the canonical position does seem to give the correct account of why we attribute such anthropomorphic qualities to natural objects, it is far from clear, for the reasons given above, that it gives an adequate account of why we attribute them to artworks.

In opposition to the canonical position, Sircello proposes that there is an important class of expressive properties that we attribute to artworks in virtue of what the artist *does in the work*. For example, he suggests that Raphael's painting *La Belle Jardinière* is calm and serene partly because Raphael views his subjects calmly and serenely in the way he paints them; that "The Love Song of J. Alfred Prufrock" is a compassionate poem because T. S. Eliot compassionately portrays the "hero" of the poem; that *Wedding Dance in the Open Air* is an ironic painting because the artist (Pieter Brueghel the Elder) treats the gaiety of the wedding scene ironically, and so on.[29] Whether Sircello is right in his assessments of these individual works of art does not matter; what is important is his general idea that we experience and assign many of the expressive qualities of artworks on the basis of how artists handle their materials. If this is right, then we should view artworks as the result of what Sircello calls artistic acts, and much of the expressiveness of the works would result from the nature of the act, that is, from *how* the artists did what they did in the works.

Like the similarity theory, Sircello's theory seems to account for only some expressive properties. For example, it is difficult to see how we could give an illuminating explanation of the mournful, agonized, and gloomy feelings of the *Eroica* by talking about how Beethoven handled the musical notes. In Beethoven—though not in all composers—it seems more reasonable to say that some tonal intervals strike us as tense rather than to claim that we experience a tense handling of intervals (as we might with Bartok). But even if Sircello is right only about some of the expressive qualities of artworks, his theory still implies that we cannot give an adequate account of expressive properties without bringing the artist back into the equation.

Another argument for the importance of the artist comes from cultural relativism. A great mountain (Mount Fuji, Grand Teton) would probably strike us as noble and strong, or expressive of nobility and strength, but it is perfectly conceivable that it might strike an observer from an alien culture as comical or agonized. In the case of a natural object, such as a mountain, such relativity of perception is no real problem, because the mountain itself isn't really noble or comical. We can only say that there are different ways to regard the mountain. These ways are based on different perceived similarities or the application of different, even incompatible, metaphors (to follow Nelson Goodman). Such relativism is a natural but palatable outcome of the belief that we assign expressive qualities according to the perceived similarities between the subject and whatever such attributions are based on (for example human behavior).

However, it is harder to swallow such relativism when it comes to the expressive properties of artworks. Nelson Goodman quotes a passage from Aldous Huxley that illustrates this point. Upon hearing some supposedly solemn music in India, Huxley had to

> confess that, listen as I might, I was unable to hear anything particularly mournful or serious, anything specially suggestive of self-sacrifice in the piece. To my Western ears it sounded much more cheerful than the dance which followed it.
>
> Emotions are everywhere the same; but the artistic expression of them varies from age to age and from country to country.[30]

Is it reasonable to contend that the Indian music is not actually solemn and that its expressive properties vary according to which culture the listener comes from? It hardly seems so.[31] It seems more plausible to say that Huxley was simply unfamiliar with the musical idiom to which he was listening. His perceptions are no more authoritative than those of the aborigine who is reported to have run from a concert of Handel's *Messiah* because he felt the music was threatening. What I am suggesting is that the emotional qualities that artworks express are not dispensable facts about them, although emotional qualities *are* dispensable facts about natural objects. On the contrary, emotional qualities are centrally important aspects of what artworks are about, and to hold that these qualities validly vary with perceivers from different cultures is to give up important determining features of the artwork. Edvard Munch's *The Scream* (see Figure 9.4) is truly frightening; it truly expresses some sort of inner psychic pain that affects the whole world (as Munch said, "I felt as though a scream went through nature."[32]). The second movement of Beethoven's *Eroica* symphony truly contains, among other things, intense negative feelings of grief and gloom. The fact that *The Scream* might strike a viewer from another culture as cheerful or that the *Eroica* might strike an alien listener as soothing should not make us think that *The Scream* is a cheerful painting or that the *Eroica is* a soothing symphony or—even worse—that there is in fact *no* feeling involved at all.[33]

Can a theory that regards the qualities of artworks as independent of the artist account for the nonrelativity of expressive properties? The answer seems to be no. As Sircello argues, the canonical theory treats works of art as though they had expressive qualities in just the same way as natural objects have them. Hence, a canonical theory (for example, the similarity theory) would have to accept the relativism inherent in the application of expressive terms to natural objects. Just as there is no real fact of the matter about whether Mount Fuji is noble or whether it is comical, so there would be no fact of the matter about whether *The Scream* is frightening or cheerful. This consequence seems absurd.

The argument just given does not deny that works of art have expressive qualities, but it insists that such qualities cannot be grounded just in the work itself. Why, in fact, do we experience artworks so readily and strongly as expressions of emotional qualities? Why do we seem so committed to the reality of expressive qualities? One obvious difference between artworks and natural objects may be relevant, namely, that artworks are intentionally made by artists. And, contrary to the critics of expression theory, don't we experience them as the expression of someone, and isn't that why they seem expressive? Not only do I take an artwork as the expression of someone, but I can and do identify with the author, painter, or musician. If I identify with the author, painter, or musician, I experience the artwork as an expression *of* a person from our culture, or at least from a culture I understand. Otherwise I would not be able to experience it as possessing expressive qualities. That seems to be the most plausible explanation for the grounding of expressive qualities.

Artists produce their works as members of particular cultures at particular times. This guarantees that there is a correct interpretation of the expressive qualities involved in the work, namely, how the work would have struck other members of the same culture, including the artist. (This argument does not exclude the possibility that works could be ambiguous.) It is because *The Scream* was painted by someone in our culture that it has definite expressive properties for us. This implies the same conclusion as Sircello argues for, but far more generally: the expressive properties of artworks may, perhaps must, derive from the artist; we experience the work of art as an expression of an artist. We may get the expression wrong — as Huxley did — but we cannot forego this presupposition and still make sense of our commitment to the idea that works of art possess real expressive properties.

The Formulation Theory of Expression

Let's return to the theme of artworks as expressive products of artists. We have now seen that some versions of expression theory are problematic, but we have also seen that there are substantial problems with theories of expression that try to dispense with the artist. Works of art do seem to have expressive properties, which are very central to what the works are about and why we care about them. Yet we have not discovered how to account for these properties without regarding the artwork as an expressive product of someone. In this section, we examine the view — principally extracted from R. G. Collingwood's *Principles of Art* (see the Readings) — that the central mechanism of expression lies in the relation of artist to artwork.

Tolstoy actually combines two common explanations of expression in his communication model. One very crude theory of expression would have it that A (an artwork) expresses E (an emotion) if A was made by an artist because he or she felt E; in short, this is the boiling-over theory of expression mocked by Collingwood. Another, less crude, theory of expression would have it that A expresses E if A typically arouses E in the audience; in short, this is an *arousal* theory of expression. Tolstoy

> I do but hide under these notes, like embers, every spark of that which has consumed me.
>
> — Sir Edward Elgar on his Second Symphony[34]

circumvents both crude versions by bolting them together to create what neither is separately: a communication model of art. In spite of this, Tolstoy does make arousal by the artist an essential part of his model of art. This component of Tolstoy's theory has drawn much fire from critics. Although a few writers[35] allow that this is one legitimate notion of expression (as in "The music expresses sadness" means "It makes me sad"), Collingwood finds this notion entirely unacceptable. Collingwood formulates his theory in direct opposition to the notion that real art—what he calls "art proper"—can have as its aim the arousal of emotions in an audience.

Like other expression theorists, Collingwood never doubts that we must view the work of art as an intentional product of the artist. But he focuses his ire on the idea that artists who intend to create genuine art do so by *intending to produce an emotional effect in an audience*. It isn't that such intentional arousal of emotion in an audience is not possible: comedians, preachers, politicians, and advertisers carry on such activity all the time. Moreover, it is obvious that the arts are often used in this way. Consider, for example, the use of national anthems to evoke emotions of patriotism. Nor does Collingwood morally object to such a process because it is manipulative. To Collingwood, such intentional arousal of emotion is a psychological craft that can be used for good or for ill. For example, it is used for good when the moralist exhorts us to aid those who are suffering from famine and for ill when the advertiser makes us feel that we will be cool if we drink beer.

Tolstoy has an inkling of a problem concerning the inherent manipulativeness of intentional emotional arousal of an audience. So he insists on the artist's sincerity; it is all right for the artist to arouse emotions in an audience provided that the artist feels the same emotions. Tolstoy would have to accept as legitimate art, then, the speeches of Hitler, which successfully influenced the German people to extreme emotions of racial purity and superiority, provided that Hitler was just as fanatical about these ideas as those he influenced.

Collingwood objects that the calculation required to intentionally evoke emotions is not any part of art nor of what is involved in the activity of expressing emotion. We saw in Chapter 7 that there are significant differences between art and craft: craft requires a prior knowledge of the result and mastery of a technique for achieving this result. If the result is the arousal of particular emotions in an audience, the artist would have to conceive those emotions—according to Tolstoy's theory—prior to creating the art, and then the artist would have to know how to arouse those emotions in the intended audiences. Collingwood objects that this has nothing to do with *expressing* emotion.

It is not that artworks do not involve intense planning and craft. For Collingwood, great works of art, such as Eliot's *The Waste Land* or Dante's *Inferno*, clearly exhibit high degrees of both. Planning, craft, and technique provide a framework for the expression of emotion, but expression itself cannot be planned in the same way, for we do not have a knowledge of the end of the process until we express our feelings.

Expressing emotions, in Collingwood's view, is a process of externalizing our inner feelings; it is a process, managed by our consciousness, of converting our unarticulated feelings into an articulation, which then becomes an object of consciousness. Expression is, accordingly, a relation between our unarticulated feelings and an external articulation. It is not a labeling of our feelings. Indeed, it cannot be that, for there is no way to know our specific feelings, in Collingwood's view, other than to articulate them; there is no way to know them other than to raise them from their unconscious state to a conscious formulation. This, he holds, is the very activity and the function of art. In saying that our feelings are unconscious until we express them, Collingwood is not embracing a Freudian explanation of art or a Freudian notion of "the unconscious." Rather, Collingwood's notion is that our feelings are unconscious in the sense that they are not objects of conscious awareness until we express them. This claim is analogous to the idea that our thoughts are "unconscious" until we give them explicit formulation in language. Accordingly I call this the formulation theory of expression. The function of art, then, is to formulate external expressions of our emotions, thus making us conscious of them.

On this view, our emotions are not just lying around below our conscious awareness like objects to be noticed and labeled as soon as we take the time to introspect. (This is the picture of emotions Tolstoy's theory suggests.) Labeling or describing feeling, Collingwood argues, *generalizes*; it categorizes feeling as a feeling of a certain kind. Collingwood argues that such labeling is both crude and the very opposite of expressing feeling:

> To describe a thing is to call it a thing of such and such a kind: to bring it under a conception, to classify it. Expression, on the contrary, individualizes. The anger which I feel here and now, with a certain person, for a certain cause, is no doubt an instance of anger, and in describing it as anger one is telling truth about it; but it is much more than anger: it is a particular anger, not quite like any anger that I ever felt before. . . . To become fully conscious of it means becoming conscious of it not merely as an instance of anger, but as this quite peculiar anger. (p. 360)

If the function of art is to express our feelings, we can now see why Collingwood challenges the arousal view. The requirements for the arousal account are antithetical to actual expression. Arousal requires a prior knowledge of the emotion to be aroused; this emotion would have to be a categorized type of emotion such as fear of a wolf or mournfulness: "So an 'artist' setting out to produce a certain emotion in his audience is setting out to produce not an individual emotion, but an emotion of a certain kind" (p. 360). But since real emotions are in fact individual and contextual, this process falsifies emotion; it is therefore not a process of expressing emotion. Tolstoy's version of the arousal view requires that artists possess knowledge of their own emotions before expressing them, and in Collingwood's view this would be impossible:

> The artist proper is a person who, grappling with the problem of expressing a certain emotion, says, "I want to get this clear." It is no use to him to get something else clear, however like it this other thing may be. . . . He does not want a thing of a certain kind, he wants a certain thing. (p. 360)

Having expressed their emotions, artists gain emotional understanding. It is not necessary that expression lead to the same emotions in those who observe the expression or in those to whom the expression is aimed. What it must lead to is *understanding*—not intellectual understanding, but the emotional understanding that occurs in experiencing the externalized formulation (the artwork) as an *expression* of emotions. If someone expresses anger to me about something toward which I feel very differently, I can still strongly feel that expression as an expression of that particular anger; this does not mean that I will become angry in the same way as the other person, but it does mean that I have the emotional capacity to *feel* this expression: "If a poet expresses, for example, a certain kind of fear, the only hearers who can understand him are those who are capable of experiencing that kind of fear themselves" (p. 362).

On the one hand, it is not merely that I recognize intellectually and unemotionally that the other person feels a certain way. Nor, on the other hand, is it that I must actually possess the other person's feelings, in the sense that I will now feel the same way that he does about the object of his emotions. If I share enough of the artist's world view (knowledge, beliefs, attitudes, culture), I can identify with the artist and accordingly express those feelings myself. Collingwood concludes that with respect to expression both artist and audience are equals: "Thus, if art is the activity of expressing emotions, the reader is an artist as well as the writer. There is no distinction of kind between artist and audience" (p. 362).

This leads to an important contrast between Tolstoy's and Collingwood's views concerning the role of the audience in art. For Tolstoy, an audience is essential to expression; it is inconceivable that one would intend to make an artwork, that is, intend to express one's feelings, without having in mind an audience for the artwork to affect. For Collingwood, by contrast, expression is a relation between the artist's feelings and the artwork that formulates or embodies these feelings. An audience is not necessary for artists to express their emotions successfully, on his theory. Usually, of course, there is an intended audience, but the role of this audience is to understand the emotions expressed. If the audience does not understand, that is, does not feel an expression of the artist's emotions in the work, then the expression may not be understandable, may not be honest, and therefore may not be real expression. Collingwood hypothesizes that consciousness is often reluctant to create an honest expression of emotions — he calls this "corruption of consciousness" — and so the fault may lie with the artist, whose attempt to express his emotions is unsuccessful, or with the audience, which is unwilling to experience the expression of such emotions.

In what sense do we *have* the emotions prior to the experience of the artwork? In a Tolstoyan theory, the artist has the emotions before the artwork is created, whereas the audience does not. Collingwood's theory alters both sides of this equation. We can understand this better if we draw a distinction between conscious feelings and dispositional feelings. Conscious feelings, we can say, are emotional experiences we go through in the course of our lives — for example, the time I was angry for five minutes at Mr. Jones or was afraid of the wolf while running through the forest — which involve objects of the emotions that we are *consciously* aware of while we are going through the emotion. We can contrast such feelings with those that we would or might have *if* we had thought about or had some other imaginary experience pertaining to that subject. These I call dispositional emotions. Let's examine these further.

We may feel deeply about certain situations, issues, or objects without experiencing those feelings at all times or even without ever having consciously experienced those exact feelings. That is, we may be *disposed* to have certain feelings about a subject *if* we were to think about it. It is also often true that it is not clear how we would feel about something if we explored it in more detail, or if we knew more about it, or if we looked at it from an unexpected perspective. We could have certain feelings based on these additional perspectives, and in these cases, too, we could speak of our dispositions to have emotions. Did we have those feelings before we experienced an artwork that explored them? Only potentially, and this is true of the artist as well. Art, on this view, is a process of discovery. What artists discover is our capacity to feel particular emotions about particular subjects and situations.

On Collingwood's theory, the experience of art is the exploration of dispositional emotional experience from a particular perspective; the experience of art is neither the calculated arousal of emotion in an audience nor the preestablished formulation of certain categorized (thus even stereotyped) emotions in the artwork.

Poems readily illustrate dispositional emotions and our capacity to feel emotion. Even if we have not experienced the death of a father, for example, we can experience Dylan Thomas's expression of emotion at his father's death in his famous poem "Do Not Go Gentle into That Good Night." We experience the poet's rage—and thus express our own emotions—when he exhorts his father to "Rage, rage against the dying of the light." The poet's exhortation expresses not only rage at death and his own powerlessness, but also perhaps frustration with a father who is different from his son—perhaps he is a father who never rages at anything, whereas his son rages at life itself. These are emotions most of us can understand and feel even if we have never thought about them or expressed them before we read the poem.

By contrast to the universal experience of death that Dylan Thomas's poem illustrates, consider Rainer Maria Rilke's poem "Moving Forward":

The deep parts of my life pour onward,
as if the river shores were opening out.
It seems that things are more like me now,
that I can see farther into paintings.
I feel closer to what language can't reach.
With my senses, as with birds, I climb
into the windy heaven, out of the oak,
and in the ponds broken off from the sky
my feeling sinks, as if standing on fishes.[36]

This poem vividly expresses a sort of mystical experience: an experience of unity with nature[37] (climbing with the birds, standing on fishes) as well as the experience of intuitions that transcend conventional thought (what language *can't* reach). This experience is unusual and not one most of us will ever have. Nonetheless, by compelling us with images and language, the poet enables the reader to experience, that is, "express," some of the feeling connected to such experience.

It is also possible for artists to explore various perspectives and personalities not their own, again depending on our capacity to feel the world imaginatively from different perspectives. For example, the song "Psycho Killer" by the Talking Heads is a powerful evocation of mental instability ("I can't sleep 'cause my bed's on fire") and threatened violence ("I hate people when they're not polite. . . . Better run run run run run run run away.") This song is clearly not autobiographical of any one band member, and, moreover, it was in fact written by three of them; yet, it is one of the most convincing evocations of mental disturbance in all of rock and roll.

There are many such examples in the arts, and they lead us to ask this question: Are there limits to our capacity to feel from extended or hypothetical perspectives? If there are, does this not suggest that there may be limits to the extent to which an audience can understand an artwork? In particular, what about artworks that express particular racial, ethnic, or gender perspectives—not to mention perspectives from the past or other cultures? This is more of an issue for the formulation theory than for other theories of art, because the formulation theory focuses on artworks as expressions of the inner emotions of artists and requires that the audience share the same capacity for feeling as the artist. Is this an objection to the formulation theory, or is it a virtue of the theory that it highlights the issue?

The received "canon" of masterpieces in literature, painting, and so forth has been criticized in recent years from feminist and ethnic perspectives as embodying a particular biased perspective: that of white Western males. Collingwood might very well agree with this critique. Every real work of art, on his theory, must involve a particular perspective from which the world is emotionally experienced. What remains undecided is this: (*a*) whether this is grounds for finding fault with the artworks in the "canon," and (*b*) whether it is true that we can emotionally understand only those artworks that express our own narrow life experiences. There seems to be considerable evidence that art expands our emotional resources much farther than they would otherwise reach in the normal course of our lives. But how far is unclear. Consider, for example, the difficult case of male bias in classic rock and roll. In one of the Beatles' most popular songs, "Run for Your Life," John Lennon threatens his girlfriend with violence if she is unfaithful: "I'd rather see you dead little girl than to be with another man. . . . Catch you with another man, that's the end, little girl." Lennon's tone of jealousy and swaggering macho threats—for example, referring to his girlfriend as "little girl"—may be difficult for female listeners to accept emotionally. Although Lennon and like-minded males can express their feelings through this song, do female listeners also express these emotions? It may be that the formulation theory shows us important constraints on the experience of art that more "objective" approaches to art do not acknowledge.

> The writing has changed, in your hands, and in a twinkling, from an expression of your notions to an epistemological tool.
>
> — Annie Dillard, *The Writing Life*[38]

Like Tolstoy, Collingwood claims that art is of fundamental importance to society. He devotes the last third of *The Principles of Art* to several speculative claims concerning the function and value of expression of emotion as he conceives it. Collingwood distinguishes non-art, which does not attempt to express emotion, from bad art, which is the failed attempt to make art; that is, "the unsuccessful attempt to become conscious of a given emotion. . . . a consciousness which thus fails to grasp its own emotions is a corrupt or untruthful consciousness" (p. 366). He uses these ideas to claim that expression of emotion is necessary to foster mental health and to provide the foundation for our moral assessment of the world:

> Art is not a luxury, and bad art not a thing we can afford to tolerate. To know ourselves is the foundation of all life. . . . Unless consciousness does its work successfully, the facts which it offers to intellect, the only things upon which intellect can build its fabric of thought, are false from the beginning. . . . In so far as consciousness is corrupted, the very wells of truth are poisoned. . . . Moral ideals are castles in the air. . . . Even common sanity and bodily health are no longer secure. (p. 367)

The issues are emotional honesty and emotional truth. The function of expression—and thus the primary function of art—is to secure these important commodities. Collingwood connects these claims with a further idea implicit throughout his book: Art, that is, emotional expression, is, when successful, a form of self-knowledge. He suggests that artists not only come to know themselves but also make themselves and their world through their art. Because expression is the only mechanism society possesses that can enable it to know its own emotions, it is easy to see that a society needs art if it is to experience the emotional truths about its world. Although these claims are large, they are not implausible; similar claims concerning self-knowledge and social reality are frequently made on behalf of individual artworks, especially for the masterpieces of art history.

Clearly, although the formulation theory has many attractions, it leaves many issues to be worked out. Let me briefly mention three additional issues.

1. The theory will seem too broad to many thinkers. A reflection of this broadness is Collingwood's extreme statement, "Every utterance and every gesture that each one of us makes is a work of art" (p. 368). He probably means to claim that the difference between art and ordinary activities is a matter of degree. Nonetheless, he does not address the question of whether there are essential differences between everyday activities and art. And so, like other expression theorists, he leaves the impression that he may be missing what is unique about art.

2. As we have seen, Collingwood's theory is also a communication theory, although of a very different sort than Tolstoy's. Collingwood emphasizes the uniqueness of each emotion and emotional context, so what guarantees that the audience will be able to understand and express their emotions through the artwork? If Tolstoy's approach to emotions is too crude and universal, isn't Collingwood's approach too individualistic? Would the logical consequence of Collingwood's thought be that each artwork is only about the artist?[39] Collingwood categorically rejects this view of art ("It would be tedious to enumerate the tangles of misunderstanding which this nonsense about self-expression has generated" [p. 415]), but how is it to be avoided on his theory? (For more on this issue, see Chapter 12.)

Arthur Danto (see the Readings for Chapter 12) gives voice to this implication of the formulation theory: "conceivably each artist could express himself in his own way, so that one vocabulary, as it were, would be incommensurable with another. . . . In any case we must understand each work, each corpus, in the terms that define that particular artist we are studying, and what is true of De Kooning need have nothing to do with what is true of anyone else" (p. 404). Here Danto questions not only our ability to understand the individual artwork, but also the general relevance of any artwork to anyone else on the formulation theory.[40]

Certainly some art — notably the art of the insane — appears to be on the boundary of intelligibility. (The formulation theory provides no obvious way to exclude works of insane people from being considered artworks.) Consider the avant-garde artworks mentioned in Chapter 5, for example, the performances of Stelarc, who hangs naked, suspended from hooks through his skin. Can normal people really understand the very unique emotions he is expressing?

3. Finally, the formulation theory has difficulty explaining *how* artworks can formulate or embody emotions. If a main objection to the causal-communication theory is that it ignores the artwork — treating it as a mere causal intermediary — a main problem for a formulation theory is to explain how the artwork itself can formulate or embody emotions. How is this to be explained, and how much art can be covered by this explanation? Although this is a large problem, it is not clear that we need a single broad explanation of how all art formulates emotions; it is more probable that the explanation would have to be made on a case-by-case basis. The explanation would no doubt include a cluster of factors, such as the history of art, the societal context, and the artist's personal history and artistic progress; and certainly the explanation must also include the observer's ability to "read" and experience the expression thus projected into the work.

An example that shows the contribution of an art genre to the expressive possibilities of individual artworks is Meyer Schapiro's sensitive analysis of the still-life (see the Readings).

(Figure 11.1, Cézanne's *Basket of Apples*, is a striking example of this genre.) Schapiro argues that, as a genre, still-life

> consists of objects that, whether artificial or natural, are subordinate to man as elements of use, manipulation and enjoyment; these objects are smaller than ourselves, within arm's reach, and owe their presence and place to a human action, a purpose. They convey man's sense of his power over things in making or utilizing them. . . . (p. 372)

Schapiro points out the enormous and special expressive possibilities of still-life:

> The still-life comes to stand then for sober objectivity, and an artist who struggles to attain that posture after having renounced a habitual impulsiveness or fantasy, can adopt the still-life as a calming or redemptive modest task . . . ; it signifies to him the commitment to the given, the simple and dispassionate. . . . It can appeal to artists of different temperament who are able through the painting of small objects to express without action of gesture the intimate and personal. They may be instruments of passion as well as of cool meditation. (p. 372)

Vincent van Gogh's art, by contrast, illustrates how an artist can project feeling onto artworks through the interrelation of his various works. In April 1882, van Gogh produced a drawing called *Sorrow* (Figure 11.2). It is easy to see how this drawing developed as an expression of van Gogh's feelings of resignation and despair. Van Gogh depicts the bent-over pregnant woman, her face hidden in an attitude of sadness and even despair, with a harsh realistic style of angular drawing. The critic Bernard Zurcher connects this drawing to several later works produced by van Gogh, all of which involve: "limbs deformed by the extreme abstraction of the sinuous lines and reduced to a . . . cipher of anguish; they all derive from *Sorrow*, the matrix of the human misery that spreads like a plague through the world and from which Vincent himself . . . could not be saved."[41] What Zurcher describes here is Vincent's own inability to escape from such an experience of the world, from the feelings that ultimately drove him to suicide.

Van Gogh's ability to express misery in this drawing is a function not only of his talent and feeling but also of the artistic tradition that clearly prepared the way for such expression. What is even more interesting is the way that van Gogh extends the style and the feelings he expresses in this drawing to his portrayal of nature. Shortly after drawing *Sorrow*, he sent it, together with a drawing of tree roots (see Figure 11.3 for a comparable drawing from the same period), to his brother, Theo. He wrote to Theo:

> I have now tried to put the same sentiment in the landscape as I have in the figure. It shows the grim tenacity and passionate intensity with which they hold onto the earth although they are half uprooted by gales. I wanted to express the struggle for life in both that white, slender figure of the woman and those angry, gnarled, black roots.[42]

This quotation helps us see how van Gogh extends to his experience of nature the feelings he associates with and expresses through the drawing of the nude figure; thus, his angular and harsh drawing of branches manages also to express an intense strength that lies at the heart of adversity.

We can also see that van Gogh was just a small step away from total abstraction, and thus we can also see how abstract art, in one sort of case, can express an artist's feelings. We should

FIGURE 11.1 *Basket of Apples* (1890–94) by Paul Cézanne (1839–1906). A painting that subtly illustrates Cézanne's attempts to undermine conventional visual perspective, it also illustrates the intimate and sensual emotions that can be associated with the still-life as a genre. Meyer Schapiro describes the still-life thus: "At first commonplace in appearance, it may become in the course of that contemplation a mystery, a source of metaphysical wonder."

note that abstract art is harder to explain on Collingwood's theory than on Tolstoy's: Tolstoy's theory requires only that emotions be *caused* by sounds or colors, and although this might be a hopelessly crude way to understand a Kandinsky painting or a Brahms symphony, at least the basic mechanism is as familiar as the idea that waving a red flag at a bull makes him mad. But that colors and forms or tones and sound and rhythmic structures actually *formulate* or *embody* emotions is a more difficult idea. Nonetheless, many accounts have been offered to explain how this is possible.

One highly developed theory of how visual elements can embody (rather than cause) moods and feelings was elaborated by the famous artist Paul Klee (1879–1940). Klee, along with Kandinsky, was a teacher at the Bauhaus in the 1920s. He published several books and lectures (for example, "Creative Credo" [1920][43], "The Jena Lecture" [1924][44], and *Pedagogical Sketchbook* [1924][45]), in which he correlates the visual properties of points, lines,

FIGURE 11.2 *Sorrow* (1882) by Vincent van Gogh (1853–90). In this drawing, van Gogh believed he made a breakthrough in his ability to express emotion, in this case, a woman's sorrow. He associated the drawing with a quotation: "How can it be that there is on earth a woman alone, forsaken?"

FIGURE 11.3 *Study of a Tree* (1882) by Vincent van Gogh. Done shortly after *Sorrow*, this drawing extends to landscape van Gogh's ability to project emotion in his line. He said of a similar drawing that he had "tried to put the same sentiment in the landscape as I have in the figure . . . I wanted to express the struggle for life in both that white slender figure of the woman and those angry, gnarled, black roots."

planes, and colors with the viewer's psychological and emotional responses (see Plate 10). For example, he formulates many ideas about how lines can be active or passive and how they can express dynamism and emotional qualities. Similarly, colors and their combinations can have emotional qualities. Klee often treated colors like musical tones.

Klee viewed the artist as an intermediary between nature and the work of art. He likened the artwork to the crown of a tree whose roots (below the level of consciousness) represent the relation of the artist — who is the trunk of the tree — to life and nature. Just as we do not expect the crown of a tree to look like its roots, so the artwork will naturally look very different from its origins in nature. This is because the pictorial elements have their own vital tendencies (Klee said that, "pictures look at us"[46]). Klee believed in a parallel between the creative forces in the universe and those inside the artist. Since the artwork is the artist's transformation of natural forces into visual form, it becomes a model of the cosmos for Klee: "Art is a simile of the Creation. Each work of art is an example, just as the terrestrial is an example of the cosmic."[47] Although he formulates a system that delineates the psychological effects of line and color, he holds that intellectual understanding can only go so far in deciphering the mysteries of art: "In the highest circle an ultimate mystery lurks behind the mystery, and the wretched light of intellect is of no avail!"[48] Many of Klee's mature pieces are entirely abstract (nonrepresentational) grids of colored squares, which use his ideas about the emotional significance of color tonality and harmonies.

The problem of explaining abstract arts with expression theory seems more a matter of working out a satisfactory explanation for each art form than an objection in principle to the very possibility of making nonrepresentational artworks that formulate emotional experiences.

> I never played a
> note I didn't
> mean.
> — Stan Getz[49]

Can the formulation theory explain art of a less expressionistic bent? Can it, for example, explain conceptual art? Surprisingly, it can accommodate intellectual art because Collingwood firmly rejects any division between intellectual matters and feelings. We have emotions about intellectual matters. He does not view emotions as primitive inner psychic forces but as feelings that can attach themselves to any subject matter, including highly abstract subject matter:

> The poet converts human experience into poetry not by first expurgating it, cutting out the intellectual elements and preserving the emotional, and then expressing the residue; but by fusing thought itself into emotion: thinking in a certain way and then expressing how it feels to think in that way. Thus Dante has fused the Thomistic philosophy into a poem expressing what it feels like to be a Thomist. (p. 371)

So, we may conceive that in *Fountain* (see Chapter 5) Duchamp expresses emotions concerning the making of art, the artificiality of the boundaries between artworks and other artifacts, humor at the pomposity of museums, and so on. All the abstract ideas and esoteric experiences that are commonly associated with conceptual art can be incorporated into Collingwood's framework once we drop two habitual assumptions about emotions and expression: (*a*) that ideas are antithetical to emotions and therefore that art motivated by intellectual concerns cannot also express emotions; and (*b*) the Tolstoyan view that the aim of the artist is to arouse specified emotions in an audience; the activity of arousal would seem antithetical to an art motivated by its own intellectual explorations. To sum up: There remain many problems to solve concerning an adequate theory of emotional expression and the application of such a theory to explain art. Nevertheless, the problems are intriguing and the prospects enticing. To make genuine progress, however, we also need to make progress in philosophy of mind and in the psychology of emotion; for, of all the major theories of art, expression theory is the most dependent on the development of knowledge in disciplines outside the arts. This is perhaps the central axiom of expression theory, and the one axiom denied by other traditional aesthetic theories: that the arts cannot be understood in isolation from assumptions about human nature, human psychology, and human society.

READINGS FOR CHAPTER 11

Leo Tolstoy, from *What is Art?*
R. G. Collingwood, from *The Principles of Art*
Meyer Schapiro, from "The Apples of Cézanne: An Essay on the Meaning of Still-Life"
Jerrold Levinson, "Music and Negative Emotion"

from *What is Art?*

Leo Tolstoy

Chapter Five

What is art—if we put aside the conception of beauty, which confuses the whole matter? The latest and most comprehensible definitions of art, apart from the conception of beauty, are the following: (1) Art is an activity arising even in the animal kingdom, *a*, springing from sexual desire and the propensity to play (Schiller, Darwin, Spencer), and *b*, accompanied by a pleasurable excitement of the nervous system (Grant Allen). This is the physiological-evolutionary definition. (2) Art is the external manifestation by means of lines, colors, movements, sounds, or words, of emotions felt by man (Véron). This is the experimental definition. According to the very latest definition, (3) Art is "the production of some permanent object or passing action, which is fitted, not only to supply an active enjoyment to the producer, but to convey a pleasurable impression to a number of spectators or listeners, quite apart from any personal advantage to be derived from it" (Sully).

Notwithstanding the superiority of these definitions to the metaphysical definitions which depended on the conception of beauty, they are yet far from exact. The first, the physiological-evolutionary definition (1*a*), is inexact because, instead of speaking about the artistic activity itself, which is the real matter in hand, it treats of the derivation of art. The modification of it (1*b*), based on the physiological effects on the human organism, is inexact because within the limits of such definition many other human activities can be included, as has occurred in the neo-aesthetic theories, which reckon as art the preparation of handsome clothes, pleasant scents, and even victuals.

The experimental definition (2), which makes art consist in the expression of emotions, is inexact because a man may express his emotions by means of lines, colors, sounds, or words, and yet may not act on others by such expression, and then the manifestation of his emotions is not art.

The third definition (that of Sully) is inexact because in the production of objects or actions affording pleasure to the producer and a pleasant emotion to the spectators or hearers, apart from personal advantage, may be included the showing of conjuring tricks or gymnastic exercises and other activities which are not art. And further, many things, the production of which does not afford pleasure to the producer and the sensation received from which is unpleasant, such as gloomy, heartrending scenes in a poetic description or a play, may nevertheless be undoubted works of art.

The inaccuracy of all these definitions arises from the fact that in them all (as also in the metaphysical definitions) the object considered is the pleasure art may give, and not the purpose it may serve in the life of man and of humanity.

In order correctly to define art, it is necessary, first of all, to cease to consider it as a means to pleasure and to consider it as one of the conditions of human life. Viewing it in this way we cannot fail to observe that art is one of the means of intercourse between man and man.

Every work of art causes the receiver to enter into a certain kind of relationship both with him who produced, or is producing, the art, and with all those who, simultaneously, previously, or subsequently, receive the same artistic impression.

Speech, transmitting the thoughts and experiences of men, serves as a means of union among them, and art acts in a similar manner. The peculiarity of this latter means of intercourse, distinguishing it from intercourse by means of words, consists in this, that whereas by words a man transmits his thoughts to another, by means of art he transmits his feelings.

The activity of art is based on the fact that a man, receiving through his sense of hearing or sight another man's expression of feeling, is capable of experiencing the emotion which moved the man who expressed it. To take the simplest example: one man laughs, and another who hears becomes merry; or a man weeps, and another who hears feels sorrow. A man is excited or irritated, and another man seeing him comes to a similar state of mind. By his movements or by the sounds of his voice, a man expresses courage and determination or sadness and calmness, and this state of mind passes on to others. A man suffers, expressing his sufferings by groans and spasms, and this suffering transmits itself to other people; a man expresses his feeling of admiration, devotion, fear, respect, or love to certain objects, persons, or phenomena, and others are infected by the same feelings of admiration, devotion, fear, respect, or love to the same objects, persons, and phenomena.

And it is upon this capacity of man to receive another man's expression of feeling and experience those feelings himself, that the activity of art is based.

If a man infects another or others directly, immediately, by his appearance or by the sounds he gives vent to at the very time he experiences the feeling; if he causes another man to yawn when he himself cannot help yawning, or to laugh or cry when he himself is obliged to laugh or cry, or to suffer when he himself is suffering — that does not amount to art.

Art begins when one person, with the object of joining another or others to himself in one and the same feeling, expresses that feeling by certain external indications. To take the simplest example: a boy, having experienced, let us say, fear on encountering a wolf, relates that encounter; and, in order to evoke in others the feeling he has experienced, describes himself, his condition before the encounter, the surroundings, the wood, his own lightheartedness, and then the wolf's appearance, its movements, the distance between himself and the wolf, etc. All this, if only the boy, when telling the story, again experiences the feelings he had lived through and infects the hearers and compels them to feel what the narrator had experienced, is art. If even the boy had not seen a wolf but had frequently been afraid of one, and if, wishing to evoke in others, the fear he had felt, he invented an encounter with a wolf and recounted it so as to make his hearers share the feelings he experienced when he feared the wolf, that also would be art. And just in the same way it is art if a man, having experienced either the fear of suffering or the attraction of enjoyment (whether in reality or in imagination), expresses these feelings on canvas or in marble so that others are infected by them. And it is also art if a man feels or imagines to himself feelings of delight, gladness, sorrow, despair, courage, or despondency and the transition from one to another of these feelings, and expresses these feelings by sounds so that the hearers are infected by them and experience them as they were experienced by the composer.

The feelings with which the artist infects others may be most various — very strong or very weak, very important or very insignificant, very bad or very good: feelings of love for one's own country, self-devotion and submission to fate or to God expressed in a drama, raptures of lovers described in a novel, feelings of voluptuousness expressed in a picture, courage expressed in a triumphal march, merriment evoked by a dance, humor evoked by a funny story, the feeling of quietness transmitted by an evening landscape or by a lullaby, or the feeling of admiration evoked by a beautiful arabesque — it is all art.

If only the spectators or auditors are infected by the feelings which the author has felt, it is art.

To evoke in oneself a feeling one has once experienced, and having evoked it in oneself, then, by means of movements, lines, colors, sounds, or forms expressed in words, so to transmit that feeling that others may experience the same feeling — this is the activity of art.

Art is a human activity consisting in this, that one man consciously, by means of certain external signs, hands on to others feelings he has lived through, and that other people are infected by these feelings and also experience them.

Art is not, as the metaphysicians say, the manifestation of some mysterious Idea of beauty or God; it is not, as the aesthetical physiologists say, a game in which man lets off his excess of stored-up energy; it is not the expression of man's emotions by external signs; it is not the production of pleasing objects; and, above all, it is not pleasure; but it is a means of union among men, joining them together in the same feelings, and indispensable for the life and progress toward well-being of individuals and of humanity.

As, thanks to man's capacity to express thoughts by words, every man may know all that has been done for him in the realms of thought by all humanity before his day, and can in the present, thanks to this capacity to understand the thoughts of others, become a sharer in their activity and can himself hand on to his contemporaries and descendants the thoughts he has assimilated from others, as well as those which have arisen within himself; so, thanks to man's capacity to be infected with the feelings of others by means of art, all that is being lived through by his contemporaries is accessible to him, as well as the feelings experienced by men thousands of years ago, and he has also the possibility of transmitting his own feelings to others.

If people lacked this capacity to receive the thoughts conceived by the men who preceded them and to pass on to others their own thoughts, men would be like wild beasts, or like Kaspar Hauser.[1]

And if men lacked this other capacity of being infected by art, people might be almost more savage still, and, above all, more separated from, and more hostile to, one another.

And therefore the activity of art is a most important one, as important as the activity of speech itself and as generally diffused.

We are accustomed to understand art to be only what we hear and see in theaters, concerts, and exhibitions, together with buildings, statues, poems, novels. . . . But all this is but the smallest part of the art by which we communicate with each other in life. All human life is filled with works of art of every kind — from cradlesong, jest, mimicry, the ornamentation of houses, dress, and utensils, up to church services, buildings, monuments, and triumphal processions. It is all artistic activity. So that by art, in the limited sense of the word, we do not mean all human activity transmitting feelings, but only that part which we for some reason select from it and to which we attach special importance.

This special importance has always been given by all men to that part of this activity which transmits feelings flowing from their religious perception, and this small part of art they have specifically called art, attaching to it the full meaning of the word.

That was how men of old — Socrates, Plato, and Aristotle — looked on art. Thus did the Hebrew prophets and the ancient Christians regard art; thus it was, and still is, understood by the Mohammedans, and thus it still is understood by religious folk among our own peasantry.

Some teachers of mankind — as Plato in his *Republic* and people such as the primitive Christians, the strict Mohammedans, and the Buddhists — have gone so far as to repudiate all art.

---

[1] "The foundling of Nuremberg," found in the market-place of that town on May 26, 1828, apparently some sixteen years old. He spoke little and was almost totally ignorant even of common objects. He subsequently explained that he had been brought up in confinement underground and visited by only one man, whom he seldom saw. — TR.

People viewing art in this way (in contradiction to the prevalent view of today which regards any art as good if only it affords pleasure) considered, and consider, that art (as contrasted with speech, which need not be listened to) is so highly dangerous in its power to infect people against their wills that mankind will lose far less by banishing all art than by tolerating each and every art.

Evidently such people were wrong in repudiating all art, for they denied that which cannot be denied — one of the indispensable means of communication, without which mankind could not exist. But not less wrong are the people of civilized European society of our class and day in favoring any art if it but serves beauty, i.e., gives people pleasure.

Formerly people feared lest among the works of art there might chance to be some causing corruption, and they prohibited art altogether. Now they only fear lest they should be deprived of any enjoyment art can afford, and patronize any art. And I think the last error is much grosser than the first and its consequences are far more harmful. . . .

Chapter Fifteen

Art, in our society, has been so perverted that not only has bad art come to be considered good, but even the very perception of what art really is has been lost. In order to be able to speak about the art of our society, it is, therefore, first of all necessary to distinguish art from counterfeit art.

There is one indubitable indication distinguishing real art from its counterfeit, namely, the infectiousness of art. If a man, without exercising effort and without altering his standpoint on reading, hearing, or seeing another man's work, experiences a mental condition which unites him with that man and with other people who also partake of that work of art, then the object evoking that condition is a work of art. And however poetical, realistic, effectful, or interesting a work may be, it is not a work of art if it does not evoke that feeling (quite distinct from all other feelings) of joy and of spiritual union with another (the author) and with others (those who are also infected by it).

It is true that this indication is an *internal* one, and that there are people who have forgotten what the action of real art is, who expect something else from art (in our society the great majority are in this state), and that therefore such people may mistake for this aesthetic feeling the feeling of diversion and a certain excitement which they receive from counterfeits of art. But though it is impossible to undeceive these people, just as it is impossible to convince a man suffering from "Daltonism"[1] that green is not red, yet, for all that, this indication remains perfectly definite to those whose feeling for art is neither perverted nor atrophied, and it clearly distinguishes the feeling produced by art from all other feelings.

The chief peculiarity of this feeling is that the receiver of a true artistic impression is so united to the artist that he feels as if the work were his own and not someone else's — as if what it expresses were just what he had long been wishing to express. A real work of art destroys, in the consciousness of the receiver, the separation between himself and the artist — not that alone, but also between himself and all whose minds receive this work of art. In this freeing of our personality from its separation and isolation, in this uniting of it with others, lies the chief characteristic and the great attractive force of art.

If a man is infected by the author's condition of soul, if he feels this emotion and this union with others, then the object which has effected this is art; but if there be no such infection, if there be not this union with the author and with others who are moved by the same work — then it is not art. And not only is infection a sure sign of art, but the degree of infectiousness is also the sole measure of excellence in art.

The stronger the infection, the better is the art as art, speaking now apart from its subject mat-

---

[1][A kind of color blindness discovered by John Dalton. — Ed.]

ter, i.e., not considering the quality of the feelings it transmits.

And the degree of the infectiousness of art depends on three conditions:

1. on the greater or lesser individuality of the feeling transmitted;
2. on the greater or lesser clearness with which the feeling is transmitted;
3. on the sincerity of the artist, i.e., on the greater or lesser force with which the artist himself feels the emotion he transmits.

The more individual the feeling transmitted the more strongly does it act on the receiver; the more individual the state of soul into which he is transferred, the more pleasure does the receiver obtain, and therefore the more readily and strongly does he join in it.

The clearness of expression assists infection because the receiver, who mingles in consciousness with the author, is the better satisfied the more clearly the feeling is transmitted, which, as it seems to him, he has long known and felt, and for which he has only now found expression.

But most of all is the degree of infectiousness of art increased by the degree of sincerity in the artist. As soon as the spectator, hearer, or reader feels that the artist is infected by his own production, and writes, sings, or plays for himself, and not merely to act on others, this mental condition of the artist infects the receiver; and contrariwise, as soon as the spectator, reader, or hearer feels that the author is not writing, singing, or playing for his own satisfaction — does not himself feel what he wishes to express — but is doing it for him, the receiver, a resistance immediately springs up, and the most individual and the newest feelings and the cleverest technique not only fail to produce any infection but actually repel.

I have mentioned three conditions of contagiousness in art, but they may be all summed up into one, the last, sincerity, i.e., that the artist should be impelled by an inner need to express his feeling. That condition includes the first; for if the artist is sincere he will express the feeling as he experienced it. And as each man is different from everyone else, his feeling will be individual for everyone else; and the more individual it is — the more the artist has drawn it from the depths of his nature — the more sympathetic and sincere will it be. And this same sincerity will impel the artist to find a clear expression of the feeling which he wishes to transmit.

Therefore this third condition — sincerity — is the most important of the three. It is always complied with in peasant art, and this explains why such art always acts so powerfully; but it is a condition almost entirely absent from our upper-class art, which is continually produced by artists actuated by personal aims of covetousness or vanity.

Such are the three conditions which divide art from its counterfeits, and which also decide the quality of every work of art apart from its subject matter.

The absence of any one of these conditions excludes a work from the category of art and relegates it to that of art's counterfeits. If the work does not transmit the artist's peculiarity of feeling and is therefore not individual, if it is unintelligibly expressed, or if it has not proceeded from the author's inner need for expression — it is not a work of art. If all these conditions are present, even in the smallest degree, then the work, even if a weak one, is yet a work of art.

The presence in various degrees of these three conditions — individuality, clearness, and sincerity — decides the merit of a work of art as art, apart from subject matter. All works of art take rank of merit according to the degree in which they fulfil the first, the second, and the third of these conditions. In one the individuality of the feeling transmitted may predominate; in another, clearness of expression; in a third, sincerity; while a fourth may have sincerity and individuality but be deficient in clearness; a fifth, individuality and clearness but less sincerity; and so forth, in all possible degrees and combinations.

Thus is art divided from that which is not art, and thus is the quality of art as art decided, independently of its subject matter, i.e., apart from whether the feelings it transmits are good or bad.

But how are we to define good and bad art with reference to its subject matter?

Chapter Sixteen

How are we to decide what is good or bad in the subject matter of art?

Art, like speech, is a means of communication, and therefore of progress, i.e., of the movement of humanity forward toward perfection. Speech renders accessible to men of the latest generations all the knowledge discovered by the experience and reflection, both of preceding generations and of the best and foremost men of their own times; art renders accessible to men of the latest generations all the feelings experienced by their predecessors, and those also which are being felt by their best and foremost contemporaries. And as the evolution of knowledge proceeds by truer and more necessary knowledge, dislodging and replacing what is mistaken and unnecessary, so the evolution of feeling proceeds through art — feelings less kind and less needful for the well-being of mankind are replaced by others kinder and more needful for that end. That is the purpose of art. And, speaking now of its subject matter, the more art fulfils that purpose the better the art, and the less it fulfils it, the worse the art.

And the appraisement of feelings (i.e., the acknowledgment of these or those feelings as being more or less good, more or less necessary for the well-being of mankind) is made by the religious perception of the age.

In every period of history, and in every human society, there exists an understanding of the meaning of life which represents the highest level to which men of that society have attained, an understanding defining the highest good at which that society aims. And this understanding is the religious perception of the given time and society. And this religious perception is always clearly expressed by some advanced men, and more or less vividly perceived by all the members of the society. Such a religious perception and its corresponding expression exists always in every society. If it appears to us that in our society there is no religious perception, this is not because there really is none, but only because we do not want to see it. And we often wish not to see it because it exposes the fact that our life is inconsistent with that religious perception.

Religious perception in a society is like the direction of a flowing river. If the river flows at all, it must have a direction. If a society lives, there must be a religious perception indicating the direction in which, more or less consciously, all its members tend.

And so there always has been, and there is, a religious perception in every society. And it is by the standard of this religious perception that the feelings transmitted by art have always been estimated. Only on the basis of this religious perception of their age have men always chosen from the endlessly varied spheres of art that art which transmitted feelings making religious perception operative in actual life. And such art has always been highly valued and encouraged, while art transmitting feelings already outlived, flowing from the antiquated religious perceptions of a former age, has always been condemned and despised. All the rest of art, transmitting those most diverse feelings by means of which people commune together, was not condemned, and was tolerated, if only it did not transmit feelings contrary to religious perception. Thus, for instance, among the Greeks art transmitting the feeling of beauty, strength, and courage (Hesiod, Homer, Phidias) was chosen, approved, and encouraged, while art transmitting feelings of rude sensuality, despondency, and effeminacy was condemned and despised. Among the Jews, art transmitting feelings of devotion and submission to the God of the Hebrews and to His will (the epic of Genesis, the prophets, the Psalms) was chosen and encouraged, while art transmitting feelings of idolatry (the golden calf) was condemned and despised.

All the rest of art — stories, songs, dances, ornamentation of houses, of utensils, and of clothes — which was not contrary to religious perception was neither distinguished nor discussed. Thus, in regard to its subject matter, has art been appraised always and everywhere, and thus it should be appraised; for this attitude toward art proceeds from the fundamental characteristics of human nature, and those characteristics do not change. . . .

from *The Principles of Art*

R. G. Collingwood

Reprinted by permission of Oxford University Press.

Chapter VI: Art Proper
(1) As Expression

§ 2. EXPRESSING EMOTION AND AROUSING EMOTION

Our first question is this. Since the artist proper has something to do with emotion, and what he does with it is not to arouse it, what is it that he does? It will be remembered that the kind of answer we expect to this question is an answer derived from what we all know and all habitually say; nothing original or recondite, but something entirely commonplace.

Nothing could be more entirely commonplace than to say he expresses them. The idea is familiar to every artist, and to every one else who has any acquaintance with the arts. To state it is not to state a philosophical theory or definition of art; it is to state a fact or supposed fact about which, when we have sufficiently identified it, we shall have later to theorize philosophically. For the present it does not matter whether the fact that is alleged, when it is said that the artist expresses emotion, is really a fact or only supposed to be one. Whichever it is, we have to identify it, that is, to decide what it is that people are saying when they use the phrase. Later on, we shall have to see whether it will fit into a coherent theory.

They are referring to a situation, real or supposed, of a definite kind. When a man is said to express emotion, what is being said about him comes to this. At first, he is conscious of having an emotion, but not conscious of what this emotion is. All he is conscious of is a perturbation or excitement, which he feels going on within him, but of whose nature he is ignorant. While in this state, all he can say about his emotion is "I feel . . . I don't know what I feel." From this helpless and oppressed condition he extricates himself by doing something which we call expressing himself. This is an activity which has something to do with the thing we call language: he expresses himself by speaking. It has also something to do with consciousness: the emotion expressed is an emotion of whose nature the person who feels it is no longer unconscious. It has also something to do with the way in which he feels the emotion. As unexpressed, he feels it in what we have called a helpless and oppressed way; as expressed, he feels it in a way from which this sense of oppression has vanished. His mind is somehow lightened and eased.

This lightening of emotions which is somehow connected with the expression of them has a certain resemblance to the "catharsis" by which emotions are earthed through being discharged into a make-believe situation; but the two things are not the same. Suppose the emotion is one of anger. If it is effectively earthed, for example by fancying oneself kicking some one down stairs, it is thereafter no longer present in the mind as anger at all: we have worked it off and are rid of it. If it is expressed, for example by putting it into hot and bitter words, it does not disappear from the mind; we remain angry; but instead of the sense of oppression which accompanies an emotion of anger not yet recognized as such, we have that sense of alleviation which comes when we are conscious of our own emotion as anger, instead of being conscious of it only as an unidentified perturbation. This is what we refer to when we say that it "does us good" to express our emotions.

The expression of an emotion by speech may be addressed to some one; but if so it is not done with the intention of arousing a like emotion in him. If there is any effect which we wish to produce in the hearer, it is only the effect which we call making him understand how we feel. But, as we have already seen, this is just the effect which expressing our emotions has on ourselves. It makes us, as well as the people to whom we talk, understand how we feel. A person arousing emotion sets out to affect his audience in a way in which he himself is not necessarily affected. He and his audience stand in quite different relations to the act, very much as physician and patient stand in quite different relations towards a drug administered by the one and taken by the other. A person expressing emotion, on the contrary, is treating himself and his audience in the same kind of way; he is making his emotions clear to his audience, and that is what he is doing to himself.

It follows from this that the expression of emotion, simply as expression, is not addressed to any particular audience. It is addressed primarily to the speaker himself, and secondarily to any one who can understand. Here again, the speaker's attitude towards his audience is quite unlike that of a person desiring to arouse in his audience a certain emotion. If that is what he wishes to do, he must know the audience he is addressing. He must know what type of stimulus will produce the desired kind of reaction in people of that particular sort; and he must adapt his language to his audience in the sense of making sure that it contains stimuli appropriate to their peculiarities. If what he wishes to do is to express his emotions intelligibly, he has to express them in such a way as to be intelligible to himself; his audience is then in the position of persons who overhear him doing this. Thus the stimulus-and-reaction terminology has no applicability to the situation.

The means-and-end, or technique, terminology too is inapplicable. Until a man has expressed his emotion, he does not yet know what emotion it is. The act of expressing it is therefore an exploration of his own emotions. He is trying to find out what these emotions are. There is certainly here a directed process: an effort, that is, directed upon a certain end; but the end is not something foreseen and preconceived, to which appropriate means can be thought out in the light of our knowledge of its special character. Expression is an activity of which there can be no technique.

§ 3. EXPRESSION AND INDIVIDUALIZATION

Expressing an emotion is not the same thing as describing it. To say "I am angry" is to describe one's emotion, not to express it. The words in which it is expressed need not contain any reference to anger as such at all. Indeed, so far as they simply and solely express it, they cannot contain any such reference. The curse of Ernulphus, as invoked by Dr. Slop on the unknown person who tied certain knots, is a classical and supreme expression of anger; but it does not contain a single word descriptive of the emotion it expresses.

This is why, as literary critics well know, the use of epithets in poetry, or even in prose where expressiveness is aimed at, is a danger. If you want to express the terror which something causes, you must not give it an epithet like "dreadful." For that describes the emotion instead of expressing it, and your language becomes frigid, that is inexpressive, at once. A genuine poet, in his moments of genuine poetry, never mentions by name the emotions he is expressing.

Some people have thought that a poet who wishes to express a great variety of subtly differentiated emotions might be hampered by the lack of a vocabulary rich in words referring to the distinctions between them; and that psychology, by working out such a vocabulary, might render a valuable service to poetry. This is the opposite of the truth. The poet needs no such words at all; the existence or nonexistence of a scientific terminology describing the emotions he wishes to express is to him a matter of perfect indifference. If such a terminology, where it exists, is allowed to affect his own use of language, it affects it for the worse.

The reason why description, so far from helping expression, actually damages it, is that description generalizes. To describe a thing is to call it a thing of such and such a kind: to bring it under a conception, to classify it. Expression, on the contrary, individualizes. The anger which I feel here and now, with a certain person, for a certain cause, is no doubt an instance of anger, and in describing it as anger one is telling the truth about it; but it is much more than mere anger: it is a peculiar anger, not quite like any anger that I ever felt before, and probably not quite like any anger I shall ever feel again. To become fully conscious of it means becoming conscious of it not merely as an instance of anger, but as this quite peculiar anger. Expressing it, we saw, has something to do with becoming conscious of it; therefore, if being fully conscious of it means being conscious of all its peculiarities, fully expressing it means expressing all its peculiarities. The poet, therefore, in proportion as he understands his business, gets as far away as possible from merely labelling his emotions as instances of this or that general kind, and takes enormous pains to individualize them by expressing them in terms which reveal their difference from any other emotion of the same sort.

This is a point in which art proper, as the expression of emotion, differs sharply and obviously from any craft whose aim it is to arouse emotion. The end which a craft sets out to realize is always conceived in general terms, never individualized. However accurately defined it may be, it is always defined as the production of a thing having characteristics that could be shared by other things. A joiner, making a table out of these pieces of wood and no others, makes it to measurements and specifications which, even if actually shared by no other table, might in principle be shared by other tables. A physician treating a patient for a certain complaint is trying to produce in him a condition which might be, and probably has been, often produced in others, namely, the condition of recovering from that complaint. So an "artist" setting out to produce a certain emotion in his audience is setting out to produce not an individual emotion, but an emotion of a certain kind. It follows that the means appropriate to its production will be not individual means but means of a certain kind: that is to say, means which are always in principle replaceable by other similar means. As every good craftsman insists, there is always a "right way" of performing any operation. A "way" of acting is a general pattern to which various individual actions may conform. In order that the "work of art" should produce its intended psychological effect, therefore, whether this effect be magical or merely amusing, what is necessary is that it should satisfy certain conditions, possess certain characteristics: in other words be, not this work and no other, but a work of this kind and of no other.

This explains the meaning of the generalization which Aristotle and others have ascribed to art. We have already seen that Aristotle's *Poetics* is concerned not with art proper but with representative art, and representative art of one definite kind. He is not analysing the religious drama of a hundred years before, he is analysing the amusement literature of the fourth century, and giving rules for its composition. The end being not individual but general (the production of an emotion of a certain kind) the means too are general (the portrayal, not of this individual act, but of an act of this sort; not, as he himself puts it, what Alcibiades did, but what anybody of a certain kind would do). Sir Joshua Reynolds's idea of generalization is in principle the same; he expounds it in connexion with what he calls "the grand style," which means a style intended to produce emotions of a certain type. He is quite right; if you want to produce a typical case of a certain emotion, the way to do it is to put before your audience a representation of the typical features belonging to the kind of thing that produces it: make your kings very royal, your soldiers very soldierly, your women very feminine, your cottages very cottagesque, your oak-trees very oakish, and so on.

Art proper, as expression of emotion, has nothing to do with all this. The artist proper is a person who, grappling with the problem of expressing a certain emotion, says, "I want to get this clear." It is no use to him to get something else clear, however like it this other thing may be. Nothing will serve as a substitute. He does not want a thing of a certain kind, he wants a certain thing. This is why the kind of person who takes his literature as psychology, saying "How admirably this writer depicts the feelings of women, or busdrivers, or homosexuals . . . ," necessarily misunderstands every real work of art with which he comes into contact, and takes for good art, with infallible precision, what is not art at all.

§ 4. SELECTION AND AESTHETIC EMOTION

It has sometimes been asked whether emotions can be divided into those suitable for expression by artists and those unsuitable. If by art one means art proper, and identifies this with expression, the only possible answer is that there can be no such distinction. Whatever is expressible is expressible. There may be ulterior motives in special cases which make it desirable to express some emotions and not others; but only if by "express" one means express publicly, that is, allow people to overhear one expressing oneself. This is because one cannot possibly decide that a certain emotion is one which for some reason it would be undesirable to express thus publicly, unless one first becomes conscious of it; and doing this, as we saw, is somehow bound up with expressing it. If art means the expression of emotion, the artist as such must be absolutely candid; his speech must be absolutely free. This is not a precept, it is a statement. It does not mean that the artist ought to be candid, it means that he is an artist only in so far as he is candid. Any kind of selection, any decision to express this emotion and not that, is inartistic not in the sense that it damages the perfect sincerity which distinguishes good art from bad, but in the sense that it represents a further process of a non-artistic kind, carried out when the work of expression proper is already complete. For until that work is complete one does not know what emotions one feels; and is

therefore not in a position to pick and choose, and give one of them preferential treatment.

From these considerations a certain corollary follows about the division of art into distinct arts. Two such divisions are current; one according to the medium in which the artist works, into painting, poetry, music, and the like; the other according to the kind of emotion he expresses, into tragic, comic, and so forth. We are concerned with the second. If the difference between tragedy and comedy is a difference between the emotions they express, it is not a difference that can be present to the artist's mind when he is beginning his work; if it were, he would know what emotion he was going to express before he had expressed it. No artist, therefore, so far as he is an artist proper, can set out to write a comedy, a tragedy, an elegy, or the like. So far as he is an artist proper, he is just as likely to write any one of these as any other; which is the truth that Socrates was heard expounding towards the dawn, among the sleeping figures in Agathon's dining-room. These distinctions, therefore, have only a very limited value. They can be properly used in two ways. (1) When a work of art is complete, it can be labelled *ex post facto* as tragic, comic, or the like, according to the character of the emotions chiefly expressed in it. But understood in that sense the distinction is of no real importance. (2) If we are talking about representational art, the case is very different. Here the so-called artist knows in advance what kind of emotion he wishes to excite, and will construct works of different kinds according to the different kinds of effect they are to produce. In the case of representational art, therefore, distinctions of this kind are not only admissible as an *ex post facto* classification of things to which in their origin it is alien; they are present from the beginning as a determining factor in the so-called artist's plan of work.

The same considerations provide an answer to the question whether there is such a thing as a specific "aesthetic emotion." If it is said that there is such an emotion independently of its expression in art, and that the business of artists is to express it, we must answer that such a view is nonsense. It implies, first, that artists have emotions of various kinds, among which is this peculiar aesthetic emotion; secondly, that they select this aesthetic emotion for expression. If the first proposition were true, the second would have to be false. If artists only find out what their emotions are in the course of finding out how to express them, they cannot begin the work of expression by deciding what emotion to express.

In a different sense, however, it is true that there is a specific aesthetic emotion. As we have seen, an unexpressed emotion is accompanied by a feeling of oppression; when it is expressed and thus comes into consciousness the same emotion is accompanied by a new feeling of alleviation or easement, the sense that this oppression is removed. It resembles the feeling of relief that comes when a burdensome intellectual or moral problem has been solved. We may call it, if we like, the specific feeling of having successfully expressed ourselves; and there is no reason why it should not be called a specific aesthetic emotion. But it is not a specific kind of emotion pre-existing to the expression of it, and having the peculiarity that when it comes to be expressed it is expressed artistically. It is an emotional colouring which attends the expression of any emotion whatever.

§ 5. THE ARTIST AND THE ORDINARY MAN

I have been speaking of "the artist," in the present chapter, as if artists were persons of a special kind, differing somehow either in mental endowment or at least in the way they use their endowment from the ordinary persons who make up their audience. But this segregation of artists from ordinary human beings belongs to the conception of art as craft; it cannot be reconciled with the conception of art as expression. If art were a kind of craft, it would follow as a matter of course. Any craft is a specialized form of skill, and those who possess it are thereby marked out from the rest of mankind. If art is the skill to amuse people, or in general to arouse emotions in them, the amusers and the amused form two different classes, differing in their respectively active and

passive relation to the craft of exciting determinate emotions; and this difference will be due, according to whether the artist is "born" or "made," either to a specific mental endowment in the artist, which in theories of this type has gone by the name of "genius," or to a specific training.

If art is not a kind of craft, but the expression of emotion, this distinction of kind between artist and audience disappears. For the artist has an audience only in so far as people hear him expressing himself, and understand what they hear him saying. Now, if one person says something by way of expressing what is in his mind, and another hears and understands him, the hearer who understands him has that same thing in his mind. The question whether he would have had it if the first had not spoken need not here be raised; however it is answered, what has just been said is equally true. If some one says "Twice two is four" in the hearing of some one incapable of carrying out the simplest arithmetical operation, he will be understood by himself, but not by his hearer. The hearer can understand only if he can add two and two in his own mind. Whether he could do it before he heard the speaker say those words makes no difference. What is here said of expressing thoughts is equally true of expressing emotions. If a poet expresses, for example, a certain kind of fear, the only hearers who can understand him are those who are capable of experiencing that kind of fear themselves. Hence, when some one reads and understands a poem, he is not merely understanding the poet's expression of his, the poet's, emotions, he is expressing emotions of his own in the poet's words, which have thus become his own words. As Coleridge put it, we know a man for a poet by the fact that he makes us poets. We know that he is expressing his emotions by the fact that he is enabling us to express ours.

Thus, if art is the activity of expressing emotions, the reader is an artist as well as the writer. There is no distinction of kind between artist and audience. This does not mean that there is no distinction at all. When Pope wrote that the poet's business was to say "what all have felt but none so well express'd," we may interpret his words as meaning (whether or no Pope himself consciously meant this when he wrote them) that the poet's difference from his audience lies in the fact that, though both do exactly the same thing, namely express this particular emotion in these particular words, the poet is a man who can solve for himself the problem of expressing it, whereas the audience can express it only when the poet has shown them how. The poet is not singular either in his having that emotion or in his power of expressing it; he is singular in his ability to take the initiative in expressing what all feel, and all can express.

§ 6. THE CURSE OF THE IVORY TOWER

I have already had occasion to criticize the view that artists can or should form a special order or caste, marked off by special genius or special training from the rest of the community. That view, we have seen, was a by-product of the technical theory of art. This criticism can now be reinforced by pointing out that a segregation of this kind is not only unnecessary but fatal to the artist's real function. If artists are really to express "what all have felt," they must share the emotions of all. Their experiences, the general attitude they express towards life, must be of the same kind as that of the persons among whom they hope to find an audience. If they form themselves into a special clique, the emotions they express will be the emotions of that clique; and the consequence will be that their work becomes intelligible only to their fellow artists. This is in fact what happened to a great extent during the nineteenth century, when the segregation of artists from the rest of mankind reached its culmination.

If art had really been a craft, like medicine or warfare, the effect of this segregation would have been all to the good, for a craft only becomes more efficient if it organizes itself into the shape of a community devoted to serving the interests of the public in a specialized way, and planning its whole life with an eye to the conditions of this service. Because it is not a craft, but the expression of emotions, the effect was the opposite of

this. A situation arose in which novelists, for example, found themselves hardly at their ease except in writing novels about novelists, which appealed to nobody except other novelists. This vicious circle was most conspicuous in certain continental writers like Anatole France or D'Annunzio, whose subject-matter often seemed to be limited by the limits of the segregated clique of "intellectuals." The corporate life of the artistic community became a kind of ivory tower whose prisoners could think and talk of nothing except themselves, and had only one another for audience.

Transplanted into the more individualistic atmosphere of England, the result was different. Instead of a single (though no doubt subdivided) clique of artists, all inhabiting the same ivory tower, the tendency was for each artist to construct an ivory tower of his own: to live, that is to say, in a world of his own devising, cut off not only from the ordinary world of common people but even from the corresponding worlds of other artists. Thus Burne-Jones lived in a world whose contents were ungraciously defined by a journalist as "green light and gawky girls"; Leighton in a world of sham Hellenism; and it was the call of practical life that rescued Yeats from the sham world of his youthful Celtic twilight, forced him into the clear air of real Celtic life, and made him a great poet.

In these ivory towers art languished. The reason is not hard to understand. A man might easily have been born and bred within the confines of a society as narrow and specialized as any nineteenth-century artistic coterie, thinking its thoughts and feeling its emotions because his experience contained no others. Such a man, in so far as he expressed these emotions, would be genuinely expressing his own experience. The narrowness or wideness of the experience which an artist expresses has nothing to do with the merits of his art. A Jane Austen, born and bred in an atmosphere of village gossip, can make great art out of the emotions that atmosphere generates. But a person who shuts himself up in the limits of a narrow coterie has an experience which includes the emotions of the larger world in which he was born and bred, as well as those of the little society he has chosen to join. If he decides to express only the emotions that pass current within the limits of that little society, he is selecting certain of his emotions for expression. The reason why this inevitably produces bad art is that, as we have already seen, it can only be done when the person selecting already knows what his emotions are; that is, has already expressed them. His real work as an artist is a work which, as a member of his artistic coterie, he repudiates. Thus the literature of the ivory tower is a literature whose only possible value is an amusement value by which persons imprisoned within that tower, whether by their misfortune or their fault, help themselves and each other to pass their time without dying of boredom or of homesickness for the world they have left behind; together with a magical value by which they persuade themselves and each other that imprisonment in such a place and in such company is a high privilege. Artistic value it has none.

§ 7. EXPRESSING EMOTION AND BETRAYING EMOTION

Finally, the expressing of emotion must not be confused with what may be called the betraying of it, that is, exhibiting symptoms of it. When it is said that the artist in the proper sense of that word is a person who expresses his emotions, this does not mean that if he is afraid he turns pale and stammers; if he is angry he turns red and bellows; and so forth. These things are no doubt called expressions; but just as we distinguish proper and improper senses of the word "art," so we must distinguish proper and improper senses of the word "expression," and in the context of a discussion about art this sense of expression is an improper sense. The characteristic mark of expression proper is lucidity or intelligibility; a person who expresses something thereby becomes conscious of what it is that he is expressing, and enables others to become conscious of it in himself and in them. Turning pale and stammering is a natural accompaniment of fear, but a

person who in addition to being afraid also turns pale and stammers does not thereby become conscious of the precise quality of his emotion. About that he is as much in the dark as he would be if (were that possible) he could feel fear without also exhibiting these symptoms of it.

Confusion between these two senses of the word "expression" may easily lead to false critical estimates, and so to false aesthetic theory. It is sometimes thought a merit in an actress that when she is acting a pathetic scene she can work herself up to such an extent as to weep real tears. There may be some ground for that opinion if acting is not an art but a craft, and if the actress's object in that scene is to produce grief in her audience; and even then the conclusion would follow only if it were true that grief cannot be produced in the audience unless symptoms of grief are exhibited by the performer. And no doubt this is how most people think of the actor's work. But if his business is not amusement but art, the object at which he is aiming is not to produce a preconceived emotional effect on his audience but by means of a system of expressions, or language, composed partly of speech and partly of gesture, to explore his own emotions: to discover emotions in himself of which he was unaware, and, by permitting the audience to witness the discovery, enable them to make a similar discovery about themselves. In that case it is not her ability to weep real tears that would mark out a good actress; it is her ability to make it clear to herself and her audience what the tears are about.

This applies to every kind of art. The artist never rants. A person who writes or paints or the like in order to blow off steam, using the traditional materials of art as means for exhibiting the symptoms of emotion, may deserve praise as an exhibitionist, but loses for the moment all claim to the title of artist. Exhibitionists have their uses; they may serve as an amusement, or they may be doing magic. The second category will contain, for example, those young men who, learning in the torment of their own bodies and minds what war is like, have stammered their indignation in verses, and published them in the hope of infecting others and causing them to abolish it. But these verses have nothing to do with poetry.

Thomas Hardy, at the end of a fine and tragic novel in which he has magnificently expressed his sorrow and indignation for the suffering inflicted by callous sentimentalism on trusting innocence, spoils everything by a last paragraph fastening his accusation upon "the president of the immortals." The note rings false, not because it is blasphemous (it offends no piety worthy of the name), but because it is rant. The case against God, so far as it exists, is complete already. The concluding paragraph adds nothing to it. All it does is to spoil the effect of the indictment by betraying a symptom of the emotion which the whole book has already expressed; as if a prosecuting counsel, at the end of his speech, spat in the prisoner's face.

The same fault is especially common in Beethoven. He was confirmed in it, no doubt, by his deafness; but the cause of it was not his deafness but a temperamental inclination to rant. It shows itself in the way his music screams and mutters instead of speaking, as in the soprano part of the Mass in D, or the layout of the opening page in the *Hammerklavier* Sonata. He must have known his failing and tried to overcome it, or he would never have spent so many of his ripest years among string quartets, where screaming and muttering are almost, one might say, physically impossible. Yet even there, the old Adam struts out in certain passages of the *Grosse Fuge*.

It does not, of course, follow that a dramatic writer may not rant in character. The tremendous rant at the end of *The Ascent of F6*, like the Shakespearian[1] ranting on which it is modelled, is done with tongue in cheek. It is not the author who is ranting, but the unbalanced character he depicts; the emotion the author is expressing is the emotion with which he contemplates that character; or rather, the emotion he has towards that secret and disowned part of himself for which the character stands.

Chapter XII: Art as Language

§ 3. GOOD ART AND BAD ART

The definition of any given kind of thing is also the definition of a good thing of that kind: for a thing that is good in its kind is only a thing which possesses the attributes of that kind. To call things good and bad is to imply success and failure. When we call things good or bad not in themselves but relatively to us, as when we speak of a good harvest or a bad thunderstorm, the success or failure implied is our own; we mean that these things enable us to realize our purposes, or prevent us from doing so. When we call things good or bad in themselves, the success or failure implied is theirs. We are implying that they acquire the attributes of their kind by an effort on their own part, and that this effort may be either more or less successful.

I am not raising the question whether it is true, as the Greeks thought, that there are natural kinds, and that what we call a dog is something that is trying to be a dog. For all my present argument is concerned, either that view may be true (in which case dogs can be good or bad in themselves), or the alternative view may be true, that the idea of a dog is only a way in which we choose to classify the things we come across, in which case dogs can be good or bad only in relation to us. I am only concerned with good and bad works of art. Now, a work of art is an activity of a certain kind; the agent is trying to do something definite, and in that attempt he may succeed or he may fail. It is, moreover, a conscious activity; the agent is not only trying to do something definite, he also knows what it is that he is trying to do; though knowing here does not necessarily imply being able to describe, since to describe is to generalize, and generalizing is the function of the intellect, and consciousness does not, as such, involve intellect.

[1]Shakespeare's characters rant (1) when they are characters in which he takes no interest at all, but which he uses simply as pegs on which to hang what the public wants, like Henry V; (2) when they are meant to be despicable, like Pistol; or (3) when they have lost their heads, like Hamlet in the graveyard.

A work of art, therefore, may be either a good one or a bad one. And because the agent is necessarily a conscious agent, he necessarily knows which it is. Or rather, he necessarily knows this so far as his consciousness in respect of this work of art is uncorrupted; for . . . there is such a thing as untruthful or corrupt consciousness.

Any theory of art should be required to show, if it wishes to be taken seriously, how an artist, in pursuing his artistic labour, is able to tell whether he is pursuing it successfully or unsuccessfully: how, for example, it is possible for him to say, "I am not satisfied with that line; let us try it this way . . . and this way . . . and this way . . . there! that will do." A theory which pushes the artistic experience too far down the scale, to a point below the region where experience has the character of knowledge, is unable to meet this demand. It can only evade it by pretending that the artist in such cases is acting not as an artist, but as a critic and even (if criticism of art is identified with philosophy of art) as a philosopher. But this pretence should deceive nobody. The watching of his own work with a vigilant and discriminating eye, which decides at every moment of the process whether it is being successful or not, is not a critical activity subsequent to, and reflective upon, the artistic work, it is an integral part of that work itself. A person who can doubt this, if he has any grounds at all for his doubt, is presumably confusing the way an artist works with the way an incompetent student in an art-school works; painting blindly, and waiting for the master to show him what it is that he has been doing. In point of fact, what a student learns in an art-school is not so much to paint as to watch himself painting: to raise the psycho-physical activity of painting to the level of art by becoming conscious of it, and so converting it from a psychical experience into an imaginative one.

What the artist is trying to do is to express a given emotion. To express it, and to express it well, are the same thing. To express it badly is not one way of expressing it . . . , it is failing to express it. A bad work of art is an activity in which the agent tries to express a given emotion, but fails. This is the difference between bad art and art falsely so called. . . . In art falsely so called there is no failure to express, because there is no attempt at expression; there is only an attempt (whether successful or not) to do something else.

But expressing an emotion is the same thing as becoming conscious of it. A bad work of art is the unsuccessful attempt to become conscious of a given emotion: it is what Spinoza calls an inadequate idea of an affection. Now, a consciousness which thus fails to grasp its own emotions is a corrupt or untruthful consciousness. For its failure (like any other failure) is not a mere blankness; it is not a doing nothing; it is a misdoing something; it is activity, but blundering or frustrated activity. A person who tries to become conscious of a given emotion, and fails, is no longer in a state of sheer unconsciousness or innocence about that emotion; he has done something about it, but that something is not to express it. What he has done is either to shirk it or dodge it: to disguise it from himself by pretending either that the emotion he feels is not that one but a different one, or that the person who feels it is not himself, but some one else: two alternatives which are so far from being mutually exclusive that in fact they are always concurrent and correlative.

If we ask whether this pretence is conscious or unconscious, the answer is, neither. It is a process which occurs not in the region below consciousness (where it could not, of course, take place, since consciousness is involved in the process itself), nor yet in the region of consciousness (where equally it could not take place, because a man cannot literally tell himself a lie; in so far as he is conscious of the truth he cannot literally deceive himself about it); it occurs on the threshold that divides the psychical level of experience from the conscious level. It is the malperformance of the act which converts what is merely psychic (impression) into what is conscious (idea).

The corruption of consciousness in virtue of which a man fails to express a given emotion makes him at the same time unable to know whether he has expressed it or not. He is, therefore, for one and the same reason, a bad artist and a bad judge of his own art. A person who is capable of producing bad art cannot, so far as he is capable of producing it, recognize it for what it is. He cannot, on the other hand, really think it good art; he cannot think that he has expressed himself when he has not. To mistake bad art for good art would imply having in one's mind an idea of what good art is, and one has such an idea only so far as one knows what it is to have an uncorrupt consciousness; but no one can know this except a person who possesses one. An insincere mind, so far as it is insincere, has no conception of sincerity.

But nobody's consciousness can be wholly corrupt. If it were, he would be in a condition as much worse than the most complete insanity we can discover or imagine, as that is worse than the most complete sanity we can conceive. He would suffer simultaneously every possible kind of mental derangement, and every bodily disease that such derangements can bring in their train. Corruptions of consciousness are always partial and temporary lapses in an activity which, on the whole, is successful in doing what it tries to do. A person who on one occasion fails to express himself is a person quite accustomed to express himself successfully on other occasions, and to know that he is doing it. Through comparison of this occasion with his memory of these others, therefore, he ought to be able to see that he has failed, this time, to express himself. And this is precisely what every artist is doing when he says, "This line won't do." He remembers what the experience of expressing himself is like, and in the light of that memory he realizes that the attempt embodied in this particular line has been a failure. Corruption of consciousness is not a recondite sin or a remote calamity which overcomes only an unfortunate or accursed few; it is a constant experience in the life of every artist, and his life is a constant and, on the whole, a successful warfare against it. But this warfare always involves a very present possibility

of defeat; and then a certain corruption becomes inveterate.

What we recognize as definite kinds of bad art are such inveterate corruptions of consciousness. Bad art is never the result of expressing what is in itself evil, or what is innocent perhaps in itself, but in a given society a thing inexpedient to be publicly said. Every one of us feels emotions which, if his neighbours became aware of them, would make them shrink from him with horror: emotions which, if he became aware of them, would make him horrified at himself. It is not the expression of these emotions that is bad art. Nor is it the expression of the horror they excite. On the contrary, bad art arises when instead of expressing these emotions we disown them, wishing to think ourselves innocent of the emotions that horrify us, or wishing to think ourselves too broad-minded to be horrified by them.

Art is not a luxury, and bad art not a thing we can afford to tolerate. To know ourselves is the foundation of all life that develops beyond the merely psychical level of experience. Unless consciousness does its work successfully, the facts which it offers to intellect, the only things upon which intellect can build its fabric of thought, are false from the beginning. A truthful consciousness gives intellect a firm foundation upon which to build; a corrupt consciousness forces intellect to build on a quicksand. The falsehoods which an untruthful consciousness imposes on the intellect are falsehoods which intellect can never correct for itself. In so far as consciousness is corrupted, the very wells of truth are poisoned. Intellect can build nothing firm. Moral ideals are castles in the air. Political and economic systems are mere cobwebs. Even common sanity and bodily health are no longer secure. But corruption of consciousness is the same thing as bad art.

I do not speak of these grave issues in order to magnify the office of any small section in our communities which arrogates to itself the name of artists. That would be absurd. Just as the life of a community depends for its very existence on honest dealing between man and man, the guardianship of this honesty being vested not in any one class or section, but in all and sundry, so the effort towards expression of emotions, the effort to overcome corruption of consciousness, is an effort that has to be made not by specialists only but by every one who uses language, whenever he uses it. Every utterance and every gesture that each one of us makes is a work of art. It is important to each one of us that in making them, however much he deceives others, he should not deceive himself. If he deceives himself in this matter, he has sown in himself a seed which, unless he roots it up again, may grow into any kind of wickedness, any kind of mental disease, any kind of stupidity and folly and insanity. Bad art, the corrupt consciousness, is the true *radix malorum.**

Chapter XIII: Art and Truth

§ 2. ART AS THEORY AND ART AS PRACTICE

Art is knowledge; knowledge of the individual. It is not on that account a purely "theoretical" activity as distinct from a "practical." The distinction between theoretical and practical activities has, of course, a certain value, but it must not be applied indiscriminately. We are accustomed to apply it, and to find that it makes sense, in cases where we are concerned with a relation between ourselves and our environment. An activity in ourselves which produces a change in us but none in our environment we call theoretical; one which produces a change in our environment but none in ourselves we call practical. But there are plenty of cases in which we are either unaware of any distinction between ourselves and our environment, or in which, if we are aware of it, we are not concerned with it.

When we really begin to understand the problems of morality, for example, we find that they have nothing to do with changes we can produce in the world around us, ourselves remaining unchanged. They have to do with changes to be

produced in ourselves. Thus, the question whether I shall return a book to the man I borrowed it from, or keep it and deny having borrowed it if he asks me to give it back, raises no serious moral problem. Which of the two things I shall in fact do depends on the kind of man I am. But the question whether I shall be an honest man or a dishonest one is a question that raises moral problems of the most acute kind. If I find myself to be dishonest, and decide to become honest, I am tackling, or setting out to tackle, a genuinely moral difficulty. But if I solve this difficulty the result will not be a change in myself only. It will involve changes in my environment too; for out of the new character which I shall acquire there will flow actions which will certainly to some extent alter my world. Hence morality belongs to a region of experience which is neither theoretical nor practical, but both at once. It is theoretical because it consists in part of finding things out about ourselves; not merely doing things, but thinking what we are doing. It is practical because it consists not merely of thinking, but of putting our thoughts into practice.

In the case of art, the distinction between theory and practice or thought and action has not been left behind, as it has in the case of any morality that deserves the name (I say nothing of the petty moralities that often usurp it); that distinction has not yet arisen. Such a distinction only presents itself to us when, by the abstractive work of intellect, we learn to dissect a given experience into two parts, one belonging to "the subject" and the other to "the object." The individual of which art is the knowledge is an individual situation in which we find ourselves. We are only conscious of the situation as our situation, and we are only conscious of ourselves as involved in the situation. Other people may be involved in it too, but these, like ourselves, are present to our consciousness only as factors in the situation, not as persons who outside the situation have lives of their own.

Because the artistic consciousness (that is, consciousness as such) does not distinguish between

*[root of evils]

itself and its world, its world being for it simply what is here and now experienced, and itself being simply the fact that this is here and now experienced, its distinctive activity is properly neither theoretical nor practical. For a person cannot properly be said to act either theoretically or practically except in so far as he thinks of himself as so acting. To an observer, the artist appears as acting both theoretically and practically; to himself, he appears as acting in neither way, because either way of acting implies distinctions which, as artist, he does not draw. All that we, as aesthetic theorists, can do is to recognize features in his activity which we should call theoretical, and others which we should call practical, and at the same time recognize that for him the distinction does not arise.

Theoretically, the artist is a person who comes to know himself, to know his own emotion. This is also knowing his world, that is, the sights and sounds and so forth which together make up his total imaginative experience. The two knowledges are to him one knowledge, because these sights and sounds are to him steeped in the emotion with which he contemplates them: they are the language in which that emotion utters itself to his consciousness. His world is his language. What it says to him it says about himself; his imaginative vision of it is his self-knowledge.

But this knowing of himself is a making of himself. At first he is mere psyche, the possessor of merely psychical experiences or impressions. The act of coming to know himself is the act of converting his impressions into ideas, and so of converting himself from mere psyche into consciousness. The coming to know his emotions is the coming to dominate them, to assert himself as their master. He has not yet, it is true, entered upon the life of morality; but he has taken an indispensable step forward towards it. He has learnt to acquire by his own efforts a new set of mental endowments. That is an accomplishment which must be learnt first, if later he is to acquire by his own effort mental endowments whose possession will bring him nearer to his moral ideal.

Moreover, his knowing of this new world is also the making of the new world which he is coming to know. The world he has come to know is a world consisting of language; a world where everything has the property of expressing emotion. In so far as this world is thus expressive or significant, it is he that has made it so. He has not, of course, made it "out of nothing." He is not God, but a finite mind still at a very elementary stage in the development of its powers. He has made it 'out of' what is presented to him in the still more elementary stage of purely psychical experience: colours, sounds, and so forth. I know that many readers, in loyalty to certain brands of metaphysic now popular, will wish to deny this. It might seem advisable for me to consider their denials, which are very familiar, and refute them, which would be very easy. But I will not do this. I am writing not to make converts, but to say what I think. If any reader thinks he knows better, I would rather he went on working out his own lines of thought than tried to adopt mine.

To return. The aesthetic experience, as we look back at it from a point of view where we distinguish theoretical from practical activity, thus presents characteristics of both kinds. It is a knowing of oneself and of one's world, these two knowns and knowings being not yet distinguished, so that the self is expressed in the world, the world consisting of language whose meaning is that emotional experience which constitutes the self, and the self consisting of emotions which are known only as expressed in the language which is the world. It is also a making of oneself and of one's world, the self which was psyche being remade in the shape of consciousness, and the world, which was crude sensa, being remade in the shape of language, or sensa converted into imagery and charged with emotional significance. The step forward in the development of experience which leads from the psychic level to the level of consciousness (and that step is the specific achievement of art) is thus a step forward both in theory and in practice, although it is one step only and not two; as a progress along a railway-line towards a certain junction is a progress towards both the regions served by the two lines which divide at that junction. For that matter, it is also a progress towards the region in which, later, those two lines reunite.

§ 3. ART AND INTELLECT

Art as such contains nothing that is due to intellect. Its essence is that of an activity by which we become conscious of our own emotions. Now, there are emotions which exist in us, but of which we are not yet conscious, at the level of psychical experience. Therefore art finds in purely psychical experience a situation of the type with which it essentially deals, and a problem of the kind which its essential business is to solve.

This might seem to be not only a problem such as art exists to solve, but the only problem which it can solve. It might seem, in other words, that psychical emotions are the only emotions which art can express. For all other emotions are generated at levels of experience subsequent to the emergence of consciousness, and therefore (it might be thought) under the eyes of consciousness. They are born, it might seem, in the light of consciousness, with expressions ready-made for them at birth. There can, therefore, be no need to express them through works of art.

The logical consequence of this argument would be that no work of art, if it is a genuine work of art, can contain in its subject-matter anything that is due to the work of intellect. This is not what I said in the first sentence of this section. Art as such might contain nothing that is due to intellect, and yet certain works of art might contain much that is due to intellect, not because they are works of art, but because they are works of a certain kind; that is, because they express emotions of a certain kind, namely, emotions that can arise only as the emotional charges upon intellectual activities.

Here, then, we have two alternatives. Either the subject-matter of a work of art (that is, the emotion it expresses) is drawn exclusively from the psychical level of experience, because that is the only level at which there exists any experience of which we are not conscious; or it may also include elements drawn from other levels, in which case these levels, too, will contain elements of which, until we find expression for them, we are not conscious.

If these two alternatives are considered in the light of the question: what emotions do this and that work of art actually express? it will hardly be doubted, I think, that the second alternative is right. If we examine almost any work of art we like to choose, and consider what emotions it expresses, we shall find that they include some, and those not the least important, which are intellectual emotions: emotions which can only be felt by an intellectual being, and are in fact felt because such a being uses his intellect in certain ways. They are the emotional charges not upon a merely psychical experience, nor upon experience at the level of mere consciousness, but upon intellectual experience or thought in the narrower sense of the word.

And this, if we come to think of it, is inevitable. For even if a certain emotion is, as I put it, endowed at birth with its own proper expression, this is only a way of saying that the work of expression has already been done in its case; and if done, done by the artistic consciousness. And every emotion is, if not born with the silver spoon of expression in its mouth, at least reborn in that state on the occasion of its second birth as idea, as distinct from impression. Since the emotional life of the conscious and intellectual levels of experience is far richer than that of the merely psychical level, therefore . . . it is only natural that the emotional subject-matter of works of art should be drawn mostly from emotions belonging to these higher levels.

For example, Romeo and Juliet form the subject of a play not because they are two organisms sexually attracted, however powerfully, to each other; nor because they are two human beings experiencing this attraction and conscious of the experience, that is, two human beings in love; but because their love is woven into the fabric of a complicated social and political situation, and is broken by the strains to which that situation subjects it. The emotion experienced by Shakespeare and expressed by him in the play is not an emotion arising simply out of sexual passion or his sympathy with it, but an emotion arising out of his (intellectual) apprehension of the way in which passion may thus cut across social and political conditions. Similarly, Lear is envisaged, by Shakespeare and by ourselves, not simply as an old man suffering cold and hunger, but as a father suffering these things at the hands of his daughters. Apart from the idea of the family, intellectually conceived as a principle of social morality, the tragedy of Lear would not exist. The emotions expressed in these plays are thus emotions arising out of a situation which could not generate them unless it were intellectually apprehended.

The poet converts human experience into poetry not by first expurgating it, cutting out the intellectual elements and preserving the emotional, and then expressing this residue; but by fusing thought itself into emotion: thinking in a certain way and then expressing how it feels to think in that way. Thus Dante has fused the Thomistic philosophy into a poem expressing what it feels like to be a Thomist. Shelley, when he made the earth say, "I spin beneath my pyramid of night," expressed what it feels like to be a Copernican. Donne (and this is why he has become so congenial to ourselves in the last twenty or thirty years) has expressed how it feels to live in a world full of shattered ideas, *disjecta membra* of old systems of life and thought, where intellectual activity is itself correspondingly shattered into momentary fulgurations of thinking, related to each other only by an absence of all logical connexion, and where the prevailing emotional tone of thought is simply the sense of this shatteredness: a tone expressed over and over again in his poems, for example in "The Glasse," and in the shape of a moral idea by his many verses in praise of inconstancy. And Mr. Eliot, in the one great English poem of this century, has expressed his idea (not his alone) of the decay of our civilization, manifested outwardly as a break-down of social structures and inwardly as a drying-up of the emotional springs of life. . . .

The Apples of Cézanne: An Essay on the Meaning of Still-Life

Meyer Schapiro

. . . Still-life as a type of theme in painting corresponds, it is clear, like landscape, genre and portraiture, to a field of interest outside art; and we sense this, without having to refer to a particular cause, when we note the separation of still-life as an independent subject (or object) matter in the sixteenth century. Landscape, too, was disengaged then as a major theme with its own completeness after having served for centuries as a setting for human figures. The objects chosen for still-life painting — the table with food and drink, the vessels, the musical instruments, the pipe and tobacco, the articles of costume, the books, tools, playing cards, *objets d'art*, flowers, skulls, etc. — belong to specific fields of value: the private, the domestic, the gustatory, the convivial, the artistic, the vocation and avocation, the decorative and sumptuous, and — less often — in a negative mood, objects offered to meditation as symbols of vanity, mementos of the ephemeral and death. There is, besides, in still-life a range of qualities congenial to a broad outlook which is less distinctly embodied in other kinds of themes. Simply to note these qualities is to suggest a kind of world-view. Still-life, I have written elsewhere, consists of objects that, whether artificial or natural, are subordinate to man as elements of use, manipulation and enjoyment; these objects are smaller than ourselves, within arm's reach, and

owe their presence and place to a human action, a purpose. They convey man's sense of his power over things in making or utilizing them; they are instruments as well as products of his skills, his thoughts and appetites. While favored by an art that celebrates the visual as such, they appeal to all the senses and especially to touch and taste. They are the themes *par excellence* of an empirical standpoint wherein our knowledge of proximate objects, and especially of the instrumental, is the model or ground of all knowledge. It is in this sense that the American philosopher, George H. Mead, has said: "The reality of what we see is what we can handle."

Often associated with a style that explores patiently and minutely the appearance of nearby things — their textures, lights, reflections and shadows — the still-life objects bring to awareness the complexity of the phenomenal and the subtle interplay of perception and artifice in representation.

The still-life comes to stand then for a sober objectivity, and an artist who struggles to attain that posture after having renounced a habitual impulsiveness or fantasy, can adopt the still-life as a calming or redemptive modest task, a means of self-discipline and concentration; it signifies to him the commitment to the given, the simple and dispassionate — the impersonal universe of matter. In the mid-nineteenth century, in reaction against the anecdote in Salon painting, one said that a pebble could serve as a sufficient theme in painting.

Once established as a model domain of the objective in art, still-life is open to an endless variety of feelings and thoughts, even of a disturbing intensity. It can appeal to artists of different temperament who are able through the painting of small objects to express without action or gesture the intimate and personal. They may be instruments of a passion as well as of cool meditation.

Still-life engages the painter (and also the observer who can surmount the habit of casual perception) in a steady looking that discloses new and elusive aspects of the stable object. At first commonplace in appearance, it may become in the course of that contemplation a mystery, a source of metaphysical wonder. Completely secular and stripped of all conventional symbolism, the still-life object, as the meeting-point of boundless forces of atmosphere and light, may evoke a mystical mood like Jakob Boehme's illumination through the glint on a metal ewer.

(I shall not go into the question of how far the vogue of still-life in Western art depends on the point of view of the bourgeois whose strong interest in portable possessions and inclination toward the concrete and practical should make still-life an appealing theme in art. The description I have given of still-life, while it ranges beyond those aspects, will suggest to some readers a connection with other features of a bourgeois outlook. Yet even where the bourgeois has been dominant for centuries and the belief in the dignity of still-life and landscape as themes and their equality to historical subjects has appeared as a democratizing trend in art that gives a positive significance to the everyday world and the environment, even there still-life painting has not been specially favored by middle class patrons of art. It has become important mainly through the achievements of Chardin, Cézanne and the Cubists. The still-life painters have had to contend with the prejudice that their art is of a lower order because of the intrinsic inferiority of its objects; noble and idealized themes, like idealistic philosophies, have won more approval even after all kinds of themes were admitted in principle to be equal and value was located in the quality of the painter's art. One should not conclude from this fact that the growth of still-life painting has been independent of the conditions of social life. An art like Chardin's or Cézanne's is unthinkable outside of Western bourgeois society. The great difference between ancient Roman still-life painting, with its bare and indeterminate space, and that of later times which has a broader range of personal objects located in an intimate domestic or other private space shaped by the viewpoint of a real observer, reflects the changed character of society.)

Early in our own century still-life was a preferred theme of an art of painting that aimed at a salient concreteness of the medium through a more tangible brush-stroke and surface, even attaching real objects to the canvas beside the traditional pigment—a culmination of a tendency to view the painting itself as a material thing and to erase by various means the boundaries between reality and representation. The work of art then is itself an ostensible object of handling like certain of the simulated and real objects that compose it. Without a fixed place in nature and submitted to arbitrary and often accidental manipulation, the still-life on the table is an objective example of the formed but constantly re-arranged, the freely disposable in reality and therefore connate with an idea of artistic liberty. The still-life picture, to a greater degree than the landscape or historical painting, owes its composition to the painter, yet more than these seems to represent a piece of everyday reality. . . .

Music and Negative Emotion

Jerrold Levinson

Reprinted by permission of the *Pacific Philosophical Quarterly*.

1

A grown man, of sound mind and body, manipulates the controls of an electronic apparatus. He settles into an easy chair, full of expectancy. Then it begins. For the next hour or so this man is subjected to an unyielding bombardment of stimuli, producing in him a number of states which prima facie are extremely unpleasant, and which one would normally go to some lengths to avoid. He appears upset, pained, and at turns a small sigh or a shudder passes through his body. Yet at the end of this ordeal our subject seems pleased. He avers that the past hour and a half has been a highly rewarding one. He declares his intention to repeat this sort of experience in the near future.

What has our man been doing, and more interestingly, why has he been doing it? He has been listening to music — just that. It turns out that his fare on this occasion was the *Marcia Funebre* of Beethoven's *Eroica* Symphony, the Scriabin Etude op. 42, no. 5, the third movement of Brahm's Third Symphony, Mozart's Adagio and Fugue in C Minor, K. 546, and the opening of Mahler's Second Symphony, all neatly assembled, with suitable pauses, on a reel of recording tape. What he experienced can be described — at least *provisionally* — as intense grief, unrequited passion, sobbing melancholy, tragic resolve, and angry despair. But why would anyone in effect torture himself in this manner? What could induce a sane person to purposely arrange for himself occasions of ostensibly painful experience?

My object in this essay is to give a comprehensive answer to this query. The general question can be formulated thus: Why do many sensitive people find the experience of negative emotion through music a rewarding or valuable one, and, what is especially paradoxical, rewarding or valuable partly in itself? Not only do appreciators of music appear to regard such experiences as instrumentally good or worthwhile — which itself needs much explaining — but they standardly seek them out and relish them for their own sakes, enjoying them or pleasuring in them, if truth be told.

At this point many readers will have ready some favorite wand for dissolving this paradox with a wave of the hand. But I do not intend to encourage them. While admitting that my initial description of the phenomenon will need to be modified somewhat, I maintain that even when all niceties on the aesthetic and psychological fronts have been attended to, the phenomenon, in essence, remains.

2

In its general form, of course, the problem of the value and desirability of the negative or unpleasant in art is one of the hoariest in aesthetics. It is the problem Aristotle raises for the appreciation of tragedy, evocative of pity and terror, and which he answers with the doctrine of catharsis. It is the problem of the sublime in eighteenth- and nineteenth-century thought, the "delightful horror" analyzed among others by Burke and Schopenhauer, which a spectator feels face to face with some threatening aspect of life as embodied in a work of art. But in the case of music the problem is generated in the absence of any representational content, and so answers to it must be framed accordingly.

We see in the following more recent writers a concern with the specific paradox of enjoyment of emotionally distressing music. It is interesting to note the virtual consensus of these writers that negative emotion is not actually evoked in the attuned listener by even the most intense of musical works.

If to hear the intense grief of the fugal passages of the Eroica *required real tears and adrenal secretions, then an anomalous if not impossible psychological state would have to prevail. The gorgeous clash of dissonant minor seconds which brings the tremendous but short fugue to an incomplete close — several measures of almost unbearable anguish — has been a source of supreme delight to countless lovers of music. How can a listener be at once pleased and pained?*[1]

Why should I ever wish to hear . . . (sad music)? Sad experiences, such as suffering personal bereavement or keen disappointment, are not the kind of thing we wish to repeat or prolong. Yet sad music does not affect us in this way; it may bring relief, pleasure, even happiness. Strange kind of sadness that brings pleasure![2]

The most unpleasant emotions imaginable are perceived in music; and if that meant our feeling these emotions, it would be utterly inexplicable why anyone would willfully submit himself to the music. Tristan und Isolde is full of music expressive of deep anguish. None, I would think, except the masochists among us, would listen to such music if indeed it were anguish-producing.[3]

I agree with these writers, on the bottom line, that full-fledged emotions of the paradigm sort fail to

be aroused by music in the course of aesthetically respectable auditionings. But I want to stress that this failure in many cases is only a marginal one, and thus that the paradox of desirable-though-unpleasant experience in music remains despite this admission. Something *very much like* the arousal of negative emotions is accomplished by *some* music, and so there is indeed something to explain in our avidity for such experience.

Before essaying explanations of my own, it will help to review a number of responses to the problem which attempt to solve it, roughly, by dissolving it. This will occupy me for the succeeding six sections. These responses in effect deny the phenomenon while introducing in its stead harmless replacement. Such moves are inadequate, however, to resolve the paradox of musical masochism limned in the opening illustration.

It is best to forestall at the outset a possible misunderstanding. In defending the reality and importance of emotional response to music I imply no position on the proper analysis of emotional expressiveness in music. The three writers quoted above are all concerned to undercut the equation of expression in music with evocation by music. In that they are certainly right. What a passage expresses and what it standardly evokes are, for an assortment of reasons, rarely (if ever) quite identical. But while I reject an evocation theory of expression, I am unwilling to see emotional response to music — particularly of a "dark" sort — exorcised so completely in the name of it. One can reject the evocation theory without regarding every instance of negative emotional response to music — whatever the work and whatever the conditions of listening — as either illusory or aesthetically inapropos. It seems to me that there are indeed compositions that can, when listened to in certain appreciatively admissible frames of mind, produce in one real feelings of both the positive and negative variety.

It is our attitude toward the latter that seems puzzling. One can be on the musical rack — one can hear the screws turn — and yet like it. This is what we must explain.

[1] Carroll C. Pratt, Introduction to *The Meaning of Music* (New York: McGraw-Hill, 1970), pp. 3–4.
[2] John Hospers, "The Concept of Artistic Expression," in *Introductory Readings in Aesthetics*, ed. J. Hospers (New York: Free Press, 1969), p. 152.
[3] Peter Kivy, *The Corded Shell* (Princeton: Princeton University Press, 1980), p. 23.

3

One hypothesis concerning the effect of music would, if accepted, neatly defuse the paradox which concerns us. This hypothesis, less popular today than at some earlier times, is that of a special "aesthetic emotion," totally different from the emotions of life and occasioned only by the perception of works of art. This view is identified with Clive Bell in its general form, but its foremost exponent with specific application to music is the English psychologist Edmund Gurney.[4] According to Gurney, there is a unique, sui generis "musical emotion" that is raised in listeners by all pieces of "impressive" (i.e., beautiful) music, and only by such. This unvarying effect of impressive music is either a kind of pleasure itself, or else something the experience of which is pleasurable. Clearly, if the chief result of music that was both impressive and, say, anguished was the arousal of such a "musical emotion," there would be little difficulty in understanding how such music could be enjoyable.

There is, however, little else to be said for the view that appreciative response to music consists of but one type of emotion, a music-specific, invariably pleasant one. The effects of different sorts of music are too different from one another, and too reminiscent of life emotions, for this view to carry much plausibility. Our manifest interest in a multiplicity of musical works and experiences begins to seem puzzling if the primary benefit to be derived from any or all of them is this selfsame "musical emotion." It just is not the case that all good or impressive music induces a single positive emotion in listeners.

This is not to say that there could not be something specifically musical, and perhaps unduplicatable, in the experience of a particular piece of music. The total experience — perceptual, emotional, cognitive — of listening to a given work may indeed be unique to it, and this fact not without aesthetic relevance. But one can maintain that without adopting the hypothesis of an invari-

ant and specifically musical emotional element in each such experience.

4

Another approach to our paradox is implicit in some reflections on music by the composer Paul Hindemith. Hindemith denies that music has an emotional effect on listeners, properly speaking. One of his main reasons for this denial seems to be the rapidity with which the typical musical composition changes its emotional character, coupled with a reasonable assumption of emotional inertia on the part of human beings. Hindemith believes that since a person cannot change emotional states as quickly as music changes its expression, it is implausible to think the music is evocative of real emotion in him.

> There is not doubt that listeners, performers, and composers alike can be profoundly moved by perceiving, performing, or imagining music, and consequently music must touch on something in their emotional life that brings them into this state of excitation. But if these mental reactions were feelings, they could not change as rapidly as they do, and they would not begin and end with the musical stimulus that aroused them. . . . Real feelings need a certain interval of time to develop, to reach a climax, and to fade out again; but reactions to music may change as fast as musical phrases do, they may spring up in full intensity at any given movement and disappear entirely when the musical pattern that provokes them ends or changes.[5]

Instead of emotions themselves, Hindemith claims that musical passages evoke in the listener merely memories or images of emotions that the listener has experienced in the past. It follows that there can be no emotional reaction to music which is not strongly rooted in emotional experience in life. On Hindemith's view listening to music becomes an occasion for a selective tour of

---

[4]His chief work, *The Power of Sound*, was published in 1880.

[5]Paul Hindemith, *A Composer's World* (New York: Doubleday, 1961), pp. 44–45.

one's gallery of emotional remembrances, with some sonata or symphony functioning as guide.

The musicologist Deryck Cooke offered two replies to Hindemith's remarks which are worth recalling.[6] The first is that even admitting a certain inertia in the average person's emotional responsiveness, the rapid changes of character from passage to passage in a musical work do not themselves insure that no emotions are raised in the course of it, for we need not assume that such reactions come abruptly to an end when the passages that stimulate them are over. According to Cooke, the response elicited by a passage will often linger and develop after the passage is no longer heard, instead of being entirely obliterated or erased by succeeding passages or completion of the piece.

Second, Cooke very plausibly maintains that our reactions to music cannot all consist of memory images of prior experiences, since it appears that music (some music) has the power to make us feel in ways that we simply have not felt before. The feeling raised in me by certain auditions of the finale of Schumann's piano concerto was distinct from any I had encountered in ordinary life before those hearings. It may have been related in complex ways to particular prior experiences of mine, but it was clearly not equivalent to a memory replay of them either singly or collectively.

Furthermore, if what we can neutrally call a *sadness-reaction* to sad music typically consisted of some memory image of a particular earlier sadness, it seems we would generally be conscious while listening of the particulars of that occasion—the time, place, object, and reasons of it. But we are not. Listeners' capacities for feeling sadness from music will be exercised and deepened by their experiences of sadness in life, to be sure, but there is little reason to think either that listeners could not possibly be saddened by music if they had not been saddened outside of music or more important, that their sadness-reactions

could only be the recollection of particular experiences of sadness in their pasts.

Two other observations on Hindemith's remarks are in order with respect to the problem of negative emotional response in music. First, if it is doubtful whether the listener's response to varied, swiftly changing musical works can be a coherently emotional one, we can focus attention instead on extended parts of sections thereof which are emotionally relatively homogeneous. There is certainly enough time in the course of the sustained *Eroica* Funeral March to build up a substantial feeling of grief leavened with little else. Our paradox remains even if only a small number of compositions have sufficient continuity and depth to properly elicit these ostensibly undesirable affects.

Second, even were Hindemith right that emotional response to music is simply a matter of the reviving of old emotions in memory, this would not really dispel the paradox of why we should desire to hear music that revives memories that are of negative emotional experiences. If it is puzzling that one should want to be *made* sad, it is only a little less puzzling that one should want to *remember* particular occasions of having been sad. For memories of sad occasions are often sad themselves; that is to say, summoning them up often reawakens the sadness they encode. Memories are not only records, but repositories as well. To revive a memory of sadness often is in part to relive that sadness. Experiential memories standardly preserve and transmit the affective tone of the original experience.[7]

Thus, we will no more find a solution to our puzzle in Hindemith's hypothesis than in Gurney's.

5

In order to discuss certain other approaches to our problem we must pursue the analysis of emotion somewhat further. It is by now orthodoxy

[6]Deryck Cooke, *The Language of Music* (London: Oxford University Press, 1959), chap. 1.

[7]See on this Richard Wollheim, "On Persons and Their Lives," in *Explaining Emotions*, ed. Amelie O. Rorty (Berkeley: University of California Press, 1980), pp. 299–321.

among philosophers of mind that emotions are more than simply states of inner feeling.[8] Although there is not absolute accord on what all the components of an emotion are, and on which, if any, are essential to the emotion, most writers agree at least that emotions contain a *cognitive* component in addition to an *affective* one. This may be expressed in the form of a belief, attitude, desire, or evaluation, focused on and identifying the *object* of the emotion. Thus, if one is afraid, one feels a certain (rather unpleasant) way, and feels that way *toward* some object that one believes to be dangerous and wants to avoid. If one hopes, one feels a certain (rather more pleasant) way, and feels that way *about* some situation that one believes may possibly obtain, and that one desires to obtain. The presence of an intentional object on which thought and feeling are directed, then, is taken as central to the paradigm of an emotion.

In addition to affective and cognitive components, a case can be made that emotions have *behavioral* and *physiological* components as well. Being afraid may typically involve cowering, shaking, or the like, and perhaps necessarily a tendency or disposition to flee in the presence of the feared object. Being afraid may require, in addition to anything one is subjectively experiencing, a certain state of the endocrine or circulatory systems.

Concerning the affective component — that part of an emotion which consists in what one *feels* in a narrow sense — there is some question as to how this should be conceived. On one view, the affective component of emotion consists in a certain overall coloring of consciousness, a certain quality of inner feeling, of which pleasurable/painful is an important, though not the only, dimension. On another view, the affective component is simply a set of internal sensations of bodily changes — e.g., sensations registering lumps in the throat, goosebumps on the skin, churnings in the stomach, and tension across muscles of the head. I am inclined to think that the feeling component of emotion is best understood as involving both sorts of things. I will accordingly refer to these, respectively, as the *phenomenological* and the *sensational* aspects of the affective (or feeling) component of an emotion.

It is time to say clearly that the standard emotional response to a musical work — e.g., what I have called a sadness-reaction — is not in truth a case of *full-fledged* emotion. This is mainly because music neither supplies an appropriate object for an emotion to be directed on, nor generates the associated beliefs, desires, or attitudes regarding an object which are essential to an emotion being what it is. When a symphonic adagio "saddens" me, I am not sad at or about the music, nor do I regard the adagio as something I would wish to be otherwise. Furthermore, this weakening of the cognitive component in emotional response to music generally results in the inhibition of most characteristic behaviors and in the significant lessening of behavioral tendencies.

Yet the purely physiological and, more important, affective components are occasionally, it seems, retained in something like full force. If music inevitably fails to induce by itself a proper, contextually embedded *emotion* of sadness,[9] still, some music appears fully capable of inducing at least the characteristic *feeling* of sadness. This is enough, I take it, for the problem of negative emotional response to music to resist complete solution by any of the proposals shortly to be

---

[8]See the discussions in William Alston, "Emotion and Feeling," in *The Encyclopedia of Philosophy*, ed. Paul Edwards (New York: Macmillan, 1967); Georges Rey, "Functionalism and the Emotions," in *Explaining Emotions*; Moreland Perkins, "Emotions and Feeling," *Philosophical Review*, 75 (1966); Patricia S. Greenspan, "Ambivalence and the Logic of Emotion," in *Explaining Emotions*; and Malcolm Budd, "The Repudiation of Emotion: Hanslick on Music," *British Journal of Aesthetics*, 20 (1980). The first two essays include rather extended analysis of the concept of an emotion, and I am particularly indebted to them for some distinctions I employ in this essay.

[9]It is helpful to keep in mind a distinction between the inducing and the reviving of emotions. Music does not by itself normally *induce* full-fledged emotions, but it can sometimes *revive* ones had earlier so that they are reexperienced — beliefs, desires, feelings, and all. (More often it will simply *recall* such emotions — i.e., revive the *memory* of them.) But the objects and cognitive contents of revived emotions will have been supplied on earlier, nonmusical occasions.

considered. I shall have occasion to distinguish between *emotions* (including cognitive elements) and associated *feelings* (lacking cognitive elements) in what follows. And when I speak subsequently of "emotional response" to music, this should be understood as an experience produced in a listener which is *at least* the characteristic feeling of some emotion, but which is short of a complete emotion per se.

I am going to assume for the purposes of this essay that the majority of common emotions have affective components (comprising both phenomenological and sensational aspects) which are more or less distinctive of them, apart from the cognitive components that are perhaps the logically distinctive ones. That is to say, I will assume there are introspectible differences between common emotions. Evidence for this is provided by cases in which persons suddenly realize that they are sad, happy, depressed, anxious, or in love without recognizing explicitly that they hold certain beliefs, desires, or evaluations, and thus apparently on the basis of quality of feeling. There is, granted, some psychological research that appears to suggest that common emotions are not much differentiated in inner feeling or affect, but this research strikes me as inconclusive and as somewhat questionable in its method.[10] In any event, it is undeniable that negative affect is integrally involved in a number of emotional conditions, and that there is at least *some* range of qualitative difference in affect across the spectrum of negative emotions. The persistence of our problem and the viability of certain answers to it that we shall entertain actually require nothing more than that.

6

Those who are skeptical of the claim that music often induces familiar emotions in listeners sometimes maintain that what is induced is neither one special aesthetic emotion nor memory images of past emotions, but instead musical *analogs* of the familiar emotions of life. There are two questions that arise here. One is the respects in which these music-emotions differ from ordinary emotions. The second is the respects in which they are the same and which presumably justify calling them by a common name.

John Hospers, in a well-known essay on expression in art, suggests that the emotional response to sad music is indeed not real sadness, but only music-sadness. Here is Hospers's explication of this phenomenon:

Sadness expressed in music is a very different thing from sadness in life; it is only by a kind of analogy that we use the same word for both. . . . Sadness in music is depersonalized; it is taken out of or abstracted from, the particular personal situation in which we ordinarily feel it, such as the death of a loved one or the shattering of one's hopes. In music we get what is sometimes called the "essence" of sadness without all the accompanying accidents, or causal conditions which usually bring it into being. In view of this, it is said, we can continue to say that music expresses sadness, but we should distinguish the music-sadness, *which is a happy experience, from* life-sadness, *which is not.*[11]

We may interpret Hospers as saying that music-sadness feels (narrow sense) like life-sadness but (1) lacks an object or situational context, and (2) lacks the usual causal conditions of sadness. What it has in common with life-sadness, then, is presumably a certain mode of feeling, possibly lessened in intensity, and certain underlying physiological disturbances.

It is not obvious that the invocation of music-emotions — muted, objectless analogs of life-emotions — is of itself any help in understanding why negative emotional response in music should be

[10]For example, one might draw this conclusion from S. Schacter and J. E. Singer, "Cognitive, Social and Physiological Determinants of Emotional State," *Psychological Review*, 69 (1962). However, that paper barely recognizes the possibility of an affective component in emotional states distinct from that of purely physiological arousal, and is mainly concerned to establish the *necessity* of cognitive components in emotion.

[11]Hospers, "Concept of Artistic Expression," p. 152. In this paragraph Hospers is considering evocation theories of expression, and so the assumption that expression equals evocation is in effect.

so sought after. The prick of a needle hurts less than the stab of a knife, but it is not for that reason to be desired. One would not go out of one's way to have it administered, even if all consciousness of perpetrating agent, physical environment, and lasting effect were eliminated. The appeal to weaker, cognitively impoverished forms of the normal negative emotions faces the following dilemma: If music-φness involves the same mode of inner feeling as life-φness, however muted in strength, then its prima facie unpleasantness would seem to make it something to avoid. On the other hand, if music-φness and life-φness involve different modes of inner feeling, then it becomes unclear what connection there is between them at all, and unconvincing that emotional response in music consists in something so wholly unrelated to the ordinary emotion by which we are disposed to denominate it. In short, if there is such a thing as music-sadness, resembling life-sadness and evoked by sad music, it has not yet been shown how this can be a "happy experience."

Another suggestion worth considering here is that when we are "saddened" by music we are not made really sad, but only make-believedly so.[12] That is to say, music raises certain states of feeling in us, which we then make believe to be emotions in the full sense, by ourselves supplying the requisite cognitive filling out.

Our response to the previous suggestion would seem to apply here as well. If the feeling component of, say, make-believe anger were the same as that of real anger, then given its unpleasant tone, it is unclear why make-believe anger should be any more pursued than real anger. Why should make believing that I am angry, given an appropriate state of inner agitation, provide me with satisfaction? Furthermore, to the extent that the make-believe is effective, the *more* distressed I would seem to become, imagining not only that I felt (narrowly) a certain unpleasant way, but that all the undesirable life consequences and accompaniments of being truly angry were also in the offing.

In addition, I am skeptical that in the cases we are interested in, those of deep emotional response to music, we in fact standardly make believe that we are truly possessed of various emotions — at least if this requires that we do so in an *explicit and fully determinate* manner. It seems our imaginative responses to music are typically not so definite as that. When we are "saddened" by sad music, or "frightened" by fearful music, we generally are not making believe that there is a particular object, with particular characteristics, for us to be sad about or frightened of. Nor do we make believe that we have certain attitudes or desires toward such determinate intentional objects. Emotional response to music does not have the same degree of cognitive structure as emotional response to well-delineated entities of fictional worlds. To maintain otherwise is to exaggerate the extent to which listeners intellectually augment their basic affective responses to music. On the other hand, this is not to deny that a listener may, in a less concrete way, imaginatively assume an emotional state in virtue of identifying with music that is engaging him. I shall return to this point in section 9.

7

Another possible way around the question of emotional response to music, and thus around the problem of negative emotion in music, is to claim that the appearance of emotional response is simply a well-buttressed illusion, founded on a confusion between perceiving and feeling. The proper aesthetic response to music, it will be said, is a purely *cognitive* one, consisting in among other things the recognition and appreciation of emotional qualities in music. What occasionally seems to us to be the experiencing of something like sorrow, while listening in anything like a correct manner, is in fact always only the vivid grasping of sorrowfulness in music.

I regard this line as highly implausible. Of course, the exclusively cognitive response to expression in music is a possible mode of aesthetic

---

[12]A suggestion like this might be drawn from Kendall Walton, "Fearing Fictions," *Journal of Philosophy*, 75 (1978): 5–27.

involvement—the detached, critical mode of the auditory connoisseur. To be sure, one can detect expression without being moved, and one can come to understand a work's moods without necessarily mirroring them. But the detached mode of involvement is just one mode among several which can be adopted, and is hardly the only aesthetically recommendable one. Its aesthetic superiority over a more open and inclusive mode of involvement—in which one both registers *and* reacts to emotion in music—is at least questionable.

Responding emotionally to music is clearly consistent with perceiving emotional qualities in it. But what is more, these activities may be subtly interdependent ones. What we seem to perceive influences what we feel, and what we feel influences what we say we perceive. On the one hand, part of what inclines us to describe a quality of music with a given emotional term is a sense of what emotion the music tends to evoke in us; but on the other hand, part of the reason we have an emotional reaction to music is perception of a corresponding emotional quality in it, provisionally identified on the basis of physiognomic resemblance—analogy to expressive behavior—or conventional associations. We are saddened in part by perception of a quality in a passage which we construe as sadness, but we in part denominate that quality "sadness"—or confirm such denomination of it—in virtue of being saddened by the music or sensing its capacity to sadden us under somewhat different conditions. Recognizing emotion in music and experiencing emotion from music may not be as separable in principle as one might have liked. If this is so, the suggestion that in aesthetic appreciation of music we simply cognize emotional attributes without feeling anything corresponding to them may be conceptually problematic as well as empirically incredible.

8

Nelson Goodman, certainly, does not make the error of representing the perception of expression in music as an emotionless undertaking. On the contrary, he emphasizes the role of feeling as an essential aid in determining what expressive properties a work actually has. In his now familiar words, "In aesthetic experience the emotions function cognitively."[13] Their chief role is to inform us about the character of the works we are involved with.

But can this by itself explain the attraction that negative music has for us? Goodman tells us that "in aesthetic experience, emotion positive or negative is a mode of sensitivity to a work."[14] The value of despairing or sorrowing response to music, then, is that it is requisite to our correctly discerning the emotional qualities of the music. So by this account we let ourselves in for often considerable distress solely in order to learn accurately the characteristics of the object that is tormenting us. What seems puzzling is why we should be so committed to ascertaining the properties of works of art that put us in unpleasant states. Do we have a duty to all artistic objects to discern their characters correctly, whatever the cost? Surely not. Does the cognitive reward we derive from perceiving rightly that a movement is, say, anguished outweigh the anguish we may feel in the course of that perception? It would not seem so. Getting to know a work's dark qualities may be a partial justification for suffering from it, but it cannot be the whole story. Two things in particular seem insufficiently explained. One is the depth to which we often want to feel negative emotion in music, beyond what could plausibly be required as an assist to cognitive assessment; the other is the fact that the Goodmanian observation, as far as it goes, accounts more for the instrumental value than for the peculiar desirability of negative emotion from music.

9

In this section I describe more fully what I take the typical strong emotional response to music to consist in. Sketching the outline of this experience in greater detail will aid us in determining what

[13]Nelson Goodman, *Languages of Art* (Indianapolis: Bobbs-Merrill, 1968), p. 248.
[14]Ibid., p. 250.

value it has that has not been adequately explained on any of the perspectives canvassed above.

I begin by stating the conditions of listening that conduce to a response of this kind. For clearly not every audition of an emotionally powerful work will affect a listener in that way, nor would one want it to. The first condition would seem to be that a work be in a familiar style, and that the work itself be rather familiar to the listener, so that its specific flow and character have been registered internally, but not so familiar that there is anything of boredom in hearing it unfold on the given occasion. This occurs when a piece is well known though not tiresome, when expectations are firmly aroused in the course of it but denouements remain uncertain.[15]

The second condition is generally taken to be central to the "aesthetic attitude" on any account of that frame of mind. And that is a mode of attention closely focused on the music, its structure, progression, and emergent character, with a consequent inattention to, or reduced consciousness of, the extramusical world and one's present situation in it.

A third condition is one of emotional openness to the content of music, as opposed to distant contemplation of the same. One must be willing to identify with music, to put oneself in its shoes. One must allow oneself to be moved in a receptive manner by the emotion one hears, as opposed to merely noting or even marveling at it.

Such a listener is not, however, moved straight into a slough of feelings and as a result into oblivion of the music itself. On the contrary, deep emotional response to music typically arises as a product of the most intense musical perception. It is generally in virtue of the *recognition* of emotions expressed in music, or of emotion-laden gestures embodied in musical movement, that an emotional reaction occurs.[16] Usually what happens is of an *empathetic* or *mirroring* nature. When we identify with music that we are perceiving—or perhaps better, with the person whom we imagine owns the emotions or emotional gestures we hear in the music—we share in and adopt those emotions as our own, for the course of the audition.[17] And so we end up feeling as, in imagination, the music does. The point to note here about this phenomenon is that cognition is central to it. If I don't perceive what emotions are in the music by attending to it intently, I have nothing to properly identify and empathize with.[18]

Now, what I am maintaining is simply that when the three conditions indicated above are fulfilled, then for certain musical compositions there is often an empathetic emotional response that consists in something very like experience of the emotion expressed in the music. As noted earlier, this experience includes at its core the characteristic physiological disturbances of the emotion

[15]An interesting account of the point of "optimum appreciation" for a musical work, from an information theoretical perspective, can be found in Leonard Meyer, "On Rehearing Music," in *Music, the Arts, and Ideas* (Chicago: University of Chicago Press, 1967), pp. 42–53.

[16]I leave out of account, for simplicity, the extent to which identification of emotional expression in music and evocation of feeling by music may be mutually dependent (see section 7).

[17]Of course, it is possible to have an emotional response to music that is not *empathetic*, but rather *reactive* in nature. Instead of identifying with music, we may just react directly to a quality the music is literally possessed of, or we may imaginatively regard music as an other and react to it from the outside, instead of equating ourselves with it emotionally. Examples of the former sort would be amusement at humorous music, indignation at plagiaristic music, annoyance at badly constructed music. In such response the music serves not only as the cause but as the proper object of the emotion aroused. Examples of the latter sort would be a fearful response to a threatening passage imaginatively taken to be a threatening individual, or a pitying response to an agonized passage that one imaginatively regards as a person in agony. To deal further with reactive emotional responses to music would take us too far afield. It should be obvious, however, that some of these responses pose the same problem of negative emotion in music as empathetic ones when they are ostensibly unpleasant in feeling tone.

[18]There is, naturally, much more that could be said to fill in the basic picture of how affective response to music is generated. For a description of the mirroring response to emotion characteristics in music, see S. Davies, "The Expression of Emotion in Music," *Mind*, 89 (1980): 67–86. On the mechanism of identifying with music, see the insightful discussion in R. K. Elliott, "Aesthetic Theory and the Experience of Art," in *Aesthetics*, ed. H. Osborne (London: Oxford University Press, 1972), pp. 145–57.

and its characteristic inner affect. The crucial falling off from bona fide emotion occurs in the cognitive dimension; music-emotions lack objects and associated thoughts about them.

This is not to say, however, that emotional responses to music have *no* cognitive (or thought-like) component. They do, but it is *etiolated* by comparison to that of real-life emotion. Say the emotion expressed in the music is sadness. Then in an empathetic response, in addition to physiological and affective elements, there is, in the first place, the general *idea* (or *concept*) of sadness. Since a listener is standardly made sad by apprehending and then identifying with sadness in the music, naturally the thought of that emotion is present to the mind concurrent with whatever is felt. In the second place, identifying with the music involves initially the cognitive act of imagining that the music is either *itself* a sad individual or else the *audible expression* of somebody's sadness. In the third place, such identification involves subsequently a cognitive act of imagining that one, too, is sad — that it is *one's own* sadness the music expresses — and thus, however amorphously, that one has something to be sad about.

Let us look at this last phase more closely. When one hears sad music, begins to feel sad, and imagines that one is actually sad, one must, according to the logic of the concept, be imagining that there is an object for one's sadness and that one holds certain evaluative beliefs (or attitudes) regarding it. The point, though, is that this latter imagining generally remains *indeterminate*. That is to say, one does not actually imagine a *particular* object for one's sadness and does not imaginarily hold beliefs about it. In imagining that I have actually become sad by virtue of hearing some music I allow only that my feeling has *some* focus, but without going on to specify this any further. In other words, the object of an empathetic sadness response to music is a largely formal one. When through identification with music I am saddened by the *poco allegretto* of Brahms's Third Symphony, my "sadness" is not directed on

the music, or on any real-life situation of concern to me, but instead on some featureless object posited vaguely by my imagination.[19]

Summing up, then, empathetic emotional responses to music of the sort we are interested in — the sort that our anecdotal hero underwent at the beginning of this essay — typically comprise the following: physiological and affective components of the emotion that is embodied in the music; the thought or idea of this emotion; and the imagination, through identification with the music, of oneself as actually experiencing this emotion, though without the usual determinateness of focus.

10

We are now, I think, in a decent position to offer explanations of the appeal of negative emotional response to music, the nature of which I have been attempting to make clear. I begin by acknowledging two contributions to a complete answer which emerge from views mentioned earlier. The first is the Goodmanian observation that emotional response facilitates our grasp, assessment, and description of the expression in a musical work. This is doubtless true, and even if it can hardly account totally for our willingness to suffer negative emotion from a sonata, neither should it be ignored.

The second is the Aristotelian element of catharsis. Surely in some circumstances the virtue of, say, a grief-response to music is that it allows one to bleed off in a controlled manner a certain amount of harmful emotion with which one is afflicted. One "grieves" while listening, in a pure and limited way, thus purging oneself to some extent of real grief that one has either been consciously yielding to, in typical unruly fashion, or else has been suppressing in the oubliettes of the

---

[19]It might be suggested that the imagined object of my sadness is just whatever is the object of the sadness of the sad person "in the music" with whom I am identifying. I think this may sometimes be so, but it does not really affect the matter of indeterminacy I am addressing since this object, too, remains completely unspecified, only formally indicated.

unconscious. From a cathartic perspective, negative emotional response to music is desirable because it conduces to mental health, improving the listener's future self by administering momentarily painful doses of emotional medicine in the present. There seems no denying that dark music can be therapeutic in this way; the thing to notice, though, is that the cathartic explanation applies strictly to listeners currently in the grip of unhealthy emotions, whether on a conscious or unconscious level. Yet it seems that negative emotional response has appeal for, and offers rewards to, listeners for whom this is not the case. I may seek out and relish grief, longing, and anguish from music when I am neither overwrought by these emotions nor occupied by them in subterranean fashion. Furthermore, just the raising of such emotions seems to provide satisfaction prior to any siphoning off that may ultimately ensue. Cathartic benefits, while occasionally very real, seem too indirect and prudential to be the whole or even the largest part of why we crave the experience of negative emotion from music.

11

The first point to be noted in arriving at the more comprehensive solution we seek is that emotional response to music and emotion in ordinary life differ in one crucial and obvious respect, connected to the attenuation of cognitive content in the former. Emotional responses to music typically *have no life-implications*, in contrast to their real counterparts. The "sadness" one may be made to feel by sympathetically attending to music has no basis in one's extramusical life, signals no enduring state of negative affect, indicates no problem requiring action, calls forth no persisting pattern of behavior, and in general bodes no ill for one's future. One does not really believe—though one may intermittently imagine—that one's sadness-response is objectively apt, that some situation exists in one's life which is to be bemoaned. On the other hand, if one is truly sad one must believe this, and will, accordingly, both expect one's feeling to persist until objective

conditions are changed and be disposed to take action to remedy one's unhappy state. The person having a sadness-response to music is generally free, however, from this expectation and disposition. The experience of sadness from music consists primarily of a feeling under a conception, but bracketed from and unfettered by the demands and involvements of the corresponding emotion in life.

Since negative emotional response to music is devoid of the contextual implications of such as sadness, grief, anger, we are able to focus more fully on just the feeling involved in these emotions. This opens the way for three benefits which we may reap by allowing ourselves to mirror darkly emotional music. These are benefits of enjoyment, of understanding, and of self-assurance.

To make out the first requires a somewhat startling claim, but it is one without which we cannot, I think, wholly resolve the paradox we have been addressing. This claim is that emotive affect itself, divorced from all psychological and behavioral consequences, is in virtually all cases something that we are capable of taking satisfaction in. That is to say, the pure feeling component of just about any emotion—providing it is not too violent or intense—is something we can, on balance, enjoy experiencing.

When feelings are made available to us isolated, backgroundless, and inherently limited in duration—as they are through music—we can approach them as if we were wine tasters, sampling the delights of various vintages, or like Des Esseintes, the hero of Huysmans's *À Rebours*, reveling in the flavors conveyed by a mouth organ fitted with a variety of liqueurs. We become cognoscenti of feeling, savoring the qualitative aspect of emotional life for its own sake.

This is not to say that the pure feeling has nothing unpleasant about it. If in itself it did not possess a negative tone it could hardly count as the feeling of some negative emotion. But in the detached context of musical response, it becomes possible for us to savor the feeling for its special character, since we are for once spared the additional distress that accompanies its occurrence in the context of life. The characteristic feeling at the core of, say, grief or despair has an irreducibly painful aspect, to be sure, but the distastefulness and undesirability of the emotion as a whole springs at least as much from the beliefs involved in it regarding the real existence of an evil and the consequent persistence of negative affect. An uncomfortable state that we know will not last and that testifies to no fault in our world does not pain us as it would if we had no such assurance. It is not so much the resulting feeling that we mind in grief or despair as the *significance* of that feeling, which is carried by the associated beliefs or attitudes. When these are absent, as in emotional response to music, we find ourselves able to a large extent to appreciate feelings — even negatively toned feelings — for themselves. We relish the particular qualities of such feelings to a degree sufficient to compensate us for the element of painfulness they still contain. The undistracted experience of affects of just about any sort, when free of practical consequence, appears to have intrinsic appeal for many of us. I will label this the reward of Savoring Feeling.

The second reward attaching to negative emotional response to music in virtue of its contextual freedom is that of greater understanding of the condition of feeling involved in some recognized emotion. It is notoriously difficult to say what the knowledge of how an emotion feels consists in, but I think it is clear that such knowledge, whatever it amounts to, can be augmented by emotional experiences during or after occasions of music listening. At such times we have an opportunity to introspectively scrutinize and ponder the inner affective dimension of an emotion — say, anguish — whose idea is before the mind, in a manner not open to the individual who is caught in the throes of real anguish. We can attain insight into what the feeling of anguish is *like*, not in the sense that we learn what it resembles, but in the sense that we perceive and register it more clearly. This in turn cashes out in an improved ability to recognize and to recollectively contemplate this

feeling in future. One can deepen or reinforce one's image of what it is to feel melancholy by experiencing the *poco allegretto* of Brahms's Third, or of what it is to feel hopeless passion by responding to Scriabin's C-sharp Minor Etude. Note, finally, that the cognitive reward attested to here, that of Understanding Feeling, is distinct from (though not unrelated to) the Goodmanian one mentioned earlier, that of Apprehending Expression.

The third of the rewards announced above relates directly to a person's self-respect or sense of dignity as a human being. Central to most people's ideal image of themselves is the capacity to feel deeply a range of emotions. We like to think of ourselves as able to be stirred profoundly, and in various ways, by appropriate occurrences. The individual whose emotional faculty is inactive, shallow, or one-dimensional seems to us less of a person. Since music has the power to put us into the feeling state of a negative emotion without its unwanted life consequences, it allows us to partly reassure ourselves in a nondestructive manner of the depth and breadth of our ability to feel. Having a negative emotional response to music is like giving our emotional engines a "dry run." If there is something wrong with the plane it is better to find this out on the runway than in the air. Although one would not opt to try on real grief just to see if one were capable of it, confirmation of this of a sort can perhaps be had less riskily by involvement with music. Whether such confirmation can legitimately be had in this way is not clearly to the point; for even if it is epistemically flawed, its psychological effect is real enough. Furthermore, in exercising our feeling capacities on music we might be said to tone them up, or get them into shape, thus readying ourselves for intenser and more focused reactions to situations in life. It is worth noting that this reward of emotional response to music is more naturally associated with negative than with positive emotions. It is usually not emotions like joy, amusement, or excitement that we have a need of proving ourselves equal to and prepared for feeling, and it is generally not the ability to feel those emotions which has the most weight in the common idea of an emotionally developed individual. Call this the reward of Emotional Assurance.

12

So far we have reckoned up certain rewards of negative emotional response to music which accrue to it regarded as an experience of pure feeling concurrent with the mere idea of a corresponding emotion. We must now turn to the rewards of imagining, through identification, that one is in the full emotional condition, while knowing throughout that one is not.

These are collectively as important as the rewards already considered. There seem to be at least three of them, which I will address in turn. The first is of special relevance to the paradox we have been concerned with in that it, unlike any of the other rewards mentioned, attaches almost exclusively to negative as opposed to positive emotional response to music.

If I empathetically experience feelings of despair or anguish from a despairing or anguished piece of music and also regard the music as the unfolding expression of someone's despair or anguish, then I may begin to identify with that someone and consequently to imagine, in a fashion described earlier, that I am myself in actual despair or anguish. I may even have the impression that I am generating the music de profundis as an expression of the despair or anguish I imagine I am now experiencing. In any case, since my imagined emotion is one with that of the music's persona, it will partake in the destiny and vicissitudes of that emotion as conveyed by the development of the music.

Since I have identified my emotional state with that expressed in the music, I can feel that what seems to happen to that emotion in the course of the music is happening to me as well. And this, because of the way in which emotional content is carried by musical structure, is often a source of satisfaction, especially where unpleasant or difficult emotions are involved.

Emotions presented in and imaginatively experienced through music, unlike those encountered in real life, have a character of inevitability, purposiveness, and finality about them. This is undoubtedly because they seem so intimately connected with the progress of musical substance itself as to be inseparable from it. Thus what primarily or initially characterizes musical movement or development comes to seem as well an attribute of the emotional content it underpins. Emotion in a musical composition, because of its construction, so often strikes us as having been resolved, transformed, transfigured, or triumphed over when the music is done.

When the first section in C minor of Brahms's *poco allegretto* gives way smoothly to a trio in A-flat major, we can imagine our sobbing melancholy melting into a mood of hesitant gaiety. When the main material of the *Marcia Funebre* breaks at midpoint into a stately fugue on the same themes, we can imagine our bottomless grief as metamorphosed, diffracted into shining fragments of a more easily borne pathos. And when the extended musical logic of the finale of Dvořák's Seventh Symphony in D Minor eventuates in a dissonant though shortly resolved brass-dominated yawp in the final measures, one can share in its experience of stern tragedy culminating in hard-won, reluctant resignation.

By imaginatively identifying our state with that of the music, we derive from a suitably constructed composition a sense of mastery and control over — or at least accommodation with — emotions that in the extramusical setting are thoroughly upsetting, and over which we hope to be victorious when and if the time comes. And emotional response, it should be emphasized, seems necessary to reap this benefit. Unless one actually feels something as the music is heard, and projects oneself into its condition, one will not be entitled to think: "That was my emotion, that is how I dealt with it, that is what became of it." This clearly helps compensate us for whatever additional distress derives from allowing in imagination that we are melancholy, despairing, grieving, or the like. Call this the reward of Emotional Resolution.

The second reward of identifying with music to the point of imagining oneself possessed of real negative emotion is simpler than and in a sense prior to that just discussed. If one begins to regard music as the expression of one's own current emotional state, it will begin to seem as if it issues from oneself, as if it pours forth from one's innermost being.[20] It is then very natural for one to receive an impression of expressive power — of freedom and ease in externalizing and embodying what one feels. The sense one has of the richness and spontaneity with which one's inner life is unfolding itself, even where the feelings involved are of the negative kind, is a source of undeniable joy. The unpleasant aspect of certain emotions we imagine ourselves to experience through music is balanced by the adequacy, grace, and splendor of the exposition we feel ourselves to be according that emotion. Of course we do not really have such expressive ability — that which we seem to ourselves to have while identifying with music is obviously founded in the musical abilities of the composer. But we are not actually deceiving ourselves. We do not literally believe we are creators of music. The composer's musical genius makes possible the imaginative experience described above, and we can remain aware of that throughout. But this does not take away the resulting satisfaction. The coat may be borrowed, but it is just as warm. Call this the reward of Expressive Potency.

[20]Cf. Elliot, "Aesthetic Theory," on the experience of hearing music "from within."

The last reward of imagining negative emotion I will discuss arises most clearly when a listener is willing to entertain what I call the Expressionist assumption concerning the emotional content of what he is hearing. On the Expression theory of music, espoused by Tolstoy and Cooke among others, emotion heard in a sonata is always emotion experienced by the composer on an earlier occasion, which has now been transmuted into music. The sonata is a vehicle for conveying a particular sort of emotional experience from one person to another. Now, it seems that without subscribing to the obviously inadequate Expression theory itself, we may sometimes as listeners adopt the Expressionist assumption — that the emotion expressed in a particular piece belongs to its composer's biography — while imagining ourselves to be possessed of the full emotion whose feeling has been aroused within us. If we do so we are in effect imagining that we are sharing in the precise emotional experience of another human being, the man or woman responsible for the music we hear. This, as Tolstoy so well appreciated, carried with it a decided reward — the reward of intimacy — which accrues whether the emotion is positive or negative in tone. The sense of intimate contact with the mind and soul of another, the sense that one is manifestly not alone in the emotional universe, goes a long way toward counterbalancing the possibly distressing aspect of the grief, sorrow, or anger one imagines oneself to have. The emotional separateness and alienation which occur frequently in daily living are here miraculously swept aside in imaginative identification with the composer whose feelings are, on the Expressionist assumption, plainly revealed for any listener to hear and to mirror. Call this the reward of Emotional Communion. . . .

SUGGESTED ADDITIONAL READINGS

Monroe Beardsley, *Aesthetics: Problems in the Philosophy of Criticism* 2d ed. (Indianapolis: Hackett, 1981).

H. Gene Blocker, *Philosophy of Art* (New York: Scribners, 1979). Chapter 3 includes a sympathetic discussion of expression in art.

R. G. Collingwood, *The Principles of Art*, Ch. 14. See Readings for Chapter 12.

Renee Cox, "Varieties of Musical Expressionism," in George Dickie, Richard Sclafani, and Ronald Roblin, eds., *Aesthetics: A Critical Anthology* 2d ed. (New York: St. Martin's Press, 1989).

R. K. Eliot, "Aesthetic Theory and the Experience of Art," *Proceedings of the Aristotelian Society*, n.s. 67 (1966–67): 111–26.

Nelson Goodman, *The Languages of Art* (Indianapolis: Bobbs-Merrill, 19C8).

John Hospers, "The Concept of Artistic Expression," in *Introductory Readings in Aesthetics*, ed. John Hospers (New York: Free Press, 1969). This essay delineates traditional arguments against different possible formulations of expression theory. A later version of Hospers's arguments is presented in Chapter 4 of his *Understanding the Arts* (Englewood Cliffs, N.J.: Prentice-Hall, 1982).

Guy Sircello, *Mind and Art: An Essay on the Varieties of Expression* (Princeton: Princeton University Press, 1972).

Alan Tormey, *The Concept of Expression: A Study in Philosophical Psychology and Aesthetics* (Princeton: Princeton University Press, 1971).

NOTES

1. Nelson Goodman, *The Languages of Art* (Indianapolis: Bobbs-Merrill, 1968), p. 94.

2. Alan Tormey, *The Concept of Expression: A Study in Philosophical Psychology and Aesthetics* (Princeton: Princeton University Press, 1971), p. 97.

3. John Hospers, "The Concept of Artistic Expression," in *Introductory Readings in Aesthetics*, ed. John Hospers (New York: Free Press, 1969), p. 142. Originally published in *The Proceedings of the Aristotelian Society* 55 (1954–55).

4. Leo Tolstoy, *What is Art?*, trans. Almyer Maude (Indianapolis: Bobbs-Merrill, 1960), p. 47.

5. Annie Dillard, *The Writing Life* (New York: Harper, 1989), p. 11.

6. Another expression theorist, the famous American philosopher John Dewey, draws a similar distinction. He notes (*Art as Experience* [New York: Minton, Balch & Co., 1934], p. 61) that the "mere giving way to an impulse . . . is expressive not in itself but only in reflective interpretation on the part of some observer — as the nurse may interpret the sneeze as the sign of an impending cold. As far as the act itself is concerned, it is, if purely impulsive, just a boiling over."

7. See Christine Battersby, *Gender and Genius: Towards a Feminist Aesthetics* (Bloomington, Ind.: Indiana University Press, 1989) for an illuminating discussion of the historical association of genius with the male gender.

8. Tolstoy, *What is Art?*, p. 152.

9. Tolstoy, *What is Art?*, p. 113.

10. See Hayden Herrera's *Frida: A Biography of Frida Kahlo* (New York: Harper & Row, 1983) for these and other details about this painting. Herrera gives an impressive interpretation of this quite complicated painting, which relates the painting to the issues in Frida Kahlo's life and to her emotional state.

11. Edward Tatnall Canby, jacket notes, Wolfgang A. Mozart, Symphony no. 40 in G Minor and Symphony in D Major, cond. Günther Wand, Gürzenich Orchestra of Cologne, Nonesuch H-71047, n.d.

12. Michael Levey, *The Life and Death of Mozart* (New York: Stein and Day, 1971), p. 204.

13. Levey, *Life and Death of Mozart*, p. 208.

14. Another common interpretation of expression theory is that it is meant to account for the expressive properties of artworks (for example, the sadness of the music). In that case, the failure of artists to have the same emotions as their works allegedly express is a closely

related objection. Marcia Eaton gives the nice example of a self-portrait by Rembrandt that expresses happiness, even though indirect evidence suggests that he could not have been happy when he painted it. See *Basic Issues in Aesthetics* (Belmont, Calif.: Wadsworth, 1988), p. 25.

15. Hospers, "Artistic Expression," p. 146.

16. Eduard Hanslick, *On the Beautiful in Music*, trans. Gustav Cohen (Indianapolis: Bobbs-Merrill, 1957), p. 22.

17. In *Emotions and Reasons: An Inquiry into Emotional Justification* (New York: Routledge & Kegan Paul, 1988), Patricia S. Greenspan takes issue with Levinson's position. She agrees that we experience emotions in response to the arts, and she claims that we experience real emotion even in response to nonrepresentational arts, such as instrumental music. She argues, however, that in such cases there is an *indefinite* intentional object for the emotion, i.e., that one feels grief or tenderness toward a vague "something or other" that one could not specify in any concrete terms.

18. Many philosophers simply *assume* that expressive properties are fundamental when they claim that the purpose of expression theories is to explain the propositional form "X (an artwork) expresses Y (a feeling)." For example, Marcia Eaton considers various versions of expression theory as analyses (or explanations) of "X expresses Y if and only if . . ." For example, she considers the proposition that "X expresses Y if and only if X causes (evokes or elicits) Y in the audience" (*Basic Issues in Aesthetics*, pp. 25ff.).

19. Pierre Boulez, jacket notes, *Boulez Conducts Debussy: La Mer, L'Après-midi d'un Faune, Jeux*, Columbia MS 7561, n.d.

20. Monroe Beardsley, "Postscript 1980," in *Aesthetics: Problems in the Philosophy of Criticism* (Indianapolis: Hackett Publishing Co., 1981), p. xi.

21. The most sophisticated discussion to address the former as well as the latter issue is given by Nelson Goodman in chapter 2 of *The Languages of Art*.

22. Goodman, *Languages of Art*, p. 85.

23. Guy Sircello, "Expressive Properties of Art," in Joseph Margolis, ed., *Philosophy Looks at the Arts* (Philadelphia: Temple University Press, 1987), p. 401.

24. As Nelson Goodman comments, "Finding a disjunction of conjunctions of ordinary literal properties of pictures that is even approximately equivalent to metaphorical sadness would give us a good deal of trouble" (*Languages of Art*, p. 93).

25. Benjamin Boretz, "Nelson Goodman's *Languages of Art* form a Musical Point of View," *Journal of Philosophy* 67 (1979): 548.

26. This theory is usually attributed to O. K. Bouwsma. See his essay "The Expression Theory of Art," in *Philosophical Analysis*, ed. Max Black (Ithaca, N.Y.: Cornell University Press, 1950).

27. See John Hospers, "The Concept of Artistic Expression," for a detailed critique of this theory.

28. Sircello, "Expressive Properties," p. 402.

29. Sircello, "Expressive Properties," p. 406.

30. Quoted in Goodman, *Languages of Art*, pp. 89–90.

31. Nelson Goodman claims in *The Languages of Art* that artworks do actually have expressive properties, but only metaphorically. This seems to imply that just the relativism I am suggesting is not sustainable, for we are free to apply many different metaphors to the same work. Goodman fails to consider that some of these metaphors might be incompatible with each other; in which case, what can it mean to say that the artwork "actually" possesses the (metaphorical) property?

32. Quoted in Robert Hughes, *The Shock of the New* (New York: Knopf, 1981), p. 285.

33. This is exactly the conclusion that Eduard Hanslick wants to draw, because the artwork cannot have incompatible properties. See Chapter 10.

34. Elgar is quoting the poet Percy Bysshe Shelley, from *Julian and Maddalo*. See Michael Kennedy, *Portrait of Elgar* (New York: Oxford University Press, 1968).

35. See Marcia Eaton, *Basic Issues in Aesthetics*, pp. 30–31.

36. *Selected Poems of Rainer Maria Rilke*, trans. Robert Bly (New York: Harper & Row, 1981), p. 101. Copyright © 1981 by Robert Bly. Reprinted by permission of HarperCollins Publishers.

37. Or perhaps the poem is an expression of a special experience of unity with a painting, of "seeing farther into" a painting with a sky and ponds, birds and fishes. In this sense, the poem is a vivid metaphor for our experience of all art.

38. Dillard, *Writing Life*, p. 3.

39. Stan Getz, the great tenor sax player, is quoted as saying, "Everything that has happened to me has made my music what it is" (Joseph Hooper, "Stan Getz through the Years," *New York Times Magazine* 9 June 1991, p. 79). Does this mean that his music is just about him, that his music can emotionally communicate only with Stan Getz? Not necessarily; it could mean that his life has given him a unique perspective on a wide range of life experiences and feelings that he senses in others and shares with them.

40. Danto also brings up the epistemological issue that afflicts all expression theories: How do we know we are attributing the right expression to the work? Danto hypothesizes that we would have to follow a "subtractionist stance"; that is, deviations from correct representation — supposing the artwork is representational — would be explained as due to the distortion caused by the artist's emotional expression. So, subtracting the correct representation from the work would yield the emotional expression. However, such an approach, as he points out, could lead to mistakes. Like several of the other objections I have mentioned, it is not clear whether this problem is a genuine objection to the theory or merely reflects the state of art.

41. Bernard Zurcher, *Vincent van Gogh* (New York: Rizzoli, 1985), p. 42.

42. Vincent van Gogh, Letter 195, quoted in Jan Hulsker, *The Complete van Gogh: Paintings, Drawings, Sketches* (New York: Abrams, 1980), p. 42.

43. Paul Klee, "Creative Credo," published in English translation by Norbert Guterman in *The Inward Vision: Watercolors, Drawings and Writings by Paul Klee* (New York: Abrams, 1959), excerpted in Herschel B. Chipp, *Theories of Modern Art: A Source Book by Artists and Critics* (Berkeley: University of California Press, 1968), pp. 182–86.

44. Paul Klee, "The Jena Lecture," published in translation by Paul Findlay as *On Modern Art* (London: Faber & Faber, 1948).

45. Paul Klee, *Pedagogical Sketchbook*, trans. Sibyl Moholy-Nagy (New York: Praeger, 1953).

46. Quoted in G. Di San Lazzaro, *Klee: A Study of his Life and Work*, trans. Stuart Hood (New York: Praeger, 1957), p. 127.

47. Klee, "Creative Credo," in Chipp, *Theories of Modern Art*, p. 186.

48. Klee, "Creative Credo," in Chipp, *Theories of Modern Art*, p. 185.

49. Quoted in Joseph Hooper, "Stan Getz through the Years," *New York Times Magazine*, 9 June 1991, p. 81.

CHAPTER **12**

Conclusion: The Future of Art

◀ *The Bride Stripped Bare by Her Bachelors, Even* (1915–23), by Marcel Duchamp. Also known as *The Large Glass, The Bride* occupied Duchamp for almost a decade. It is a summation of images and themes that run throughout Duchamp's work. There are hundreds of pages of notes and a story that the glass illustrates involving the bachelor male figures on the lower left and the schematic female figure in the upper left (the bride). Indeed, parts of the painting were never completed and are even supposed to be imagined! As such, *The Bride* illustrates a direction art has traveled in the twentieth century toward an intellectual complexity in which the work becomes an idea that transcends its physical embodiment.

Art is the community's medicine for the worst disease of
mind, the corruption of consciousness.

— R. G. Collingwood

THE PRESENT

In "Modernist Painting," the critic Clement Greenberg (see the Readings for Chapter 6)
suggests that at the end of the eighteenth century the arts were in danger of losing their status:

> At first glance the arts might seem to have been in a situation like religion's. Having
> been denied by the Enlightenment all tasks they could take seriously, they looked as
> though they were going to be assimilated to entertainment pure and simple, and
> entertainment itself looked as though it were going to be assimilated, like religion, to
> therapy. The arts could save themselves from this leveling down only by demonstrat-
> ing that the kind of experience they provided was valuable in its own right and not to
> be obtained from any other kind of activity. (p. 155)

The arts are in even greater danger today. After two centuries of lofty status and massive
experimentation, the high arts are threatened on all sides, especially in the United States,
where the roots of art in mass society seem to be very shallow (see the Readings for Chapter 2).

Movements to suppress and censor artworks, whether public sculpture, rock and roll
songs, or art photographs, have grown strong in recent years. For example, in September
1990 the Cincinnati Arts Center and its director were prosecuted under local antiobscenity
statutes for mounting a show (in April 1990) of the homosexual erotic photographs of Robert
Mapplethorpe — a show that traveled around the country and was mounted in many other
museums without any public outcry. Although the jury acquitted the defendants, this episode
marks the first time an American art museum or official was prosecuted for the contents of an
art show.[1] (See Figure 4.1.) Earlier, in June 1989, the prestigious Corcoran Gallery of Art in
Washington, D.C., canceled a major retrospective exhibition of Robert Mapplethorpe's
photographs to avoid the controversy surrounding his work. Andres Serrano is another
photographer who incensed some members of the public with his now infamous photograph
of a plastic crucifix in urine, *Piss Christ*. The works of Mapplethorpe and Serrano were a focal
point for attacks on the National Endowment for the Arts (NEA), which had funded
institutions that displayed their artworks.

Indeed, the NEA has been the principal target of attempts to control the production and
display of offensive artworks. Various controversial artworks became the center of attention
in 1989, including the photographs of Mapplethorpe and Serrano. Since then, some politicians have made a systematic attempt either to eliminate the NEA or to control the content of
what it subsidizes. The efforts are ongoing in skirmishes among Congress, which authorizes
NEA funding, the NEA itself, which funds grants through a peer panel system, and the courts.
In 1989, for instance, Congress placed a ban on funding obscene art, and the Senate proposed

to ban for five years all NEA funding for two institutions that had exhibited Mapplethorpe and Serrano photographs.[2] The NEA then required a sort of loyalty oath, a no-obscenity pledge, from artists and institutions receiving grants. As a result, many artists and institutions, including dance and theater companies, university presses, art reviews and poetry magazines, public radio stations, and universities, declined the grants. Some of these recipients took the issue to court, and the pledge was ruled unconstitutional.[3] Meanwhile, in reauthorizing the NEA for 1991, Congress replaced the antiobscenity clause with a phrase requiring all NEA grants to conform to "general standards of decency and to show respect for the diverse beliefs and values of the American public."[4] This seems a clear recipe for eliminating funding for controversial art of any sort.

Those in favor of controlling the contents of arts that are funded argue that the public has a right to control what it pays for; this is not censorship, they say. Those against such restrictions argue that it will lead — indeed, in the case of the Corcoran, already has led — to self-censorship as artists and institutions avoid topics and points of view that are controversial or that some members of the public might deem offensive. It certainly seems true that because most major cultural institutions depend at least in part on public subsidies for their existence, bans on funding institutions that display controversial or offensive art would effectively make such works largely inaccessible to the general public.

Public funds for the arts are also in great danger from economic hard times, which have led many people to demand that spending be limited only to those activities perceived to have a high priority to society. The symphony orchestras of several American cities have gone bankrupt since the 1970s, for example, and there are many fewer alternative performance spaces than there were in the 1970s. Meanwhile, composers of classical music have discarded the most advanced twelve-tone music in favor of minimalist and romantic styles from the past, seemingly to win back audiences who could not accept the more difficult music of the twentieth century. It is unclear, however, that composers have developed any new style that will either have the public appeal of earlier forms of music or preserve the intellectual content of twelve-tone music or the avant-garde experiments of such leading twentieth-century composers as John Cage, Karlheinz Stockhausen, Pierre Boulez, and Milton Babbitt. Parallel stories can be told about the other arts as each draws back from experimentation in favor of public support. Clearly, recent events vividly demonstrate the naïveté of taking for granted what was once universally assumed without argument: the high status of the arts and automatic public and political support for art.

The political forces that are advocating limits on the arts are a symptom of the isolation of the artworld from much of the general culture. The cause of this isolation is very complex; clearly it is the result of a combination of cultural and political factors. But we cannot ignore in this equation trends within the artworld, both trends in the arts themselves and trends in art *theory*. The fact is that contemporary aesthetic theory, whether "modernist" or "postmodernist," American or European, *assumes* the value of art — without any discussion, entirely ignoring pressing issues about the purpose and direction of art today. Value questions have been consistently ignored or obscured by every tradition of recent art writing. As an example of the way questions have been obscured we need only note how Clement Greenberg follows up his trenchant characterization of the nineteenth-century crisis in the arts. He argues that modernism solved the problem by promoting an exploration of the essence of each art form: "What had to be exhibited and made explicit was that which was unique and irreducible not only in art in general, but also in each particular art" (p. 155). But, as we saw, Greenberg quite rightly specifies *two* demonstrations that must be made, only one of which is the demonstration of the uniqueness of art. The other is the demonstration of how the experience of each art is *valuable in its own right*. This, which is surely the more important requirement, does not follow from uniqueness. Some experiences, and some kinds of artifacts, are unique but not valuable (or desirable) at all. Greenberg concentrates, however, on the uniqueness of each art—that is what modernism is to him—forgetting entirely the question: what is the *value* of these unique experiences?

These trends in art theory have been dominant since the 1940s. They have been coupled with skepticism at or even disdain for traditional theories of art, both in critical writing and in aesthetic theorizing. This has contributed to a crisis of theory in the arts, for, as we have seen in the last three chapters, the traditional theories of art do address the pressing value questions with plausible and sometimes persuasive answers. If we are once again to address the value questions, we will need to start with the traditional accounts. They tend to converge on a few basic elements: emotional communication of some sort; expression of feelings that cannot be done in any other way; truthful but subjective perspectives on the external world; insights into the nature of our socially experienced world. In short, truth, feeling, and form, and perhaps even beauty, are central, as are the notions that truth, feeling, and form are related to the world outside the artwork and that the truth, feeling, and form comprising art cannot be duplicated by any discursive or scientific activities or representations. This is how art is both unique and valuable.

Unless the theories on which these value claims are based are hopelessly flawed, we can reasonably expect that these are the elements with which to answer the challenges we delineated in our beginning chapters. It is thus mandatory that thinkers who reject the traditional theories actually demonstrate that they are untenable. Critics of the traditional theories also owe us something else, then: a positive account of the value of art. It will require ingenuity to produce such an account, for it will not be based on appeals to emotion or expression, nor to beauty or form, nor to insights (formal or substantive) into reality that only artworks can provide.

THE FUTURE

The weight of the discussion throughout this book has made clear that the relation of art to society is a crucial question. Having insisted on that general question, we can turn to two fascinating sub-questions.

1. What *should* the relation of art to society be, that is, what is the *ideal* relation of art to society? Is there an ideal relation or role for art to fill?
2. What will that relation in fact be in the future? Will the relation of art to society remain the same in the future as it has been in the past?

Both questions concern the place of art in society. In "The End of Art" (see the Readings) Arthur Danto addresses the second question, arguing, very disturbingly, that we are at the end of art. For him, Art with a capital *A* is a historically conditioned concept that may now be coming to an end. The era of artworks as special artifacts with special meanings determined by their place in the historical context is probably over, according to him. Artworks of a sort will still be made: "Decoration, self-expression, entertainment are, of course, abiding human needs. There will always be a service for art to perform, if artists are content with that"

(p. 410). But because decoration or entertainment have never been considered "elevated" qualities or functions that are unique to art, Danto implies that the meaning and high value of art will be given up in the future, whether we like it or not.

Danto's vision is historicist. He believes that art is tied to a particular historical context and gains its meaning from that context; the meaning of artworks up until now has been determined by the place they occupy in the ongoing historical development of art. But if art has run its historical course, art works will no longer exist in a meaning-conferring context. R. G. Collingwood formulates a strongly opposing view based on his distinctive version of expression theory (see Chapter 11). Collingwood addresses the question of the relation of the artist to society in the last few chapters of *The Principles of Art* (see the Readings). What art really is, for Collingwood, is also what it *ought* to be. Perhaps this is best summed up by his claim that the artist is the conscience of the community: "The artist must prophesy not in the sense that he foretells things to come, but in the sense that he tells his audience, at risk of their displeasure, the secrets of their own hearts" (p. 420). The function of art — *real* art — is so important that there will always be an essential place for the arts as long as there is need to express emotional truths that the community needs to know. The importance of truthful expression, Collingwood contends, does not reside in the place of the artwork in the history of art but, rather, in its place in the common personal history of the artist and his or her audience and their real life together.

We can relate these divergent views about the future of art to the fundamental question of whether art is or is not an autonomous realm. Danto's view grows out of a belief that the arts are autonomous, whereas Collingwood's is strongly anti-autonomous. Those who believe that the arts are independent of social and psychological functions find it possible to conceive of an end to art — nothing, after all, *requires* us to have art — but those who consider the arts as a "condition of life," as Tolstoy puts it, naturally see them going on as long as life does.

The artwork, for Collingwood, is not to be treated as an object independent of the emotional lives and truths about the artist and his or her community. In the last chapters of *The Principles of Art*, he rejects the seeming consequence of expression theories generally, namely, that they reinforce an individualistic view of art. According to this individualistic view, art is simply about artists and their feelings, and audiences merely overhear these expressions, which they may or may not find relevant to themselves. On this view, artists do not need audiences, and audiences do not need artists. Collingwood — as does Tolstoy in a different way — strongly objects to this understanding of expression theory.

The crux of Collingwood's argument against this interpretation of expression theory is his denial of what he calls "individualistic" psychology. As we learned in Chapter 11, the function of real art, for Collingwood, is self-discovery; the artwork formulates specific emotional truth about a particular subject matter. The outcome of real art is self-knowledge. This does not, however, imply that the artwork is relevant only to the artist, unless we also assume that the artist is a unique and isolated individual — that his self-knowledge is unique to him. But this is what Collingwood denies. Collingwood suggests not only that artists ought to see it as their business to express, that is, discover, the emotions of the communities of which they are members, but also that the audience as a whole is an essential collaborator in the expression of the artists' own feelings. No artist, for Collingwood, is an isolated and self-sufficient creator: "But a man, in his art as in everything else, is a finite being. Everything that he does is done in relation to others like himself" (p. 415). The artist inherits most of what he feels and thinks and the means to express these from the community and from other artists and the artistic tradition. Hence artists are not the sole authors of their expressions. Rather, they collaborate with the preceding artistic tradition, with other artists, and with their audience, whether they acknowledge this fact or not. To know whether the artist's expression is authentic or whether it is the victim of "corrupt consciousness" (self-deception), it is essential that the audience be brought in to see if the expression is genuine, for it must be their expression as well.[5] The constant process of becoming aware of oneself, which is art for Collingwood, requires the reactions of others to validate that the awareness is true, that the feelings expressed are *our* real feelings: "If he has a new thought, he must explain it to others, in order that, finding them able to understand it, he may be sure it is a good one. If he has a new emotion, he must express it to others, in order that, finding them able to share it, he may be sure his consciousness of it is not corrupt" (p. 415). Thus to the extent that we need to overcome our tendency to emotional self-deception as a community, real art will be a necessary component of our social life.

READINGS FOR CHAPTER 12

Arthur Danto, "The End of Art"
R. G. Collingwood, from *The Principles of Art*

The End of Art

Arthur Danto

There are philosophical visions of history which allow, or even demand, a speculation regarding the future of art. Such a speculation concerns the question of whether art has a future, and must be distinguished from one which merely concerns the art of the future, if we suppose art will go on and on. Indeed, the latter speculation is more difficult in a way, just because of the difficulties which go with trying to imagine what the artworks of the future will look like or how they will be appreciated. Just think how out of the question it would have been, in 1865, to predict the forms of Post-Impressionist painting, or to have anticipated, as late as 1910, that there would be, only five years in the future, a work such as Duchamp's *In Advance of the Broken Arm*, which, even when accepted as a work of art, retained its identity as a quite ordinary snow shovel. Comparable examples can be drawn from the other arts, especially as we approach our own century, when music and poetry and dance have yielded exemplars which could not have been perceived as art had anything like them appeared in earlier times, as sets of words or sounds or movements. The visionary artist Albert Robida began in 1882 the serial publication of *Le vingtième siècle*. It meant to show the world as it would be in 1952. His pictures are filled with wonders to come: *le téléphonoscope*, flying machines, television, underwater metropolises, but the pictures themselves are unmistakably of their own era, as is the way much of what they show is shown. Robida imagined there would be restau-

rants in the sky to which customers would come in airborne vehicles. But the boldly anticipated eating places are put together of ornamental ironworks of the sort we associate with Les Halles and the Gare St. Lazare, and look a lot like the steamboats that floated the Mississippi at that time, in proportion and in decorative fretwork. They are patronized by gentlemen in top hats and ladies in bustles, served by waiters wearing long aprons from the Belle Epoque, and they arrive in balloons Montgolfier would recognize. We may be certain that were Robida to have depicted an underwater art museum, its most advanced works would be Impressionist paintings, if Robida had eyes even for those. In 1952, the most advanced galleries were showing Pollock, De Kooning, Gottlieb, and Klein, which would have been temporally unimaginable in 1882. Nothing so much belongs to its own time as an age's glimpses into the future: Buck Rogers carries the decorative idioms of the 1930s into the twenty-first century, and *now* looks at home with Rockefeller Center and the Cord automobile; the science fiction novels of the 1950s project the sexual moralities of the Eisenhower era, along with the dry martini, into distant eons, and the technical clothing worn by its spacemen belong to that era's haberdashery. So were *we* to depict an interplanetary art gallery, it would display works which, however up to the minute they look to us, will belong to the history of art by the time there are such galleries, just as the mod clothing we put on the people we show will belong to the history of costume in no time at all. The future is a kind of mirror in which we can show only ourselves, though it seems to us a window through which we may see things to come. Leonardo's wonderful saying, that *ogni dipintore dipinge se*,* implies an unintended historical limitation, as may be seen from Leonardo's own visionary drawings, so profoundly part of their own time. We may imagine *that* all sorts of things will come to be. But when we seek to *imagine* those things, they inevitably will look like things that *have* come to be, for we have only the forms we know to give them.

Even so, we may speculate historically on the future of art without committing ourselves on what the artworks of the future are to be like, if there are to be any; and it is even possible to suppose that art itself has no future, though artworks may still be produced post-historically, as it were, in the aftershock of a vanished vitality. Such indeed was a thesis of Hegel, certain of whose views have inspired the present essay, for Hegel said quite unequivocally that art as such, or at least at its highest vocation, is quite finished with as a historical moment, though he did not commit himself to the prediction that there would be no more works of art. He might have argued that, certain as he was that his astonishing thesis was true, he had nothing to say about those works to come, which might, perhaps must, be produced in ways he could not anticipate and enjoyed in ways he could not understand. I find it an extraordinary thought that the world should have gone through what one might term the Age of Art, parallel to the way in which, according to a theological speculation of the Christian theorist Joachim of Flores, the Age of the Father came to an end with the birth of His Son, and the Age of the Son with the Age of the Holy Spirit. Joachim did not claim that those whose historical fulfillment lay in the Age of the Father will become extinct or that their forms of life will abruptly disappear in the Age of the Son: they may continue to exist past the moment of their historical mission, historical fossils, so to speak, as Joachim

would have supposed the Jews to be, whose time on the stage of history he believed over with. So though there will be Jews in time to come, whose forms of life may evolve in unforeseeable ways, still, their history will no longer be coincident with the history of History itself, conceived of as Joachim did, in the grandest philosophical manner.

In almost precisely this way, Hegel's thought was that for a period of time the energies of history coincided with the energies of art, but now history and art must go in different directions, and though art may continue to exist in what I have termed a post-historical fashion, its existence carries no historical significance whatever. Now such a thesis can hardly be pondered outside the framework of a philosophy of history it would be difficult to take seriously were the urgency of art's future not somehow raised from within the artworld itself, which can be seen today as having lost any historical direction, and we have to ask whether this is temporary, whether art will regain the path of history — or whether this destructured condition *is* its future: a kind of cultural entropy. So whatever comes next will not matter because the concept of art is internally exhausted. Our institutions — museums, galleries, collectors, art journals, and the like — exist against the assumption of a significant, even a brilliant, future. There is an inevitable commercial interest in what is to come now, and who are to be the important practitioners in movements next to come. It is very much in the spirit of Joachim that the English sculptor William Tucker has said, "The 60's was the age of the critic. Now it's the age of the dealer." But suppose it *has* really all come to an end, and that a point has been reached where there can be change without development, where the engines of artistic production can only combine and recombine known forms, though external pressures may favor this or that combination? Suppose it is no longer a historical possibility that art should continue to astonish us, that in this sense the Age of Art is internally worn out, and that in Hegel's stunning and melancholy phrase, a form of life has grown old?

*[Every painter paints himself.]

Is it possible that the wild effervescence of the artworld in the past seven or eight decades has been a terminal fermentation of something the historical chemistry of which remains to be understood? I want to take Hegel quite seriously, and to sketch a model of the history of art in which something like it may even be said to make sense. Better to appreciate the sense it does make, I shall first sketch two rather more familiar models of art history, for the model which will finally interest me presupposes them in a striking and almost dialectical way. It is an interesting fact that though the first model has application primarily to mimetic art, to painting and sculpture and moving pictures, the second model will include them and include a great deal more of art than mimesis can easily characterize. The final model will apply to art in so comprehensive a way that the question of whether art has come to an end will have as wide a reference as the term "art" itself has, though its most dramatic reference will be to the objects purveyed in what is narrowly known as "the artworld." Indeed, part of the explanation lies in the fact that the boundaries between painting and the other arts — poetry and performance, music and dance — have become radically unstable. It is an instability induced by the factors which make my final model historically possible, and which enables the dismal question to be put. I will conclude by asking how we are to adapt to the fact that the question has an affirmative answer, that art really is over with, having become transmuted into philosophy.

· · · · · · · · · · · · · · · · · · · ·

Whatever the case, it has always been possible to imagine, at least grossly, the future of art construed in terms of representational progress. One knew in principle what the agenda was, and hence what progress would have to be if there was to be progress. Visionaries could say such things as "Someday pictures will move," without knowing how it was to be achieved, just as not long ago they could say, "Someday men will walk on the moon," without knowing, again, quite how *this* was to be achieved. But then, and this has been the main reason for canvassing this entire theory,

it would be possible to speak of the end of art, at least as a progressive discipline. When, for every perceptual range R, an equivalent could be technically generated, then art would be over with, just as science would be over with when, as was thought to be a genuine possibility in the nineteenth century, everything was known. In the nineteenth century, for example, it was believed that logic was a finished science, and even that physics was, with a few nagging details to mop up. But there is no internal reason for us to think that science, or art, has to be endless, and so there was always a question that would have to be faced, as to what post-progressive life would be like. To be sure, we have more or less abandoned this model in art, since the production of perceptual equivalence no longer much dazzles us, and in any case there are certain definite limits set when narrativization becomes an artistic fact. Even so, as we shall see, the model has an oblique pertinence even today.

Before coming to that, however, I want to raise a philosophical point. So long as the philosophy of art was articulated in terms of success or failure in technologies of perceptual equivalence, it would have been difficult to get an interestingly general definition of art. Aristotle widened the notion of imitation to include the imitation of an action, in order to bring narrative drama into the scope of that concept, but at that point the theory of mimesis parts company with the concept of perceptual equivalences, since it is far from plain that drama presents us with merely perceptual equivalences to what a sort of eyewitness to the action would perceive. And while this is, in the case of dramatic presentations, a mistakenly entertainable ideal, it is not so at all when we consider *fiction* as the description of an action. And when we think of description as against mimesis, we may immediately notice that it is not at all clear that there is any room for the concept of progress or of technological transformations at all. Let me explain this.

Thinkers have, from Lao Tzu to the present, lamented or celebrated the inadequacies of language. It is felt that there are descriptive limits, and then important things beyond these limits which language cannot express. But to the degree that this is true, no expansion of representational possibilities, say by introducing new terms into the language, will remedy the situation, largely because the complaint is against descriptivity itself, which simply is too distant from reality to give us the experience reality itself affords. And it is a mark of the natural languages that whatever can be said in one can be said in any (and what *cannot* be said in one cannot be said in any), allowing always for differences of felicity and degrees of roundaboutness. So there cannot ever have been a technological problem of expanding the descriptive resources of the natural languages: they are equivalently universal.

I do not mean to imply that there are no limits to language, but only that whatever they are, nothing is going to count as progress toward their overcoming, since this would still be within language as a representational system. So there is no logical room for the concept of progress. At no point in the history of literature, for example, would visionaries have been able to prophesy that someday men will be able to say certain things — in part perhaps because in saying what men will be able to say, it is *already* said. Of course someone might have been able to say that someday men will be able to talk about things then forbidden, sex perhaps, or be able to use language to criticize institutions which they are not able to do now. But this would be a matter of moral progress, or political progress, if it is that, and would have as much application to pictures as to words. Whatever the value of doing so, we can today see things in movies it would have been unthinkable to show a generation ago — the star's breasts, say. But this is not *technological* advance.

The linear or progressive model of the history of art thus finds it best examples in painting and sculpture, then in movies and talkies and, if you wish, feelies. There has never been a problem of *describing* motion, or depth, or for that matter palpability. "Her soft and yielding flesh" describes a perceptual experience for which there is no mimetic equivalent. Our next model will make a more general definition possible, since it is not thwarted by the differences between words and pictures. But then it eliminates those factors from the essence of art which made it possible to think of art as a progressive discipline.

I like to surmise that a confirmation of my historical thesis — that the task of art to produce equivalences to perceptual experiences passed, in the late nineteenth and early twentieth centuries, from the activities of painting and sculpture to those of cinematography — [lies] in the fact that painters and sculptors began conspicuously to abandon this goal at just about the same time that all the basic strategies for narrative cinema were in place. By about 1905, almost every cinematic strategy since employed had been discovered, and it was just about then that painters and sculptors began asking, if only through their actions, the question of what could be left for *them* to do, now that the torch had, as it were, been taken up by other technologies. I suppose that the history of artistic progress could be run backward: we can imagine the projected end state as having been achieved, but now it seems a good idea, for whatever reason, to replace perceptual equivalences with cues to inference — perhaps because a greater value gets put on inference (= Reason) than on perception. Bit by bit cinematography gets replaced with the cues to kinematic motion of the sort we find in Rosa Bonheur or Rodin, and so on, until, I suppose, perceptual equivalence disappears from art altogether and we get an art of pure descriptivity, where words replace perceptual stimuli. And who knows, this may seem too closely tied to experience and the next move might be music. But given the way progress itself *was* conceived, about 1905 it appeared that painters and sculptors could only justify their activities by redefining art in ways which had to be shocking indeed to those who continued to judge painting and sculpture by the criteria of the progressive paradigm, not realizing that a transformation in technology now made practices appropriate to those criteria more and more archaic.

The Fauves are good examples. Consider the portrait by Matisse of his wife done in 1906, in which Madame Matisse is shown with a green stripe down her nose (indeed, the title of the painting is *The Green Stripe*). Chiang Yee told me of a painting done by a Jesuit artist of a Chinese emperor's favorite concubine, which shocked her, since she knew her face was not half black and *he* used shadows. Instruction on how the world really looks would have made her recognize that *she* really looked the way he had shown her, given the realities of light and shade. But nothing of that sort is going to redeem Matisse's painting for the history of perceptual equivalences, not even if there happened to be a greenish shadow along his subject's nose — for it would not have been *that* particular green. Nor were ladies at that time using nose shadow as those of our time use eye shadow. Nor was she suffering nasal gangrene. So one could only conclude (as people did) that Matisse had forgotten how to paint, had remembered how to paint but had gone crazy, was sane but was perverting his skills to the end of shocking the bourgeoisie, or trying to put something over on the collectors, critics, and curators (who are the three C's of the artworld).

These would have been standard rationalizations of objects, beginning to appear in epidemic quantity just then, which were unquestionably *paintings*, but which fell short by so considerable a degree of perceptual equivalence to anything in either the real world or the artworld, that some explanation of their existence seemed imperative. Until, that is, it began to be grasped that only relative to a theory which may have been put to a challenge was there any discrepancy at all, and that if there was one, well, it might be the fault of the theory. In science, ideally at least, we don't blame the world when our theories don't work — we change the theories until they do work. And so it was with Post-Impressionist painting. It became increasingly clear that a new theory was urgently required, that the artists were not failing to yield up perceptual equivalences but were after something not to be understood in those terms primarily or at all. It is to the credit of aesthetics that its practitioners responded to this with theories which, however inadequate, recognized the need, and a good example of at least a suitable theory was that painters were not so much represent-

ing as expressing. Croce's *Estetica come scienza dell'espressione* appeared in 1902. Suppose then that *The Green Stripe* tries to get us to see how Matisse felt about the subject shown, his own wife, calling for a complex act of interpretation on the part of the viewer.

This account is remarkable for the fact that it incorporates the theory of perceptual equivalences in the sense that it presupposes the discrepancies, which it then explains as due to feelings. It acknowledges, as it were, the intensional character of emotional states, that feelings are *about*, or *toward*, some object or state of affairs; and since Croce supposes art to be a kind of language, and language a form of communication, the communication of feeling will succeed to just the extent that the work can show what object it is toward which the feeling is expressed — e.g., the artist's wife. Then the discrepancies between the way this object is in fact shown and the way it would be shown were mere perceptual equivalence aimed at, no longer marks a distance to be covered by the progress of art or by the artist's mastery of illusionist technique, but rather consists in the externalization or objectification of the artist's feelings toward what he shows. The feeling is then communicated to the viewer to just the degree that the viewer can infer it on the basis of the discrepancies. Indeed, the viewer must generate some hypothesis to the effect that the object is shown in the way it is because the artist feels about the object the way he does. Thus De Kooning paints a woman as the locus of slashes. El Greco paints saints as stretched verticalities, Giacometti molds figures as impossibly emaciated, not for optical reasons nor because there really are women, saints, or persons like these, but because the artists respectively reveal feelings of aggressiveness, spiritual longing, or compassion. It would be very difficult to suppose De Kooning is expressing compassion, let alone spirituality, or that El Greco is expressing aggression. But of course the ascription of feelings is always epistemologically delicate.

It becomes particularly delicate when the theory recommends the view that the object represented by the work becomes the occasion for expressing something about it, and we then begin to reconstitute the history of art along these new lines. For we now have to decide to what degree the discrepancies with an ideal perceptual equivalence are a matter of technical shortfall, and to what degree a matter of expression. Obviously we are not to read all discrepancies as expressive, for then the concept of progress no longer applies: we must assume that in a great many cases an artist would eliminate discrepancies if he but knew how. Even so, certain discrepancies which would be laughable from the point of view of representation become artistically fundamental from that of expression. At the time of the Fauves, the deviations emphasized by apologists of the new art and subscribers to the new theory were made acceptable by pointing to the fact that the artist after all could *draw*: one pointed in evidence to Matisse's academic exercises, or to Picasso's amazing canvases of his sixteenth year. But these anxious questions lost their force after a time as expression seemed more and more to carry the definitional properties of art. Objects became less and less recognizable and finally disappeared altogether in Abstract Expressionism, which of course meant that interpretation of purely expressionist work required reference to objectless feelings: joy, depression, generalized excitement, etc. What was interesting was the fact that since there could be paintings which were purely expressive and hence not explicitly representational at all, representationality must disappear from the definition of art. But even *more* interesting from our perspective is the fact that the *history* of art acquires a totally different structure.

It does so because there is no longer any reason to think of art as having a progressive history: there simply is not the possibility of a developmental sequence with the concept of expression as there is with the concept of mimetic representation. There is not because there is no mediating technology of expression. I do not mean to imply that novel technologies of representation may not admit novel modes of expression: beyond question there are expressive possibilities in cinema that simply had no parallel in the kind of art cinema transformed. But these new possibilities would not constitute a progressive development—viz., there would be no basis for saying that we now can express what we could express badly or not at all before, as we could say that we now can show things we could only show badly or not at all before. So the history of art has no future of the sort that can be extrapolated as it can against the paradigm of progress: it sunders into a sequence of individual acts, one after another. Of course there may be feelings one dare not express at a given time but which in time one can express, but the raising or lowering of the thresholds of expressive inhibition belong to the history of morality. And of course there may be a history of *learning* to express feelings, as through a kind of therapy, but then this would belong to the general history of freedom, with no particular application to art. Heidegger has said that not one step has been taken since Aristotle's *Rhetoric* in the philosophical analysis of feelings—but this surely is because the range of human feelings can be very little different from what it was in ancient times. There may be new objects for these feelings, even new ways of expressing them—but once more this is not a development history.

There is a further point. Once art becomes construed as expression, the work of art must send us ultimately to the state of mind of its maker, if we are to interpret it. Realistically speaking, artists of a given period share a certain expressive vocabulary, which is why, right or wrong, my casual interpretations of De Kooning, El Greco, and Giacometti seem at least natural. Even so, this seems to me a quite external fact, not at all necessary to the concept of expression, and conceivably each artist could express himself in his own way, so that one vocabulary, as it were, would be incommensurable with another, which makes possible a radically discontinuous view of the history of art, in which one style of art follows another, as in an archipelago, and we might in principle imagine any sequence we choose. In any case we must understand each work, each corpus, in the terms that define that particular artist we are studying, and what is true of De Kooning need have nothing to do with what is true of anyone else. The concept of expression makes such a view possible, relativizing art, as it does, to individual artists. The history of art is just the lives of the artists, one after another.

It is striking that the history of science is thought of somewhat along these lines today — not, as in the optimism of the nineteenth century, as a linear, inevitable progression toward an end state of total cognitive representation, but as a discontinuous sequence of phases between which there is a radical incommensurability. It is almost as though the semantics of scientific terms were like the semantics of terms like "pain," where each user is referring to something different and speaking in a private idiom — so that to the degree that we understand one another at all, we do so on our own terms. Thus "mass" means something different in each phase of science, in part because it is redefined with each theory that employs it, so that synonymy between theory and theory is ruled out. But even if we stop short of this extreme lexical radicalism, the mere structure of history might insure some degree of incommensurability. Imagine the history of art reversed, so that it begins with Picasso and Matisse, passes through Impressionism and the Baroque, suffers a decline with Giotto, only to reach its pinnacle with the original of the *Apollo Belvedere*, beyond which it would be impossible to imagine a further advance. Strictly speaking, the works in question *could* have been produced in that order. But they could not have the interpretation, nor hence the structure, we perceive them as having under the present chronology. Picasso, only for example, is constantly referring to the history of art he systematically deconstructs, and so presupposes those past works. And something of the same sort is true of science. Even if scientists are not as conscious of their history as artists are, in truth there are intertheoretic references which assure a degree of incommensurability, if only because we know Galileo and he could not have known us, and to the degree that our uses refer to his, the terms we use cannot have the same meanings his

did. So there is an important respect in which we *have* to understand the past in our *own* terms, and there can in consequence be no uniform usage from phase to phase.

There have been philosophies of history which have made these incommensurabilites central, if not for precisely the reasons I have sketched. I am thinking just now of Spengler, who dissolved what had been assumed to be the linear history of the West into three distinct and self-contained historical periods, Classical, Magian, and Faustian, each with its own vocabulary of cultural forms, between which no commensurability of meaning could be assumed. The classical temple, the domed basilica, the vaulted cathedral are less three moments in a linear history than three distinct expressions in the medium of architecture of distinct underlying cultural spirits. In some absolute sense the three periods succeed one another, but only in the way in which one generation succeeds another, with the specific analogy to be drawn that each generation reaches and expresses its maturity in its own way. Each of them defines a different world, and it is the worlds that are incommensurable. Spengler's book was notoriously titled *The Decline of the West*, and it was reckoned exceedingly pessimistic when it first appeared, in part because of the biological metaphors Spengler employed, which required each of his civilizations to go through its own cycle of youth, maturity, decline, and death. So the future of *our* art is very dim, if we accept his premises, but — and how optimistic he after all was — a new cycle will begin, with its own peaks, and we can no more imagine it than *we* could have been imagined from an earlier cycle. So *art* will have a future, it is only that *our* art will not. *Ours* is a form of life that has grown old. So you could look on Spengler as saying something dark or something bright, depending upon how you feel about your own culture within the framework of the severe relativism it, as indeed all the views I have been discussing in this section, presupposes.

And the reason I am stressing this relativism here is that the question I began with, whether art has a future, clearly is antirelativistic in that it really does presuppose a linear history in some sense. This has an absolutely profound philosophical implication, in that it requires an internal connection between the way we define art and the way we think of the history of art. Only, for instance, if we first think of art as representation can we then think of art as having the sort of history which fulfills the progressive model. If, on the other hand, we think of art as simply being expression, or the communication of feelings, as Croce did, well, it just can't have a history of that sort and the question of the end of art can have no application, just because the concept of expression goes with that sort of incommensurability in which one thing just comes after another thing. So that even if it is a fact that artists express feelings, well, this is only a fact, and cannot be the essence of art *if* art has the kind of history within which the question of its coming to an end makes sense. That art is the business of perceptual equivalence is consistent with its having that sort of history, but then, as we saw, it is insufficiently general as a definition of art. So what emerges from this dialectic is that if we are to think of art as having an end, we need a conception of art history which is linear, but a theory of art which is general enough to include representations other than the sort illusionistic painting exemplifies best: literary representations, for example, and even music.

Now Hegel's theory meets all these demands. His thought requires that there be genuine historical continuity, and indeed a kind of progress. The progress in question is not that of an increasingly refined technology of perceptual equivalence. Rather, there is a kind of *cognitive* progress, where it is understood that art progressively approaches that kind of cognition. When the cognition is achieved, there really is no longer any point to or need for art. Art is a transitional stage in the coming of a certain kind of knowledge. The question then is what sort of cognition this can be, and the answer, disappointing as it must sound at first, is the knowledge of what art is. Just as we saw is required, there is an internal connection between the nature and the history of

art. History ends with the advent of self-consciousness, or better, self-knowledge. I suppose in a way our personal histories have that structure, or at least our educational histories do, in that they end with maturity, where maturity is understood as knowing — and accepting — what or even who we are. Art ends with the advent of its own philosophy. I shall now tell this last story by returning to the history of past perceptual art.

The success of the Expression Theory of art is also the failure of the Expression Theory of art. Its success consisted in the fact that it was able to explain all of art in a uniform way — i.e., as the expression of feelings. Its failure consisted in the fact that it has only one way of explaining all of art. When discontinuities first appeared as puzzling phenomena in the progressive history of representation, it was a genuine insight that perhaps artists were trying to express rather than primarily to represent. But after about 1906, the history of art simply seemed to be the history of discontinuities. To be sure, this could be accommodated to the theory. Each of us has his or her own feelings, so it is to be expected that these will be expressed in individual ways, and even in incommensurable ways. Most of us, of course, express our feelings in very similar ways, and there are forms of expression which must in fact be understood in evolutionary, not to say physiological, terms: we are built to express feelings in ways we all recognize. But then the theory is that these are artists and artists are defined in part through the uniqueness of their feelings. The artist is different from the rest of us. But the trouble with this plausible if romantic account lay in the fact that each new movement, from Fauvism down, let alone the Post-Impressionism from which that derived, seem to require some kind of *theoretical* understanding to which the language and the psychology of emotions seemed less and less adequate.

Just think of the dazzling succession of art movements in our century: Fauvism, the Cubisms, Futurism, Vorticism, Synchronism, Abstractionism, Surrealism, Dada, Expressionism,

Abstract Expressionism, Pop, Op, Minimalism, Post-Minimalism, Conceptualism, Photorealism, Abstract Realism, Neo-Expressionism — simply to list some of the more familiar ones. Fauvism lasted about two years, and there was a time when a whole period of art history seemed destined to endure about five months, or half a season. Creativity at that time seemed more to consist in making a period than in making a work. The imperatives of art were virtually historical imperatives — Make an art-historical period! — and success consisted in producing an accepted innovation. If you were successful, you had the monopoly on producing works no one else could, since no one else had made the period with which you and perhaps a few collaborators were from now on to be identified. With this went a certain financial security, inasmuch as museums, wedded to historical structure and the kind of completeness which went with having examples from each period, would want an example from you if you were a suitable period. As innovative an artist as De Kooning was never especially allowed to evolve, and De Chirico, who understood these mechanisms exactly, painted de chiricos throughout his life, since that's what the market wanted. Who would want a Utrillo that looked like Mondrian, or a Marie Laurencin that looked like Grace Hartigan, or a Modigliani like Franz Kline? And each period required a certain amount of quite complex theory in order that the often very minimal objects could be transacted onto the plane of art. In the face of this deep interplay between historical location and theoretical enfranchisement, the appeal to feeling and expression seemed just less and less convincing. Even today we hardly know what Cubism was really about, but I am certain that there is a great deal more to it than Braque and Picasso ventilating their surprisingly congruent feelings toward guitars.

The Expression Theory, while too thin by far to account for this rich profusion of artistic styles and genres, has nevertheless the great merit of having approached works of art as constituting a natural kind, surface variations notwithstanding,

and to have responded in the spirit of science to what has been a brooding question since Plato — namely, What is Art? The question became urgent in the twentieth century, when the received model collapsed, though that was not even a good model when no one could tell that it was not. But the inadequacy of the theory became year by year — or, if I may, period by period — more apparent as each movement raised the question afresh, offering itself as a possible final answer. The question indeed accompanied each new artform as the Cogito, according to a great thesis of Kant's, accompanies each judgment, as though each judgment raises about itself the question of What is Thought? And it began to seem as though the whole main point of art in our century was to pursue the question of its own identity while rejecting all available answers as insufficiently general. It was as though, to paraphrase a famous formula of Kant, art were something conceptuable without satisfying any specific concept.

It is this way of looking at things which suggests another model of art history altogether, a model narratively exemplified by the *Bildungsroman*, the novel of self-education which climaxes in the self's recognition of the self. This is a genre recently and, I think, not inappropriately to be mainly found in feminist literature, where the question the heroine raises, for reader and for herself, is at once who is she and what is it to be a woman. The great philosophical work which has this form is Hegel's astonishing *Phenomenology of Spirit*, a work whose hero is the spirit of the world — whom Hegel names *Geist* — the stages of whose development toward self-knowledge, and toward self-realization through self-knowledge, Hegel traces dialectically. Art is one of these stages — indeed, one of the nearly final stages of spirit's return to spirit through spirit — but it is a stage which must be gone through in the painful ascent toward the final redeeming cognition.

The culmination of Geist's quest and destiny is, as it happens, philosophy, according to Hegel's scheme, largely because philosophy is essentially reflexive, in the sense that the question of what it is is part of what it is, its own nature being one of its major problems. Indeed, the history of philosophy may be read as the story of philosophy's mistaken identities, and of its failures in seeing through and to itself. It is possible to read Hegel as claiming that art's philosophical history consists in its being absorbed ultimately into its own philosophy, demonstrating then that self-theoretization is a genuine possibility and guarantee that there is something whose identity consists in self-understanding. So the great drama of history, which in Hegel is a divine comedy of the mind, can end in a moment of final self-enlightenment, where the enlightenment consists in itself. The historical importance of art then lies in the fact that it makes philosophy of art possible and important. Now if we look at the art of our recent past in these terms, grandiose as they are, what we see is something which depends more and more upon theory for its existence as art, so that theory is not something external to a world it seeks to understand, so that in understanding its object it has to understand itself. But there is another feature exhibited by these late productions which is that the objects approach zero as their theory approaches infinity, so that virtually all there is at the end *is* theory, art having finally become vaporized in a dazzle of pure thought about itself, and remaining, as it were, solely as the object of its own theoretical consciousness.

If something like this view has the remotest chance of being plausible, it is possible to suppose that art had come to an end. Of course, there will go on being art-making. But art-makers, living in what I like to call the post-historical period of art, will bring into existence works which lack the historical importance or meaning we have for a very long time come to expect. The historical stage of art is done with when it is known what art is and means. The artists have made the way open for philosophy, and the moment has arrived at which the task must be transferred finally into the hands of philosophers. Let me conclude by spelling this out in a way which might make it acceptable.

"The end of history" is a phrase which carries ominous overtones at a time when we hold it in our power to end everything, to expel mankind explosively from being. Apocalypse has always been a possible vision, but has seldom seemed so close to actuality as it is today. When there is nothing left to make history — i.e., no more human beings — there will be no more history. But the great meta-historians of the nineteenth century, with their essentially religious readings of history, had rather something more benign in mind, even if, in the case of Karl Marx, violence was to be the engine of this benign culmination. For these thinkers, history was some kind of necessary agony through which the end of history was somehow to be earned, and the end of history then meant the end of that agony. History comes to an end, but not mankind — as the story comes to an end, but not the characters, who live on, happily ever after, doing whatever they do in their post-narrational insignificance. Whatever they do and whatever now happens to them is not part of the story lived through them, as though they were the vehicle and it the subject.

Here is a pertinent summation by that profound and influential commentator on Hegel, Alexandre Kojève:

> *In point of fact, the end of human time, or History — that is, the definitive annihilation of Man, properly speaking, or of the free and historical individual — means quite simply the cessation of action in the full sense of the term. Practically, this means the disappearance of wars and bloody revolutions. And also the disappearance of Philosophy. For since Man no longer changes essentially, there is no reason to change the (true) principles which are at the basis of his understanding of the world and himself. But all the rest can be preserved indefinitely: art, love, play, etc.: in short, everything that makes man happy.*

And Marx, in a famous passage upon which there can be little doubt that Kojève based his, describes the life of man when all the contradictions that define history, and which are expressed socially as the class wars so ominously specified in *The Communist Manifesto*, have worked themselves out through the agony of history, so that society is now classless and there is nothing left to generate more history, and man is deposited on the promised shores of utopia, a paradise of nonalienation and nonspecialization. There, Marx tells us, I can be a hunter in the morning and a fisher in the afternoon and a critical critic in the evening. Posthistorical life, for Hegel as for Marx, will have the form of a kind of philosophical *Club mediterranée*, or what used to be known as heaven, where there is nothing left for us to do but — in the phrase of our adolescents — hang out. Or, to take another image, this time from Plato, where, at the end of his *Republic*, he depicts a choosing situation, in which men, purged in the afterlife and ready to reenter the world, have arrayed before them the variety of lives from which they may pick one: and the canny Odysseus chooses a life of quiet obscurity, the sort of life most people live most of the time, the simple dumb existence of the sitcom, village life, domestic life, the kind of life lamented, in a painful episode, by Achilles in the underworld. Only, in Marx and in Hegel, there is no history to rumble beyond the distant horizons. The storms have abated forever. And now we can do what we like, heeding that imperative that is no imperative at all: *Fay çe que voudras* — "Do whatever you want."

The End of History coincides, and is indeed identical, with what Hegel speaks of as the advent of Absolute Knowledge. Knowledge is absolute when there is no gap between knowledge and its object, or knowledge is its own object, hence subject and object at once. The closing paragraph of the *Phenomenology* suitably characterizes the philosophical closure of the subject it treats of, by saying that it "consists in perfectly knowing itself, in knowing what it is." Nothing is now outside knowledge, nor opaque to the light of cognitive intuition. Such a conception of knowledge is, I believe, fatally flawed. But if anything comes close to exemplifying it, art in our times does — for the object in which the artwork consists is so irradiated by theoretical consciousness that the division between object and subject is all but overcome, and it little matters whether art is philosophy in action or philosophy is art in thought. "It is no doubt the case," Hegel writes in his *Philosophy of the Fine Arts*, "that art can be

utilized as a mere pastime and entertainment, either in the embellishment of our surroundings, the imprinting of a life-enhancing surface to the external conditions of our life, or the emphasis placed by decoration on other subjects." Some such function must be what Kojève has in mind when he speaks of art as among the things that will make men happy in the post-historical time. It is a kind of play. But this kind of art, Hegel contends, is not really free, "since subservient to other objects." Art is truly free, he goes on to say, only when "it has established itself in a sphere it shares with religion and philosophy, becoming thereby one mode more and form through which . . . the spiritual truths of widest range are brought home to consciousness." All this and, being Hegel, a good bit more having been said, he concludes, dismally or not I leave it to the reader to determine, "Art is and remains for us a thing of the past." And: "On the side of its highest possibilities [art] has lost its genuine truth and life, and is rather transported to our world of *ideas* than is able to maintain its former necessity and its superior place in reality." So a "science of art," or *Kunstwissenschaft* — by which certainly Hegel meant nothing remotely like art history as practiced as an academic discipline today, but rather instead a sort of cultural philosophy of the sort he himself was working out — a "science of art is a far more urgent necessity in our own times than in times in which art sufficed by itself alone to give full satisfaction." And further on in this utterly amazing passage he says, "We are invited by art to contemplate it reflectively . . . in order to ascertain scientifically its nature." And this is hardly something art history as we know it attempts to do, though I am certain that the present rather anemic discipline grew out of something as robust in its conception as Hegel meant for it to be. But it is also possible that art history has the form we know because art as we knew it is finished.

Well.

As Marx might say, you can be an abstractionist in the morning, a photorealist in the afternoon, a minimal minimalist in the evening. Or you can cut out paper dolls or do what you damned please. The age of pluralism is upon us. It does not matter any longer what you do, which is what pluralism means. When one direction is a good as another direction, there is no concept of direction any longer to apply. Decoration, self-expression, entertainment are, of course, abiding human needs. There will always be a service for art to perform, if artists are content with that. Freedom ends in its own fulfillment. A subservient art has always been with us. The institutions of the art-world — galleries, collectors, exhibitions, journalism — which are predicated upon history and hence marking what is new, will bit by bit wither away. How happy happiness will make us is difficult to foretell, but just think of the difference the rage of gourmet cooking has made in common American life. On the other hand, it has been an immense privilege to have lived in history.

from *The Principles of Art*

R. G. Collingwood

Reprinted by permission of Oxford University Press.

Chapter XIV: The Artist and the Community

§ 4. THE AUDIENCE AS UNDERSTANDER

What is meant by saying that the painter "records" in his picture the experience which he had in painting it? With this question we come to the subject of the audience, for the audience consists of anybody and everybody to whom such records are significant.

It means that the picture, when seen by some one else or by the painter himself subsequently, produces in him (we need not ask how) sensuous-emotional or psychical experiences which, when raised from impressions to ideas by the activity of the spectator's consciousness, are transmuted into a total imaginative experience identical with that of the painter. This experience of the spectator's does not repeat the comparatively poor experience of a person who merely looks at the subject; it repeats the richer and more highly organized experience of a person who has not only looked at it but has painted it as well.

That is why, as so many people have observed, we "see more in" a really good picture of a given subject than we do in the subject itself. That is why, too, many people prefer what is called "nature" or "real life" to the finest pictures, because they prefer not to be shown so much, in order to keep their apprehensions at a lower and more manageable level, where they can embroider what they see with likes and dislikes, fancies and emotions of their own, not intrinsically connected with the subject. A great portrait painter, in the time it takes him to paint a sitter, intensely active in absorbing impressions and converting them into an imaginative vision of the man, may easily see through the mask that is good enough to deceive a less active and less pertinacious observer, and detect in a mouth or an eye or the turn of a head things that have long been concealed. There is nothing mysterious about this insight. Every one judges men by the impressions he gets of them and his power of becoming aware of these impressions; and the artist is a man whose life's work consists in doing that. The wonder is rather that so few artists do it revealingly. That is perhaps because people do not want it done, and artists fall in with their desire for what is called a good likeness, a picture that reveals nothing new, but only recalls what they have already felt in the sitter's presence.

How is any one to know that the imaginative experience which the spectator, by the work of his consciousness, makes out of the sensations he receives from a painting "repeats," or is "identical" with, the experience which the artist had in painting it? That question has already been raised about language in general . . . and answered by saying that there is no possibility of an absolute assurance; the only assurance we can have "is an empirical and relative assurance, becoming progressively stronger as conversation proceeds, and based on the fact that neither party seems to the other to be talking nonsense." The same answer holds good here. We can never absolutely know that the imaginative experience we obtain from a work of art is identical with that of the artist. In proportion as the artist is a great one, we can be pretty certain that we have only caught his meaning partially and imperfectly. But the same applies to any case in which we hear what a man says or read what he writes. And a partial and imperfect understanding is not the same thing as a complete failure to understand.

For example, a man reading the first canto of the *Inferno* may have no idea what Dante meant by the three beasts. Are they deadly sins, or are they potentates, or what are they? he may ask. In that perplexity, however, he has not completely lost contact with his author. There is still a great deal in the canto which he can understand, that is to say, transmute from impression into idea by the work of his consciousness; and all this, he can be fairly confident, he grasps as Dante meant it. And even the three beasts, though he does not understand them completely (something remains obstinately a mere untransmuted impression) he understands in part; he sees that they are something the poet dreads, and he imaginatively experiences the dread, though he does not know what it is that is dreaded.

Or take (since Dante may be ruled out as allegorical and therefore unfair) an example from modern poetry. I do not know how many readers of Mr. Eliot's poem *Sweeney among the Nightingales* have the least idea what precisely the situation is which the poet is depicting. I have never heard or read any expression of such an idea. Sweeney has dropped asleep in a restaurant, vaguely puzzled by the fact that the Convent of the Sacred Heart, next door, has reminded him of something, he cannot tell what. A wounded Heart, and waiting husbandless women. As he snores all through the second verse a prostitute in a long cloak comes and sits on his knees, and at that moment he dreams the answer. It is Agamemnon's cry — "O, I am wounded mortally to the heart" — wounded to death at his homecoming by the false wife he had left behind. He wakes, stretching and laughing (tilting the girl off his knee), as he realizes that in the queer working of his mind the hooded husbandless nuns and the cloaked husbandless girl, waiting there like a spi-

der for her prey, are both Klytaemnestra, the faithless wife who threw her cloak (the "net of death") round her lord and stabbed him.

I quote this case because I had known and enjoyed the poem for years before I saw that this was what it was all about; and nevertheless I understood enough to value it highly. And I am willing to believe that the distinguished critic who thinks that the "liquid siftings" of the nightingales were not their excrement, but their songs, values it highly too, and not everywhere so unintelligently as that sample would suggest.[1]

The imaginative experience contained in a work of art is not a closed whole. There is no sense in putting the dilemma that a man either understands it (that is, has made that entire experience his own) or does not. Understanding it is always a complex business, consisting of many phases, each complete in itself but each leading on to the next. A determined and intelligent audience will penetrate into this complex far enough, if the work of art is a good one, to get something of value; but it need not on that account think it has extracted "the" meaning of the work, for there is no such thing. The doctrine of a plurality of meanings, expounded for the case of holy scripture by St. Thomas Aquinas, is in principle perfectly sound: as he states it, the only trouble is that it does not go far enough. In some shape or other, it is true of all language.

§ 5 . THE AUDIENCE AS COLLABORATOR

The audience as understander, attempting an exact reconstruction in its own mind of the artist's imaginative experience, is engaged on an endless quest. It can carry out this reconstruction only in part. This looks as if the artist were a kind of transcendent genius whose meaning is always too profound for his audience of humbler mortals to grasp in a more than fragmentary way. And an artist inclined to give himself airs will no doubt interpret the situation like that. But another interpretation is possible. The artist may take his audi-

[1] And it was not until a few days after I had written the above, that I recognized "gloomy Orion" as a borrowing from Marlowe's *Dido* — another tragedy about a husbandless woman.

ence's limitations into account when composing his work; in which case they will appear to him not as limitations on the extent to which his work will prove comprehensible, but as conditions determining the subject-matter or meaning of the work itself. In so far as the artist feels himself at one with his audience, this will involve no condescension on his part; it will mean that he takes it as his business to express not his own private emotions, irrespectively of whether any one else feels them or not, but the emotions he shares with his audience. Instead of conceiving himself as a mystagogue, leading his audience as far as it can follow along the dark and difficult paths of his own mind, he will conceive himself as his audience's spokesman, saying for it the things it wants to say but cannot say unaided. Instead of setting up for the great man who (as Hegel said) imposes upon the world the task of understanding him, he will be a humbler person, imposing upon himself the task of understanding his world, and thus enabling it to understand itself.

In this case his relation to his audience will no longer be a mere by-product of his aesthetic experience, as it still was in the situation described in the preceding section; it will be an integral part of that experience itself. If what he is trying to do is to express emotions that are not his own merely, but his audience's as well, his success in doing this will be tested by his audience's reception of what he has to say. What he says will be something that his audience says through his mouth; and his satisfaction in having expressed what he feels will be at the same time, in so far as he communicates this expression to them, their satisfaction in having expressed what they feel. There will thus be something more than mere communication from artist to audience, there will be collaboration between audience and artist.

We have inherited a long tradition, beginning in the late eighteenth century with the cult of "genius," and lasting all through the nineteenth, which is inimical to this second alternative. But I have already said that this tradition is dying away. Artists are less inclined to give themselves airs than they used to be; and there are many indications that they are more willing than they were, even a generation ago, to regard their audiences as collaborators. It is perhaps no longer foolish to hope that this way of conceiving the relation between artist and audience may be worth discussing.

There are grounds for thinking that this idea of the relation is the right one. . . . we must look at the facts; and we shall find that, whatever airs they may give themselves, artists have always been in the habit of treating the public as collaborators. On a technical theory of art, this is, in a sense, comprehensible. If the artist is trying to arouse certain emotions in his audience, a refusal on the part of the audience to develop these emotions proves that the artist has failed. But this is one of the many points in which the technical theory does not so much miss the truth as misrepresent it. An artist need not be a slave to the technical theory, in order to feel that his audience's approbation is relevant to the question whether he has done his work well or ill. There have been painters who would not exhibit, poets who would not publish, musicians who would not have their works performed; but those who have made this great refusal, so far as one knows them, have not been of the highest quality. There has been a lack of genuineness about their work, corresponding to this strain of secretiveness in their character, which is inconsistent with good art. The man who feels that he has something to say is not only willing to say it in public: he craves to say it in public, and feels that until it has been thus said it has not been said at all. The public is always, no doubt, a circumscribed one: it may consist only of a few friends, and at most it includes only people who can buy or borrow a book or get hold of a theatre ticket; but every artist knows that publication of some kind is a necessity to him.

Every artist knows, too, that the reception he gets from his public is not a matter of indifference to him. He may train himself to take rebuffs with a stiff lip, and go on working in spite of bad sales and hostile reviews. He must so train himself, if he is to do his best work; because with the best will in the world (quite apart from venality in reviewers and frivolity in readers) no one enjoys having his unconscious emotions dragged into the light of consciousness, and consequently there is often a strongly painful element in a genuine aesthetic experience, and a strong temptation to reject it. But the reason why the artist finds it so hard to train himself in this way is because these rebuffs wound him not in his personal vanity, but in his judgement as to the soundness of the work he has done.

Here we come to the point. One might suppose that the artist by himself is in his own eyes a sufficient judge of his work's value. If he is satisfied with it, why should he mind what others think? But things do not work like that. The artist, like any one else who comes before an audience, must put a bold face on it; he must do the best he can, and pretend that he knows it is good. But probably no artist has ever been so conceited as to be wholly taken in by his own pretence. Unless he sees his own proclamation, "This is good," echoed on the faces of his audience — "Yes, that is good" — he wonders whether he was speaking the truth or not. He thought he had enjoyed and recorded a genuine aesthetic experience, but has he? Was he suffering from a corruption of consciousness? Has his audience judged him better than he judged himself?

These are facts which no artist, I think, will deny, unless in that feverish way in which we all deny what we know to be true and will not accept. If they are facts, they prove that, in spite of all disclaimers, artists do look upon their audiences as collaborators with themselves in the attempt to answer the question: is this a genuine work of art or not? But this is the thin end of a wedge. Once the audience's collaboration is admitted thus far, it must be admitted farther.

The artist's business is to express emotions; and the only emotions he can express are those which he feels, namely, his own. No one can judge whether he has expressed them except some one who feels them. If they are his own and no one else's, there is no one except himself who can judge whether he has expressed them or not. If he

attaches any importance to the judgement of his audience, it can only be because he thinks that the emotions he has tried to express are emotions not peculiar to himself, but shared by his audience, and that the expression of them he has achieved (if indeed he has achieved it) is as valid for the audience as it is for himself. In other words, he undertakes his artistic labour not as a personal effort on his own private behalf, but as a public labour on behalf of the community to which he belongs. Whatever statement of emotion he utters is prefaced by the implicit rubric, not "I feel," but "we feel." And it is not strictly even a labour undertaken by himself on behalf of the community. It is a labour in which he invites the community to participate; for their function as audience is not passively to accept his work, but to do it over again for themselves. If he invites them to do this, it is because he has reason to think they will accept his invitation, that is, because he thinks he is inviting them to do what they already want to do.

In so far as the artist feels all this (and an artist who did not feel it would not feel the craving to publish his work, or take seriously the public's opinion of it), he feels it not only after his work is completed, but from its inception and throughout its composition. The audience is perpetually present to him as a factor in his artistic labour; not as an anti-aesthetic factor, corrupting the sincerity of his work by considerations of reputation and reward, but as an aesthetic factor, defining what the problem is which as an artist he is trying to solve — what emotions he is to express — and what constitutes a solution of it. The audience which the artist thus feels as collaborating with himself may be a large one or a small one, but it is never absent.

§ 6. AESTHETIC INDIVIDUALISM

The understanding of the audience's function as collaborator is a matter of importance for the future both of aesthetic theory and of art itself. The obstacle to understanding it is a traditional individualistic psychology through which, as through distorting glasses, we are in the habit of looking at artistic work. We think of the artist as a self-contained personality, sole author of everything he does: of the emotions he expresses as his personal emotions, and of his expression of them as his personal expression. We even forget what it is that he thus expresses, and speak of his work as "self-expression," persuading ourselves that what makes a poem great is the fact that it "expresses a great personality," whereas, if self-expression is the order of the day, whatever value we set on such a poem is due to its expressing not the poet — what is Shakespeare to us, or we to Shakespeare? — but ourselves.

It would be tedious to enumerate the tangles of misunderstanding which this nonsense about self-expression has generated. To take one such only: it has set us off looking for "the man Shakespeare" in his poems, and trying to reconstruct his life and opinions from them, as if that were possible, or as if, were it possible, it would help us to appreciate his work. It has degraded criticism to the level of personal gossip, and confused art with exhibitionism. What I prefer to attempt is not a tale of misdeeds, but a refutation.

In principle, this refutation is simple. Individualism conceives a man as if he were God, a self-contained and self-sufficient creative power whose only task is to be himself and to exhibit his nature in whatever works are appropriate to it. But a man, in his art as in everything else, is a finite being. Everything that he does is done in relation to others like himself. As artist, he is a speaker; but a man speaks as he has been taught; he speaks the tongue in which he was born. The musician did not invent his scale or his instruments; even if he invents a new scale or a new instrument he is only modifying what he has learnt from others. The painter did not invent the idea of painting pictures or the pigments and brushes with which he paints them. Even the most precocious poet hears and reads poetry before he writes it. Moreover, just as every artist stands in relation to other artists from whom he has acquired his art, so he stands in relation to some audience to whom he addresses it. The child learning his mother tongue, as we have seen, learns simultaneously to be a speaker and to be a listener; he listens to others speaking, and speaks to others listening. It is the same with artists. They become poets or painters or musicians not by some process of development from within, as they grow beards; but by living in a society where these languages are current. Like other speakers, they speak to those who understand.

The aesthetic activity is the activity of speaking. Speech is speech only so far as it is both spoken and heard. A man may, no doubt, speak to himself and be his own hearer; but what he says to himself is in principle capable of being said to any one sharing his language. As a finite being, man becomes aware of himself as a person only so far as he finds himself standing in relation to others of whom he simultaneously becomes aware as persons. And there is no point in his life at which a man has finished becoming aware of himself as a person. That awareness is constantly being reinforced, developed, applied in new ways. On every such occasion the old appeal must be made: he must find others whom he can recognize as persons in this new fashion, or he cannot as a finite being assure himself that this new phase of personality is genuinely in his possession. If he has a new thought, he must explain it to others, in order that, finding them able to understand it, he may be sure it is a good one. If he has a new emotion, he must express it to others, in order that, finding them able to share it, he may be sure his consciousness of it is not corrupt.

This is not inconsistent with the doctrine, stated elsewhere in this book, that the aesthetic experience or aesthetic activity is one which goes on in the artist's mind. The experience of being listened to is an experience which goes on in the mind of the speaker, although in order to its existence a listener is necessary, so that the activity is a collaboration. Mutual love is a collaborative activity; but the experience of this activity in the mind of each lover taken singly is a different experience from that of loving and being spurned.

A final refutation of aesthetic individualism will, therefore, turn on analysis of the relation between the artist and his audience, developing the view stated in the last section that this is a case of collaboration. But I propose to lead up to this by way of two other arguments. I shall try to show that the individualistic theory of artistic creation is false (1) as regards the relation between a given artist and those fellow artists who in terms of the individualistic theory are said to "influence" him; (2) as regards his relation with those who are said to "perform his works"; and (3) as regards his relation with the persons known as his "audience." In each case, I shall maintain, the relation is really collaborative.

§ 7. COLLABORATION BETWEEN ARTISTS

Individualism would have it that the work of a genuine artist is altogether "original," that is to say, purely his own work and not in any way that of other artists. The emotions expressed must be simply and solely his own, and so must his way of expressing them. It is a shock to persons labouring under this prejudice when they find that Shakespeare's plays, and notably *Hamlet*, that happy hunting-ground of self-expressionists, are merely adaptations of plays by other writers, scraps of Holinshed, Lives by Plutarch, or excerpts from the *Gesta Romanorum*; that Handel copied out into his own works whole movements by Arne; that the Scherzo of Beethoven's C minor Symphony begins by reproducing the Finale of Mozart's G minor, differently barred; or that Turner was in the habit of lifting his composition from the works of Claude Lorrain. Shakespeare or Handel or Beethoven or Turner would have thought it odd that anybody should be shocked. All artists have modelled their style upon that of others, used subjects that others have used, and treated them as others have treated them already. A work of art so constructed is a work of collaboration. It is partly by the man whose name it bears, partly by those from whom he has borrowed. What we call the works of Shakespeare, for example, proceed in this way not simply and solely from the individual mind of the man William Shakespeare of Stratford (or, for that matter, the man Francis Bacon of Verulam) but partly from Kyd, partly from Marlowe, and so forth.

The individualistic theory of authorship would lead to the most absurd conclusions. If we regard the *Iliad* as a fine poem, the question whether it was written by one man or by many is automatically, for us, settled. If we regard Chartres cathedral as a work of art, we must contradict the architects who tell us that one spire was built in the twelfth century and the other in the sixteenth, and convince ourselves that it was all built at once. Or again: English prose of the early seventeenth century may be admired when it is original; but not the Authorized Version, for that is a translation, and a translation, because no one man is solely responsible for it, cannot be a work of art. I am very willing to allow with Descartes that "often there is less perfection in works put together out of several parts, and made by the hands of different masters, than in those at which one only has worked"; but not to replace his "often" by "always." I am very willing to recognize that, under the reign of nineteenth-century individualism, good artist have seldom been willing to translate, because they have gone chasing after "originality"; but not to deny the name of poetry to Catullus's rendering of Sappho merely because I happen to know it for a translation.

If we look candidly at the history of art, or even the little of it that we happen to know, we shall see that collaboration between artists has always been the rule. I refer especially to that kind of collaboration in which one artist grafts his own work upon that of another, or (if you wish to be abusive) plagiarizes another's for incorporation in his own. A new code of artistic morality grew up in the nineteenth century, according to which plagiarism was a crime. I will not ask how much that had to do, whether as cause or as effect, with the artistic barrenness and mediocrity of the age (though it is obvious, I think, that a man who can be annoyed with another for stealing his ideas must be pretty poor in ideas, as well as much less concerned for the intrinsic value of what ideas he has than for his own reputation); I will only say that this fooling about personal property must cease. Let painters and writers and musicians steal with both hands whatever they can use, wherever they can find it. And if any one objects to having his own precious ideas borrowed by others, the remedy is easy. He can keep them to himself by not publishing; and the public will probably have cause to thank him.

§ 8. COLLABORATION BETWEEN AUTHOR AND PERFORMER

Certain kinds of artist, notably the dramatist and the musician, compose for performance. Individualism would maintain that their works, however "influenced," as the phrase goes, by those of other artists, issue from the writer's pen complete and finished; they are plays by Shakespeare and symphonies by Beethoven, and these men are great artists, who have written on their own responsibility a text which, as the work of a great artist, imposes on the theatre and the orchestra a duty to perform it exactly as it stands.

But the book of a play or the score of a symphony, however cumbered with stage-directions, expression-marks, metronome figures, and so forth, cannot possibly indicate in every detail how the work is to be performed. Tell the performer that he must perform the thing exactly as it is written, and he knows you are talking nonsense. He knows that however much he tries to obey you there are still countless points he must decide for himself. And the author, if he is qualified to write a play or a symphony, knows it too, and reckons on it. He demands of his performers a spirit of constructive and intelligent co-operation. He recognizes that what he is putting on paper is not a play or a symphony, or even complete directions for performing one, but only a rough outline of such directions, where the performers, with the help, no doubt, of producer and conductor, are not only permitted but required to fill in the details. Every performer is co-author of the work he performs.

This is obvious enough, but in our tradition of the last hundred years and more we have been constantly shutting our eyes to it. Authors and performers have found themselves driven into a state of mutual suspicion and hostility. Performers have been told that they must not claim the status of collaborators, and must accept the sacred text just as they find it; authors have tried to guard against any danger of collaboration from performers by making their book or their text fool-proof. The result has been not to stop performers from collaborating (that is impossible), but to breed up a generation of performers who are not qualified to collaborate boldly and competently. When Mozart leaves it to his soloist to improvise the cadenza of a concerto, he is in effect insisting that the soloist shall be more than a mere executant; he is to be something of a composer, and therefore trained to collaborate intelligently. Authors who try to produce a fool-proof text are choosing fools as their collaborators.

§ 9. THE ARTIST AND HIS AUDIENCE

The individualism of the artist, partly broken down by collaboration with his fellow artists and still further by collaboration with his performers, where he has them, is not yet wholly vanquished. There still remains the most difficult and important problem of all, namely, that of his relation to his audience. We have seen in § 6 that this, too, must in theory be a case of collaboration; but it is one thing to argue the point in theory, and quite another to show it at work in practice. In order to do this, I will begin with the case where the artist is a collaborative unit consisting of author and performers, as in the theatre, and consider how, as a matter of empirical fact, this unit is related to the audience.

If one wants to answer this question for oneself, the best way to proceed is to attend the dress rehearsal of a play. In the rehearsal of any given passage, scenery, lighting, and dresses may all be exactly as they are at a public performance; the actors may move and speak exactly as they will "on the night"; there may be few interruptions for criticism by the producer; and yet the spectator will realize that everything is different. The company are going through the motions of acting a play, and yet no play is being acted. This is not because there have been interruptions, breaking the thread of the performance. A work of art is very tolerant of interruption. The intervals between acts at a play do not break the thread, they rest the audience. Nobody ever read the *Iliad* or the *Commedia* at a sitting, but many people know what they are like. What happens at the dress rehearsal is something quite different from interruption. It can be described by saying that every line, every gesture, falls dead in the empty house. The company is not acting a play at all; it is performing certain actions which will become a play when there is an audience present to act as a sounding-board. It becomes clear, then, that the aesthetic activity which is the play is not an activity on the part of the author and the company together, which this unit can perform in the audience's absence. It is an activity in which the audience is a partner.

Any one, probably, can learn this by watching a dress rehearsal; but the principle does not apply to the theatre alone. It applies to rehearsals by a choir or orchestra, or to a skilled and successful public speaker rehearsing a speech. A careful study of such things will convince any one who is open to conviction that the position of the audience is very far from being that of a licensed eavesdropper, overhearing something that would be complete without him. Performers know it already. They know that their audience is not passively receptive of what they give it, but is determining by its reception of them how their performance is to be carried on. A person accustomed to extempore speaking, for example, knows that if once he can make contact with his audience it will somehow tell him what he is to say, so that he finds himself saying things he had never thought of before. These are the things which, on that particular subject, he and nobody else ought to be saying to that audience and no other. People to whom this is not a familiar experience are, of course, common; but they have no business to speak in public.

It is a weakness of printed literature that this reciprocity between writer and reader is difficult to maintain. The printing-press separates the writer from his audience and fosters cross-purposes between them. The organization of the literary profession and the "technique" of good writing, as that is understood among ourselves, consist to a great extent of methods for mitigating this evil; but the evil is only mitigated and not removed. It is intensified by every new mechanization of art. The reason why gramophone music is so unsatisfactory to any one accustomed to real music is not because the mechanical reproduction of the sounds is bad—that could be easily compensated by the hearer's imagination—but because the performers and the audience are out of touch. The audience is not collaborating, it is only overhearing. The same thing happens in the cinema, where collaboration as between author and producer is intense, but as between this unit and the audience nonexistent. Performances on the wireless have the same defect. The consequence is that the gramophone, the cinema, and the wireless are perfectly serviceable as vehicles of amusement or of propaganda, for here the audience's function is merely receptive and not concreative; but as vehicles of art they are subject to all the defects of the printing-press in an aggravated form. "Why," one hears it asked, "should not the modern popular entertainment of the cinema, like the Renaissance popular entertainment of the theatre, produce a new form of great art?" The answer is simple. In the Renaissance theatre collaboration between author and actors on the one hand, and audience on the other, was a lively reality. In the cinema it is impossible.

The conclusion of this chapter may be summarized briefly. The work of artistic creation is not a work performed in any exclusive or complete fashion in the mind of the person whom we call the artist. That idea is a delusion bred of individualistic psychology, together with a false view of the relation not so much between body and mind as between experience at the psychical level and experience at the level of thought. The aesthetic activity is an activity of thought in the form of consciousness, converting into imagination an experience which, apart from being so converted, is sensuous. This activity is a corporate activity belonging not to any one human being but to a community. It is performed not only by the man whom we individualistically call the artist, but partly by all the other artists of whom we speak as "influencing" him, where we really mean collaborating with him. It is performed not only by this corporate body of artists, but (in the case of the arts of performance) by executants, who are not merely acting under the artist's orders, but are collaborating with him to produce the finished work. And even now the activity of artistic creation is not complete; for that, there must be an audience, whose function is therefore not a merely receptive one, but collaborative too. The artist (although under the spell of individualistic prejudices he may try to deny it) stands thus in collaborative relations with an entire community; not an ideal community of all human beings as such, but the actual community of fellow artists from whom he borrows, executants whom he employs, and audience to whom he speaks. By recognizing these relations and counting upon them in his work, he strengthens and enriches that work itself; by denying them he impoverishes it.

Chapter XV: Conclusion

. . . The decay of our civilization, as depicted in *The Waste Land*, is not an affair of violence and wrong-doing. It is not exhibited in the persecution of the virtuous and in the flourishing of the wicked like a green bay tree. It is not even a triumph of the meaner sins, avarice and lust. The drowned Phœnician sailor has forgotten the profit and loss; the rape of Philomel by the barbarous king is only a carved picture, a withered stump of time. These things are for remembrance, to contrast with a present where nothing is but stony rubbish, dead tree, dry rock, revealed in their nakedness by an April that breeds lilacs out of the dead land, but no new life in the dead heart of man. There is no question here of expressing private emotions; the picture to be painted is not the picture of any individual, or of any individual shadow, however lengthened into spurious history by morning or evening sun; it is the picture of a whole world of men, shadows themselves, flowing over London Bridge in the winter fog of that Limbo which involves those who, because they never lived, are equally hateful to God and to his enemies.

The picture unrolls. First the rich, the idle man and his idle mistress, surrounded by all the apparatus of luxury and learning; but in their hearts there is not even lust, nothing but fretted nerves and the exasperation of boredom. Then the public-house at night; the poor, no less empty-hearted: idle recrimination, futile longing for a good time, barren wombs and faded, fruitless youth, and an awful anonymous voice punctuating the chatter with a warning "Hurry up please it's time." Time for all these things to end; time's winged chariot, the grave a fine and private place, and mad Ophelia's good-night, the river waiting for her. And then the river itself, with its memories of idle summer love-making, futile passionless seductions, the lover whose vanity makes a welcome of indifference, the mistress brought up to expect nothing; with contrasting memories of the splendours once created by Sir Christopher Wren, the pageantry of Elizabeth, and Saint Augustine for whom lust was real and a thing worth fighting.

Enough of detail. The poem depicts a world where the wholesome flowing water of emotion, which alone fertilizes all human activity, has dried up. Passions that once ran so strongly as to threaten the defeat of prudence, the destruction of human individuality, the wreck of men's little ships, are shrunk to nothing. No one gives; no one will risk himself by sympathizing; no one has anything to control. We are imprisoned in ourselves, becalmed in a windless selfishness. The only emotion left us is fear: fear of emotion itself, fear of death by drowning in it, fear in a handful of dust.

This poem is not in the least amusing. Nor is it in the least magical. The reader who expects it to be satire, or an entertaining description of vices, is as disappointed with it as the reader who expects it to be propaganda, or an exhortation to get up and do something. To the annoyance of both parties, it contains no indictments and no proposals. To the amateurs of literature, brought up on the idea of poetry as a genteel amusement, the thing is an affront. To the little neo-Kiplings who think of poetry as an incitement to political virtue, it is even worse; for it describes an evil where no one and nothing is to blame, an evil not curable by shooting capitalists or destroying a social system, a disease which has so eaten into civilization that political remedies are about as useful as poulticing a cancer.

To readers who want not amusement or magic, but poetry, and who want to know what poetry can be, if it is to be neither of these things, *The Waste Land* supplies an answer. And by reflecting on it we can perhaps detect one more characteristic which art must have, if it is to forgo both entertainment-value and magical value, and draw a subject-matter from its audience themselves. It must be prophetic. The artist must prophesy not in the sense that he foretells things to come, but in the sense that he tells his audience, at risk of their displeasure, the secrets of their own hearts. His business as an artist is to speak out, to make a clean breast. But what he has to utter is not, as the individualistic theory of art would have us think, his own secrets. As spokesman of his community, the secrets he must utter are theirs. The reason why they need him is that no community altogether knows its own heart; and by failing in this knowledge a community deceives itself on the one subject concerning which ignorance means death. For the evils which come from that ignorance the poet as prophet suggests no remedy, because he has already given one. The remedy is the poem itself. Art is the community's medicine for the worst disease of mind, the corruption of consciousness.

SUGGESTED EXERCISE

To what extent are we separate and unique individuals, and to what extent are we communal beings whose inner lives are not unique? This is a crucial question for Collingwood and, indeed, for any expression theorist. To the extent that people are unique and different from each other, it will be difficult for Collingwood to argue that a given artist's expression is relevant to others or requires an audience to judge its genuineness; even though art would still be valuable to the individual artist, its claim to have a larger social role would be reduced. Looking at the history of the arts, which vision, individualistic or communalistic and collaborative, finds support? Write an essay exploring this question.

SUGGESTED ADDITIONAL READINGS

Leo Tolstoy, *What is Art*, trans. Almyer Maude (Indianapolis: Bobbs-Merrill, 1960). Chapter 19 addresses art of the future.

John Berger, "Problems of Socialist Art," in *Radical Perspectives in the Arts*, ed. Lee Baxandall (Baltimore: Penguin Books, 1972).

NOTES

1. See Jayne Merkal, "Art on Trial," *Art in America*, Dec. 1990, pp. 41–51.
2. See Front Page, *Art in America*, Sept. 1989, p. 33. In a related case, the Illinois state legislature cut the funding for the Chicago Art Institute from $65,000 to $1 for showing an artwork done by a student that involved placing the American flag on the floor. The work was intended to be political and to challenge patriotic attitudes, but it strongly offended many people, who demanded its removal. The Institute refused. As a result of the punitive budget cut, however, the display of artworks at the Institute will now be monitored by the administration rather than by the students or faculty. (See pp. 33 and 239.)
3. See Front Page, *Art in America*, Mar. 1991, p. 31.

4. See Front Page, *Art in America*, Feb. 1991, p. 37.
5. Collingwood implies that the audience is more likely to have corrupt consciousnesses than the artist; that is, the audience/community needs to be told the truth but may find the truth unpleasant in some way. Thus, the audience test of the genuineness of expression may seem inherently unreliable. This problem is probably what leads Collingwood to deny that we could be afflicted by corrupt consciousness most of the time. There must be some basic willingness on the part of both artists and members of the audience to deal with the emotional truth about things a significant portion of the time.

INDEX

ACKNOWLEDGMENTS

Text Credits

Page 246 e. e. cummings: "anyone lived in a pretty how town," copyright 1940 by e. e. cummings; renewed 1968 by Marion Morehouse Cummings. Reprinted from *Complete Poems 1913–1962* by e. e. cummings by permission of Liveright Publishing Co.

Illustration Credits

Page xiv *Mona Lisa*, courtesy of the Louvre, Paris; *Cuts*, © 1967 Carl Andre, courtesy of Paula Cooper Gallery

Page 30 © Erika Davidson 1990

Pages 38–39 *The Destruction of "Tilted Arc": Documents*, edited by Clara Weyergraf-Serra and Martha Buskirk. © 1991 MIT Press.

Page 72 Photographer: Robert Doisneau

Page 93 © Nancy Bless

Page 118 © 1984 Andy Freeberg

Page 122 Duchamp, *Nude Descending a Staircase, No. 2*. Philadelphia Museum of Art: Louise and Walter Annenberg Collection

Page 123 Collection Galleria Schwarz, Milan

Page 124 Marcel Duchamp, *L.H.O.O.Q.*, 1919. Pencil on print of Leonardo's *Mona Lisa*. 7¾ × 4¾". Private collection.

Page 125 © 1960 by Henmar Press Inc. Used by permission of C. F. Peters Corporation.

Page 128 Chris Burden, *Shoot*. November 19, 1971. Performance at F Space, Santa Ana, Calif. Courtesy of the artist.

Page 129 Chris Burden, *Trans-fixed*. Courtesy of the artist.

Page 146 Duchamp, *Fountain*, c. 1917. Philadelphia Museum of Art: Louise and Walter Annenberg Collection

Page 149 Walter De Maria, *The Lightning Field*, 1977. All reproduction rights reserved: copyright Dia Center for the Arts. Photo: John Cliett.

Page 162 Courtesy of Percival David Foundation of Chinese Art, London.

Page 178 *Once Upon a Time in the West*, copyright © 1969 by Paramount Pictures. All rights reserved.

Page 201 Alinari/Art Resource, by permission

Page 203 Alinari/Art Resource, by permission

Page 204 Bequest of Robert Treat Paine, 2nd Courtesy, Museum of Fine Arts, Boston

Page 206 Scala/Art Resource, by permission

Page 242 Courtesy of Soprintendenza Archeologica delle Province di Napoli e Caserta, Napoli

Page 254 Scala/Art Resource, by permission

Page 322 Scala/Art Resource, by permission

Page 347 Paul Cézanne, French, 1839–1906, *The Basket of Apples*, oil on canvas, c. 1895, 65.5 × 81.3 cm, Helen Birch Bartlett Memorial Collection 1926.252. Photograph © 1992, The Art Institute of Chicago. All rights reserved.

Page 348 Collection: State Museum Kroller-Muller, Otterlo, The Netherlands.

Page 349 The Hague, 1882. Kroller-Muller State Museum, Otterlo

Page 392 Duchamp, *Large Glass; Bride Stripped Bare by Her Bachelors*, c. 1915. Philadelphia Museum of Art: Bequest of Katherine S. Dreier.

Color Plate 1: Paris, Louvre. Courtesy of Art Resource.

Color Plate 2: Padua, Scrovegni Chapel. Courtesy of Art Resource.

Color Plate 3: *Spiral Jetty*, Great Salt Lake, 1970, by Robert Smithson; photo by Gianfranco Gorgoni. Courtesy of SYGMA.

Color Plate 4: Mondrian, Piet, *Broadway Boogie-Woogie*. 1942–43. Oil on canvas, 50 × 50″. Collection, The Museum of Modern Art, New York. Purchase.

Color Plate 5: Courtesy of Doria Pamphilj Gallery. Photographer: Araldo De Luca

Color Plate 6: *Top:* Claude Monet, French, 1840–1926, *Grainstack*, oil on canvas, 1891, 65.6 × 92 cm. Restricted gift of the Searle Family Trust; Major Acquisitions Centennial Endowment; through prior acquisitions of the Mr. and Mrs. Martin A. Ryerson and Potter Palmer collections; through prior bequest of Jerome Friedman, 1983.29. Photograph © 1992, The Art Institute of Chicago. All rights reserved. *Bottom:* 1970.253, *Grainstack (Snow Effect)*, Monet, Oscar Claude, France, 1840–1926, oil on canvas, 65.4 × 92.3 cm (25¾ × 36⅜ in.). Gift of Misses Aimee and Rosamond Lamb in memory of Mr. and Mrs. Horatio A. Lamb. Courtesy, Museum of Fine Arts, Boston.

Color Plate 7: Courtesy of Leo Castelli Photo Archives

Color Plate 8: Stedelijk Museum. Alexander Liberman © 1992.

Color Plate 9: O'Keeffe, Georgia, *Orange and Red Streak*, 1919, Philadelphia Museum of Art: The Alfred Stieglitz Collection: Bequest of Georgia O'Keeffe.

Color Plate 10: The Metropolitan Museum of Art, The Berggruen Klee Collection, 1987. (1987.455.17).

Color Plate 11: Reproducción Autorizada por El Instituto Nacional de Bellas Artes y Literatura.